The Hindu, by understa forms, symbols and festivals of Ganesha explained in this book, so rich with pictorial illustrations, becomes more devout and attached to his religion and to Ganesha. Aspiring Hindus and the many non-Hindus in the Western world, increasingly becoming interested in vegetarianism, *ahimsa, karma,* rebirth and other concepts of Hindu religion, will find useful information and explanations to remove many misconceptions and misinformation about Hindu religion and Hindu worship. The large number of Hindus living in the Western world, cut off from their roots in India and Sri Lanka, will find the book inspiring to refresh their religion and make them proud of their rich culture. Many quotations from the *Vedas, Bhagavad Gita, Mahabharata, Tirumantiram, Tirukural,* Auvaiyar, Yogaswami and other scriptures make the book a religious and literary treatise worthy of study by scholars and savants. The glossary explains many words and phrases to help the understanding of the text. This book should find a place in every Hindu home and library.

Tiru M. Arumugam, Chairman, Siva Thondan Nilayam (Yogaswami Centre); London, U.K.

Millions of Hindus around the world invoke Ganesha, the divine Remover of Obstacles. Millions of Hindus should study this book and benefit from the esteemed author's knowledge, wisdom and human warmth. It is a wonderful cornucopia of those wishing to deepen their understanding of and strengthen their faith in Lord Ganesha. A high-quality, practical and very readable volume.

Georg Feuerstein, Ph.D., author of *Encyclopedic Dictionary of Yoga* and *Wholeness and Transcendence;* Lower Lake, California

In putting this book *Loving Ganesha* together, Satguru Sivaya Subramuniyaswami has done an outstanding and encyclopedic work, especially for the benefit of Westerners interested in Hindu thought and second-generation Indian Hindus growing up in the West. Several aspects of Ganesha that are not popularly known are included. These will tend to strengthen the faith of the readers in Lord Ganesha and make their prayers to Him come from deep within and hence be more fruitful. In addition to covering the various aspects of Ganesha, Swamiji has also included several other topics of common interest. These will prove very valuable to the readers in developing clarity about Hindu thought and in adopting more meaningful things in their daily lives.

Dr. Deendayal Khandelwal, Chairman, Board of Directors, Hindu University of America, Orlando, Florida

Loving Gaṇeśa

प्रेमवान् गणेशः
सनातनधर्मवल्लभो
गजाननमहादेवः

Himalayan Academy Publications

Books in Print by Satguru Sivaya Subramuniyaswami

RISHI COLLECTION

Dancing with Śiva: Hinduism's Contemporary Catechism
Living with Śiva: Hinduism's Contemporary Culture
Loving Gaṇeśa: India's Endearing Elephant-Faced Deity
Gems of Wisdom: One Hundred and Eight Classical Hindu Meditations for Pilgrims of the Mind

THE MASTER COURSE

Śaivite Hindu Religion, A Seven-Book Illustrated Children's Course

THE SAIVITE SERIES

Saivite Calendar: A Panchangam for Hindu Temple and Home
Saivite Controversy: Monism and Pluralism in Saiva Siddhanta
Saivite Culture: Insights into Eastern Manners and Customs
Saivite Names: A Practical Manual on Becoming a Hindu
Saivite Virtue: A 7-Week Course on the Power of Celibacy for Hindu Youth
Saivite Worship: The Saiva Atmartha Puja, Traditional Hindu Liturgy for the Home Shrine

THE SATGURU SPEAKS ON:

Hindu Renaissance
Hindu Family Life

OTHER PUBLICATIONS

God's Money: Dasamamsha, the Hindu Law of Tithing
Hindu Hymnal: Devotional Songs and *Bhajans* for Temple and Home, with Simple English Translations
Holy Orders of Sannyas: A Saiva Swami's Diksha and Lifetime Vows of Renunciation
Know thy Self: Enlightenment Lessons for Discovering the Divine Within You
Monks Cookbook: Recipes from Kauai Aadheenam
Praying to the Gods: A Modern Tantra on Writing Prayers for the Sacred Temple Fire, with an Introduction to Tyaf
Shum, the Language of Meditation (available to initiated members of Śaiva Siddhānta Church)
Siva's Cosmic Dance: An Introduction to the World's Most Ancient Religion
Truth is One, Paths Are Many

Books by Other Authors

WORKS OF GURU'S OF OUR LINEAGE

Natchintanai: Songs and Sayings of Yogaswami (published by the Sivathondan Society, 1974)
Words of Our Master (published by Sivathondan Society)
Yogaswāmī's Natchintanai: Songs in English and Tamil
Tirumantiram: A Tamil Scriptural Classic by Ṛishi Tirumular (English/Tamil clothbound edition by Ramakrishna Math, Madras)

MONTHLY PUBLICATIONS

Hinduism Today: International Hindu family newspaper affirming the *dharma* and recording the modern history of nearly a billion members of a global religion in renaissance

SCRIPTURE

Vedic Experience: An Anthology of the *Vedas* for Modern Man and Contemporary Celebration, by Raimon Panikkar
The Principal Upanishads, S. Radhakrishnan
Āgama-Kosha (Āgama Encyclopaedia,

three volumnes), Kalpatharu Research Academy, Chief Editor: Daivajna K.N. Somayaji.

OTHER SELECT TITLES

Banares, City of Shiva, Rajesh Bedi, Brijbasi Printers

Hindū Marriage Saṁskāra, Marriage Rites and Rituals of Hindus, Dr. Prem Sahai

Kumbha Mela, The World's Largest Act of Faith, Jack Hebner and David Osborn, Ganesh Editions

The Penguin Book of Hindu Names, Maneka Gandhi, Viking

Ways to Siva, Life and Ritual in Hindu India, Joseph M. Dye, Philadelphia Museum of Art

Available Now or Soon On the World Wide Web

http://www.HinduismToday.kauai.hi.us/ashram/

Many of the above publications are also available on the World Wide Web along with the titles listed below which are currently not in print. The teachings are being offered mainly in English but also in other languages including Malay, Hindi, Tamil, Malayalam, Sanskṛit, French, French Creole, Japanese and German.

By Sivaya Subramuniyaswami

RISHI COLLECTION

Merging with Śiva: Hinduism's Yoga Lessons

Raja Yoga: A Down-to-Earth Manual on Spiritual Consciousness with Advanced Meditations on Purification, Energy Transmutation and the Five States of Mind

Mystic Scrolls: Hinduism's Angelic Prophecies Revealed (initiated-Church members only)

COURSES OF HIMALAYAN ACADEMY

The 1967 Master Course
- Book I: Mind, Its Five States
- Book II: Man, His Seven Aspects
- Book III Part 1: Innerversity, the Art of Meditation
- Book III Part 2: Man's Key to a Woman's Mind
- Book III Part 3: Woman's Key to a Man's Mind

The 1970 Master Course: A Twelve-Chapter Course in the Ancient Philosophy of Saiva Siddhanta (text and audio by Satguru Sivaya Subramuniyaswami)

The 1975 Master Course
- Siddhanta Course
- Vedanta Course

The 1980s' Master Course
- Hindu Sadhana: Saivite Hindu Mysticism and Spiritual Life, 63 Daily Lessons (1983)
- Hindu Metaphysics: Color, Karma and Chakras, 35 Daily Lessons (1984)

INNERSEARCH DIARIES

Personal chronicles by devotees on religious pilgrimage with Sivaya Subramuniyaswami, from the 1969 Indian Odyssey to the present

YOGA LETTERS

26 lessons composed in the late 1960s by teachers of Himalayan Academy

THE HOLY BIBLE OF THE SAIVITE HINDU RELIGION

Vol. I: Tirumantiram: A Tamil Scriptural Classic by Tirumular, English translation and editor's notes by Dr. B. Natarajan

Vol. II: The Weaver: Holy Tirukural in English

Vol. III: Vedic Experience: An Anthology of the *Vedas* for Modern Man and Contemporary Celebration, by Raimon Panikkar

Vol. IV: The Hymns of the 18th-Century Tamil Saint, Tayumanavar

ON THE PATH SERIES
The Self God (1959)
The Clear White Light (1967)
Reflections (1968)
The Lotus of the Heart (1972)
The Search Is Within (1973)
The Meditator (1973)

THE PATHFINDER'S LIBRARY
The River of Life (1958)
The Power of Affirmation (1958)
Everything Is Within You (1958)
On the Brink of the Absolute (1958)
The Fine Art of Meditation (1973)
I'm All Right, Right Now (1973)

ALOHA SERIES
Beginning to Meditate (1972)

THE INSPIRED TALK SERIES
Singing to the Gods: Hindu Hymns of Invocation (1978)
Hinduism: The Greatest Religion in the World (1978)
The Final Conclusions for All Mankind (1978)
Courage, Courage, Courage (1978)
Free Will and the Deities (1978)
Love of the Gods: Devotion in Hinduism (1978)
Tirumantiram: Fountainhead of Saiva Siddhanta (1979)
Stand Strong for Hinduism (1980)
The Hand that Rocks the Cradle Rules the World (1980)
Protect, Preserve and Promote the Saiva Dharma (1981)

JNANA DANA PAMPHLETS
Karma and Reincarnation
Dharma and Realization
Vedas and Agamas
God and Gods in Hinduism
Hindu Ethics
Four Facts of Hinduism
Nine Beliefs of Hinduism
A Saivite Hindu's Twelve Beliefs
How to Realize God

GURUDEVA'S UPADESHA ON:
Reincarnation, Death and Dying (1989)
Bhakti Yoga (1989)
Karma Yoga (1989)
Ahimsa (1989)
Japa Yoga (1990)
Anava Marga (1990)
Hatha Yoga (1990)

BOOKLETS AND SPECIAL EXCERPTS
Guru Protocol: An Ancient Text Excerpted from the *Kularnava Tantra*
How to Become a Hindu (Excerpted from Loving Gaṇeśa)
Vegetarianism: How to Win an Argument with a Meat-Eater
Nine Questions People Ask About Hinduism

HINDUISM TODAY
Current and back issues back from November 1985 and other features
Hindu Scriptures Speak on Abortion
Healing, By Doctor Devananda Tandavan MD

By Other Authors

TEACHINGS OF OUR PARAMAGURU
Message of the Heart (Sayings of Yogaswami, published by the Yogaswami Society, San Francisco)
Saint Yogaswami and the Testament of Truth, by Ratna Ma Chelliah Navaratnam, 1972

OTHER SELECT TITLES
Family Issues as Seen by Different Religions, UNESCO, 1994

For catalog and prices, write to: Himalayan Academy Publications, 107 Kaholalele Road, Kapaa, Hawaii USA, Phone: 1-808-822-3012; Fax 822-4351, or visit our World Wide Web home page for the above books and a list of available posters, postcards, sacred *pūjā* items and more.
http://www.HinduismToday.kauai.hi.us/ashram/

Loving Gaṇeśa

Hinduism's Endearing Elephant-Faced God

प्रेमवान् गणेशः
सनातनधर्मवल्लभो
गजाननमहादेवः

Satguru Sivaya
Subramuniyaswami

Published by
Himalayan Academy
India • USA

First Edition

 Designed, typeset and illustrated by the *swāmīs* of the Śaiva Siddhānta Yoga Order, 107 Kaholalele Road, Kapaa, Hawaii, 96746-9304, USA.

Published by
Himalayan Academy
India • USA

PRINTED IN USA

Library of Congress Catalog Card Number 95-080939

ISBN 0-945497-64-4

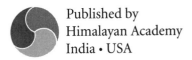

ഉ

Dedication

Samarpaṇam

समर्पणम्

IT WAS NOT SO LONG AGO THAT SEEKERS REQUESTED WE PUBLISH MORE ABOUT THIS MYSTICAL GOD, MOST BELOVED OF THEM ALL. SO we did. Now, into your hands we present a loveable *Loving Gaṇeśa.* Why did we choose that name of all names? Because everyone, young and old, thin and hefty (especially the latter) loves Gaṇeśa. Of course, He loves us all very, very much. He is the God of unfailing laws such as gravity, retributions and *karmic* responses. In matters of less gravity, He is the lover of all things sweet. He is also the Prince of Culture and Patron of the Arts. Everyone loves music, art, drama and the dance. He, in His joyous pompousness, is the Remover of Obstacles, and that is just what He did for us—He removed the obstacles we faced in publishing *Loving Gaṇeśa* and those you faced in finding it. Many, many months of research went into this gem. Help was given by Sanskṛit scholars, *paṇḍitas, swāmīs* and *āchāryas,* Gaṇeśologists, housewives and children, experts in all fields of knowledge about Hindutva's elephant-faced Lord, first to be worshiped before starting any quest. Only after the book was assembled did we come to know that He and His army of *gaṇas* must have spent not a little time in doing what they do best: implementation. We happily dedicate this book to my *satguru,* the venerable sage of Sri Lanka, Yogaswāmī, whose *āśrama* in Colombuthurai rested across the road from the Varasitthi Vinayagar Temple, in the northern Tamil domain. We pray that *Loving Gaṇeśa* brings to you a deeper, subtler appreciation of Hinduism.

Contents

Vishayasūchī

विषयसूची

On September 21, 1995, just days after I had completed the final editing of *Loving Gaṇeśa,* something quite wonderful happened. Lord Gaṇeśa began sipping milk, first in India, then in nearly every country where Hindus reside, as devotees rushed to temples and shrines to offer milk to the elephant-faced God. It was a great spiritual experience for us in Hawaii, where we publish the international monthly news journal, HINDUISM TODAY, to receive the many phone calls and fax messages with positive, uplifting testimony as to His drinking milk in so many places. As perhaps the most fitting preface to this benevolent Lord's 800-page book, we are pleased to present the story of the milk miracle—*kshīra chamatkāra*— from HINDUISM TODAY, November, 1995.

"It's a Miracle!" Rejoice Millions As Lord Gaṇeśa Receives Milk

The Supernatural Event of this Century Is Experienced Simultaneously Worldwide

IT ALL BEGAN ON SEPTEMBER 21 WHEN AN OTHERWISE ORDINARY MAN IN NEW DELHI DREAMT THAT LORD GAṆEŚA, THE ELEPHANT-HEADED GOD of Wisdom, craved a little milk. Upon awakening, he rushed in the dark before dawn to the nearest temple, where a skeptical priest allowed him to proffer a spoonful of milk to the small stone image. Both watched in astonishment as it disappeared, magically consumed by the God. What followed is unprecedented in modern Hindu history. Within hours, news had spread like a brush fire across India that Gaṇeśa was accepting milk offerings. Tens of millions of people of all ages flocked to the nation's temples. The unworldly happening brought worldly New Delhi to a standstill, and its vast stocks of milk, more than a million liters, sold out within hours. Just

NEWS □ LOCAL
Statue of Hindu God, Ganesha, drinks milk
Phenomenon witnessed in Fiji and around the world
By Hari Gaunder
Hindu women offer milk to a stone sculpture in India
Hindus Claim Milky Miracle
The Daily Teleg
Wonder of milk draws thousan
Page 23
Page 24
I cannot explain says Ramakrishna boss
'Miracles have been known to happen'
TONIGHT'S WEATHER: CLOUDY
LATE PRICES EXTRA
Evening Standard
LONDON, FRIDAY, 22 SEPTEMBER, 1995
INCORPORATING THE EVENING NEWS 30p
ES magazine
YOU COULD WIN UP TO £50,000
Pick up your new game card free with today's ES Magazine
IT'S SO EASY TO PLAY – SEE PAGE 38 OF THE PAPER FOR DETAILS AND WINNING NUMBERS
THE AMAZING MILK 'MIRACLE'
to see milk-sipping
on't believe m
Thousands flock to London Hindu temple as statues 'drink'
by TOM LEONARD
The Edmonton Jou
The Daily Post
Police begin hunt for Naitasiri thugs
A Hindu centu
Milk miracle linked to Hind
Edmonton Hindus gather around a statue of Lord Ganesha, which appeared to drink milk
A THIRST FOR MIRAC
Milk-drinking idol renews faith, joy for city's Hindu c
DON THOMAS
Journal Staff Writer
Temples mobbed after 'milk miracle'
By Rahul Bedi in New Delhi
Indiase godenbeelden zuigen melk
Tientallen miljoenen Indiërs geloven gisteren getuige te zijn geweest van een wonder
November, 1995 • Volume 17, Number 11
North America Edition
US$2.75
HINDUISM TODAY
The Hindu Family Newspaper Affirming the Dharma and Recording the Modern History of Nearly a Billion Members of a Global Religion in Renaissance
"It's a Miracle!" Rejoice Millions As Lord Ganesha Receives Milk
"The" Supernatural Event of This Century Is Experienced Simultaneously Worldwide

as suddenly as it started in India, it stopped, in just 24 hours.

But it was just beginning elsewhere as Hindus in India called their relatives in other parts of the world. Soon our HINDUISM TODAY offices were flooded with reports from around the world. Everywhere the story was the same. A teaspoonful of milk offered by touching it to Gaṇeśa's trunk, tusk or mouth would disappear in a few seconds to a few minutes—not always, but with unprecedented frequency. Reuters news service quoted Anila Premji, "I held the spoon out level, and it just disappeared. To me it was just a miracle. It gave me a sense of feeling that there is a God, a sense of Spirit on this Earth." Not only Gaṇeśa, but Śiva, Pārvatī, Nandi and the Nāga, Śiva's snake, took milk.

This "milk miracle" may go down in history as the most important event shared by Hindus this century, if not in the last millennium. It has brought about an instantaneous religious revival among nearly one billion people. No other religion has ever done that before! It is as if every Hindu who had, say "ten pounds of devotion," suddenly has twenty.

Miracles witnessed by many people happen from time to time in Hinduism as in other faiths, but they're rare. As a young boy, the tenth-century saint, Nambi Anbar Nambi, inspired Lord Gaṇeśa to actually eat the offerings placed before Him. Saint Jñaneśvara of Mahārāshṭra became famous 600 years ago for having a water buffalo recite the *Vedas* before a group of arrogant priests.

Naturally there are skeptics—10% of Hindus, according to our very unscientific poll, all of whom moved swiftly to distance themselves from the phenomenon. "Capillary action," coupled with "mass hysteria" is the correct explanation, concluded many scientists within a few hours. Aparna Chattopadhyay of New Delhi replied to these scoffers in a letter to the *Hindustan Times:* "I am a senior scientist of the Indian Agriculture Research Institute, New Delhi. I found my offerings of milk in a temple being mysteriously drunk by the Deities. How can the scientists explain the copper snake absorbing the milk I offered

Ganesha Idols Around the World 'Drink' Milk

...tees offering milk to an idol of Lord Ganesha at the ...nu Temple in Toronto PHOTO: KULDIP DHEER

By Narayanan Madhavan

NEW DELHI—Crowds swarmed into temples across India and neighboring Nepal on Sept. 21 after reports that idols of Hindu gods were drinking milk poured as sacred offerings.

Hindus packed temples as news spread that milk offered to ...

INDIA JOURNAL

...verted by what they were sure they ...

DAILY NATION

The newspaper that serves the nati...

No. 10824, Nairobi, Saturday, September 23, 1995 — Price ...

...du 'milk miracle' frenzy spr...

...Reporters ...encies

...faithful around ...ged on temples ...rd spread that ...drinking sacred

...Long Island in ...and Hong Kong

...shippers and the merely curious thronged temples hoping to witness what Indians were calling the "milk miracle".

"It is a miracle," said Srikant Ravi, the priest at New Delhi's Hanuman Temple. "The gods have come down to earth to solve all our problems."

'Milk-drinking' idol picture on page 2

Thursday with wildfire rumours that idols of the Hindu god Shiva, his consort Parvati and their ...

Ganesh, were sipping traditional milk offerings in Delhi. Word quickly spread through India.

Indian offices and homes were abuzz as even well-heeled businessmen, politicians and journalists dropped what they were doing to join the frenzy.

But by yesterday the fever had ...

were rep... feed milk... "It can... business... "Where w... One De... milk in h... ished, sw...

Patriot

NEW DELHI FRIDAY SEPTEMBER 22, 1995

The miracle of vanishing m...

India mail

London, September 28th - October 4th 1995

News — Snake venom brings nirvana to junkies Page 6

Special Feature — Indiamail's guide to winter holidays in India Pages 11, 12, 21, 22

Arts — Tamasha brings its own version of Lorca's Yerma Page 8

Millions queue to witness 'Act of God'

INDIA JOURNAL September 29, 1995

MILK MIRACLE

...entary Physics, Gullible Public ...te Mass Hysteria of Milk Feeding

...Idols' "Milk Miracle" ...ds to Indonesia

Hindu Statue "Sips Milk" in Roman Catholic Italy

Shiva Fever Spreads to London

By Alan Wheatley

"Milk Miracle" in T...

The Guardian

Homogenised, semi-skimmed, UHT: the idol had no particular preference

EVENING STANDARD

Believers thirst for a miracle from Hong Kong to Southall

by RICHARD HOLLIDAY

THE STATESMAN — METRO

Delhi witnesses frenzy of devotees

STATESMAN NEWS SERVICE

...my case such a thing happened," she added with a shrug.

"Either I am growing old and ...eyes are playing tricks with ...or else there is really a God."

...21-year-old Minnie who ...rks in a private firm in ...naught Place and had tried the "milk theory" as she calls ... "The answer which I want is ... is it possible for stone ...ues to drink milk? Where is the milk going even if the ...ole thing is a stunt", she asks ...n exasperated tone.

...r Pyare Lal, who works in a ...ate firm said, "I can't believe ...The idol 'drinks' only when ...spoon is tilted. Naturally any ...id will go down because of ...ity. The fanatics won't no... ...it."

...r Sant Sharma, a journalist, ...med that the whole pheno...non was nothing but a man...station of surface tension ...a little bit of kesar in the ... Kesar is sacred, but the idols refuse to drink that milk. I tried that out myself."

According to Mr Bhagwati ...Bhan, a private firm executive: "If God is there to drink milk ...

Cong blames BJP for mass hysteria

V.N. Gadgil, alleged that the BJP and the RSS were in the habit of exploiting such religious sentiments for political purposes.

Replying to questions, he said, "Having exhausted the Ram issue, they are now after Ganesh."

"Elections in the North have showed that people are not misguided by such things. Ram failed to come to their rescue in Madhya Pradesh, Himachal Pradesh and U.P. and Ganesh will give them the same treatment in the Lok Sabha polls," he said.

...ences, people waited patiently ...watch the Gods "drinking" ...ilk.

While many believed that a ...iracle was actually happening ...

Phenomenon leads to milk scarcity

STATESMAN NEWS SERVICE

Evening News — Saturday Sept. 23 1995

Ganesha ...

...e phenomenon of idols of ...to an artificial scarcity of ...

...nd devotees to experiment ...cepted by God or not. ...ess and by early afternoon ...s. The demand and supply ...ent haywire and milk was ...few outlets where it was ...

...by a Gujarat-based milk ...o more milk while milk in ...le outside major temples ...

...e refuted "any shortage" of ...milk supply to the Capital ...S supplies 3,00,000 litres ...

...here will be no shortage of ...e Delhi Milk Scheme and ...arrangements for supply of ...n to the normal supply.

Metro News

SUNDAY SEPTEMBER 24 1995 — INDIAN EXPRESS N...

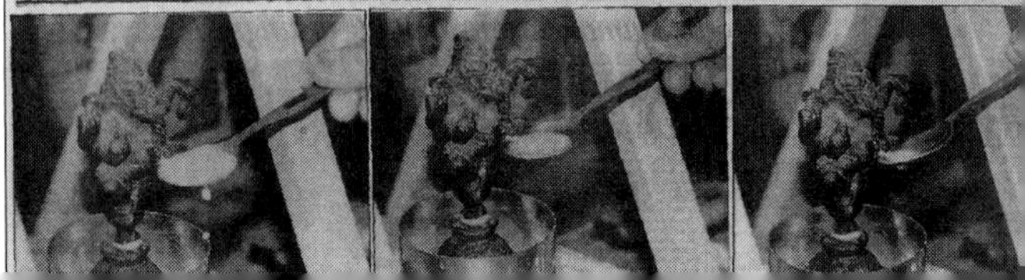

with a spoon kept at a good distance away from it?" Scientific or not, gallons of milk were disappearing with hardly a trace. A leading barrister in Malaysia was dumbfounded when he watched a metal Gaṇeśa attached to an automobile dashboard absorb six teaspoons of milk. In Nepal King Birendra himself made offerings to the God. Deities in Kenya and other countries took gallons of milk while sitting in shallow metal trays with no drains.

The worldwide press coverage has been nearly as amazing as the miracle itself. Of course, the event dominated the news in India for days. But once it started outside India, local and leading national papers, such as the *New York Times* and *Washington Post* in America, and the *Financial Times* in UK, had picked up the story. The international wire services Reuters and Associated Press carried a dozen articles a day on what had now been named the "Milk Miracle." Many in India are unaware of how warmly the Western press embraced the miracle. In many countries reporters came to the temples and personally offered milk. Of course, they too would put forward a "scientific explanation" in their report, but many otherwise-detached Western journalists shared their own joyful experience as a fact.

Ironically, the reporting inside India was a completely different matter. The English-language press in India with its Marxist-leaning political slant has never been a friend of Hinduism. Headlines heralded the attitude: "People go Berserk at 'Milk Miracle;' " "Scientists Dismiss it as Mass Hysteria," and "Milk-Drinking Deities Unleash Mass Hysteria, Scientists Ridicule Miracle Theory." Not every Indian paper was so negative: Tunku Varadarajan of *The Times* expressed his concern that, "Modern Hindus are often all too apologetic about the apparent angularities in the beliefs of their countrymen. In this, secular Indians are in danger of denying the very logic which has allowed India to be secular in the first place. If that tolerance is now under strain, the blame lies in part with those who would regard as dangers any celebrations of the country's underlying

Hindu identity."

Hinduism has its own science to apply to this miracle, that of the interpretation of *portents*—unusual or supernatural events. Portents are the specific domain of astrologers to interpret. The "milk miracle," under this analysis, is not the end in itself, but rather signals a future event of great import. Śrī K.N. Rao, one of India's most noted astrologers, explained that the involvement of Gaṇeśa means that harm will come to the "commanders of armies." The acceptance of milk, however, is an auspicious sign. Therefore the final result will be a greater good. The portent will take effect in eight months, just about the time of an eclipse in April, 1996.

H.H. Śrī Tiruchi Mahāswāmīgal of Bangalore said incidents of Deities accepting offerings occur every 100 years, usually eight or nine days after Gaṇeśa Chaturthā. Swāmījī believes it is a very good omen, as do other *swāmīs,* astrologers and *pundits* we have contacted.

Testimony of the Milk Miracle Worldwide

INDIA: It was around 7:30AM that my father came back from his morning walk and told me, "Rajiv, go to the temple. A great miracle is taking place. Lord Gaṇeśa is having milk. This is happening all over Delhi." I and my wife rushed to the Deepali temple which is next to our house. There were hundreds in a long queue waiting to offer milk. Inside the eight-by-ten-foot sanctum a dozen people at a time were offering milk in spoons to the small Gaṇeśa. My wife offered milk twice. I could clearly see the milk disappearing in a few seconds. Many temple priests said they had dreams of Gaṇeśa asking for milk, which they then offered in the early morning. The Deepali temple priest told me, "Somebody came and knocked on my door at 4:30 in the morning. He called, 'Gaṇeśa is having milk! Gaṇeśa is having milk!' The man was gone when I answered the door." Life in Delhi was almost at

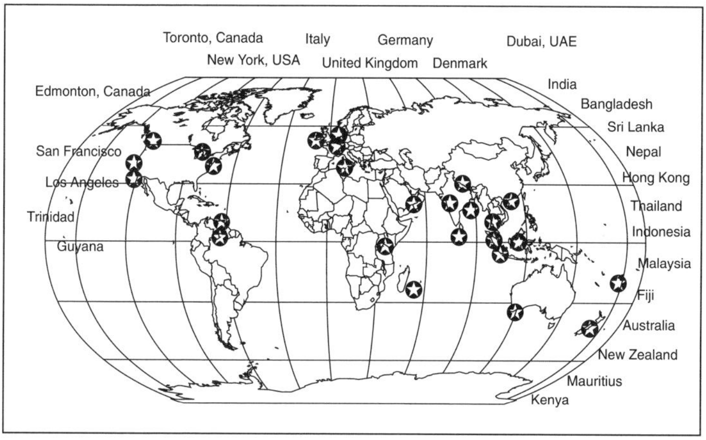

Joyous eye-witness reports of Gaṇeśa's drinking milk were received at our editorial offices from over two dozen nations and a multitude of locations.

a standstill. The markets were deserted. Banks and official institutions had very thin attendance. In the last few days I have spoken to about 100 people. Ninety percent of them told me that they had experienced it, and the milk had really been accepted by the Deity.

Rajiv Malik, New Delhi, Journalist

NEW YORK: Even in cynical, hard-edged New York, the miracle was happening. The milk was actually disappearing. Manisha Lund, a young college student, went to the Hindu temple in Queens, and says it was a virtual stampede. When she offered milk to Lord Gaṇeśa, "It was sucked up like someone was drinking it with a straw." Gaṇeśa seemed to be in a whimsical mood: sometimes He refused the spoonfuls offered by devotees and slurped up that given by nonbelievers. At the Hindu temple in Flushing, a young African-American woman who is not a Hindu but loves Hindu philosophy wondered aloud whether Śiva would accept her offering. She extended her spoon and before the eyes of many worshipers, the milk disappeared into Śiva's mouth.

Tales of faith and joy were repeated in many homes and offices where devotees offered milk to idols of stone, brass and silver. Young people seemed to have better luck, and delighted in the miracle: Pummy Singh, 14, called Indra, her mother, at work and gave her the exciting news: Gaṇeśa had taken the milk three times from her and her friends. Such was the frenzy that it was hard to gain entrance into the crowded temples, even at 2:00 in the morning.

Lavina Melwani, New York, Journalist

LOS ANGELES: "One of the devotees received a phone call from India about the miracle," recalls Bharat Shastri, priest of the Hindu temple in Norwalk. By evening he had received 600 phone calls. There was a general air of skepticism here and at other temples in Los Angeles. Only a few devotees had their milk offerings taken by Gaṇeśa at Norwalk. Nothing extraordinary happened at the Śrī Venkateshwara Temple in Calabasas, where milk was offered only by the priests. At the Chatsworth temple, the miracle seemed to have happened big time. "On Thursday morning, temple president Dinesh Lakhanpal offered milk. It disappeared. Then I offered more, and that too disappeared," said Ravi Sharan, vice president of the temple. CNN and local TV channels came and the miracle reportedly happened for them. "One reporter, Sharon Tae of Channel 5, was so excited she hugged me with tears in her eyes," said Sharan.

Archana Dongre, Los Angeles, Journalist

CANADA: The phenomenon began following the 7:30PM *pūjā,* Friday and continued unabated until about 11:45PM Sunday the 24th at the Edmonton Gaṇeśa temple. The atmosphere around the Gaṇeśa *mūrti* was scintillating. Devotees approached, bowed and offered their prayers and a spoonful of milk. They ran the gamut from sari-clad pious elderly ladies supported on either side to gum-chewing teens in

This devotee is one of thousands to offer milk to Lord Gaṇeśa at a temple in Edmonton. Unlike in India, the phenomenon continued here for days.

black leather jackets. I simply can't explain what happened to the milk. It would visibly "wick" up from the spoon to the surface of the stone of the trunk. Spoonful after spoonful was absorbed, sometimes as quickly as one could count to three, usually in 20 seconds. At the conservative rate of two teaspoons per minute for 51.5 hours (milk was offered continuously), some 7.7 gallons of milk were taken up. I could see no significant amount of milk around the Gaṇeśa *mūrti.* Of course, with the number of devotees and dripping spoons, Gaṇeśa's garments became wet on the same side as his trunk, but this didn't begin to account for the volume of milk offered. I was forced to conclude that we were all witnessing something that we could not logically explain.

Aran Veylan, Edmonton, Barrister

MAURITIUS: Today, September 25th, I've given milk to Gaṇeśa. It is happening at a temple called Tulsi Sham Temple in Beau Bassin. I rushed there, leaving all my jobs behind. I took some milk and brought it close to the trunk without spilling any. The milk was absorbed very quickly. This is something great which is happening all around the world and making us better and better Hindus.

Parmesh Pallanee, Petite Riviere, Computer Systems Advisor

KENYA: It all started with a phone call from India to a relative in Nairobi that Lord Gaṇapati's marble statue was drinking milk. Pandit Narinder Kumar Śāstrī, head priest of Shree Sānatan Dharma Temple, recounts the experience with great emotion. According to him, an unlimited amount of milk was consumed by the two Deities in the temple. People from different religions and nationalities came and made the offering. Many nonbelievers came to test. When the offering was accepted, it changed people's thinking. The miracle had a special effect on the younger generation. Panditji believes a new generation of staunch Hindus has been born as a result. It is extraordinary that the miracle occurred even on African soil, and it is equally remarkable that many African non-Hindus visited the temple and have become devotees. I stood inside the temple door for three hours and saw crowds coming and going. The atmosphere was charged and volatile, but peaceful. The people were mesmerized and were not prepared to leave the hall even after having made the offering.

In the private temple of Jyotin Arvind Bhai Patel in Nairobi, the miracle began in their temple at 4:30PM on Thursday and continued till 9:30AM on Sunday. He and Minal tried with a spoonful of milk, which disappeared. The spoon was kept under the trunk of Śrī Gaṇeśa and the milk was sucked up. Minal recalls hearing the sucking sound. In four days, 15,000 people belonging to all castes and nationalities—Hindus, Sikhs, Africans and Europeans—made offerings. As the result of the personal experience of one non-Hindu, the Patels have been offered free land to build a Śiva temple in a shopping complex.

Prabha Prabhakar Bhardwaj

My Luckiest Day

By Colonel P. C. Bhardwaj

It has taken many, many births for millions of us to witness and participate in such a miracle. I was one of the many lucky ones whom God gave the opportunity to feed Him. This miracle was needed to instill faith in people that the temple images do have powers, and to worship them is one path to reach Him. I am an engineer of long standing. The theory that capillary action caused the suction of hundreds of pints of milk by Deities of stone and metal as small as twelve by six inches is not possible. Most of the Deities are carved out of solid stone or cast of metal. Lord Gaṇeśa's trunk takes a bend and makes a twist at the tip. Its tip only has a small hole, the rest is solid mass. This tip is not capable of holding even one spoonful of milk. In some of the *mūrtis,* the trunk falls straight and the tip does not have a hole. It sucked hundred of pints of milk in a few hours. No milk was seen flowing out of the body, and no mist was formed around the *mūrtis.* What shall we call it, other than Godly miracle?

We Are So Close To God

By Jay Dubashi, a columnist for New Delhi's Organiser, *in which his article first appeared*

It was a small boy who first alerted me as to what was happening. "Come, come," he said, "Gaṇeśjī is drinking milk." We went to the nearby temple together, he and I, and the crowd was thick. A small girl, not more than three or four, was raising a spoon to the lips of Gaṇeśjī, and as we watched in awe the milk disappeared. "What did I tell you?" said the small boy. There was nothing to argue. A miracle is a miracle. Even if it was not a miracle, it is still a miracle in the eyes of those who see it. There are too many things in this world which cannot be explained by the simple theories of physics or chemistry, for the theories themselves are changing with the times.

But it is not milk that interests me. The miracle was seen not just in India, but almost all over the world, wherever Hindus congregate. And it did not take days, not even hours, probably a few minutes to spread. It shows how close the Hindu community is when it comes to things that affect its identity, even closer than the Internet. There were throngs of Hindus in temples in London and Leicester, New Jersey and Chicago, Denmark, Canada, Bangkok and Singapore. And the whole thing was breath-takingly spontaneous.

It also revealed how close the Hindus are, not only to each other but also, to their Gods. This is something nobody but a Hindu understands. To us, the Gods are not something external to us, but very much a part of our being. The relationship is affectionate and intimate, as between members of a family. There is nothing in the world as close-knit as a Hindu family, and the Gods are as much a part of this family as anyone else.

When I grew up as a small boy in Goa, we had, of course, temples and *maṭhas,* but what we liked best was the time when Gaṇeśjī came home for the Gaṇeśa Visarjana festival. We used to have made a serious-looking idol as befits a family of teachers and officials, but somehow we never thought of Gaṇeśjī as a serious person. How can anybody be serious if He chooses a small mouse to carry His plump weight? But we never asked such questions. It was enough that He was in our house for a few days, and we treated Him like a king. He wore the finest silks and ate the finest food. He was bathed in enough milk and honey to wash a grown elephant and his family. We kept Him in the house only for a day or so, and then it was time to take Him to the river for immersion. That was the hardest time for all of us, particularly for my uncle, whose job it was to prepare Him for immersion. We children went to the river, shouting all the way, but overtaken by grief

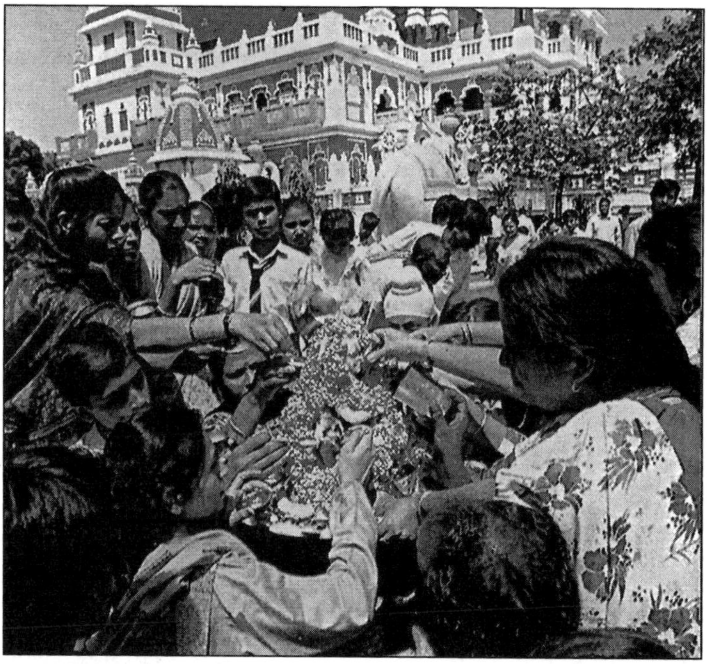

Associated Press flashed this photo worldwide of Hindus in New Delhi gathered around an image of Gaṇeśa to offer milk outside the Birla temple.

at the impending departure. After a brief *pūjā* on the bank of the river, the idol was slowly let into the swirling waters as we all wept, including my uncle, a grown man who actually ran the district. Our Gods do not ask for votes or for money. All they want is your love and affection, for that is the only bond between a Hindu and his God, like the bond between a father and son, or between brothers.

In no other religion is there such a deep and lasting bond between Gods and men as there is among Hindus. For we are, after all, descended from the Gods, and from the mountains and rivers where They stand guard and watch our holy land. And, if once in a while, they come down and sip a little milk from our spoons, why should it be a miracle? It's the most natural thing in the world.

Author's Introduction

Granthakāra Bhūmikā

ग्रन्थकारभूमिका

LORD GAṆEŚA HAS BEEN PRAYED TO, WORSHIPED AND ADORED IN ONE FORM OR ANOTHER SINCE TIME BEGAN; AND TIME ITSELF BEGAN with His creation. He, above all others, is the God, the great Mahādeva, to be invoked before every act and especially worshiped and prayed to when changes occur in our lives as we move from the old established patterns into new ones. Lord Gaṇeśa is always there to steady our minds and open the proper doors as we evolve and progress. He never, ever fails. He is always there for us when we need Him.

Hindus around the world pray to Gaṇeśa for help and guidance as He leads us out of an agricultural age through the technological and information eras and on into the new age of space. Many are still on the farms; others are in the offices and in the factories; while still others land on the moon and orbit through space. With a mind more intricate than the most complicated computers in the world all hooked together, but as simple as an on-and-off switch, Gaṇeśa knows all aspects of these transitions, in unfailing continuity, from one era to another. He is totally aware, at every point in time, of the mother in her home, the farmer in his field, the astronaut orbiting this planet, the corporate worker at his desk and the factory technician performing his tasks.

In the villages of Vedic India, Lord Gaṇeśa was for thousands of years and is today a powerful and immediate presence in everyone's lives. He was and is the one prayed to when starting a business or an enterprise of any kind. Today factory workers approach a small shrine to Him before entering for their daily work so that nothing might go wrong. Businessmen beg His help in adjusting the stock market to their advantage, and farmers, of course, chant His 108 names while planting their seeds, rice, trees and other crops. When no rain comes, images of our loving Lord are seen throughout Bhārat land submerged in water up to His neck, so that His great mind may become impressed with their crying needs. When grandma is sick or the crops are not coming in on time, when the children are growing up wrongly by adopting alien ways, Hindus diligently pray to our loving God for help in restructuring their lives. He is the supreme Lord of Dharma, and we pray to Him for guidance in the direction of our lives.

In fact, in my own experience in Sri Lanka in early years, many decades ago and in recent years as well, Śaivite *paṇḍitas* have explained that they considered Lord Gaṇeśa with all their hearts to be the one Supreme Deity, because it is through their worship of Him that they reach the holy feet of our Supreme God Śiva, thus avoiding His Rudra aspect. They explain, in their wisdom, that they begin their worship by entering Gaṇeśa's great, benevolent Being of ever-pervasive love, and then through Him, the son, they safely reach the father.

However, in modern times in the Kali Yuga (which began about the time mothers began relinquishing their *dharma* and, Gaṇeśa admonishes, it is the pure mothers of the world who will herald the next Sat Yuga), there are a great many liberal Hindus and-or Western-influenced Hindus who don't think of Gaṇeśa as a real being. To them He is a symbol, a superstition, a way of explaining philosophy to children and the uneducated. But this has not been my experience of our loving Lord. I have seen Him with my own eye. He has come to me in visions several times and convinced my lower mind of His reality. The living, loving reality of our benevolent God is the premise of the book that you hold in your hand. Believe it, for it is true.

Worship of Lord Gaṇeśa is immediate. One has but to

think of His form to contact His ever-present mind. Close your eyes for a second, visualize His large elephant head and experience the direct communication that has immediately begun. This is similar to punching in a code at a personal computer terminal which gives immediate access to the entire network of computers, large and small. On this remarkable and universal Innernet, obscure and necessary information and answers to every question are now available through the direct link with Lord Gaṇeśa. Wherever we are, whatever we are doing, we can use the computer terminal of our own brain and code in the divine image of Lord Gaṇeśa and gain complete access to His vast computer-like mind. Gaṇeśa's mind has been programmed by the history of experience over eons of time and naturally encompasses the intricacies of the universe and the cycles of life in all their ramifications and simplicities. Our great God Gaṇeśa sits contentedly upon the *mūlādhāra chakra.* This *chakra* controls the forces of memory within every creature. Worship of Him strengthens your memory, builds character and brings knowledge from the within. It also protects you from the lower forces which reside in the little-known *chakras* below the *mūlādhāra.* These darker *chakras* govern fear, anger, jealousy and the confused thinking centered around self-preservation.

The first *chakra* below the *mūlādhāra* governs the state of mind of fear and lust. The *chakra* below that governs raging anger, which comes from despair or from threats to one's self-will and can make people even angry with God. The third *chakra* below the *mūlādhāra* governs retaliatory jealousy, pride and arrogance, which are associated with feelings of inadequacy, inferiority and helplessness. At this level the only safe *sādhana* is *japa,* repetition of simple *mantras.* People who live in the consciousness of this *chakra* often deny the existence of God and are contentiously combative with one another. The fourth *chakra* down governs prolonged confusion and instinctive willfulness, the desire to get rather than to give. Those in this region of mind proclaim the existence of materialistic advancement over everything else. Hatred arises here as unwholesome *vāsanās* build one upon another. The fifth *chakra* below the *mūlādhāra* is the very home of the instinctive mind's cruel selfishness. People in the consciousness of this *chakra* are capable of actions without conscience. They see to their own well-being at all costs, think only of "I, me and mine." The sixth *chakra* down is the realm of absence of conscience which brings about theft, fraud and other dishonest dealings. People in this state of mind believe the world owes them a living and they can simply take from it what they please from whomever they please. The seventh and last *chakra* below the *mūlādhāra* governs malice, also without conscience, expressed through revenge, torture for the joy of it, murder for the sake of murder, the destruction of others' property, mind, emotion or physical body. Hatred abides here. Reason seldom reaches those who live in this state of mind.

Men and women of wisdom will work diligently to close off these lower *chakras* and the negative *karmas* they can unleash. By worship of Lord Gaṇeśa, seated upon the *mūlādhāra chakra*, you can slowly *seal* off these lower states of mind and keep awareness lifted above the animal instincts.

Wherever His devotees are—in the home, the factories, the offices, the hospitals, the marketplace, orbiting in space or tilling the soil on the farm—Lord Gaṇeśa is ever there. Intimate access is acquired by simply loving Gaṇeśa and holding His robust image in your mind. Carefully visualize the large head and ears, His long trunk, massive body, big belly and the objects He holds in His many hands. Look into Gaṇeśa's eyes. Train yourself to see Him within your own mind with your eyes closed. This is the key. Hold His form steady in your mind through the power of visualization. Now you can talk to Him. Pronounce the words mentally into His ear. He is listening, though He will never speak back but take into His vast mind your prayer and slowly work it out. You must simply speak all of your questions and your problems into His right ear. When you are finished, open your eyes. Go on with your day and go on with your life. Wherever you are, remember this simple way of making contact with Lord Gaṇeśa and, as a good seeker, exercise this *siddhi.*

Starting today and in the days to come, you will notice how He answers questions and solves problems for you through the course of your daily life. You will notice how He influences events and decisions slowly and subtly, in unseen ways. Situations will change for you, unexpected doors will open, and accustomed ones will close as you are propelled through His grace toward your inevitable glorious future. Read and reread the above formula for immediate access to Lord Gaṇeśa until it is firmly implanted in your subconscious memory patterns and then begin to make contact with Him often through each day wherever you are and whatever you are doing. Yes! Lord Gaṇeśa is immediate, and you have immediate access to Him. Wherever you are, remember this and as a seeker on the path through life's experiences exercise this *siddhi.* It is your right to do so.

All the major religions of the world, including Hinduism, have established institutions and societies to research, remodel and remold their spiritual community to be of service to their people in the fast-moving technological age. In almost every country, the various sects of Hinduism have now created temples and institutions to bring their members closer to their religion, to make it applicable to their daily modern life. Hindus have realized that those who left the farms and village guilds, the paddy fields and orchards are moving into the factories and the offices as their countries industrialize. Therefore, every effort is being made by hundreds of thousands of Hindu religious leaders to remodel and remold the presentation of our great faith to compensate during this renaissance, to establish a new era, to circumference, master and reform the ailing people of the world. Every effort is being made to make Hinduism as vital and practical in this era as it has been in more rustic times, to bring back the truant members to our religion and to vivify the Gods, for so many have put them into exile.

There is an unfortunate and totally erroneous assumption that the Gods are needed less as man pioneers new fields of science and technology and the ever-expanding field of knowledge, which is nothing other than other people's opinions and is constantly changing. Every true Hindu knows that our Gods are the essence of knowledge. They are helping us to bring through more sophisticated insights, blending scientific inquiry with spiritual intuition. They are constantly assisting us in the wise use of that knowledge for the benefit of mankind. We must teach the world's youth of the greatness of Hinduism. We must put forth our messsage to all who are ready to listen. Let them accept or reject and turn us away. It is our duty to pass on our knowledge to the generation that follows us, even if there is only a thirty-day difference in our ages. It is our *varṇāśrama dharma* to speak to those who are younger than we, to pass on everything we know to those who don't know, for no one knows the exact moment of his or her great departure. Let us dispatch our duty while we have the opportunity.

Education of the youth has been a major concern of Hindu communities around the world. During August, 1994, I was invited to preside over the *kumbabhishekam* of the Sri Subramaniya Swami Temple in Nandi Town on the island nation of Fiji. During those auspicious days the stewards of the famous South India Sanmarga Ikya Sangam (who administrate over 27 schools and colleges, and now this outstanding temple) requested us to create for them a course of lessons for children to be taught among their 17,000 students. This request birthed the Śaiva Hindu Religion children's course of seven grades. The course teaches culture, moral values, temple worship, Vedic outlook on life and more. Yes, we must teach the children, and a course to facilitate this is in progress, validated by *swāmis, pundits* and scholars worldwide with great joy. It is our *Master Course Level One,* for children five to fifteen. We urge all who are interested that the young ones get off to a *dharmic* start in life to obtain a copy. The course for Fiji is in Hindi, Tamil and English. Translations are now progressing in other language groupings as well. For Malaysia the course will be in Tamil, Malay and English. For Europe there is Tamil, German and English. Sanskrit, Kannada and English for Karnataka State in India; and combinations of French, Hindi, English and Creole for the garden island country of Mauritius.

Yes, we must teach the world's Hindu youth the greatness of their Hinduism. We must teach them they need not leave their hereditary faith to enter into science, politics or any kind of intellectual pursuit. We must teach them to seek the able assistance of Lord Gaṇeśa in all things. He is the first Ishṭa Devatā, the chosen God, of all Hindus, regardless of their sectarian position. Worship of Lord Gaṇeśa leads the devotee most naturally to the other great Gods.

Love and blessings to you from this and inner worlds,

Satguru Sivaya Subramuniyaswami
Jagadāchārya of the Nandinātha
Sampradāya's Kailāsa Paramparā,
Guru Mahāsannidhānam,
Kauai Aadheenam, Hawaii,
Gaṇeśa Chaturthī, August, 29, 1995, Hindu year 5096

Hinduism: the Greatest Religion in the World

Hindudharmaḥ Mahattamo Viśvadharmaḥ

हिन्दुधर्मः महत्तमो विश्वधर्मः

RELIGION IS MAN'S ASSOCIATION WITH THE DIVINE, AND THE ULTIMATE OBJECTIVE OF RELIGION IS REALIZATION OF TRUTH. FORMS which symbolize Truth are only indications; they are not Truth itself, which transcends all conceptualization. The mind in its efforts to understand Truth through reasoning must always fail, for Truth transcends the very mind which seeks to embrace it.

Hinduism is unique among the world's religions. We may boldly proclaim it the greatest religion in the world. To begin with, it is mankind's oldest spiritual declaration, the very fountainhead of faith on the planet. Hinduism's venerable age has seasoned it to maturity. It is the only religion, to my knowledge, which is not founded in a single historic event or prophet, but which itself precedes recorded history. Hinduism has been called the "cradle of spirituality," and the "mother of all religions," partially because it has influenced virtually every major religion and partly because it can absorb all other religions, honor and embrace their scriptures, their saints, their philosophy. This is possible because Hinduism looks compassionately on all genuine spiritual effort and knows unmistakably that all souls are evolving toward union with the Divine, and all are destined, without exception, to achieve spiritual enlightenment and liberation in this or a future life.

Of course, any religion in the world is a mind stratum within people, isn't it? It is a group of people who think consciously, subconsciously and subsuperconsciously alike and who are guided by their own superconsciousness and the superconsciousness of their leaders which make up the force field which we call a religion. It does not exist outside the mind. People of a certain religion have all been impressed with the same experiences. They have all accepted the same or similar beliefs and attitudes, and their mutual concurrence creates the bonds of fellowship and purpose, of doctrine and communion.

The people who *are* Hinduism share a mind structure. They can understand, acknowledge, accept and love the peoples of all religions, encompass them within their mind as being fine religious people. The Hindu truly believes that there is a single Eternal Path, but he does not believe that any one religion is the only valid religion or the only religion that will lead the soul to salvation. Rather, the Eternal Path is seen reflected in all religions.

To put it another way, the will of God or the Gods is at work in all genuine worship and service. It is said in Hindu scripture that "Truth is one. Paths are many." The search for Truth, for God, is called the Sanātana Dharma, or the Eternal Path, because it is inherent in the soul itself, where religion begins. This path, this return to the Source, is ever existent in man, and is at work whether he is aware of the processes or not. There is not this man's search and that man's search. Where does the impetus come from? It comes from the inside of man himself. Thus, Hinduism is ever vibrant and alive, for it depends on this original source of inspiration, this first impulse of the spirit within, giving it an energy and a vibrancy that is renewable eternally in the now.

Naturally, the Hindu feels that his faith is the broadest, the most practical and effective instrument of spiritual unfoldment, but he includes in his Hindu mind all the religions of the world as expressions of the one Eternal Path and understands each proportionately in accordance with its doctrines and dogma. He knows that certain beliefs and inner attitudes are more conducive to spiritual growth than others, and that all religions are, therefore, not the same. They differ in important ways. Yet, there is no sense whatsoever in Hinduism of an "only path." A devout Hindu is supportive of all efforts that lead to a pure and virtuous life and would consider it unthinkable to dissuade a sincere devotee from his chosen faith. This is the Hindu mind, and this is what we teach, what we practice and what we offer aspirants on the path.

We often send people back to their own religion, for Hindu doctrine would consider it an unseemly *karma* to draw someone away simply because he believed differently. To the Hindu, conduct and the inner processes of the soul's maturation are more essential than the particular religion one may be by the accidents of birth, culture or geography. The Hindu knows that he might unknowingly disturb the *dharma* of the individual if he pulls him away from his religious roots, and that would cause an unsavory *karma* for them both. He knows, too, that it is not necessary that all people believe exactly the same way or call God by the same name.

A Religion of Experience

Still, Hinduism is also extremely sectarian, altogether dogmatic in its beliefs. Its doctrines of *karma* and reincarnation, its philosophy of nonviolence and compassion, its certainty of mystical realities and experience and its universality are held with unshakable conviction. Perhaps this is due to the fact that Hinduism is a religion more of experience than of doctrine. It prefers to say to its followers, "This is the nature of Truth, and these are the means by which that Truth may be realized. Here are the traditions which have withstood time and proved most effective. Now you may test them in your own life, prove them to yourself. And we will help as we can." Hinduism will never say, "You must do or believe thusly or be condemned." In Hinduism it is believed that none is eternally condemned. That loving acceptance and unremitting faith in the goodness of life are another reason I boldly say that Hinduism is the greatest religion in the world.

Within Hinduism, as within every religious system, are the practical means of attaining the purity, the knowledge and the serenity of life. Each Hindu is enjoined to attend a *pūjā* every day, preferably at a certain and consistent time. He must observe the laws of virtue and the codes of ethics. He must serve others, support religion within his community. He should occasionally pilgrimage to sacred shrines and temples, and partake in the sacraments. If he is more advanced, an older soul, then he is expected, expects of himself, to undertake certain forms of *sādhana* and *tapas,* of discipline and asceticism.

Though it is broad and open in the freedom of the mind to inquire, Hinduism is narrowly strict in its expectations of devotees—the more awakened the soul, the higher the demands and responsibilities placed upon him. And though other systems of belief are fully acceptable mind structures within the structure of the higher mind, there is no way out of Hinduism. There is no excommunication. There is no means of severance. There's no leaving Hinduism once you have formally accepted and been accepted. Why is that? That is because Hinduism contains the whole of religion within itself. There is no "other religion" which one can adopt by leaving Hinduism, only other aspects of the one religion which is the sum of them all, the Eternal Path, the Sanātana Dharma.

I would say that, if it lacked all the qualities of openmindedness and compassion and tolerance just mentioned, Hinduism would be the greatest religion on the basis of its profound mysticism alone. No other faith boasts such a deep and enduring comprehension of the mysteries of existence, or possesses so vast a metaphysical system. The storehouse of religious revelations in Hinduism cannot be reckoned. I know of its equal nowhere. It contains the entire system of *yoga,* of meditation and contemplation and Self Realization. Nowhere else is there such insightful revelation of the inner bodies of man, the subtle *prāṇas* and the *chakras,* or psychic centers within the nerve system. Inner states of superconsciousness are explored and mapped fully in Hinduism, from the clear white light to the sights and sounds which flood the awakened inner consciousness of man. In the West it is the mystically awakened soul who is drawn to Hinduism for understanding of inner states of consciousness, discovering after ardent seeking that Hinduism possesses answers which do not exist elsewhere and is capable of guiding awareness into ever-deepening mind strata.

Hinduism's Unbounded Tolerance

In apparent conflict, the scriptures written thousands of years ago explain how we should live, and saints and *ṛishis* and seers throughout the ages have told us that it is impossible to live that way. So, Hinduism has a great tolerance for those who strive and a great forgiveness for those who fail. It looks in awe at those who succeed in living a life according to its own strict ethics. In Hinduism, we have many, many saints. You don't have to die to be acknowledged a saint in our religion, you have to live. The Hindus, perhaps beyond all other people on the earth, realize the difficulties of living in a human body and look in awe at those who achieve true spirituality.

The Hindu believes in reincarnation. He believes that he is not the body in which he lives, but the soul or awareness which takes on a body for a definite purpose. He believes he is going to get a better body in a better birth, that the process does not begin and end in a single life, that the process is continuous, reaching beyond the limits that one life may impose on inner progress. Of course, his belief in *karma* assures him that a better birth, that progress inwardly will come only if he behaves in a certain way. He knows that if he does not behave according to the natural laws, to the Hindu ethics, that he will suffer for his transgressions in a future life, or future lives, that he may by his own actions earn the necessity of a so-called inferior birth, earn the right to start over where he left off in the birth in which he failed.

The belief in *karma* and reincarnation are exclusively Hindu, and yet many people in the world today, whether they call themselves religious or not, are coming to the same conclusions, not from being told to believe but in a natural way, from the inside out. This belief in more than a single life brings to the Hindu a great sense of peace. He knows that the maturity of the soul takes many lives, perhaps hundreds of lives. If he is not perfect right now, then at least he knows that he is progressing, that there will be many opportunities for learning and growing. This eliminates anxiety, gives the serene perception that everything is all right as it is. There is no sense of a time limit, of an impending end or an ultimate judgment of his actions and attitudes. This understanding that the soul evolves gives the Hindu remarkable insight into the human condition and appreciation for all men in all stages of spiritual development.

Hinduism is so broad. Within it there is a place for the insane and a place for the saint. There is a place for the beggar and for those who support beggars. There is a place for the intelligent person and plenty of room for the fool. The beauty of Hinduism is that it does not demand of every soul perfection in this life, a necessary conclusion for those who believe in a single lifetime during which human perfection or grace must be achieved. Belief in reincarnation gives the Hindu an acceptance of every level of humanity. Some souls are simply older souls than others, but all are inherently the same, inherently immortal and of the nature of the Divine.

Hindu Views of the Divine

In Hinduism it is believed that the Gods are living, thinking, dynamic beings who live in a different world, in an inner world in the microcosm within this world in which there exists a greater macrocosm than this visible macrocosm. For the Hindu, surrender to the Divine Will that created and pervades and guides the universe is essential. The Hindu believes that these beings guide our experiences on earth, actually consciously guide the evolutionary processes. Therefore, he worships these beings as greater beings than himself, and he maintains a subjective attitude toward them, wondering if he is attuned with these grand forces of the universe, if his personal will is in phase with what these great beings would have him do. This gives birth to a great culture, a great attitude, a great tolerance and kindness one to another. It gives rise to humility in the approach to life. Not a weak or false humility, but a strong and mature sense of the grand presence and purpose of life before which the head naturally bows.

There are said to be millions of Gods in the Hindu pantheon, though only a few major Deities are actually worshiped in the temples. That God may be worshiped as the Divine Father or a Sainted Mother or the King of kings is one of the blessings of Hinduism. It offers to each a personal and significant contact, and each Hindu will choose that aspect of the Deity which most appeals to his inner needs and sensibilities. That can be confusing to some, but not to the Hindu. Within his religion is monism and dualism, monotheism and polytheism, and a rich array of other theological views.

God in Hinduism is accepted as both transcendent and immanent, both beyond the mind and the very substratum of the mind. The ideal of the Hindu is to think of God always, every moment, and to be ever conscious of God's presence. This does not mean the transcendent God, the Absolute Lord. That is for the *yogī* to ponder in his contemplative discipline. That is for the well-perfected Hindu who has worshiped faithfully in the temples, studied deeply the scriptures and found his *satguru.* For most Hindus, *God* means the Gods, one of the many personal *devas* and Mahādevas which prevail in our religion. This means a personal great soul which may never have known physical birth, a being which pervades the planet, pervades form with His mind and Being, and which guides evolution. Such a God is capable of offering protection and direction to the followers of Hinduism. The Hindu is supposed to think of God every minute of every day, to see God everywhere. Of course, most of us don't think of God even one minute a day. That's the reason that each Hindu is obliged to conduct or attend at least one religious service, one *pūjā* or ceremony, every day in his temple or home shrine. This turns his mind inward to God and the Gods.

Hinduism is an Eastern religion, and the Eastern religions are very different from those of the West. For one thing, they are more introspective. Hinduism gave birth to Buddhism, for Buddha was born and died a good Hindu. And it gave birth to other religions of the East, to Taoism, to Jainism, to Sikhism and others.

Three Pillars: Temples, Philosophy and Preceptors

There are three distinct aspects of Hinduism: the temples, the philosophy and the *satguru.* It is very fortunate that in the last two decades Hindu temples have nearly circumferenced the world. There are temples in Europe, in North America, in South America, Australia, in Africa and throughout Southeast Asia. The Hindu temple and stone images in it work as a channel for the Deity, for the Gods, who hover over the stone image and in their subtle etheric forms change people's lives through changing the nerve currents within them through their *darśana.* People come to a sanctified temple and go away, and in that process they are slowly changed from the inside out. They have changed because their very life force has changed, their mind has been changed and their emotions have undergone a subtle transformation. The temples of Hinduism are magnificent in their immensity and in their ability to canalize the three worlds, the First World of physical, outer existence and the inner Second and Third Worlds.

Hindu temples are not centered around a priest or minister, though there may be a holy man associated with a temple whose advice is cautiously and quietly sought. There is no sermon, no mediator, no director to guide the worship of pilgrims. The temple is the home of the Deities, and each devotee goes according to his own timing and for his own particular needs. Some may go to weep and seek consolation in times of sorrow, while simultaneously others will be there to rejoice in their good fortune and to sing God's name in thanksgiving. Naturally, the sacraments of name-giving and marriage and so forth are closely associated with the temple. One has only to attend a Hindu temple during festival days to capture the great energy and vitality of this ancient religion.

In its second section, of philosophy, Hinduism has influenced the deep religious thinkers of all cultures through known history. It is not a single philosophy which can be labeled "Hinduism." Rather, it is a network of many philosophies, some seeming to impertinently contradict the validity of others, yet on deeper reflection seen as integral aspects of a single radiant mind flow. In the area of philosophy must be included the enormous array of scripture, hymns, *mantras,* devotional *bhajana* and philosophical texts which are certainly unequaled in the world.

In the natural order of things, temple worship precedes philosophy. It all starts with the temple, with this sacred house of the Deities, this sanctified site where the three worlds communicate, where the inner and outer mesh and merge. It is there that devotees change. They become more like the perfect beings that live in the temple, become the voice of the Deity, writing down what is taught them from the inside, and their writings, if they are faithful to the superconscious message of the God, become scripture and make up the philosophies of Hinduism. The philosophies then stand alone as the voice of the religion. They are taught in the universities, discussed among scholars, meditated upon by *yogīs* and devout seekers. It is possible to be a good Hindu by only learning the philosophy and never going to the temple, or by simply going to the temple and never hearing of the deeper philosophies.

Hinduism has still another section within it, and that is the *guru*—the teacher, the illuminator, the spiritual preceptor. The *guru* is the remover of darkness. He is one who knows the philosophy, who knows the inner workings of the temple, and who in himself is the philosopher and the temple. The *guru* is he who can enliven the spirit within people. Like the temple and the philosophy, he stands alone, apart from the institutions of learning, apart from sites of pilgrimage. He is himself the source of knowledge, and he is himself the pilgrim's destination.

Should all the temples be destroyed, they would spring up again from the seeds of philosophy, or from the presence of a realized man. And if all the scriptures and philosophical treatises were burned, they would be written again from the same source. So, Hinduism cannot be destroyed. It can never be destroyed. It exists as the spirit of religion within each being. Its three aspects, the temple, the philosophy and the *satguru,* individually proficient, taken together make Hinduism the most vital and abundant religion in the world.

Hinduism's Fathomless Diversity

Hinduism has a grand diversity among its many sects. That diversity is itself a strength, showing how broad and encompassing Hinduism is. It does not seek to have all devotees believe exactly alike. In fact, it has no central authority, no single organized institution which could ever proclaim or enforce such sameness. There is an immense inner unity, but the real strength and wisdom of Hinduism is its diversity, its variety. There are so many sects within Hinduism that you could spend a lifetime studying them and never begin to assess them all. More is there than any single human being could assimilate in a single lifetime. Hinduism, therefore, has the magnetism to draw us back into its immensity life after life. Each sect may be said to be a full religion in its own right, with all the increments of faith, with no necessary part missing. Therefore, each sect works for the individuals within it completely, and each tolerates all the other sects. It does not totally divorce itself from the other sects, denying their beliefs, but simply separates to stress or expound a limited area of the vast philosophy, apart from all others, to be understood by the limited faculties of man.

These various sects and divisions within Hinduism all spring from a one source. Most Hindus believe in the transcendental God as well as the personal Lord or God, and yet there is within the boundaries of the faith room for the nonbeliever, for the atheist or for the agnostic who is assessing and developing his beliefs. This brings another unique asset to our religion—the absence of heresy. There is no such thing as a heretic in Hinduism, for there is no single right perspective or belief. Doctrine and *sādhana* are not considered absolutes, but the means to an absolute end, and they can be tailored to individual needs and natures. My *satguru* would say that different prescriptions are required for different ailments.

In Hinduism there is no person or spiritual authority who stands between man and God. In fact, Hinduism teaches just the opposite. The priests in the temples are the servants of the Deity, the helper, the keeper of the Gods' house. He prepares and purifies the atmosphere of the temple, but he does not intervene between the devotee and his God—whichever of the many Gods within our religion that he may be worshiping. Without a mediator, responsibility is placed fully upon the individual. There is no one to intercede on his behalf. He is responsible for his actions, for his thoughts, for his emotions, for his relationship with his God. He must work out his beliefs from the inside without undue dependence upon external influences. Of course, there is much help, as much as may be needed, from those who have previously gone through what he is now going through. It is not enough that he adopts an authorized dogma. He must study and bring the teachings to life from within himself.

Within the philosophy, each philosopher proclaims that God can be found within man if man practices the proper precepts of *yoga* and delves within himself through his *kuṇḍalinī* force. The *guru* himself teaches the awakening of that force and how God can be realized in His transcendental as well as His personal aspect within the sphere of one's own personal experience in this very lifetime if he but pursues the path and is obedient.

Hinduism is unique because God and man, mind and God, instinctive mind, intellectual mind and superconscious mind, can merge as one, according to the evolution of the individual. Each one, according to his own self-created *karma,* has his own fulfillment. Those in the first stages of evolution, whose interests and experiences are basically instinctive, who possess little intellect or mental prowess, are guided by their emotions and impulses are generally fearful. They have a personal experience of the Deity in the temple, but it is generally a fearful experience. They are afraid of God. Alongside of them during a *pūjā* is a great *ṛishi* who has had many hundreds of lives on this planet. He has his own personal experience of God, but it is an experience of love, of oneness and of union. There they are, side by side.

Each experience of God is as real to one as to the other. There is no one in-between, no arbitrator of the experience to compel the one to see God exactly as the other one does.

Within Hinduism is a Place for Everyone

Hinduism is as broad as humanity is, as diverse as people are diverse. It is for the rich and the poor, for the mystic and for the materialist. It is for the sage and the fool. None is excluded. In a Hindu temple you can find every variety of humanity. The man of accumulated wealth is there, supporting the institutions that have grown up around the temple, seeking to spend his abundance wisely and for its best purpose so that good merit may be earned for his next life. The pauper is there, begging in hopes that perhaps he will eat tomorrow and the God will inspire some devotee to give him a coin or two. So, a Hindu temple is a reflection of life, set in the midst of the life of the community. It is not making an effort to be better than the life of the village, only to serve that life and direct it to its next stage of evolution. The same Hindu mind which can consume within it all the religions of the world can and does consume within it all of the peoples of the world who are drawn to the temple by the *śakti,* the power, of the temple. Such is the great embracing compassion of our religion.

The greatness of Hinduism cannot be compared with other religions. There is no basis for comparison. Hinduism has no beginning, therefore will certainly have no end. It was never created, and therefore it cannot be destroyed. It is a God-centric religion. The center of it is God. All of the other religions are prophet-centric. The center of those religions is a great saint or sage, a prophet, a messenger or messiah, some God-Realized person who has lived on earth and died. Perhaps he was born to create that particular sect, that particular religion, needed by the people of a certain part of the world at a certain time in history. The Hindus acknowledge this and recognize all of the world's religious leaders as great prophets, as great souls, as great incarnations, perhaps, of the Gods, or as great realized beings who have through their realization and inward practices incarnated themselves into, or transformed themselves into, eminent religious leaders and attracted devotees to them to give forth the precepts of life all over again and thus guide a tribe, or a nation or a race into a better way of life.

The Hindu mind can encompass this, appreciate it, for it is firmly settled in a God-centric religion. The center of Hinduism is the Absolute, the timeless, formless, spaceless God who manifests as Pure Consciousness and as the most perfect form conceivable, the Primal Soul. He radiates out from

SHRIKANT DAMODAR PANDIT

that form as a myriad of Gods and Goddesses who inhabit the temples and bless the people, inspire the scriptures, inspire the spiritual leaders and uplift humanity in general. It is a one God in many forms. We have recently heard a *sannyāsinī* at the Gaṇeśa Temple in New York describe this in a most wonderful and profound way, "Siva is the fire. Śakti is the heat of that fire. Gaṇeśa is the red color of that fire. Murugan is the light of that fire."

There are nearly a billion Hindus in the world today. That's roughly four times the population of the entire United States. Every sixth person on the planet is a Hindu. Hinduism attends to the needs of each one. It is the only religion that has such breadth and depth. Hinduism contains the Deities and the sanctified temples, the esoteric knowledge of inner states of consciousness, *yoga* and the disciplines of meditation. It possesses a gentle compassion and a genuine tolerance and appreciation for other religions. It remains undogmatic and open to inquiry. It believes in a just world in which every soul is guided by *karma* to the ultimate goal of Self Realization, or *moksha,* freedom from rebirth. It rests content in the knowledge of the divine origin of the soul, its passage through one life and another until maturity has been reached. It offers guidance to all who take refuge in it, from the nonbeliever to the most evolved *mahāṛishi.* It cherishes the largest storehouse of scripture and philosophy on the earth, and the oldest. It is endowed with a tradition of saints and sages, of realized men and women, unrivaled on the earth. It is the sum of these, and more, which makes me boldly declare that Hinduism is the greatest religion in the world.

The above spiritual discourse was given by Satguru Sivaya Subramuniyaswami at Kauai's Hindu Monastery in Hawaii on October 15, 1979.

Sanskṛit Pronunciation

Ucchāraṇa Vyākhyā

उच्चारण व्याख्या

VOWELS
Vowels marked like ā are sounded twice as long as the short vowels. The four dipthongs, e, ai, o, au, are always sounded long, but never marked as such.

अ a as in about
आ ा ā ...tar, father
इ ि i ...fill, lily
ई ी ī ...machine
उ ु u ...full, bush
ऊ ू ū ...allude
ऋ ृ ṛi ...merrily
ॠ ॄ ṛī ...marine
ऌ ḷri ...revelry
ए े e ...prey
ऐ ै ai ...aisle
ओ ो o ...go, stone
औ ौ au ...*Haus*

GUTTURAL CONSONANTS
Sounded in the throat.

क् k ...kite, seek
ख् kh ...inkhorn
ग् g ...gamble
घ् gh ...loghouse
ङ् ṅ ...sing

PALATAL CONSONANTS
Sounded at the roof of the mouth.

च् ch ...church
छ् çh ...chain
ज् j ...jump
झ् jh ...hedgehog
ञ् ñ ...hinge

CEREBRAL CONSONANTS
Pronounced with the tongue turned up and back against the roof of the mouth. These are also known as retroflex.

ट् ṭ ...true
ठ् ṭh ...nuthook
ड् ḍ ...drum
ढ् ḍh ...redhaired
ण् ṇ ...none

DENTAL CONSONANTS
Sounded with the tip of the tongue at the back of the upper front teeth.

त् t ...tub
थ् th ...anthill
द् d ...dot
ध् dh ...adhere
न् n ...not

LABIAL CONSONANTS
Sounded at the lips.

प् p ...pot
फ् ph ...path
ब् b ...bear
भ् bh ...abhor
म् m ...map

SEMIVOWELS

य् y ...yet (palatal)
र् r ...road (cereb.)
ल् l ...lull (dental)
व् v ...voice (labial), but more like *w* when following a consonant, as in the word *swāmī*.
ह् h ...hear (gutteral)

SIBILANTS

श् ś ...sure (palatal)
ष् sh ...shut (cerebral)
स् s ...saint (dental)

ANUSVĀRA ं (ṁ)
Represents the nasal of the type of letter it precedes; e.g.: अंग = *aṅga*. Transliterated as ṁ, or the actual nasal, e.g., ñ. At the end of words it is often म् *(m)*.

AYOGAVAHA ँ ॅ
An accentuated Vedic form of *anusvāra* preceding र ष श स ह. The ँ is used following short vowels, and ॅ follows long vowels.

VISĀRGA (ः) ḥ
Pronounced like *huh* (with a short, stopping sound), or *hih*, after i, ī and e.

AVAGRAHA ऽ
Marks the deletion of initial a after e or o (because of *sandi*). Thus: तेऽब्रुवन्

DAṆḌA
। marks end of sentence.
॥ marks end of stanza.

SPECIAL CHARACTERS

ज्ञ् jñ ...a nasalized sound, like *gya* or *jya*.
क्ष् = क्+ ष् ksh

CONVENTIONS

1. च्छ is transliterated as cçh, and च्च as cch.
2. Geographical terms, e.g., *Himalaya*, generally are given without diacriticals.

Śṛī Gaṇeśasya Svabhāvaḥ

श्रीगणेशस्य स्वभावः

The Nature Of Lord Gaṇeśa

The Nature of Lord Gaṇeśa

A TRIAD OF THREE GREAT PILLARS HAVE HELD HINDUISM HIGH, CENTURY AFTER CENTURY: THE SATGURUS, THE TEMPLES AND THE scriptures. Together they echo the greatness of the loving God Gaṇeśa, the Lord of Dharma, son of Śiva. For untold millennia our *ṛishis* and sages have proclaimed the profound depths of the mind, assuring us that we, too, can and must come to know God and the Gods. It is the living presence of these *satgurus* and their spoken teachings which has brought to life the traditional practices and philosophy of the Sanātana Dharma. Now we shall delve into the nature of Lord Gaṇeśa, what He is like, what functions this great God performs and find out how each seeker can make Him a vital part of daily life's path of experience.

Once a psychic connection is made with Lord Gaṇeśa—the Deity who manifests in several forms, including the elephant-headed Lord of Categories and Remover of Obstacles—one is brought slowly into the mysteries of the Sanātana Dharma. Such an inner connection, which can be as subtle as a feeling, as tenuous as a dream or as bold as a personal visit, is also an entering into one's own *mūlādhāra chakra,* governed by the planet Mercury, for every opening into a new *chakra* is also an introduction to the Deity who governs that state of consciousness and the planet to which that *chakra* is connected.

The Sanātana Dharma, known today as Hinduism, is the only living religion on the planet that does not look to a human founder for its source of inspiration, scripture or historical beginning. It is timeless and ageless. Sanātana Dharma, the root religion of humankind, looks inward for its origins, into the subtle, superconscious realms within the microcosm, which it calls the Kāraṇaloka, Śivaloka or Third World. This great religion has no single organized headquarters on the material plane. Nor does it have a one hierarchy. Who then is in charge of Hinduism? Why, it is none other than our loving Gaṇeśa! He doesn't live in Rome, nor in Salt Lake City. Lord Gaṇeśa lives simultaneously everywhere Hindus worship and pray within themselves. He doesn't have to be reappointed from time to time, because *yugas* and *yugas* ago He was permanently and irrevocably appointed when He was created for this work.

Gaṇeśa, the Great Gatekeeper

Yes, it is the Great Gaṇeśa who is the gateway for seekers into the world's most ancient faith. He is the inner authority, the guardian, the one who grants access to the spiritual mysteries of the Sanātana Dharma. All Hindus worship Him, regardless of their sectarian or philosophical positions. He truly binds them together in His love. This great God is both the beginning of the Hindu religion and the meeting ground for all its devotees. And that is only proper inasmuch as Gaṇeśa is the personification of the material universe. The universe in all of its varied and various magnificent manifestations is nothing but the body of this pompous God.

Gaṇeśa sits on the psychic lotus of the *mūlādhāra chakra,* the ganglia of nerves at the base of the spine within everyone. This *chakra* governs time, matter and memory. As the spiritual aspirant is lifted up from fear and confusion into conscious awareness of right thought, right speech and right action, the *mūlādhāra chakra* becomes activated. It is then that the seeker, with heart filled with love, encounters the holy feet of Lord Gaṇeśa. As the spiritual seeker worships the loving elephant-faced God, clearness of mind comes more and more as he automatically and very slowly enters the Hindu path to enlightenment. Once the connection is firmly established between the devotee and Gaṇeśa, all of the currents of the devotee's mind and body become harmonized. After that strong connection is made, should he falter on the spiritual path, he has gained divine protection.

But the seeker loses one thing. He loses his free, instinctive willfulness. It is lost forever. Yet, it is not a great loss. Man's own personal willfulness, his animalistic free will, is a feeble and insignificant force when compared to Lord Gaṇeśa's divine will. When beholden to God Gaṇeśa and inwardly awakened enough to be attuned to His will, it is then quite natural that the instinctive will bows down. Personal likes and dislikes vanish. Limited faculties of reason and analysis are overpowered and subdued by a greater will, a cosmic will, the will of *dharma.* When sufficient humility has been awakened, it is easy to surrender personal, instinctive willfulness to the greater subsuperconscious will of *dharma.* It happens most naturally, but very slowly, because Lord Gaṇeśa, of all the many Gods, proceeds with methodic deliberation. He is the careful, loving guide on the inner path of all seekers.

Among all the wonderful Hindu Deities, Lord Gaṇeśa is the closest to the material plane of consciousness, most easily contacted and most able to assist us in our day-to-day life and concerns. In His hands Gaṇeśa wields a noose and a goad. With the noose He can hold you close, or hold obstacles close. Gaṇeśa can capture and confine both blessings and obstacles. With the goad Gaṇeśa can strike and repel obstacles. This Lord is called the Remover of Obstacles, but He also places obstacles in our way, for sometimes his devotees are proceeding in the wrong direction, and His obstacles block their progress and guide them slowly back onto the straight path of *dharma.* When instinctive willfulness causes the seeker to decide to step out of the boundaries of *dharma,* the Lord of Obstacles is there to block the way. His emblem is the *swastika,* symbolizing His circuitous course in guiding the seeker through life's perplexing experiences.

Adopted by the Elephant God

Seekers of Truth come from many backgrounds, many religions and have trod many paths. Having become acquainted with Lord Gaṇeśa, they may wonder how their past can participate in their present aspirations. "What am I doing worshiping an elephant-faced God and loving it?" they may wonder. "What do I do now to harmonize this unfoldment with my previous upbringing?"

There is a way to reconcile this subconscious dilemma. Let's not "pack it away in denial," as they say; let's face up to the spiritual awakening. Truth is, you have a loving friend in Gaṇeśa, who, if we may use the word, is the pope of the Hindu religion. And you are by no means alone. One fourth of the human race is acquainted with Gaṇeśa—twenty-five percent of the people on this planet—1.25 billion, and that number is growing year by year.

Our loving Gaṇeśa leads his devotees deep into the oldest religion on planet Earth. There are two ways to come into Hinduism. One is to be born into the Hindu religion and be carried in your mother's arms to the temple, there to be inwardly and psychically connected to our loving God Gaṇeśa. So strong are those early impressions and *saṁskāras* that they carry you through life. Another way is to unfold naturally to the point of being ready to formally enter Hinduism, to supplicate, to sincerely beg the guardians of that religion to allow you to be a part of that immense and ancient tradition. You have to want to be a Hindu so strongly, so sincerely, that Lord Gaṇeśa lifts you out of the fog of the materialistic conscious mind, establishing a connection and a relationship with you. This is a personal relationship with the Deity. There is nobody in-between—just you and the

God, Lord Gaṇeśa. It's like being adopted, in a way. If you were an orphan on the streets of Mexico or on the streets of Madras or on the streets of wherever there are little kids running around, you would be "free." You could go through life listening to no one and exercising unrestricted free will, free instinctive will. If you had a developed intellect, then you could exercise an intellectual will. You could do anything that you wanted to do, absolutely anything. Of course, you would find that as you attempted to fulfill your desires, you were limited, sometimes prevented, by the natural forces within and without. But you could attempt anything.

If you were fortunate enough, foster parents might come along to help you. They would adopt you and take you into their home. Your new mother would begin to lovingly guide and direct your life. She would tell you, "You can play as you like in this room, but not in the others." She is a wise mother and knows that you are accustomed to having your own way, so she lets you play freely within the confines of your own room. But if she catches you playing in another room, she might say firmly, "You may play in your room. Not here in this room." You have lost your free will in being adopted by a mother and father, you are a part of their family now, and your well-being, your education, your training all now come under their will to which you must adjust yourself and obey. They will watch over you and discipline you morning and night. They will protect you from getting into trouble with your "free will." The modern concept of freedom leads to the darker *chakras* below the *mūlādhāra chakra*. Anguish is there.

Developing a Personal Relationship

It is the same when you evolve a relationship, a personal relationship, with the Deity Lord Gaṇeśa. He will not allow you to use your free will to get into difficulties. Guiding you carefully and protecting you along your way in your natural *karma* through life is His concern. Someone once said, "I worship Lord Śiva, I worship Lord Murugan, but I have never really gotten acquainted with Lord Gaṇeśa." I responded, "You worship Śiva and Lord Murugan, and that is wonderful. But unless you have established a personal relationship with Lord Gaṇeśa, your worship of any of the Gods is probably more according to your own thoughts and fancy than true worship. Until you have established a rapport with Lord Gaṇeśa, you cannot establish a relationship with Kṛishṇa, Ayyappan, Amman, Vishṇu, Rāma, Hanuman, Lakshmī, Sitā, Rādharāṇi, Śiva or Murugan outside of your own limited concepts. It is Gaṇeśa who introduces you to the millions of Gods of the Hindu pantheon, none else. That is the way it works."

Yes, little by little, slowly, very slowly, a relationship evolves, a very personal, loving relationship, between the devotee and the elephant-faced God. Psychic protection is granted, physical protection, mental and emotional protection are all granted as boons by Him. He will not allow His devotees to use their free, instinctive willfulness to make more *kukarma* by getting into difficulties. Rather, He will guide them carefully, protecting them every moment along the way so that their natural birth *karmas* may be worked through and *sukarma* created by right living. This is His main concern. Lord Gaṇeśa loves and cares for His devotees. Once the devotee is connected to Him through the awakening of the *mūlādhāra chakra*, loneliness is never experienced.

Gaṇeśa is a truly wonderful, loving God. He has an extraordinary knack for unweaving complicated situations and making them simple. He can unweave his devotees from their *karma*, simplifying and purifying their lives. But this only happens after they have established a personal relationship with Him. Soon thereafter, changes begin to happen in their lives, and when they go through difficult times, they no longer become angry or live in fear or worry. When difficult times come, they know it is because they are being unwound from accumulated and congested, difficult *karmas* or being turned in a new direction altogether. They know that at such a time they have to consciously surrender their free, instinctive willfulness and not fight the divine happenings, but allow the God's divine will to guide their life. Such is the spiritual path of total surrender, known as *prapatti.*

The Meaning of Grace

"What about the grace of the Deity?" seekers often ask. Grace is received from the God when you are consistent in your worship, consistent in your discipline, consistent in your *bhakti,* your devotion. With such a foundation in your life, a great *śakti,* a force or power, will come from Lord Gaṇeśa. This is grace. It is uplifting. It comes unexpectedly. When grace comes, your mind may change and your heart may melt.

Your sight will become clear and penetrating. You may say, "I have been graced to see everything differently." New doors will begin to open for you, and as you go through them, your life will become more full, more wonderful. And the grace of it is that it would not have ordinarily happened to you.

Seekers also inquire, "What is the difference between grace and a boon from the Gods?" Grace is not exactly a boon. A boon comes as the result of something that you ask for and receive. A boon is quite specific. Grace comes because of the state of the soul in conjunction with its particular *karma.* It comes because we have done everything right up to a certain point in time according to the laws of *dharma.* It is then that the grace of the God comes. Grace is not for a specific need or event in our life, as a boon would be. Grace is more of a complete transformation—a metamorphosis. After receiving grace of a God, the devotee can never be the same again, never look at life again in the old way.

By grace we are directed deeper into spiritual life, pointed in the right direction, carefully guided on the San Mārga, the straight path to our supreme God. After grace has been received, our thoughts are enlivened, our life is inspired with enthusiasm and energy, and we live daily in the joyous knowledge that everything is all right, everything is happening around us in accord with our *karma,* our *dharma* and God's gracious will.

The Gods Are Real Beings, Not Mere Symbols

Many people look at the Gods as mere symbols, representations of forces or mind areas. Actually, the Gods are beings, and down through the ages ordinary men and women, great saints and sages, prophets and mystics in all cultures have inwardly seen, heard and been profoundly influenced by these superconscious, inner-plane, inner-galactic beings. Lord Gaṇeśa is just such a being. He can think just as we can think. He can see and understand and make decisions—decisions so vast in their implications and complexity that we could never comprehend them with our human faculties of limited understanding.

In recent history, missionaries and others from the Western religions have told the Indian people over and over again that their Gods are not real beings, but merely symbols of spiritual matters—and unfortunately many have begun to believe this and look at their Gods in this way. Even among Hindus there are quite a few who don't believe in innerworld beings. Their belief is restricted to the people they see in the physical world and that is all. You dare not tell them differently. It is very difficult, but not impossible, to introduce them to the grand philosophy which is based solely on worship, meditation, inner discipline and the search for Absolute Truth. But this is too high-minded for those living in the everyday materialistic consciousness. For the knowledge of inner worlds to become accepted, a personal realization has to occur, and this is a slow process for the materialist, a very slow process, and only Lord Gaṇeśa can help it along. To contact Lord Gaṇeśa, it is imperative that the materialist visit one of His temples or shrines to make initial contact. It only takes one meeting.

How to Approach the Deity

When you approach the Deity, you should believe that Gaṇeśa feels your presence, that He sees you just as you see Him. In thus seeing Him in very human terms, you will get to know Him better. You will develop a very human relationship with Him. It is especially important that you develop this relationship with Lord Gaṇeśa. It will not be difficult to nurture a friendly feeling for Him, because Gaṇeśa is the Deity who governs our instinctive-intellectual state of mind. He governs the instinctive mind of all the animals, the insects, the birds, the fish and governs as well all the forces of *prakṛiti,* nature. Lord Gaṇeśa is also the Deity who governs the higher intellectual mind, of science and profound knowledge. This is why they call Him Lord of Categories. As Lord of Categories, He organizes and clears the intellectual mind so that individual awareness can flow unhindered in the many areas of developing thought. As Lord of Obstacles, He creates and removes obstacles so that *karma* becomes more and more perfect as the refinement process of living through the experiences of life continues.

In the temples of India, even the offerings that come in through the day from pilgrims who bring silver, gold and gifts of all kinds to be placed into the *hundi* are counted at nightfall before the Deity. He sees this and is told of all that was given to him, and He knows. At night the Deity is ceremoniously put to bed. They treat Him in very human terms. In the morning, He is symbolically awakened, then bathed and dressed. The Deity is treated just as if He were a human person. Well, in the Third World that kind of dedication, intense *bhakti*, is noticed and it is appreciated.

Connecting the Three Worlds: Hindu Magic

Now, you might wonder, "Where are the inner worlds?" It is where you were just before you were conceived. They are in the nonphysical microcosm of this macrocosm. When you were conceived, you began to slowly grow a new physical body inside your mother. At that time you were living in your astral body in the nonphysical microcosm. You existed, to be sure, but not in this physical macrocosm.

The *devas* and Deities are all in that nonphysical microcosm. They actually exist inside material existence, for there are many worlds or planes of existence within the physical world. If you were to go into the physical microcosm, into a cell, and into an atom, and into the inside of that and the inside of that, you would come out in the macrocosm of the Gods. This is called the Śivaloka, or Third World. Their macrocosm is bigger than our macrocosm.

The concept of this inner space is different than we ordinarily conceive. Even though their macrocosm exists within this macrocosm, it is larger than this macrocosm. Of course, that immensity is in another dimension, another world. And each world is larger than the one before—the world of departed souls is larger than this physical world, and the world of the Gods is much larger than the heaven worlds. Therefore, in a tiny space in this physical world hundreds of thousands of *devas* exist—in a very tiny space.

Establishing the Link Through *Pūjā*

When the temple priest invokes the inner worlds and the beings within them, he is consciously trying to establish a channel of communication. When he is successful, this physical microcosm opens into the *devonic* macrocosm. In other words, through conscious effort, he connects the inner and outer worlds, even to the point that devotees may see the transfiguration of the God, or Mahādeva, superimposed over the stone image of the Deity in the temple. They can actually see the God, as He is in the inner world. Many, many awakened souls have seen such things—the eyes of the God moving, for instance—and some *gurus* can actually hear the God speak to them. The God is still in the inner world when this happens. It is the temple that has tuned into His world. This is much like live TV. Hundreds of sets can be tuned into the same station at the same time and view actual happenings as they occur.

The God, therefore, does not travel from the altar of one temple to the altar of another temple. The procedure is similar to that of dialing a friend on the telephone and bringing his voice across a vast distance into your ear. The friend can be heard quite clearly, but he has not moved to another place. The telephone could be likened to a connection between the gross and the subtle worlds, the world of matter and the worlds of spirit or *ākāśa.*

Where Do We Go When We "Die?"

Where does the soul go when a person dies? It goes into the subtle microcosm and then into a larger macrocosm, or greater world, and ceases for a time to function in this gross macrocosm because it is not living in a physical body. At death, the soul drops off the physical body and travels in and in and in to subtle worlds, inner worlds of existence that have their own expansive space, their own macrocosm.

Small children, four or five years old, who can speak but have not yet become too immersed in the learned reality of the conscious or external mind, often tell their parents that they remember when they were born and even before. I have had children tell me, "I came from a world that was bigger than this world." And they talked about the activities that go on there and described the people living there. Of course, as they grow older and become involved in the external thought processes, these memories fade away.

This is the kind of experiential knowledge that makes religion come alive in us, more real and useful. True religion should be the most real and solid and certain thing in our entire life. When we ponder these inner worlds, we learn from within ourselves how they relate and interrelate with each other.

Ponder the many visions that prophets have spoken of experiencing, of all the angels or *devas* that have graced mankind with their presence and their prophecies. Ponder the mystic human events that cannot adequately be explained by the rational intellect. Think of them all in terms of the inner worlds of existence, and all will become clear. Yes, one day it will all become clear from the inside of you to the external intellect. This is real knowing. This is the building of faith. This is true Hinduism, the bedrock of daily life. When this knowing comes from the depths of your knowing state of consciousness, the temple will be the home of the Gods to you.

A Meditation on Lord Gaṇeśa

Bhakti is a *yoga,* a definite discipline and practice to be perfected according to the aptitude of the devotee. Here is a meditation that you can follow when you worship that will, when diligently and consistently practiced, bring its own rewards. After bathing and preparing the mind, approach Lord Gaṇeśa in the shrine or temple, bringing a small gift or flower to be placed at His holy feet. Consider that you are approaching and about to meet the most important person in the world. Make your offering and prostrate. In your prostration feel the energies of love and devotion flow along your spine and out through the top of the head and into the home shrine altar or sanctum sanctorum, *garbhagṛiha,* of the temple, and offer those pure actinic energies to Lord Gaṇeśa. Rise and walk slowly three times around the sanctum, always clockwise. Sit before the Deity and bring up the images of your own father and mother, then the family *guru* and finally the *darśana* of the elephant Lord. Now meditate upon His form, His eyes, His ears, His trunk, His two tusks, His belly in which rests the whole world. The first time your mind wanders into the thought patterns of daily life, bring it back to your parents, your *guru* and the first Lord to be worshiped before proceeding on to any other of the 330 million Gods of our ancient Sanātana Dharma.

The objective is to maintain an unbroken continuity of thought and to not allow the mind to wander away from the *darśana* of the God. You can begin this meditation by pondering the obvious physical properties of the worshipful image. If it is made of stone, think of the stone. How large is it? Where was it quarried and how was it carved? What are the various parts of the Deity and what do they mean? What are his symbols and what do they mean? Recall them to memory. If it is a picture of Gaṇeśa, ponder how that picture was produced. Continue to explore the Lord Gaṇeśa with your mind. Later you can move on to less physical points of concentration. You will find that your awareness or mind will wander to unrelated areas, to concerns of the past or worries of the future. When it does, bring awareness back to your point of concentration—the Deity, Lord Gaṇeśa. Begin again your stream of thoughts toward Him, and when the mind once again wanders, use your willpower to bring it back to His *darśana.*

This may be difficult at first, but constant practice will unfold new knowledge from within you, knowledge that you never knew existed and did not learn from the outside. When that happens, concentration is strong and meditation is not far away. You should be able to have twenty, thirty or even fifty thoughts on loving Gaṇeśa in sequence without awareness being distracted into areas of the external mind. It will help if you learn to breathe diaphragmatically during these exercises. Breathe deeply but naturally, without strain or effort. As we control the *prāṇas* of the breath, we simultaneously control awareness so that it remains steady and does not move here and there. You also have to teach the body to sit still, to remain poised and not restless. All of this will come in time, not immediately. Be patient. Never become upset with yourself when distractions arise, for that is a greater distraction still. Simply accept each departure from your concentration as an opportunity to become stronger and more one-pointed, and then quietly and firmly bring awareness back to its subject, Lord Gaṇeśa.

You must teach this simple meditation to your children, and together the entire family will learn much about the Gods of our religion. It will inspire one and all to read more about Them, to study Their stories and memorize Their sacred chants. The Gods will come to life within your own mind and every member of the family as you penetrate behind the symbols and the stories and discover the true nature of Divinities. It is not necessary to practice this meditation for extended periods. A few minutes each day is enough. Once your brief meditation is finished, sit quietly in His *darśana* and enjoy His energies merging with your own *prāṇic* radiations. Take that *darśana* and that love out of the temple when you leave, spreading it among all the peoples of the world that they, too, may come to know and love the pompous God of Hinduism.

Śṛī Gaṇeśasya Patrāṇi

श्रीगणेशस्य पत्राणि

Letters from Lord Gaṇeśa

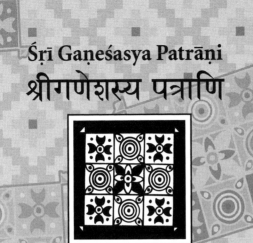

Letters from Lord Gaṇeśa

BLESSINGS FROM ONE OF THE GODS OCCASIONALLY COME TO A GREAT SEER ON EXTREMELY AUSPICIOUS DAYS IN THE FORM of a direct communication. These profound messages are *śruti*, that which is given directly by the Gods. I have received such messages through the grace of my *satguru*, Āsān Yogaswāmī. The vision that is to be described happened while looking clairvoyantly through the *ājñā chakra*, the third eye, at the site of an ancient temple where Kauai's Wailua River merges with the North Pacific Ocean, where the Hawaiian priesthood invoked Gaṇeśa by the name Lono many hundreds of years ago. In my amazement I began to see golden letters written on a great scroll in the *ākāśa*. They became clearer and clearer, until I was able to read them to a scribe. The three scrolls, revealed as letters from Lord Gaṇeśa, are released here for you to enjoy. They are unique messages, couched in exquisite prose and profound philosophy. Through reading them carefully, we may gain a deep understanding of how this great God looks at us and at the physical world.

The First Letter from Lord Gaṇeśa

Glitter, glint and gleam your temples. Clean them well. These are the twinkle that is seen by those who do not see. Guard the gilded throne of Siva's stall. Keep it well lit and open. No night doth fall upon His Holy Form. He is the Sun, both cold and warm.

Piercing vision of deep, inner spinning wheels
pierces through the twinkle and the clinkle of your
temple Ferris wheel. These enjoy the darshan
flooding out. Those caught in chain-like discs of
darker hours see only glitter and the flowers.

When we come, as puja calls, we hardly see those
who cannot see. We see those who can, clear and
crisp, their wasp-like form in the temple,
they adorn lovingly the floors.

I tell you this, Saivite brahmin souls,
have no fear to shine the sparkle all the year.
Gild the gilded forms anew so that your temples
appear just built. Appeal to every chakra wheel;
one spins one and then the other.

Gild—the base, the rudder, the anchor of it
all—doth stimulate. And sound, the one that
hears. Smell, the controller of the glands.
And so, when chakras spin all through,
your temple will be always new.

Once you realize that some see, and others do not
condescend to kneel, but stand and look with
open mouth as sight and sound rush in along with
drainage from the bath, be not afraid to open wide
the door. Those who enter will eventually prostrate
on the floor.

Keep it clean, and gild and glint anew.
That is your job, what you have to do.

Love,
Lord Ganesha

The Second Letter from Lord Gaṇeśa

Keep track of your paces, for your walk makes marks. Each mark is a reward or a stumbling block. Learn to look at the step you have made and the step you have not made yet. This brings you close to Me. I'm not doing anything. If I were any place, I would not be. You are someplace, doing something. You are not.

Insofar as this is a fact, there then is some semblance of Me in you. If you are not what you apparently are and you keep track of your paces fore and aft in your mind, the karma balancing out the dharma is nothing.

Always live as nothing, and your mission is fulfilled immediately. You do not have to live long, but live well while you live. Be sum total at any point in time.

The mind through which you think you travel, or of which you think you are, is not. The awareness of which you think doth travel, or which you think is aware, is not. Therefore, what is?

That is a mystery, to the mind, to awareness, but can be solved by you and Me coming close together. Let's do it now.

Love,
Lord Umaganesh

The Third Letter from Lord Gaṇeśa

Softness comes when you are precise, concentrated, with a sense of penuriousness. The concentration of the intellect comes from a vast, expansive ability accrued which has brought an intricate intellect into usage. Softness, therefore, and a demure countenance and approach to life and associates must be accrued through these means.

If you are not soft in your intellect toward others, refrain from speaking as well as thinking. For the true intellect is accrued from within oneself, and by listening to your guruji, who stimulates the within of you for this to occur.

Obedience is the keynote here, and the ravaging forces of emotion are rejected. And I dismay as you retreat into the devilish worlds in the plane beyond My sight. I sit waiting for your return.

Because I am here, it all exists.
The pole holds the feathers that dance in the wind of desire around it.

Therefore, the thing that we seek is countenance, precision and self-effacement. You know the rest. I wait for your return.

See Me first before each advent into another Lord. I am the gatekeeper, the Mother that cares for you and makes you just right for the Father.

I am the now that makes you ready for the then.
I am the dragon that scares away the untimely
events in your life due to the ignorance
within your dharma.

I am the innovation of your karma,
if you come to Me, My Being, your Being,
when you get here, now.

See to this. I command you. I implore you.
I do puja to you by ringing My little bell in front
of Me, by eating a ball-like sweet goody and by
lighting the fire of Siva, My Father, in My Father,
through My head, burning at the top of My head,
your head, burning there, a flickering flame
burning there on nothing except the dross forces
of your dharma, the accumulation of your karma
of this life, burns away the top of your head,
My head, Our head.

Success on the path is assured for you who have
the good fortune to hear, to see, to read or to have
been told to this message, is blessed by your good
fortune, is in tune with Me, your Self, and I
introduce you to realms beyond your limited
vision at this very moment.

Love,
Lord Ganesh

Śrī Gaṇeśasya Pañchaśaktayaḥ

श्रीगणेशस्य पञ्चशक्तयः

Gaṇeśa's Five Powers

Lord Gaṇeśa's Five Powers

COME NOW, LET US TURN OUR HEARTS AND MINDS TO THE FIVE POWERS OF LORD GAṆEŚA. DEVOTEES HAVE ASKED FOR ELUCIdation on the five profound ways in which this Great God functions in helping us from the inner worlds. For many Hindus in both the East and the West, it is this understanding of the five powerful positive powers, or *śaktis,* of Lord Gaṇeśa and their five powerful *asuric* counterforces that makes religion a working part of the devotee's life and a stabilizing force within the extended family—which embraces kindred, friends, community elders and close business and social associates. This knowledge and practical experience has helped them understand just how intimately Lord Gaṇeśa works with each of us every day in even our mundane life.

There are five great *śaktis* of Lord Gaṇeśa, as He Himself explained. Their positive vibratory rates can be felt through your astral and physical body and should always be with you. "What is this *śakti?*" you may be wondering. It is being in the presence of Divinity. All holy men and women emanate all of these *śaktis,* and you can too, some stronger than others. *Śakti* is divine radiation from the Third World through the Second World into the First. The astral body is in the Second World and lives inside the physical body. It is through the astral body that *śakti* is felt. The *śakti* comes from the Third World and permeates the astral body in the Second World. This is why the physical body sometimes seems to feel "filled up" with *śakti* from deep within, permeating out to the inside of our skin. Deeply awakened souls become so filled with the *śakti* of the Divine that it permeates as cosmic rays out through the skin to the perimeter of the aura, the colorful film of light that surrounds the body. It is felt by other people and attributed as a personal *darśana.*

Thus it can be said that Lord Gaṇeśa has five aspects to His presence. Feeling the presence of the benevolent Deity Gaṇeśa everywhere is the exemplary example of what each soul wishes to attain. His five powers could well be called "the feet of the Lord," for it is at these feet we sit and worship, bringing harmony to our home, among our relatives and friends and business associates, bringing culture, creativity and religion into our life. Crowned by a heartfelt love of God that we then give forth, we are then allowed to perform charities and, in overflowing abundance, prepare the religious edifices for the next generation. Experiencing this personally will take daily meditation.

THE FIRST ŚAKTI

The first *śakti* emanates the feeling of love and compassion that the good person naturally has for his or her immediate family. Love and harmony within the nuclear or joint family is most important to all Hindus, and the beautiful feeling when it exists is the first *śakti* of the Lord. If love abounds in the home and virtue prevails, the home is perfect and its end fulfilled.

THE SECOND ŚAKTI

The second *śakti* is the same feeling but extended to relatives, neighbors and friends, all who are part of the extended family. This is more difficult to hold, as inharmonious conditions often arise. These are called *asuric* forces, which come between people, causing misunderstanding and upsets. Through prayers and through worship, the first *śakti* can be extended beyond the circumference of the immediate family to include acquaintances, relatives and friends. When this vibration of harmony is felt, all the power of the Lord is with you, as the first *śakti* and the second *śakti* merge, bringing in abundance the onrush of the third *śakti.*

THE THIRD ŚAKTI

The third *śakti* of Lord Gaṇeśa is this same love extended to all persons one has dealings with in the external world: business associates, a casual merchant and the public at large. It is honest and harmonious relationships in conducting the business of trade and dealings in goods, finance and the dissemination of the wealth of the world. This is a most important vibration to be felt, and constantly felt. This *śakti* of the Lord is tenuous to hold onto, for worldly and materialistic forces, as you well know, militate against this kind of harmony. But once these lower powers are conquered, worries cease, concerns are alleviated and heartfelt joy comes. Such is the grace of loving Gaṇeśa. As the *Tirukural* (120) declares, "Those businessmen will prosper whose business protects as their own the interests of others."

THE FOURTH ŚAKTI

The fourth *śakti* is that of an outpouring of having held fast to the first three. It is a combination of the first two *śaktis*, stabilized by the third. The fourth *śakti* of Lord Gaṇeśa brings through the creative-intuitive mind—the love of culture and all that it brings, religious protocol and the respect and appreciation of discipline. Here we find the vibration of religion, which brings as a boon creativity in music, art, drama and the dance. It is through these refining rays that religious life is adhered to and congested forces are braided together in a harmonious pattern for a glorious future. It is through the fourth *śakti* that religious practices are performed consistently and the refinements of the past are carried into the future. It also extends to devotion toward one's ancestors and all forms of positive community participation.

THE FIFTH ŚAKTI

The fifth *śakti* of Lord Gaṇeśa is the combination of the first and the third in vibration, and it extends into the wonderful feelings obtained by the outpouring of love of this God. Loving Lord Gaṇeśa with all your heart and soul is the combined merging of these five *śaktis*. This gives the added boon of being able to be charitable, for those who love God perform charity, build shrines and temples and participate in the overflowing generosity from their abundance, earning abundant *puṇya*, fine merit, accrued for this life and passed on to the next. We can see that harmony within the immediate family and harmony extended to all business associates creates the spiritual dynamic within the individual and the group to burst forth into loving this benign God and receiving His material, emotional, intellectual and spiritual abundance.

The Hindu soul who is immersed in the love of the Lord of Obstacles knows he is not the giver, but only the channel for the giving. He is intuitively aware of the *māyā* of his existence, yet acutely aware of the necessity of sharing his natural, blissful state of having become one with this Lord through the first five *śaktis.* Such a devotee is the pillar of the temple, the protector of the *sādhaka,* the respecter of the priesthood, the obedient slave to the holy scriptures, and is seen by all as the compassionate one. Being free in mind, emotion and body, the family that lives basking in the five *śaktis* of Gaṇeśa performs daily *pūjā,* yearly pilgrimage while upholding the five obligations, the *pañcha nitya karmas,* of the Hindu with joyous ease.

The Sixth, Seventh and Eighth *Śaktis*

You may be wondering what lies beyond these first five vibratory rates. Three more śaktis are yet to be unfolded, which we shall do here but briefly.

The sixth *śakti,* entrusted to Lord Murugan, is that of *rāja yoga,* the awakening of the *kuṇḍalinī,* which should never be vied for until the first five vibratory rates of the Lord have been maintained and are a natural part of one's life. The sixth *śakti* is only felt in *yogic* meditation, when the crown of the head becomes the temple—the high-pitched eee tone ringing within it like a temple bell, and the *kuṇḍalinī* awakened, the camphor light aglow. The *yogī* thus locked in his own yoke finds himself seated on the fifth *śakti,* supported by the lotus petals of the other four. In his state of *yoga,* he then merges into *jñāna,* and answers to his deepest philosophical questions come crystal clear as the seventh *śakti* penetrates the *ākāśic* ether of his mind.

The seventh *śakti* is the great ray of the giving forth of spiritual teachings from the brink of the Absolute, at which point Lord Śiva and His son Lord Murugan merge. This great *śakti* is held by the *ṛishis* and the saints of our religion. Lord Murugan Himself is the preceptor of all of our religion. The seventh and eighth *śaktis* are the Śiva-Śakti, the great dance of creation, the eighth being that outpouring power

SHRIKANT DAMODAR PANDIT

felt when mind collects itself when it comes out of the Self, the Absolute, and then forms into manifest knowledge: the seventh śakti.

We shall not concern ourselves now with the sixth, seventh or eighth *śaktis,* for we are to meditate on and bring through the rays of the first five *śaktis* through the worship of Lord Gaṇeśa. These five *śaktis* actually form the basis for all of the religions in the world, though usually not in their entirety. What we call Gaṇeśa worship today is actually the age-old religious pattern performed through eons of time, and is found in some form in each of the eleven religions of the world and in the multitudes of faiths. The height of religious experience in many religions is to uphold these five *śaktis* for society to survive and flourish. And this is basically the extent of most of the world's religions, for once religion is secured in one's life, *rāja yoga*—finding the temple within, going into that temple, merging within the sanctum sanctorum with the Supreme Lord Himself, the father of the great God Gaṇeśa—is the next and most natural unfoldment.

The Hindu who takes such steps into the realms of Lord Murugan, God of all *yoga,* son of Śiva, can rely upon the firm foundation of the first five *śaktis,* which are maintained within him through his personal association with Lord Gaṇeśa. Thus, if he falters in his practice of *yoga,* he does not fall into an abyss. One who does not have the five *śaktis* firmly established in life should not perform the more rigorous *yogas,* lest he or she awaken and invoke the *asuric,* antagonistic forces of the lower worlds which have the power to counteract all of one's previous positive efforts.

Sealing Off the Lower Realms

The higher one climbs toward the summit of Truth, the deeper the abyss that lies below, should he stumble and fall from the path. What happens when seekers on the path detour into lower worlds of contemptuous behavior toward themselves as well as others? Low self-esteem, loneliness, fear, unfounded guilt and remorse all are symptoms of the abyss of consciousness so feared by *devas* and humans alike, and written of in scripture and protected against by spiritual preceptors. It is plain to see that the doors of the *chakras* below the *mūlādhāra* must be firmly closed, sealed off, before serious *yoga* practice is sought for or performed.

The Five-Fold Abyss

What is the abyss? It is the way of *adharma,* and the fate of those who neglect religious practices or fall from any vows they may have taken along the way. There are five abysses and they are the exact opposites in vibration to the first five *śaktis* so carefully guarded by Lord Gaṇeśa.

THE FIRST ABYSS

The first abyss is inharmonious conditions within the home, fighting and squabbling among those who are near and dear to each other. This makes strong *saṁskāras,* or scars, in the subconscious mind and begins to create a subconscious that opposes any kind of furtherance of religious life. The first, therefore, is the deepest abyss and the most difficult to rise out of.

THE SECOND ABYSS

The second abyss is inharmonious conditions and misunderstandings—allowed to exist without apology, recompense or forgiveness—between acquaintances, friends and relatives not living in the immediate home. It is easier to scale the walls of this abyss; it takes a little humility to do so, some understanding and kindness. Lord Gaṇeśa is expert in retrieving souls who invoke His guidance, for He is a Mahādeva who could well be called the master of the conscious and subconscious states of mind. Therefore, Hindus go to Him in all worldly matters. This *asuric* force, propelled by entities of the lower astral, is one which stimulates deteriorating gossip about family and social relationships outside the home. It could cause a wife to speak ill of her husband to a neighbor. It would provoke the spreading of lies about an individual to ostracize him or her from the community or social set.

THE THIRD ABYSS

The third abyss is that of worry and concern. The courts of law handle this one, the collection agencies—and displeased customers. Lack of courtesy in business affairs, the borrowing and the lending of money all together throw their power into making a luscious, comfortable, luxurious abyss of inharmonious conditions within the business world. This *asuric* force stimulates dishonest business dealings, taking advantage of goodwill and trust an establishment has extended. Not honoring commitments when expected is the devilish force that antagonizes. This force also separates people through misunderstanding, causing them to dislike one another. Many people live in this abyss throughout their entire life. It is a welcoming pit that the gravity of desire constantly leads one into. There are many *asuric* people within it to torture as they entertain. However, this abyss can be gotten out of through the careful handling of one's business affairs and consistent religious practice, seeking the help of Lord Gaṇeśa all the way. Within each of these first three pits are *asuric* people on the lower astral plane who aid in distressing the dreams at night; and the vibration within these three abysses is terrible.

THE FOURTH ABYSS

The fourth abyss is a most tenuous one, and even though someone may have avoided falling in the first three, he may still find himself in this one, turning his back on culture, away from music, art, drama and the dance, laughing at religious people and their practices, being content with the dull, drab life of mundane things. Sloth and conceit are found here, along with the smug attitudes of those that have the first three *śaktis* well under control. Here their intellect is God to them; here money is God to them. The reliance on intellect and wealth within this abyss makes it difficult to perceive that someone is there. But being graced with an educated intellect and-or wealth, and perhaps a shallow religious nature, void of deep, heartfelt understanding, the lack of creativity, refined sensibilities and love of God is the key to knowing that, indeed, the fourth abyss lays claim to the soul. This abyss of worldliness could well become the constant fulfillment of desires, one after another, only for the sake of desires and their fulfillment.

This *asuric* force and its representatives on the inner and outer planes, spiritual anacharists and, worse, mercenary terrorists with no cause for a better society, bring the breakdown of religiousness, art, culture and the heritage of the past. In the inner worlds these are well-trained entities, intelligent beings skilled in the black arts, conspiring with their physical-plane, human, counterparts to bring down the nature of humanity to a base level. They have dedicated themselves to destruction for destruction's sake. If you enter into this abyss and the others, you come under their control and become their pupils. This power breeds promiscuity between the sexes and drains the life of man, bringing him firmly into his animal nature, resulting in loss of conscience. When he loses conscience, he no longer suffers remorse or repents for his misdeeds, and hence an *asuric* culture is born for the many who participate in it. Ancestry is forgotten and the ways of the past are put down as no one has time to perfect the refinement and the arts of yesterday, bringing them into today to preserve them for tomorrow.

THE FIFTH ABYSS

The fifth abyss, of course, is that dark night of the soul the religious person goes through when devoid of the childlike spontaneity of spiritual giving. This abyss is found shrouding the soul, disabling him from spontaneously participating in all kinds of religious festivals and events as the opportunities present themselves around the years. The vibration felt by the person who feels nothing when he goes to the temple, sees the Deity as a piece of stone or metal, who observes and faults those around him is as powerful a negative feeling as that felt by the devotee standing next to him weeping because of his love of God—this is the mystery of the fifth *śakti* and its corresponding enshrouding abyss.

Consciously Tuning into the Five Śaktis

To bring religion into one's life requires the worship of Lord Gaṇeśa and the daily tuning into these five great *śaktis.* This worship brings harmony to our home, to our relatives and friends and to business associates. It brings culture, creativity and religion into our life. All this is crowned by such a heartfelt love of God that we can then give forth. We are allowed to perform charities and, in overflowing abundance, prepare the religious edifices for the next generation. This is what our daily *pūjās* and meditation, our pilgrimages and

The Five Śaktis of Lord Gaṇeśa

An Inspired Writing by a Śaiva Monk

Loving Gaṇeśa! Dear to Śiva's men,
Within whose form the world of form resides,
Who earned the mango by a ponderous ken
And made the moon to wax and wane in tides.

Aum Gaṇeśa! Loved by saints and sages,
Whose skillful arms five potent *śaktis* wield
To guide men now as in forgotten ages—
The seeker's shield, the farmer's fertile field.

Aum! Gaṇeśa's first *śakti* is home life,
Protection, harmony, fertility—
Respect becomes the man, as love the wife,
Obedience their cherished offspring's glee.

Aum! Gaṇeśa's second *śakti's* family—
By blood, by marriage and proximity.
Word and thought controlled, like minds agree,
While faithful friends preserve community.

Aum! Gaṇeśa's third *śakti's* the market,
Where commerce earns the earth stability,
Where forthright, selfless merchants, free from debt,
Conceive, produce, exchange prosperity.

Aum! Gaṇeśa's fourth *śakti* brings culture—
Refined expression, graceful artistry
In music, dance, in poetry and sculpture
Or common conduct performed consciously.

Aum! Gaṇeśa's fifth *śakti* is *dharma*—
Fair merit found in virtue's charity—
Where love of God does conquer ancient *karma*
And Śiva's slaves earn grace's rarity.

Jaya Gaṇeśa! Come, our hearts protect
From discord in the home, from strife with friend,
From business misfortune, from art's neglect,
From soul's dark night—these griefs *asuric* end.

Vijñāne Parataścha

विज्ञाने परतश्च

In Science and Beyond

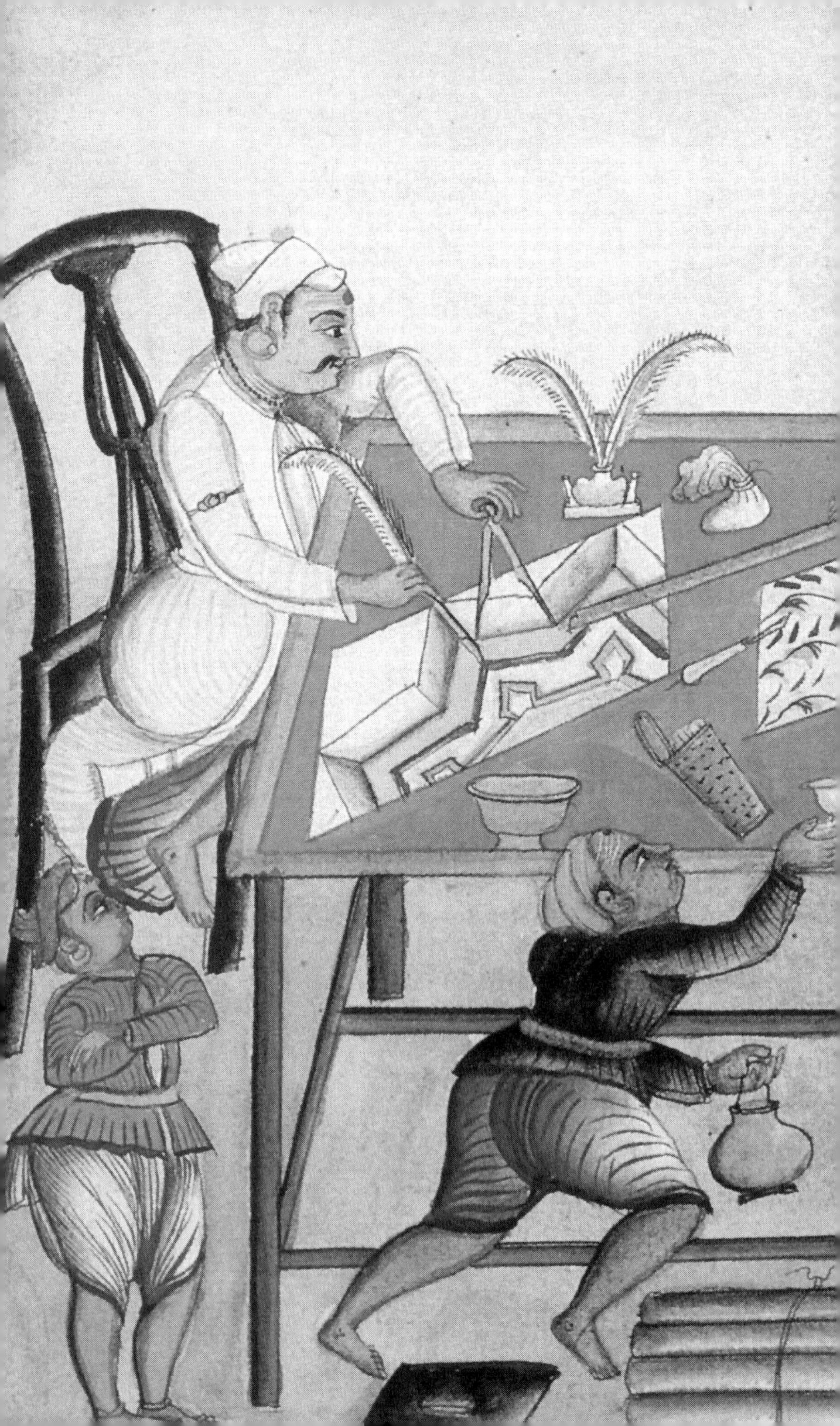

In Science and Beyond

DHARMA, SANĀTANA DHARMA, THE ETERNAL FAITH, HINDUISM, IS THE GREATEST OF ALL RELIGIONS ON THE PLANET, IN MY OPINION, not merely because it is the oldest, the root religion from which all others have sprung forth. It is the greatest because it is the most profound and mystical. No other religion offers such insight into the intricate workings of our universe. More importantly, no other religion offers the grace of a God that is within us as well as within all things outside of ourselves, that is both within form as Saguṇa Brahman and beyond form as Nirguṇa Brahman, and that may be known by the devout seeker even in this life. Little wonder that the Sanātana Dharma, the eternal path, has withstood the ravages of time and stands today as the most advanced system of philosophy and devotion on the earth. It is fully in accord with, and in fact its sages clearly anticipated, the advances of 20th-century science. Hinduism today stands as the religion of the village community as well as the urban family—an enlightened faith for all men in all times. The single most unifying force within Hinduism is Lord Gaṇeśa, son of Śiva-Śakti, beloved Deity of 900 million Hindus.

To Him we offer our reverent love and praise. It is an incontrovertible fact that Lord Gaṇeśa is real, not a mere symbol. He is a potent force in the universe, not a representation of potent universal forces. Abundantly built, Lord Gaṇeśa is said to contain within Himself all matter, all mind. He is the very personification of material existence. We look upon this physical world as the body of Lord Gaṇeśa. In seeing and understanding the varied forces at work in the physical universe, we are seeing and understanding the powers and the being of Lord Gaṇeśa. There is nothing that happens on this material plane of existence except that it is the will of God Śiva and minutely detailed by His beloved son Lord Gaṇeśa. When this is known, life becomes a daily joyous experience, for we know that all that happens—whether it brings sorrow or happiness, whether we personally wanted it to happen or not, still we know that all that happens—is right and good, for it flowed from the wisdom and benevolent kindness of our loving Gaṇeśa, the gracious Lord of Dharma. This wonderful spirit all Hindus strive to carry into daily life—a complete trust that all that happens is for the best, a full knowing that the Supreme God's will prevails everywhere and that the elephant-faced God is caring for each detail every minute of every hour of the day.

Hinduism is at the heart of science, and yet its understanding of the universe lies beyond the most advanced scientist's conceptualization. Modern science, like the Vedic *ṛishis,* describes the whole of the universe as energy in one form or another. Matter itself is merely condensed energy, as Einstein's renowned formula $E=MC^2$ proclaims in mystic brevity.

A Meditation on the Gods and Three Forms of Energy

There are three strong forces at work in the universe: gravity, electromagnetism and the nuclear force. On the following pages we offer a meditation comparing these three energies that are affecting our lives all the time to the powers of Lord Gaṇeśa, Lord Murugan and God Śiva. It is a general analogy—not meant to be theologically perfect—humbly offered as an aid to understanding the unique characteristics of the Deities.

Once Lord Gaṇeśa appeared to me as I was slumbering in a half-waking state in a family's home close to the Kumbalavalai Gaṇeśa Temple in Alaveddy in northern Sri Lanka. He pointed out that the gardener had unnecessarily broken a branch off a tree while pruning, and that this small happening had immediately affected the whole universe. Such instantaneousness is Gaṇeśa's way, and such vastness is His hallmark, as we shall soon see. We can then liken His nature to gravity, as one gravitational event in one part of the universe affects all other parts of the universe at that very instant, no matter how distant. The nine planets in this solar system affect all humans and plants in their interaction, so precise is our loving Gaṇeśa's mind, the Lord of Karma, the Lord of Dharma.

When I was trying to buy the original building that the Sri Subramuniya Ashram in Northern Sri Lanka was founded in, much opposition was experienced from the owners, but finally we prevailed. Soon after I had an early morning vision in which Gaṇesa was sitting on my knee as the baby elephant, Pillaiyar. With His soft face pressed against my cheek, He said, "We have accomplished the unaccomplishable." I knew then the building and all that was to go on within it was blessed by His loving grace. This has proven true through the many decades that followed. The doors and windows of my ashram have since opened on all continents as the devotees who learned of their religion there experienced the diaspora of Tamilians into nearly all the countries of the world. They now carry forth with great vigor all they learned at our little ashram, keeping it all in practice today as it was so many years ago.

This showed me that if you forge ahead for a good cause, even when all the forces of the universe align themselves against you, including society itself, you will succeed. It's a little like a great elephant walking through the forest, clearing all barriers for those who follow. Such blessings come to those who follow Gaṇeśa. Slowly the forces will clear, and all benefit from His grace.

Gravitational Force

Tradition describes the entire universe as being contained in Lord Gaṇeśa's big belly. Thus we look upon Him, in this meditation, as the overlord Who holds sway over the material universe, the sum of cosmic mass; and one of His potencies is gravity. Gravity is a mysterious force to the scientist, even today. It is the galactic glue which draws and holds larger mass together, and gives order to the macrocosm. It is an instantaneous force, so that when one celestial body moves in a remote corner of a galaxy, all other masses throughout the galaxy adjust simultaneously, even though it would take light at its incredible speed millions of years to travel the distance. This implies to the scientist what the Hindu knew from the beginning, that space and time are relative concepts and that there is a "something" that exists everywhere in the universe at once. Like gravity, Lord Gaṇeśa is totally predictable and known for orderliness. Without gravity, the known galactic systems could not exist. Masses would stray apart; all organization of life as we know it would be impossible. Gravity is the basis of ordered existence in the macrocosm, and our loving Gaṇeśa holds dominion over its mysteries.

Electromagnetic Force

Within and between the atoms which comprise our physical universe there reigns a second force: electromagnetism. Lord Murugan, Kārttikeya, holds sway over the forces which bind sub-atomic particles together. The electromagnetic force is many magnitudes greater than the gravitational force, but because it works in the microcosm of existence, it has less influence on our daily lives than the gravitational force. Similarly, Gaṇeśa is more involved in our day-to-day concerns than is Lord Murugan, whose power is electric, given more to change than to order, more to the unsuspected than to the predictable. Like the powerful forces that bind together the atomic systems of protons, neutrons, electrons, quanta, quarks and other sub-atomic "particles," Lord Murugan's *śakti* works deeply within us, within our spiritual sphere, within the great depths of the mind. His electric power issues forth from the *śakti vel.* Just as energy races through the universe in the form of radio, radar and light waves, x-rays, heat, gamma and cosmic rays, so does Murugan's electric *śakti* impact our life. Just as we experience light and darkness, positive and negative potential, so do the electromagnetic forces issue forth from Murugan's realm of positive and negative forces, of *devas* and their *asuric* counterparts.

Like gravity, Lord Gaṇeśa is always with us, supporting and guiding our physical existence. And just like electrostatic energy, Lord Murugan is most often invisible, working in a sphere of which we are not always conscious, present in our lives through His radiant energies and light, yet not so apparently known as Lord Gaṇeśa. The ancient *Āgamas* offer a more philosophically technical summary of the above. They declare that Gaṇeśa rules over *aśuddha māyā*, the gross energies of the odic realms from the thirteenth tattva to the 36th. Muruga's domain, they state, is *śuddhāśuddha māyā*, the realms of actinodic energy, being the sixth to the twelfth *tattvas.* Finally, they declare that Siva's domain is *śuddha māyā*, the purely spiritual realms of actinic energy, being the first to the fifth *tattvas* in the unfolding of the universe.

Atomic or Nuclear Energy

God, Śiva, is the Lord of Lords and the source of all energies in the universe. His is the most interior sphere of all—the nuclear energies within sub-atomic particles and the essence even of that. Of all energies, the nuclear energy is by far the most powerful; and of all the Hindu Gods, God Śiva reigns supreme. At the core of matter, Lord Śiva whirls through His Cosmic Dance as Naṭarāja. Never has a greater conception been seen by seers to describe the divine operations of the universe. We quote from the book, *The Tao of Physics,* by noted physicist and researcher Fritjof Capra:

> The dance of Śiva is the dancing universe; the ceaseless flow of energy going through an infinite variety of patterns that melt into one another. Modern physics has shown that the rhythm of creation and destruction is not only manifest in the turn of the seasons and in the birth and death of all living creatures, but is also the very essence of inorganic matter. According to quantum field theory, all interactions between the constituents of matter take place through the emission and absorption of virtual particles. More than that, the dance of creation and destruction is the basis of the very existence of matter, since all material particles "self-interact" by emitting and reabsorbing virtual particles. Modern physics has thus revealed that every subatomic particle not only performs an energy dance, but also *is* an energy dance—a pulsating process of creation and destruction. For the modern physicist, then, Śiva's dance is the dance of subatomic matter, a continual dance of creation and destruction involving the hole cosmos, the basis of existence and of all natural phenomena. The metaphor of the Cosmic Dance thus unifies ancient mythology, religious art and modern physics. It is indeed, as Coomaraswamy has said, "poetry, but science nonetheless."

Hinduism's Unsurpassed Cosmology

Hindus may be justifiably proud of a religion which postulated thousands of years ago a cosmology that only today is being discovered and appreciated by science through the ponderous process of reason and empirical proof. Hinduism knew the truth of the source and organization of the universe long before Newton and Einstein confirmed the validity of our world view. While many Western religious systems stand opposed to science or alter their beliefs according to its evolving conclusions, it is one of the great heritages of the Hindu perception of the all-pervasive God, soul and cosmos

that we have spiritual Truths that are in complete accord with and cannot be refuted by modern science.

When the astrophysicist ponders the expanding and contracting nature of the universe, he is contemplating the Hindu view of existence as the day and night of Brahmā, a nonlinear conception of time and space that manifests and then undergoes total absorption in *mahāpralaya,* then manifests again in unending cycles. And when that same theoretical, scientific mind contemplates the end of the cycle of contraction wherein all matter-energy is assembled together, he is contemplating the "cosmic egg," Brahmāṇḍa, of Hindu cosmology. And when high-energy technicians assembled in the 1970s in California to construct the world's largest and most powerful particle accelerator, they went to the great Swāmī Muktānanda Mahārāj of Ganeshpuri, India, and asked him to name it for them. The *siddhayoga satguru* aptly named it "Shiva." Hinduism, the Hindu-inspired faiths of Buddhism, Sikhism, Jainism and most indigenous faiths offer knowledge and insights to science; religion is once again cooperating with science in the quest for knowledge. No wonder we boldly proclaim Hinduism the greatest religion in the world.

Gaṇapateḥ Svarūpāṇi

गणपतेः स्वरूपाणि

Forms of Gaṇeśa

The Forms of Gaṇeśa

EVERYWHERE IN THE MACROCOSM IS OUR BELOVED, BENEVOLENT DEITY GAṆEŚA, AT EVERY POINT IN TIME, IN THE FORCES OF family, community, commerce and *dharma* that shape our lives, as well as in our culture—indeed all cultures of the world—in the physical universe and within our hearts. Of course, He is most present in the consecrated temple or road-side shrine from which His grace radiates out from the world of the Gods. Gaṇeśa is the Lord of beginnings, guiding the practical aspects of our lives that we may best fulfill *dharma.* For the Hindu, Gaṇeśa is easily contacted, and He is thought of as lenient of our errors and shortcomings, most understanding of our humanness. So vast is Gaṇeśa's Being that He cannot be contained by any single concept, and therefore He is portrayed in many forms. He is each of them, and He is all of them.

Gaṇeśa is a word derived from the Sanskṛit roots *gaṇa,* meaning "the hosts, multitudes or troops of demigods, especially the retinue of Lord Śiva under the rule of Gaṇeśa," and *Īśa,* meaning "ruler, lord or sovereign." This is virtually synonymous with the word *Gaṇapati.*

As Gaṇapati, Lord Gaṇeśa is the leader of the *gaṇas,* ruling over the celestial hosts, over the benign as well as the malevolent inner-plane beings. He controls them not as Lord Murugan does, through bravery and forcefulness, but by strategy and intelligence. We follow the path of Lord Gaṇeśa when we resort to discrimination and sagacity to resolve our difficulties, when we proceed past obstacles in a slow, prudent and well-planned manner. Lord Gaṇeśa is not in a hurry. He is cautious. He is patient, willing to await the right time for events to take place.

As Vighneśvara, Lord Gaṇeśa is Lord of Obstacles, creating difficulties and obstructions if the time is wrong for us to proceed and removing those same obstacles when our success is assured. It is to Vighneśvara that we supplicate before we undertake a task, plan a change in our life or begin the worship any of the other Gods.

As Ekadanta, Lord Gaṇeśa is the Single-Tusked One, the Patron of Literature who, when all others failed, Himself undertook to scribe the great epic, *Mahābhārata,* dictated to Him by sage Vyāsa. He offers us here the lesson in life that knowledge and *dharma* are of utmost importance, worth sacrificing even pride and beauty to attain.

As Siddhidātā, Lord Gaṇeśa is the Giver of Success associated with bountiful harvests and general abundance in life. It is said that Lord Gaṇeśa is the material manifestation of the *manas,* or mind, of Lord Śiva, and that He embodies the five elements—earth, air, fire, water and ether—and guides the elemental forces that produce and maintain order in the universe.

The *Mudgala Purāṇa,* an ancient text on Lord Gaṇeśa, cites eight forms of Gaṇeśa, who prevail over eight human weaknesses or demons. Ekadanta is the conquerer of Moda, arrogance. Dhumravarṇa (smoke colored) overcomes Abhimāna, pride; Vakratuṇḍa (curved trunk) is the vanquisher of Matsarya, jealousy; Mahodara (big belly) is lord of Moha, infatuation; Gajānana (elephant face) conquers Lobha, greed; Lambodara (corpulent belly) overcomes Krodha, anger; Vikaṭa (deformed) conquers Kāma, lust; Vighnarāja (king of obstacles) prevails over Mamatā (ego). So now we can see that our Loving Gaṇeśa is "there" for even the lowest of the low, that there is hope for everyone and that there really is "no intrinsic evil," only a seemingly variation of the past containing all that has to be learned to live and grow from a young soul to an older one and then mature into *ṛishi* consciousness. He is "there for us." Yes, there is hope for all, and none are damned forever. It is our Loving Gaṇeśa who eventually introduces us to His brother, our Loving Murugan, the God Who sits upon the *maṇipūra chakra,* center of willpower.

The Two Śaktis of Lord Gaṇeśa

There is a confusion regarding the two consorts of Lord Gaṇeśa: Buddhi and Siddhi, with whom He is often depicted. Buddhi is wisdom, or more precisely sagacity, the intelligent and discriminating use of knowledge. Siddhi is success, or more precisely fulfillment, accomplishment or attainment. While in North India Gaṇeśa is conceived as having two consorts, in the South He is looked upon as a *brahmachārī,* or bachelor. Esoterically, it must be stressed that none of the Gods has a wife. Their consorts are not to be considered as separate from them, but as aspects of their being, as their *śakti,* or power. The Mahādevas, who live in the inner Third World, cannot be likened to men and women who live on the earth, known as the First World. They exist in perfectly evolved soul bodies, bodies which are not properly differentiated by sex. They are pure beings made of pure consciousness and light; they are neither male nor female. To better understand these divine Gods, we sometimes conceive of them as being the man if they are strong in expression or the woman if they are gentle and compassionate. In truth, this is a misconception. There are no husbands and wives in the vast superconscious realms of the Third World, or Śivaloka. Thus, Buddhi and Siddhi are properly seen as the two *śaktis*—wisdom and success—of the great Gaṇeśa, and not as His so-called consorts. These two represent benefits or boons accrued by His worshipers. In an inner sense, Buddhi and Siddhi are the *iḍā* and *piṅgalā nāḍīs,* the female and male currents, both of which are embodied within the being of Gaṇeśa, corresponding to Vallī and Devayāni, the mythological consorts of Lord Murugan.

Thirty-Two Forms of Gaṇeśa

In temples and shrines around the planet, from Moscow to London, from Durban to Kuala Lumpur, Gaṇeśa's worshipful image, or *mūrti,* appears in many forms. The *Mudgala Purāṇa,* in addition to the above eight, lists thirty-two. We present sketches here of these on the following pages. Children will enjoy coloring them. It may interest you to know that the first sixteen *mūrtis,* the Shoḍaśa Gaṇapati, are installed in an eight-sided, chariot-shaped structure at the Śri Śaṅkara Maṇḍapam of Rameshvaram, South India, established by the late Śrī lā Śrī Chandraśekharendra Saraswatī, 68th preceptor of the Kanchi Kamakoti Pītham.

The Quiet Within

Our Loving Gaṇeśa's a powerful God
Yet, He is so quiet you might think it odd
That such a meticulous, intricate soul
Would care to guide all of our *karma* so old.

Indeed it is fortunate that He is so near
For if He were not we would hardly be here,
For He holds the base *chakra* so firmly in place
That we may thus live in this one time in space.

Pray to him dearly and truth you'll be seeing
That the quiet inside is the cave of your being
To attain through your striving, to be quiet within
That the heritage of all happy births you will win.

1

Bāla Gaṇapati

बालगणपति

Bāla Gaṇapati is the "childlike" God of golden hue. In His hands He holds a banana, mango, sugar cane and jackfruit, all representing the earth's abundance and fertility. His trunk garners His favorite sweet, the *modaka.*

2
Taruṇa Gaṇapati
तरुणगणपति

Eight-armed, Taruṇa Gaṇapati, the "youthful," holds a noose and goad, *modaka*, wood apple, rose apple, His broken tusk, a sprig of paddy and a sugar cane stalk. His brilliant red color reflects the blossoming of youth.

3

Bhakti Gaṇapati

भक्तिगणपति

Shining like the full moon during harvest season and garlanded with flowers, Bhakti Gaṇapati, dear to devotees, is indeed pleasant to look upon. He holds a banana, a mango, coconut and a bowl of sweet *pāyasa* pudding.

4

Vīra Gaṇapati

वीरगणपति

As Vīra Gaṇapati, the "valiant warrior," Gaṇeśa assumes a fierce, commanding pose, with sixteen-arms, holding every variety of weapon: a goad, discus, bow, arrow, sword, shield, spear, mace, a battleaxe, trident and more.

5
Śakti Gaṇapati
शक्तिगणपति

Four-armed and seated with one of His *śaktis* on His knee, Śakti Gaṇapati, the "powerful," of orange-red hue, guards the householder. He holds a garland, noose and goad, and bestows blessings with right hand in *abhaya mudrā*.

6

Dvija Gaṇapati

द्विजगणपति

Four-headed Dvija Gaṇapati, "the twice-born," is moon-like in color. Holding a noose, a goad, an *ola* leaf scripture, a staff, water vessel and a strand of *japa* beads, He reminds one and all of the urgency for disciplined striving.

7

Siddhi Gaṇapati

सिद्धिगणपति

Golden-yellow Siddhi Gaṇapati, the "accomplished" one, is the epitomy of achievement and self-mastery. He sits comfortably holding a bouquet of flowers, an axe, mango, sugar cane and, in His trunk, a tasty sesame sweet.

8

Ucçhishṭa Gaṇapati

उच्छिष्टगणपति

Ucçhishṭa Gaṇapati is "Lord of blessed offerings" and guardian of culture. Of blue complexion and six-armed, He sits with His Śakti, holding a *vīṇā,* pomegranate, blue lotus flower, *japa mālā* and a sprig of fresh paddy.

9

Vighna Gaṇapati

विघ्नगणपति

Vighna Gaṇapati, Lord of "obstacles," is of brilliant gold hue and bedecked in jewels. His eight arms hold a noose and goad, tusk and *modaka,* conch and discus, a bouqette of flowers, sugar cane, flower arrow and an axe.

10

Kshipra Gaṇapati

क्षिप्रगणपति

Handsome, red-hued Kshipra Gaṇapati, the "quick-acting" giver of boons, displays His broken tusk, a noose, goad and a sprig of the *kalpavṛiksha* (wish-fulfilling) tree. In His sturdy trunk He holds a tiny pot of precious jewels.

11

Heramba Gaṇapati

हेरम्बगणपति

Five-faced, white in color, Heramba Gaṇapati, "protector of the weak," rides a big lion. He bestows the gestures of protection and blessing while holding a noose, *japa* beads, axe, hammer, tusk, garland, fruit and *modaka*.

12
Lakshmī Gaṇapati
लक्ष्मीगणपति

Lakshmī Gaṇapati, pure white giver of success, sits flanked by Wisdom and Achievement. Displaying *varada mudrā,* He holds a green parrot, a pomegranate, sword, goad, noose, sprig of *kalpavṛiksha* and a water vessel.

13
Mahā Gaṇapati
महागणपति

Accompanied by one of His *śaktis*, Mahā Gaṇapati, "the great," is red-complexioned and three-eyed. He holds His tusk, a pomegranate, blue lily, sugar-cane bow, discus, noose, lotus, paddy sprig, mace and a pot of gems.

14

Vijaya Gaṇapati

विजयगणपति

Four-armed, of red hue, and riding His resourceful Mūshika, Vijaya Gaṇapati is the "victorious" bestower of success. He holds His broken tusk, the elephant goad, a noose and a delicious, golden mango, His favorite fruit of all.

15
Nṛitya Gaṇapati
नृत्यगणपति

The happy "dancer," Nṛitya Gaṇapati, is a four-armed golden *mūrti*, with rings on His fingers, holding a tusk, goad, noose and *modaka* sweet. He prances under the *kalpavṛiksha* tree, epitomizing lively activity and joy.

16

Ūrdhva Gaṇapati

ऊर्ध्वगणपति

Seated with one of His *śaktis* on His left knee, Ūrdhva Gaṇapati is the "elevated" Lord of golden hue. In His six hands He holds a sprig of paddy, a lotus, the sugar cane bow, an arrow, His broken ivory tusk and a blue water lily.

17

Ekākshara Gaṇapati

एकाक्षरगणपति

Ekākshara, of "single-lettered" (*gaṁ*), is three-eyed, of red complexion and attire. Crescent moon on His crown, He sits in lotus pose upon Mūshika, offers the boon-giving gesture and holds a pomegranate, noose and goad.

18

Varada Gaṇapati

वरदगणपति

Varada Gaṇapati, the boon-giver with prominent third eye of wisdom, holds a dish of honey, the noose and the goad and conceals a pot of jewels in His trunk. His *śakti* is at His side, and the crescent moon adorns His crown.

19

Tryakshara Gaṇapati

त्र्यक्षरगणपति

Tryakshara Gaṇapati, the Lord of "three letters" (A-U-M), is gold in color and has fly whisks in His big floppy ears. He carries the broken tusk, goad, noose and mango, and is often seen holding a delicious *modaka* in His trunk.

20

Kshipra Prasāda Gaṇapati

क्षिप्र प्रसादगणपति

Kshipra Prasāda Gaṇapati, the "quick rewarder," presides from a *kusha*-grass throne. His big belly symbolizes the manifest universe. He holds a noose, goad, tusk, lotus flower, pomegranate and a twig of the wish-fulfilling tree.

21

Haridrā Gaṇapati

हरिद्रागणपति

Haridrā Gaṇapati, the golden one dressed in bright yellow vestments, sits calmly on a posh, regal throne. Along with His tusk and a *modaka,* He wields a noose to hold devotees close and a sharp goad to inspire them onward.

22
Ekadanta Gaṇapati
एकदन्तगणपति

Ekadanta, He of "single tusk," is known for His blue color and large pot belly. This *mūrti* of the elephant God holds an axe for cutting the bonds of ignorance, prayer beads for *japa*, a *laḍḍu* sweet and His broken right tusk.

23

Sṛishṭi Gaṇapati

सृष्टिगणपति

Riding on His large friendly mouse, Sṛishṭi Gaṇapati is the Lord of happy "manifestation." This active God, of red complexion, holds His noose and goad, His tusk, representing selfless sacrifice, and a perfect mango.

24
Uddaṇḍa Gaṇapati
उद्दण्डगणपति

Uddaṇḍa Ganapati is the bold "enforcer" of *dharma,* the laws of being. His ten hands hold a pot of gems, a blue lily, sugar cane, a mace, a lotus flower, a sprig of paddy, a pomegranate, noose, garland and His broken tusk.

25

Ṛiṇamochana Gaṇapati

ऋणमोचनगणपति

As Ṛiṇamochana Gaṇapati, the elephant God is the remover of humanity's bondage, dressed in red silk with skin of white crystalline hue. He bears a noose and a goad, His milk-white tusk and a choice fruit, the rose apple.

26
Ḍhuṇḍhi Gaṇapati
ढुण्ढिगणपति

Red-hued Ḍhuṇḍhi Gaṇapati, "the sought after," holds a strand of *rudrāksha* beads, His broken tusk, an axe and a small pot of precious gems thought to represent the treasury of awakenings He saves for all ardent devotees.

27

Dvimukha Gaṇapati

द्विमुखगणपति

Dvimukha Gaṇapati's two faces remind us that the elephant God sees in all directions. His lovely blue-green form is dressed in red silk, He wears a jewel-studded crown and holds a noose, goad, His tusk and a pot of gems.

28
Trimukha Gaṇapati
त्रिमुखगणपति

Trimukha Gaṇapati, the contemplative "three-faced" Lord of red hue, sits on a golden lotus flower, telling His beads, holding a noose, goad and vessel of nectar. He gestures protection with a right hand and blessings with a left.

29

Sinha Gaṇapati

सिंहगणपति

Sinha Gaṇapati, white in color, rides astride a lion and displays another in one hand, symbolizing strength and fearlessness. He also holds a *kalpavṛiksha* sprig, the *vīṇā,* a lotus blossom, flower bouquet and a *kumbha* of jewels.

30
Yoga Gaṇapati
योगगणपति

Yoga Gaṇapati is engaged in *mantra japa,* knees strapped in meditative pose, hands holding a *yoga* staff, sugar cane stalk, a noose and prayer beads. His color is like the morning sun, and blue garments adorn His form.

31

Durga Gaṇapati

दुर्गगणपति

Durga Gaṇapati, the "savior," waves the flag of victory over darkness. This magnificent *mūrti* is of deep gold hue, dressed in red, holding a bow and arrow, noose and goad, prayer beads, broken tusk and a rose apple.

32

Saṅkaṭahara Gaṇapati

संकटहरगणपति

Saṅkaṭahara Gaṇapati, the "dispeller of sorrow," is of sunlike hue, dressed in blue, seated on a red lotus flower. He holds a bowl of pudding, a goad and noose while gesturing the boon-granting *varada mudrā* with one right hand.

Gaṇeśa Iconography

By Dr. L.S. Madhava Rao,
From "Gaṇeśa As Primus Inter Pares,"
Published in the Organiser, *September 18, 1994*

In every Hindu function, invocation to Lord Gaṇeśa for His blessings takes precedence over all other Gods to ward off any mishap. This has been the practice from the Vedic times. Every part of Gaṇeśa's body, such as ear, nose, eyes, trunk, has some significance. One has only to know it, believe in it and follow it. His intellect is par excellence. A critical examination of the various names of the Deities will enable us to know and trace the features of religious development and understand the religious tendencies of the people. Here an attempt is made to highlight how Lord Gaṇeśa in His different *bhaṅgimas* (postures and attitudes) is worshiped in *Āgamic* temples.

1. Icons without headdress in the sitting pose and with two arms: To this class belong two variations. The first is the prevalent *utkuṭakāsana* ["sitting on the hams" with one or both knees raised] see illustration, page 93). Second is Gaṇeśa seated in *padmāsana,* lotus pose, with legs crossed, which is quite rare.
2. Gaṇeśa icons with two arms and headdress: These images are mostly carved out of stone and normally belong to a period between the 9th and 12th centuries. These are represented in the usual *utkuṭaka* pose, and the proboscus is shown taking a left turn and eating from a bowl of pudding held in the left hand.
3. Four-armed figures without *alaṅkāra* [ornamentation] and *prabhāvalī* [shrouding arch]: These are discernable specimens of early Gaṇapati sculpture with four arms, devoid of any kind of ornamentation and with little proportion.
4. Gaṇapati icons with four arms, ribbon-like *prabhāvalī,*

jaṭāmukuṭa [crown of matted hair] and *udarabandha* [waist band]: These figures are usually ascribed to the period between the 9th and 12th centuries. They are mostly carved out of hard granite, and they present a pleasant and elegant form.

5. Gaṇapati icons with four arms and with bowl-like *kinita* or with conical or *karaṇḍa mukuṭa* [basket-shaped crown]: This type of Gaṇapati image is ascribable to the 10th, 11th or 12th centuries. They may not have the mount or profusion of *alaṅkara*. The *prabhāvalī* resembles a semicircular tape or is flame-like.
6. Gaṇapati icons representing the Hoysala type: These figures are known for their profusion in ornamentation, delicacy of taste and elegance.
7. Gaṇapati icons with the usual *nāgabandha, vāhana, karaṇḍa mukuṭa* and conventionalized form of details: These figures are assigned to the period between the 14th and 18th centuries. They represent the various forms of Gaṇapati according to the textual prescription.
8. 

   Gaṇapati icons in *tribhaṅga:* Hitherto, four bronzes have been discovered in the *tribhaṅga* pose. Three are ascribed to the 10th century. [At left is an example of *tribhaṅga* in *nṛitya* (dancing) pose, from a *sthapati's* sketch on a workshop wall in Mahabalipuram, Tamil Nadu.]
9. Nṛitya Gaṇeśa, the dancing form: Only two [ancient] icons of this type have come to light so far. One is a small (20cm high) stone icon at Hariharakshetra, Subrahmanya. The other is a bronze in the Raghavendra Maṭha in Udīpi. The latter is a bronze of considerable iconographic interest. In features, although it presents conventional forms, its theological background is rather unique.

Gaṇeśa's Seating and Standing Poses

Illustrations of Poses
In Gaṇeśa Representation

Utkuṭ akāsana
Seven variations of Gaṇeśa's usual sitting pose, with one or both knees raised.

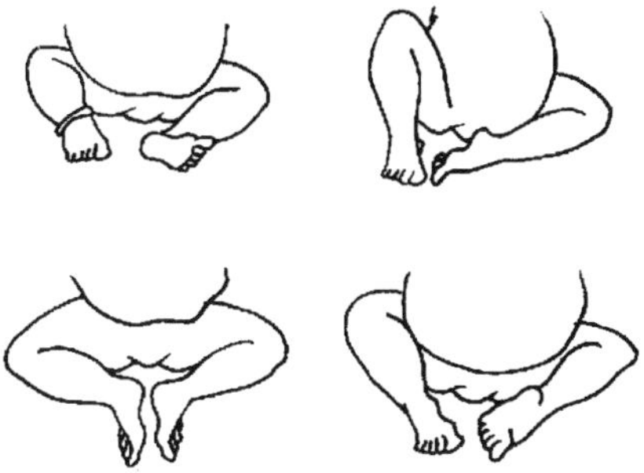

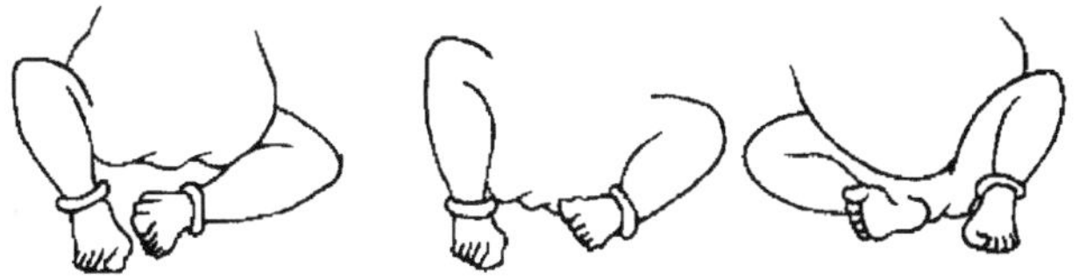

Lalitāsana: Playful, charming poses.

Nṛitya
Three dancing poses, the last in *tribhaṅga.*

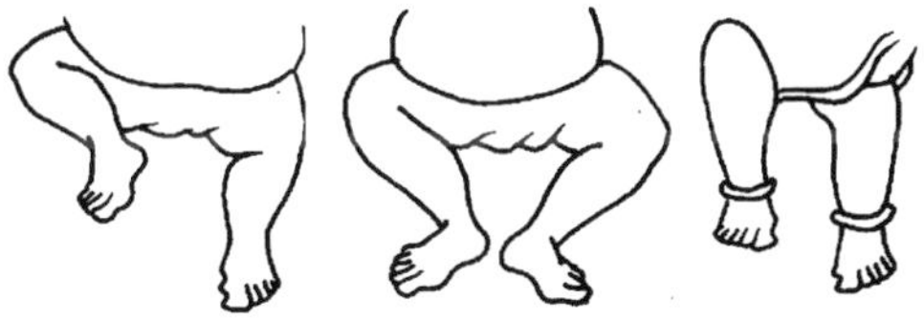

Other Seated Postures

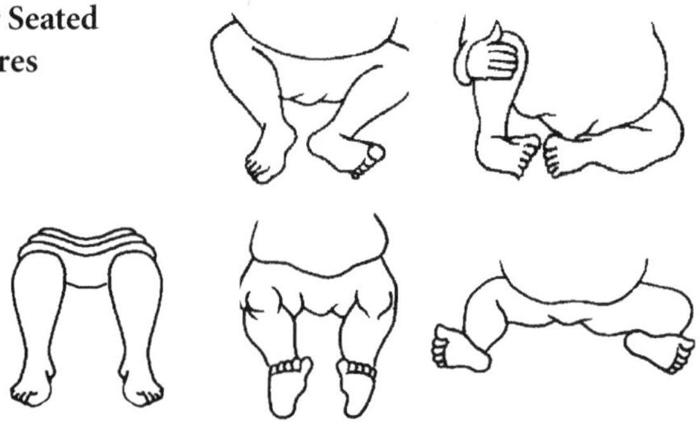

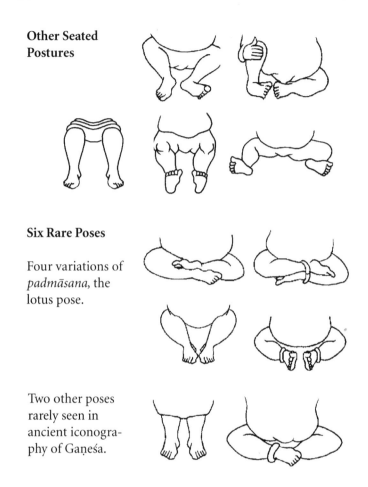

Six Rare Poses

Four variations of *padmāsana*, the lotus pose.

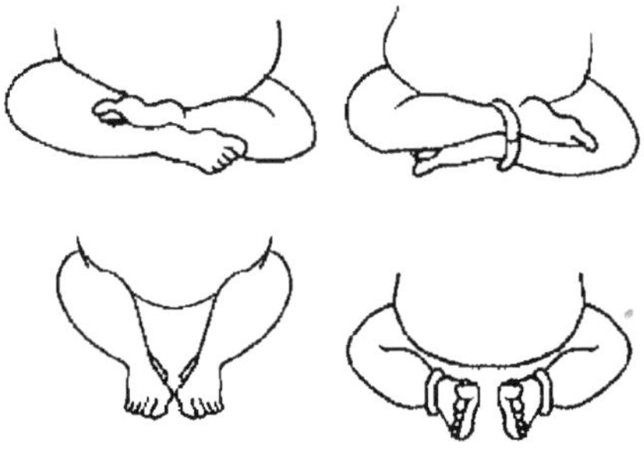

Two other poses rarely seen in ancient iconography of Gaṇeśa.

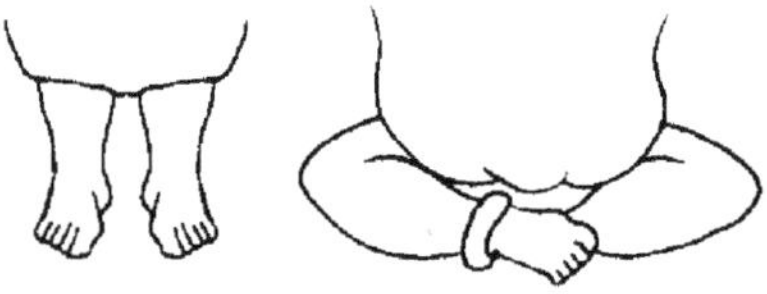

Gaṇeśa's Trunk Poses

On the page to the right are numerous trunk poses. The first group are examples of *valampuri* (turning to the right). Group two are *edampuri* (turning left). In most icons of Loving Ganeśa the trunk is turned toward the left (from the perspective of the Deity). Only in rare cases is it turned to the right.

Valampuri Pose
Trunk turning to the Deity's right. This form is very rare.

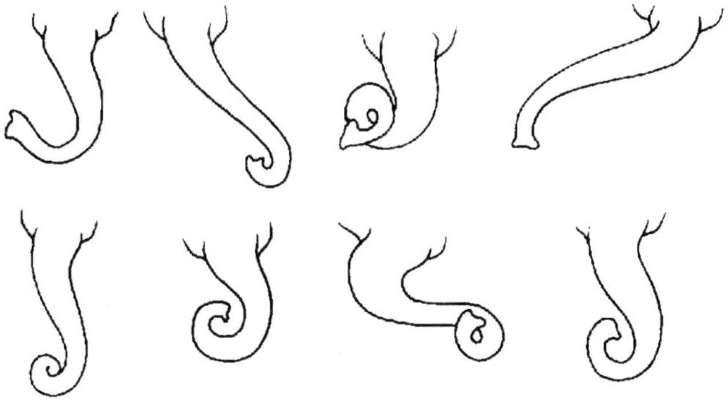

Edampuri Pose
Trunk turning to the Deity's left. This is the common form.

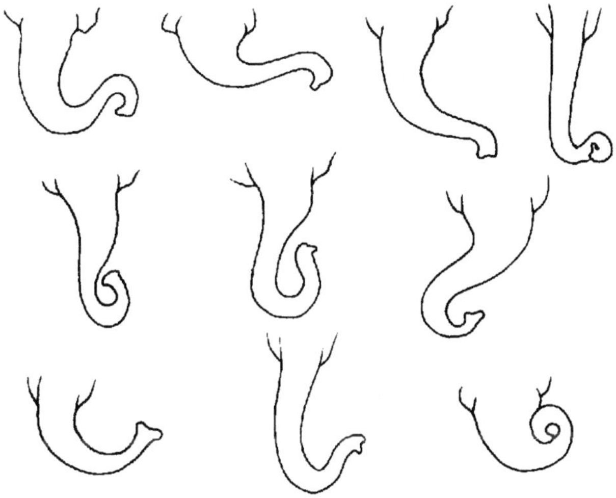

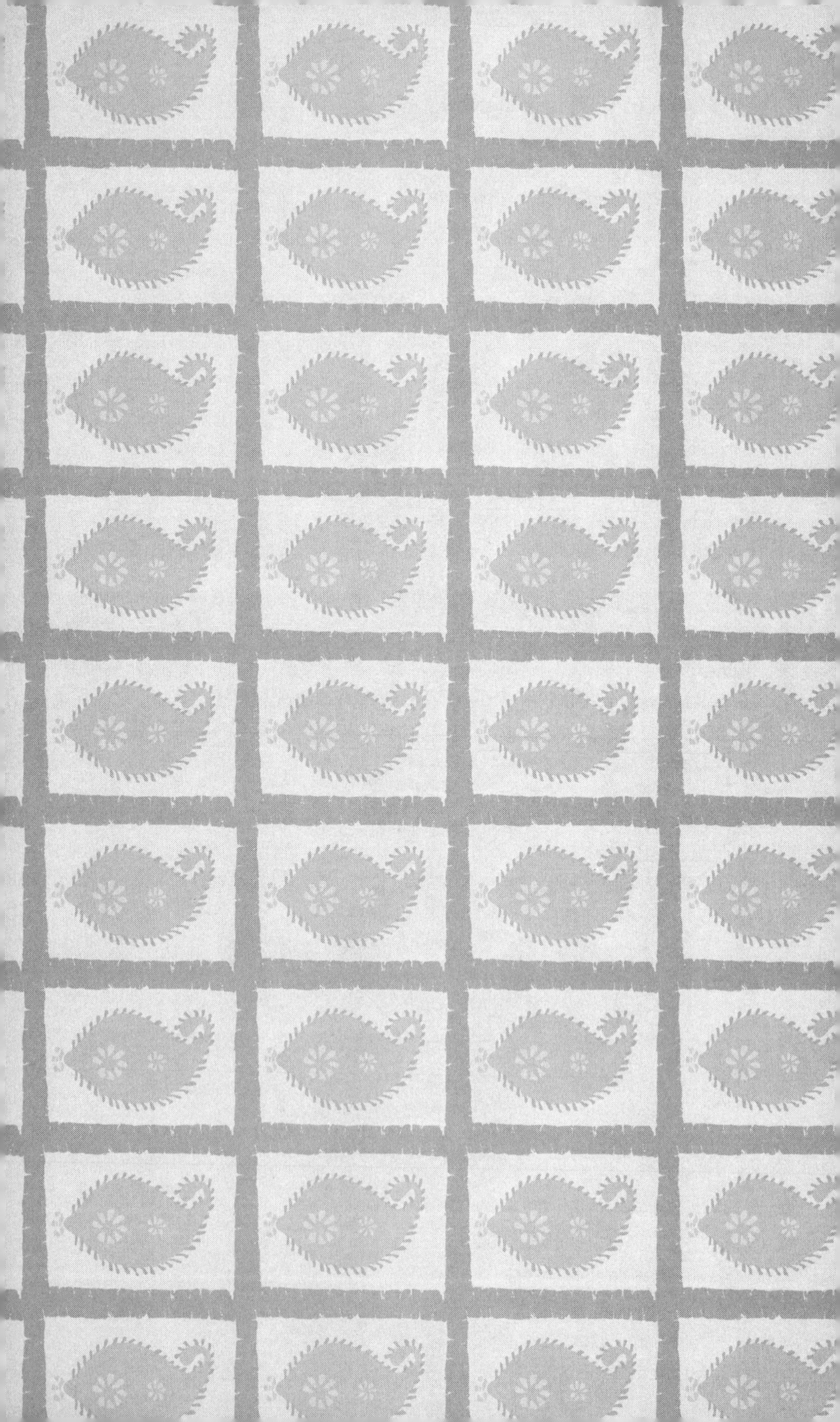

Puṇyalakshaṇāni
पुण्यलक्षणानि

Sacred Symbols

Sacred Symbols

FELICITOUS ICONS ARE ASSOCIATED WITH EACH OF THE HINDU GODS, SYMBOLS THAT SEEK TO DESCRIBE THE MANIFEST POWERS of that particular Third World Mahādeva. The *vitarka mudrā,* the "gesture of debate," is associated with Lord Gaṇeśa, as are red and yellow flowers. Everywhere the elephant symbolizes strength, intelligence and majestic poise. So honored was the elephant among the creatures, that they were used in kingly days to select a successor to the throne. In ancient Bharat the superiority of a *mahārāja's* army was measured by the strength of his elephant brigade—the largest kraal on record being 5,000. In India, the white elephant is a symbol of purity (elephants, despite their size, are pure vegetarians), and its birth was said to usher in an era of prosperity and plenitude for the entire nation. There are many stories surrounding visions of a white elephant, including that which the mother of Prince Siddhārtha had before his birth. In this section of *Loving Gaṇeśa* we describe briefly some of the traditional Indian symbols and their meanings.

"His four arms stand for His immense power in helping humanity. The noose and the goad borne in two of His hands stand for His all-pervasiveness and grace. The broken tusk held in the right hand shows that He is the refuge for all. His huge belly is indicative of His tolerance and also signifies that all things, the entire Universe, are contained in Him. His feet stand for the bestowal of *siddhi* and *buddhi,* attainment of desires and knowledge. The *modaka* (sweet goody) in His hand is symbolic of *jñāna,* conferring bliss. His mount, the shrew, represents the worldly desires which are to be overcome" (M. Arunachalam, *Festivals of Tamil Nadu,* 1980, page 112).

Śaṅkha, Conch

शङ्ख

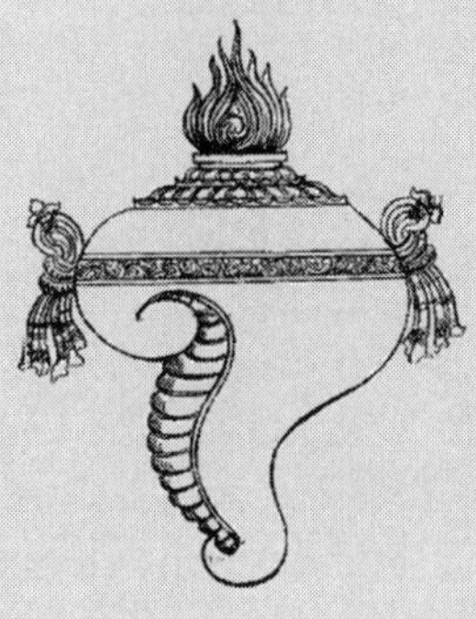

Loving Gaṇeśa listens to the *pūjā's* conch sound loudly, reminding Him of elephants calling happily in the jungle. He declares, "Come hither to be with Me and pray."

Aṅkuśa, Goad

अंकुश

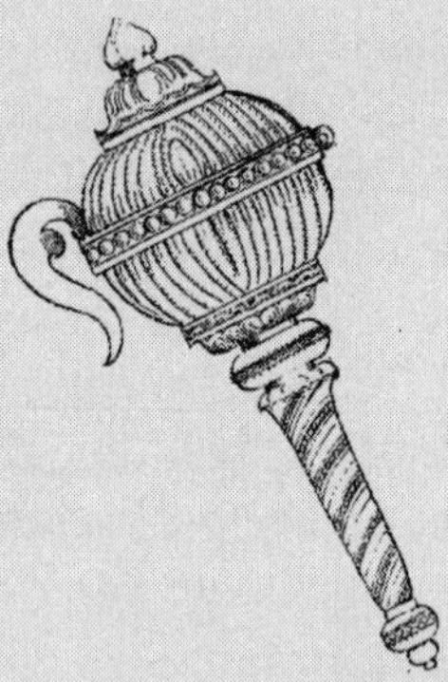

Loving Gaṇeśa's deliberate mind moves dullards ahead in their birth *karmas* whenever they tarry. He goads on with His *aṅkuśa* all souls who are moving too slowly.

Paraśu, Axe

परशु

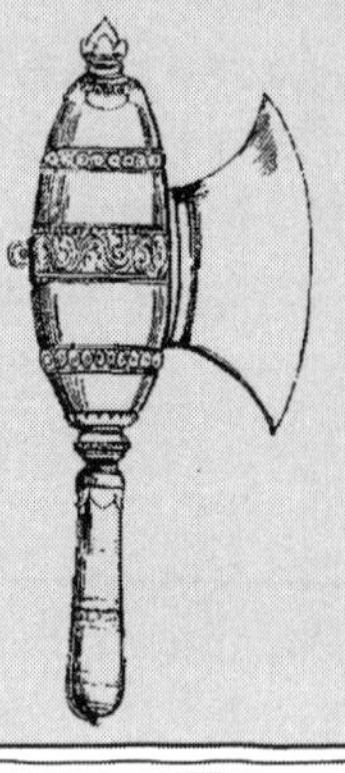

Loving Gaṇeśa knows there are difficult times ahead for some of His devotees. He protects them with His *paraśu* in gentle ways from evils they have attracted.

Pāśa, Noose

पाश

Loving Gaṇesa's magnificent mind, like the noose, draws close those He loves most dearly and reaches out to encircle and save strayed ones in extraordinary ways.

Vajratriśūla, Lightning Bolt

वज्रत्रिशूल

Loving Gaṇeśa, like His brother Murugan, holds a great power, the lightning bolt: spirit over mind, mind over matter, controlling both the higher and lower *chakras.*

Chakra, Discus

चक्र

Loving Gaṇeśa holds the discus, symbol of the sun and of the mind, as the moon symbolizes the emotions. Wielded as a weapon, it is the intellect divinely empowered.

Modakapātra, Bowl of Sweets

मोदकपात्र

Loving Gaṇeśa is said to have a sweet tooth, or tusk. But the *modaka* ball is a symbol of what He loves most, *moksha*, liberation, the sweetest of all things sweet.

Gadā, Mace

गदा

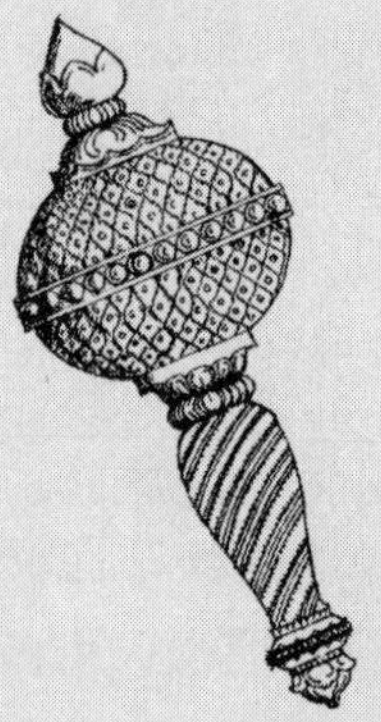

Loving Gaṇeśa is definite and commanding as symbolized by *gadā*, His mace. He casts *karmas* back on devotees for resolution, never letting up until completion.

Çhuri, Dagger

छुरि

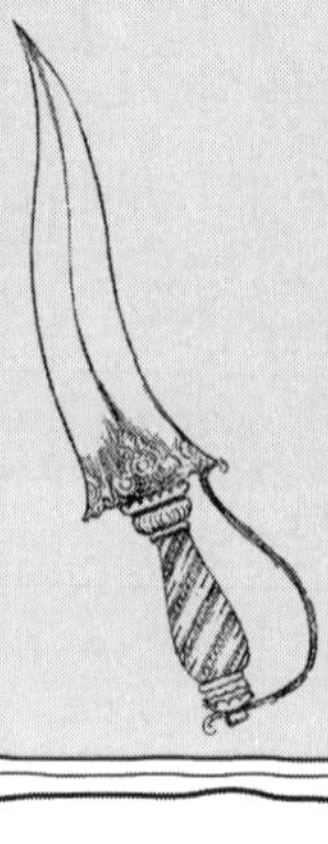

Loving Gaṇeśa sometimes holds the dagger, keenly sharp, likened to the "razor's edge," the narrow and sometimes difficult path the spiritual aspirant must walk.

रुद्राक्ष माला

Rudrāksha Mālā, Prayer Beads

Loving Gaṇeśa sits at Lord Siva's holy feet with *japa mālā,* His prayer beads, in hand, waiting for instruction from the Supreme Lord of all the Gods, His father.

पुष्पशर

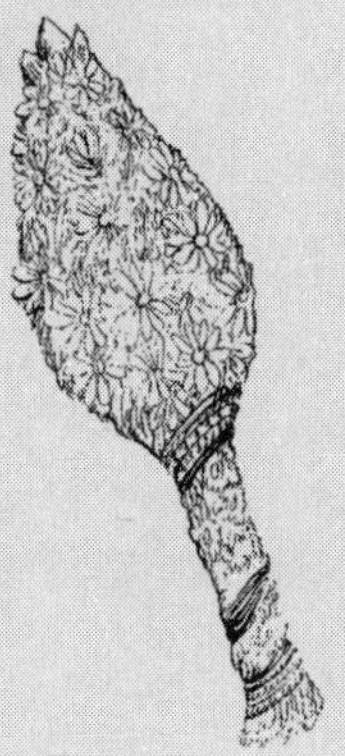

Pushpaśara, Flower Arrow

Loving Gaṇeśa shoots flower-covered arrows from His sugar cane bow in guidance to devotees so they will not wander too far from *dharma's* path of true fulfillment.

अमृतकुम्भ

Amṛitakumbha, Pot of Nectar

Loving Gaṇeśa receives a bath each time the temples are knocked with arms crossed. The *amṛita* flows from your *sahasrāra* down to His seat at *mūlādhāra's* base.

Padma, Lotus

पद्म

Loving Gaṇeśa wants all minds to be as the lotus flower's taught potential: "coming from the depths of the mud into the opening of the bud high above the water's edge."

Ikshukārmuka, Sugar Cane Bow

इक्षुकार्मुक

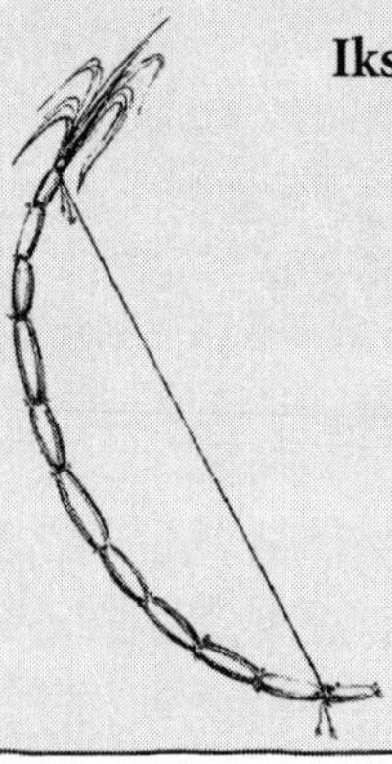

Loving Gaṇeśa shows His generous nature of giving all that is good to devotees. His sugar cane bow shoots the kindest arrows, which are projections of His thought.

Śara, Arrow

शर

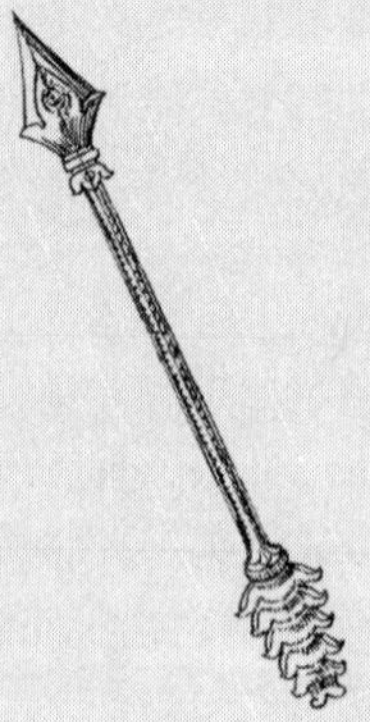

Loving Gaṇeśa has power over thought and each one hits its mark. Bow drawn, arrow aimed, He teaches us to precisely begin all beginnings with good intentions.

वीणा

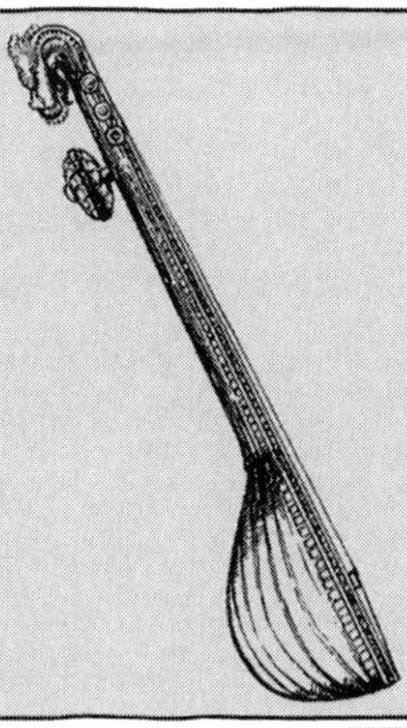

Vīṇā, Indian Lute

Loving Gaṇeśa is sound in all its beauty and meaning. Śiva is the ocean; Gaṇeśa is its sound. Śiva, the wind God; Gaṇeśa its sound. Listen to the *vīṇā* within and hear.

असुर

Asura, Goblin

Loving Gaṇeśa is not beyond frightening those who live in the *chakra* of fear by sending His *gaṇas* to lift them into a better life. Sometimes fear is a helpmate in need.

दण्ड

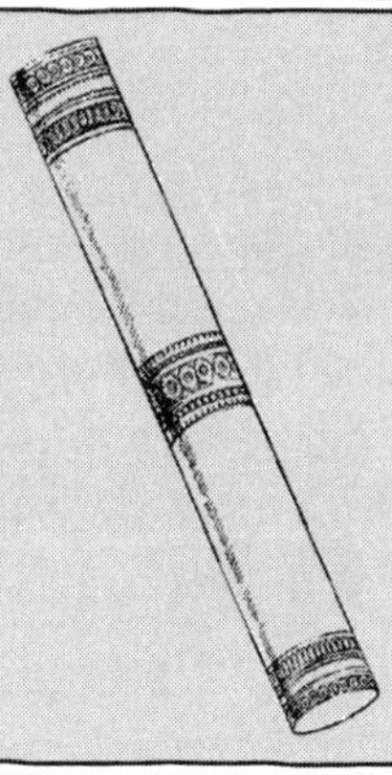

Daṇḍa, Stick

Loving Gaṇeśa carries a short stick, a sign of authority, warning all not to threaten the noble ways of *dharma* and controlling those who have even the thought to do so.

चामर

Chāmara, Fly-Whisk Fan

Loving Gaṇeśa sits, as He always does, whisking away the past within the minds of devotees, young and old, rich and poor, educated and practical. Yes, is He wise?

कमण्डलु

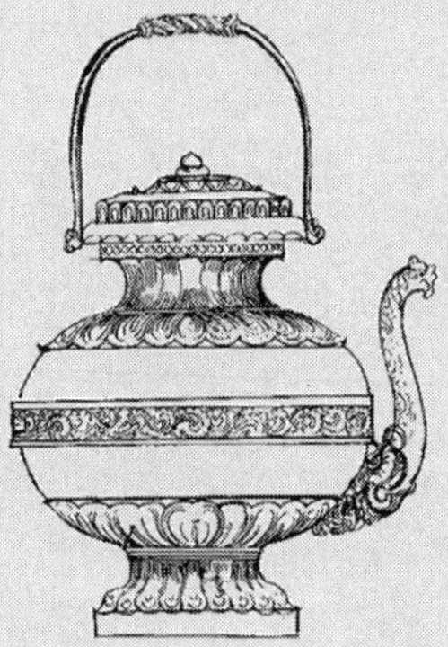

Kamaṇḍalu, Water Vessel

Loving Gaṇeśa, dear to *sannyāsins,* has their water vessel. Symbol of fullness, giving devotees all needs, *kamaṇḍalu* eternally pours, never needing to be filled.

धनुष

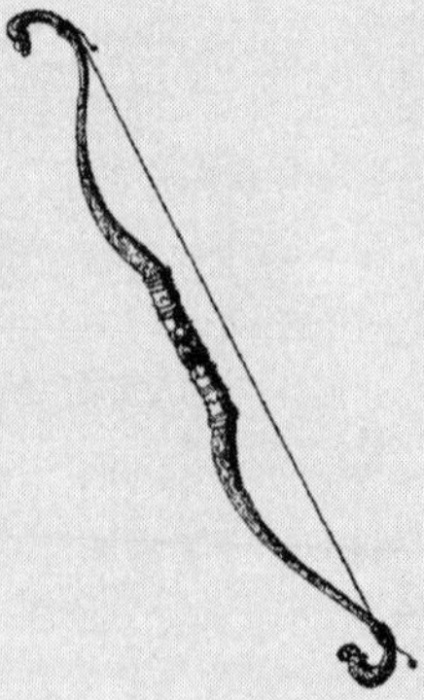

Dhanush, Bow

Loving Gaṇeśa is stealthy as He draws His bow and bends His thoughts into forms most helpful to dear devotees. They all cherish all attentions with great ecstasy.

नाग

Nāga, Serpent

Loving Gaṇeśa has a snake as His pet. Many are afraid of such creatures, but He tells us that it is the *kuṇḍalinī* within all and each one can rise above all adversity.

शालिपल्लव

Śālipallava, Rice Sprig

Loving Gaṇeśa knows rice is the life-sustainer of villagers and city folk alike. Holding a sprig of paddy, He assure us rains will come and all will be well at harvest time.

मुद्गर

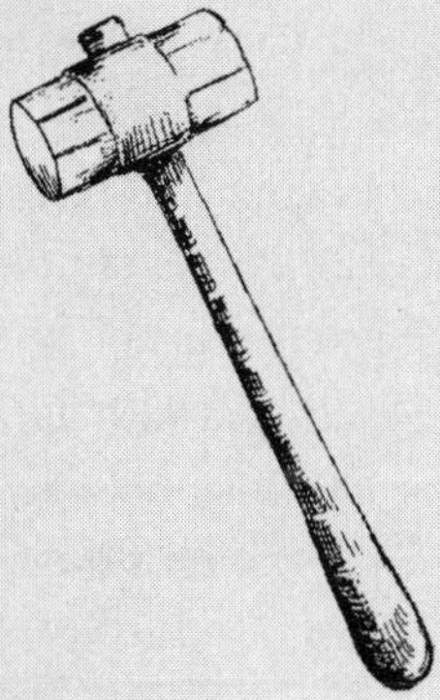

Mudgara, Hammer

Loving Gaṇeśa wields a mallet, sign of His position as Patron of Arts and Crafts, supporter of all who build and shape, chisel and sculpt the many needs of society.

शास्त्र

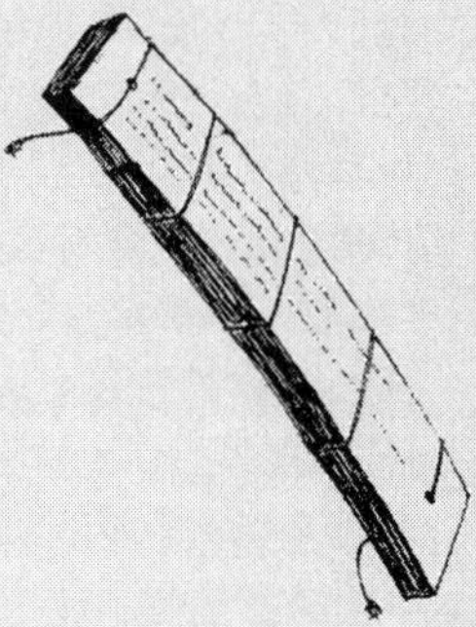

Śāstra, Scripture

Loving Gaṇeśa studiously edits all the scriptures on this planet and on others, too. His is the potent pen that writes and edits life and brings forth deeper meanings.

कल्पवृक्ष

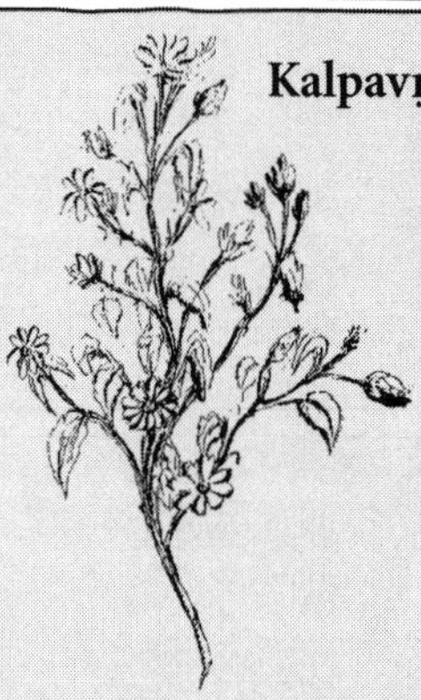

Kalpavṛiksha, Wish-Fulfilling Tree

Loving Gaṇeśa holds a sprig of the wish-fulfilling tree to tell us that all our wishes will be gratified. We have but to tell Him our needs, that is all, just tell Him.

परश्वध

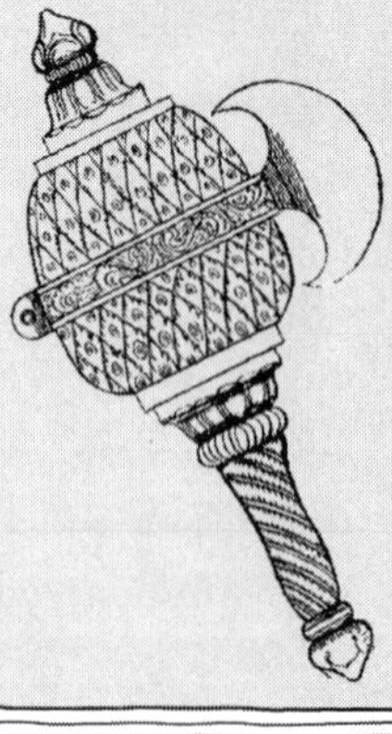

Paraśvadha, Battleaxe

Loving Gaṇeśa knows sometimes strong measures must be taken to fulfill a righteous goal, like crashing through a jungle. He uses a battleaxe as forceful mind.

महापरशु

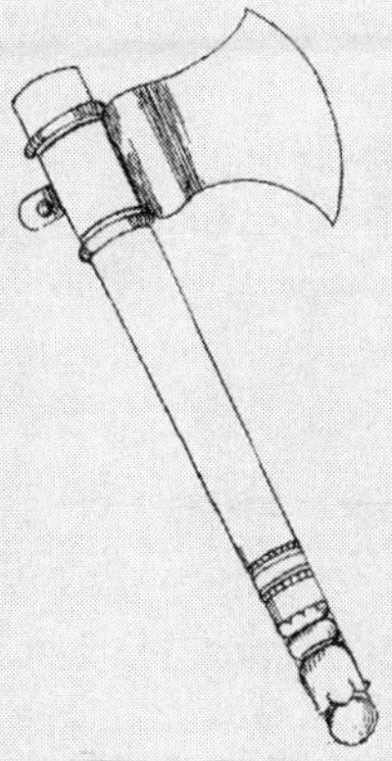

Mahāparaśu, Large Axe

Loving Gaṇeśa often wields a big axe. This great *mahāparaśu* frightens off *asuras* and banishes unwanted thoughts of those who intend harm to His chosen ones.

त्रिशूल

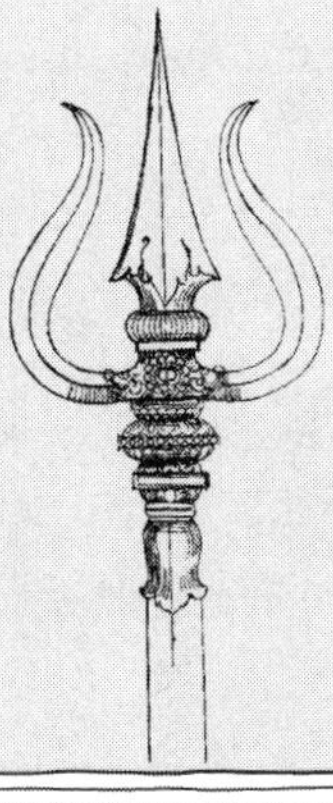

Triśūla, Trident

Loving Gaṇeśa makes His way through the mind's vast complexities with His abilities represented by *triśūla,* His three-fold power: Love, Wisdom and Action.

नारिकेल

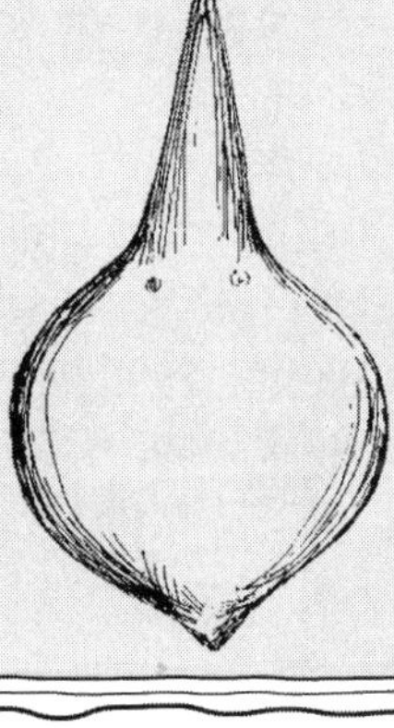

Nārikela, Coconut

Loving Gaṇeśa holds the coconut, symbol of the ego, soft and sweet inside, hard and rough outside. When we break a coconut to Him, we break the ego's hold on us.

Dhvaja, Banner

ध्वज

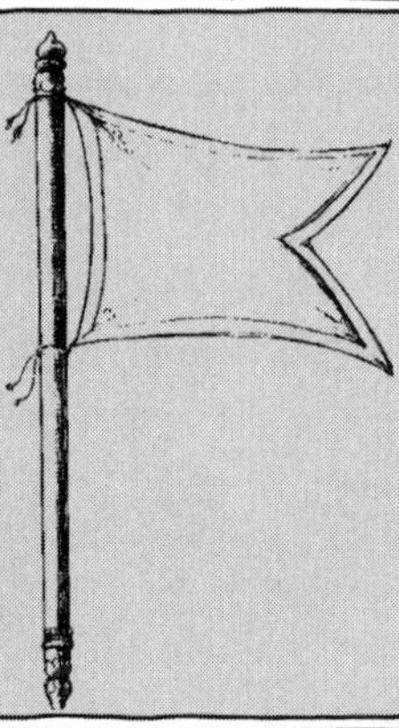

Loving Gaṇeśa is the spirit of mirth. On festival days Hindutva *dhvaja* flies above all His many temples and shrines, bringing souls from afar near and nearer.

Bhagnadanta, Broken Tusk

भग्नदन्त

Loving Gaṇeśa broke His beautiful right tusk in a sacrificial act, using it as a stylus to get the job done. By this act He demonstrates that what we begin we must finish.

Pāshāṇadāraṇa, Pick Axe

पाषाणदारण

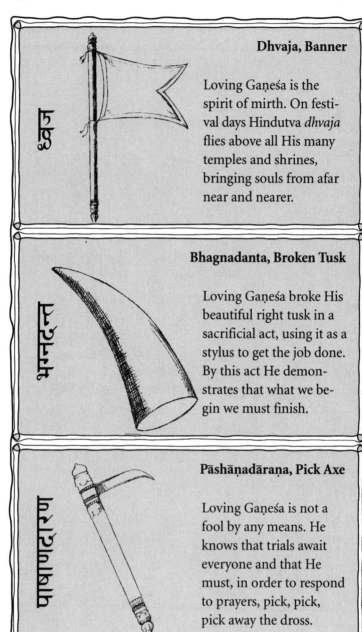

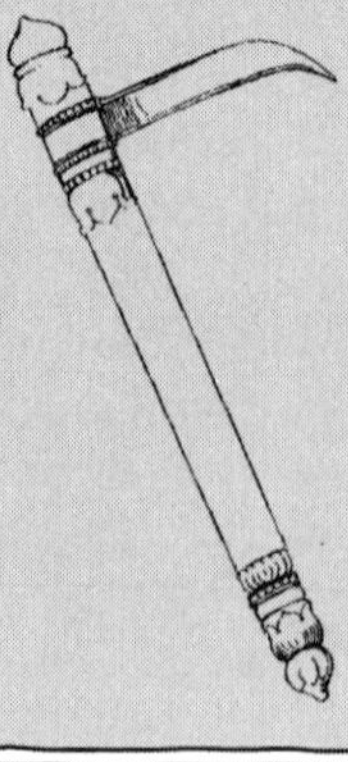

Loving Gaṇeśa is not a fool by any means. He knows that trials await everyone and that He must, in order to respond to prayers, pick, pick, pick away the dross.

अग्नि

Agni, Fire

Loving Gaṇeśa gives access to His fiery powers, capable of consuming our dross, destroying residual *karmas,* if we but offer our confessions into its flames.

खड्ग

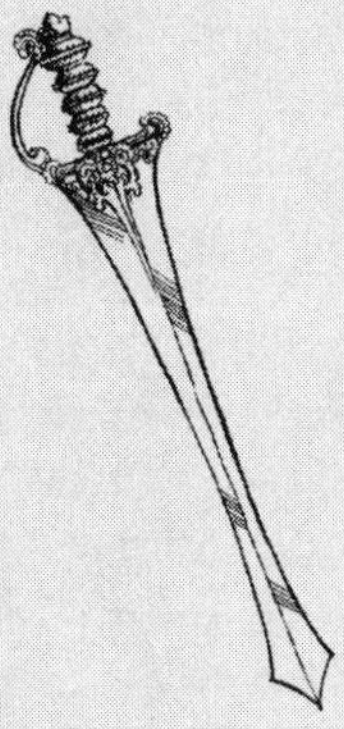

Khaḍga, Sword

Loving Gaṇeśa has a sword bejeweled with precious gems. It communicates to those who only respond to fear His defiance of crime and His abhorrence of hurt.

फल

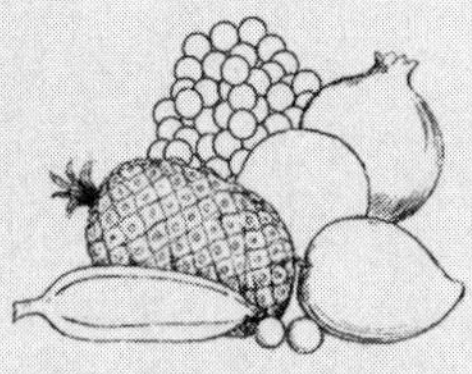

Phala, Fruits

Loving Gaṇeśa, dweller in the forest, enjoys all the earth's many life-giving fruits. He wants parents and children alike to keep healthy by eating lots of fruits.

Mūlaka, Radish

मूलक

Loving Gaṇeśa makes us grow food that is good for us to eat by the desire for the simple radish. He knows we will grow to please Him maybe more than for ourselves.

Kheṭaka, Shield

खेटक

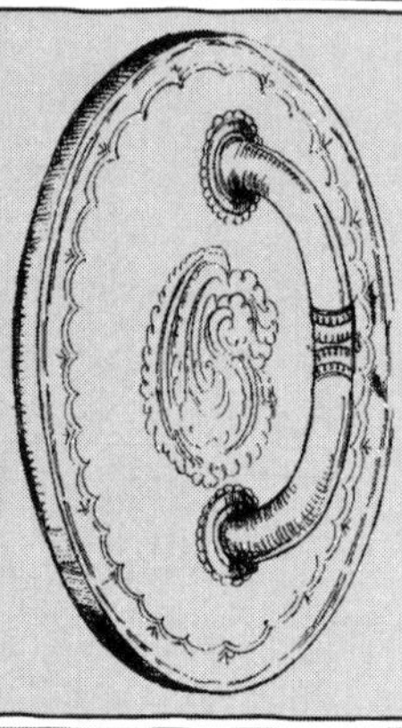

Loving Gaṇeśa holds the shield of divine security, symbol of His power to defend lands of the upright, to preserve traditions, to protect all souls on the spiritual path.

Āmra, Mango

आम्र

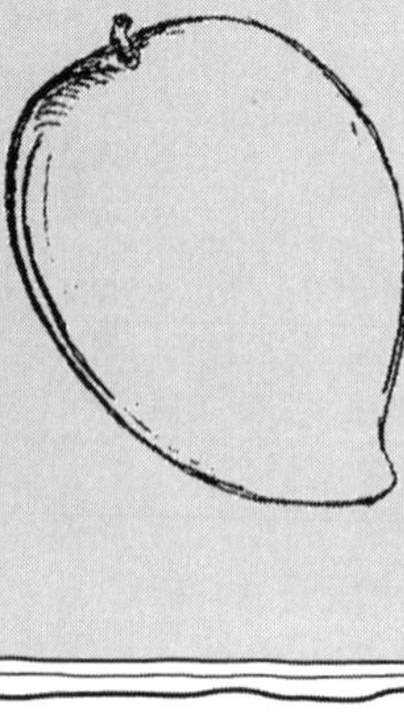

Loving Gaṇeśa tells of the mango: "It was given to Me from Lord Śiva's own hand after performing My first wisdom act. It represents the highest spiritual fruition."

तृतीयाक्षि

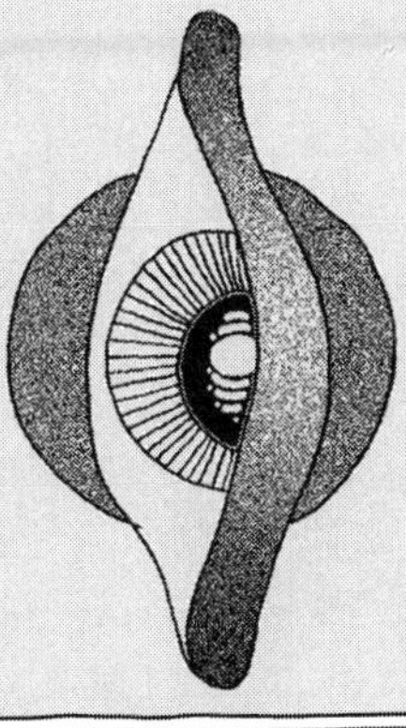

Tṛitīyākshi, Third Eye

Loving Gaṇeśa, as do we all, has three eyes, not two, the third being the eye of the mind, of spiritual sight. With this eye He sees the reality behind the world's seeming.

रत्नकुम्भ

Ratnakumbha, Pot of Gems

Loving Gaṇeśa knows the power resident in precious gems. Diamonds, rubies, emeralds are like human souls, each with a different color, faceting and loveliness.

गारित्र

Gāritra, Grains

Loving Gaṇeśa knows that there are many kinds of people, and they need variety in their diet. He protects the kingdom of all kinds of grains that make their bodies strong.

इक्षुकाण्ड

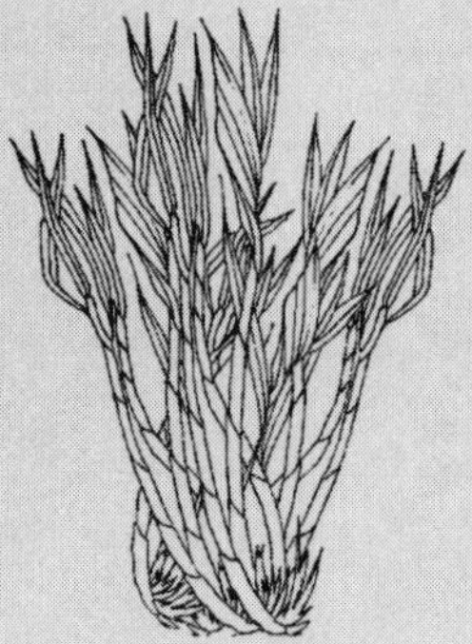

Ikshukāṇḍa, Sugar Cane

Loving Gaṇeśa is taken by sugar cane, in fact, by anything sweet. Being the Lord all children adore, it is His joy to see their beautiful eyes light up when offering sugar cane.

मधुकुम्भ

Madhukumbha, Pot of Honey

Loving Gaṇeśa wears a side smile across His face when offered a pot of sticky honey. It is, to Him, like *moksha* itself, the sweetest of all things sweet, worth any effort.

कदलीफल

Kadalīphala, Banana

Loving Gaṇeśa has in His hand the banana, ripe and ready to eat. He looks at it longingly yet would give it up in a moment should a devotee smell its perfume.

योगदण्ड

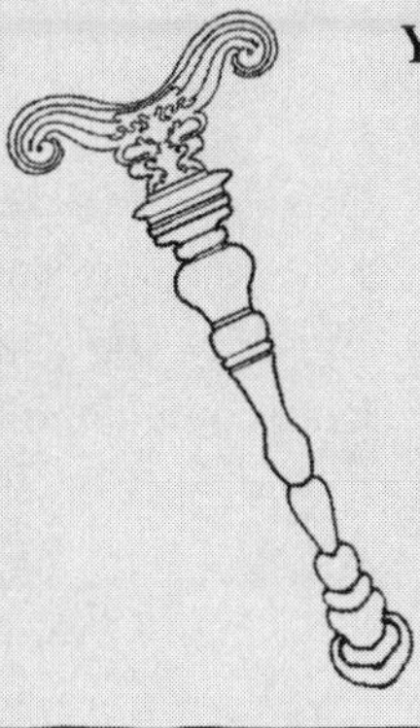

Yogadaṇḍa, Meditation Staff

Loving Gaṇeśa rests His arm upon a short staff when talking to devotees and when in deep *samādhi.* He finds it lets Him meditate more effortlessly, more deeply.

तृण

Tṛiṇa, Grasses

Loving Gaṇeśa knows that there are many kinds of little animals and big ones, too. Each needs special foods, so He protects the grasses, little flowers and seeds.

तिल गोल

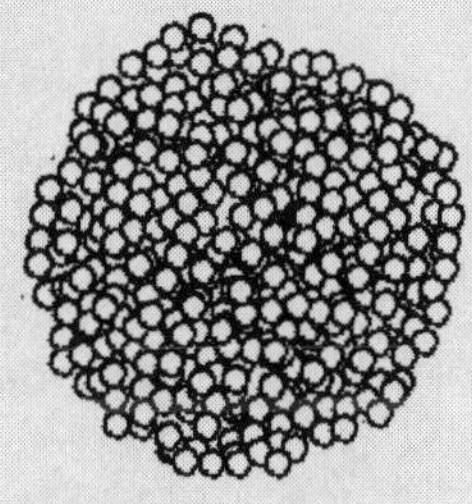

Tila Gola, Sesame Ball

Loving Gaṇeśa teaches us that size may be immense but there is nothing too small to overlook. In His trunk is a sweet made of tiny sesame seeds, and He rides on a tiny mouse.

शुक

Śuka, Parrot

Loving Gaṇeśa is pleased when Śuka talks and shows he is happy. Perched in Gaṇeśa's hand, he watches all who come and go, giving his opinion when they are alone.

अननस

Ananasa, Pineapple

Loving Gaṇeśa holds the pineapple and is ready to slice it to share with those in His aura. Giving and sharing is our lesson from the sweet pineapple that He gives us.

मूषिक

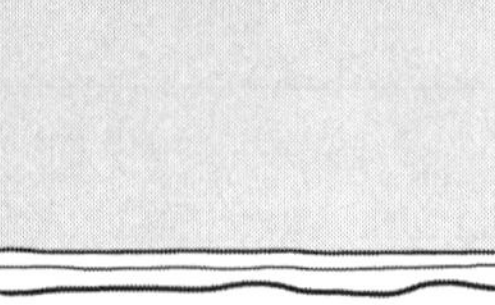

Mūshika, Mouse

Loving Gaṇeśa's tiny mouse attests to the all-pervasiveness of the elephant God. As His *vāhana*, or mount, Mūshika, carries His grace into every nook and cranny.

Lambodara, Big Belly

लम्बोदर

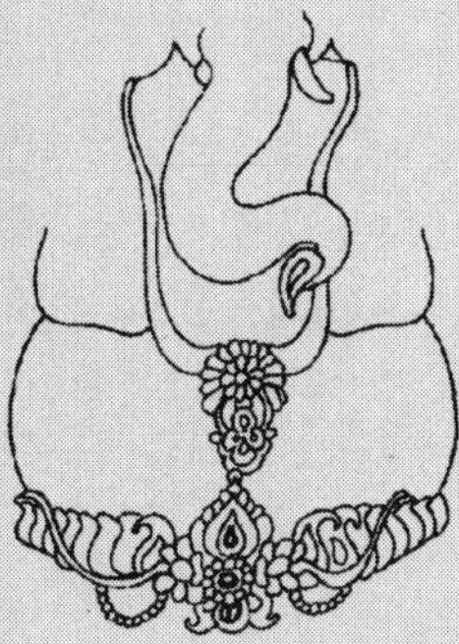

Loving Gaṇeśa has this world in His abundant belly as well as all the galaxies, all known and unknown universes are contained within His prodigious stomach.

Swastika, Mark of Auspiciousness

स्वस्तिक

Loving Gaṇeśa's good fortunes are represented by the *swastika,* a sign of luck and auspiciousness. Its crooked arms show how life is filled with change and indirection.

Jambira, Lime

जम्बिर

Loving Gaṇeśa is a practical God, and it is His wish that all who know Him use the juice from one of His favorite fruits. He wants them to be healthy and enjoy life.

Aum, Cosmic Sound

ॐ

Loving Gaṇeśa is Aum. He is the A, the base sound of the universe, He is the U, the sound of the galaxies and He is the M, the sound of the planets and the littlest stars.

Śuṇḍā, Elephant Trunk

शुण्डा

Loving Gaṇeśa has a great trunk, and He makes it known that it is a symbol of His ability to always love His devotees. With it He reaches out to touch each of them.

Nīlapadma, Blue Water Lily

नीलपद्म

Loving Gaṇeśa often sits upon the side of a lily pond, pondering the current state of the universe. His *lila* is to see all remains in order until the next Mahāpralaya.

पनसफल

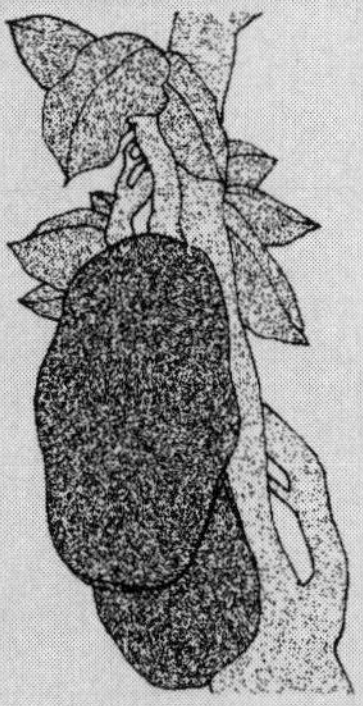

Panasa Phala, Jackfruit

Loving Gaṇeśa's favorite jackfruit is a potato-like vegetable, a chewy nut and sweet yellow fruit all in one. Like the jack's stem, our attachments though small are strong.

प्रभावली

Prabhāvalī, Fiery Arch

Loving Gaṇeśa sits within an arch depicting creation, preservation and fiery dissolution. Above is the God of time, Mahākāla, who ultimately claims everything.

दाडिम

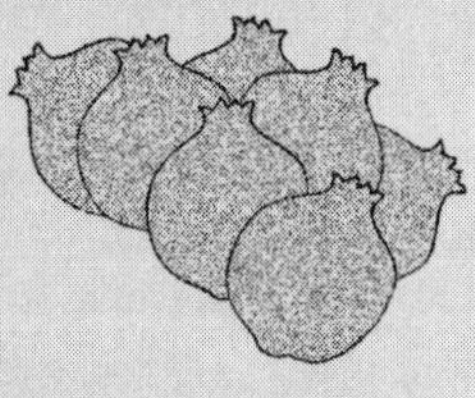

Dāḍima, Pomegranate

Loving Gaṇeśa knows we may be led astray by ways of worldly people who eat meat. He offers us red *dāḍimas* saying: "Its many pink seeds are much better than flesh."

Nāgapāśa, Snake Cord

नागपाश

Loving Gaṇeśa wears a snake around Him to tell us all that we have to be like Him and control our instinctive, animal mind. Yes, it is possible through the grace of this God.

Kapittha, Wood Apple

कपित्थ

Loving Gaṇeśa loves wood apples, *kapittha,* called the elephant fruit. Sweet to eat, packaged in a tough shell, it is a pharmacy of *āyurveda's* secret medicinal potencies.

Laḍḍu, Milk Sweet

लड्डु

Loving Gaṇeśa was never accused of turning down a *laḍḍu,* rich with milk, flour and sugar. Maybe it reminds Him of being young. Every young one loves sweets.

Kavacha, Armour

कवच

Loving Gaṇeśa's granite form in temple and shrine worldwide is enhanced by silver and gold look-a-likes placed over them on festival days. He does appreciate adulation.

Śaśikalā, Crescent Moon

शशिकला

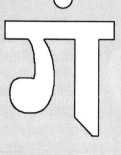

Loving Gaṇeśa, as does His father, wears the crescent moon on His great head. It is a symbol of time's passing, of auspicious moments and of the powers of the mind.

Gaṁ Mantra

गं मन्त्र

Loving Gaṇeśa is called by devotees through this mystery *mantra*. Upon hearing it, He immediately responds. There is no love greater than receiving it from Him.

Yajñopavīta, Sacred Thread

यज्ञोपवीत

Loving Gaṇeśa wears across a massive shoulder the holy cord to remind us that we, too, can be twice born through His grace, that none is low and none is high.

Jambu, Rose Apple

जम्बु

Loving Gaṇeśa loves the rose apple among many other wonderful fruits and vegetables. He shows us the path to good health, harmlessness to creatures and love.

Pāyasa, Pudding

पायस

Loving Gaṇeśa is seen from time to time enjoying sweet tapioca pudding, likened to the love and kindness that comes from caring for others as one's very own self.

शक्ति

Śakti, Consort

Loving Gaṇeśa is often seen with two female consorts, or *śaktis.* They represent *iḍā* and *piṅgalā,* the two life currents, emotion and intellect, that hold us close to Earth.

मूलाधार चक्र

Mūlādhāra Chakra, Base Center

Loving Gaṇeśa, sitting on the four petalled *mūlādhāra,* rules memory and knowledge as the gatekeeper to the six *chakras* above and the guard of the seven below.

वृक्ष

Vṛiksha, Trees

Loving Gaṇeśa is the giver of gifts from healing trees, the professor of *āyurveda.* He is the great doctor who helps us gain the knowledge of health from His many trees.

Swastikam

स्वस्तिकम्

Symbol of Auspiciousness

Symbol of Auspiciousness

GO BACK FIVE THOUSAND YEARS IN HISTORY. AT THE LOTHAL PORT ON THE COAST OF INDIA'S NORTHERN ARABIAN SEA, TONS OF cargo lines the wharves. A trader, inspecting his goods before voyaging to the Sumerian cities on the Tigris River, turns an imprinting seal over in his hands, feeling its upraised image of a cross with arms sweeping ninety degrees leftward from each endpoint of the cross. Swiftly he turns the seal over and presses it into a soft clay tag anchored to a bundle of cotton. The impression is a mirror image of the seal, a right-hand facing *swastika.* The symbol, so evocative of unending auspiciousness, is sewn into his sails, as the *swastika* would later also adorn the sails of a ship described in the *Rāmāyaṇa.* The trader is from Hinduism's most ancient known civilization: the Indus Valley in Northwest India. The seal rests today in a museum and is the oldest surviving representation of the *swastika,* a Sanskṛit word that means "good being, fortune or augury," literally "conducive to well-being," derived from *su,* "well" and *asti,* "it is."

For Hindus, the *swastika* is a lucky cross associated with the good fortunes given by Lord Gaṇeśa. It also represents the sun and the cycle of life. This ancient benevolent symbol is used today by housewives to guard thresholds and doors, by priests to sanctify ceremonies and offerings and by businessmen to bless the opening pages of account books each New Year's day. No ceremony or sacrifice is considered complete without it, for it is believed to have the power to ward off misfortune and negative forces. A series of small *swastikas* is a favorite border pattern for textiles. In Mahārāshṭra, the rainy season is especially devoted to its honor, when it is drawn on the floor in elaborate patterns using colorful powders and flower petals.

It is said that the *swastika's* right-angled arms reflect the fact that the path toward our objectives is often not straight, but takes unexpected turns. They denote also the indirect way in which Divinity is reached—through intuition and not by intellect. Symbolically, the *swastika's* cross is said to represent God and creation. The four bent arms stand for the four human aims, called *purushārtha:* righteousness, *dharma;* wealth, *artha*; love, *kāma*; and liberation, *moksha.* Thus it is a potent emblem of Sanātana Dharma, the eternal truth. It also represents the world wheel, eternally changing around a fixed center, God. The *swastika* is regarded as a symbol of the *mūlādhāra chakra,* the center of consciousness at the base of the spine, and in some *yoga* schools with the *maṇipūra chakra* at the navel, the center of the microcosmic sun *(sūrya).*

Found Throughout Earth's Cultures

The *swastika* is a sacred sign of prosperity and auspiciousness, perhaps the single most common emblem in earth cultures. As the *Encyclopedia Britannica* explains, "It was a favorite symbol on ancient Mesopotamian coinage; it appeared in early Christian and Byzantine art (where it became known as the gammadion cross because its arms resemble the Greek letter gamma); and it occurred in South and Central America (among the Mayans) and in North America (principally among the Navajos). In India it continues to be the most widely used auspicious symbol of Hindus, Jainas and Buddhists."

When Buddhism emerged from India's spiritual wellspring, it inherited the right-angled emblem. Carried by monks, the good-luck design journeyed north over the Himalayas into China, often carved in statues into Buddha's feet and splayed into a spectrum of decorative meandering or interconnecting *swastikas.* On the other side of the planet,

American Indians inscribed the spoked sign of good luck into salmon-colored seashells, healing sticks, pottery, woven garments and blankets. Two thousand miles south, the Mayans of the Yucatan chiseled it into temple diagrams. Once moored to the ancient highland cultures of Asia Minor, the emblem later voyaged around the Mediterranean, through Egypt and Greece, northward into Saxon lands, Scandinavia and west to Scotland and Ireland.

Nineteenth-century Americans picked up the symbol from the American Indians. Boy Scouts wore brassy *swastika* belt buckles, and a US World's Fair early this century minted flashy *swastika* commemorative coins. It was displayed in jewelry, inscribed on souvenirs, light fixtures, post cards and playing cards. In the 1920s and early 30s the *swastika* was the emblem of the United States' 45th Infantry Division, proudly worn by soldiers on their left shoulder as an ancient good-luck symbol, in yellow on a square red background. The emblem was changed to an Indian thunderbird during the 1930s. Canada has a town called Swastika, 360 miles north of Toronto, named in 1911 after a rich gold mine. When WWII broke out, the townsfolk withstood pressures from the federal government to change the name to Winston.

Use by the German Nazis

In the 1930s, when Adolf Hitler's Nazi Third Reich rose to power in Germany and engulfed the planet in World War II, the fortunes of the *swastika* declined. From September 1935 to the fall of the Nazis in 1945, it was displayed on the Reich's official flag, a black *swastika* in a white circle against a red field. In the West it became an infamous, hated symbol of fascism and anti-Semitism, banned by the Allied Command at the war's end, though the *swastika's* history is as extensive in the West as in Asia.

Tracking the *Swastika's* Left and Right Forms

The *swastika* has throughout history mutated into a wide diversity of forms and meanings, but in its Hindu usage the right-hand *swastika* is far more prevalent and ancient than its left-hand counterpart.

Next to the Indus seal, the oldest Indian *swastika* motif appears abundantly on the early Buddhist sculptures, a period when Buddha was not depicted in human form—only his foot prints surrounded by dozens of right-hand *swastikas.* Similarly, the Jain emblem for their seventh TīrthaṀkara (path finder) is the symbol of the sun, the right-facing *swastika.* In Malaysia, the Sikh shrines all have right-hand *swastikas* as mystical ornamentation.

In some sources, neither *swastika* was assigned a negative connotation: the right-hand was a spring solar, male symbol, the left was an autumn solar, female icon. As the *tantric* sciences of Śaivism and Śāktism bifurcated into a left-hand and right-hand path—the *vāma* and *dakshiṇa*—the *swastika* may have followed into black or white mysticism and magic.

The search for a pre-World War II text on the *swastika* struck gold with a book entitled *The Swastika: the Earliest Known Symbol and its Migrations,* by Thomas Wilson, a curator of the US National Museum. It was written in 1894 for the Smithsonian Institute. The work opens with a right-hand *swastika* on the title page and presents an exhaustive survey of the global dispersion of this symbol from the Navajo tribes of North America to Egypt, ancient Troy and the Taoists of China.

Among a cadre of Oriental scholars referenced in the book is Prof. Max Muller, the German *Veda* translator who introduced the word *Aryan* to the European intelligentsia. It was through Muller that *Aryan* was first imbued with a sense of race rather than an attribute of virtuous, spiritual nobility. Wilson writes, "Prof. Max Muller makes the symbol different according as the arms are bent to the right or left. That bent to the right he denominates the true *swastika,* that bent to the left he calls *suavastika,* but he gives no authority for the statement." Further, after examining all the positions of dozens of scholars Wilson concludes, "Therefore, the normal *swastika* would seem to be that with the ends bent to the right."

Wilson's book pictorially surveys the dispersion of the *swastika* symbol region by region. Indeed, so broadly cast is the symbol in the early ages of human society that Wilson determines it is impossible to trace the *swastika's* origin. Wilson's exploration of European use of the *swastika* prior to 1894 is an eye-opener. Under the section "Germany and Austria," we are treated to ten samples of the *swastika* (now displayed in museums) that are designed into filigree screens, ornament burial urns and spearheads, and fashioned into broach and pin jewelry. They orient both right and left, with a preference to the right. The entirety of runic Europe was covered with *swastikas,* both in ornamentation and in some of their best-preserved Teutonic inscriptions to the old Gods.

The Right-Hand *Swastika*

The *swastika* is an emblem of geometric perfection. In the mind's eye, it can be stable and still or whirl in perpetual motion, its arms rotating one after another like a cosmic pinwheel. It is unknown why and how the term *swastika,* "it is good," was wedded to this most ancient and pervasive of symbols. Most authorities designate the right-hand *swastika* as a solar emblem, capturing the sun's path from east to west, a clockwise motion. One theory says it represents the outward dispersion of the universe. One of its finest meanings is that transcendent reality is not attained directly through the logic of the mind, but indirectly and mysteriously through the intuitive, cosmic mind. Though Hindus use the *swastika* straight up and down, other cultures rotated it at various angles.

The Left-Handed *Swastika*

The left-hand *swastika* appears in many cultures, including Hindu. It often is used interchangeably with the right-hand version, though the majority of Hindus employ the right-facing form. One school sees this *swastika* as that which rotates clockwise because a wind blowing across its face would catch the arms and rotate it to the right. But this is an unusual interpretation. Most see it as rotating anti-clockwise as the arms point as such. Some say this form signifies the universe imploding back into its essence. It has been associated with the *vāma*, left-handed, mystic path that employs sensual indulgence and powerful Śākta rites, with night, with the Goddess, Kālī, and magical practices. Another interpretation is that it represents the autumn solar route, a time of dormancy.

The *Swastika* After Hitler

Because of its association with the Third Reich, the *swastika* was and still is feared by many inside and outside of Germany, still held in contempt and misunderstanding, which itself is understandable though unfortunate. Now is a time for this to change, for a return to this solar symbol's pure and happy beginnings. Ironically, even now Hindus managing temples in Germany innocently display on walls and entryways the *swastika,* symbol of Lord Gaṇeśa and hated insignia of Nazism, alongside the *shaḍkona,* six-pointed star, symbol of Lord Kārttikeya and Star of David, cherished emblem of Judaism.

The *Swastika* and the *Chakras*

From a mystically occult point of view, the *swastika* is a type of *yantra,* a psychic diagram representing the four-petalled *mūlādhāra chakra* located at the base of the spine within everyone. The *chakras* are nerve plexuses or centers of force and consciousness located within the inner bodies of man. In the physical body there are corresponding nerve plexuses, ganglia and glands. The seven principal *chakras* can be seen psychically as colorful, multi-petalled wheels or lotuses situated along the spinal cord. The seven lower *chakras,* barely visible, exist below the spine. The following is a list of the fourteen *chakras*, their main attributes and location in the body.

CHAKRAS ABOVE THE BASE OF THE SPINE

14) *sahasrāra*	crown of head	illumination
13) *ājñā*	third eye	divine sight
12) *viśuddha*	throat	divine love
11) *anāhata*	heart center	direct cognition
10) *maṇipūra*	solar plexus	willpower
9) *svādhishṭhāna*	navel	reason
8) *mūlādhāra*	base of spine	memory/time/space

CHAKRAS BELOW THE BASE OF THE SPINE

7) *atala*	hips	fear and lust
6) *vitala*	thighs	raging anger
5) *sutala*	knees	retaliatory jealousy
4) *talātala*	calves	prolonged confusion
3) *rasātala*	ankles	selfishness
2) *mahātala*	feet	absence of conscience
1) *pātāla*	soles of feet	malice and murder

Śivāchārya priests, adept in temple mysticism, testify that when they tap the sides of their head with their fists several times at the outset of *pūjā* they are actually causing the *amṛita,* the divine nectar, to flow from the *sahasrāra chakra* at the top of their head, thus giving *abhisheka,* ritual anointment, to Lord Gaṇeśa seated upon the *mūlādhāra chakra* at the base of the spine.

Meditating on the right-facing *swastika,* visualized as spinning clockwise, is a key to ascending to the seven higher *chakras,* which likewise spin clockwise. Meditating on the left-facing *swastika,* spinning counterclockwise, takes consciousness into the seven lower *chakras,* which spin counterclockwise.

The Soul's Evolution through the *Chakras*

Devotees sometimes ask, "Why is it that some souls are apparently more advanced than others, less prone to the lower emotions that are attributes of the lower *chakras?*" The answer is that souls are not created all at once. Lord Śiva is continually creating souls. Souls created a long time ago are old souls. Souls created not so long ago are young souls. We recognize an old soul as being refined, selfless, compassionate, virtuous, controlled in body, mind and emotions, radiating goodness in thought, word and deed. We recognize a young soul by his strong instinctive nature, selfishness, lack of understanding and absence of physical, mental and emotional refinement.

At any given time there are souls of every level of evolution. My *satguru,* Sage Yogaswāmī, taught that "The world is a training school. Some are in kindergarten. Some are in the BA class." Each soul is created in the Third World, and evolves by taking on denser and denser bodies until it has a physical body and lives in the First World, the physical plane. Then as it matures, it drops off these denser bodies and returns to the Second and Third Worlds, the astral and causal planes.

This process of maturation, occurring over many, many lifetimes, is the unfoldment of consciousness through the *chakras.* First, the young soul slowly matures through the *pātāla, mahātala, rasātala* and the *talātala chakras.* Such individuals plague established society with their erratic, *adharmic* ways. Between births, on the astral plane, they are naturally among the *asuras,* making mischief and taking joy in the torment of others. When lifted up into jealousy, in the *sutāla chakra,* there is some focus of consciousness, and the desires of malice subside. Finally, the *pātāla chakra* sleeps. Later, when the *sutāla* forces of jealousy are thwarted, the young soul arises into anger, experiencing fits of rage at the slightest provocation. As a result of being disciplined by society, through its laws and customs, the individual slowly gains control of his forces, and a conscience begins to develop. It is at this stage that a fear of God and the Gods begins to manifest. Now, totally lifted up into the *atala chakra,* seventh of the fourteen force centers, the individual emerges into the consciousness of the *mūlādhāra,* the seat of the Elephant God, and several of the *chakras* below cease to function. Here begins the long process of unfoldment through the higher *chakras,* a process outlined in Śaiva Siddhanta as the progressive path of *charyā, kriyā, yoga* and *jñāna.*

Thus, through hundreds of lifetimes and hundreds of periods between births, the *asura* becomes the *deva* and the *deva* becomes the Mahādeva until complete and ultimate merger with Śiva, *viśvagrāsa.* Individuality is lost as the soul becomes Śiva, the creator, preserver, destroyer, veiler and revealer. Individual identity expands into universality.

Our loving Gaṇeśa, sitting on the *mūlādhāra chakra,* signified by the *swastika,* is "there for us" throughout our evolution from one set of four *chakras* to the next until all seven of the highest are functioning properly. He and His brother, Lord Murugan, work closely together to bring us all to Lord Śiva's feet, into His heart, until *jīva* becomes Śiva.

Gaṇeśaḥ Praṇavātmakaḥ

गणेशः प्रणवात्मकः

Gaṇeśa as The Primal Sound

Gaṇeśa as Primal Sound

By Ratna Ma Navarātnam,
From Om Gaṇeśa: the Peace of God

HYMNS OF THE *VEDAS* EXTOL GAṆAPATI, THE LORD OF THE GAṆAS, THE ATTENDANTS OF ŚIVA. THE MOST FAMOUS VERSE TO THE elephant-faced Lord is found in the Śrī Rudram in the *Yajur Veda Saṁhitā* (and *Ṛig Veda* 2.23.1).

> Gaṇānām tvā gaṇapatiṅg havāmahe
> [traditionally chanted *gaṇapati gm]*
> kaviṅkavīnām upamaśravastamam,
> jyeshṭharājam brahmaṇām brahmaṇaspata
> ā naḥ śṛiṇvannūtibhiḥ sīda sādanam

The Deity who is hailed as the chief of the celestial hosts (Gaṇapati) here is referred to as Brahmaṇaspati. However, the descriptive epithets applied to Him are apposite to the elephant-faced God as Kaviṅkavīnām, the Seer of seers, Gaṇapati being the God of wisdom par excellence, and Jyeshṭharājam, the Vināyaka commanding precedence over others.

Also, in the *Gaṇeśa Pañcharatna* by Śrī Śrī Śrī Ādi Śaṅkara if found the line: *kalādharāvataṁsakam,* "He who dons the crescent," which attribute is also applied to Śiva. The *Vedas* assign Him a special place amongst the Gods. He was propitiated to bestow success and enjoyment and to avert obstacles and calamities. Various prayers to Gaṇeśa are found in the Vedic texts. He is invoked as the Law of laws, the Seers of seers and the Principal of principals in the verse above, as translated below:

> O Gaṇapati, the Seer of seers, unrivalled in wealth, King of elders, Principal of principals. Hear us and take Thy place, bringing with Thee all enjoyments.

In *Śatapatha Brāhmaṇa* 10.4.56, the Son of God, "a second myself," *dvitiya ātma,* is spoken of as *mithuna:* the "word not spoken." God's unspoken word is internal and unmanifest. Gaṇeśa thus came to be recognized as the "God Word." The Son is the testimony of the immanence of God being generated eternally. Gaṇeśa reflects the wisdom of His Father and is the repository of the word of God Śiva.

In the *Taittirīya Āraṇyaka* is a clear reference to Gaṇapati as Dantim (tusker). This word occurs in the Gāyatrī sacred to Gaṇapati:

> *Tanno dantiḥ pracodayāt.*
> Let that Tusker illumine our thoughts.

In the beginning is the Word. That Word is Aum, and the resonance of Aum is heard everywhere. *Aum Tat Sat.* That is what It is. So declare the *Vedāgamas.*

> That word is Aum.
> This syllable is the imperishable spirit,
> This indeed is the highest end.
> Knowing this syllable, truly indeed,
> Whatsoever one desires will be his....
> That is the Supreme Support,
> Knowing that support,
> One becomes happy in the Brahma world.
>
> *Kaṭha Upanishad* 2.15-16

> This audible symbol Aum serves as a support of contemplation. One infers the unseen in the seen, the unheard in the heard.
>
> *Dr. Ananda Coomaraswamy*

> We sing in praise of Him
> Who is the essence of Omkāram.
>
> *Satguru Yogaswāmī's Natchintanai*

The Causal Word, Aum, represents the divine thought, the source of existence. It corresponds to the power of will, known as Śiva Intention, or *icçhā śakti.* The power of knowledge known as Vishṇu Formulation, or *jñāna śakti,* and the power of action known as Brahma Expression, or *kriyā śakti,* also express the Causal Word, Aum.

Omkāra signifies the Supreme Śiva, being both *vyashṭi* (individual) and *samashṭi* (cosmic). Thus, Gaṇeśa Aum, the divine son of Śiva, is the support of the whole universe. His sound-symbol Aum is indestructible in past, present and future. It is immortal and ageless. He is ever Pillaiyar, the cherished child of Umā-Parameśvara. By meditating on Him in the three aspects of A-U-M, devotees can realize the reality of the Godhead. The *mahāvākya* Aum Tat Sat implies "That is what it is," and it is transmuted into the form of Gaṇeśa. He embodies the Truth of Tat Tvam Asi, "Thou art That."

Everything that our mind can grasp can be expressed in terms of kind, or category. So, category is a fundamental element of existence. All that can be counted or comprehended is a category *(gaṇa).* The principle of classifications through which the relations can be understood between different orders of things, between the macrocosm and the microcosm, is called the Lord of Categories. He is Gaṇapati.

Mahāgaṇapati is the ruler of all the categories and can be identified with Divinity in its perceptible manifestation. He guards the first approach to life and all its manifold unfoldment. The principle of categories transcends intellect. As the Lord of categories, Gaṇapati rules over the universal intellect, and the principles of the elements *(tattvas)* derived from it.

It is noteworthy that Gaṇapati is sometimes identified with Bṛihaspati, the patron of letters. Mythologically, He is the scribe who writes down the scriptures. He figures as the scribe of Sage Vyāsa, the author of the *Mahābhārata.*

You, leader of categories,
are the writer of this *Mahābhārata.*"

Mahābhārata 1.1.77

Microcosm and Macrocosm

In Gaṇeśa Hindus perceive one of the basic concepts of Hindu mythological symbolism: the identity of the macrocosm and the microcosm. In our religious tradition, the remembrance of the divinity of man and the immanence of God must be present before the doer of any action. In this way a Hindu learns to bow to Gaṇeśa at every turn. Not only is He worshiped at the beginning of every undertaking, but He guards the entrance of every house, of every temple and business establishment in the land of the Hindus. Aum Gaṇeśa is what He is: the master guide of devotees to realize their Divinity.

This identity of the macrocosm and the microcosm can be observed in the permanence of the relations formed as the substratum of all the aspects of the perceptible universe. Pillaiyar, as he is fondly called by the Śaivites, is represented as elephant-headed to express the unity of the small being, the microcosm that is man, and the great being, the macrocosm. The word *Gaja,* meaning elephant, is taken to mean "the origin and the goal." The stage reached by the reintegrated being, the *yogī,* in his experience of ultimate identification *(samādhi)* is called *Ga,* the goal; and the principle called *Ja,* the origin, is that from which the syllable *AUM* is said to be issued through a process of multifold reflection.

The man-part of Gaṇapati, representing the manifest principle, is subordinate to the unmanifest, shown as the elephant, which is the head. In symbols depicting Divinity, opposites can coexist. Hence man and elephant are combined in Gaṇapati's symbol, which leads to its essential meaning of *Praṇava.* The elephant is also a symbol of the stage whence existence begins *(Brahma Sūtra* 1.1.4) and whence the syllable *Aum* issues. From *Aum* issues the *Veda*, the universal law, and from the *Veda*, the universe. *Prāṇa* is the life current, and Va is the energy of Śiva named Chit *Śakti*. When they mingle in the vibration of *Prāṇa Va*, Gaṇeśa reveals Himself. *Aum Tat Sat Aum* is His sacred message. The living beings are the visible form of That, the Supreme Reality. Human existence denotes the coordination of the Absolute and the relative, of That and Thou.

> That (Tat) represents, the limitless, transcendent principle whose (nature) is Truth and Knowledge."
>
> *Taittirīya Āraṇyaka* 8.1.1

The Letters of Aum

True knowledge is the realization of this unity which Gaṇeśa signifies. *Aum* is commonly attributed to the form of Gaṇeśa, the Lord of the Praṇava Mantra, even though the three letters A-U-M signify a number of God's names when taken separately. *A* stands for Virat, Agni, and Viśva. *U* stands for Hiraṇyagarbha, Vāyu and Taijasa. *M* represents Īśvara, Āditya and Prajña.

Virat is the all-comprehensive universe of being. Agni is the primary source of all sacrificial ceremonies. *Viśva* means God Śiva, since the whole universe and the objects in the universe are manifested and are sheltered in Him. He pervades all of them. Hiraṇyagarbha is One who is the source and support of all light and luminous bodies as the sun, moon and stars. *Vāyu* means one who is the life and support of the universe, the cause of its dissolution. Taijasa is one who is resplendent and gives light to the sun and other luminous bodies. Īśvara is one whose knowledge and power are infinite. *Āditya* means immortal. *Prajña* means one whose knowledge is perfect and one who is omniscient.

Thus, the sacred syllable *Aum* combines within itself some of the most sublime names of the Supreme Being, and connotes His omnipotent and omniscient nature and attributes. *Aum* thus represents, in its fullest connotation, God Śiva, the Supreme Being.

> Aksharam Brahma Paramam
> Svabhavo Adhyātmamuchyate.
>
> *Bhagavad Gītā* 8.3

Brahman is spoken of as Akshara: that which is imperishable and inexhaustible. Saint Auvaiyar also referred to Akshara, meaning eternal wisdom, in her famous poem on Vināyaka. Kṛishṇa tells Arjuna in the following verse that he who leaves the body reflecting on *Aum* reaches the goal of beatific bliss, *paramam gatira.*

> Aum Ityekāksharam Brahma
> Vyaharan mam anusmaran
> Ya: prayati tyajan deham sa
> Yati paramam gatim.
>
> *Bhagavad Gītā* 8.13

Aum is the Ekākshara, the one lettered *mantra* of the Para Śivato, the word not spoken. *Mantra* is that which redeems when contemplated upon:

> Mananat thrayate itimantra.
>
> The Son of Śiva, Gaṇeśa, being "a second myself," came to be recognized as the God Word *Aum.*

When we chant the Praṇava Aum—the harmonious combination of the three basic sounds, *akara, ukara* and *makara*—the microcosmic activity links with the entire macrocosmic activity of the cosmos, which represents the all-pervading Reality of Paraśiva.

Akara sound is produced from the base of the spinal cord, where the *kuṇḍalinī* is posited, and rises to the throat. The supreme consciousness *(chaitanya)* functioning through the gross body in the waking state in the individual is called *vaiśvānara,* and is represented by the first syllable, *A. Ukara* is the second stage, where the sound from the throat is rolled outwards to the tip of the tongue. The same supreme consciousness functioning through the subtle body in the dream state in the individual is called *taijasa,* and is represented by the second syllable, *U. Makara* sound is concentrated at the lips. This same supreme consciousness functioning through the causal body in the deep sleep state in the individual is called *prajña,* and is represented by the final syllable, *M,* in *AUM.*

The significance of the *Aum mantra* is also brought out lucidly in the *sīkshāvalli* of the *Taittirīya Upanishad:*

> Aum iti Brahmā, Aum iti iḍām sarvam
> Aum ityedad anukṛiti, Aum iti samani gayanti (1.8).

And in the *Çhandogya Upanishad:*

> Aum ityetadāksharam Udgitham upasita
> Aum iti Hyudgayati tasyopa Vyakhyanam (2.23.3).

Śvetāśvatāra Upanishad exclaims:

> O Revealer of the Vedic truths, deign to make propitious that arrow which thou holdest in thy hand for shooting at somebody. O protector of devotees, do not destroy that benign personal form of thine which has manifested as the Universe (3.6).

The Praṇava, or the mystic syllable *Aum,* represented by the arrow reveals the form of the chosen ideal, Ishṭa Devatā. The Praṇava here means both the Impersonal (Nirguṇa) and Personal (Saguṇa) Brahman. That He holds the arrow in His hand shows that Gaṇeśa is ever ready to reveal Himself unto His devotees, if they repeat and contemplate on the *mantra Aum.*

The image of Gaṇapati and His *mantra Aum* constantly

remind us of the reality of the great identity. Man truly is the image of the cosmos. All realization lies within himself. Through the study of his inner impulses and of his inner structure, he can understand the nature of the universe. Lord Vighneśvara assures the freedom from fear. He instills the knowledge necessary to remove the fear inherent in time and duration. What power lies hidden in the mystic *Aum,* the sound symbol of Gaṇapati, and which is uttered at the beginning of every rite. Its meaning is expressed in Aum Tat Sat, and represents the fundamental identity of the macrocosm and the microcosm.

Aum Symbols of Gaṇeśa

The *swastika* reflects the graphic symbol of Gaṇapati. It is represented by a cross, being the development of the multiple from the basic unity, the central point, but each of its branches is bent so that it does not aim at the center. This is intended to show that man cannot reach the basic unity directly through the outward forms of the universe.

Gaṇeśa's trunk is bent because Divinity cannot be directly understood and also because He is master of obstacles. The noose in His hand destroys *moha,* delusion, the enemy of all seekers. The driving hook is the insignia of the ruler of the universe. The hand granting boons fulfills all desires, and the other hand allays all fears. Man seeks Gaṇeśa's protection at every turn in order that the Great Being may establish itself in his midst, and he may become one with It.

That Transcendental One is Aum Gaṇeśa. That Immanent One is Aum Gaṇeśa. The living beings are Gaṇeśa Aum. Thus do we raise the chant of concord, *Aum Gaṇeśa Tat Sat Aum.* It is through the worship of Lord Gaṇeśa that we come to know the venerable Lord Murugan, and lastly Supreme God Śiva, their Creator, our Father-Mother God, Lord of all creation, preservation and dissolution. *Aum Tat Sat Aum.*

> Aum is the one Eternal Syllable of which
> all that exists is but the development.
> The past, present and the future are
> all included in this one sound,
> and all that exists beyond the forms of time
> is also implied in the word Aum.
>
> *Māṇḍūkya Upanishad*

A Graphic Collection of Thirty-Six Aums

On the following pages we have assembled a special collection of Aums gathered at our Kauai monastery over the past few years. They are mostly in Sanskṛit, but also in some of India's regional languages. Of all the sacred symbols from India's rich spiritual heritage, none is more widely used and loved than the Aum. It is Divinity incarnate, and so it is natural that calligraphers and artists, designers and wall painters use it again and again to express the highest Truth.

From many hundreds of styles, our editors chose a few dozen and scanned them into Adobe's Illustrator program. There they fine-tuned them, removing some of the rough edges occasioned by printing in Bharat, then added a few embellishments where needed. The scrolls themselves were produced in Adobe's Photoshop program, which was also the tool used to create the embossed effects.

We take great joy in trading Aums (and other Indian art forms, like Gaṇeśas, village logos and more) and will release rights to anyone who shares their Aum collection with us. Send us a few Aums you epecially like, and we will send you a few back. Send a pile, and receive a treasure from our years of collecting. Mail your contributions (photocopies are fine) to Acharya Palaniswami, Himalayan Academy, 107 Kaholalele Road, Kapaa, Hawaii 96746-9304.

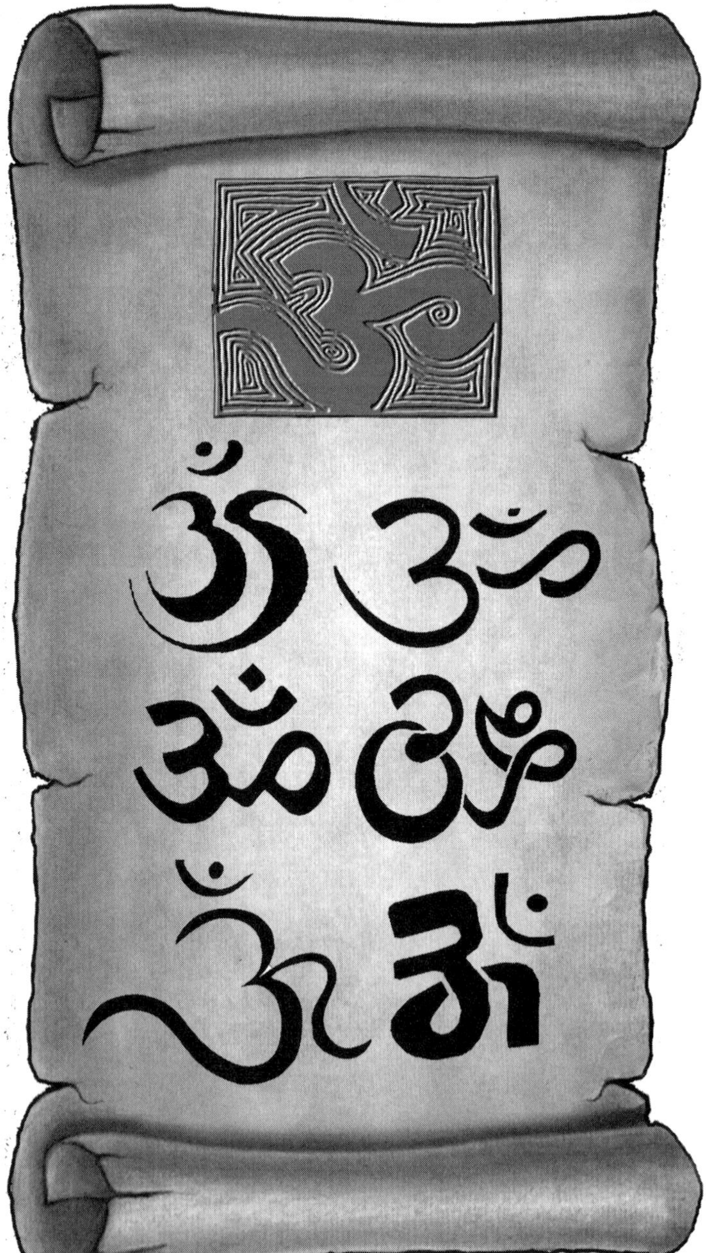

आर्य वर्णरिंतदृन्तरम् ।
रतः। अर्धेन्दुलसितम्।
एतत्तव अनुस्वरूपम्...गै...

गणादिं पूर्वमुद्धार्य वर्णरिंतदृन्तरम् ।
अनुस्वारः परतः। अर्धेन्दुलसितम्।
तारेण श्रेष्ठम एतत्तव अनुस्वरूपम्...गै...

गणा
अनु
तारेण

आर्य वर्णरिंतदृन्तरम् ।
रतः। अर्धेन्दुलसितम्।
एतत्तव अनुस्वरूपम्...गै...

गणादिं पूर्वमुद्धार्य वर्णरिंतदृन्तरम् ।
अनुस्वारः परतः। अर्धेन्दुलसितम्।
तारेण श्रेष्ठम एतत्तव अनुस्वरूपम्...गै...

गणा
अनु
तारेण

आर्य वर्णरिंतदृन्तरम् ।
रतः। अर्धेन्दुलसितम्।
एतत्तव अनुस्वरूपम्...गै...

गणादिं पूर्वमुद्धार्य वर्णरिंतदृन्तरम् ।
अनुस्वारः परतः। अर्धेन्दुलसितम्।
तारेण श्रेष्ठम एतत्तव अनुस्वरूपम्...गै...

गणा
अनु
तारेण

आर्य वर्णरिंतदृन्तरम् ।
रतः। अर्धेन्दुलसितम्।
एतत्तव अनुस्वरूपम्...गै...

गणादिं पूर्वमुद्धार्य वर्णरिंतदृन्तरम् ।
अनुस्वारः परतः। अर्धेन्दुलसितम्।
तारेण श्रेष्ठम एतत्तव अनुस्वरूपम्...गै...

गणा
अनु
तारेण

आर्य वर्णरिंतदृन्तरम् ।
रतः। अर्धेन्दुलसितम्।
एतत्तव अनुस्वरूपम्...गै...

गणादिं पूर्वमुद्धार्य वर्णरिंतदृन्तरम् ।
अनुस्वारः परतः। अर्धेन्दुलसितम्।
तारेण श्रेष्ठम एतत्तव अनुस्वरूपम्...गै...

गणा
अनु
तारेण

आर्य वर्णरिंतदृन्तरम् ।
रतः। अर्धेन्दुलसितम्।

Bṛihaspatiḥ

बृहस्पतिः

Master of the Word

Gaṇeśa, Master of the Word

From Tattvāloka, February-March, 1990

IN THE PRIMORDIAL THROB, *ADYA SPANDA*, THE *TANTRA* SAYS, INHERE A SERIES OF VIBRATIONS THAT TAKE THE FORM OF SOUND, *nāda*. This is the word, the Word Eternal, *nityavak*, of the *Veda*, which itself became all the worlds. *Vāk* descends for the purpose of creation with Her four cosmic steps. The *Veda* says that all speech is measured out in four steps or planes, impelled by the mind, and these are known to the knowers of Brahman. The first three are hidden in secrecy while the fourth step is human speech, that is, the ordinary word.

These four steps are *sthūla*, the physical substance of matter; *sūkshma*, the vital life force supporting and circumferencing it; *kāraṇa*, the causal, the mind principle; and *mahākāraṇa*, the great causal, the high Supernal, where abides the Word with all the original rhythm. And these again correspond to the four states of consciousness: *jāgrat*, the waking state; *svapna*, the dream state; *sushupti*, deep sleep; and *turīya*, the fourth, that which is beyond these three states.

The *tantrikas*, while admitting the principle of the division, apply it for practical purposes, dealing with the subject from a psycho-physical and psycho-spiritual point of view. Naturally, therefore, since the subtle centers play a vital part in their *yoga*, they locate the *vāk* of the states in the nervous system. They name it *para, pasyānti, madhyama* and *vaikharī*. The first and the supreme force—the primordial *paravāk*—is beyond. It is unmanifest but turned towards manifestation. It is the great causal *mahākāraṇa*, and as such its center is at the base of the spinal column that supports the nervous system. This bottom is *mūlādhāra*, the root center of the physical being. Next is *pasyānti vāk*, the word that perceives, and this is the causal, located in the navel center. Then is *madhyama vāk,* the middle, the word in the intermediate, subtle region between the navel and the throat, which is the region for the expression of speech, called *vaikharī vāk.* Gaṇapati as Brahmaṇaspati is the Master of the Word, the Lord of Satya Mantra. And so, the *Tantra* conceives Him having His abode in the *mūlādhāra* of beings, from where speech originates in the form of *paravāk.*

Seat of *Mūlādhāra*

It is said in the *Veda* that Brahmaṇaspati descends deep down into the inconscient waters to bring about in creation something stable and solid. In the macrocosm, His whole process of creation starts from the bottom. His action applies equally to the microcosm. In the microcosm, in the human being, there are different planes and parts of being which are governed by conscious centers and sources of the dynamic powers of the being, which again act as focal points for the consciousness to operate. These centers, picturesquely described as *chakras* (wheels of power), or *padmas* (lotuses) ready to unfold, are situated in the subtle body and are arranged one above the other in an ascending series from the lowest physical to the highest mind center and spiritual center. The lowest physical is represented by the bottom-most center, *mūlādhāra,* and Gaṇapati operates from there as the unmanifest word.

There is an ancient Tamil classic known as *Vināyaka Ahaval,* attributed to Auvaiyar, which is in praise of Gaṇapati. Fittingly, it starts with the words *sitak kalabhach chentamarippum padachilambu pala isai pada,* which means superficially, "the various notes raised by the anklets adorning the lotus feet of the Lord which are as cool as sandalpaste." The cool sandal *gandha* is the measure, *tanmatra,* of the earth element, *pṛithivī tattva,* and *sentāmarai* is the red lotus. Obviously, the *mūlādhāra* center is indicated, which is known as the *kulam,* where the earth element, the lowest *physical,* abides. Similarly, by *padachilambu* is indicated the quarter of speech, *paravāk.* At the outset of itself, the ancient Tamil classic praises Gaṇapati as the form of *paravāk,* having his abode in *mūlādhāra.*

In the *mūlādhāra* is the potential energy picturesquely represented as the sleeping serpent power *kuṇḍalinī śakti.* There is a fire there which in its gross form is *jaṭharāgni,* the physical fire, the fire that cooks all food, digests it and transforms it to sustain the physical. The other form is *vaiśvānara,* the soul in the heart of every being, the *jīva,* the Self, the Skanda of the *Purāṇas.* Still another form is the *vaidyuta,* electric energy, from which speech arises, thereby representing Gaṇapati. When Gaṇapati becomes active in the *mūlādhāra,* when His grace is felt, the *kuṇḍalinī śakti* wakes up, the fire shoots up its flames, opening the centre at the summit and filling the whole system with a downpour of nectar-like bliss. Then one is able to realize the Godhead in the *mantra* and know the sign of the Lord in the conscious mind—"Sattattil sadāśivam katti, cittattil Śivaliṅgam katti," as the Tamil classic says.

Powers and Personalities

Many are the powers and personalities of Gaṇapati. The universe is created in the form of groups *(gaṇas),* and for each *gaṇa* there is a Gaṇapati, collective head. Thus, there are innumerable *Gaṇanāthas* and *Vināyakas.* At least in the *Mahāśodha Nyāsa* in the *Śākta Tantra,* there are as many Gaṇeśas as there are *mātṛikāksharas,* letters of the alphabet, that is, 51. Gaṇapati in the form of an infant, *Bāla,* indicated possibilities of growth and future unfoldment for the aspirant. Gaṇapati as a dancer indicates dynamic, harmonious activity geared towards progress.

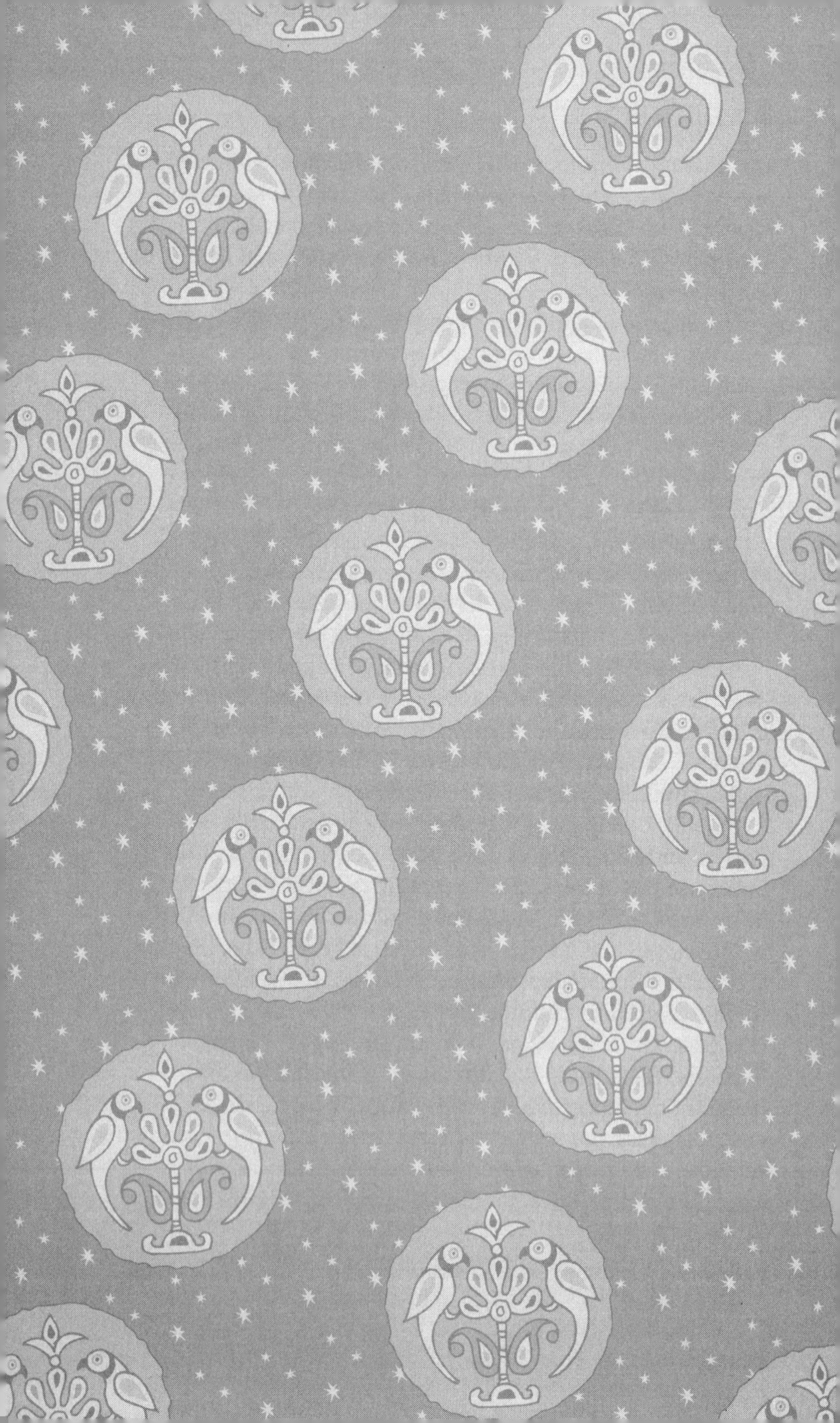

Gaṇapati Japaḥ

गणपति जपः

Mantra Recitation

ਰਾਮਕਲੀ
ਮਾਰੂ

Mantra Recitation

J*APA*, OR RECITATION, IS THE SPIRITUAL PRACTICE OF DEVOTEDLY REPEATING A *MANTRA*, GENERALLY A SPECIFIED NUMBER OF TIMES, such as 108, often while counting on a strand of beads, called a *japa mālā*, while conscientiously concentrating on the meaning of the *mantra*. The repetition should be dutifully slow. This brings *puṇya*, merit, to the devotee. It should not be thoughtlessly mechanical or the hurried, so-called rapid-fire or machine-gun *japa*, which demonstrate ignorance of the *tantras*. Such arrogance and disregard for contemplative traditions brings *pāpa*, demerit, to the devotee, creating internal strife, community opposition and turmoil for all concerned.

Japa is a form of devotional worship, invocation, supplication, praise, adoration, meditation and direct, experiential communion. Unless we are actually in a state of *samādhi* (total absorption), which is rare for most people, *japa* provides a means to disengage from our racing thoughts and our memories of the past—mostly the bad ones. The repetition of positive, uplifting, spiritual *mantras* over and over again lifts consciousness and causes the *mūlādhāra chakra* to spin clockwise. We feel uplifted. Life does not look so bad, and neither does the past. A sense of forgiveness comes and the future looms bright. The past is forgiven and forgotten.

The power of thought and mind is embodied in sound form, that is, in the Word. The ancient *ṛishis* made this knowledge of the Word into a science and turned their minds toward the inner worlds, invoking the beings therein and offering their thoughts to the Deities and *devas* through Vedic hymns, prayers and *mantras*. According to the *Vedas*, the holy scripture that forms the basis of Hinduism, out of the mind of the Deity came the Word, *vāk*. Its evolutes precede and give rise to the forms of the inner mind—the astral forms. These subtle forms in turn give rise to the outer, material forms that we see.

> By that Word of His, by that Self, He created all this, whatever there is.
>
> *Śukla Yajur Veda, Śatapatha Brāhmaṇa* 10.6.5.5. VE, 106

> This [in the beginning], was only the Lord of the universe. His Word was with Him. This Word was His second. He contemplated. He said, "I will deliver this Word so that she will produce and bring into being all this world."
>
> *Sāma Veda, Tāṇḍya Mahā Brāhmaṇa* 20.14.2. VE, 107

> The Word is infinite, immense, beyond all this.... All the Gods, the celestial spirits, men and animals live in the Word. In the Word all the worlds find their support.
>
> *Kṛishṇa Yajur Veda, Taittirīya Brāhmaṇa* 2.8.8.4. VE, 107

The Vedic view brings increasing confirmation that modern physics is on the right track. Quantum electromagnetic field theories tell us that, in fact, there is no such thing as matter. There are only force fields of time and space that are observable as varying intensities. Thus, a carbon atom is not a bit of matter; it is a time-space-energy force field of a particular intensity.

Nuclear physicists can change the energy force fields in a chamber and change one element to another. If we knew the carbon *mantra* and could say it properly, we would cause the particular time-space-energy force field to occur, and some carbon would precipitate. Certain occult practitioners can actually do this with their minds and cause objects to appear.

Such magic does show the correspondence that there is between mind, sound and form. This is the basic mystical reality behind *mantras.* What is important for us to realize is that each Mahādeva can be experienced, expressed, in a *mantra* form that corresponds to that Being. This phenomenon is akin to remembering someone by their name rather than their face. When we utter such a *mantra,* we call forth the Mahādeva or cause a particular inner truth to rise up in our minds. Then we feel His presence and enjoy.

Two Classes of *Mantras*

There are two basic kinds of *mantras.* One class is a very powerful set that causes immediate, direct changes to occur in the force fields around us, whether we know the meanings of the sounds or not. These *mantras* should only be used after initiation and proper instruction, because if they are mispronounced they can do us serious harm. The *mantra* singers of the Navajo Indians of North America used very powerful healing *mantras* that would last for days and days. Even in recent times, a Navajo singer wrongly chanted on the fifth day of a nine-day chant and crippled himself physically. This is a documented occurrence. He had to resort to less powerful *mantras* after that.

The second kind of *mantras* are either weaker, or the strong vibrations they produce cannot be distorted by misuse or mispronunciation. With this class of *mantras*, it is the power of our own minds concentrated upon the inner-plane being or concept that makes the *mantra* most beneficial. If we are not concentrated, still the energy of the *mantra* can evoke only one vibration or image. The majority of the Vedic *mantras*, all the names of the Gods and the Gāyatrīs fall into this category. Most of the Vedic chants are simply short hymns and prayers, while the Sanskṛit language itself causes positive, uplifting force fields that penetrate immediately into the inner realms.

My *satguru*, Sage Yogaswāmī placed tremendous emphasis on the performance of *japa*, repeating the name of the Lord with concentration and feeling. This great *jñānī* explained, "May we not forget that *mantram* is life, that *mantram* is action, that *mantram* is love and that the repetition of *mantram*, *japa*, bursts forth wisdom from within. *Japa yoga* is the first *yoga* to be performed toward the goal of *jñāna*. In the temple perform *japa*. Under the sacred tree perform *japa*. I performed *japa* all this life as a silent *sādhana*. It is automatic now."

Sage Yogaswāmī enjoined his Śaivite devotees to "Wear *rudrāksha* beads and repeat the Pañchākshara. Let your heart grow soft and melt. Chant the Letters Five and in love you will discover His will. Chant so that impurities, anxieties and doubts are purged. All hail Namaḥ Śivāya!"

Repeating *mantras* slowly purifies the mind, like running fresh water continually into a container of discolored water. A fresh stream of water causes the mud at the bottom of a container to rise and flow out over the top edges, eventually to be completely replaced by crystal-clear water. Similarly, *japa* cleanses the mind of impurities as the pure vibrations of the *mantras* loosen and wash away the impure vibrations.

Aum Japa

Lord Gaṇeśa is invoked through the *mantra Aum.* The *Māṇḍūkya Upanishad* elucidates the inner meaning of *Aum,* which embodies the highest wisdom. *Aum* has three syllables. *A* represents the waking state. *U* represents the dreaming state. *M* represents the state of deep sleep. *Aum* in its entirety, plus the moment of silence which follows it, represents the *śānti,* the peace beyond understanding. Thus, Aum *japa* performed as an invocation to Lord Gaṇeśa, the Lord of Wisdom and Knowledge—while love is welling up from our hearts and tears are for no reason flowing simultaneously—calls forth the knowledge of the entirety of our existence in these four categories of consciousness. These are realms that God Gaṇeśa rules over as Lord of Categories and this is the knowledge that He can grant devotees who perform Aum *japa* and meditation on the meaning of Aum.

For Aum *japa* to be effective, the *mantra* must be pronounced correctly. The first syllable is *A,* pronounced as the English word "awe," but prolonged: "aaa." The second syllable is *U,* as in "roof," pronounced "oo" but prolonged: "ooo." The third syllable is *M,* pronounced "mm" with the front teeth gently touching and the sound prolonged: "mmmm." Each repetition is sounded for about seven seconds, with two seconds on *A,* two seconds on *U* and three seconds on *M,* with a silence of about two seconds before the next repetition. The three syllables are run together: AAUUMM (silence), AAUUMM (silence), AAUUMM (silence). On the first syllable, *A,* we feel the solar plexus and chest vibrating. On the second syllable, *U,* the throat vibrates. The third syllable, *M,* vibrates the top of the head. Thus, proper chanting of Aum also is a high form of *yoga,* moving energy from the lower *chakras* of the body up to the highest *chakra,* or energy center—the *sahasrāra chakra* at the crown of the head.

Another traditional way to do this *japa* is to take a full breath and then chant the AUM three times as you exhale.

The first repetition is audible, the second is more quiet and the third is barely audible, as you concentrate within. Then inhale slowly as you visualize the image of our loving Lord Gaṇeśa in your mind. Then repeat the AUM again three times as you exhale. The breathing should not be forced, but natural, slow, gentle and rhythmical. We can use a *japa mālā* with 108 beads and pass over one bead for each repetition, or do the *japa* for a prearranged period of time.

Two Famous Gaṇeśa *Mantras*

Two other Gaṇeśa *mantras* are commonly used. One is *Aum Śrī Gaṇeśāya Namaḥ,* meaning "Praise to Lord Gaṇeśa." This is the *mantra* of invocation, adoration and worship. It is repeated at the beginning of *pūjās* and it can be used for *japa,* to invoke Gaṇeśa's blessings for the auspicious beginning of a task, project, change of life, community undertaking or simply to offer Him our praise.

Another very special *mantra* is *Aum Gaṁ Gaṇapataye Namaḥ.* This is Lord Gaṇeśa's *mūla* ("root") *mantra.* It is also known as His *bīja mantra,* for it combines Gaṇeśa's *bīja* ("seed") sound, "gam," with the phrase, "Praise be to Gaṇapati." This *mantra* is used for *yoga sādhana* in which we invoke Gaṇeśa and merge ourself with His supreme knowledge and peace. These two *mantras* are not harmful if mispronounced, as sometimes happens, though they should be sounded as properly as possible to be most effective. Most importantly, they must be chanted at the same time each day, and this means exactly the same time, for full *devonic* support.

When the *gaṇas* and *devas* of Lord Gaṇeśa are finally attracted to the home shrine, the room will feel filled with actinodic energy even if it is a closet or a small sacred alcove. The energy will come out of seeming nowhere into the room. This feeling indicates that Ganeśa's *gaṇas* are present, eager and willing to do whatever they can to maintain *śānti,* peace, within the home and bind the family together. Nothing bad, hurtful or harmful will ever be performed by them, even if fervently prayed for. Only good and goodness will be their actions. They do not condone revenge. They do not deny anything to anyone who is within *dharma's* calling. And they do work within the *prārabdha karmas* of each individual within the family. Theirs is a calculated job in doing what they have to do to maintain family togetherness, even at great distances.

These *gaṇas* are numbered in the trillions, and they are available in every home to serve the devout. Today in China, Japan and nearly every country of the world they work to improve family togetherness, for this is their mission, given to them detail by detail by our loving Gaṇeśa. Because of them, family life goes smoothly, protection is immanent, immediate, and all members of the family enjoy the secure vibration of being bound in love, good feelings for one and all and support for each other by every other member. This intricate working of the *prāṇas* within the home is what the *gaṇas* of our Lord do tirelessly day after day, year after year, generation after generation. By doing so they earn their rewards within the heaven of heavens. After all, humans are tribal and don't do well on their own, unless they are mature, renunciate *sannyāsins* of austere orders who thrive on their own bliss.

It is Gaṇeśa's *gaṇas* who keep the extended families together, perpetuating the wealth from generation to generation, on into the future of futures. Invoke Lord Gaṇeśa through the proper *sādhanas* the same time each day, and He will send his *gaṇas* to reward you. Feed them milk and honey and all things sweet, placed upon your altar. This will be pleasing and considered a reward for good works well performed for you, your family and other loved ones.

Three Gaṇeśa Gāyatrī Mantras

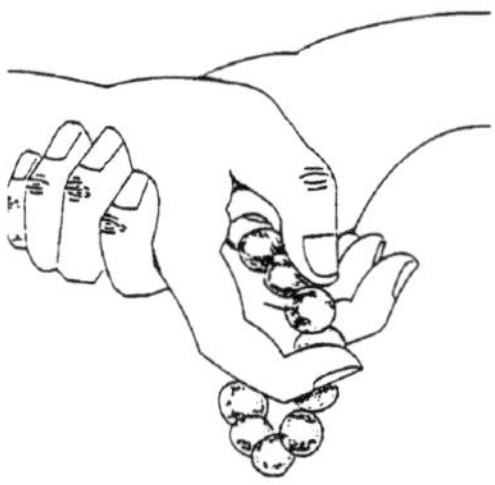

Gāyatrī refers to a special three-line *Vedic* meter used in *mantras* for invoking and focusing consciousness on the Deity. The three *Gāyatrīs* below are intoned during *pūjās* and *yajñas.* They may also be recited as powerful *japa*—repeated again and again, while gently regulating the breath according to systematic rhythms given by one's *guru* to establish a deep inner connection with Lord Gaṇeśa.

ॐ एकदन्ताय विद्महे
वक्रतुण्डाय धीमहि
तन्नो दन्तिः प्रचोदयात्

Aum ekadantāya vidmahe
vakratuṇḍāya dhīmahi
tanno dantiḥ prachodayāt

We devote our thought to the one-tusked Lord.
We meditate upon Him who has a curved-trunk.
May the tusked One guide us on the right path.

Gaṇapati Upanishad

ॐ तत्पुरुषाय विद्महे
वक्रतुण्डाय धीमहि
तन्नो दन्तिः प्रचोदयात्

Aum tatpurushāya vidmahe
vakratuṇḍāya dhīmahi
tanno dantiḥ prachodayāt

We devote our thought to that supreme person.
We meditate upon Him who has a curved-trunk.
May the tusked One guide us on the right path.

Nārāyaṇa Upanishad

ॐ तत् कराताय विद्महे
हस्तिमुखाय धीमहि
तन्नो दन्तिः प्रचोदयात्

Aum tat karātāya vidmahe
hasti mukhāya dhīmahi
tanno dantiḥ prachodayāt

I know the mysterious Lord.
May His elephant face guide me.
May the tusked One guide us on the right path.

Maitrāyaṇi Saṁhitā 2.6-9

A Special Collection of Gaṇeśa Mantras

From Sadguru Sant Keshavadas' Book, Lord Gaṇeśa.

Gaṇeśa *mantras* are *siddhi mantras.* Each *mantra* contains certain specific powers of Lord Gaṇeśa. When chanted with the proper *prāṇāyāma* (rhythmic breathing) and sincere devotion, they will yield good results. In general, Gaṇeśa *mantras* will ward off all evil and bless the devotee with abundance, prudence and success. Evil spirits dare not enter the home or the mind of the devotee where Gaṇeśa *mantras* are recited. Those so mystically inclined and knowledgeable of the seven *chakras* below the *mūlādhāra* use these powerful incantantions under the direction of the *guru* to close off these regions of the mind one by one and free consciousness from deep depression, confusion, jealousy, rage, lingering anger and fear. Some such *mantras* are given below for the spiritual benefit of the readers.

One more point to remember is that one should bathe or wash the limbs before sitting for repetition of the *mantra.* Also, one should do three or more *prāṇāyāma* before beginning the *mantra.* The minimum repetition of the *mantra* should be one full *mālā,* or 108 times. When this is done at a fixed hour and place regularly for 48 days, it becomes an *upāsanā,* which means intense meditation, which will yield *siddhi,* or spiritual powers. The warning given is that one should use those powers only for healing the sick and other such selfless actions for the benefit of mankind. These powers should not be misused. Misuse of power may bring the curse of the *asuras.*

ॐ गम् गणपतये नमः

Aum gaṁ gaṇapataye namaḥ

This is a *mantra* from *Gaṇapati Upanishad.* One may always use it before beginning a journey, a new course in school, new career or job, or before entering into any new contract or business so that impediments are removed and your endeavor may be crowned with success.

ॐ नमो भगवते गजाननाय नमः

Aum namo bhagavate gajānanāya namaḥ

This is a devotional *mantra* personifying the all-pervading consciousness of Gaṇeśa. This *mantra* is very efficacious to have the *darśana* of Gaṇeśa or to feel His immediate presence as a person.

ॐ श्री गणेशाय नमः

Aum śrī gaṇeśāya namaḥ

This *mantra* is usually taught to children for their good education. It increases their memory power, and they become successful in their examinations. Of course, people of any age may use this *mantra* when taking courses in a school or university and for success in attaining their degree.

ॐ वक्रतुण्डाय हुं

Aum vakratuṇḍāya hum

This is a very powerful *mantra* as discussed in the *Gaṇeśa Purāṇa.* When something is not working properly, individually or universally, nationally or internationally, or when the minds of the people get curved and negative, the attention of Gaṇeśa may be drawn by this *mantra* to straighten their ways. The HUM symbolizes "Delay no more, my Lord, in straightening the paths of the curve-minded ones." This *mantra* is used many times in the *Gaṇeśa Purāṇa* to curb the atrocities of cruel demons. In addition, this *mantra* could also be used for healing any spinal deficiency, such as curvature of the spine or curved limbs. Dedicate 1,008 repetitions of this holy word to straighten and heal such deficiencies.

ॐ क्षिप्रप्रसादाय नमः

Aum kshipra prasādāya namaḥ

Kshipra means instantaneous. If some danger or negative energy is coming your way and you don't know how to get rid of that trouble, with true devotion, practice this *mantra* for quick blessing and purification of one's aura.

ॐश्रीं ह्रीं क्लीं ग्लौं गं

गणपतये वर वरद् सर्व

जनम्मे वषमानाय स्वाहा

Aum śrīṁ hrīṁ klīṁ glauṁ gaṁ
gaṇapataye vara varada sarva
janamme vashamānāya svāhā

There are several *bīja* (seed) *mantras* in this *mantra*. Among other things, it means "shower Your blessings, I offer my ego as an oblation."

ॐ सुमुखाय नमः

Aum sumukhāya namaḥ

This *mantra* has a lot of meaning, but to make it simple, it means you will be always very beautiful in soul, in spirit, in face, everything. By meditating on that *mantra*, very pleasing manners and a beauty comes on you. Along with that comes peace, which constantly dances in your eyes, and the words you speak are all filled with that power of love.

ॐ एकदन्ताय नमः

Aum ekadantāya namaḥ

Ekadanta refers to one tusk in the elephant face, which means God broke the duality and made you to have a one-pointed mind. Whoever has that oneness of mind and single-minded devotion will achieve everything.

ॐ कपिलाय नमः

Aum kapilāya namaḥ

Kapila means that you are able to give color therapy. You are able to create colors around yourself and around others, bathe them in that color and heal them. As per the *mantra* you create, so will you create the colors. Another meaning is "wish cow," the "cow of plenty." It means that whatever you wish, that comes true. There is a wish-cow inside you. Whatever you wish, especially for healing others, comes true immediately.

ॐ गजकर्णिकाय नमः

Aum gajakarṇikāya namaḥ

The ears of Gaṇeśa, the elephant, are constant fanning, which means people may talk a lot, but you are not receiving inside anything other than that which is important. It also means that you can sit anywhere and tune this cosmic television (the body) with seven channels *(chakras)* and all 72,000 *nāḍīs,* to any *loka* and be able to hear ancestors, angels, the voice of God or the voice of prophets. That kind of inner ear you will develop through this *mantra.*

ॐ लम्बोदराय नमः

Aum lambodarāya namaḥ

This means you feel that you are this universe. It means that all the universes are within you. Like an entire tree is in the seed, the whole universe is in the sound of creation, which is Aum, and that Aum consciousness in you makes you feel that you are the universe. Therefore, if you say, realizing the oneness with the universe, "*śānti,*" to the world every day, then the grace of God will come and there will be world peace, universal peace. It is the universes within Aum and Aum within you.

ॐ विकटाय नमः

Aum vikaṭāya namaḥ

This means realizing this world as a dream or a drama. When you are in that high consciousness, this whole world looks like a dream. All of us have taken a role. We have to play our role in life as wife or husband or kids or citizens as per the role which we have taken. When an actor bitten by a sponge cobra which is brought on the stage falls, the entire audience cries, but that boy who has fallen knows that it was not a real cobra and that he is not dead. Life is a drama—definitely life in this material world, this physical world of ego, is a drama. But inside, like the boy on the stage who is very happy knowing that he didn't die by the bite of the sponge cobra, like that, the truth never dies in us; it is immortal. So everything else you consider as drama. That consciousness comes to you by knowing this *mantra.*

ॐ विघ्ननाशनाय नमः

Aum vighna nāśanāya namaḥ

This *mantra* invokes the Lord Gaṇeśa to remove every impediment in your life and in your works. By constantly knowing this *mantra,* all obstacles and blocked energy in you also are released.

ॐ विनायकाय नमः

Aum vināyakāya namaḥ

Vināyaka is the name of Gaṇeśa in the golden age. So by realizing this *mantra,* your life will have a golden age. In your office, in your work, you'll be the boss. Vināyaka means something under control. Vināyaka means the Lord of problems.

ॐ धुम्रकेतवे नमः

Aum dhumrakatuve namaḥ

Halley's Comet is called Dhumraketu in the *Vedas.* Whenever Halley's Comet appears, on the whole planet Earth, and in other places also, there will be fear and terror. The guiding masters and those who have the wisdom to face it will all withdraw to the higher worlds. Important people die during that time, and bloodshed and various other problems come. To overcome that, it's important for us to remember this *mantra* for world peace.

ॐ गणाध्यक्षाय नमः

Aum gaṇādhyakshāya namaḥ

This *mantra* is so important. Suppose you have a group, a country, neighbors, or any kind of group therapy, group healing or a whole country needing healing, then you have to bring that entire group to your mind's arena and say this *mantra.* A group healing takes place by this *mantra.*

ॐ भालचन्द्राय नमः

Aum bhālachandrāya namaḥ

In Sanskṛit, *bhāla* means the forehead center. *Chandra* means the crescent moon. *Bhālachandra* means that *chakra* from where the nectar drips. That is the secret of all healing. It is to feel yourself as Śiva, identifying yourself with the Truth and feeling constantly that you are carrying the crescent moon, the symbol of growth and nectar and peace.

ॐ गजाननाय नमः

Aum gajānanāya namaḥ

This means the ego is cut off and in its place you have the memory of an elephant, a place where AUM is kept. Gajānana is the leader of righteous happenings, one who makes changes according to *dharma.* Whenever this *mantra* is invoked, the head is filled with infinite consciousness.

Gaṇapati Prārthanāḥ

गणपति-प्रार्थनाः

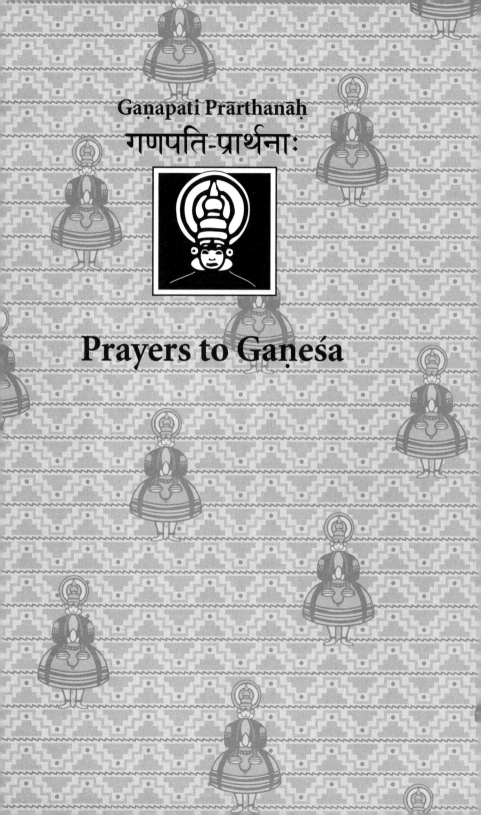

Prayers to Gaṇeśa

Prayers to Lord Gaṇeśa

KNEELING OR STANDING, SITTING IN *PADMĀSANA* OR WALKING ALONE, DEVOTEES DISCOVER IN PRAYER ONE OF THE MOST powerful forms of communication with inner worlds. Through praying with concentrated feeling, or *bhāva,* we can share our inmost sensibilities with Lord Gaṇapati. Thus we establish a connection with the Deity. One of the finest explanations of prayer from the Hindu perspective was given by the renowned Swāmī Sivānanda of Ṛishikesh, North India, in one of his books on Deity worship:

"The entire process of spiritual ascent is from start to finish one of earnest practice. There is no other road except *abhyāsa* (dedicated striving and practice). One may have the best feeling, the best heart, the most sublime *bhāva,* but unless and until every part of this is put into actual practice, there is no hope. *Abhyāsa* is the keynote of the life of *sādhana.* Without it, *sādhana* will not go towards its fruition of *anubhūti,* or experience. Thus, we have the celestials standing at the door of Mahādeva. They hymn Him, glorify Him and pray unto Him; and this is our next cue. It is the law of prayer that is now given to us as our sole guide upon the path. Prayer means, first and foremost, a perfect belief in a higher power. It means the desire and willingness to submit our *abhimāna,* or ego, at the feet of a higher power. Thus, the acquisition of *śraddhā* (faith) is now pointed out to us. The submission of our personal ego, or *abhimāna,* is next pointed out to us. Herein its natural corollary, the cultivation of the supreme virtue of absolute humility, also is indicated. The *devas* prayed not that they may get power to win over the *asuras.* There is the attitude of willing self-abnegation, self-effacement, a standing aside so that the fullest manifestation of the divine power may stand in front and take over the stand from them. This indicates the recognition of the nondoership of the individual self and the Supreme doership of the one doer, the Supreme God. It indicates that the *sādhaka*, or the seeker, is but a mere instrument; and it is the Lord Himself, the Indweller in the individual, who takes over the *sādhana* and actually does it. When the seeker begins to feel that even this *sādhana* is not done by him, but that it is the Divine *śākti* that works within him and enables the *sādhana* to be worked out and which achieves the ultimate fulfillment of the Divine Will, then he starts on the real upward march and rapid ascent toward triumphant divinity.

"Thus, the second aspect of prayer unfolds itself before us. We completely allow the Divine to take charge of our personality. The seeker recedes into the background and there is total resignation to the will of the Divine. 'I am nothing; Thy will be done.' This is the formula that keeps tune to every beat of his heart, every pulsation in his body. The seeker becomes a transformed being" (*Lord Shanmukha and His Worship*, page xiii-xv).

Using Various Kinds of Prayers

When we go to the temple in distress or when we go in great joy and thankfulness, our prayers may flow spontaneously up from our hearts. Some find it very natural to speak out in words, bringing their gratitude, adoration or troubles into a form that can be offered to Lord Gaṇeśa. Others may just stand, feeling but not knowing what to say in their own minds or hearts. Others may not yet feel at all close to the Mahādeva but still yearn to open the door to religious communion with the Deity. In other words, many people want to learn how to pray.

We are indeed fortunate if we have been raised to learn the ancient Hindu hymns or the songs and prayers of the *sants.* These can be spoken in their original Indian language, or voiced in the translation to other tongues. There are many types of prayer. There are prayers of invocation performed prior to worship or important actions. There are prayers of entreaty, requesting *devonic* aid in times of decision, trouble or turmoil. There are prayers of praise, giving thanks for God's grace and the fulfillment of our needs. And, perhaps most importantly, there are prayers specially written for the children, messages that make them aware of their innate intimacy with the Divine. On the following pages, we offer a wide variety of prayers to Lord Gaṇeśa, composed in recent times in the English language, along with several famous invocations from the Sanskṛit tradition.

By memorizing prayers, we make them immediately available to put into use wherever we are. In the temple with God Gaṇeśa before us or by ourselves with the Lord in our mind, we can repeat them with a strong, concentrated feeling which will carry our thoughts into the inner world of the Gods. As our worship matures into an open relationship with the Deity, these prayers will come automatically to mind as our way of talking with the Lord. They are especially useful during and after Gaṇeśa *pūjā,* when the Lord is present and listening and we are in close touch with Him. Of course, prayer can be used at any time to make us aware of our being in the mind of Lord Gaṇeśa. As we come to know God Gaṇeśa better, our communication with Him will take on more the spirit of talking with one's intimates, parents or close friends, and our own spontaneous words may mix freely with formal prayers.

Prayers of Invocation

Invocations are chants and prayers by which we "invoke" the presence of the Deity. The God is being called. The God and the devotee are being brought together, in touch. Prayers of invocation often sing out the greatness of the Deity, His known attributes and qualities. Vedic *ṛishis* and holy sages of olden times were masters of invocation. They could immediately call up the *devatā* through the strength of their *mantras.* In the *pūjā* and *japa* chapters of this book there are many chants which also serve as powerful invocations. "Aum Śrī Gaṇeśāya Namaḥ" is an invocation in itself. We begin this section on prayers with a famous, *śloka* to Lord Gaṇeśa from the root scripture of all denominations of Sanātana Dharma, the *Vedas.* It has been chanted by billions of Hindus down-through the ages, uttering five attributes of Gaṇeśa and invoking His all-powerful protection.

Aum śuklāmbaradharaṁ vishṇum
Śaśivarṇaṁ chaturbhujam
Prasanna vadanaṁ dhyāyet
Sarva vighnopa śāntaye

Aum, attired in white and all-pervading,
O moon-hued, four-shouldered One
with smiling face so pleasing,
upon You we meditate
for removing all obstacles.

Śrī Ādi Śaṅkara prayed in his *Gaṇeśa Bhujaṅgam* the following invocation. It is particularly suitable for recitation before *japa* and deep meditation on the highest wisdom of Lord Gaṇeśa, the incomparable Lord:

To You whom the wise exclaim
as the single-syllabled, Supreme sound,
stainless and peerless,
bliss, formless, unconditioned—
the Indweller in the core of
sacred tradition—to that
Primeval One I bow in adoration.

Prayers of Supplication

Prayers of supplication are requests, pleadings or entreaties presented to the Deity in the spirit of personal surrender and loving devotion. Something specific is being asked for, a specific problem is being laid at the Lord's Holy Feet. Such supplications to the one-tusked Lord are given unconditionally, with full trust that He will do what is best for us, though not necessarily what *we* might think is best. We do not demand of the Lord, for He, like a parent, provides not as we desire, but as we truly need. Prayers of supplication may come forth in the natural language of our hearts.

Leaving a problem at His holy feet means we let it be there and do not carry it home with us. Nor do we worry or wonder about how it will be handled, when it will be taken care of, or if it will be taken care of at all. In full unquenchable faith we leave the matter there, at the feet of the God, and walk away from the temple or shrine, feeling that release has started and solution will be forthcoming. We must have this kind of faith for religion to work within us. To carry home with us the same problems, fears and worries would be to take back the offering we have given the Deity to dissolve. This is like the rich and famous who buy with gifts and do not give at all, slyly expecting more than something in exchange, gaining *pāpa* rather than *puṇya* and not knowing the difference. The course of events will later show how He works for our ultimate spiritual welfare.

MOMENTS OF DECISION

Aum, Śrī Gaṇeśāya *namaḥ*—Great Lord of Wisdom, here I stand with so many decisions to make, with so many ways to turn. I beg for Your grace. Fill me with righteous judgment and clear discrimination as I lay all confusion at Your holy feet and immerse myself solely in You. Aum, Gaṇeśa *śaraṇam, śaraṇam* Gaṇeśa.

RELEASE FROM WORLDLINESS

Aum, Śrī Gaṇeśāya *namaḥ*—Lord Vināyaka, You are the Destroyer of all sin. I need you; help me. How long I've spent thinking only of worldly pursuits, caring not for the children of the future. How often I forget your eternal presence. I beg for Your noose to hold me close, and Your goad to spur me on. Give me faith in God, Gods and *satgurus.* Gaṇeśa *śaraṇam, śaraṇam* Gaṇeśa.

TIMES OF NEED

Aum, Śrī Gaṇeśāya *namaḥ*—Gaṇapati, Lord of Gaṇas. I, too, am a *deva* under Your command. I know I can never ever separate myself from the intricate mind of the supreme intelligence. O Lord who destroys the obstacles of His devotees, grant me protection, guidance and help in this hour of need. (Devotee states his need or trouble.) Aum, Gaṇeśa *śaraṇam.* Grant me Your grace, *śaraṇam* Gaṇeśa.

FAMILY WELFARE

O Lord Gaṇeśa, holder of the noose and goad, sweets, fruits and sugarcane, please provide for the welfare of my family. Guide prosperity and abundance to our door. But while we wait and mostly see only our wants and needs, please help us feel within our home Your goodness and Divinity, which no calamity can conceal. Gaṇeśa *śaraṇam, śaraṇam* Gaṇeśa.

FREEDOM FROM FEAR AND ANGER

Omnipresent Lambodara, pure and peaceful doer of all good. Take away my fear and anger. Let me see Thee everywhere and at all times. Show me the truth that there is no intrinsic evil. Remove all

barriers in my mind to understanding, true trust and love. Guide me to a harmonious life and righteous success in the fulfillment of my *dharma.*
Gaṇeśa *śaraṇam, śaraṇam* Gaṇeśa.

RELEASE FROM EGOITY

Aum, Śrī Gaṇeśāya *namaḥ!* O keeper of the gate to the life of Sanātana Dharma, open that gate for me to feel Your intricate mind moving all things toward the world of the Gods. Open the gate for me to a life of continuous worship. Let me enter a new world where my ego is not my God. Open the gate, let me through to Your blissful world of trust, love and harmony.
Gaṇeśa *śaraṇam, śaraṇam* Gaṇeśa.

Praise, Adoration and Thankfulness

In prayers of praise, adoration and thankfulness we do not ask for anything, but simply offer our feelings of love and recognition to Lord Gaṇeśa when our heart is full of His grace. The more we worship and come to understand Him, the more we realize the greatness of His work in our life and see His presence all around us. It is from this perspective that the great *bhaktas* of the past sang many of their songs to God. Such prayers confirm our relationship with Lord Gaṇeśa and draw us ever closer to His mind.

JOYOUS PRAISE

Aum, Śrī Gaṇeśāya *namaḥ!* Thank You, Umagaṇeśa, for the wonderful fulfillment You have brought into my life. I show gratitude by giving abundant *dāna* to the temple where You received and answered my prayers. Your *śakti* is the blossoming origin of love. Praise to You who are the source of all sweetness. I take refuge in grateful surrender at Your holy feet. Aum, *jai* Gaṇeśa!

OFFERING GIFTS

Aum, Śrī Gaṇeśāya *namaḥ!* O my grand and gracious Lord Gaṇeśa. Here I am, with only You in my mind. My body's life is Your warmth. Your fire is my comfort. Now, with *pūjā* flames we offer that fire back to You. These fruits and flowers are Yours to enjoy. My very mind, too, is Yours to direct. O peaceful One, praise to You. Take these offerings and take, too, a place in my humble life, in Your heart. Gaṇeśa *śaraṇam, śaraṇam* Gaṇeśa.

APPRECIATION

Aum, Śrī Gaṇeśāya *namaḥ!* Peerless One, industrious indweller in all, we see You in the full warmth of the Sun, in the full life of Earth and the orderliness of all the turning planets. O Lord and lover of intellect, You are the intricate knowledge blossoming in the mind of the people. O Lord who rules the mind of each and all who worship You, because of You, chaos never was nor will it ever be. Gaṇeśa *śaraṇam, śaraṇam* Gaṇeśa.

Here is a prayer that has been used for centuries wherever Gaṇapati is the principal Deity of the home.

TRADITIONAL SALUTATION

Praise be to elephant-faced Gaṇeśa, the incomprehensible one with a sharp tusk, three eyes and capacious belly, king of all beings, the eternal one of blood-red hue, Whose forehead is illuminated by the new moon, son of Śiva-Śakti, remover of all difficulties. Gaṇeśa *śaraṇam, śaraṇam* Gaṇeśa.

Daily Prayers for Children

Teaching children prayers to recite at regular times during the day is a wonderful practice through which we fulfill our duty of passing our religion on to coming generations. Parents are encouraged to sit and say these prayers with them until they enter the spirit of talking with Lord Gaṇeśa themselves.

MORNING PRAYER

Aum, Lord Gaṇeśa, You make the flowers grow, You keep the Earth going around the Sun. All day You keep things going right. You are Lord of the *devas.* I am one of Your *devas,* too. Help me to think of the needs of others, and to be kind to everyone I meet. Help me to think of You first before beginning something new and to always do what is right and kind. Gaṇeśa *śaraṇam, śaraṇam* Gaṇeśa.

NOON PRAYER

Aum, Lord Gaṇeśa, You have kept my heart beating. You have guarded me from wrongdoing. Make my love for my family and friends grow stronger each day. Make me careful and wise. Help me to respect and heed the remindings of our *kulaguru,* to be respectful to my parents and remember above all the wisdom of the *Vedas.* Gaṇeśa, that is a lot for me to do. Please help me succeed. Gaṇeśa *śaraṇam, śaraṇam* Gaṇeśa.

BEDTIME PRAYER

Aum, Lord Gaṇeśa, nighttime is here and the moon is in the sky above, reminding me of Your crescent tusk. Remain with me, Gaṇeśa, through the night, in my deepest sleep, in my inner experiences, as You have remained with me during my daytime, outer encounters. Let me never forget You, even in my dreams. May we as a family be guided by Your loving wisdom, even there. Gaṇeśa *saraṇam, śaraṇam* Gaṇeśa.

MEALTIME PRAYER

Aum, Lord Gaṇeśa, all is within You. God Śiva has given You dominion over the material universe. Let me remember to always share my food with others. May the *prasāda* You have given me today make all my *prāṇas* and subtle currents flow in perfect harmony, making my body healthy and strong so that I may serve You well. Gaṇeśa *śaraṇam, śaraṇam* Gaṇeśa.

We close this section with a prayer to Lord Vighnarāja, Ruler of Obstacles, for guidance and inspiration. This is something we all need to persevere through life's offerings of its many challenges to the supreme goal of *moksha.*

FOR GUIDANCE AND INSPIRATION

O Lord and ruler of many *gaṇas,* O Peaceful One who loves pomp and ceremony, patron of the arts and perserver of the best of ancient cultures, the one worshiped by all sages, use Your mighty trunk to hold us close to Your majestic mind, our purest state. Respond to our entreaties for clarity and direction, for this we supplicate. Protect us from beguiling ways and sternly direct us in the ways of our forefathers' traditions, forging for us new patterns to bring forth the old in the world of today. Keep us resolute to live the Sanātana Dharma. We prostrate at Your holy feet. Please grant us your grace. Gaṇeśa *śaraṇam, śaraṇam* Gaṇeśa.

Śrī Gaṇeśa Upanishad

Excerpts from Gaṇapatyatharśīrsham,
Translated from Sankṛit by Dr. Vasant Lad

Aum! Let us listen with our ears to that which is auspicious, adorable one. Let us perceive with our eyes what is holy and auspicious. With strong, stable body and limbs, may we seek the divine grace and accept the noble order of all our life.

I surrender to you, Lord Gaṇeśa. You are the speaker. You are the listener. You are the giver. You are the sustainer. I am your disciple. Protect me from the front and back. Protect me from the north and the south, from above and below. Protect me from all directions.

You are full of perfect knowledge of truth and awareness. You are full of bliss and pure consciousness. You are truth, consciousness and bliss. You are the absolute awareness. You are full of supreme wisdom and knowledge.

You are the earth, water, fire, air and the space. You are the root foundation of speech. You are beyond the three *guṇas: sattva, rajas* and *tamas.* You are beyond the physical, mental and causal bodies. You are beyond the three aspects of time: past, present and future. You are eternally established in the *mūlādhāra chakra.* You have three *śaktis:* action, knowledge and will.

Salutation to the Gaṇapati whose seed *mantra* is *Aum Gaṁ.* We know Ekadanta, the One-tusked God, the unique God. We meditate upon Vakratuṇḍa, the curved-trunk God. May that unique elephant God illumine our consciousness and direct us along the right track.

One should meditate upon Lord Gaṇeśa having one tusk and four arms; holding the noose and goad with two of them; with the other two indicating *varada,* the giving of boons and blessings, and *abhaya mudrā,* the fear removing gesture; having a mouse as the emblem on his ensign; possessing a big, beautiful belly and large, lovely ears which look like winnowing baskets; having a red cloth and His whole body covered with red sandalwood paste. He should be worshiped with red flowers. He manifests Himself as the universe and is beyond *prakṛiti,* matter, and Purusha, the manifest God. One who worships Gaṇeśa in this way forever is the best of *yogīs.*

Prostrations to Vrātapataye, the Lord of Plenty. Prostrations to Gaṇapataye, the Lord of various groups of Gods. Prostrations to Pramathapataye, the Lord of Śiva's hosts. Prostrations to Lambodara, the full-bellied God with a single tusk, destroyer of obstacles, the Son of Śiva, the Bestower of all Blessings.

He who chants this *Gaṇapati Upanishad* will verily get established in Brahman, the pure awareness. He will never encounter any obstacles. He will be happy everywhere. He will be free from the five great sins and lesser ones. By reciting this in the evening, the day's sins are destroyed.

By reciting this in the early morning, one becomes free from the sins committed at night in dreams. Reciting this morning and evening, one becomes totally free from all sins. He becomes totally free from all obstacles. He achieves the four divine ends of life: *dharma, artha, kāma* and *moksha*: virtue, wealth, pleasure and liberation. Aum Gaṇeśa *śaraṇam, śaraṇam* Gaṇeśa.

Mahā Gaṇeśa Pañcharatna Stotram

महागणेशपञ्चरत्नस्तोत्रम् ॥

A Renowned Five-Jeweled Hymn by Śrī Ādi Śaṅkara (798-820), with a Free-Flowing Translation by J. Sethuraman

मुदा करात्तमोदकं सदा विमुक्तिसाधकं
कलाधरावतंसकं विलासिलोकरक्षकम् ।
अनायकैकनायकं विनाशितेभदैत्यकं
नताशुभाशुनाशकं नमामि तं विनायकम् ॥१॥

नमामि तं विनायकम् I bow to Vināyaka, मुदा करात्तमोदकम् who, with glee, holds a half-eaten *modakam* in His hand, सदा विमुक्तिसाधकम् who is the ever-present means of *moksha*, कलाधरावतंसकम् who has the moon as an ear ornament, विलासिलोकरक्षकम् who protects all the worlds, अनायकैकनायकम् who is the single leader for those who have been left leaderless (i.e. are lost without anybody to help them,) विनाशितेभदैत्यकम् who destroyed the elephant demon and नताशुभाशुनाशकम् who swiftly removes the blemishes of those who bow to Him.

नतेतरातिभीकरं नवोदितार्कभास्वरं
नमत्सुरारिनिर्जरं नताधिकापदुद्धरम् ।
सुरेश्वरं निधीश्वरं गजेश्वरं गणेश्वरं
सुरेश्वरं समाश्रये परात्परं निरन्तरम् ॥२॥

सुरेश्वरं समाश्रये I seek refuge of the great Lord (Vināyaka), परात्परं who is higher than the highest, निरन्तरम् who is everlasting, नतेतरातिभीकरम् who is ferocious to others than those that bow to Him, नवोदितार्कभास्वरम् who is resplendent as the newly rising sun, नमत्सुरारिनिर्जरम् worshiped by both demons and Gods, नताधिकापदुद्धरम् the savior of those that bow to Him from all their miseries, सुरेश्वरम् the lord of all the Gods, निधीश्वरम् the lord of all wealth, गजेश्वरम् the elephant God, and गणेश्वरम् Gaṇeśvara, the lord of the *gaṇas.*

समस्तलोकशङ्करं निरस्तदैत्यकुञ्जरं
दरेतरोदरं वरं वरेभवक्त्रमक्षरम् ।
कृपाकरं क्षमाकरं मुदाकरं यशस्करं
मनस्करं नमस्कृतां नमस्करोमि भास्वरम् ॥३॥

नमस्करोमि भास्वरम् I bow to the resplendent one समस्तलोकशङ्करम् who bestows peace to all the worlds, निरस्तदैत्यकुञ्जरम् who conquered the elephant demon, दरेतरोदरम् who has not a small belly, वरम् the excellent one वरेभवक्त्रम् who has a beautiful elephant face, अक्षरम् who is eternal कृपाकरम्, who is kind, क्षमाकरं who is forgiving, मुदाकरम् who gives happiness, यशस्करम् who bestows fame and नमस्कृतां मनस्करम् who satisfies every wish of those that bow to Him.

अकिञ्चनार्तिभाजनं चिरन्तनोक्तिभाजनं
पुरारिपूर्वनन्दनं सुरारिगर्वचर्वणम् ।
प्रपञ्चनाशभीषणं धनञ्जयादिभूषणं
कपोलदानवारणं भजे पुराणवारणम् ॥४॥

भजे पुराणवारणम् I worship the ancient elephant God, अकिञ्चनार्तिभाजनम् who shares the misery of the poor, चिरन्तनोक्तिभाजनम् the fit receptacle of all the ancient prayers, पुरारिपूर्वनन्दनम् the first son of the enemy of the three cities (Śiva), सुरारिगर्वचर्वणम् the shatterer of the pride of the demons, प्रपञ्चनाशभीषणम् the fierce destroyer of the worlds, धनञ्जयादिभूषणम् decorated by fire and other elements, and कपोलदानवारणम् whose elephant cheeks are flowing with must (the rut that flows from the cheeks of male elephants.)

नितान्तकान्तदन्तकान्तिमन्तकान्तकात्मजं
अचिन्त्यरूपमन्तहीनमन्तरायकृन्तनम् ।
हृदन्तरे निरन्तरं वसन्तमेव योगिनां
तमेकदन्तमेव तं विचिन्तयामि सन्ततम् ॥ ८ ॥

तमेकदन्तमेव तं विचिन्तयामि सन्ततम् I constantly think of Him alone, the single-tusked one, नितान्तकान्तदन्तकान्तिम् with a lovingly brilliant tusk, अन्तकान्तकात्मजम् the son of the destroyer of the sacrifice (Śiva), अचिन्त्यरूपम् with a form that cannot be comprehended, अन्तहीनम् with no end, अन्तरायकृन्तनम् who tears asunder all doubts, and योगिनां हृदन्तरे निरन्तरं वसन्तमेव who is verily like spring to the *yogīs* who hold Him in their hearts all the time.

महागणेशपञ्चरत्नमादरेण योऽन्वहं
प्रजल्पति प्रभातके (प्रदोषके)
हृदि स्मरन् गणेश्वरम् ।
अरोगतामदोषतां सुहासतां सुपुत्रतां
समाहितायुरष्टभूतिमभ्युपैति सोऽचिरात् ॥ ६ ॥

योऽन्वहम् प्रजल्पति One who repeats every day महागणेशपञ्चरत्नस्तोत्रम् the Mahā Gaṇeśa Pañcharatna Stotram आदरेण with reverence, प्रभातके (प्रदोषके) हृदि स्मरन् गणेश्वरम् in the mornings (evenings) while holding Gaṇeśvara in his heart, सोऽचिरात् he, very quickly, अभ्युपैति will be joined by अरोगतामदोषतां सुसहासतीं सुपुत्रतां समाहितायुरष्टभूतिम् good health, blemishlessness, good fellowship, good children, long life and the eight *vibhūtis* (powers, or *ashṭavibhūti, animā, mahimā, lagimā, garimā, etc.)*

॥ महागणेशपञ्चरत्नस्तोत्रं संपूर्णम् ॥

Gaṇeśa Invocation

गणेशमन्त्रम्

An Invocation to Lord Gaṇapati
Ṛig Veda 2.23.1

ॐ गणानां त्वा गणपतिं हवामहे
कविङ्कवीनामुपमश्रवस्तमम् ।
ज्येष्ठराजं ब्रह्मणां ब्रह्मणस्पत
आनःशृण्वन्नूतिभिः सीदसादनम् ॥

Aum gaṇānā ṁ tvā gaṇapatiṅg
(traditionally chanted gaṇapati gm) havāmahe
kaviṅkavīnāmupamaśravastamam
jyeshṭharājam brahmaṇām brahmaṇaspata
ānaḥ śṛiṇvan nūtibhiḥ sīdasādanam

May we worship Gaṇapati,
the Protector of Noble People,
the Best Poet,
the Most Honorable,
the Greatest Ruler and
the Treasure of all Knowledge.
O Gaṇapati! Please listen to us
and take Your seat in our heart.

Food-Blessing Chant

भोजनमन्त्रम्

A Prayer of Gratitude to the Source of Sustenance.
Lines 1-4 are from Śrī Śaṅkarāchārya's Annapūrṇāshṭakam.
Lines 5-6 are the Īśa Upanishad *invocation.*
Lines 7-8 are a traditional Śaivite closing.

ॐ अन्नपूर्णे सदापूर्णे शङ्करप्राणवल्लभे ।
ज्ञानवैराग्यसिद्ध्यर्थं भिक्षां देहि च पार्वती ॥
माता च पार्वती देवी पिता देवो महेश्वरः ।
बान्धवाः शिवभक्ताश्च स्वदेशो भुवनत्रयम् ॥
ॐ पूर्णमदः पूर्णमिदं पूर्णात्पूर्णमुदच्यते ।
पूर्णस्य पूर्णमादाय पूर्णमेवावशिष्यते ॥
ॐ शान्तिः शान्तिः शान्तिः ॥ ॐ
शिवार्पणमस्तु ॥

Aum annapūrṇe sadāpūrṇe śaṅkaraprāṇa vallabhe;
Jñanavairāgya siddhyartham bhikshām dehi cha pārvatī.
Mātā cha pārvatī devi pitā devo maheśvaraḥ
bāndhavāḥ śiva bhaktāścha svadeśo bhuvanatrayam.
Aum pūrṇamadaḥ pūrṇamidam pūrṇātpūrṇamudachyate,
Pūrṇasya pūrṇamādāya pūrṇame vāva śishyate.
Aum śāntiḥ śāntiḥ śāntiḥ. Aum śivārpaṇamastu.

Aum, beloved Śakti of Śiva, Fullness everlasting and fully manifest as this food; O, Mother of the universe, nourish us with this gift of food so that we may attain knowledge, dispassion and spiritual perfection. Goddess Pārvatī is my mother. God Maheśvara is my father. All devotees of Śiva are my family. All three worlds are my home. Aum, Śiva is Fullness. Creation is fullness. From Śiva's Fullness flows this world's fullness. This fullness issues from that Fullness, yet that Fullness remains full. Aum, peace, peace, peace. Aum, this I offer unto Śiva.

Prayer for Offering Incense

धूपमन्त्रम्

दशाङ्गं गुग्गुलोपेतं सुगन्धं सुमनोहरम्
आघ्रेयःसर्वदेवानां धूपोऽयं प्रतिगृह्यताम्

daśāṅgaṁ guggulopetaṁ
sugandhaṁ sumanoharam
āghreyaḥ-sarvadevānāṁ
dhūpo-yam pratigṛihyatām

O Lord! here is offered the incense
made of sweet-smelling herbs.
This is meant for the *devas.*
Please accept it.

Peace Invocation
शान्तिमन्त्रम्

A Prayer for Peace and Clarity
intoned to begin and end teaching sessions,
meetings and other group activities.
Krishṇa Yajur Veda, Taittirīya Upanishad 2.1.1

ॐ स॒ह ना॑ववतु ।
स॒ह नौ॑ भुनक्तु ।
स॒ह वी॒र्यं᳚ करवावहै ।
ते॒ज॒स्विना॒वधी॑तमस्तु ।
मा वि॑द्विषा॒वहै᳚ ।
ॐ शान्ति॒ः शान्ति॒ः शान्ति॑ः ॥

Aum saha nā̍ vavatu,
saha nau̍ bhunaktu,
saha vī̱ryam̍ karavāvahai,
tejasvinā̱v adhi̍tamastu,
mā vi̍dvishā̱vahai̍,
Aum śāntih̤, śāntih̤, śānti̍h̤.

Aum, may He protect us. May He be pleased with us.
May we work together with vigor. May our studies
illumine us. May we have no contention or hostility
between us. Aum, peace, peace, peace.

Gaṇapati Pūjā

गणपति पूजा

Gaṇeśa Home Liturgy

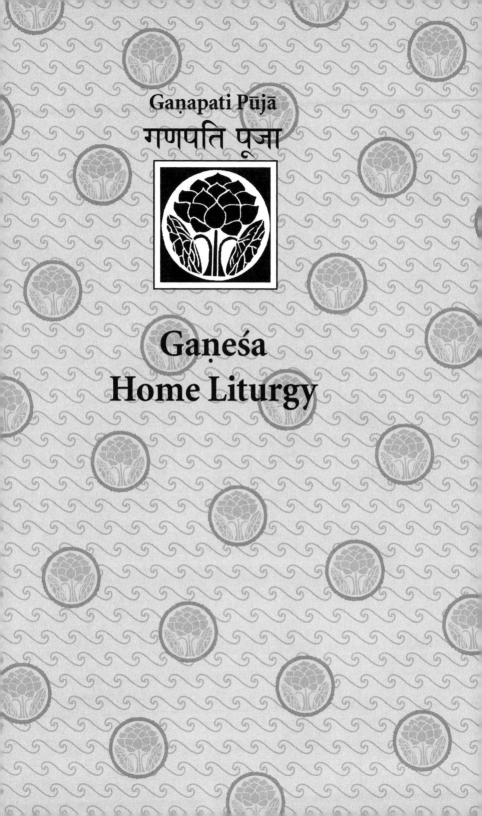

Gaṇeśa Home Liturgy

LOVE AND JOY COME TO HINDU FAMILIES WHO WORSHIP LORD GAṆEŚA IN THEIR HOME THROUGH THE TRADITIONAL CEREmony known as *pūjā*. Through such sacred rites and the divine energies invoked, each family makes their house a sacred sanctuary, a refuge from the concerns and worries of the world. *Pūjās* can be as simple as lighting a lamp and offering a flower at the Lord's holy feet, or they can be most elaborate and detailed, with many Sanskṛit chants and offerings. The essential and indispensable part of any *pūjā* is devotion. Without love and reverence in the heart, outer performance is of little value. But with true devotion even simple gestures become sacred ritual. On the following pages, we present a simple *pūjā* which anyone desirous of invoking our loving Gaṇeśa can perform in his or her home shrine room. One need not be initiated to perform this *pūjā*. All that is required is that the celebrant believe in the laws of *karma* and reincarnation, which are the cornerstones of Hindu ethical and philosophical doctrine. Gaṇeśa worship is enjoyed by all, Hindus and non-Hindus alike, as He is the first God to be worshiped. He permits those from alien faiths and those who have no religion at all to fully enter Sanātana Dharma through Him. It is not wise for an *ardha*-Hindu, or half-Hindu, to centralize worship on Śiva or Murugan or another of the Gods until full commitment has been made through receiving the traditional sacraments, called *saṁskāras*. Home *pūjā* is performed at least once a day, usually in the early morning, but also in the afternoon or evening. It is a common practice to not partake of food at least three hours before *pūjā*, which means that *pūjā* is usually done prior to the daily meals.

The Sanctity of the Home Shrine

All Hindus attend *pūjā* at their local temple at least once a week and maintain a sacred shrine at home, which esoterically functions as an extension of the temple. The shrine room is meticulously cared for and not used for purposes other than worship, prayer, scriptural study and meditation. Here *pūjā,* home liturgy, is performed daily, generally by the head of the house. All members of the family attend.

Establishing a Home Shrine

Creating a home shrine is not difficult. The altar should be close to the floor, since most of the *pūjā* is performed while seated, or when there are small children in the home it is often higher, out of their reach. For a Gaṇeśa shrine, an image, or *mūrti,* of Lord Gaṇeśa is placed at the center of the altar. A metal or stone image is best, but if not available there are two traditional alternatives: 1) a framed picture, preferably with a sheet of copper on the back, or 2) A *kumbha,* which is a symbol of Gaṇeśa made by placing a coconut on a brass pot of water with five mango leaves inserted between the coconut and the pot. The coconut should be husked but still have the fibers on the top. (See illustration on page 224.) Bathing the God's image, or *mūrti,* is part of the *pūjā.* For this, special arrangements may need to be made. Most simply, the *mūrti* may be placed in a deep tray to catch the water. After the bath, the tray is removed and the *mūrti* dried off, then dressed and decorated. More elaborately, a drain may be set up so the water flows into a pot at the side of the altar. This blessed water is later served by the *pujārī,* who places a small spoonful in each devotee's right palm.

Pūjā Items

Pūjā implements for the shrine are kept on a large and ideally metal tray. On it are arranged *ghee* lamps, bells, cups, spoons and small pots to hold the various sacraments. Available from Indian shops, these are dedicated articles, never used for purposes other than *pūjā.* The necessary items are:

1. two water cups and a small spoon for offering water;
2. a brass vessel of unbroken, uncooked rice mixed with enough turmeric to turn the rice yellow;
3. a tray or basket of freshly picked flowers (without stems) or loose flower petals;
4. a standing oil lamp, *dīpastambha,* which remains lit throughout the *pūjā;* ideally kept lit through the day.
5. a *dīpa* (lamp with cotton string wick) for waving light before the Deity;
6. a small metal bell, *ghaṇṭā;*
7. incense burner and a few sticks of incense, *agarbhatti;*
8. a container of holy ash, *vibhūti;*
9. a small vessel of sandalwood paste, *chandana;*
10. a small container of red powder, *kuṅkuma;*
11. *naivedya,* fresh fruit and-or a covered dish of freshly cooked food (most often rice) to offer the Deity;
12. a camphor (*karpura)* burner for passing the sacred flame before the God at the height of the *pūjā.*
13. Additional items may include: small Indian pots for bathing the *mūrti,* colorful clothing for dressing the *mūrti,* garlands and additional oil lamps to light and decorate the room, and a CD or tape player.

Restrictions from Entering a Shrine

Before entering the shrine room, all attending the ceremony bathe, dress in clean clothes and bring a small offering of flowers or fruit (prepared before the bath). It is traditional for women during their monthly period to refrain from attending *pūjā,* entering the home shrine or temple or approaching *swāmīs* or other holy men. Also during this time women do not help in *pūjā* preparation, such as picking flowers or making *prasāda* for the Deity. At this time of retreat, ladies are allowed to rest and perform private *sādhanas*, such as *haṭha yoga, japa, prāṇāyāma,* meditation and reading the holy texts.

This same rule applies to men or women with injuries that are in the process of healing; minor scratches do not apply. Cuts, injuries, internal bleeding and operations create psychic openings in the aura that allow vulnerability for lower astral *naraka* people to enter or to draw energy from and do damage with that energy. The period of retreat extends until the bleeding stops and there is no more danger of infection. A minor cut or scratch may reach this point within a few hours. A deeper cut will generally take two or three days to knit to the point that no restriction is required. A severe wound may take ten days or longer. A major operation, such as heart surgery, caesarean section or appendicitis, might require several weeks or even longer, until the person feels whole again. This means that you do not go to a Hindu temple to get healed from injuries such as these, though loved ones can go to pray on your behalf.

When I was in Jaffna in 1948 and 1949, living as a guest in the homes of strict Śaivite Hindus, I was impressed that they had a small house made of thatched *cajan* at the far end of the family compound where the women of the household went for three or four days or more each month until their period was over. During this time they did not cook for the family or perform any of their regular duties. They had a time of complete solitude. No sexual intercourse was engaged in during that time. Before reentering the family home, clothing and cloth that had blood on it were burned. Women bathed, donning new clothes when they were ready to return to the home, shrine room and normal duties. This all made a strong *saṁskāra* on my mind. The same custom was followed by the Hawaiians and other ancient ethnic communities. The custom protects the temple from *asuric* intrusion.

There is another important form of retreat followed by all knowledgeable Hindus. I have codified this restriction in *sūtra* 269 of *Living with Śiva:* "All followers must observe a period of thirty-one days following the birth or death of a family member during which they do not enter temples or home shrines, perform worship rites or attend auspicious events." *Japa* and other personal *sādhanas* can and should be continued during this time. The judgment of who is part of the family rests on the shoulders of the family itself.

Special Offerings to Lord Gaṇeśa

During festivals and special *pūjās,* it is customary to decorate the offering tray, altar and shrine room with sugar cane stalks, whole saffron plants with root attached, coconuts and banana leaves or even whole banana trees. Every variety of fruit is acceptable, notably bananas, mangos, limes, pomegranates and jackfruit. The elephant comes from the forest, and so the elephant-faced Deity's temple or shrine is made to look like a small forest on festival days sacred to Him. Of course, *modaka* balls and other sweets are Lord Gaṇeśa's favorite treat.

Thiru M. Arunachalam provides some insights into Gaṇeśa's most traditional flower offerings: "In the matter of floral worship, two articles are considered very important to Gaṇeśa. One is the *aruhu* grass blade. The tip of the grass shoot is collected in sufficient quantities for floral *archana* [chanting the names of the Lord while offering flowers]. *Aruhu* is the most common grass, a weed in the cultivated gardens. It is the common *hariali* grass *(durva* in Sanskṛit and botanically *Cynodon dactylon).* It is generally collected for worship with three blades or five blades. Sometimes it is made into a wreath and placed on the shoulders of Gaṇeśa. The second is the *erukku (Calotropis)* flower.... *Erukku* flowers are stringed together and placed round the crown and neck of Gaṇeśa (*Festivals of Tamil Nadu,* page 117)."

Instructions for Pūjā

In performing the *pūjā,* preparation is of utmost importance—gathering flowers, cleaning the altar and *pūjā* tray, making ready the oil lamps and preparing the fruit and-or cooked food offering. It is common to chant the 108 or 1,008 holy names of our loving Gaṇeśa or to softly sing devotional songs while performing these tasks. This quiets the mind of the devotees and brings their awareness close to Him. Indeed, all this preparation is an integral part of worship.

Before beginning the *pūjā,* check the altar to make sure all necessary articles are there—for having to get a missing item later would disrupt the flow of *pūjā.* Hold the attitude that you are the servant of the Gods as *pujārī,* a channel for the spiritual energies. Only thoughts of God are on your mind as you perform *pūjā,* thus allowing the outpouring of Divine blessings.

All items are arranged the same way for each *pūjā* so they can be reached automatically when needed, with the most frequently used items closest to hand. Tradition provides a caution: you should never perform *pūjā* during or shortly after experiencing anger, deep emotional upset or crying, but it would be all right to attend. *Pūjā* is a *yoga,* or link, between this and inner worlds. Therefore, you must be at your best in mood and emotion to assist in making this connection.

Before performing *pūjā* you should be freshly dressed, clean and undistracted by concerns of the day. Having bathed beforehand, enter the shrine room and prostrate, this being the only time you prostrate until the conclusion of the *pūjā.*

The form of prostration differs for men and women. Men perform "eight-limbed obeisance," *ashṭāṅga praṇāma,*

a fully prone pose in which hands, chest, forehead, knees and feet touch the ground. Women perform "five-limbed obeisance," *pañchāṅga praṇāma,* a kneeling pose in which hands, head and legs touch the ground (with ankles crossed, right over the left). Another term for prostration is *praṇipāta,* "falling down in obeisance."

Pūjā Procedures

When everything is ready, take your seat in a cross-legged posture (never kneeling) in front of and to the left of the altar (or on the Deity's right), facing the Deity but turned slightly to the right. Close your eyes, sit quietly for a moment and tune your nerve system to God Gaṇeśa and the sacred *pūjā* you are about to perform. If others are attending your *pūjā,* be careful not to sit directly in front of the Deity thereby blocking their view of the altar. Generally one remains seated throughout the ritual, though in some shrines it may be more comfortable to stand during the *āratī* or throughout the *pūjā.* When small children are in the home, the shrine room is locked so they do not disturb the contents. If a lockable room is not available, the altar is raised so as to be out of reach, and the *pūjā* is performed standing up. Those attending will usually sit during most of the ceremony, then stand during the main *āratī.* However, this again may be left to individual discretion in consideration of the height of the shrine.

During the ritual, you will be making many offerings to the God. All offerings are made with the right hand, never the left, though there are occasions when both hands are used and the left hand is held under the right hand, as if supporting it. When done correctly, this makes a beautiful gesture of sincere offering.

Offering of Food

The offering of food is an important part of *pūjā.* Traditionally, a simple dish of cooked rice is prepared especially for the Deity, with cooking utensils reserved for this purpose alone. If cooked food is not offered, then freshly cut fruit may be substituted. Keep the offering covered until the point in the *pūjā* when the *prāṇas* (life energies) of the food are offered to the Deity. Keeping the food covered helps to preserve purity and contain the *prāṇas,* which the Gods and *devas* can see and absorb and enjoy and reflect back into the auras of devotees to cleanse them. After the *pūjā,* the food offerings (along with holy ash, *vibhūti*; sacred water, *tīrtha;* sandalwood paste, *chandana;* red powder, *kuṅkuma;* and flowers, *pushpa*) are passed out and enjoyed as *prasāda.*

A recording of sacred chanting from the *Vedas* is played softly before the *pūjā.* At the high point, as the *āratī* is presented, loud drums and *nāgasvaras* resound. As the sacraments are passed out by the *pujārī,* the divine *rāgas* are heard softly played on the *vīṇā,* as everyone enjoys quiet meditation, internalizing their worship.

Meditating After the Pūjā

After the sacraments are passed out, ask everyone present to chant *Aum* three times and then to sit quietly and internalize worship on God within them. Externalized worship traditionally is followed by internalized worship in the Siddhānta tradition. This is because all the *prāṇas* invoked during the *pūjā* must be transferred into the devotees. This is accomplished by *japa yoga* which quiets the external mind and brings one into a state of meditation, awareness aware of itself without distraction. This simple practice of mentally chanting Aum many, many times followed by a period of meditation and self-reflection alone make devotees strong enough to face the external world with enhanced willpower, true confidence, a heart filled with love, realizing that we are truly one world, one family.

Visualize Gaṇeśa sitting on the *mūlādhāra chakra,* Murugan on the *maṇipūra chakra* and Śiva on the *sahasrāra chakra.* This *chakra bhakti* makes everyone strong, prepares them inwardly to face with confidence the *karmas* of the day. Encourage everyone to sit quietly for a while to enjoy the *śakti* of the *sānnidhya,* the ever-present divine feeling that the God, Gods, inner-plane *gurus* and *devas* leave in the shrine room. For during the *pūjā,* you and all attending had lost physical, emotional and intellectual consciousness, having been so intently focused upon the God you were devotionally invoking. Now, everyone should be encouraged by you to turn awareness within to the true Self. While holding within your mind the image of the God you have been worshiping, become conscious of the God Consciousness of all your bodies' energy, of the movement of the breath, of the light that lights your thoughts, of the divine energy that pervades the universe, and of the high-pitched eee sound that is heard ringing in the head like a million temple bells. Intuit these five as coming directly from God within. When you have experienced all these at at the same time, you have attained the five-fold God consciousness.

Internalizing worship in this way gives you and all members of the family strength to face the outside world, its daily challenges and, yes, school exams. Internalizing worship is the core of the Sanātana Dharma. It is the root, stem and blossom of the highest *chakra,* the 1,000-petalled lotus. It is the force that gives the strength to resist temptation, to turn others from their bad ways and to face up to and live through birth *karmas, prārabdha karmas,* that are brought with you in this life. It gives the courage to resist making new, especially unwanted, *karmas* to be faced at a later date. It gives the willpower needed in this Kali Yuga to survive. It gives the love which provokes the understanding to overlook and forgive then forget. Finally, internalized worship gives the peace of mind, the *śānti,* in which all saints, sages, *mahātmas* and great seers dwell, in their *jñāna* of how things work in their universe of which we are a vital part.

Gaṇeśa Pūjā for the Home Shrine

The Gaṇeśa Pūjā presented here consists of several chants to be intoned while performing the indicated actions and visualizations. Each chant is given in three forms, first in *devanāgarī* script, second in transliterated English, and third in a freely-rendered English translation. To the left of the transliteration are brief instructional cues. Each translation is followed by more detailed explanations.

There are few restrictions on the performance of the *pūjā* to Loving Gaṇeśa. There are more temples, roadside and home shrines to Him than to any other of the 330 million Gods in the pantheon of Sanātana Dharma. He understands life as it is. Fathers, mothers, children, grandparents, widows, divorcees and divorcé's all may perform His worship in home shrines where no *yantra* has ceremoniously been installed through the traditional *bālasthāpana*. He knows the world and all its worldliness even though He is a *śākāhāra*, or vegetarian, even though He is a virgin. He is literate in every language of the world at every given time. He enjoys the worship of His devotees, even those who serve meat, fish, fowl, eggs or bugs to humans in their home, those who are unknowing of languages and those who have enjoyed the pleasures of promiscuity. He, our loving Gaṇeśa, is the God of humans and all sentient beings. But beware, He will guide them slowly in inscrutable ways. The druggies will become drugless, the meat eaters will become veggies and none will ever know what has happened. He will prick their conscience, so that guilt comes up, and lift their soul to heights sublime. Therefore, even if you do not know Sanskṛit, His favorite language among all His other favorite languages, you may perform this worship to Him in English or in any other language it would be easily translated into, and He will hear. Yes, He will hear.

Mastering Sanskṛit Pronunciation

The chants of the simple Gaṇeśa *pūjā* given here are in Sanskṛit, Hinduism's ancient scriptural language. How well you pronounce Sanskṛit depends entirely on how well you learn the 48 basic sounds of the alphabet. No amount of memorization or practice of the *pūjā* verses alone will take the place of learning the alphabet, because without mastering the sounds, your chanting will not be perfect. Time spent mastering the pronunciation is time well spent. You will then be able to read and chant the verses properly. The best way to approach the study is through learning to read the Devanāgarī, the Sanskṛit script, because it most perfectly conveys the nuances of the language. However, many people find the chants more approachable in the transliterated English. A key to Sanskṛit pronunciation for the transliteration system used in this book is given on page xix.

Our Sacred Hindu Temple Priesthoods

An additional word here about those refined souls who have guided the worshipful ways of Hindus for so many centuries may be useful. Our priesthood in Hinduism is trained from birth to be exceedingly loving, overly giving and softly humble. They live, as they are taught, an unworldly existence, and there are some people, sad to say, who take advantage of their unassuming ways. Our priests are raised as children in ancestral schools called *pāṭhaśālas.* All temples throughout the world have priests who are well trained in performing the arts of *Parārtha Pūjā* (temple liturgy), consecration of temples, *saṁskāras* (sacraments), home blessings, purification of new properties and more.

These priests, when approached in the proper attitude, will be happy to teach you the Sanskṛit alphabet and how to perform this Gaṇeśa *pūjā* properly. Most if not all will say their service is freely given and they expect nothing. But, by tradition, it is the duty of the recipient to give a *dakshiṇā,* gifts from you periodically as your study progresses and a larger one at the end, which is mandatory. However, the priest has been trained to say no three times and then accept in great reluctance. Just because he says no once or twice does not mean that you can keep your gift and go home with it.

This protocol must be gone through. A subtle way is to give a fruit offering with a gift of money in an envelope tucked in among the fruits. He will readily accept the tray and offer the fruits to the God and keep the envelope for himself as his *dakshiṇā.* Culturally, this refined mode of compensation is very different from hiring and paying a salary to a person. The Indian spiritual tradition avoids the sense of employer-employee relationship in an attempt to keep the relationship highly spiritual, elevated beyond the business of the day. Knowing this, it becomes the responsibility of the community to abundantly compensate priests, who will never ask for a penny more than what they are given, not a penny more than what God provides them through you, for you are a channel for God's abundance to them. God will, through the unfailing law of *karma,* eventually pay you back double what you gave.

This *dakshiṇā* is an important part of their livelihood. As a gentle guideline for giving *dakshiṇā,* the amount should be pro-rated according to how many hours they have served or taught you. The per-hour rate must be comparable to the pay rate of a highly skilled person within your community. It is not, for instance, equitable to pay a small pittance in U.K. pounds with the explanation that this is more than the priest would make in Madras. Service in the U.K. is rightly given in accordance with British wages, not wages in India.

It should be very clear that priests are not the servants of the devotees or of temple managers. Their knowledge, their skills and their spirit of devotion are what attract devotees to the temple. Imagine a temple with no priest in it. It would be a silent museum or art gallery—nothing more. There is a magic that happens during *pūjā* that no one can really explain. It is a parapsychology that happens beyond the boundaries of the intellect.

You too can create this magic within your own home shrine. Proceed with confidence. If you don't know the Sanskṛit, perform the *pūjā* in English until you have learned the Vedic chants, the language of the Gods. On the next few pages, we include eight illustrations and brief explanations of important aspects of Hindu worship in the home and the temple.

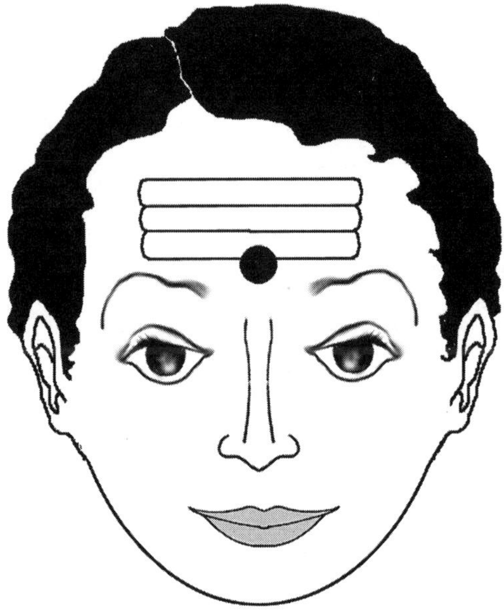

VIBHŪTI, HOLY ASH

Holy ash, *vibhūti*, connotes purity, and is a reminder to us of life's precious transitoriness. It is prepared by burning cow dung into a whitish ash. An essential sacrament at Śaiva *pūjā*, men wear it as the *tripuṇḍra*, a sectarian mark of three lines across the forehead, signifying the burning away of *pāśa*—the bonds of *āṇava* (veil of duality), *karma* (effects of past deeds) and *māyā* (the world). Women often wear a light film of ash across the forehead. Seen from *devonic* realms, holy ash has a bright phosphorescent glow, and wearing it helps the *devas* and the Deities see devotees more clearly.

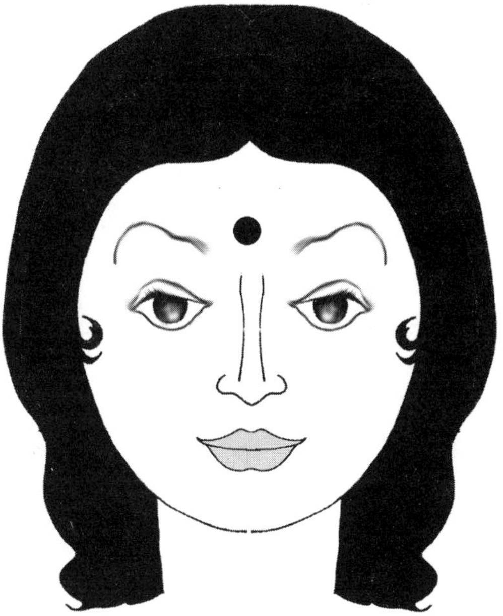

POTTU OR BINDU, THE FOREHEAD DOT

The *bindu,* "dot," worn between the eyebrows, or in the middle of the forehead, identifies one as a Hindu. It is made of red powder *(kuṅkuma),* sandalpaste, clay, cosmetics or other substance. Mystically, it represents the "third eye," our inner, superconscious vision, which sees what the physical eyes cannot see, reminding us to cultivate our higher, spiritual faculties and insight. The *bindu (pottu* in Tamil) is also a beauty mark for Hindu women, the color red generally a sign of marriage. Unmarried women usually wear a small black *pottu* with a short horizontal stroke of *vibhūti* just above.

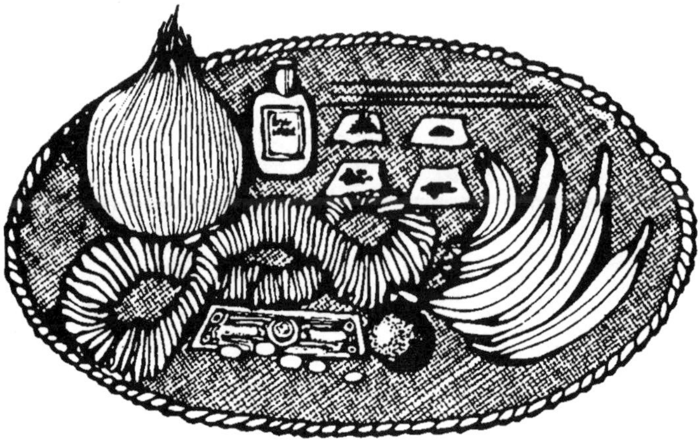

TEMPLE OFFERING TRAY

When journeying to a temple to attend *pūjā,* devotees bring a sacred offering tray or basket. The offerings can be prepared at home or sometimes purchased in small stalls near the temple entrance. Traditionally, the offerings include: 1) a fresh, husked coconut; 2) a garland of fresh flowers; 3) a few sticks of incense; 4) fresh fruits, e.g., banana, lime, mango; 5) a package of *vibhūti* (holy ash); 6) *kuṅkuma* (red powder); 7) sandalwood powder; 8) a packet of camphor; 9) a small bottle of rosewater; 10) a *modaka* or other sweet (optional); 11) and a financial contribution for the temple or its priests.

PRADAKSHIṆA, CIRCUMAMBULATION

Before worship, and sometimes during the *pūjā,* we walk three times around the Deity, the shrine or the temple. This is called *pradakshiṇa,* "right-facing," referring to keeping the Deity to our right by walking clockwise, never counterclockwise. By this custom we deliberately withdraw our awareness from worldly matters and direct it toward the Divine. As we circle the God, subtle psychic worldly bonds that naturally accumulate during the day in the human aura are broken. Thus, circumambulating the Lord three times brings us into a pure, one-pointed, worshipful state of consciousness.

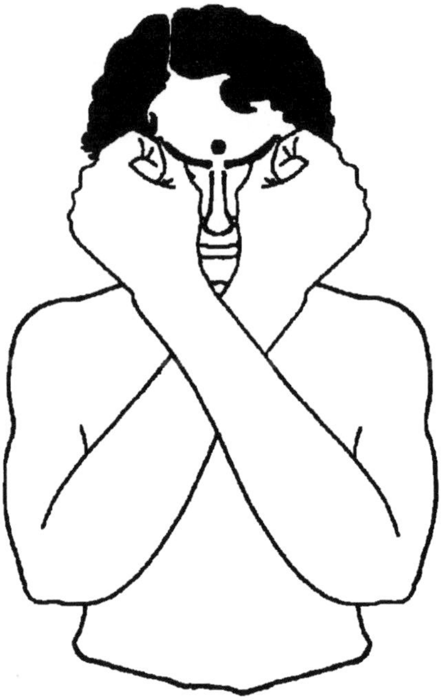

ŚAṄKHAPRAHATI, KNOCKING THE TEMPLES

When worshiping Lord Gaṇeśa, standing before His shrine, devotees may tap the temples gently three times with the knuckles, fists closed and arms crossed in front of the face. Esoterically, this action is said to stimulate certain nerves within the head to catalyze the flow of *amṛita* (nectar) from the *sahasrāra chakra* at the crown of the head, giving *abhisheka* (ritual bath) to Lord Gaṇeśa Who sits on the *mūlādhāra chakra* at the base of the spine. It is a gesture of submission, beeseeching forgiveness for errors, remembrance of Gaṇeśa's presence and supplication of the grace of this loving God.

PĀLĪKARSHA, PULLING THE EARS

After knocking the temples lightly, devotees will often pull gently on the ear lobes with arms crossed, while bobbing up and down by bending the knees and bowing forward slightly. This rather humorous gesture is an expression of humility, a recognition that all souls are like children in the eyes of God. Pulling the ears is done to draw Lord Gaṇeśa's loving attention to His self-effacing, self-erasing servant, and sumission of transgressions at His holy feet. Mystically, it stimulates important *nāḍīs,* inner nerve currents to help internalize awareness for ritual worship, *pūjā,* and meditation, *dhyāna.*

GAṆAPATI KALAŚA—WATER POT AND COCONUT

The *kalaśa* (or *kumbha)*, a water pot topped with mango leaves and a husked coconut, may represent the Deity on home altars and at special *pūjās* in the temple. Coconuts are especially sacred to Lord Gaṇeśa, and many are broken and offered at His temples and shrines. Breaking a coconut during prayer symbolizes the shattering of the ego, which must be surrendered lest it obstruct true worship through its desires and intrigues. Breaking the coconut's rough, hard shell to reveal the ripe fruit within is likened to shattering our brittle shell of ignorance to reveal the sweet spiritual truths inside.

HUṆḌI, THE TEMPLE OFFERING BOX

In the Hindu temple there is always a small or large strongbox into which devotees may offer a sacrifice to perpetuate the temple and its charitable works. When our prayers are answered, when God has shown us His grace and we seek to support His home on earth, we place money or other valuables, such as jewels, gold and silver, into the *huṇḍi.* In many temples, the donations are counted before the Deity each evening. To support the priests and their families, we place a separate and usually smaller contribution, called *dakshiṇā,* on the offering tray, traditionally wrapped in *betel* leaf.

Gaṇeśa Pūjā

गणेश पूजा

A TRADITIONAL DAILY WORSHIP CEREMONY PERFORMED IN THE HOME SHRINE TO BESEECH GOD GAṆEŚA'S BLESSINGS AND PROTECTION.

आचमनम् ***āchamanam*** Water sipping	ओं सुमुखाय स्वाहा ओं एकदन्ताय स्वाहा ओं गजकर्णकाय स्वाहा
Rinse, sip 3 times, then rinse again.	Aum sumukhāya svāhā Aum ekadantāya svāhā Aum gajakarṇakāya svāhā

Aum! Hail to the God whose face is always shining!
Aum! Hail to the God who has only one tusk!
Aum! Hail to the God with huge elephant ears!

Holding the spoon with your left hand, pour a spoonful of water from the cup into the right palm to rinse the hand, letting the excess fall onto the floor or a tray. Put another spoonful of water into the right hand, pronounce "Aum sumukhāya svāhā" and sip the water. Repeat for the second and third lines, then rinse the right hand again as above.

विघ्नेश्वर प्रार्थना
Vighneśvara Prārthanā

Ganeśa Invocation

Namaskāram,* knock temples, *namaskāram.

ॐ शुक्लांबरधरं विष्णुं
शशिवर्णं चतुर्भुजम् ।
प्रसन्नवदनं ध्यायेत्
सर्वविघ्नोपशान्तये ॥

Aum śuklāmbaradharam vishṇum
śaśivarṇaṁ caturbhujam
prasannavadanaṁ dhyāyet
sarvavighnopaśāntaye

Aum. O Lord dressed in splendid white, pervading all the universe, shining radiantly like the ivory rays of the full moon, having four mighty shoulders and a charming, happy face. We meditate on you, Lord, that all obstacles may be quelled.

Salute Lord Gaṇeśa on the altar by holding your hands in *añjali mudrā,* the prayerful pose. Then, while reciting the above verse, cross your arms before your face and tap your temples lightly with your knuckles three times, the left hand tapping the right temple and vice versa. This is a traditional way of supplicating Lord Gaṇapati. The place to knock is the bony, protruding part toward the front. Return your hands to *añjali mudrā* while reciting the last words of the chant.

संकल्पम्

Saṅkalpam

Dedication of *pūjā* and statement of purpose

ॐ अद्य पूर्वोक्त एवंगुणसकल
विशेषेण विशिष्टायां अस्यां शुभतिथौ
ॐ महागणेश्वर उद्दिश्य
महागणेश्वरप्रीत्यर्थं
महागणेश्वरप्रसादसिद्ध्यर्थं
यथा शक्ति (chant period of day)
ध्यानावाहनादि गणेशपूजां करिष्ये ।
ॐ अप उपस्पृश्य

Five periods of the day (insert one in the chant).

उषः काल	ushaḥ kāla, dawn
प्रातः काल	prātaḥ kāla—morning
मध्याह्नकाल	madhyāhnakāla, noon
सायङ्काल	sāyaṅkāla, evening
ऊर्ध्वयामकाल	ūrdhvayāmakāla, night

Hold rice and flower in closed right hand at chest.	Aum adya pūrvokta evaṁguṇasakala viśesheṇa viśishṭāyām asyāṁ śubhatithau Aum Mahāgaṇeśvara-uddiśya Mahāgaṇeśvara prītyartham Mahāgaṇeśvara prasāda siddhyartham yathā śakti (insert the time of day)
Toss rice and flower. Rinse hands.	dhyānāvāhanādi Gaṇeśa pūjāṁ karishye Aum apa upaspṛiśya

Now, at this particularly auspicious moment, time and place, on this wholly auspicious day, so that we may realize the fullness of your grace, to the best of our ability this (insert time of day) Gaṇeśa *pūjā* we shall now perform. Aum. By touching pure water we become pure.

While reciting the above statement of purpose, take a pinch of rice and hold it in your closed right palm at chest height. Depending on when you are performing the *pūjā*, insert the time of day where indicated. As you chant the last word, *karishye,* gently toss the rice toward the base of the image. Then, with the left hand, place a spoonful of water into the right palm, return the spoon to the cup and ritually wash both hands with the water by wiping the palms together a few times as you recite "Aum apa upa spṛiśya." Once the *saṅkalpam* has been chanted, the *pūjā* must not be interrupted or abandoned until the concluding *mantras* are recited.

ध्यानम् ***Dhyānam*** **Meditation**	ध्यायामि । आवाहयामि । रत्नसिंहासनं समर्पयामि ।
Offer rice three times.	dhyāyāmi āvāhayāmi ratnasiṁhāsanaṁ samarpayāmi

We now meditate on Lord Gaṇeśa. In all splendor we have prepared for you a jewel-studded, lion-footed throne to sit upon, Lord Gaṇeśa.

> Offer a pinch of rice to the Deity as you chant each line of the above meditation and invocation. Visualize God Gaṇeśa seated on a golden throne before you, smiling, full of blessings, waiting to be honored as a guest in the home of His devotee.

अर्घ्यम् ***Arghyam*** Bathing the feet and hands of God Gaṇeśa	पादयोः पाद्यं पाद्यं समर्पयामि । हस्तयोः अर्घ्यं अर्घ्यं समर्पयामि ।
Offer water two times into the *tīrtha* cup.	pādayoḥ pādyam pādyam samarpayāmi hastayoḥ arghyam arghyam samarpayāmi

We now humbly bathe each of your white lotus feet and gently wash each of your precious hands, Lord Gaṇeśa.

With your right hand offer a spoonful of pure water by holding it up before the Deity momentarily and then placing it in the *tīrtha* cup. This is how all water offering is done throughout the *pūjā*. As you chant the first line, visualize yourself bathing the feet of Gaṇeśa. Offer a second spoonful of pure water as you intone the next line and visualize yourself washing His hands.

आचमनम्

Āchamanam

ॐ भूर्भुवः स्वः
आचमनीयं समर्पयामि ।

Offer water.

Aum bhūr-bhuvaḥ svaḥ
āchamanīyaṁ samarpayāmi

Aum! In the presence of all three worlds, O Lord Gaṇeśa, we humbly offer you fresh, pure water for sipping.

Offer a spoonful of pure water to Gaṇeśa. This time visualize Him accepting it in His Hand and sipping it.

अभिषेकम्

Abhishekam

Bathing the Lord with pure water

स्नपयामि ।
इमं मे गङ्गे यमुने सरस्वति
शुतुद्रि स्तोम ꣳ सचता
परुष्ण्या असिक्न्या मंरुद्वृधे
वितस्तयाऽऽर्जीकीये शृणुह्या सुषोमंया ।
गङ्गास्नानं समर्पयामि ।

Ring bell,
hold flower and
sprinkle *mūrti.*
Set bell down.

snapayāmi
imam me gaṅge yamune sarasvatī
śutudri stomagm (stomaṅg) sachatā
parushṇyā asiknyā marudvṛidhe
vitastayār-jikīye śṛiṇuhyā sushomayā
gaṅgāsnānam samarpayāmi

We now bathe you, beloved Lord, calling forth all the sacred rivers in the holy land—the swift-flowing Gaṅgā, the twin-streamed Yamuṇā, the Sarasvatī flowing in a hundred streams. These we praise highly, O Gaṇeśa, along with the river Śutudrī, twisting and rushing, the Parushṇī, whose water runs dark, the rivers Jīkīye and Sushomā. We have bathed you in sacred Gaṅgā water, Lord Gaṇeśa,

While ringing the bell and reciting this auspicious, purifying hymn, dip a flower into the *tīrtha* water and gently sprinkle the Deity. Do this three times or more. Hold the flower in your right hand in the *mṛigi mudrā,* the stem between your third and fourth fingers. If the altar design allows, you may pour water over the *mūrti,* rather than sprinkling it during this chant.

अलङ्कारम्
Alaṅkāram

Adornment
and prayer
for prosperity

गन्धद्वारां दुराधर्षां
नित्यपुष्टां करीषिणीम् ।
ईश्वरीꣳ सर्वभूतानां
तामिहोपह्वये श्रियं ॥
दिव्य परिमल विभूति
कुंकुम चन्दनं समर्पयामि ।

Adorn the Deity with flowers, garlands, clothing, and jewels.	gandhadvārām durādharshām nityapushṭām karīshiṇīm īśvarīṅg sarvabhūtānām tāmihopahvaye śriyam (repeat while decorating)
Apply *vibhūti*, sandalwood paste and *kuṅkuma.*	divya parimala vibhūti kuṅkuma chandanaṁ samarpayāmi

May this divine fragrance be the means to boldly and permanently open the doors of wealth, abundance and well-being. May it cause material wealth and abundance to flood out in never-ending supply. O Lord of all living creatures, as one lost in the dark would call for light, I call upon you, God Gaṇeśa. Now we anoint you with divine and supremely pure white *vibhūti*, exceedingly fragrant sandalwood paste and red, red *kuṅkuma.*

During this chant, decorate the *mūrti* or picture and adorn it with the traditional *pūjā* sacraments. The first four lines of the verse may be repeated again and again until the adornment is completed. The last two lines are recited once while applying *vibhūti* (holy ash), *chandana* (sandalpaste) and *kuṅkuma* (red powder).

मङ्गलाक्षतान् ***Mangalākshatān*** ***Offering rice and flowers***	तदुपरि मङ्गलाक्षतान् समर्पयामि । पूजार्थे नानाविधपत्र पुष्पाणि समर्पयामि ।
Offer rice, then flower(s) or more rice.	tadupari maṅgalākshatām samarpayāmi pūjārthe nānāvidhapatra pushpāṇi samarpayāmi

We now offer this auspicious unbroken rice. And for the fulfillment of our devotion, we offer fresh, blooming flowers for your enjoyment, our peerless Lord.

A pinch of rice is offered with the first line. A handful of flowers, a single flower or a pinch of rice is offered with the second.

धूपम् *Dhūpam—Offering Incense*

ॐ वनस्पत्युद्भवैः दिव्यैः नानागन्धसमन्वितैः
आघ्रेयधूपदीपनं धूपोऽयं प्रतिगृह्यताम्
धूपमाघ्रापयामि ।
धूपानन्तरमाचमनीयं समर्पयामि ।
मङ्गलाक्षतान् समर्पयामि ।

Ring bell, pass incense in 3 circles, then trace Aum with light (in Sanskṛit, Tamil, Gujarati, etc.)	Aum vanaspatyudbhavaiḥ divyaiḥ nānāgandhasamanvitaiḥ āghreyadhūpadīpanam dhūpo-yam pratigṛihyatām
Ring bell loudly.	dhūpamāghrāpayāmi
Offer water.	dhūpānantaramāchamanīyam samarpayāmi
Offer rice.	maṅgalākshatān samarpayāmi

The finest incense, of magical qualities, of full and varied fragrances, for your enjoyment, Lord Gaṇeśa, we set aflame and offer to you in this, our home. This fine incense we have duly offered for your pleasure. And in the proper order, we again offer you cool, sweet water for sipping and auspicious unbroken rice.

During the above chant, make three circles before the Deity with lighted incense held in the right hand while ringing the bell with the left hand. With practice, you will complete the third circle as you chant the fifth line, *dhūpamāghrāpayāmi.* At that point the incense is raised higher and the bell rung louder. Putting the incense down, the next two lines are recited. With the first, water is offered, with the second, a pinch of rice.

दीपम् ***Dīpam—Offering the Light***

उद्दी॑प्यस्व जात॑वेदोप॒घ्न निर्ऋ॑ति॒ं मम॑ ।
प॒शूँ᳚ श्च॒ मह्य॒माव॑ह॒ जीव॑नं च॒ दिशो॑ द॒श ।
मा नो॑ हिंग्॒सीज्ञात॑वेदो॒ गामश्वं॒ पुरु॑ष॒ञ्जग॑त्
अबि॑भ्र॒दग्न॒ आग॑हि श्री॒यामा॒ परि॑पात॒य ॥

दिव्य मङ्गल दीपं सन्दर्शयामि ।
दीपानन्तरमाचमनीयं समर्पयामि ।
मङ्गलाक्षतान् समर्पयामि ।

Ring bell, pass lamp in 3 circles, then trace Aum.	uddīpyasva jātavedopaghnan nirṛitim mama paśūgumścha (paśūṅgścha) mahyamāvaha jīvanañ cha dīśo daśa mā no higumsījjātavedo (hiṅgsījjātavedo) gāmaśvam purushañjagat abibhradagna āgahi śrīyāmā paripātaya
Ring loudly.	divya maṅgala dīpaṁ sandarśayāmi
Offer water.	dīpānantaramāchamanīyaṁ samarpayāmi
Offer rice.	maṅgalākshatān samarpayāmi

Within fire is spiritual knowledge, our refuge. Because of it, no harm can befall us. In our home, cows are honored and highly respected, which enlivens the nations in all directions. Let us not forget right knowledge, culture and religious rites, O matchless Lord! Nor may any soul living in this world so forget! Spreading before and around us, purity and peace abound, as this holy flame illumines all with clarity. This divine flame we have shown you, Lord Gaṇeśa, and dutifully, in proper order. That all may receive your grace, we again offer you cool, sweet water for sipping and auspicious unbroken rice.

Offer the oil light to Gaṇeśa and ring the bell as you chant this Vedic hymn. As with the incense, circle three times then draw the Aum with the flame. While chanting the line beginning with *divya*, raise the flame and ring the bell louder, then stop ringing. With the last two lines, offer water, then a pinch of rice or a flower.

नैवेद्यम्

Naivedyam

Food offering

सत्यं त्वर्तेन (chant in morning)

ऋतं त्वा सत्येन (in evening)

परिषिञ्चामि ।

ॐ अमृतमस्तु

अमृतोपस्तरणमसि स्वाहा ।

Ring bell, stop, satyaṁ tvartena (chant if in morning)
ṛitaṁ tvā satyena (if evening)

Offer water. parishiñchāmi

Offer water. Aum amṛitamastu
amṛitopastaraṇamasi svāhā

Aum. We add Truth to Truth. Aum. May this sweet and pungent food be transformed into nectar, O Gaṇeśa.

While reciting the first part of the *mantra,* uncover the food offering. Then, ringing the bell, take a spoonful of water and circle it clockwise above the food. During the second part *(Aum amṛitamastu…),* without ringing the bell, offer a spoonful of water.

आसमर्पणम्

Āsamarpaṇam

Offering the *prāṇic* essence of the food

ॐ प्रा॒णाय॒ स्वाहा᳚ ।

ॐ अ॒पा॒नाय॒ स्वाहा᳚ ।

ॐ व्या॒नाय॒ स्वाहा᳚ ।

ॐ उ॒दा॒नाय॒ स्वाहा᳚ ।

ॐ स॒मा॒नाय॒ स्वाहा᳚ ।

ॐ ब्रह्म॑णे॒ स्वाहा᳚ ।

Waft flower over food while chanting each line.

Aum prā̱ṇāya̱ svāhā̎
Aum a̱pānāya̱ svāhā̎
Aum vyā̱nāya̱ svāhā̎
Aum u̱dānāya̱ svāhā̎
Aum sa̱mānāya̱ svāhā̎
Aum brahma̍ṇe̱ svāhā̎

Aum, the vital ascending life force, *prāṇa,* that sustains inhalation and exhalation, we offer to You, O Gaṇeśa.

Aum, the vital descending energy *apāna prāṇa,* that control the functions of elimination, we offer to You, O Gaṇeśa.

Aum, the vital diffuse life force, *vyāna,* that circulates through all the limbs, we offer to You, O Gaṇeśa.

Aum, the vital transcending life force, *udāna,* that sustains speech and ascent into higher consciousness, we offer to You, O Gaṇeśa.

Aum, the vital assimilating life force, *samāna,* that sustains digestion we offer to You, O Gaṇeśa.

Aum. The divine, all-pervading energy, Brahma *prāṇa,* that sustains all life we offer to You, O Gaṇeśa.

For the above, while holding the bell but not ringing it, gently waft the aroma and vital essences of the food or fruit toward the Deity. Do this by sweeping the right hand over the food (one wave for each *prāṇa* offered) with a flower held between your fingers, stem upward. The palm is facing downward as it moves over the food, then rotates upward as the sweep approaches the Deity, bringing the fragrance and *prāṇas* into His nose and mouth. As you complete the last line, gently toss the flower toward the feet of the Deity by releasing it at the end of the sweep with all the love in your heart.

Begging the Lord to accept our food offering

ॐ आवाहिताभ्यः सर्वाभ्यः
देवताभ्यो नमः ।
नानाविधमहानैवेद्यं निवेदयामि ।
यथाशक्त्यासमर्पितमहानैवेद्यम्
कृपया स्वीकुरु ।

Ring bell loudly, pick up rice or flower. Toss rice and flower, then stop ringing.

Aum āvāhitābhyaḥ sarvābhyaḥ
devatābhyo namaḥ
nānā vidha mahānaivedyaṁ
nivedayāmi
yathāśaktyā samarpita mahānaivedyam
kṛipayā svīkuru

Aum! Salutations to all the Gods and *devas* present! Because we are offering you our very best, Lord Gaṇeśa, in all sincerity and love, the essence of this humble plate of food must be counted among the finest meals you have ever received. To the best of our ability in the worship of you, we offer the sacred essence of this food and humbly beg that you will receive it.

Ringing the bell loudly as you recite the above chant, pick up a flower or a pinch of rice and hold it at chest height in the fingertips of the right hand. As the last word is spoken, gently release the rice or flower at the feet of the Deity. Then put down the bell and raise both hands above your head in devout prayer that Gaṇeśa will accept the meal. While your hands are raised, close your eyes and hold a clear visualization of Gaṇeśa accepting and partaking of the meal. After a moment, lower your hands and intone Aum quietly.

विघ्नेश्वराष्टोत्तर शतनामावलिः

Viggneśvarāshṭottara Śatanāmāvaliḥ

Chanting the 108 Names of Lord Gaṇeśa

In this section of the *pūjā,* chant the Vigneśvarāshṭottara Śatanāmāvali, "garland of Gaṇeśa's 108 names. As you intone each name, offer with your right hand a flower, some flower petals or a pinch of rice. The names are attributes of the Deity, each one delineating an aspect of His infinite and indescribable nature. Hold the flower basket in your left hand if you are standing, and in your lap if sitting. The bell is not rung. The names may be recited at any pace, depending on your time and ability. Each name is preceded by the *mantra Aum* and followed by *namaḥ,* meaning "obeisance, praise, adoration or homage to."

1 ॐ विनायकाय नमः Aum Vināyakāya Namaḥ
Adoration to the remover (of obstacles)

2 ॐ विघ्नराजाय नमः Aum Vighnarājāya Namaḥ
Adoration to the ruler of obstacles

3 ॐ गौरीपुत्राय नमः Aum Gaurīputrāya Namaḥ
Adoration to the son of Gaurī

4 ॐ गणेश्वराय नमः Aum Gaṇeśvarāya Namaḥ
Adoration to the lord of categories

5 ॐ स्कन्दाग्रजाय नमः Aum Skandāgrajāya Namaḥ
Adoration to Skanda's elder brother

6 ॐ अव्ययाय नमः Aum Avyayāya Namaḥ
Adoration to the inexhaustible one

7 ॐ पूताय नमः Aum Pūtāya Namaḥ
Adoration to the pure one

8 ॐ दक्षाय नमः Aum Dakshāya Namaḥ
Adoration to the skillful one

9 ॐ अध्यक्षाय नमः Aum Adhyakshāya Namaḥ
Adoration to the great presider

10 ॐ द्विजप्रियाय नमः Aum Dvijapriyāya Namaḥ
Adoration to Him who loves the twice-born

11 ॐ अग्निगर्वच्छिदे नमः Aum Agnigarvacçhide Namaḥ
Adoration to Him who destroyed the ego of the fire

12 ॐ इन्द्रश्रीप्रदाय नमः Aum Indraśrīpradāya Namaḥ
Adoration to the restorer of Indra's wealth

13 ॐ वाणीप्रदाय नमः Aum Vāṇīpradāya Namaḥ
Adoration to Him who gives the power of speech

14 ॐ अव्ययाय नमः Aum Avyayāya Namaḥ
Adoration to the inexhaustible one

15 ॐ सर्वसिद्धिप्रदाय नमः Aum Sarvasiddhipradāya Namaḥ
Adoration to the bestower of all fulfillment

16 ॐ सर्वतनयाय नमः Aum Sarvatanayāya Namaḥ
Adoration to the son of Śiva

17 ॐ शर्वरीप्रियाय नमः Aum Śarvarīpriyāya Namaḥ
Adoration to Him who is loved by Pārvatī

18 ॐ सर्वात्मकाय नमः Aum Sarvātmakāya Namaḥ
Adoration to Him who is the soul of all

19 ॐ सृष्टिकर्त्रे नमः Aum Sṛishṭikartre Namaḥ
Adoration to the Creator

20 ॐ देवाय नमः Aum Devāya Namaḥ
Adoration to the Resplendent One

21 ॐ अनेकार्चिताय नमः Aum Anekārchitāya Namaḥ
Adoration to the one worshiped by multitudes

22 ॐ शिवाय नमः Aum Śivāya Namaḥ
Adoration to the auspicious one

23 ॐ शुद्धाय नमः Aum Śuddhāya Namaḥ
Adoration to the pure one

24 ॐ बुद्धिप्रियाय नमः Aum Buddhipriyāya Namaḥ
Adoration to Him who is fond of intelligence

25 ॐ शान्ताय नमः Aum Śāntāya Namaḥ
Adoration to the peaceful one

26 ॐ ब्रह्मचारिणे नमः Aum Brahmachāriṇe Namaḥ
Adoration to Him who is celibate

27 ॐ गजाननाय नमः Aum Gajānanāya Namaḥ
Adoration to Him who has an elephant's face

28 ॐ द्वैमातुराय नमः Aum Dvaimāturāya Namaḥ
Adoration to Him who has two mothers

29 ॐ मुनिस्तुताय नमः Aum Munistutāya Namaḥ
Adoration to Him who is praised by sages

30 ॐ भक्तविघ्नविनाशनाय नमः Aum Bhaktavighna-vināśanāya Namaḥ
Adoration to the destroyer of devotees' obstacles

31 ॐ एकदन्ताय नमः Aum Ekadantāya Namaḥ
Adoration to Him who has one tusk

32 ॐ चतुर्बाहवे नमः Aum Chaturbāhave Namaḥ
Adoration to Him who has four arms

33 ॐ चतुराय नमः Aum Chaturāya Namaḥ
Adoration to the ingenious one

34 ॐ शक्तिसंयुताय नमः Aum Śaktisaṁyutāya Namaḥ
Adoration to Him who is united with power

35 ॐ लंबोदराय नमः Aum Lambodarāya Namaḥ
Adoration to Him who has a large belly

36 ॐ शूर्पकर्णाय नमः Aum Śūrpakarṇāya Namaḥ
Adoration to Him with ears like winnowing fans

37 ॐ हरये नमः Aum Haraye Namaḥ
Adoration to Him who destroys evil with lion-like courage

38 ॐ ब्रह्मविदुत्तमाय नमः Aum Brahmaviduttamāya Namaḥ
Adoration to the foremost knower of the supreme God

39 ॐ कालाय नमः Aum Kālāya Namaḥ
Adoration to the master of destiny

40 ॐ ग्रहपतये नमः Aum Grahapataye Namaḥ
Adoration to the lord of all planets and galaxies

41 ॐ कामिने नमः Aum Kāmine Namaḥ
Adoration to Him who is love

42 ॐ सोमसूर्याग्निलोचनाय नमः Aum Somasūryāgni-lochanāya Namaḥ
Adoration to Him whose eyes are the moon, sun and fire

43 ॐ पाशाङ्कुशधराय नमः Aum Pāśāṅkuśadharāya Namaḥ
Adoration to the One who holds a noose and goad

44 ॐ चण्डाय नमः Aum Chaṇḍāya Namaḥ
Adoration to the One who appears fearsome

45 ॐ गुणातीताय नमः Aum Guṇātītāya Namaḥ
Adoration to Him who transcends qualities

46 ॐ निरञ्जनाय नमः Aum Nirañjanāya Namaḥ
Adoration to Him who is without blemish

47 ॐ अकल्मषाय नमः Aum Akalmashāya Namaḥ
Adoration to Him who is without impurity

48 ॐ स्वयंसिद्धाय नमः Aum Svayaṁsiddhāya Namaḥ
Adoration to Him who is self-fulfilled and perfect

49 ॐ सिद्धार्चितपदाम्बुजाय नमः Aum Siddhārchita-padāmbujāya Namaḥ
Adoration to Him whose lotus feet sages worship

50 ॐ बीजपूरफलासक्ताय नमः Aum Bījapūraphalā-saktāya Namaḥ
Adoration to Him who is fond of pomegranates

51 ॐ वरदाय नमः Aum Varadāya Namaḥ
Adoration to the bestower of boons

52 ॐ शाश्वताय नमः Aum Śāśvatāya Namaḥ
Adoration to the eternal, unchanging one

53 ॐ कृतिने नमः Aum Kṛitine Namaḥ
Adoration to the skillfully accomplished one

54 ॐ द्विजप्रियाय नमः Aum Dvijapriyāya Namaḥ
Adoration to Him who is fond of the twice-born

55 ॐ वीतभयाय नमः Aum Vītabhayāya Namaḥ
Adoration to Him who is free from fear

56 ॐ गदिने नमः Aum Gadine Namaḥ
Adoration to Him whose weapon is the mace or club

57 ॐ चक्रिणे नमः Aum Chakriṇe Namaḥ
Adoration to Him whose weapon is the discus

58 ॐ इक्षुचापधृते नमः Aum Ikshuchāpadhṛite Namaḥ

Adoration to Him who holds the sugarcane bow

59 ॐ श्रीदाय नमः Aum Śrīdāya Namaḥ

Adoration to the bestower of great wealth

60 ॐ अजाय नमः Aum Ajāya Namaḥ

Adoration to the unborn one

61 ॐ उत्पलकराय नमः Aum Utpalakarāya Namaḥ

Hail to Him who holds the upright blue lotus flower

62 ॐ श्रीपतये नमः Aum Śrīpataye Namaḥ

Adoration to the Lord of overflowing wealth

63 ॐ स्तुतिहर्षिताय नमः Aum Stutiharshitāya Namaḥ

Adoration to Him who delights in praise

64 ॐ कुलाद्रिभृते नमः Aum Kulādribhṛite Namaḥ

Adoration to Him who supports Himālaya, His family's mountain

65 ॐ जटिलाय नमः Aum Jaṭilāya Namaḥ

Adoration to Him who wears distinguished matted hair

66 ॐ कलिकल्मषनाशनाय नमः Aum Kalikalmasha-nāśanāya Namaḥ

Adoration to Him who destroys sins in the Kaliyuga

67 ॐ चन्द्रचूडामणये नमः Aum Chandrachūḍā-maṇaye Namaḥ

Adoration to Him who wears a moon upon his head

68 ॐ कान्ताय नमः Aum Kāntāya Namaḥ

Adoration to the beloved, loving one

69 ॐ पापहारिणे नमः Aum Pāpahāriṇe Namaḥ

Adoration to the destroyer of sins

70 ॐ समाहिताय नमः Aum Samāhitāya Namaḥ
Adoration to Him who is absorbed in meditation

71 ॐ आश्रिताय नमः Aum Āśritāya Namaḥ
Adoration to Him who is our refuge

72 ॐ श्रीकराय नमः Aum Śrīkarāya Namaḥ
Adoration to Him who manifests prosperity

73 ॐ सौम्याय नमः Aum Saumyāya Namaḥ
Adoration to the pleasant one

74 ॐ भक्तवाञ्छितदायकाय नमः Aum Bhaktavāñ-çhitadāyakāya Namaḥ
Adoration to the grantor of devotees' desires

75 ॐ शान्ताय नमः Aum Śāntāya Namaḥ
Adoration to the peaceful one

76 ॐ कैवल्यसुखदाय नमः Aum Kaivalyasukhadāya Namaḥ
Adoration to the bestower of unsullied liberation

77 ॐ सच्चिदानन्दविग्रहाय नमः Aum Sacchidānanda-vigrahāya Namaḥ
Adoration to the embodiment of existence-knowledge-bliss

78 ॐ ज्ञानिने नमः Aum Jñānine Namaḥ
Adoration to the great wisdom

79 ॐ दयायुताय नमः Aum Dayāyutāya Namaḥ
Adoration to Him who is full of compassion

80 ॐ दान्ताय नमः Aum Dāntāya Namaḥ
Adoration to Him who has self-control

81 ॐ ब्रह्मद्वेषविवर्जिताय नमः Aum Brahmadvesha-vivarjitāya Namaḥ
Adoration to Him who is free from aversion to knowledge

82 ॐ प्रमत्तदैत्यभयदाय नमः Aum Pramattadaitya-bhayadāya Namaḥ
Adoration to Him who brings terror to power-intoxicated demons

83 ॐ श्रीकण्ठाय नमः Aum Śrīkaṇṭhāya Namaḥ
Adoration to Him whose throat is beautiful

84 ॐ विबुधेश्वराय नमः Aum Vibudheśvarāya Namaḥ
Adoration to the Lord of the Wise

85 ॐ रामार्चिताय नमः Aum Rāmārchitāya Namaḥ
Adoration to Him who is worshiped by Rāma

86 ॐ विधये नमः Aum Vidhaye Namaḥ
Adoration to Him who is the destiny of all

87 ॐ नागराजयज्ञोपवीतवते नमः Aum Nāgarājayajño-pavītavate Namaḥ
Adoration to Him whose sacred thread is a king cobra

88 ॐ स्थूलकण्ठाय नमः Aum Sthūlakaṇṭhāya Namaḥ
Adoration to Him who has a stout neck, representing tremendous will and compassion

89 ॐ स्वयं कर्त्रे नमः Aum Svayaṁkartre Namaḥ
Adoration to Him who is the cause of himself

90 ॐ सामघोषप्रियाय नमः Aum Sāmaghoshapriyāya Namaḥ
Adoration to Him who loves the sound of Sāma Veda

91 ॐ परस्मै नमः Aum Parasmai Namaḥ
Adoration to Him who is supreme

92 ॐ स्थूलतुण्डाय नमः Aum Sthūlatuṇḍāya Namaḥ
Adoration to Him who has a stout, unpredictable trunk

93 ॐ अग्रण्ये नमः Aum Agraṇye Namaḥ
Adoration to Him, the first-born of Śiva

94 ॐ धीराय नमः Aum Dhīrāya Namaḥ
Adoration to the courageous one

95 ॐ वागीशाय नमः Aum Vāgīśāya Namaḥ
Adoration to the Lord of speech

96 ॐ सिद्धिदायकाय नमः Aum Siddhidāyakāya Namaḥ
Adoration to the bestower of fulfillment

97 ॐ दूर्वाबिल्वप्रियाय नमः Aum Dūrvābilvapriyāya Namaḥ
Adoration to Him who loves dūrvā grass and bilva leaves

98 ॐ अव्यक्तमूर्तये नमः Aum Avyaktamūrtaye Namaḥ
Adoration to the manifestation of the Unmanifest

99 ॐ अद्भुतमूर्तिमते नमः Aum Adbhutamūrtimate Namaḥ
Adoration to Him of wondrous form

100 ॐ शैलेन्द्रतनुजोत्सङ्गखेलनोत्सुकमानसाय नमः
Aum Śailendratanujotsaṅga khelanotsukamānasāya Namaḥ
Adoration to Him who is fond of playing in the lap of His mother, Pārvatī daughter of the mountain Lord [Himavat]

101 ॐ स्वलावण्यसुधासारजितमन्मथविग्रहाय नमः
Aum Svalāvaṇyasudhāsārajita manmathavigrahāya Namaḥ
Adoration to Him who defeated Manmatha, the God of love, by His sweet beauty

102 ॐ समस्तजगदाधाराय नमः Aum Samastajagadādhārāya Namaḥ
Adoration to the supporter of all the worlds

103 ॐ मायिने नमः Aum Māyine Namaḥ
Adoration to the source of illusory power

104 ॐ मूषिकवाहनाय नमः Aum Mūshikavāhanāya Namaḥ
Adoration to Him who rides the abundance-gathering mouse

105 ॐ हृष्टाय नमः Aum Hṛīshṭāya Namaḥ
Adoration to the rapturously joyful one

106 ॐ तुष्टाय नमः Aum Tushṭāya Namaḥ
Adoration to the contented one who has it all in control

107 ॐ प्रसन्नात्मने नमः Aum Prasannātmane Namaḥ
Adoration to the bright loving kindly-souled one

108 ॐ सर्वसिद्धिप्रदायकाय नमः Aum Sarvasiddhi-pradāyakāya Namaḥ
Adoration to the grantor of all fulfillment

मन्त्र पुष्पम्

Mantra Pushpam

Blessing and worshiping with flowers

यो॑ऽपां पुष्पं॒ वेद॑ ।
पुष्प॑वान् प्र॒जावा᳚न् प॒शुमा॑न् भ॑वति ।
च॒न्द्रमा॒ वा अ॒पां पुष्प᳚म् ।
पुष्प॑वान् प्र॒जावा᳚न् प॒शुमा॑न् भ॑वति ।
य ए॒वं वेद॑ । यो॑ऽपामा॒यत॑नं॒ वेद॑ ।
आ॒यत॑नवान् भवति ॥

ॐ श्री महागणेश्वराय नमः
मन्त्रपुष्पाञ्जलिं समर्पयामि ।

Hold a double handful of flowers or rice in *namaskāram.*

yopām pushpaṁ veda
pushpavān prajāvān paśūmān bhavati
chandramāvā apām pushpam
pushpavān prajāvān paśumān bhavati
ya evaṁ veda yopāmāyatanaṁ veda
āyatanavān bhavati

Toss flowers over *mūrtis.*

Aum Śrī Mahāgaṇeśvarāya namaḥ
mantra pushpāñjalin samarpayāmi

The one who understands the beauty of the blooming Powers of the Supreme Being is blessed with beautiful blooming life, progeny and cattle. The moon is certainly the bloom of those Powers. One who realizes the qualities of the moon, which are nothing but the blooming Divine Powers, is blessed with a blooming, beautiful life of perfection, progeny and cattle. One who realizes this principle and realizes the Source from Whom all these powers have come himself becomes the abode of those Divine Powers.

While chanting the above *mantra,* hold an offering of flowers before you in *añjali mudrā,* hands cupped loosely around the flowers at chest height. If no flowers are available, uncooked unbroken rice may be offered, held in the closed right hand, palm down, supported by the open left hand. Recite the verses with adoration. As you intone the last word, *samarpayāmi,* throw the flowers into the air above the altar, sending a shower of blossoms or rice upon the God with the feeling of total release, of giving in loving devotion.

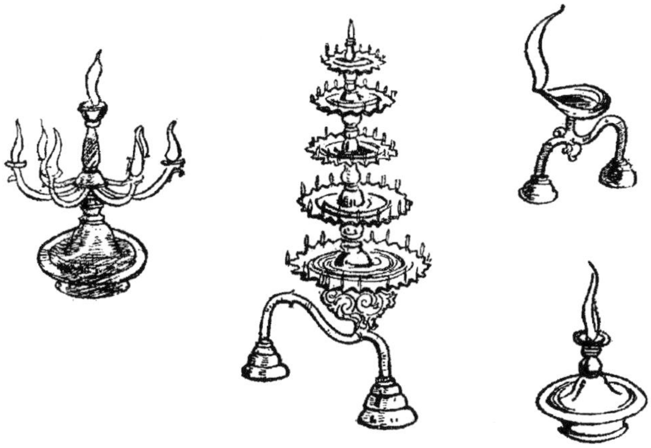

आरती

Āratī

Worship with flame

ॐ ग॒णानां॑ त्वा ग॒णप॑तिꣳ हवामहे
क॒विङ्क॑वी॒नामु॑प॒मश्र॑वस्तमम् ।
ज्ये॒ष्ठ॒राज॒ं ब्रह्म॑णां ब्रह्मणस्पत॒
आ नः॑ शृ॒ण्वन्नू॒तिभिः॑ सीद॒ साद॑नम् ॥

ॐ आवाहिताभ्यः सर्वाभ्यो
देवताभ्यो नमः ।
दिव्य मङ्गलदीपारतिक्यं सन्दर्शयामि ।
आचमनीयं समर्पयामि ।
मङ्गलाक्षतान् समर्पयामि ।

Ring bell, draw three circles and Tamil Aum.

Aum gaṇānāṁ tvā gaṇapatigm
(gaṇapatiṅg) havāmahe
kaviṅkavīnāmupamaśravastamam,
jyeshṭharājam

Ring bell loudly.

brahmaṇām brahmaṇaspata
ā naḥ śṛiṇvan nūtibhiḥ sīda sādanam

Keep ringing loudly.	Aum āvāhitābhyaḥ sarvābhyo devatābhyo namaḥ divya maṅgaladīpāratikyaṁ sandarśayāmi
Offer water.	āchamanīyaṁ samarpayāmi
Offer rice.	maṅgalākshatān samarpayāmi

May we pray to the Lord Gaṇapati: the master and protector of noble, righteous people, the wisest among the wise, preeminent among the renowned, the greatest ruler, protector of the knowledge of all knowledgeable people. O Lord Gaṇapati, please hear our prayers and protect us with your powers. We have prepared the best seats for you in ourselves. Please come and grace them.

Adoration to all Gods we have invited for this *pūjā*. To them I offer this divine Light of camphor *arati* flame. I offer holy water for sipping and auspicious unbroken rice grains to grant me blessings.

With the above chant, hold the lit camphor burner (or oil lamp) in your right hand and the bell in your left. While ringing the bell and reciting the *āratī mantra,* slowly make three circles clockwise before Gaṇeśa with the flame. Stop at the top of the third circle, lower the lamp slightly and trace the symbol of Aum in Sanskṛit or in your native language. Then lift the flame slightly above the Aum that you placed in the *ākāśic* ether and ring the bell louder for all three worlds to hear. Keep ringing loudly while chanting the above four-line salutation to the *devas (āvāhitābhyaḥ...)*. Put down the bell and the lamp and then, with the flame still burning, offer a spoonful of water with "*āchamanīyaṁ...*," then a pinch of rice with "*maṅgalākshatān....*"

रक्षधारणम्	इन्द्र स्तोमेन पञ्चदशेन
Rakshadhāraṇam	मध्यमिदं वातेन सगरेण
Prayer to Indra	रक्ष रक्ष धारयामि ।

Set lamp down,	indra-stomena pañchadaśena
circle 3 times	madhyamidaṁ vātena sagareṇa
with flower	raksha raksha dhārayāmi

O Indra, Lord of material and spiritual prosperity! Please protect the space between the heavens and earth as well as the mind between the body and the soul with the help of fifteen noble powers and virtures (five *prāṇas,* five *jñānendriyas* and five *karmendriyas).* The space is filled with the air and moisture, while the mind is filled with *prāṇa* and devotion and love for you. I wear this garment of your protection and blessings.

As you recite this *mantra,* make three circles above the burning flame with a flower held in the right hand, stem upward. With the last words, toss the flower gently toward the Deity and place your hands in *namaskāra* while facing the altar.

Now pass the flame to the others present. Offer it in front of each person at chest level. They, in turn "take the flame" by passing the fingers of both hands through it and lightly touching the eyes. The Gods and *devas* can see us through the sacred flame and send their blessings. If any especially honored persons are present, such as one's *guru,* parents or teacher, take the flame first to

them. Then proceed clockwise, offering it to all others present. In some cases, the *pujārī* may stand near the altar while devotees come forward themselves to take the blessings of the *ārati* flame. If no one is attending the *pūjā*, then you may take the flame yourself, but not otherwise. Finally, "present" the flame once more to the Deity on the altar, then extinguish it with a wave of the right hand or by snuffing it out with a flower. When the flame is camphor, it is best to let it burn clean of itself.

अर्पणम्

Arpaṇam

Final consecration and surrender to the Lord

अनया यथाशक्ति कृत
(state period of day)
पूजया भगवान् सर्वदेवात्मकः
श्रीमहागणेश्वरः सुप्रीतः
सुप्रसन्नो वरदो भवतु ।

Five periods of the day

Chant appropriate period at line two above.

उषः काल	ushaḥ kāla, dawn
प्रातः काल	prātaḥ kāla, morning
मध्याह्नकाल	madhyāhnakāla, noon
सायङ्काल	sāyaṅkāla, evening
ऊर्ध्वयामकाल	ūrdhvayāmakāla, night

Rice and water in hand, offer before the Deity.

anayā yathā śaktī kṛita
(state period of day from list above)
pūjayā bhagavān sarva devātmakaḥ
śrī mahā gaṇeśvaraḥ suprītaḥ
suprasanno varado bhavatu

Now to the best of our ability we have performed this (state time of day) *pūjā* and worshiped You, dear Lord, the brightest of all the Gods. May it please You. May it be enjoyed by You. Surrounded by Your presence, we place ourselves in Your care, loving Gaṇeśa.

Before reciting the above verse, place a pinch of rice in your left palm, then immediately transfer it to the right palm. Add to the rice three spoonfuls of water and close the hand. Hold the rice before you as you face the Deity, the left hand under the right hand, and recite the *mantra*. As you intone the last words, let the rice and water fall into the *tīrtha* cup. The sacraments may then be given out in the following order: *vibhūti, tīrtha, chandana, kuṅkuma, naivedya* and flowers. If no one is attending the *pūjā*, you may partake of the sacraments yourself, but not otherwise. If many devotees are attending, a second person may help pass out the sacraments, except for the *vibhūti* which is always given by the person who performed the *pūjā*.

विसर्जनम् Visarjanam—Farewell and Apologies

Hold hands in *añjali mudrā*. Prostrate after completing the chant.

ॐ आवाहनं न जानामि न जानामि विसर्जनम् ।
पूजांचैव न जानामि क्षम्यतां परमेश्वर ॥
मन्त्रहीनम् क्रियाहीनम् भक्तिहीनम् सुरेश्वर ।
यत् पूजितं मया देव परिपूर्णं तदस्तु मे ।
अन्यथा शरणम् नास्ति त्वमेव शरणम् मम ।
तस्मात् कारुण्यभावेन रक्ष रक्ष गणेश्वर ॥
ॐ तत् सत् ॐ

Aum āvāhanaṁ na jānāmi na jānāmi visarjanam
pūjāñchaiva na jānāmi kshamyatām parameśvara
mantrahīnaṁ kriyāhīnam bhaktihīnaṁ sureśvara
yat pūjitam mayādeva paripūrṇam tadastume
anyathā śaraṇaṁ nāsti tvameva śaraṇam mama
tasmāt kāruṇyabhāvena raksha raksha gaṇeśvara
Aum tat sat Aum.

O beloved Lord Gaṇeśa, we really do not know the proper means of invoking You or communicating with You as You are. A full knowledge of priestly rites has not been imparted, so You must overlook and forgive any mistakes or omissions. We know little of *mantras* or pious conduct, and we are strangers to true *bhakti*. Nonetheless, You must forgive us and, whatsoever worship we have been able to do, accept it as exact and complete—because You are our only refuge our loving Gaṇeśa. With your blissful nature, Lord Gaṇeśa, please protect those who pray. Aum Tat Sat Aum.

This concluding apology is recited with hands in *namaskāram, añjali mudrā.* It is a formal and devout end to the worship service. As the final words, "Aum Tat Sat Aum," are spoken, it is customary for yourself and others present to clap the hands together softly three times. You may now prostrate. Having completed the *pūjā,* it is customary to sit in internalized worship, realizing our loving Gaṇeśa within ourselves.

To meditate for a few minutes after the *pūjā* is very traditional. There is great personal benefit in taking in to the soul level the refined feelings, the *prāṇa,* that the *pūjā* has created and which still remains in the room. Externalized worship is the *kriyā* path; internalized worship is the *yoga* path. Both together make the complete circle that sustains devotees in their spiritual life, making them strong and kindly in moving the forces of the world in their daily life. It is the very foundation for the final goal of all seekers: *moksha,* freedom from rebirth.

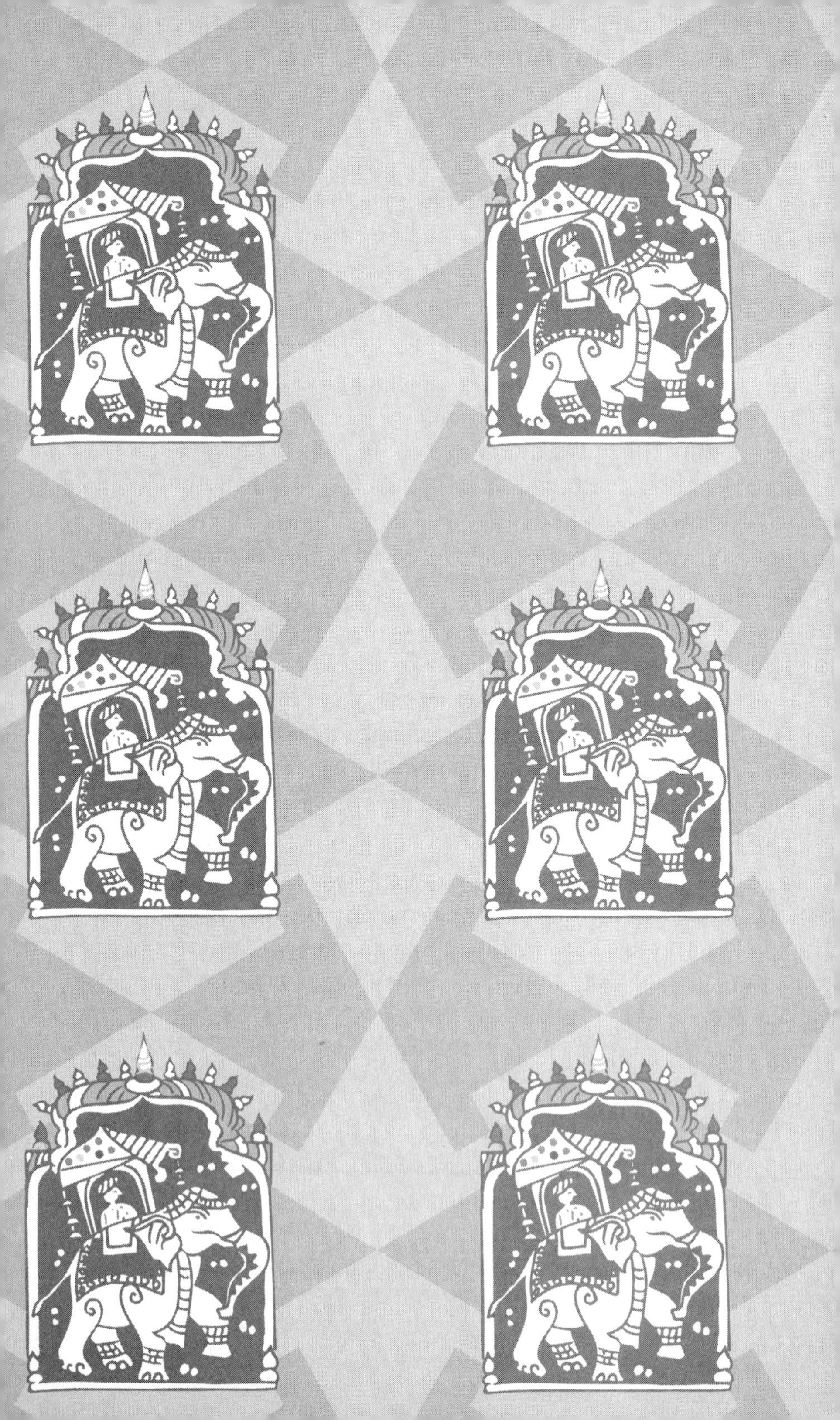

Paribhuvanam

परिभुवनम्

Around the World

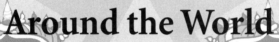

Around the World

MAHĀ GAṆAPATI, OF COURSE, BELONGS TO ALL MANKIND, NOT TO HINDUS ALONE, THOUGH NOT ALL PEOPLE ON THE PLANET CALL HIM by our endearing name, Preman Gaṇeśa. To the Chinese He is embodied in the form of a massive dragon, whose physical immensity depicts His incredible and irresistible force. To some Chinese He is Kuan-shi t'ien or Ho Tei, the large-bellied God of Happiness. To the Polynesians He is God Lono.

The South Indian and Sri Lankan Tamils call him by the affectionate term Pillaiyar, "Noble Child." The Tibetans know Him as ts'ogsbdag, and the Burmese worship Maha-Pienne. In Mongolia His name is Totkharour Khaghan. Cambodians offer worship to Prah Kenes, and the Japanese supplicate Vinayaksa or Sho-ten. By some He is envisioned as the feminine Mother Nature, and even nonbelievers seek to understand Him through personifying His great powers as Fate, Destiny or Numen. The Greeks called Him Janus and sought His blessings at the outset of any new venture. In the West He is revered as the corpulent Santa Claus, the giver of boons and gifts who knows our thoughts, words and deeds and bestows rewards accordingly. The Buddhists and Jains also honor Gaṇeśa. In one form or another, Lord Gaṇeśa is honored throughout the world.

As the respected author, Ratna Ma Navaratnam, devotee of Sage Yogaswāmī of Colombuturai Sri Lanka, wrote, "Gaṇeśa worship is most effective in illumining consciousness, and hence He is sought after and propitiated by the Śaivites, Vaishṇavites, Śāktas, Smārtas, Kumāras, Jains and Buddhists as the Dispeller of Obstacles" *(Aum Gaṇeśa, The Peace of God,* page 176).

Hindus worship the great God Gaṇeśa at countless *pūjās* performed daily on every continent. In temples and home shrines Lord Gaṇeśa is worshiped today in India, Sri Lanka, Nepal, Malaysia, Java, Bali, Borneo, Tibet, Myanmar, Siam, Afganistan, the Middle East, China, Indo-China, Japan, the Caribbean, Trinidad and Tobago, Hawaii and the Pacific

Islands, Africa, Mauritius, Reunion, European Community, Australia, Canada, South America, the United States and elsewhere.

Every Hindu village and community has an image of the God Gaṇeśa, and one of the many forms of Gaṇeśa is found in every Hindu temple. The eminent scholar M. Arunachalam wrote, "Gaṇeśa is usually installed at the entrance to the central sanctum, at the south, and also at the southwestern corner in the first court, of every Śiva temple. Besides, he is placed on the first eastern *goshṭa* (niche) on the other southern wall of the *ardha maṇḍapa* [secondary hall] in the dancing pose, known as Nartana Gaṇapati, in many temples. The tip of His trunk will curve to the left and touch the *modaka,* generally held in the left hand. In a few rare cases, the trunk will curve to the right to touch the *modaka* on a right hand. Here He is called Valampuri (right turned) Vināyaga" *(Festivals of Tamil Nadu,* 1980, page 112).

Roadside Shrines

While Gaṇeśa shrines are found at all Hindu temples, they often stand alone as well. They are often quite humble, not uncommonly a simple roadside shrine such as the one between Jaffna and Anuradhapura in Sri Lanka or along the road sides here and there in South India. Here travelers stop to break a coconut and burn a bit of camphor before the Lord of Obstacles to pray for a safe and successful journey. There is a similar shrine near the university in Madras. Many years ago a young man discovered a tree that formed the shape of Gaṇeśa head in its gnarled trunk. He began worshiping and soon took a vow not to leave the site. He has been there, serving as a priest and doing *sādhana* for several decades now, without leaving the tiny compound. Travelers and students about to take their exams come to the shrine to seek Lord Gaṇeśa's blessings. Such tree shrines enjoy the patronage of thousands of worshipers annually.

Historically, His image is often found in places of danger, such as steep slopes, river crossings or where two roads cross. Here His *mūrti* may be a rough-hewn stone or even a trunk of a bo or banyan tree which has taken the form of the God Gaṇeśa. A natural stone, or *svayambhū* ("self-created") *mūrti,* may also be the object of worship. Researcher Alice Getty wrote: "The most celebrated *svayambhū mūrtis* of Gaṇeśa are found in Kashmir, where there are three famous and most powerful formless stones which from ancient times have drawn pilgrims to their shrines. One, which is near the village of Gaṇeś-bal, is in the river Lidar near its right bank, and is still an important place of pilgrimage.... Another rock in Kashmir which has been worshiped from most ancient times as a symbol of Gaṇeśa under the name of Bhimasvamin is at the foot of the hill Hari-Parbat near Srinagar....The most remarkable of these *svayambhū mūrtis* in Kashmir is the one on a cliff along the Kishen-Gaṅgā known as Gaṇeś-Gati" *(Gaṇeśa, A Monograph on the Elephant-Faced God,* by Alice Getty, 1971, page 22-23).

Renowned Gaṇeśa Temples

Perhaps the most famous Gaṇeśa temple in India is the Uchi Pillaiyar Koyil at Trichy. *Uchi* means "at the top." This large temple (also known as the Rock Fort Temple) is built on a hilltop and commands a breathtaking view of the city and of the river Kāverī. Another large Gaṇeśa temple is the Pillaiyarpatti Temple near Karaikudi in Rāmanāthapuram District, also in Tamil Nadu. In New Delhi there is the Siddhi Buddhi Vināyagar temple situated in Vināya Nagar. The Mukkuruni Pillaiyar inside the huge Meenakshi Temple complex in Madurai, India, is also quite famous. This *mūrti* is ten to twelve feet tall. *Mukkuruni* refers to a large measure of rice (about forty pounds). Here the priests cook a huge *modaka* ball for Gaṇeśa using this measure. Hence the name Mukkuruni Pillaiyar. Also in Madurai, Lord Gaṇeśa is worshiped as Vyāghrapāda Gaṇeśanī, in female form with tiger feet. The Gaṇeśanī *mūrti* in *sukhāsana* pose resides at Suchindram. There are two other temples in India with the female Gaṇeśa form. One is at a tenth-century temple dedicated to sixty-four *yoginīs* in Bheraghat, a village near Jabalpur. The other is the Tanumalaya Swami Temple in Suchindrum, Kerala. In Tibet, She is worshiped as Gajānanī.

A five-headed Gaṇeśa mounted on a lion resides at Nagapattinam. At Vellore, India, Gaṇeśa is enshrined as Valampuri Vināyakar, with his trunk turned to the right instead of to the left. This *mūrti* is considered very auspicious. Highly revered Gaṇeśa shrines are also found in the precincts of the Śiva temple of Tirunelveli, in the Kanyākumārī temple at the southern tip of India, and in Rāmeshvaram and Chidambaram. Our loving Gaṇeśa is especially beloved in Mahārāshṭra, where eight temples form one of His most sacred pilgrimages, and dozens of other sites are designated for his adoration. At the end of this chapter we offer a list of fifty of India's most prominent Gaṇeśa citadels. It is said that to make a visit on hardship pilgrimage (third-class on trains, on foot or by crawling) to 108 Gaṇeśa temples and roadside shrines is most auspicious to smooth out the *karmas* of the future by, through His grace, dissolving the negative *karmas* and mistakes of the past, made knowingly or unknowingly. Penance of this sort deliberately condenses into a short period, or puts all in one place, the suffering that would otherwise be encountered over a long span of time.

The garden island of Sri Lanka has fourteen well-known Gaṇeśa temples. There is an unusual Vināyaka at the Śiva temple in Central Java, which is presently an archeological tourist site being restored by the Indonesian government. Lord Gaṇeśa here sits with the soles of His feet pressed together, much like a child would sit, or as a *yogī* would sit in deep *samādhi*.

Archeological Discoveries

Śrī H. Kṛishṇamūrthi writes in *Tattvāloka* (Feb.-March 1990): "Several images of Gaṇeśa have been discovered in the excavations of Central America and Mexico. It is said that in Mexico the name of Gaṇeśa is Virakośa." Recently India's Birla Science Institute announced a new find: "A piece of evidence was connected with the legend of Gaṇeśa's writing down the epic to the dictation of Vyāsa. A metal plate depicting the elephant-headed Deity holding a quill has been found in Luristan in Western Iran and has been dated to around 1200 BCE *(Motilal Banarsidass Newsletter* Dec. 1993)."

In Malaysia and Elsewhere

Among the most renowned of God Gaṇeśa's temples in Malaysia are the Siddhi Vināyagar temple of Petaling Jaya and the Kotta Malai Pillaiyar Temple of Kuala Lumpur on the busy street of Paduraya. The latter is a very small temple, but extremely powerful and said to be the most popular Gaṇeśa temple in the land. Also notable are the Jalan Pudu (Pasar Road) Pillaiyar Temple and the Poyyata Vināyagar Temple of Melaka. In Hawaii our Kadavul Hindu Temple for monastics and initiated members has a three-ton, six-foot-tall Gaṇeśa. And we have installed a five-ton, nine-foot tall, five-faced *mūrti* of Gaṇeśa, Pañchamukha Gaṇapati, in a mango orchard at the Śaiva Dharmaśāla of Riviere du Rempart, Mauritius. In Edmonton, Canada, and Nandi, Fiji, there are two exquisite stone *mūrtis* of the elephant-faced God, established to begin new temples. In Great Britain, Gaṇeśa is enshrined at each of the nation's several new temples and is the presiding Deity at the Shree Gaṇapati Temple in Wimbledon and at temples in Switzerland, Germany, Denmark.

Lord Gaṇeśa in America

The religion of the earliest known North American Indians was apparently the offspring of, and virtually the same as, our own venerable Sanātana Dharma, a fact that is evidenced by their rituals and religious beliefs and symbols. One of Lord Gaṇeśa's oldest symbols, the *swastika,* was one of the central motifs used in the designs and patterns of many American Indian tribes and is still seen today in their beautiful blankets and pottery. So, the great God Gaṇeśa is not new to the Western countries, but old. His recent coming into prominence is more our remembering Him in lands where He has always been. But it is in this twentieth century, in the decades of the '70s and '80s, that Lord Gaṇeśa has come to be traditionally enshrined in magnificent multi-million-dollar Hindu temples. We find Him in New York,

Pittsburgh, Chicago, Concord, Livermore, Fremont, Denver, Houston, Nashville, Edmonton in Canada and hundreds of other places. These shrines have brought forth the *mūrti,* or physical image, of Gaṇeśa as *Gajānana,* the Elephant-Faced. His strong footing now in all the major Hindu communities in the West is a great blessing and a joyous time for all. Gaṇeśa's presence in North America at the beginning of the growth of Āgamic Hinduism in the West ensures its success.

As Hinduism emerged in North America in the twentieth century, Gaṇeśa led the way. One of the first traditional temples to be built was the large Mahā Gaṇapati Temple in Flushing, New York. As each community sought guidance and direction in establishing religious roots, I constantly urged the trustees of each temple society, who came seeking guidance from Kauai's Hindu Monastery in the Hawaiian Island chain, to first begin their congregations in the worship of Gaṇeśa in order for their temple to come up quickly. We would often present the group with large or small stone images of the great God and give them the blessings for His worship to begin. Thus, at many new temple site, a Gaṇeśa image was established in a small shrine while construction and fund raising proceeded. This occurred in Fiji, Edmonton, Livermore, Fremont, Salt Lake City, Houston, Denver, Chicago, Lansing, Bethesda, London, Germany and elsewhere. Priests were brought from India, devotees flocked to the shrines, the worship began, and the funds to construct the temple began to flow. This practice has now become a tradition in the West as Hindus have learned from experience that once Lord Gaṇeśa is worshiped, it is actually He who builds the temple in a most wonderful and inspiring way, and they are his helpers.

Visions of Lord Gaṇeśa

Lord Gaṇeśa's vivified presence in the Western world has already culminated in many special visions of Him by both born and formally converted Hindus living in North and South America. In hopes of spiriting onward the worldwide fellowship of Hindus around the globe, a few such visions will be included here anonymously.

Lord Gaṇeśa has been worshiped here and there in North and South America in many small ways by devotees from India for many years since the turn of the century. But not until events in the early 1970s brought about the building of a large and very expensive Gaṇeśa temple in New York did Lord Gaṇeśa take up a formal public residence. The sequence of events leading up to this temple affirmed for our modern times the ancient tradition wherein the Deity Himself decides when and where His temple is to be built. It is not a man or a woman or a group of people who make that decision on the whim of personal inspiration. Rather, the Deity, the God, informs us that the time has come for His temple to come up and then we, in turn, proceed to help Him manifest it in the material world. The message from the God containing the direction of when and where to build His home is traditionally given by Him to holy men, *gurus, swāmīs, sants* who are respected by the community and are in personal touch with the Gods. Such religious leaders also have spiritual insight into the religious progress of the community. Lord Gaṇeśa may strengthen the instructions of such holy men through a dream or vision to a devotee.

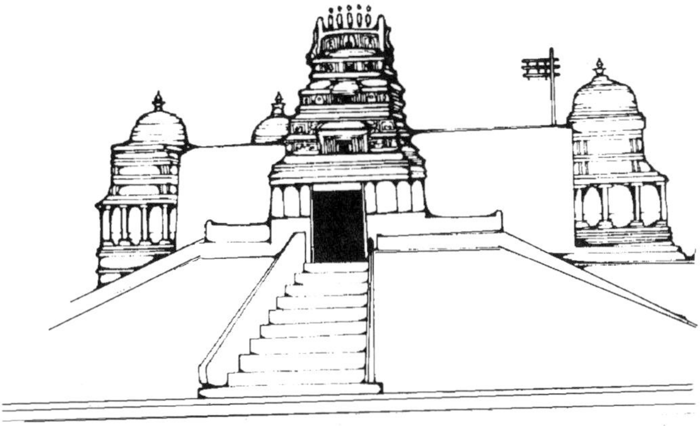

The Mahā Gaṇapati Temple in Flushing, New York, began with two gentlemen from India who had been living in New York for several years. One of these hailed from a long line of temple builders, the other was a devout man who performed regular religious and *yoga sādhana.* This man had returned to India. He had a vision one night. He found himself soaring high above New York City until he came above an abandoned church in an area near his former residence. He came over the steeple which opened as he moved down to land in front of the altar. Lo! there on the altar was Lord Gaṇapati Himself who said nothing to him but just smiled. Immediately upon awakening, with his heart filled with love and the vision of the Great God still fresh in his inner mind, this *sant* phoned the temple builder who was then serving at the United Nations in New York. The temple builder asked him to come to New York right away. Travel arrangements were made, and within 24 hours the two of them were driving around the Queens section of New York in search of Lord Gaṇapati's new home. They finally came upon the old Christian church that was the very one seen in the vision and which was for sale at the time! There could be no doubt that Lord Gaṇeśa had come and had shown where to put His temple. The building was subsequently purchased. After many years of hard work, with the blessings and sanction of Śrīlaśrī Pandrimalaiswāmī, Lord Gaṇeśa was installed and consecrated in an orthodox shrine to receive traditional public worship.

Meanwhile, nearly halfway around the world on the Kona coast of the island of Hawaii in the Pacific Ocean, a small *mūrti* of Lord Gaṇeśa was being worshiped at a seashore shrine by my Śaiva Siddhānta devotees. A sixteen-year-old *kumārī* girl who lived nearby had been performing regular daily *pūjā* and chanting at the site. Her devotion was blessed with several visions of the Deities Gaṇeśa and Murugan. During April of 1980, at the time that new *mūrtis* of Lord Gaṇeśa and Lord Murugan were being delivered to their temporary residence at another devotee's home farther down the hillside, this young lady looked out from her home and saw the Lords Gaṇeśa and Murugan walking in a circle of blue light up toward the seashore shrine. She described them as completely bedecked with flowers, Gaṇeśa dressed in white and Murugan in orange. The Murugan *mūrti* was that of Palani, the renunciate, and this is how He appeared in the vision. She also reported having seen Lord Gaṇeśa on two other occasions sitting serenely at the site of His new shrine, gazing silently at her with doe-like eyes.

Just a few months later, another of my devotees in Hawaii, an older woman who had been doing *sādhana,* was sitting in meditation when her *satguru* appeared before her. He started to ascend upward in this vision and she clutched his robes and went up with him until her strength failed and she fell back down. Before she landed, Lord Gaṇeśa caught her in His trunk and took her back up to where her *satguru* was seated in front of two large golden doors which opened into the world of the Gods. Lord Gaṇeśa gently set her down on the threshold next to her beloved *guru,* she said.

Since 1972 many other devotees have seen Lord Gaṇeśa in their visions and dreams. For example, several pilgrims on the 1981 India Odyssey, a spiritual pilgrimage to the holy lands of ancient Bhārat (today's India), had life-altering visions of Lord Gaṇeśa at the Śrī Kumbalavalai Temple in Jaffna, Sri Lanka. Such visions of Lord Gaṇeśa clarify much about the way this great Lord works. While the visions took place within the subtle minds of His devotees, or our microcosm, this subtle space is in fact enormous and quite a macrocosm of its own.

Just as Lord Gaṇeśa's vehicle, the tiny rodent, ferrets out every secret space and hidden area of the house, so does this Great Mahādeva have the ability to move within the seemingly most obscure and intricate areas of our minds. He is the master of both the big and the small, the macrocosm and the microcosm. Lord Gaṇeśa's great belly is the entire manifestation of all that is, of the five elements of earth, air, fire, water and ether. Thus, He pervades all, not from the outside in but from the inside out. He does not move to pervade, for all form in its purest state is together, not far apart. Seated unmoving on the broad, four-petalled lotus of the *mūlā-*

dhāra chakra, Lord Gaṇeśa records and governs the movements of vast inner oceans of *actinodic* energy that appear to our physical eyes to manifest as forms so many millions of miles apart. He is at work through all the outwardly gross forms of nature, and yet mounted on his tiny mouse He can, in utter minuteness, travel about within His devotees' minds as if they were great, well-lit caverns. Such is the mystery of the pompous elephant-faced God, the embodiment of form who rides the mouse.

During *pūjā* at the Madhaya Kailāsa Temple in Madras devotees saw and continue to see Gaṇeśa, the elephant God, and Hanuman, the monkey God, merging into one, as the alpha and omega of existence. To honor this unusual form, in 1993 a five-metal image half Gaṇeśa and half Hanuman was created and enshrined. It all started with a series of early-morning visions that graced devotees of the two unusual and somewhat similar Gods in the great Hindu pantheon of 330 million.

The final vision to recite is one that I had in the mid-1980s of Lord Ganeśa walking from His temple attended by two priests. He was about to take a bath in the beautiful Indian Ocean in the country of Mauritius where the river meets the sea. I was standing in the water with several sharks swimming around me. Lord Gaṇeśa, accompanied by two priests, looked at me and said, "Just rub some oil on their noses and they will not harm you." This vivid mystic experience is illustrated on the next page.

Remember, such visions of this great Lord do not come only to the meditating *yogīs,* but to sincere *bhaktas* as well—those who by virtue of their *sukarma* receive this special grace at particularly auspicious times in their lives.

Our Loving Gaṇeśa

Loving Gaṇeśa is our friend indeed.
He is our protector,
The God we go to when in need.

Loving Gaṇeśa knows our future and past.
He is our conscience,
The God we go to when we want to move fast.

Loving Gaṇeśa is the God on our side.
He is immediate,
The God we pray to when we want to abide.

Loving Gaṇeśa is our loving Lord.
He is our All,
The God that we shall all look toward.

The Favorite God Of Mahārāshṭra

BY DR. S. SRINIVASAN, FROM *TATTVĀLOKA, FEB/MAR 1990*

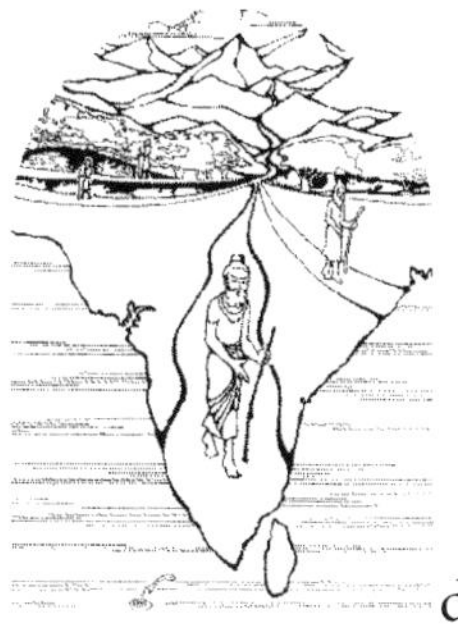

No other state in India dotes on its presiding Deity the way Mahārāshṭra does with Lord Gaṇeśa. Every year the whole state reverberates with rhythm and music in praise of the Lord for ten days, starting with Gaṇeśa Chaturthī and culminating in a grand, pompous immersion ceremony on Ananta Chaturdaśi day. No wonder Mahārāshṭrians cherish visiting the eight sacred temples of Vināyaka, known as Ashṭavināyaka, where the Lord's image is said to have sprung up naturally, true to the word *svayambhū*. Logically, the images are devoid of elaborate ornamentation. They are simple pieces of stone showing only the broadest outlines of Lord Gaṇeśa's tusked face and trunk, heavily smeared with red *sindūr* applied layer over layer for centuries.

Lord Gaṇeśa was brought to the heart of every Mahārāshṭrian by Bal Gaṅgādhara Tilak decades ago as part of a socio-cultural movement directed against alien rulers. The momentum it has gathered is now for all to see. Despite intrusion by modern tastes and living habits of the younger generation, the deep roots that Gaṇapati worship has struck in the ethos of this tradition-loving state appear well set to stay for eternity. The eight icons are located in scenic spots scattered over three or four districts of Western Mahārāshṭra. In the good old days, with transport system not so well developed, visiting all of them took eight days or more, but today one can complete the pilgrimage in three days. There are several travel agencies in Pune that arrange safe and comfortable trips for the pilgrims. A brief resume of the shrines follows. Pilgrimage can be arranged through India embassies worldwide, each of which has access to efficient travel bureaus, and friendly help in arranging the pilgrimage will be gladly provided.

1. Morgaon Temple to Śri Mayūreśvara

Let us begin with the most important of the eight holy places, Morgaon, situated about 65 KM southeast of Pune and 16 KM from the nearest railway station, Jejuri. Enclosed by tall stone walls forming a quadrangle, the temple here bears some semblance to Islamic architecture characterized by minaret-like towers in the four corners. Apparently it enjoyed the support of a benevolent Muslim chieftain for awhile. An interesting feature of this temple is the giant-sized stone Nandi positioned in front of the Lord. It is said that centuries ago as the Nandi was being transported to a Śiva temple nearby, it decided to settle in front of Lord Gaṇeśa and just would not move. Within the quadrangle surrounding the temple there are eight smaller temples with Gaṇapati idols by the names Ekadanta, Mahodhara, Gajānana, Lambodara, Vikaṭa, Naṭarāja, Dhūmravarṇa and Vakratuṇḍa. There are also 23 other idols of various Gods from the Hindu pantheon, besides two sacred perennial trees: *bilva* and *shamī*. The sanctum sanctorum houses Mayūreśvara [Peacock Lord], a primordial idol with a left-sided trunk, fully smeared with saffron and protected by the hood of a cobra. It is said that the actual image is quite small but it looks big due to the thick layer of saffron, which falls off once in a century or so. The local people believe that this happened last in 1882 and prior to that in 1788.

2. Thevoor Temple to Śrī Chintāmaṇi

Situated 22 kilometers from Pune, this village became the spiritual retreat of many a Peshāwar ruler of Pune, especially Mādhavarao the senior. Lord Gaṇeśa here is known as Chintāmaṇi [jewel of consciousness]. The story behind this name relates to the Lord's retrieving a precious stone *(chintāmaṇi)* for one of his devotees, Kapila Muni, from a greedy king, Gaṇa. By then, however, Kapila Muni would rather have his Lord than the precious stone. The Lord thus chose to stay with his devotee as Chintāmaṇi himself. The conjoint river Mūlā-Muthā flows by the village as it winds its way to join Chandrabhāgā which in turn flows past Pandharpur to eventually join the Tuṅgabhadrā and the Kṛishṇā. Morya Gosavi, the great Gaṇeśa devotee, used to pass through Thevoor on his trips between Chinchwad and Morgaon. The Lord's icon, again smeared with *sindūr,* is not much different from the others of the Ashṭavināyaka group, with the features hardly being visible, except the elephant head and trunk. But the divine impact on the devotees is there as ever.

3. Siddhatek Village Temple to Śrī Siddhivināyaka

This village is 13 kilometers northeast of Daund railway junction, but one has to cross the Bhīma River by boat. Years ago, before a downstream dam was built, one could walk across the dry river bed, but today the waters are too deep. The idol of Gaṇeśa here is right-tusked. Devotees are enjoined to be extra careful about the rituals and austerity while worshiping a right-tusked Gaṇapati [Siddhi Vināyaka, Masterful Remover]. The temple complex is atop a hill which stretches over a kilometer on the other side. Devotees seeking a favor from the Lord go around the entire hill seven times in *pradakshiṇa.* With no footpath or road and with thorny bushes all around, this exercise—covering several kilometers of rough terrain—ought to bring the Lord's mercy to the seeker!

4. Ranjangaon Shrine to Śrī Gaṇapati

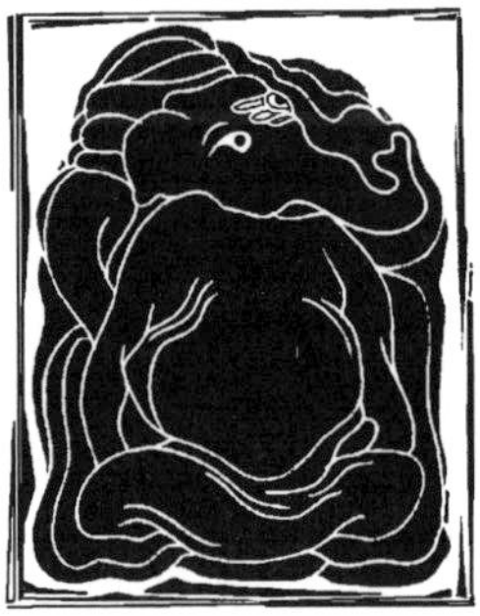

Located on the highway connecting Pune and Ahmednagar is the home of Śrī Mahāgaṇapati [Great Lord of Hosts]. Flanked by *Buddhi* and *Siddhi,* as his consorts are popularly known in Mahārāshṭra, Śrī Mahāgaṇapati of Ranjangaon can even enjoy the direct rays of the sun around noon time, thanks to the way the sanctum sanctorum is constructed. The icon of a ten-headed Gaṇapati known as Mahotkata is also housed in the temple complex but hidden from the view of most devotees. Some believe that this was the main idol once upon a time, but it was put away fearing destruction by invaders.

5. Ojhar Kshetra to Śrī Vighneśvara

Just off the Pune-Nasik highway, this *kshetra* is ruled by Śrī Vighneśvara [Lord of Obstacles], again flanked by *Buddhi* and *Siddhi.* Two smart *dvārapālakas* (sentries), a wide two-tiered *prakāram,* a well-polished figure of a *mūshika* (mouse, the vehicle of Lord Gaṇeśa) and two giant *dīpastambhas* (lamp posts) all made of stone are the noteworthy features of this temple.

6. Lenyadhri Cave to Śrī Girijātmaja

The name indicates a cave in a mountain. Gaṇeśa as Śrī Girijātmaja [mountain-born] enjoys a picturesque view of the landscape dotted with hills all around, merging into a mountain range beyond, and the Pushpavatī river winding its way in-between, glistening in the sunlight. After climbing 283 steps, one enters the temple, a single large room, about 57 feet long and 51 feet wide cut into the rock, with no supporting pillars anywhere. There are 18 other caves of Buddhist architecture in this hill. This icon of Gaṇeśa has even less distinct features than the others. The locals believe that it is only the back of Gaṇeśa that is visible to the devotees and that the face is on the other side of the hill which is unapproachable. Some Peshāwar rulers who tried to locate it were reportedly thwarted in their attempts.

7. Mahad Hamlet Temple to Śrī Varada Vināyaka

This is a tiny hamlet close to the Bombay-Pune highway near Khopoli, an industrial center. It is not to be confused with Mahad, a township on the way to Goa from Bombay. The temple is located next to a tank that tends to go dry during summer, but the green fields and trees provide abundant cool air and a quiet atmosphere conducive to introspection and prayer. The sanctum is open to the public and, true to Mahārāshṭrian tradition, many devotees place their head right on the feet of the icon to seek blessings [of Varada Vināyaka, Lord of Boons]. An interesting feature of this temple is an *anantadīpa* (eternal flame) that has been kept alight since 1892.

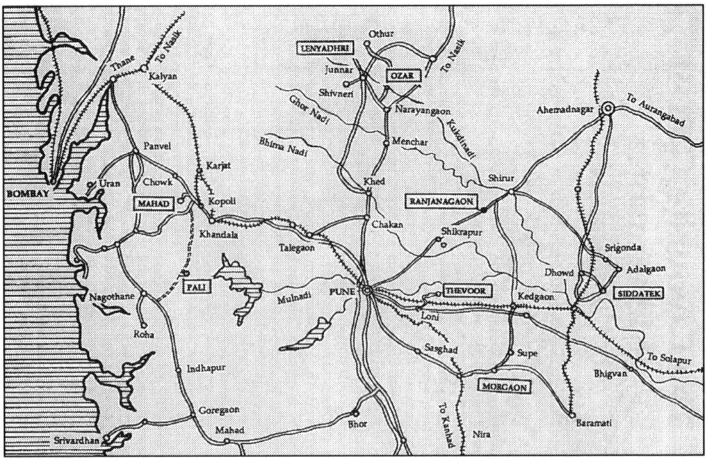

8. Pali Temple to Śrī Ballaleśvara

About 8 kilometers off the Bombay-Goa highway, again set amidst a pleasant countryside dotted with hills and criss-crossed by rivers, one finds the village of Śrī Ballaleśvara. The name comes from Lord Gaṇeśa saving a boy named Ballala who even as a child spent all his time praying to Him. Angered by the boy's obsessive behavior, the villagers beat him up mercilessly, and it was Lord Gaṇeśa who intervened to save his life. There are two Gaṇeśa temples here. One has first to visit Śrī Dhundivināyaka, the idol which Ballala worshiped, before proceeding to Śrī Ballaleśvara in the main temple. The idol in the latter is unusually broad and enjoys early-morning sun rays, as it sits facing the east, right at the foot of a steep hill. During the usually heavy monsoon months, waterfalls streak the landscape all around. A huge *pañchadhātu* (five-metal) bell adorns the temple. Its sweet chimes add a special touch of music to the various *āratīs* performed for the Lord.

Mahārāshṭra's Other Gaṇeśa Temples

In addition to the famous Ashṭavināyakas, Mahārāshṭra boasts a bounty of Gaṇeśa temples in every nook and corner, some famous, others not so. The more important ones include Śrī Siddhivināyaka of Bombay; Śrī Mahāgaṇapati (famous as a matrimonial matchmaker) at Titwala, 75 KM from Bombay; Śrī Maṅgala Mūrti at Chinchwad, a suburb of Pune; Śrī Kasva Gaṇapati and Śrī Sarasbag Gaṇapati, both of Pune city. On the Arabian seacoast, just off Ratnagiri, Gaṇapatipule houses a temple that is literally kept washed by the waves every day, an attraction for tourists and devotees. Other well-known temples are Dasabhuja Gaṇapati near Chiplun on the coastal belt, Siddhivināyaka at Nandgaon, Vighnāyana Gaṇapati at Rakshasabhuvan in Marathwada, Modakeśvara at Nasik and Śrī Gaṇapati at Seetabardi, Nagpur. Pilgrims who visit all the temples here-in named during a single *tīrthayātrā,* spiritual outing, are said to have gained the ultimate blessing of the five-armed Lord. Those rare souls who add more visits to His other abodes to this list are kept in His heart forever, enjoying the bliss of all sweet things when in the hereafter, between births.

A List of Gaṇeśa Temples Worldwide

Three great pillars have held Hinduism high millenia after millenia: the *satgurus*, scriptures and the temples. Listed here are significant Gaṇeśa temples we know of around the world, with place name followed by temple name or the *mūrti* inside the temple. We welcome submissions to expand this list for future printings of *Loving Gaṇeśa.*

Maharashtra

Eight-Temple Pilgrimage

MORGAON
Mayūreśvara—India's foremost Gaṇeśa pilgrimage

SIDDITEK
Siddhi Vināyaka

PALI
Ballāla Vināyaka

MADHA
Varada Vināyaka

OJHAR
Vighneśvara

LENYADRI
Girijātmajā

RANJANGAON
Mahā Gaṇapati

THEUR
Chintāmaṇi

Other Maharashtrian Sites

ADOSHA, NAGAPUR AREA
Śamī Vighneśa

BEROLA
Laksha Vināyaka

JETHA KAPAD MKT, BOMBAY
Siddhi Vināyaka

KALAMBA
Cintāmaṇi Gaṇeśa

KANAKESVARA
Rāma Siddha Vināyaka

KASVA
Jayate Gaṇeśa

NAGAJHARI RIVER
Triśuṇḍa

NAMALGAON
Amalāśramakshetra (famous for prayers)

NANDED
Citrakūṭa Gaṇeśa

NASIK
Higalyaka Gaṇapati

PADMALAYA
Pravālakshetra with two Gaṇeśa *murtis*

PRABHA DEVI, BOMBAY
Siddhi Vināyaka

RAJUR
Rājasadanakshetra

RAKSHASABHUVAN
Vijña Gaṇeśa

SANGLI, KRISHNA RIVER
Gaṇeśa
(a *svayambhū* Gaṇeśa installed over a Śivaliṅga)

TITWALA
Siddhi Vināyaka Mahā Gaṇapati (a place of miracles)

Uttar Pradesh

PRAYAGA
Oṁkara Gaṇapati

VARANASI
Ḍhuṇḍhirāja Gaṇeśa

Orissa

CHANDIKHOLE, CUTTACK
Mahā Vināyaka

Kerala

TIRUVANANTHAPURAM
Śrī Agrasala Gaṇapathy

Tamil Nadu

AMBAL
Suddu Vināyaka

ANBILALANTURAI
Sevisaitta Pillaiyar

CHIDAMBARAM
Katpaka Vināyaka

KUDANTAI KIRKKODDAM
Gaṅgai Gaṇapati

KALATI
Mañjanti Vināyaka

KANCHIPURAM
Valampuri Vināyaka,
Vikada Chakra Vināyaka

MADRAS, PERIAMEDU
Śrī Varasiddhi Vināyaka

MADURAI
Mukkuruni Pillaiyar
Siddhi Vināyaka

MAYURAPURAM
Mayureśa Vināyaka

NAGAPADDINAM
Pañcha Mukha Vināyaka

PONDICHERRY
Manakkula Pillaiyar

SENPAKKAM
Temple of eleven *svayambhū* Gaṇeśas

SIRGALI
Aapattukatta Vināyaka

TIRUCHIRAPPALLI
Uchi Pillaiyar

TIRUINNAMPAR
Nirutana Vināyaka

TIRUKKACHYUR
Tālamūla Vināyaka,
Karukkadi Vināyaka

TIRUKKADAVUR
Kallavarana Pillaiyar

TIRUKKARUVIL
Kadukkai Vināyaka

TIRUKODDAIYUR
Kodi Vināyaka

TIRUKOKARNAM
Mahā Gaṇapati

TIRUMAKARAL
Poyyā Vināyaka

TIRUMALAPADI
Sundara Gaṇapati

TIRUMARAIKADU
Veeragati Vināyaka

TIRUMURUGANPUNDI
Kūppidu Pillaiyar

TIRUNADDIYATANKUDI
Kaikaddi Vināyaka

TIRUNALLUR
Salakkirāma Vināyaka

TIRUNALLARU
Sorna Vināyaka

TIRUNARAIYUR
Polla Pillaiyar

TIRUNTUTEVANKUDI
Karkadaka Vināyaka

TIRUPATTUR
Maya Pillaiyar

TIRUPPANAIYUR
Tunaiyirunta Pillaiyar
TIRUPPURAMPAYAM
Piralayangkātta Pillaiyar
TIRUVAIYARU
Ādi Vināyaka
TIRUVALAM
Valam Vanda Vināyaka
TIRUVALAMSULI
Vellai Pillaiyar
TIRUVARUR
Vātāpi Vināyaka
TIRUVAVADUTURAI
Śivaprākasa Vināyaka
TIRUVETIKUDI
Veta Pillaiyar
TIRUVIDAIMARUTUR
Ānda Vināyaka
TIRUVILIMILALAI
Padikkāsu Vināyaka
TIRUVUSATANAM
Kutavana Pillaiyar
VALLAM
Varasiddhi Vināyaka
VIRUTTASALAM
Mattru Uraita Pillaiyar

Sri Lanka

Jaffna

CHULIPURAM
Kannaikothikakkai Pillaiyar
INUVIL
Karunakara Pillaiyar
MANIPAY
Maruthady Vināyagar
MURUKANDI
Murukandi Pillaiyar
NALLUR
Kailāsa Pillaiyar
NEERVELY
Arasakesari Pillaiyar

Outside Jaffna

ALAVEDDY
Kumbalavalai Pillaiyar
BATTICALOA
Mamaṅga Pillaiyar
COLOMBO, CHETTY STREET
Śri Muthu Vināyaga Temple
COLOMBO, BAMBALAPITIYA
New Kathiresan Temple
KANDY
Selva Vināyaka
KATIRAGAMA
Manikka Vināyaka

Nepal

BHATAGAON NEAR KATHMANDU
Sūryavināyaka Gaṇeśa
GORKHA
Vijaya Gaṇapati
JANAKPUR
Rāma Temple
Siddha Gaṇeśa
PHULAHARA
Rāma/Jānakī Temple
Girijā Gaṇeśa

Cambodia

KANDALA
Padmāsana Gaṇeśa

Malaysia

Kuala Lumpur Vicinity

JALAN BRUNEI/PASAR
Śrī Siddhi Vināyaka
JALAN IPOH
Śrī Paranjothi Vināyaka

KUALA KUBU BARU
Śrī Sithivināyaka
JALAN PUDU LAMA
Śrī Gaṇeśan

Outside Kuala Lumpur

BEHRANG ULU, PERAK
Siddhi Vināyaka
IPOH
Śrī Mahā Gaṇapati
KLANG
Siddhi Vināyaka
SANDAKAN, SABAH
Siddhi Vināyaka

Singapore

CEYLON ROAD
Śrī Senpaga Vināyaka
KEONG SIAK ROAD
Śrī Vināyaka

Australia

MAGILL
Gaṇeśa
MELBOURNE
Vakratuṇḍa Vināyaka

South Africa

DURBAN, NATAL
Sithi Vinayaka
LADYSMITH, NATAL
Gaṇeśer
MT. EDGECOMBE, NATAL
Gaṇeśa

Germany

HAMM
Siddhi Vināyaka
HALTINGEN
Vara Siddhi Vināyaka
HEILBRONN
Vināyaka

France

PARIS
Śrī Manikkavināyakar Alayam

United Kingdom

LONDON, EFFRA ROAD
Śrī Gaṇapati

United States

FLUSHING, NEW YORK
Śrī Mahā Vallabha Gaṇapati Devasthanam
NASHVILLE, TENNESSEE
Gaṇeśa

Canada

EDMONTON
Mahā Gaṇapati

Indochina

Gaṇeśa has few of his own temples in these lands, tens of thousands of small Gaṇeśa images are found everywhere, and one or two larger images. He was worshiped in the Śaivite tradition that covered these areas as early as 400 CE.

Java/Indonesia

While we do not find temples dedicated specifically to Gaṇeśa, He is found in almost every Śiva shrine throughout the country.

Praśnottarī

प्रश्नोत्तरी

Questions and Answers

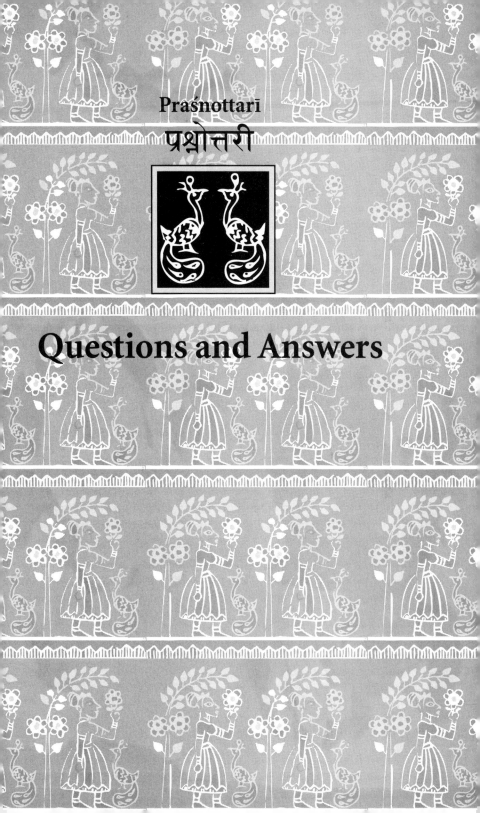

Questions and Answers

NOW IT MAY BE HELPFUL IN OUR EXPLORATION TOGETHER OF THE WONDERFUL BEING, LORD GAṆEŚA, TO SHARE WITH YOU answers to some of the questions most commonly asked about Him by the many devotees worldwide. Hopefully these insights will inspire you to draw closer to Him and learn about His grace and His ever giving boons through your own experiences. Yes, Lord Gaṇapati is a mysterious God to most adults, but not to children. We too must be like little children to really enjoy and understand His majesty, mirth, wisdom and simple complexities. The God whose symbol is the *swastika,* who moves in many directions all at once, is truly, to a child, as simple as a digital on-and-off switch. Children who grow up in the ten arms of Him who has no second are intricate of mind, agile to change, not affected by wealth or poverty, adjustable and secure in His daily *darśana* before they worship other Lords of their choice.

Devotee: *What is the nature of Lord Gaṇeśa?*
Gurudeva: Lord Gaṇeśa is a Mahādeva, a Great God, created by Lord Śiva to assist souls in their evolution. He is the elephant-faced Patron of Art and Science, the Lord of Obstacles and Guardian of Dharma, the first son of Śiva. His will prevails as the force of righteousness, the embodiment of Śiva's *karmic* law in all three worlds.

My *satguru,* Sage Yogaswāmī, proclaimed: "The God with the elephant's face I shall never forget—Śaṅkara's Son, with massive belly and the ring in His ear, the Lord who gave His grace to Indra, of whom *mantra* is His very form." I often explain Lord Gaṇeśa in this way: "Lord Śiva, the Almighty Power, created heaven and earth and the God, Lord

Gaṇeśa, to oversee the intricate *karmas* and *dharmas* within the heavens and all the earths. Lord Gaṇeśa was created as a governor and interplanetary, intergalactic Lord. His knowledge is infinite His judgment is just. It is none other than Lord Gaṇeśa and His mighty band of *gaṇas* that gently help souls out of the Naraka abyss and adjust them into higher consciousness after due penance has been paid, guiding them on the right path toward *dharmic* destiny. He, is intricate of mind, loving pomp, delighting in all things sweet and enjoying adulation. Lord Śiva proclaimed that this son be worshiped first, even before Himself. Verily, He is the Lord of Karma. All Mahādevas, minor Gods, *devas* and sentient beings must worship Lord Gaṇeśa before any responsible act could hope to be successful. Those who do not are subject to their own barriers. Yea, worship of Him sets the pattern of one's destiny. Thus, this mighty ruler is truly a great God. The 2,000-year old South Indian scripture *Tirumantiram* says, "Five-armed is He, elephant-faced with tusks protruding, crescent-shaped, son of Śiva, wisdom's flower, in heart enshrined, His feet I praise."

Devotee: *What is Lord Gaṇeśa's special duty?*
Gurudeva: He is Vighneśvara, Lord of Obstacles. As such, He controls our evolution by preventing or permitting events to happen in our life.

Lord Gaṇeśa holds the architect's plans of the divine masterpiece of universal past and future of this small world and all the galaxies. They were entrusted to Him when He took office by command of God Śiva. His rule is compassionate, His disciplines strong. He is equally feared and loved. His law is just, for justice is His mind. He enjoys adulations, festivity, hearing of His name, for this brings the devotee into His court, into His presence, close to Him. Only good comes from Lord Gaṇeśa, who by taking the form of an elephant distinguishes Himself from other Gods. He staves off misfortune for those who perform penance in His name. He is within us and not otherwise, closer than our heartbeat, guiding our *karma* through the timing of events. Our Lord of Obstacles prevents us from hurting ourselves through living under an incomplete concept or making a request unneeded or beginning an endeavor not well thought out. He expects us to use all of our intellectual and intuitive faculties and resources, to wield the knowledge available to us before submitting our petitions to Him. It is for us to try to arrive at the right decision, the one that He Himself would have made in granting the acquisition. Thus, this Mahādeva, wise and all-powerful, truly is a great God. The ancient *Āgamas* declare, "These Lords who, it is said, on the pure path, attend to the various duties deriving from a higher realm of *māyā* are at the prow of the effects of the higher realm of *māyā*."

Devotee: *Why must we supplicate Lord Gaṇeśa before beginning any worship or task?*
Gurudeva: At the command of God Śiva Himself, we supplicate, that is, humbly request, Lord Gaṇeśa to clear obstacles from the path of our endeavor, if it be His will. As Lord of Obstacles, Gaṇeśa wields the noose and the goad, icons of His benevolent power of preventing or permitting events to happen in our life. Thus, we invoke His grace and wisdom before any worship or task.

My *satguru,* Sage Yogaswāmī, proclaimed: "May the Supreme Guru, who bestows on me His grace, be my protection! May the elephant-faced God be my protection! May the fair child who wields the shapely lance be my protection!" I have answered this question in this way: "The father and mother, in a properly conducted home, govern their children and prepare them to be fine citizens. The children ask permission from their parents before beginning any new endeavor. The employee asks permission from the employer before beginning any new endeavor. The subjects in a realm ask permission from the monarch before beginning any new endeavor. Why wonder we about asking permission from His Majesty, Lord Gaṇeśa, governor of this world, head, chieftain of our religion, before beginning any new endeavor? He of intricate mind and power is immediate and aware of any form of sincere prayer and supplication, humble requests to clear obstacles from the path of our endeavors, but only if that be His will. Thus, this loving God rules our lives, commanding acknowledgment and adulation—a truly great God is He.

Devotee: *If an obstacle is encountered despite our sincere supplication of Lord Gaṇeśa, what does it mean?*
Gurudeva: It may mean that the time, the means or the goal itself is not right for our *karma* and *dharma.* The architect presents his finished plans to the engineer. They are rejected for one technical reason or another. The executive presents a completed letter to the president. It is rejected as not being explicit enough in the third paragraph. The architect and the executive were equally sincere in presenting their work. The engineer and the president were performing their duty as well. Lord Gaṇeśa loves us. He is a loving God who guides, governs and controls with speed and accuracy when the plan is perfect, deliberates long and rejects often when the plan needs revision. Take the plan back into your mind. Search your own superconsciousness for the greater ideas and revise your efforts with confidence. Seek for the right timing and proceed with confidence when you know the timing to be right. "When the will rises and commands, even the Gods are willing to obey," or to give immediate cooperation, to guide and enhance our efforts. We must work our minds in close cooperation with the mind of Lord Gaṇeśa, and then success is certain. Thus, this God is called Bhaktavighnavināsana, He who destroys the obstacles of the devotees.

If you worship the elephant-faced Vināyaka,
your life will expand bountifully.
If you worship the white-tusked Vināyaka,
your desires and doubts will flee.
Therefore, worship Him
with love-offerings of jack, hoppers,
plantain and mango fruits
and thus mitigate the burden of deeds.

Saint Auvaiyar

O, Elephant-Faced One!
You are so near and we are far from You.
You are in and we are out;
You are at home, while I'm a stranger.
Yet, You have destroyed my egoity.
I shall sing Your praise forever
and lay my garland of songs at Your feet.

Saint Nambiandiyadigal

He is worshiped with red flowers.
Unfailing, merciful, the origin of the worlds,
He appears at the beginning of creation,
alone, beyond Nature, beyond the Cosmic Person.
He who meditates on His form
becomes great among the *yogīs.*

Gaṇapati Upanishad

Gaja, the elephant, is the origin and the goal.
The stage reached by the *yogī* in his
experience of *samādhi* is called *ga,* the "goal,"
and the principle called *ja,* the "origin,"
is that from which the syllable
of obeisance, Aum,
is said to be issued.

Brahma Sūtras

Puṇyotsavāḥ

पुण्योत्सवाः

Sacred Festivals

Sacred Festivals

OPULENT HINDU FESTIVALS ARE TIMES OF JOYOUS CELEBRATION MARKED BY SPECIAL OBSERVANCES. THERE ARE MANY FESTIVALS each year, several to each of the Gods. In this section we present the major festivals that honor Lord Gaṇeśa. Some are celebrated in the temple and others primarily in the home and village. Each of Hinduism's major denominations has its special festivals, and all share in certain celebrations. Each festival occurs at approximately the same time of year, varying slightly according to astrological calculations, usually based on the lunar calendar. Festivals are characterized by acts of piety—penance, fasting, pilgrimage—and spiritual rejoicing: singing, dancing, musical performance, parades, storytelling, scripture-reading and elaborate *pūjās.*

M. Arunachalam wrote in his book *Festivals of Tamil Nadu,* "There are three aspects to every festival in the land. The first is the ritualistic aspect—the various steps of its celebration,...performance of a *pūjā,* preliminary arrangements, etc. The second is the legend aspect—the ancient stories which had grown round it....The third is the philosophical or esoteric aspect which gives significance to the celebration and has kept it alive through so many centuries."

Gaṇeśa Chaturthī

Gaṇeśa Chaturthī, also known as Vināyaka Chaturthī, is the festival day celebrating the birth of Lord Gaṇeśa. One of the great national festivals of India, and the foremost annual festival to Gaṇeśa, it is celebrated on the *chaturthī* or "fourth day" after the new moon in the Tamil month of Avani (August-September). We decorate the temple and home shrine with banana leaves, sugarcane and strings of mango leaves, making it look like a small forest. We bring baskets of fruits and sweets, especially modaka balls, and place them before the sanctum of Lord Gaṇeśa. He receives special *pūjās* throughout the day and often a festival parade. Each year we obtain or make a small or large soft clay image of Gaṇapati and use it for worship at home for two to ten days after Gaṇeśa Chaturthī. Pundit M. Arunachalam noted, "In Karnataka, India, young people make a ritual of seeing 108 Vināyakas on this occasion, so they go about visiting their friends' and relatives' houses on this day.... The worship of Gaṇeśa on this day is supposed to confer advancement in learning to the young student and success in any enterprise undertaken" *(Festivals of Tamil Nadu,* page 110-121).

Śrī Arunachalam continues with a description of the Chaturthī Pūjā itself: "The worship, or *pūjā,* is done as usual towards the close of the forenoon. The whole house and the entrance are decorated with *kolam.* Festoons are hung 'round the place of worship, making it into a sort of decorated *maṇḍapam,* or hall. Tender coconut leaves, split and artistically designed, white in color, mango leaves dark green, lilies in white, and pink and crimson festoons, present a colorful appearance. The newly-made clay image is placed facing east in a convenient place in the northern part of the house on a pedestal decorated in *kolam* design of an eight-petalled *padma* (lotus flower). On the *padma,* a small quantity of paddy (uncooked rice) is spread and the Gaṇeśa image is placed on it over a plantain leaf. Only white flowers are used for the worship. *Aruhu* and *erukku* are special favorites. Then all the *pūjā* rituals are gone through fully.

"Besides, the fruits of the season, such as the wood apple and *jambu* (naval), are also offered in plenty along with the customary plantain fruits and coconuts.... Usually in the rural parts, a *pūjā* is performed again the next morning or noon *(punarpūjā)* with fresh food offerings. In the evening, the Gaṇeśa image is carried by the boys, along with the flowers, and consigned to a running stream or to a good water pool or tank. So, Gaṇeśa who was shaped out of the earth, is now returned to the same earth." This is a day for rejoicing and for seeking the blessings of the Lord of Obstacles to bring wealth and success into our life.

Gaṇeśa Visarjana

Gaṇeśa Visarjana (a Sanskṛit word meaning "departure") names the Gaṇeśa Chaturthī immersion ceremony. Especially in Mahārāshṭra state, it takes place ten days after Gaṇeśa Chaturthī, though in some areas, Visarjana is done even on the Chaturthī day itself. It is a ceremony of fond farewell to a beloved God. On Chaturthī day we celebrate Gaṇeśa's birthday and then honor Him as our beloved guest for ten days. Then on the tenth day, called *chaturdaśi,* we bid Him fond farewell at the ocean shore or banks of a river or babbling brook of love and watch Him float off on the conveyance we have prepared for Him until He finally disappears from sight into the waters. We honor His departure with a grand parade, as we carry Him on a palanquin bedecked with flowers and accompanied by *pūjā,* music, dancing and celebration. Clay images of Gaṇeśa specifically prepared for the event are ceremoniously dissolved in the ocean or other body of water at this time by devotees all over the world, signifying Gaṇeśa's withdrawal into all-pervasive consciousness. Though the Visarjana has been celebrated as a religious festival for thousands of years, it became especially popular early in this century.

Śrī S.K. Deodhar explained the popularity of the Visarjana festival in HINDUISM TODAY, JULY, 1988: "Lokmanya Tilak from Mahārāshṭra, who first raised the banner for Indian independence and freedom from British rule, gave the call around 1910 to celebrate the Gaṇeśa festival as a public *pūjā,* so as to mobilize people to come together to build up a strong, united India, based on her holy traditions and scriptural teachings. Since then, people observe the festival, both

at home and in public, with options of one and one-half days to 5, 7 or 10 days. The tenth day is Ananta Chaturdaśi, which coincides with the *pūjā* to Ananta, the Holy Serpent.

"The tenth-day immersion procession is truly spectacular in many cities, when thousands of idols are taken to the sea or river with a lot of music, dance, rejoicing, street-chariots and decorations. These continue often throughout the tenth night, up to the eleventh day morning. The celebration consists of bringing an earthen idol from the market and doing *pūjā* in the traditional style as you would do for a respected guest who comes to your home. When it is time for a guest to depart, we offer him gifts and food for his travel. Then we accompany him up to the border of the village, which is often a small stream or rivulet. As the guest enters the water of the stream, we bid him goodbye and return home. ;mersing the earthen idol in the river, sea or tank. The observance was originally for one and one-half days; bringing the idol on the first day, doing the *pūjā*, rejoicing and immersing it on the second day. But later many people increased the period to celebrate the festival with more joy, devotion, music, religious talks, etc. The Indian state of Mahārashṭra is renowned for its Visarjana festivals which each year draw millions of participants, most notably in the cities of Bombay and Pune." (Śrī Deodhar's description was translated from Gujarati by Śrī Vināyak Vishwanāth Gokhale.)

It is well known that Lord Gaṇeśa has a knack for bringing devotees together, and the Visarjana is one of the ways that He does this. All forget their daily concerns, worries and personal lives during this celebration and gather with others in the fun. In 1988 Gaṇeśa broke new ground in his public relations when Visarjana was held in the United States. It was the first large-scale interdenominational public Hindu festival held in US history. It was indeed an historic event. Almost two thousand Hindus gathered in San Francisco, California, on September 25 for a grand festival culminating ten days of worship and festivities begun on Gaṇeśa Chaturthī. More than twenty Hindu organizations of various traditions participated against the majestic backdrop of the Golden Gate Bridge. Horns sounded, drums played and bells rang out *pūjās* as hundreds of images of Gaṇeśa were dramatically conveyed to the Pacific Ocean. Many worshipers stated with delight that they felt as if they were back in India. The celebration proved to one and all that Hinduism had reached a new level of maturity in the US, as devotees boldly proclaimed their faith in such a grand public ceremony. The festival has been held in the Bay Area every year since its inception. Australia followed suit a few years later, and now yearly parades are held on the streets of Sidney by all Hindu groups joining together in public worship.

Making Clay Gaṇeśas

Pundit M. Arunachalam provides the following excellent description of the joyful activity of making clay Gaṇeśas: "The form of Gaṇeśa is a delight not only to the artist and the sculptor but also to the children....Almost all the children try their hand at producing the complete form of Gaṇeśa in clay with their own hands—the full elephant face with its trunk curved at the tip, four hands, the uplifted ones carrying the goad and the noose, the left hand carrying the *modaka*, the right in the pose of offering benediction, the big belly with the sacred thread thrown across the left shoulder, the two stumpy legs, and not omitting His mount, the little shrew [mouse]. The scarlet black-eyed seeds of the creeper *kunrimani* (the crab's eye, *Abrus precatorius*) serve as the eyes of Gaṇeśa. In places like Madras, a slender, paper umbrella is added.

"The clay image is made at the moment in the morning. In urban areas, people purchase it. But in the rural parts, it is the pride of the urchins to make the image each for the family worship. The boys vie with one another in making the image perfect, i.e., in making it conform to what is known as the Ravi Varma picture as closely as possible. Rules lay down that the image is made out of the mud of the ants' hill. In urban areas, hand-made supply cannot keep up with the demand. So, the makers have wooden moulds on which they hand-press the kneaded clay and cast the images."

THE PROPER ATTITUDE

Making an image of the God must be done in the right spirit. Swāmī Satyānanda Saraswati of Devī Mandir in California contributed the following instruction.

"Take all of the love in your heart, all the longing to see God face to face, the totality of your aspiration for Self Realization, mix it with straw and earth and watch as the divine image takes shape within your very proximity.

"Give form to your longing, that heartfelt desire to know the Divine immediately and directly, to experience the divine presence in intimate contemplation, and see how all the elements—earth, water, fire and air—unite from the infinite expanse of nature in order to form an image of Divinity, the reflection of God.

"Please remember the difference between trying to make a statue and praying for the *mūrti* of God to manifest through us. Meditate upon the various attributes, and put your mind into the fullness of *bhāva,* the attitude of the Deity.

"Let all the peace, all the light, all the goodness which the Deity inspires become part and parcel of your being. Inwardly worship the Deity, reciting the *mantras* and contemplating His subtle form.

"Smile at that internal *mūrti* and with the utmost sincerity request permission from God to make that divine form manifest in a manner all can perceive.

"When the image takes form, find all the love and devotion you can offer and breathe the soul of life into your image of God, praying for the blessings of wisdom and peace for all."

A SIMPLE METHOD FOR A WOOD-BASED GAṆEŚA

By Śrī Sateesh N. Apte M.D. of Danville, California

The materials needed for a wood-based clay Ganeśa are: 1) clay, either the professional sculptor's clay or that gathered from a river bed) or *papier maché;* 2) latex or other water-based paint in yellow, red, black and flesh colors; 3) gold-leaf paint, 4) aluminum foil, 5) paint brushes, 6) sandpaper, 7) putty or joint compound, 8) miscellaneous ornaments and cloth for dressing the *mūrti.*

INSTRUCTIONS

1. Mix clay or *papier maché* to a firm but homogeneously wet consistency.
2. Make an armature (skeleton) of wood, styrofoam or similar material.
3. Create the image by covering the armature with clay.
4. Brush the exterior smooth with a wet brush.
5. Let the image dry in a cool place, away from the sunlight. (Drying time is usually one month for every foot in height for a clay image, three weeks for *papier maché.*)
6. When dry, sand with coarse, then fine sandpaper.
7. Fill cracks with putty or joint compound. Sand again.
8. Apply a white primer and sand with very fine sandpaper.
9. Make the image dust-free.
10. Paint the torso, head, trunk and limbs in flesh color.
11. Place appropriate dress (traditionally white or red silk) upon the image.
12. Paint the crown gold and the hair and eyes black.
13. Draw three stripes of *vibhūti* on the forehead and a *swastika* and an Aum on the abdomen with red paint and a fine brush.
14. Make implements for each hand out of aluminum foil.
15. Decorate the image with ornaments, flowers, etc.

Vināyaka Vratam

Vināyaka Vratam is a 21-day festival honoring Lord Gaṇeśa beginning on the full moon day in the month of Kārt-tikai—November/December. During these days Vināyaka Purāṇa, or stories, are recited in the temples, and special *pūjās* are conducted at every Gaṇeśa temple. Many devotees observe the *vrata* ("vow") of attending daily *pūjā* at a Gaṇeśa temple and taking only one meal a day, in the evening.

Mārkali Pillaiyar

Mārkali Pillaiyar is a month-long home religious festival held in honor of Lord Gaṇeśa. For untold thousands of years winter festivities and ceremonies have been held in honor of Lord Gaṇeśa. During the Tamil month of Mārkali—from the middle of December to the middle of January—we wor-ship Lord Pillaiyar, the Noble Child, with special devotion, prayers and *japa* of His names. This month is the most spiritual time of the year, and we meditate diligently, especially between four and six in the morning. Traditionally, all worship, prayer, spiritual disciplines, or *sādhanas*, are commenced during the month of Mārkali, and the home is cleaned each day.

Pañcha Gaṇapati

Pañcha Gaṇapati is a modern Hindu festival of the Five-Faced (*pañcha* means "five") Mahāgaṇapati—Lord of Categories. This festival falls during the thirty days of the Mārkali Pillaiyar home festival and lasts for five days—from December 21st through 25th.

The winter solstice has always been a festive time of year in all countries, religions and among Hindus especially, for it is a traditional season for the worship of Lord Gaṇeśa. In Hindu Vedic Astrology this time of year marks the end of the sun's southward movement and the beginning of its movement north, the change from *dakshiṇāyane* to *uttarāyane.* Since Hindus do not celebrate Christmas, they often find it difficult to relate in a meaningful way to those who do. Their children are often embarrassed when asked why they do not receive gifts on December 25th. Adults feel the need to give gifts and mail greeting cards as well as receive them from their relatives, neighbors, friends and business associates. Pañcha Gaṇapati is a Hindu expression of this natural season of worship, gift-giving and celebration.

December 25th and the days that precede and follow it have truly become a special time of year for people of many religions and for non-religious people as well. In fact, this season has become so universally popular that it has virtually become a secular cultural holiday in addition to its observance by specific religions. Recognizing this fact, the U.S. Supreme Court ruled Christmas a secular, social holiday. This is because it has become a time for everyone to rejoice, give and share their abundance, each in his own way.

CREATING THE PAÑCHA GAṆAPATI SHRINE

Pañcha Gaṇapati is not a temple *utsava;* it is a contemporary home observance. Because of the importance of this festival as a new beginning and mending of all mistakes of the past, a festive shrine is created especially for the five-day event in the main living room of the home. At the center of the shrine is placed a large wooden or bronze five-faced *mūrti* of Lord Pañcha Gaṇapati. But if this is not available, then a large picture of Lord Gaṇeśa will do. The home shrine is decorated in the spirit of this festive season. Lord Gaṇeśa is often depicted as coming from the forest; therefore, pine boughs (or banana leaves) may be used. *Dūrvā* grass, sugarcane, garlands of sweet *modaka* balls are used to decorate the home shrine. Flashing lights, tinsel and colorful hanging ornaments may also be added.

Pañcha Gaṇapati is dressed anew each morning, preferably by the children, in a special color for that particular day. His five *śaktis* are loved and adored by all members of the family. He appears in golden yellow on December 21st. A regal gown of royal blue is presented to Him on December 22nd and one of ruby red on the 23rd. On December 24th He appears in emerald green, and on the final day Lord Pañcha Gaṇapati comes forth in brilliant orange to bless all who visit Him, bestowing 365 days of wealth and abundance until returning again next year in the form of Pañcha Gaṇapati.

Pañcha Gaṇapati should be celebrated in a distinctly Hindu way. The items which should not be used are Christmas trees, Santa Claus or symbols of other religions. These symbols carry connotations that are to be avoided in Hindu worship. Season's greeting cards should be Hindu in design and content. Season's greetings to friends in other religions can continue with thoughts of Hindu wisdom or quotes from Hindu scripture. If properly chosen they will be appreciated and cherished.

PAÑCHA GAṆAPATI ACTIVITIES

Pañcha Gaṇapati is a joyous time for the family and should include outings, picnics, holiday feasts, exchange of cards and gifts with relatives, friends and business associates. Each day a traditional offering tray of sweets, fruits and incense is offered to Pañcha Gaṇapati. It may be prepared and presented by the children of the home. Gifts should be given to the children each day during these five days. They place them unopened before Pañcha Gaṇapati. After each *pūjā*, the sweets are given to them from the offering tray as *prasāda.*

During each of the five days of Pañcha Gaṇapati, chants, songs, hymns and *bhajanas* are sung in His praise. A different family *sādhana* each day is focused upon. The first *sādhana* begins on the morning of December 21st and each day thereafter until the fifth and final day, December 25th. The *sādhanas* to be performed are as follows.

DECEMBER 21

The family *sādhana* for the first day of Pañcha Gaṇapati is to create a vibration of love and harmony among the immediate family members. The day begins early and the entire family works together to design and decorate the shrine with

traditional symbols, *raṅgoli,* lamps and more. When it is finished, a grand *pūjā* is performed invoking the spirit of Pañcha Gaṇapati. The *sādhana* of the day now begins. The family sits together for the purpose of easing strained relationships that have arisen during the year. They make amends one with another for misdeeds performed, insults given, mental pain and injuries caused and suffered. When forgiveness is offered to all by one and all, they speak of each other's good qualities and resolve that in the days ahead they will remember the futility of trying to change another and the practicality of changing one's self to be the silent example for all to witness. Gifts are then exchanged and placed unopened before Pañcha Gaṇapati. Family harmony is important to all Hindus. This *sādhana* must be taken seriously.

DECEMBER 22

The family *sādhana* for the second day of Pañcha Gaṇapati is to create a vibration of love and harmony among neighbors, relatives and close friends. This is the day for presenting gifts to next-door neighbors, relatives that live in the area and close friends. The *sādhana* of the day is to offer apologies and clear up misunderstandings. Relatives and friends living in far off places are written to or called, forgiveness is sought, apologies made and tensions released. All gifts received today are placed unopened before Pañcha Gaṇapati.

DECEMBER 23

The family *sādhana* for the third day of Pañcha Gaṇapati is to create a vibration of love and harmony among business associates, the casual merchant and the public at large. This is the day for presenting gifts to merchants, customers and to honor employers and employees with gifts and appreciation. The *sādhana* today is the settling of all debts and disputes. All gifts received today are placed unopened before Pañcha Gaṇapati.

DECEMBER 24

The family *sādhana* for the fourth day of Pañcha Gaṇapati is to create a vibration of love and harmony, bringing forth the vibration of joy that comes from music, art, drama and the dance. The family, relatives and friends gather for *satsaṅga* to share and enjoy their individual artistic gifts. When the program is over, all sit together discussing the traditional values of the Hindu Dharma. Then, before Pañcha Gaṇapati, Patron of the Arts and Guardian of Culture, plans are made for the year ahead to bring more of these refinements of living into the home. All gifts received today are placed unopened before Pañcha Gaṇapati.

DECEMBER 25

The family *sādhana* for the fifth and final day of Pañcha Gaṇapati is to bring forth love and harmony within all three worlds. Because of *sādhanas* well performed during the first four days, the family members are now more open and aware of His Grace. Their love for Him is now overflowing. On this day the entire family experiences a climax of an outpouring of love and tranquility from the God Himself. His blessings fill the home and the hearts of everyone within it, inspiring them anew for the coming year. This exchange of affection between all members of the family and the Lord is invoked and perpetuated through the day by performing five special *pūjās*. The first *pūjā* is at 6AM. Before the *pūjā*, personal offering trays are prepared and placed before His shrine. After the *pūjā*, each one gives verbal testimony about prayers that were answered during the past year. Hearing testimonies strengthens the faith of everyone. Then vows of sacrifice can be verbally made. Vows should improve the quality of the life of the individual, such as giving up smoking or correcting other harmful habits.

The second *pūjā* is at 9AM, and the third at 12 noon. The fourth *pūjā* is held at 3PM. At 6PM the fifth and final *pūjā* of the day is held. These five *pūjās* to Pañcha Gaṇapati solicit help from His *devas* in the home and establish the patterns for improvement in family life. The overflowing love that is felt today will inspire generosity in the year to come, bringing in return abundance and good fortune. All gifts received during the day are placed unopened before Pañcha Gaṇapati.

The evening *pūjā*, held at six o'clock, is the long awaited time. The five *sādhanas* have been completed. Peace, love and harmony among everyone has been restored. After the *pūjā* and before the great feast that follows, Lord Pañchamukha Gaṇapati Himself gives His final *darśana* and *prasāda* to one and all. Gifts are distributed and joyously opened. Happy children. Happy parents. Happy God.

A FAMILY PRAYER FOR AFTER PAÑCHA GAṆAPATI

Enjoy this prayer during the next 360 days after Pañcha Gaṇapati. May His blessings flood your home with bounteous joy. May you and your family experience His boons of abundance, culture and sensitivity to the feelings of others that He will grant through the months ahead. Repeat the following prayer together after each *pūjā* in your shrine until Lord Gaṇeśa returns again next year as Pañcha Gaṇapati.

Om bhur bhuvaḥ suvaḥ
Ekadantāya vidmahe

Oh divine beings of all three worlds,
let us bring our minds to rest in
the *darśana* of Him who has one tusk.

Vakratuṇḍāya dhīmahi

Let us meditate upon Him who has the
form of an elephant with a curved trunk.

Tanno dantiḥ prachodayāt
May He guide us always along the right path.

Jai Gaṇeśa!
Jai Pañchamukha Gaṇapati!
Jai Gaṇeśa! Jai! Jai!
Aum Śāntiḥ, Śāntiḥ, Śāntiḥ, Aum.

Victory to the Lord of Celestials!
Hail to the Five-Faced Lord of *gaṇas!*
Victory to the Lord of Celestials!
Hail to Gaṇeśa. *Jai, jai.*
Aum, peace, peace, peace, Aum.

An Elephant Prayer

Everyone's heard of an elephant walk
And a few have listened to an elephant talk,
But this is a poem more special, more rare,
Than an African doo made of elephant hair.

Two hands on the head beat an elephant prayer.
It's a gesture of hope when we tap ourselves there.
While onlookers see but a strange little knock,
Devotees swear it breaks any deadlock.

So, if you should worry or anguish or balk
When life gets you down or you meet a big block,
Whisper an Aum, and if you but dare,
Call on loving Gaṇeśa Who always is there.

Mishṭānnanaivedyam

मिष्टान्ननैवेद्यम्

Sweet Offerings

Sweet Offerings

PILLAIYAR HAS A SWEET TOOTH, JUST LIKE EVERYONE ELSE. FOR EACH SPECIAL PŪJĀ TO HIM, GOODIES ARE CAREFULLY PREPARED in a worshipful mood while chanting *mantras. Modaka* balls are presented among other sweets on trays before Lord Gaṇeśa in temples and home shrines in over 120 countries, especially during festivals. Of course, foods for *pūjā* are never tasted or smelled during preparation or before being offered. They are enjoyed only after the *pūjā,* as *prasāda.* The spirit of *modaka* offering is captured in the following poem by one of Gaṇeśa's dearest devotees, Tirumati S.K. Jagadeswari of Bangalore, South India.

Mudakaratta Modaka

Aum Gaṇapati Aum.
Aum Gaṁ Gaṇapataye Namaḥ.
Vināyaka!—What is dear to Thee,
That will I offer Thee! With what fondness
Thou hold *kolukattai* in Thy Hand!
I know Thou like it. Thou art sweetness.
Mudakaratta modaka, with smooth rice dough,
Will I envelop and wrap
Jaggery sweet mix with sesame powder,
Cook in steam—that I serve Thee with devotion.

Recipe One: *Modaka*

Ball-Like Sweets

The following recipe will make approximately 20 lime-sized *modakas,* a treat for the children and a traditional offering in the temple. It takes about two hours to make them.

Ingredients and Utensils

1 lb. rice flour
2 cups jaggery (or 2 cups brown sugar
with four tbsp. dark molasses added)
2 cups raw sesame seeds
2 grated coconuts (optional)
2 cups melted *ghee* or drawn butter
1 tsp. salt
banana leaf or waxed paper
a flour sifter or fine sieve
an *iddli* or vegetable steamer

Directions

Roast the sesame seeds in a pan, without oil, until golden brown (5 to 10 minutes). Crack the seeds by rolling with a rolling pin or pounding. Add 4 tbsp. *ghee* to the jaggery to soften it, then mix in the sesame seeds and coconut thoroughly. (This mix may be refrigerated in jars for making quick sweets simply by adding a bit of *ghee* and squeezing the dough into balls.)

Next sift the rice flour and toast it without oil until it browns slightly—about 5 to 7 minutes. Spread it out on a tray or table top when done and allow to cool completely. While the rice flour is cooling, bring approximately a half gallon of water, with a tsp. of salt, to a rolling boil. Turn off heat and, stirring constantly, slowly add the cooled rice flour, blending it into a paste as it cooks. If two people are present, one can stir and one can add the flour. When all the flour is stirred in well, cover the pot and cook on low heat for a few minutes, stirring frequently. Turn off heat when the dough has cooked to a sticky paste. It should be moist but not wet when you put it out on the table or breadboard.

Next, place water in the bottom of the *iddli* steamer and bring to a full boil. Spread a thin coating of *ghee* or oil on a piece of banana leaf or waxed paper. Take a lump of dough half the size of a lime and work it in your hands for a moment to remove the air and then pat it out flat and round on the leaf, about as wide across as your palm. Make it a uniform thickness so it will cook evenly. Place a lump of the sesame-jaggery-coconut mixture into the center and wrap the dough up around the mixture. Pinch the dough into a cone-shape over the stuffing and wrap the leaf or paper up around it. (The *modakas* can also be round if desired.) Repeat until you have enough to fill your steamer. Place the assembled *modakas* in the steamer, spaced so as to not touch one another. Cover and steam until done (15 to 20 minutes). While they cook you can prepare the next batch. When cool enough to handle, dip the *modakas* in melted ghee. Now they are ready to offer.

Recipe Two: *Pudi Kolukattai*

Sweet Rice Flour Roll

Ingredients and Utensils

2 cups rice flour
1 cup jaggery or brown sugar
1 shredded coconut
1 tsp. salt
an *iddli* or vegetable steamer
a pan for toasting the flour
banana leaf or tray

Directions

Heat the rice flour in a dry skillet until lightly toasted, then spread it out on a tray or table top to cool. Sprinkle a little water on it and add the salt, jaggery and coconut. Mix together, adding water only as needed. When it is well kneaded and firm, pinch the dough off into as many lime-sized balls as it will make. Roll into balls, or squeeze in the right hand to create a fist-shaped *kolukattai*. Bring water in the steamer to a boil and arrange the *kolukattais* in it, wrapped in banana leaves as in recipe #1. Steam until the balls are a light brown in color. Arrange on a banana leaf or tray and serve to Lord Gaṇeśa.

Recipe Three: *Yallu Kolukattai*

Sesame Seed and Sweet Rice Roll

This type of *kolukattai* is commonly prepared in South India for Gaṇeśa Chaturthī festivals.

Ingredients and Utensils

1 cup sesame seeds
1 cup jaggery or brown sugar
4 cups rice flour
1 tsp. salt
oil or *ghee*
8 cups water
a steamer with flat rack
a skillet for toasting flour
a small piece of cheesecloth
a mortar and pestle, rolling pin or blender
banana leaf or tray

Directions

Fry the sesame seeds, without oil, until light brown, then mix with the jaggery. Then, using a pestle and mortar, rolling pin or blender, powder this mixture and set it aside. Heat the rice flour until lightly toasted and spread it out on a tray or table top to cool. While it cools, add the salt to 8 cups of water in a pan and bring to a strong boil. Stirring rapidly, slowly add in the rice flour. The flour must not be allowed to lump together, but be stirred and cooked into a paste, even and smooth. When all the flour has been stirred in, turn the heat very low and continue to stir for 5 to 10 minutes until the rice is completely cooked. When done, spread the resulting dough on the table to cool. When it can be handled, squeeze the dough into lime-sized balls and set them aside.

Smear a bit of oil or *ghee* on a banana leaf, tray or table top and roll or knead one of the dough balls out on it to a patty about 3 inches in diameter. Place a full tablespoon of the sesame and sugar mixture in the middle and fold the patty over in a crescent shape, pinching it closed where the edges meet. Repeat the process for the rest of the balls.

Bring the water in your vegetable or *iddli* steamer to a boil and insert the steaming rack or a plate with small holes in it. The rack should be fairly flat and be covered over with a layer of cheesecloth or cotton weave. Arrange the *kolukattai* on the flat rack, as many as will fit without touching. Cover and steam for 15 to 20 minutes, or until done, depending on the size of your steamer. When finished, transfer them to a plate or banana leaf and allow to cool. Serve to Gaṇeśa as His fondest sweet. With any remaining sesame-sugar mixture you may make small Gaṇeśa figures. Keep them along with the cooked ones for *pūjā*. *Betel* leaves, nuts and fruits may be offered with these.

Sādhvī Auvaiyār Mā

साध्वी औवैयार् मा

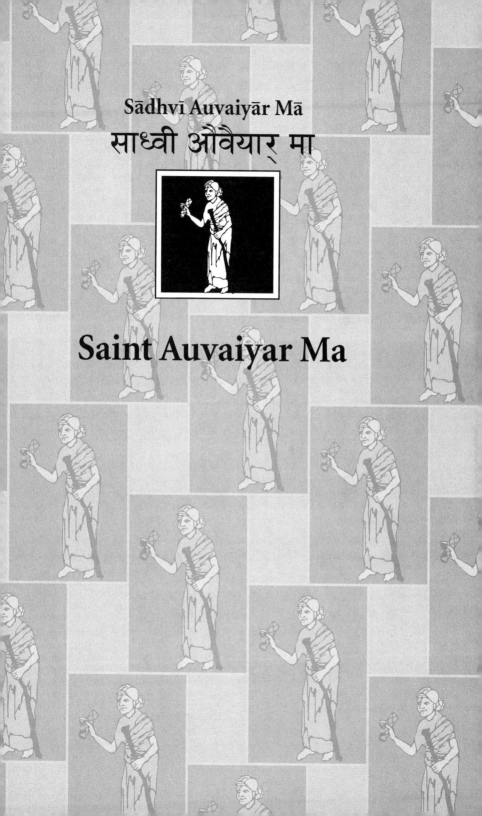

Saint Auvaiyar Ma

The Story of Saint Auvaiyar Ma

QUITE A LONG TIME AGO, IN THE NINTH CENTURY, THERE LIVED IN THE SOUTH INDIAN TAMIL LAND A WOMAN SAINT KNOWN AS Auvai or Auvaiyar, a Tamil word meaning a respected older woman. Abandoned by her parents at birth, Auvaiyar was raised by a family of Panars, who were wandering minstrels. As a young girl, she was deeply devoted to religion and literary pursuits and wanted to serve the people. Known for her intelligence and extraordinary beauty, she had many aristocratic suitors, and pressure was brought to bear for arranging her marriage. While most young women would welcome such attention, it was for Auvaiyar more threat than opportunity. Her interests were philosophical and devotional, and her life revolved around her love of Śiva. She did not want to make a man the center of that universe. Faced with the impending marriage her family would surely arrange, Auvaiyar wept and prayed before her chosen Deity, Vighneśvara, to save her from this fate: "Oh, my Lord, these people are only after my youth and beauty; but I want to dedicate myself to the Goddess of learning and to the spread of learning. Please take away my youth and my beauty so that I can have peace and follow my chosen way of life." Gaṇeśa heard her prayer, and in the days that followed her skin wrinkled, hair grayed, eyes dulled, limbs stiffened and breasts sagged. Looking at her reflection in the village well, the maiden was overcome with joy, knowing she was safe from the world, knowing that her loving Gaṇeśa had graced her prayers .

Auvaiyar left the shelter of home, where most people find security, and wandered far and wide in the palmyra-covered Tamil kingdoms of Chola, Pāṇḍya and Chera. Her life was simple, dedicated to the practice of *yoga* and to following her *guru's* instructions. As her spiritual *sādhana* bore fruit, she slowly matured into spreading the *tantras,* the mystical teachings of the *siddhars,* the wisdom of God Śiva and the Gods. Her innumerable literary and philosophical works, both for children and elders, cover the entire gamut of human experience and testify to her profound wisdom. Her royal benefactors, among whom were Śrī, Śrī, Śrī Adiyaman, Pari, Kari and Seraman, are historical figures distinguished by their bravery and benevolence. These *mahārājas* patronized her cultural works so that her fame spread far and wide. She is now acclaimed as the wisest woman of all ages in the chronicles of Indian culture.

Auvaiyar Ma was a contemporary and close associate of two noble Śiva *bhaktas,* Sundarar and Seraman Perumal, ruler of the Chera kingdom, both extolled as great Śaiva saints in Sekkilar's epic hagiography, the *Periyapurāṇam.* One day, near the end of her life, it is said that Auvaiyar was in the midst of her daily worship of her beloved Gaṇeśa. She had a vision in which Saint Sundarar was proceeding to Mount Kailāsa, Śiva's abode, with his comrade King Seraman. Sundarar was riding a white elephant, and Seraman was on a white horse. They were as aware of her as she was of them. She became disturbed, and tried to rush her worship, filled with a yearning to join her spiritual friends on their last journey. But Lord Gaṇeśa appeared and told her to finish her rituals calmly and without haste, with the promise that she would be taken to Kailāsa ahead of her two friends. Thereupon, she entered her trance even more deeply and sang the renowned hymn of praise entitled *Vināyaka Ahaval.* (This great song of religious devotion to Gaṇeśa is sung to this day throughout the Tamil land at the time of Gaṇeśa worship, particularly during the annual Gaṇeśa Chaturthī festival.) As she finished her worship and placed the sacramental offering at His gracious feet, Vināyaka appeared before her, lifted her in His gentle trunk and delivered her to the Śivaloka, to Mount Kailāsa, before the two friends arrived. When Seraman Perumal inquired how it was that she had arrived ahead of them, she sang this in her unique and charming Tamil:

O king, is there anything unattainable
To them who intensely contemplate
On the fragrant feet of the son
Of Ummaiyal, of sweet and comely speech?
The thunderous thud of the swift elephant
And that of the agile horse must give place
To that of the rider of this old dame!
He is none other than the mighty Mahāgaṇapati.

Vināyaka Ahaval
Adoration to the Remover of Obstacles

Translated from Tamil by Professor K. Swamināthan
(Originally Published in Om Gaṇeśa, the Peace of God)

Cool, fragrant lotus feet
With anklets tinkling sweet,
Gold girdle, flower-soft garment
Setting off the comely hips,
Pot-belly and big, heavy tusk,
Elephant-face with the bright red mark,
Five hands, the goad, the noose,
Blue body dwelling in the heart,
Pendulous jaws, four mighty shoulders,
Three eyes and the three required marks,
Two ears, the gold crown gleaming,
The breast aglow with the triple thread,
O Being, bright and beautiful!
Wish-yielding elephant, born of the
Master of Mystery in Mount Kailāsa,

Mouse-rider fond of the three famed fruits;
Desiring to make me yours this instant,
You like a mother have appeared before me
And cut the delusion of unending births.
You have come and entered my heart
Imprinting clear the five prime letters;
Set foot in the world in the form of a *guru,*
Declared the final Truth is this,
Gladly, graciously shown the way
Of life unfading.
With that unfailing weapon, Your glance,
You have put an end to my heinous sins,
Poured in my ear uncloying precepts;
Laid bare for me the clarity
Of ever-fresh awareness;
Sweetly given me your sweet grace
For firm control of the senses five;
Taught how to still the organs of action,
Snapped my two-fold *karma* and dispelled
My darkness; giving, out of grace,
A place for me in all four states;
Dissolved the illusion of triple filth;
Taught me how to shut the five
Sense-gates of the nine-door temple;
Fixed me firm in the six *yogic* centers;
Stilled my speech; taught me
The writ of *iḍā* and *piṅgalā,*
Shown me at last the head of *sushumṇā;*
To the tongue of the serpent that sinks and soars
Have brought the force sustaining the three
Bright spheres of sun and moon and fire,
The *mantra* unspoken asleep in the snake,
And explicitly uttered it;
Imparted the skill of raising by breath
The raging flame of *mūlādhāra;*

Explained the secret of immortality,
The sun's movement and the charm
Of the moon, the water lily's friend,
The sixteen states of the *prasāda mantra;*
Revealed to me in thoughtful wise
The six-faced form and the meanings four;
Discovered to me the subtle body
And the eight separate modes of being;
The orifice of Brahman opened,
Giving me miraculous powers,
By your sweet grace, and *mukti,* too;
Revealed my Self to me, and by Your grace
Swept away accumulated *karma;*
Stilled my mind in tranquil calm
Beyond speech and thought;
Clarified my intellect, plunged me
In bliss which is the common ground
Of light and darkness;
Boundless beatitude You have given me,
Ended all affliction, shown the way of grace,
Śiva eternal at the core of sound,
Śivaliṅga within the heart,
Atom within atom, vast beyond all vastness!
Sweetness hid in the hardened node,
You have steadied me clear in human form
All besmeared with holy ashes;
Added me to the congregation
Of Your servants true and trusty;
Made me experience in my heart
The inmost meaning of the five letters;
Restored my real state to me,
And rule me now, O Master of Wisdom,
Vināyaka; Your feet alone,
Your feet alone are my sole refuge.

Saint Auvaiyar's Approach to Vināyaka

BY RATNA MA NAVARATNAM

Saint Auvaiyar's *ahaval* (poem) on Vināyaka is one of the most popular canonical hymns of adoration and is noted for its poetic diction, vivid imagery and *yogic* insights. It is a work of paramount importance, as it communicates the quintessence of the worship of Gaṇeśa. He confers power and peace of the Supreme Para-Śiva to His votaries.

O Master of wisdom, Vināyaka,
Your feet alone are my sole refuge.

In the *ahaval*, lines 1-14 delineate the form of Vināyaka. Lines 15-72 depict the detailed action of divine grace bestowed on His devotees. Saint Auvaiyar addresses Gaṇeśa in three places only in the whole poem. "Oh wish-fulfilling elephant!" is followed by "The one who rides on the mouse," and finally comes "The peerless Vināyaka, Master of Wisdom." She describes in great detail the way in which His grace worked on her and transformed her life. She shares her experience of grace with the world just before she departs from this life. The symbol of divine grace is conveyed by the image of the feet of Gaṇeśa. She commences her poem by extolling the feet in words that vibrate with melody. Right in the middle and at the end of the poem, too, we find the allusion to the sacred feet of grace, signifying thereby that the poem has been based on the foundation of grace, outflowing from the elder son of Śiva, Vittaka Vināyaka.

Thus, the hymn *Vināyaka Ahaval* is a highly mystical

work. It consists of seventy-two lines of poetry. The author begins the poem with a salutation to the holy feet of Gaṇapati. His feet are mystically placed at the tail end of the spinal column called *mūlādhāra,* which emits the heat necessary for the functioning of the inner organs. His feet guard, as it were, the source of the bodily energy from extinction and are a symbol of grace. From His feet emanate the seven modulations of the musical notes, giving rise to the succinct vibrations of *mantras.* The primordial vibration from the *mūlādhāra,* the eternal substratum, gives rise to the cosmic dance full of dynamic motion around and within. So potent are His lotus feet of grace. Meditating on His feet, the poetess describes the vision of the beauteous formation of the body of Gaṇeśa, so symmetrical and subdued, radiating light with the golden hip-chain and white, silken attire. He is a living presence to Mother Auvai and not an image of stone.

Ma Auvai sees, in her *yogic* perception, the impressive nature of Vināyaka's countenance. She sees one tusk broken and kept in one of His hands, while the other tusk adorns His comely elephant face and is the source of mitigating countless malicious forces. *"Eka dantāye vighna vināśine."* Gaṇeśa's elephant face adorned with the red mark on the forehead beams with beauteous smile at the votary who sings His praise. The twinkle in His eye symbolizes His auspicious nature. His five hands signify the five-fold activities of the manifested cosmos. There is ceaseless creation, vigilant preservation followed by dissolution of all that is transient. Then occurs the phase of involution, a subtle veiling leading to the stage of *anugraha,* revelation. It is the reemergence through grace with sound and light. It permeates the outer cosmos as well as the inner realm of "being."

In this context, the divine mother views Gaṇeśa's five arms. She sees in one hand the displaced tusk ready to be used as a writing *stylus,* symbolizing the creative function. The other hand holding the sweet called *modaka* indicates the ever-watchful, protective care and the assurance of the reward of fulfillment. The goad and the noose in the other two hands are the deterrent weapons to safeguard man from the pitfalls of disillusionment caused by vicious desires and egoism. The lofty trunk is the fifth hand which holds the water pot in an act of oblation, signifying His perennial grace and the Pure Awareness of the One in many.

His countenance glows in sky-blue hue. His shoulders appear strong and balanced. The gleam of the sun, moon and fire emanates from His triple eyes, illuminating the caverns of the heart and the crevices of the outer world. The light of Truth radiates in His countenance as the principle of delusion recedes, leaving its pronounced marks on the face of Gaṇeśa. How wonderful are His expansive ears, reminding us that, "Heard melodies are sweet, but those unheard are sweeter." So muses the saintly poetess who experiences the wordless music of the primordial *Aum,* wafting from His fan-like ears and awakening her to the sublime awareness of Reality. The splendor of His crown and the insignia of the triple strand of initiation on His chest mark the extending vistas of light and sound mingling in the oneness of Gaṇeśa.

Auvaiyar Ma thus is transported in bliss at the vision of the wish-fulfilling elephant-faced form of Vināyaka. Lest the grandeur of the supernal light dazzle her, she turns her gaze at His immanent form again. Ma views Him enjoying the triple delicious fruits, and is amazed at the incongruity of Pillaiyar riding on His rat mount! It reminds her that life is a bundle of contradictions and contrasts. The massive elephant with His immense strength and prudence is no less important than the humble mouse. All come within the purview of the all-knowing God Śiva, and are either scourged or saved by their own actions. His main intent is to wean the heart of man from the darkness of ignorance to the light of wisdom and Truth. The divine mother recollects the immense love bestowed on her by Gaṇeśa. He pointed the way, and, fortified with the mystic *mantra* of the *guru,* she communicates the inevitable bliss of realization when she exclaims "He, my true Self, filled my whole being."

In this poem, mother Auvai melts in love like that of Saint Manikkavasagar as she recalls in tranquility her *yogic* vision and the experience of the inner self mingling in the greater Self! To experience the Reality of the supreme Self and communicate it to the world of suffering humanity—here where men sit and hear each other groan—is the noblest service of all the realized seers in the fold of Hinduism.

Problems arising from the origins of Lord Gaṇapati, son of Śiva, His place in the Hindu pantheon and the truth of the many legends that have grown up around Him all pale into insignificance before the living testimony of the noble poetess Auvaiyar in her wonderful praise of Vināyaka. Who can deny the truth of her awareness of the Supreme Being and dismiss her translucent experience as ephemeral outpouring of an overworked mind?

Mother Auvai is the witness, and her poem is the living testament of Gaṇeśa's grace and how He came into her inner being as a *guru* and endowed her with insight of truth by placing His gracious feet on her head. Faithfully has she recorded the steps of the religious practice *(sādhana)* that took her from the grip of the mundane world to the absorption in bliss divine. Deep concentration is the secret of mastering the avenues of the deluding senses. And the more she meditates on the oppressive limitations exercised by the principles of time and space and the sway of the thirty-six categories *(tattvas)* of manifestation, the more is her withdrawal into the interior of her being, where the phantom of duality ceases to lure her. The mystic *mantra* Aum permeates her whole being. Her *japa* is impregnated with ceaseless remembrance of the vibrant word.

We follow her from behind, rapt in mute wonder, as step by step she leads us into the mysteries of the *yoga mārga,* so ably propounded by sages like Patañjali, Vaśishṭha and Nārada. The dormant *śakti,* once ignited by the grace of Gaṇeśa, floods all the six psychic centers of consciousness within Auvai Ma and consummates in the supreme awareness of the Self. Such is the mystic import of the mother's poem on Vināyaka, which starts like a catalog of His iconographical details and consummates in the highest communion with Aum Gaṇeśa.

From lines fifty-five to the end, the pendulum of the individual being swings in harmony to the symphony of the universal being. Neither discord nor limitation nor separation can be sensed in the experience of the divine mother from this stage. Auvai Ma's descriptions from this stage of illumination are highly mystical and elude the comprehension of those who have not yet experienced such *yogic* fulfillment. Yet, her communication of the intangible rings of sincerity and sublimity. The steps to control the inhalation and exhalation by suitable chanting of *mantras,* leading the vital force from one center of consciousness to the other centers gradually, have all been made so vividly clear to Mother, that her perception intuits through the *yogic* cord to the highest center at the crown of the head. The serpent power, the *kuṇḍalinī śakti,* as this subtle fire is termed, once awakened, can effect wondrous transformation in the personality. The tongue is made so potent as to experience infinite power of expression. Yet, at the same time, the inexpressible, inaudible *mantra,* known as *ajapa,* is also made vividly clear to her, as the gravitational *prāṇa,* or life force. Beyond *Aum* is the silent melody of *ajapa,* heard and yet unheard, in the vibration of inhaling, retention and exhaling of the life breath every fractional second of our existence. That is He. The ever-elusive, life-giving, immortal and immaculate Gaṇeśa.

Many have been the expositions on this aspect of meditation by the rhythmic modulation of the life breath. Mother Auvai reveals in unmistakable terms of poesy the indefinable and subtlest of the subtle aspects of experiential awareness of the Supreme Sat. The fire in its dormant state has been ignited by the spark that blazoned from the inhaling breath. We perceive the awakened *kuṇḍalinī* in Auvai Ma arising as a coiled snake at the touch of the flame. It ascends up the mystic center of consciousness, experiencing the most inexplicable powers at each of the centers. Finally, it reaches the zenith, where bliss ineffable transmutes her whole being into the radiance of light eternal, whence the light of the sun, moon and stars appear but reflections of the true glory of the effulgent Self. Blessed is the saint whose attainment is so absolute and perfect.

The Mother resumes her normal consciousness and recalls her vision of ecstasy. What has my Gaṇeśa done to me? She ponders and is filled with an unquenchable devotion, as she proclaims the greatest of her utterances in the whole of this magnificent poem:

> Given me miraculous powers
> By your sweet grace, and *mukti* too.
> Revealed myself to me,
> Stilled my mind in tranquil calm.

The perplexing question of who am I, which has baffled humanity down the ages, has been solved by Saint Auvaiyar:

> By His grace beatific, He makes me know my Self.
> That art nondual, eternal, real, pure existence,
> pure consciousness and everlasting bliss.

Gone forever are the network of limitations exercised by actions of past births, and the roots are exterminated forever and ever by the power of Gaṇeśa. Mother Auvai finds herself in tranquil quiescence: "speechless, mindless, immersed in the glory of illumination within." No more opposing factors of dualism, no more darkness in the transcendent luminosity of Gaṇeśa! Absorbed in divine bliss, afflictions recede. It is the way of grace, and we follow her from afar as she ascends on wings of self-knowledge. The immanent and all pervading intermingle in Auvaiyar Ma's cosmic vision as she swims in the ineffable experience of the undifferentiated Supreme. She can only communicate with us in the language of symbols. "Sweeter than ambrosia and subtler than the subtlest of the atoms is it."

Who can know the Real? Only those who have experienced it. Having entered into the beatific bliss of the "liberated," it is in the nature of such experience to seek and abide in an everlasting allegiance with all who have attained. Their insignia of renunciation and purity are self-evident. Saint Auvaiyar's outpourings, embodied in the purest form of poesy, tug at our heart strings, as her worship of the image of Gaṇapati transcends from the physical and subtle phases to the state of supreme awareness of Oneness. The radiant wisdom has been her priceless boon from the one-pointed worship of Gaṇeśa. It overwhelms Auvaiyar with such a surging love for humanity that she communicates the incommunicable by the assurance so positive and veritable to take up the incantation of the *mantra* of the Five Letters, Pañchākshara. It is the panacea for the ills of human existence.

Gaṇeśa will be the illuminator, the *guru,* who can effect this transfiguration. Therefore, the mother bids one and all to surrender all at the gracious feet of the Lord of Wisdom. All the Hindu seers proclaim the one supreme Truth of realization by the act of self-surrender before the self-luminous Śiva—one of whose rays divine is Pillaiyar, the honored son with manifold names who is testified in diverse forms of worship. Thus the worship of Aum Gaṇeśa by the renowned seer Auvaiyar reveals the wondrous Truth that the self has been illumined by the Self and abides in the Self. Then all appearances of otherness and of dualism *(dvaita)* vanish. There only remains the real Self within as well as outside the ego-self.

Divine Mother Auvai's poem on Vināyaka gives a super-experience *(anubhava)* of reality by means of the spiritual practice enjoined in the *yoga* pathway. The sun is hidden from our sight by the clouds. So, too, the reality of the Self is obscured by illusion. The ego can hide our real Self from our consciousness. Yet, human life cannot exist without our real Self, even though apparently hidden, just as day cannot exist without the diffused light of the sun, however hidden by fog or mist. The dominance of the ego by thoughts raised by the mind *(manas)* can conceal the real Self from our consciousness. The ego is the I-maker *(ahaṁkāra)* and is inseparable from the Self *(ātma)*. *Aum* is the symbol of reality when we start from the inner being, and *Namaḥ Śivāya* is the reality when we start from man's experience of the outer world. The Mother's incantation in her immortal poem validates her experience of the truth of *paśu*-Pati. Their common symbol is *Aum*, and the form is that of *Gaṇeśa.*

Mother Auvai portrays in her poem that Gaṇeśa is the Deity of *yogīs*. He typifies the coupling of two mutually complementary elements yoked together with a view to obtaining unity in being and in action, the unification of the respective individual and universal aspects, of the *jivātma* and the Paramātma. It is the drawing together of man to his inner ruler *(antaryāmin)* enthroned in his own Self.

The theme of *kuṇḍalinī* is intimately connected with the cult of Gaṇapati worship. The human body consists of the five elements, and these merge into one another by the control of the breath, and through the reciting of the formulae, until consciousness dissolves into the original matter.

Yoga is the disciplined effort that draws the individuality of man, united with his personality, to the Lord (Īśa) pervading beyond and to the all-Knower *(ayamātma)* who comprehends from within. He who reaches this end is a *yogī*. According to Satguru Auvaiyar Ma, consciousness in the form of a serpent sleeps within the body and can be awakened by *japa* techniques to penetrate, one after another, the six *chakras,* or superimposed circles of the body, until it reaches the opening of *brahmarandhra,* on top of the head, where it brings about the union of the being with Śiva. The vital power of the vibration of the litany of Oṁkara, the word symbol of Gaṇeśa, brings about the cooperation of the Divine and effects the union with Śiva at *sahasrāra.* It is the goal of all types of *yoga.* The way of *yoga* leads to the immortality of the liberated one, supplemented by the infusion of *bhakti.* Saint Auvaiyar Ma attempted the *yoga,* the *bhakti* and the *jñāna* pathway in the worship of loving Gaṇeśa in order to gain the apperception of Reality.

We discern in the poem on Vināyaka the underlying principle of the One in the many, and the many converging into the One. The iconography of Lord Gaṇeśa accentuates the resonance of the sacred syllable Aum culminating in the experience of the oneness of Truth. Ṛishi Tirumular, who lived before Saint Auvaiyar, had given immortal expression to the efficacy of the *mantra* Aum in a gem of *Tirumantiram.*

Oṁkara abides as the Primal Word,
Oṁkara manifests in the many forms,
Oṁkara activates all true experiences,
Oṁkara leads to final liberation.

By the Grace of Gaṇeśa, the Supreme is revealed to Auvaiyar as self-luminous and self-evident. His grace is the alchemy that transforms the wise language into wisdom itself, where all means of expression merge into "That which is," Aum Tat Sat. The Divine Mother Auvaiyar attained the goal of the highest awareness of the Supreme Śiva by her earnest worship of Vināyaka. In the footsteps of this votary, let us with one accord sing her litany of love and walk in the presence of Pillaiyar, the Son of Śiva, and realize His grace within our own real Self.

Pillaiyar Stutiḥ

पिल्लैयर स्तुतिः

In Praise of Pillaiyar

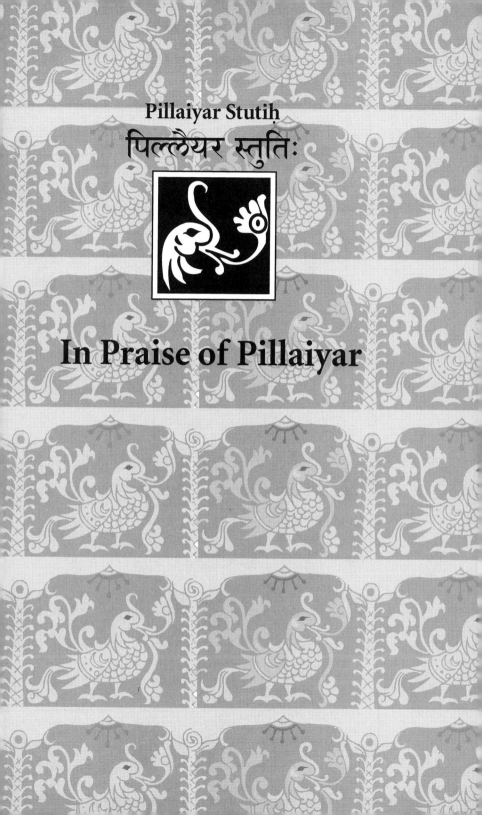

In Praise of Pillaiyar

A Collection of Tamil Devotional Poetry Rendered Into English by Saṅgaratna Dr. S.M. Ponniah

RANGING FROM TIRUMULAR TO KASSIAPPA ŚIVĀCHĀRYA, FIFTEEN DIFFERENT DEVOTEES HAVE COMPOSED THIS ANTHOLOGY OF Tamil hymns in praise of Gaṇapati, the Lord of Hosts, popularly known as Pillaiyar. They are sung daily in Hindu homes and temples where Tamil is spoken. An attempt has been made to give their meanings in English, but they need to be sung in prescribed Tamil tunes to attain maximum effect. In accordance with Āgamic tradition, all cultural concerts, literary endeavors and religious rites and rituals must begin with an invocatory verse seeking the grace of the Lord Gaṇapati to ensure success. The hymns of invocation found here help strengthen the belief that through love and devotion and ultimate surrender to God, man can attain *moksha.*

TIRUMANTIRAM, INVOCATION

ஐந்து கரத்தனை ஆனை முகத்தனை
இந்து இளம்பிறை போலும் எயிற்றனை
நந்தி மகன்தனை, ஞானக் கொழுந்தினைப்
புந்தியில் வைத்தடி போற்றுகின் றேனே.
திருமூலர் திருமந்திரம்

Implant in your intelligence the worshipful feet of Umā-Śaṅkara's son, the first-born, five-handed, elephant-faced elegant One with twin, white tusks, curved like the crescent-moon. He is wisdom's embodiment.

TIRUMANTIRAM

கணபதி என்றிடக் கலங்கும் வல்வினை
கணபதி என்றிடக் காலனும் கைதொழும்
கணபதி என்றிடக் கரும மாதலால்
கணபதி என்றிடக் கரும மில்லையே.

If you but utter *Gaṇapati,* our Lord's name, the gaunt *karmic* ills that bind us fast will become loose; the Lord of Death himself will in submission raise his hands in worship. Therefore, dutifully utter daily Gaṇapati's gracious name which will, without fail, your *karmic* bonds sever.

TIRUJÑĀNA SAMBANDAR'S TIRUKKATAIKKAPPU

பிடியதன் உருவுமை கொளமிகு கரியது
வடிகொடு தனதடி வழிபடு மவரிடர்
கடி கண பதிவர அருளினன் மிகுகொடை
வடிவினர் பயில் வலி வலமுறை இறையே.

The bountiful being who reigns over Vallivalam's shrine, united with Umā-Maheśvarī, the Mother of the Universe, manifesting in manifold forms, bestowed upon His devotees the elephant-visaged God in order to remove their obstacles and impediments and to confer His grace upon all who follow the eternal Śaivite path.

FROM ARATAMPATIYA PERUNTEVANAR

ஓத வினை அகலும்; ஓங்கு புகழ் பெருகும்
காதற் பொருள் அனைத்தும் கைகூடும் - சீதப்
பனிக் கோட்டு மால்வரை மேல் பாரதப்போர் தீட்டும்
தனிக் கோட்டு வாரணத்தின் தாள்!

Those who worship the redeeming feet of the single-tusked, elephant-visaged Lord of the heavenly hosts, who recorded with His tusk the *Mahābhārata* battle upon the snow-capped hills of the Himālayan mountains, will gain great glory, attain their hearts' desires and become freed from the fetters of *karma.*

SAINT AUVAIYAR

வாக்குண்டாம், நல்லமனமுண்டாம், மாமலராள்
நோக்குண்டாம், மேனி நுடங்காது பூக்கொண்டு
துப்பார் திருமேனித் தும்பிக்கையான் பாதம்
தப்பாமல் சார்வார் தமக்கு.

Those who worship without fail the grace-granting feet of Gaṇeśa with flowers fresh and fragrant shall acquire eloquence of speech, fruitful friendship—besides gaining the graceful glance of the lotus-seated Lakshmī's eyes, which will ensure every human happiness on earth.

SAINT AUVAIYAR

பாலும் தெளிதேனும், பாகும் பருப்பு மிவை
நாலும் கலந்துனக்கு நான் தருவேன் கோலஞ்செய்
துங்கக் கரிமுகத்து தூமணியே, நீ எனக்குச்
சங்கத்தமிழ் மூன்றுந் தா

I shall offer to you, O Lord, the delicacies four: fresh milk, pure honey, cane sugar with cereals mixed, O elephant-visaged, bright-jewelled Lord of the Universe, if you will enrich me with the treasured-triple Tamil tongue acclaimed by the ancient academies.

KABILADEVAR'S IRATTAI MANI MALAI

விநாயகனே வெவ்வினையை வேரறுக்க வல்லான்
விநாயகனே வேட்கை தணிவிப்பான், விநாயகனே
விண்ணிற்கும் மண்ணிற்கும் நாதனுமாம்
தன்மையினால் கண்ணிற் பணிமின் கனிந்து.

Vināyaka cuts asunder the very roots of all human suffering and sorrow. Vināyaka destroys all desires. Vināyaka is Lord indeed of heaven and earth. Surrender, therefore, unto Him with hearts that melt with devotion.

KABILADEVAR'S IRATTAI MANI MALAI

திருவாக்கும், செய்கருமமும் கைகூட்டும் செஞ்சொல்
பெருவாக்கும், பீடும் பெருக்கும் உருவாக்கும்
ஆதலால், வானோரும் ஆனைமுகத்தானைக்
காதலால் கூப்புவர் தம்கை.

Your words and deeds shall with success meet. Eloquence and eminence shall be your rewards. Therefore, worship Him even as the celestials raise their hands high in adoration and love of the elephant-visaged Vināyaka, the matchless Lord.

KABILADEVAR'S IRATTAI MANI MALAI

கணங்கொண்ட வல்வினைகள் கண்கொண்ட நெற்றிப
பணங்கொண்ட பாந்தட் சடைமேல் - மணங்கொண்ட
தாதகத்த தேன்முரலுங் கொன்றையான் தந்தளித்த
போதகத்தின் தாள் பணியப் போம்.

Your burdensome bonds of *karma* will but disintegrate and dissolve if you but worship the grace-granting feet of Gaṇapati, the Lord of Hosts bestowed upon us all by the triple-eyed Lord Śiva whose ruddy locks are entwined by a serpent strand, whose head is adorned by honey-rich, golden-bright *konrai* blooms which fill the air around with their fragrance.

NAKKIRADEVA NAYANAR'S VINĀYAKA AHAVAL

வெண்ணீ றணியும் விமலன் புதல்வா
பெண்ணு முமையாள் பெற்றிடுந் தேவே
அரிதிரு மருகா அறுமுகன் துணைவா
கரிமுக வாரணக் கணபதி சரணம்
குருவே சரணம் குணமே சரணம்
பெருவயிற் றோனே பொற்றாள் சரணம்

கண்ணே மணியே கதியே சரணம்
விண்ணே யொளியே வேந்தே சரணம்.

O first born son of Śiva who adorns His head with sacred ashes, beloved of Umāsundarī, Kumāran's companion, beloved of Hari! O dark-hued, elephant-visaged, elegant Lord of heavenly hosts, my divine *guru*, unto you, O Lord, I surrender myself. O matchless Lord! Embodiment of wisdom and all excellence—O portly Gaṇapati, unto your golden feet I surrender myself. O precious jewel bright! O heavenly light! O Lord of the universe, I surrender unto you.

FROM NAMBI ANDAR NAMBI

தந்தையும் நீயே தாயும் நீயே
எமரும் நீயே ஈசனும் நீயே
போத ஞானப் பொருளும் நீயே
நாதமும் நீயே நான்மறை நீயே
அரியும் நீயே அயனும் நீயே
திரிபுர தகனஞ் செய்தவன் நீயே
சத்தியும் நீயே சதாசிவம் நீயே
புத்தியும் நீயே புராந்தகன் நீயே
பத்தியும் நீயே பந்தமும் நீயே
முத்தியும் நீயே மோக்ஷமும் நீயே
ஏகமும் நீயே என்னுயிர் நீயே
தேகமும் நீயே தேகியும் நீயே
உன்னரு ளன்றி யுயிர்த்துணை காணேன்
பின்னொரு தெய்வம் பேசவு மறியேன்.

You are indeed my father and mother both, my kith and kin—the infinite Lord, wisdom's embodiment, substance of all sound and the *Vedas* four. You are indeed Hari and the lotus-seated Brahma, Śakti and Sadāśiva, the triune beings. The dauntless destroyer of the roving cities three, that dared to defy you! You are the Lord of heaven and earth, devotion and its binding force, *moksha* and its meaning. O matchless Lord! My life is yours, and you are my sole support. But for your grace, friends I've none. O Indwelling Lord, I'll speak only of your glory!

NAMBI ANDAR NAMBI

என்னை நினைந்து அடிமை கொண்டு என் இடர்
கெடுத்துத்
தன்னை நினையத் தருகின்றான் - புன்னை
விரசு மகிழ் சோலை, வியன் நாரையூர் முக்கண்
அரசு மகிழ் அத்தி முகத்தான்.

The triple-eyed Pillaiyar, enshrined under the shade of the flower-filled *punnai* tree in splendid Naraiyur Park, thinking of me, enslaved me, removed all my ills and impediments and conferred upon me His infinite grace. My thoughts are of Him and none else on earth.

SEKKILAR'S PERIYAPURĀṆAM

எடுக்கும் மாக்கதை இன்தமிழ்ச் செய்யுளாய்
நடக்கும் மேன்மை நமக்கருள் செய்திடத்
தடக்கை ஐந்துடைத் தாள்செவி நீள்முடிக்
கடக் களிற்றைக் கருத்துள் இருத்துவாம்.

Before I venture to narrate in vivid Tamil verse the moving great story of the ennobling lives of the saintly sixty-three enslaved by the Lord Śiva, I shall first retain in my mind the guiding hand of the dark-hued, high-crowned, five-handed Gaṇapati, in order that we may all gain by His divine grace the enriching rewards of this endeavor.

UMĀPATI ŚIVAM

வானுலகும் மண்ணுலகும் வாழ மறைவாழப்
பான்மை தருசெய்ய தமிழ் பார்மிசை விளங்க
ஞானமத, ஐந்துகர மூன்றுவிழி, நால்வாய்
ஆனைமுகனைப் பரவி அஞ்சலி செய்கிற்பாம்.

In order that, O man, the heavens and earth may prosper and thrive, the Vedic ways endure, the sacred Tamil tongue be renowned the world over, worship without fail the sagacious, five-handed, triple-eyed, elephant-visaged Vināyaka of victory.

KUMARA GURUPARAR

சீர்கொண்ட காசிநகர் சேர்துண்டி ராஜனெனும்
பேர்கொண்ட வைங்கரற்குப் பேசுபுகழ்த் -
தார்கொண்ட
நற்றிருப்பாட் டீரைந்தும் ஞாலமிசைத்
தொண்டரெலாங்
கற்றிருப்பார் மேலாங் கதி.

Those who sing with devotion this garland of twice-five hymns in praise of the elephant enshrined at famed Varāṇasī washed by the sacred Gaṅgā—known by His devotees as Ḍhuṇḍhirāja Gaṇapati, the five-handed Lord—shall surely attain in time the heavenly abode above.

KASSIYAPPA ŚIVĀCHĀRYA'S KANDAPURĀṆAM

மண்ணுலகத்தினிற் பிறவிமாசற
எண்ணிய பொருள் எல்லாம் எளிதின் முற்றுறக்
கண்ணுதல் உடையதோர் களிற்றுமாமுகப்
பண்ணவன் மலரடி பணிந்து போற்றுவோம்.

In order that your birth becomes free of its fetter, and you attain with ease human perfection on earth, worship, O man, with devotion true the flower-like feet of the triple-eyed, elephant-visaged divine *guru,* Mahāgaṇapati, who grants without fail all your wishes.

ARUNAGIRINĀTHAR'S TIRUPUGAL

உம்பர்தருத் தேனுமணிக் கசிவாகி
ஒண் கடலிற் றேனமுதத் துணிர்வூறி

இன்பரசத் தேபருகிப் பலகாலும்
என்றனுயிர்க் காதரவுற் றருள்வாயே
தம்பிதனக் காகவனத் தணை வோனே
தந்தைவலத் தாலருள்கைக் கனியோனே
அன்பர்தமக் கானநிலைப் பொருளோனே
ஐந்து கரத்தானை முகப் பெருமானே.

O five-handed Lord! By your innate wisdom you gained the coveted fruit from Umāśaṅkara's hand. O matchless Lord who relishes the nectar churned by the celestials out of the shimmering sea, did you not venture forth your beloved brother to help wed the doe-eyed Valli upon the Kuruñchi hill? O refuge of your devotees! My labored life on earth you must support and sustain. Enslave me by your grace.

ARUNAGIRINĀTHAR'S TIRUPUGAL

கைத்தல நிறைகனி அப்பமோ டவல்பொரி
கப்பிய கரிமுகன் அடிபேணிக்
கற்றிடும டியவர் புத்தியி லுறைபவ
கற்பக மெனவினை கடிதேகும்
மத்தமு மதியமும் வைத்திடு மரன்மகன்
மற்பொரு திரள்புய மதயானை
மத்தள வயிறனை உத்தமி புதல்வனை
மட்டவிழ் மலர்கொடு பணிவேனே
முத்தமி ழடைவினை முற்படு கிரிதனில்
முற்பட எழுதிய முதல்வோனே
முப்புரம் எரிசெய்த அச்சிவ னுறைரதம்
அச்சது பொடிசெய்த அதிதீரா
அத்துய ரதுகொடு சுப்பிர மணிபடும்
அப்புன மதனிடை இபமாகி
அக்குற மகளுட னச்சிறு முருகனை
அக்கண மணமருள் பெருமாளே.

I'll seek in worship the feet of the one who dwells within the minds of the learned—one whose firm hand is filled with the pomegranate fruit and delicacies sweet.

I'll offer flowers fresh for the one who destroys the inherited *karmic* ills of all His devotees—the broad-shouldered being born of Umāśaṅkara whose head is adorned by the crescent moon and the *konrai's* bloom.

I'll offer fragrant flowers unto the redeeming feet of portly Gaṇapati, born of Gaurīśaṅkara, the first-born, who did inscribe with His own tusk the *Mahābhārata* epic.

Upon the Himālayan peaks I'll worship true the redeeming feet of the valiant one who dared to break the chariot wheel of the three-eyed Lord whose mere laughter destroyed the roving cities three of the *adharmic asuras.*

I'll worship the feet Of the wise being who by His timely intervention on Bālasubramaṇya's behalf performed the marriage rites of youthful Kumaran and the doe-eyed Valli upon the Kuruñchi Hill.

ABHIRAMI PATTAR'S ABHIRAMI ANTATI

தாரமர் கொன்றையும் சண்பக
மாலையும் சாத்தும் தில்லை
ஊரர்தம் பாகத்து உமைமைந்த
னேஉல(கு) ஏழும்பெற்ற
சீரபி ராமி அந் தாதிஎப்
போதும்என் சிந்தையுள்ளே
காரமர் மேனிக் கணபதி
யேநிற்கக் கட்டுரையே.

O dark-hued Gaṇapati, son of Umāsundarī who mothered the seven worlds and is ensconced in the Lord of Tillai, He who is ever adorned by bright *konrai* blooms and *chempaka* garlands. Dwell you must, O Lord, within my mind and being as I sing of Abhirami, the paragon of beauty, in this anthology of a hundred hymns by your benign grace.

RĀMALIṄGA ADIGAL'S TIRU ARUTPA

முன்னவனே யானைமுகத்தவனே, முத்தி நலம்
சொன்னவனே, தூய்மைச் சுகத்தவனே -
மன்னவனே
சிற்பரனே, ஐங்கரனே, செஞ்சடையஞ் சேகரனே
தற்பரனே நின்தாள் சரண்.

O first-born, elephant-visaged harbinger for good tidings who guides mankind unto the attainment of *mukti;* the immanent Lord, five-handed son of Śiva of the sacred tresses, unto your feet I surrender myself.

TIRUPPALLANDU, BY SENTHANAR

குழல்ஒலி யாழ்ஒலி கூத்தொலி ஏத்தொலி
எங்கும் குழாம் பெருகி
விழல்ஒலி விண்ணளவும் சென்று விம்மி
மிகு திருவாரூரின்
மழவிடையார்க்கு வழிவழி ஆளாய்
மனஞ்செய் குடிப்பிறந்த
பழவடியாரொடுங் கூடி எம்மானுக்கே
பல்லாண்டு கூறுதுமே.

Your devotees, O Lord, are gathered in groups to dance in joy and sing your praise. The music of the flute and the *vīṇā's* string resound in the heavens in praise of you who rides the white bull and rules over Tiru-arur. We've come to join your dear devotees who've enslaved themselves for succeeding generations. We are gathered to sing your eternal glory.

SEKKILAR'S PERIYAPURĀṆAM

ஐந்து பேரறிவுங் கண்களே
கொள்ள வளப்பருங் கரணங்களுற்கும்
சிந்தையேயாக குணமொரு மூன்றுந்
திருந்து சாத்து விகமேயாக
இந்து வாழ் சடையானுடு மாணந்த வெல்லேயில்
தனிப் பெருங்கூத்தின் வந்து பேரின்ப
வெள்ளத்துள் திளேத்து மாறிலாமகிழ்ச்சியில்
மலர்ந்தார்.

The throbbing senses five become by the eyes absorbed, the intrinsic organs four become in the mind absorbed and the innate *guṇas* three become transformed into one *sattvic* state for those who behold the singular dance of joy by Him who adorns in His tresses long with the crescent moon, delighting in everlasting bliss, immersed in an ocean of love.

BENEDICTORY VERSE BY KASSIAPPA ŚIVĀCHĀRYA

வான் முகில் வழாது பெய்க, மலிவளம்
சுரக்க மன்னன்
கோன்முறை அரசு செய்க, குறைவிலாது
உயிர்கள் வாழ்க
நான் மறை அறங்கள் ஓங்க, நற்றவம்
வேள்வி மல்க
மேன்மை கொள் சைவநீதி விளங்குக
உலகம் எல்லாம்.

May the rain-rich clouds descend without fail and enrich this earth. May the monarchs rule this resplendent earth with unfailing justice. May all living beings of this enduring earth live without want. May all righteous deeds, governed by the *Vedas* four, prevail upon this earth. May the sacrificial fires and deeds of penance grow in abundance. May the glorious Śaivite truths become renowned the world over.

Gaṇeśa Bhajanam

गणेश भजनम्

Singing to Gaṇeśa

Singing to Gaṇeśa

SOMETIMES WE FEEL A GREAT LOVE OF GOD; SOMETIMES THE GRACE OF GAṆEŚA FILLS US WITH SUCH INSIGHT AND JOY THAT our heart bursts in an overflowing expression of devotion. Our *bhakti* turns the word into song which in turn is offered back to the Deity whence came this gift of divine love and bliss. There may also be other times when our heart is dry, our mind distracted; we feel forlorn and distant from Gaṇeśa. At such times devotional singing is a simple, sure way to raise our spirits up to a level where we can commune with Gaṇeśa once again. Or we may find ourself together with other Hindus who want to join in fellowship to joyfully affirm our religion and praise the Gods that guide us. So we join together in song. In Hinduism this form of worship, called *bhajana* or *kīrtana,* is an age-old tradition, ranging from simple melodious repetition of the names of the Lord to the singing of inspired song/poems of great devotees. Presented here are a few songs in modern notation to aid international group participation. But remember that Hindu music has never been rigid like Western classical music, where a small deviation is viewed as error. In Hindu music melodies often vary from one village to another, singer to singer, one *satsaṅga* to another. Infinite diversity, tolerance and flexibility is a central theme of Hinduism and its sacred music as well. Deep devotion is the standard. Particular notes, in time, in tune or not are hardly noticed. If you are singing with genuine feelings and awareness, then even the song itself will be transcended. Before presenting some of these hymns for us all to use together, let us first consider the deeper meaning of *bhajana* as elucidated in a talk I gave at Kauai Aadheenam in Hawaii on October 16, 1978.

Singing to the Gods: Hindu Hymns of Invocation

AN INSPIRED TALK ON THE POWER OF SATSAṄGA

The Hindu approach to God is well-defined and mystically oriented. It confidently proclaims that every soul is created by God and is destined to return to God; and it provides through its vast cultural and scriptural heritage both the intellectual insight and the pragmatic means for following that path and attaining life's ultimate objective, spiritual realization. One of the legacies inherited by all Hindus is the rich and varied collection of sacred hymns, sung alone in the privacy of early morning worship or in gatherings of like-minded devotees whose combined invocations bring forth in each participant heightened communion with the Divine. There are many ways that Hindus offer devotion through chanting and song. Through the *sādhana* of *japa yoga,* the holy names of the Deities and sacred *mantras* are chanted both silently and aloud as a constant remembering. Pilgrims to the temple will assemble in the outer chambers to hear skilled musicians and singers well-versed in age-old devotional arts, fully capable of turning the mind toward God and away from the world through the subtlety and beauty of their lyrical offerings. Religious epics and stories filled with history and with parable are related to large congregations through dramatic choral presentation. Devotees gather in small and large groups throughout the world to chant in unison, generally led in turn by one among them and then another, singing their praises to the Gods to the accompaniment of the harmonium, drums, *tambūrā* and cymbals. This is called *bhajana.* It is certainly the most popular form of

Hindu devotional singing.

For thousands of years Hindus have gathered in conclave to share hours of the outpouring of their love of the Gods. Their chants have filled the temple chambers, the village hall and the private courtyard, but mostly it has filled and thrilled those who participated with a full heart. In the advanced stages of *bhakti* it matters little whether we are alone or with others when chanting the names of the Lord, for that mature state is steadfast in the higher devotional sensibilities, unruffled by the external world of name and form. Yet few have attained the serene heights of perfect devotion, and fewer still are steady enough to maintain such states once reached. The steadying support of others who also share spiritual goals in life can enhance the individual aspirant's efforts, keeping him firmly on the Sanātana Dharma, the Eternal Path. When these sacred gatherings are regular, either daily or weekly, they generate a spiritual dynamic in the lives of all who participate, a shared energy to which all contribute and from which all can draw.

The Working Together of Three Worlds

Bhajana is an essential part of the Hindu religious life. My *satguru*, Sage Yogaswāmī of Columbuthurai, Sri Lanka, placed great importance on chanting. He would say, "Sing, sing, sing. Morning, noon and evening we will chant with joyful hearts the blessed name of Śiva. Sing always of the Lord and meditate on Him who bestows virtue, wealth, happiness and liberation."

We join a revered band of devotees when we chant the praises of God. Hindus sing to God, to the Gods, to the multitudes of *devas* within their temples and home shrines who will gather around devotees when they congregate together almost anywhere. Each Hindu has his or her own guardian *devas* who are never far away, always available and willing to assist from an inner world of consciousness, from the Second World, or astral plane. These guardian *devas* attend Hindus from the time of birth or from a previous birth or from a ceremony or event occurring anytime in life when he or she enters the great tribe known as the Hindu religion. When two or more Hindus gather, each brings to that assembly—depending upon the personal *sādhana* that the Hindu has performed in this life and in past lives—his own *devas* to add to the throng.

As sincere devotees meet, the inner-plane *devas* form a conclave in the same room, invisible to the physical sight but fully visible to the inner sight and sensed through the feeling of sanctity that pervades the atmosphere of the room. As the singing of the Hindu hymns commences, other Second World *devas* are drawn according to the sum of devotional intensity. These *devas* sing together in the inner planes in concert with the First World *bhajana,* and that calls others, until a multitude of beings in the Second World join in the same chorus as is being sung in the First World.

Sincerity of Purpose

We must realize that when we sing *bhajana* the *devas* of the Second World and even the Gods of the Third World hear our intonations and are aware too of the depth of our devotion. They are fully aware of us though we may be only partially aware of them. They know and appreciate the meaning of the words that we chant. For this reason it is very necessary that each one deeply understand the meaning of the words, even when those words are in Sanskṛit. The meaning, the tones of the voice, the thought behind the meaning, the feeling behind the thought—all these give power to the *bhajana,* add their beauty to the sounds that radiate out from our love and devotion, taking that meaning, thought, feeling and sound from this macrocosm into the microcosm of the *de-*

vonic world and through that into a greater macrocosm where the Gods live. High tones penetrate deepest, piercing through the microcosm into the great macrocosm that we know as the inner worlds. Also, concentration of mind, awareness of meaning and sincerity of inner feeling add to the ability of the chant to penetrate to spiritual depths or, in their absence, to remain little more than a sweet song hardly distinguishable from any other song.

Singing is Prayer and Thanksgiving

Most Hindu chants are a joyous praising of the Divine. They can also be a reminder that there are subtle inner worlds of existence, a pleading that we may be more aware of them and more in harmony with their great beauties and truths, and an invocation of the Gods and even of certain benefits which they are empowered to bestow. Our hymns are a thanksgiving of all that we have, for all the good that has been granted to us in life by our Gods, or during an immediate time span. Of course, we are only capable of such thanksgiving when we inwardly feel grateful, content within ourselves and not dissatisfied with our *dharma,* not struggling to oppose our *karma* in this life but to fulfill it by bringing it into harmony with our religion. True thanks must be offered or true petitions made with the mind and emotions and thought in a single accord as the Sanskṛit lyrics are enunciated. How would the God perceive a devotee who is chanting something to him, pleading to him through the tones of his voice but simultaneously thinking about something totally different and unrelated, or if he or she is not thinking at all but merely mouthing meaningless syllables? Obviously the devotee will be inwardly seen as insincere and shallow, saying things that he doesn't really mean. It would be unwise to assume that the Gods are incapable of perceiving such states of mind. They are, in fact, more fully aware of the devotee's inner feeling and thinking states during *bhajana* than the

devotee himself.

One bathes before coming to *satsaṅga* or *bhajana.* One prepares the mind and the emotion, knowing that he is, in a sense, on stage and performing before beings of great intelligence who are able from their microcosm to look into this macrocosm. These Gods are being invoked, and they will attend if the invocation is properly and sincerely performed with a devout heart and a mind that is one-pointed in spiritual pursuit. The *devas* in the Second World—which is the world of astral or mental bodies—will respond because their function, their fulfillment and *dharma* on their plane of consciousness is to help evolution in the First World, physical plane, and thereby further evolve themselves. They are spiritual helpers, working with the First World to open it up to the Third World. All the worlds work together when Hindu devotees gather together. The astral beings who work on the lower astral plane contact more evolved beings in the higher Second World who are able to themselves work with the individual and to invoke the Third World. The Personal Deity is thus reached, and the blessings flood forth from within.

It is very important that we are sincere when we chant these holy hymns that have reverberated in the nerve systems of uncounted seekers and sages down through the millennia. We would not want to be seen as insincere or inattentive, saying one thing and thinking another, or saying and thinking one thing and feeling another. Presenting ourselves to the Gods through prayerful song or just appearing before them in the temple precincts, we want to be in a most pious and profound state of mind. Ordinary affairs must be temporarily relinquished along with ordinary feelings and thoughts. Yet, you would not want to pretend either. If you are unhappy when you come to the temple, they must see that unhappiness, and you must not try to cloud or conceal it from them or yourself. Then they can help. The Gods are going to see you the way you are from their vantage point in the microcosm looking out and into this macrocosm.

Depth of Meaning and Feeling

For those of you who may not know the Sanskṛit language, it is necessary to make a special effort to understand in English or in the language with which you are most familiar what is being chanted in Sanskṛit during *bhajana.* When we chant together "Gaṇeśa Śaraṇam," it is essential that we know that it means "I take refuge in the *darśana* of Lord Gaṇeśa." Even knowing the meaning is not enough. You must actually take refuge in the overpowering feeling of Gaṇeśa's presence as you visualize His *mūrti* or form. You must also be able to awaken to the higher emotional realms, to rise to a devotional mood as you are singing to the Gods, a mood that itself carries you into Gaṇeśa's protective refuge, a mood that awakens you to the presence of Gaṇeśa's love and compassion. If you are singing to the Gods with such genuine feelings, then the song itself has been transcended even while you are in the midst of your lyrical worship. Now this is very important. That makes your chanting truly beneficial, beneficial not only for yourself and those who are with you but for all mankind.

You could be singing "Gaṇeśa śaraṇam, śaraṇam Gaṇeśa" most beautifully with no thought deeper than enjoying the sounds and realizing that you were on key and another in the room was not. Or you could be singing and at the same time thinking about some problem that came up during the day or an event that will take place in the days to come.

Little benefit is to be derived from such an approach to *bhajana*. Similarly, when the time comes at a later date for you to be initiated into the art of meditation there will be no real meditation if the mind is allowed to wander aimlessly, mulling over things of the past and imaginings of the future. *Bhajana* too, is a *sādhana* that requires preparation, attention and concentration. It is not an external performance meant to entertain the participants. It is an internal performance that invokes the inner-plane Gods and draws awareness deep within. Approach your chanting as a devotional *sādhana*. Let it be a time of communion with the deepest strata of consciousness within you and a communication with the Gods. Study the chants. Memorize their meanings so that as your voice goes out into the physical room your awareness simultaneously pierces into inner dimensions.

From your own experience in the world you can understand how the Gods naturally perceive an aspirant whose body is joining in the *bhajana* but whose mind is elsewhere. People have come to you and said things that they did not mean. People have talked with you and you knew that they were thinking about something entirely different and thinking only absent-mindedly about the conversation. You have observed the results when people approach anything half-heartedly, perhaps preferring that they were somewhere else doing something else. Nothing permanent and valuable is ever accomplished even on the gross physical plane by such an approach. Then how much more important is it that the subtle worlds, the deeper states of consciousness, be approached with mindfulness?

The Group Helps the Individual

A group that is chanting regularly, singing to the Gods day after day after day, gives the *devas* great power, a channel through which they can reach out and help other Hindus in the community and around the world. Within a hundred-mile radius inner-plane helpers assigned to guide Hindus, who are perhaps not religious Hindus, would come to the *bhajana* on the astral plane and be renewed themselves. Inner-plane helpers may also be renewed and inspired.

A large *satsaṅga* or *bhajana* conducted regularly at the same time can summon these thousands and thousands of guardian *devas* together in a single conclave, renewing and inspiring them. Then they go back to the First World Hindu whom they are bound to guard and guide and in turn uplift and inspire him. He may be lifted out of the fog of the outer mind in its morass of confusions and become inspired to pay closer attention to his religion. He may awaken a desire to go to the temple, to serve others more selflessly, and on and on. Such things can happen just because a group of devotees get together and sing to God, feel what they are singing, know the meaning of the words they are saying and the implications within the meaning of the words. Of course, children love to sing, and *bhajana* is universally enjoyed by children of all ages, providing one of the most wonderful ways to bring your sons and daughters fully into the religion. They should attend group *bhajana*s often. The family itself can chant together in the shrine room each day for at least a few minutes.

We want to take it all in, take in the tone, take in the thought, take in the feeling, take in the knowledge—take it all back to the source, back to the microcosm where you were living ten months before you were born in this physical world. You were there in the microcosm, fully aware, fully matured, working out your own spiritual destiny through helping those on this plane, awaiting another birth that would catapult you into an even greater evolution when you returned to the microcosm. So the microcosm is nothing with which you are not familiar. You came out of the microcosm and will return to it after the purpose of this birth has been fulfilled. It is really more your home than any structure on this earth could ever be. So you are just contacting home when you invoke the Second World. It is nothing difficult. It is relatively easy, and you can do it night after night after night as you sing here to the Gods. Know that there are people listening, people just like you, people on the lower astral plane and people on the higher astral planes. They too join in the chanting where they are. If you had an inner ear, you could stop chanting and they would all be heard chanting simultaneously. This has been done; these inner-plane chants have been heard. The more regular the *bhajana*, the deeper it penetrates into the inner worlds. We believe that religion is the working together of the three worlds, and in our *bhajana* this working together is a joyous ritual simultaneously celebrated on all planes of consciousness.

Association with Other Devotees

One of the great benefits to be derived from *bhajana* is the association with other devotees, others of your religion who believe as you do and whose strength is added to your own. This is known as *satsaṅga*. *Satsaṅga* is the traditional meeting of Hindu Truth-seekers, gathered often to read from scripture or to receive *upadeśa* from a *swāmī* or their own *satguru.* The company of good men and women who themselves exemplify the Hindu ideals, who are striving, who are devout and virtuous is to be sought after. Such association will immeasurably enhance your own efforts.

It is very important in the world today that Hindu people gather together and express themselves in a religious way. *Satsaṅga* groups are enjoyed all over the world wherever Hindus are found. The greatness of Hinduism lies in its diversity, and this diversity is also its greatest strength. This applies to the religion as a whole as well as to various groups within it. No single *satsaṅga* group will be quite like another, yet those within it must be in agreement on at least the major points of the philosophy that it represents.

When you join a *satsaṅga* group this becomes your religious experience and focus. It is different than the experience of worship in the temple, and it is different than private meditation and devotions in your home shrine. When you go to worship in the temple, you are there alone even though others may be present. It is a most sacred and individual experience, a time set aside for communion with your personal Deity. Within the *satsaṅga* group, however, within that kind of *saṅga,* you are sharing your devotion with others. You temporarily set aside your own mind, your *karma,* for a period of time and work your mind within the context of the group, which is the combined mind or *karma* of those present. This by no means should be taken to be a total involvement or entangling of the various *karmas,* but is a temporary combining or merging of *karmas* for those few hours each week when the *satsaṅga* meets together.

I have often said that the individual helps the group and the group helps the individual. This is to be clearly seen in the working of group devotions and chanting in *satsaṅga* groups. We are inspired, lifted above our personal concerns and able to give our thoughts entirely to the high purposes of the *satsaṅga,* and with everyone present doing this, a dynamic vibration is created, an environment that is conducive to further progress on the spiritual path.

Sharing Individual *Karmas*

There are many religious groups throughout the world sharing the same philosophy and beliefs, chanting the same *bhajanas* and meeting together regularly. Some of these groups are productive, while others are unproductive. The actual results which manifest as a consequence of the gathering of a *satsaṅga* group are totally dependent upon the combined *karma* of the group as a whole.

The one mind of the group is made up of both the positive and negative *karmas* of each member. This does not mean that if a group is unproductive or unhappy that certain members should be singled out and sent away, for that would only serve to create yet a greater unseemly *karma* for the outcast as well as for the group that inadvisedly cast him out. Rather this indicates that the group must perform a deeper *sādhana,* a greater disciplined effort, that it must make a special effort to feel inwardly the meaning of the words as they are chanted and be in tune with the extraterrestrial vibratory rate of the *devonic* world. The group may also ponder whether the social period is excessively long, whether too much emphasis is being placed on the foods being served and whether one or more members are bringing their personal *karmic* implications and involvements into the group rather than taking these matters to the feet of the Lord. Above all, the group should realize that a problem exists within the mind of the group, which is no particular individual's fault or problem. It is simply an effect of accumulated and combined *karmas* of the entire membership and must be faced in this impersonal way.

A productive group is also a harmonious group, a useful group. Its members will want to distribute religious literature as a natural overflow of the energies that well up from within them during the *satsaṅga.* They will want to give food to the hungry. They will not be able to neglect the needy. They will naturally want to host a Hindu family newly arrived in their community, to visit Hindus in the hospital, to write letters for them, talk to them and see that they are properly cared for. There are so many practical things that a *satsaṅga* group can and should involve itself with, but this is possible only when all members are of a one mind, a one harmony.

If the group is an unproductive group, it will be found to be a group that is inharmonious and argumentative, one in which the *asuric* forces are perhaps more prevalent than the *devonic* forces. This must be dealt with positively, not run away from or avoided. If *asuric* forces have penetrated the group, it is best to chant sitting in a circle, thereby creating enough magnetism to lift the consciousness of the entire *satsaṅga* simultaneously. If the group is a harmonious group, then all may sit, as at traditional Hindu gatherings, with the women on one side of the room and the men on the other. It is always preferable to sit on the floor, for that releases certain forces from within the body that can greatly enhance the spiritual life of man. When we worship in a temple, we receive individual attention from the great beings of the Second and Third Worlds. That is our time for personal communication with the inner worlds, with the inner realms of our own being. But *satsaṅga* is different, and that difference should be realized by all present. It is a group religious experience. It enhances both the personal *karma* of every member as well as the collective *karma* of the one mind which is the *saṅga* itself.

I urge each *satsaṅga* group to look sincerely into its productivity and to seek creative ways that it can be useful to its members and to the community in which it lives. It is important that we use our energies well, that we do not waste energy, do not waste our lives. *Satsaṅga* groups can search out ways to help the many thousands of Hindus who have migrated from the Holy Land to all parts of the world and would benefit from a kind word and a compassionate smile.

Conducting *Satsaṅga*

There are many ways that *satsaṅga* groups can be conducted, and there will be established groups with their own routines. New groups just being formed may wish to follow our schedule of twenty minutes of *bhajana* followed by twenty

minutes of scriptural reading or *upadeśa* and then another twenty minutes of *bhajana*, making a total of one hour. It is customary to have *satsaṅga* groups move from one home to another each week or each month, and of course the leader and host of the *satsaṅga* that week is always the person in whose home the group is meeting. He or she would select the reading or recording to be used that week, or arrange for a talk by a *swāmī* or other spiritual leader. The host would also arrange the room, preparing a small altar which could have a picture of the Deity—Lord Gaṇeśa is agreeable to all—and pictures of the *gurus* of the various members of the *satsaṅga*, for all will not necessarily share the same preceptor. As a *satsaṅga* group grows in strength and maturity, these and other ways of helping our fellow man will blossom forth. That is the first sign that the *satsaṅga* has done its work on the inside, has begun to fulfill its purpose.

A Special Collection Of Hymns to Lord Gaṇeśa

FOR YOUNG AND OLD ALIKE

On the following pages, we have assembled several hymns for individual or group singing and chanting. We have put the chants into Western musical notation so they can be played easily on a harmonium. A free translation of the Sanskṛit into English has also been added to inspire high-minded thought and visualization based on the meaning of the songs. Usually one person leads the group, and then another, with the leader chanting the verse initially, then the entire group repeating that verse once. The leader then chants the second verse, and so on. Often the leader, if he or she is musically adept, will make embellishments on the musical line, but the group generally repeats the verse in its simple form. Many chants start off slowly and gradually pick up in both speed and volume. The length of the chant is left to the leader's discretion, but usually is best when limited to five or ten minutes.

These songs may be used during formal *bhajana* and informally to yourself at other times during the day. Sing them during your morning meditations and silently to yourself throughout the day. Sing them before meals and to the children just before they go to sleep. Sing them as you work and in the car as you travel. When you are discouraged, sing. When you are inspired and creative, sing. When you are upset, sing. When you find yourself waiting somewhere and feeling there is nothing to do, sing to the Gods. Sing with a full heart. As you sing, listen for the silence within the sounds, for that silence is itself the voice of God.

Gitā

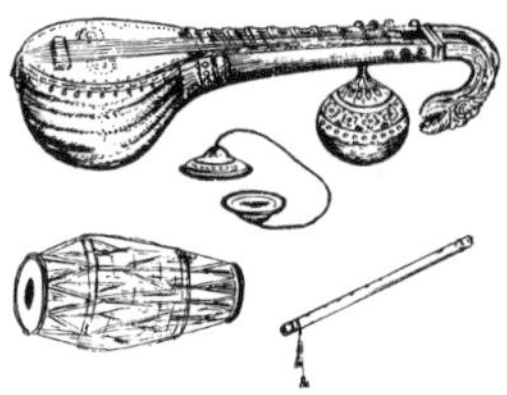

Gītā means song. *Gītās* can be sung solo or in unison by a group. The pace is relaxed. The words aid in devotional visualization. We seek to invoke the *darśana* and *śakti* of Lord Gaṇeśa, picturing Him in our minds while concentrating on His divine attributes. A deep communion with the joyous Lord is attained. "Vighneśvara Gītā" is often the first taught to beginning students of Hindu music. Sing with all your heart this ode to our Loving Gaṇeśa. He will hear. Yes, He will hear. It is important to realize that with His big ears and His astute mind that He knows everything at every point in time, even when eating a *modaka*. This is amusing. So, sing out loud, sing boldly His songs, and His grace will pour upon you with all the abundance under His control (which is, actually, all abundance).

SONG TO THE LORD OF OBSTACLES

VERSE 1 O Gaṇeśa, You are the red-colored leader
of the *gaṇas,* the ocean of compassion,
O elephant-faced Lord.

VERSE 2 The *siddhas* and *chāraṇas* ever in Your service,
the grantor of all attainment. O Vināyaka, we
bow to You again and again.

VERSE 3 Master of all arts and knowledge, the best
one of all, we bow to You again and again.

REFRAIN Big-bellied Lord who blesses all with prosperity,
Pārvatī's son, you are praised by all the Gods.

VIGHNEŚVARA GĪTĀ

Composed by Pūrandaradāsa

Malahari Rāga **Rūpaka Tāla**

AROHANA: S R_1 M_1 P D_1 Ṡ AVAROHANA: Ṡ D_1 P M_1 G_3 R_1 S

Dhyānam

Dhyānam means *meditation.* This form of song is usually done solo, slowly, in free time, with no instruments other than a drone. More prayer than music, the words of a *dhyānam* are often from our ancient Sanskṛit scriptures. For singers, it is a devotional offering. For listeners, the words direct the mind to commune silently with Loving Gaṇeśa. A short meditative silence following any *dhyānam* is traditional. Not enough can be said about meditation. It is the perfection of the peaceful mind. What makes the mind not peaceful? Well, Gaṇeśa would explain in His exemplary way, "Among the realms beyond My reach, one is fear." Still, He can help, for fear is within His control, even though it resides as the emotion within the *chakra* directly below the *mūlādhāra chakra* upon which He sits: the four-petalled lotus of great beauty and strength rising above the waters of memory. Further below Him is the *chakra* of anger and rage in which the mind gives up its control to *asuric* forces. He, our loving Lord, prays for those in the state of anger, because mind and emotions out of control seals us from His grace. So, sing the song to lift up the *purusha* into its own pristine glory and begin to change. That is the message of our loving God: "address *śānti,*" invoke peace, as the perfect performance to live up to as actors on the stage of life and make hence for a reality "off stage," within the home.

MEDITATION ON THE LORD OF OBSTACLES

Translation: O elephant-faced Lord Who is served by all creatures and satisfied with the juice of *kapittha* and *jambu* fruits, son of Umā, remover of sufferings and pains, O Lord of all Obstacles, I bow at Your lotus feet.

GAṆEŚA DHYĀNAM

Hamsadhwani Rāga **Free Time**

AROHANA: S R_2 G_3 P N_3 Ṡ AVAROHANA: Ṡ N_3 P G_3 R_2 S

Bhajana

Bhajana means *adoration* or *worship,* often by responsive group singing. A leader sings a phrase, the group repeats it exactly. *Bhajanas* usually have a strong rhythm, sometimes slow and steady and then fast, sparking attention, and raising the group energy. *Bhajana* is dynamic *japa.* The goal is concentrated communion with the God. Three *bhajanas* follow, two from tradition and one from recent times.

GAṆEŚA ŚARAṆAM

"Lord Gaṇeśa, you are my refuge."

Hamsadhwani Rāga **Ādi Tāla**

AROHANA: S R_2 G_3 P N_3 Ṡ AVAROHANA: Ṡ N_3 P G_3 R_2 S

JAYA GAṆAPATI AUM

Popular Melody **Ādi Tāla**

"Be Victorious, Gaṇapati!
Lord Gaṇapati, Victory unto Thee!"

PAÑCHAMUKHA GAṆAPATI

This song was inspired by the eight-foot-tall granite statue of Pañchamukha Gaṇapati that we installed on the north shore of Mauritius, the Pearl of the Indian Ocean. This majestic five-faced, ten-armed Gaṇapati looks East toward India over azure blue seas—a towering reminder of the original home of the nation's Hindus and of the importance of harmony in life. The greatest linguist of all time is He who holds time in ten hands, balancing it moment to moment by slightly moving His magnificent trunk. Yes, language is no mystery to our loving Lord. He knows them all. The island's official language, French, and its sweet child Creole are perfect mediums for *bhajana.* All *creoles* of the world are dear to His ears. They are languages of the heart.

VERSES: O Five-faced Lord of Gaṇas, let there be harmony in the family, in society and in all our business affairs. Long live culture and our religion. Grant us love of God and charity for all.

REFRAIN: O Elephant-Lord, protect and heal us.

INVOCATION DE CINQ GAṆEŚA ŚAKTIS

Nattai Rāga **Ādi Tāla**

AROHANA: S G_3 M_1 P N_3 Ṡ AVAROHANA: Ṡ N_3 P M_1 G_3 M_1R_3 S

R, R R S | P N N | S; |
Ra ksha Ra ksha Ga jā na na—
P, M R; | S G M | P; |
L'har mo nie dan la fa mille
L'har mo nie en so cie té
L'har mo nie dans les af fairs
Vivela culture et la re li gion
L'amour Di vine et la cha ri té
M M M M P P P P | M M M | R M R S |
Pañ cha mu kha Ga ṇa pa ti Ga jā na na
Pañ cha mu kha Ga ṇa pa ti Gajava da na
Pañ cha mu kha Ga ṇa pa ti Ga jā na na
Pañ cha mu kha Ga ṇa pa ti Gajava da na
Pañ cha mu kha Ga ṇa pa ti Ga jā na na
R, R R S, | P N N | S; ||
L'har mo nie dan la fa mille
L'har mo nie en so cie té
L'har mo nie dans les af fairs
Vive la culture et la re li gion
L'amour Di vine et la cha ri té

Natchintanai

The venerable sage, Āsān Yogaswāmī of Jaffna, Sri Lanka, sang many songs of God, Gods and his beloved *guru* which contained profound religious and metaphysical teachings. These songs were called *Natchintanai,* meaning "good thoughts." In one famous ode to the One God Śiva, Yogaswāmī invokes Gaṇeśa in the first verse, before proceeding to sing of the One. Using traditional images, he alludes to a famous story where Lord Gaṇeśa gave His grace to Lord Indra, king of the Vedic *devas.* He also speaks of the ancient mystery teaching that Lord Gaṇeśa's form is the *mantra* Aum itself. Thus did Yogaswāmī affirm the teaching to worship our loving Lord Gaṇeśa first before beginning any worship or task.

Invocation of the Elephant-Faced Lord

O elephant-faced Lord, son of Śaṅkara
with abundant belly and earrings, who granted
grace to Indra, the king of the *devas.*
You who are of *mantra* form I will never forget.

Throughout time Lord Gaṇeśa as Aum has come into the lives of the elemental beings, men, women, children and even the Gods themselves. For His is the office of gatekeeper. Nothing can begin without a nod of approval and nothing can end without giving thanks and showing appreciation to Him, for every end is a new beginning. Loving Gaṇeśa has a mystical symbol, the *swastika.* It represents the power of the matured mind. A mind that has flexibility. A mind that has resilience. A mind that has compassion. A mind that has the twice-born strength to finish what has been begun. A mind that is in touch with the divine above, below and to either side. The *swastika* represents Gaṇeśa, to be sure.

TANDI MUKHAN TANAI

Nattai Rāga **Ādi Tāla**

AROHANA: S G_3 M_1 P N_3 Ṡ AVAROHANA: Ṡ N_3 P M_1 G_3 M_1R_3 S

Gaṇapati Prahelikāḥ

गणपति प्रहेलिका:

Gaṇeśa Puzzles

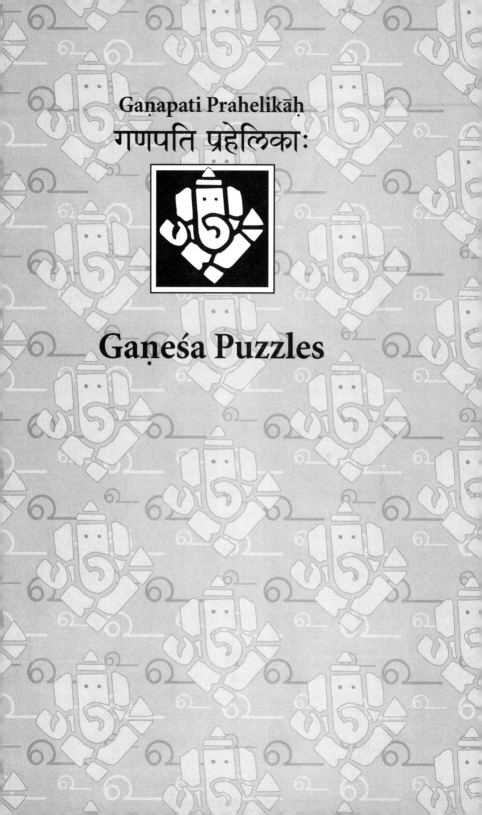

Gaṇeśa Puzzles

THE PLAYFUL, POWERFUL CHILD OF UMĀ IS BĀLA GAṆEŚA, ONE OF LORD GAṆEŚA'S FAVORITE FORMS. HERE WE OFFER A FEW FORays into the world of highminded fun and wordful frolic. Enjoy. This is playful *svadhyāya. Svadhyāya* is a key concept in Hinduism, one of the classical *yamas,* or cardinal guidelines of conduct, expounded by the ancient Nātha Ṛishi Patañjali and others. It is the deliberate focused activity of self-upliftment through scriptural study, memorization of holy verses and reading elevating tales of spiritual giants, listening to religious discourses. We use our time involving the mind and intellect in pursuits that lead us onward toward the goal of moksha, rather than dispersing consciousness through pointless ramification. But it need not be all so serious. For children and youthful minds, play can also be *svadhyāya*—recreation that fills the mind with religious impressions. Hindu art and culture overflows with an unsurpassed richness of spiritual play. This chapter is a small contribution to that vast river of *dharma's* fun and games.

Lord Gaṇeśa rules the *mūlādhāra,* the *chakra* of memory. Yogic insight shows that memorization of spiritual teachings, chants and concepts, a seemingly mere rote process, in fact works a transformation of the energies of the *mūlādhāra.* We actively remold the contents of the subconscious, refining the nature, sublimating and transmuting instinctive energies. May these few games invoke and indelibly stamp upon our minds the great teachings and culture of *dharma* held in the mind of our beloved Lord Gaṇeśa. Seers say even heavenly *devas* delight in word play of a spiritual nature.

The Puzzle of the Guardian of Bhārat

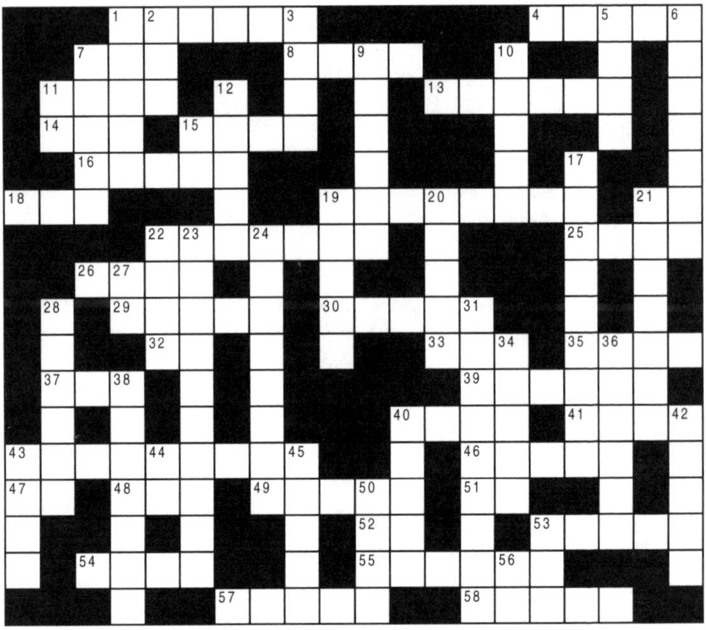

Across

1. Sacred syllables chanted by Hindus.
4. The *chakra* that Gaṇeśa sits upon is a four-petalled ______ .
7. Gaṇeśa's *vāhana* (vehicle)
8. Gaṇeśa is full of _____.
11. ______ fields are sacred to Lord Gaṇeśa.
13. Gaṇeśa is sometimes called the Lord of _______.
14. Gaṇeśa is very ____.
15. Gaṇeśa has four _____.
16. Gaṇeśa uses a _____ and a goad to help him do his work.
18. Divine servant. Used at the end of a devotee's name.
19. What you say to Gaṇeśa when he answers your prayer.

Down

1. The fruit Gaṇeśa won in a contest with his brother.
2. Gaṇeśa ___ too many *modaka* balls one day.
3. Gifts to the poor and crippled.
5. Devotees who are having a special Gaṇeśa *archana* often carry their offerings on a ______.
6. Gaṇeśa _____ the *Mahābhārata* with one of his tusks.
7. The monsoons of Southeast Asia bring severe tropical _____.
9. The traditional Hindu wedding is called a _________ ceremony.
10. Just look at the *mūrti* of Gaṇeśa makes you feel _______.
11. First and last letters of bean pod that tastes like chocolate.

Across Continued

21. A Śiva temple facing ___ is a fire-temple. (Abbreviation!)
22. The God we always worship first.
25. Hindus pray to Gaṇeśa to ___ them in good and happy ways.
26. Gaṇeśa loves all the animals in all the _____ in the world.
29. Gaṇeśa works slowly and patiently, never in _____.
30. The Gaṅga is a sacred _____ to all Hindus.
32. Twice.
33. Hindus worship Gaṇeśa with ___ and yellow flowers.
35. Another name for Vishṇu.
37. Gaṇeśa is even brighter than the ____.
39. Gaṇeśa's favorite sweet.
40. _____ gather honey from flowers.
41. Gaṇeśa always makes careful decisions, never a ____ decision.
43. Kailāsa is in the Himālayan _________.
46. The lower instinctive mind, seat of desire and governor of sensory and motor organs.
47. Gaṇeśa pūjās start as early as 3:00 __ in the morning.
48. Gaṇeśa is Lord Śiva's eldest ____.
49. Indian variety of basil often used for *japa* beads.
51. Having two.
52. First two letters of the number of most famous Gaṇeśa temples in Maharashtra.
53. Kolam designs are ______ on the floor in front of Gaṇeśa shrines.
54. Gaṇeśa pūjās fill you with ____.
55. Gaṇeśa's ______ flows through our minds and all form.
57. Indian women wear _______.
58. Incense has a beautiful ______.

Down Continued

12. Cane fields are _______.
15. Gaṇeśa is known __ the Lord of Obstacles.
17. The big *chakra* that Gaṇeśa sits upon deep in the microcosm.
19. Lord Gaṇeśa lives in the _____ World.
20. Gaṇeśa _______ forgets the prayers of His close devotees.
21. Hindu holy scriptures in Sanskṛit.
22. The weapon Gaṇeśa uses to knock obstacles out of our path and spur us onward.
23. A big world for "help."
24. Gaṇeśa has the head of an _______.
27. OH.
28. Gaṇeśa always knows how to answer our prayers just right because His ________ is so great.
31. Gaṇeśa's memory is so great He _________ things that happened millions of years ago.
34. Indian thin flour pancake.
36. The subtle inner ethers.
38. When Murugan tried to win the contest with His brother, He flew around the world _______.
40. Gaṇeśa's _____ is bigger than any computer in the world.
42. The *nāgaswara* and conch are two types of temple _____.
43. Lord Gaṇeśa is a ____deva.
44. The first two letters of the first finger on your foot.
45. Gaṇeśa likes a lot of ______ in His sweet goodies.
50. Even though Gaṇeśa has little eyes, He still ____ everything.
53. Many different organic substances are used to ___ the beautifully colored Indian fabrics.
56. The first initial of Śiva's two sons.

The Puzzle of the Lord of Dharma

[Mahā Clue for this whole puzzle: All words are Sanskṛit.]

Across

1. Lord Gaṇeśa's seed *mantra.*
5. Good karma, righteous action, merit.
8. Eternal, something which should be done without fail always at the right time.
10. The second goal of human existence, wealth.
11. The first goal of human existence, love, pleasure.
16. "Demon place." Hindu concept of hell; lower realm of the Second World in which souls temporarily experience self-created hellish states of mind.
18. What you are when you always follow *dharma.* A person good enough to go to the temple and do *pūjā.*
20. Our most important scriptures.
22. The inert, dark, heavy, dull, ignorant quality of nature.
24. A hall, generally in a temple or monastery.
25. Same as *moksha.*

Down

2. The third-eye *chakra.*
3. Spiritual practice of devotedly repeating a *mantra,* generally a specified number of daily repetitions while counting on a *mālā.*
4. A name of Supreme God as "The Auspicious One."
5. Bad *karma,* sin, wrong-doing.
6. A pot of water on which a husked coconut is nested on five mango leaves.
7. The soul.
9. Lord Gaṇeśa's *vāhana,* the mouse, traditionally associated with abundance.
12. Delusion, fascination with and attachment to material existence.
13. Individual or group singing of devotional songs, hymns.
14. Rosary for performing *japa,* recitation of holy names.
15. A round sweet goody made of rice, coconut, sugar, etc. Esoterically, it corresponds to *siddhi* (attainment or fulfillment) the gladdening fulfillment of pure joy.
17. The Deity of fire.
19. The Primal Sound.
21. The name of the light that is waved during *pūjā.*
22. That, pure Being.
23. Immanent Truth.

The Puzzle of the Fruit of Truth

Across

3. Same as *moksha.*
4. Merging the individual mind with the universal mind of God within.
5. Peace.
8. A Mahādeva, or great God, created by Lord Śiva to assist souls in their evolution. The elephant-faced Patron of Art and Science, first son of Śiva, Remover of Obstacles.
10. Teacher, guide, remover of darkness.
13. Loving Gaṇeśa holds a sprig of this wish-fulfilling tree to tell us that all our wishes will be gratified. We have but to tell Him our needs, that is all, just tell Him.
17. Loving Gaṇeśa has this snake as His pet. Many are afraid of such creatures, but He tells us that it is the kuṇḍalinī within all and each one can rise above all adversity.
20. Symbolic hand gestures used in pūjā, dance and *haṭha yoga.*
21. Dedicated striving and practice.
23. A stringed instrument with two round dried pumpkins on the ends, that makes heavenly music.

Down

1. A period of time that spans many ages.
2. Loving Gaṇeśa uses this instrument to move dullards ahead in their birth *karmas* whenever they tarry.
6. "Without qualities." Refers to the Absolute God, Paraśiva or Parabrahman.
7. "Accomplished or skillful one." Someone who is dedicated to spiritual practices is usually celibate, wears white and is not a sannyāsin.
9. Loving Gaṇeśa knows there are difficult times ahead for some of His devotees. He protects them with this implement in gentle ways from evils they have attracted.
11. Householder; family man or woman. The period of human life after *brahmacharya,* or studentship, is over, the individual establishing of a career, home and family.
12. The calm, quiescent, peaceful, still quality of nature.
14. A word meaning "of the stars." Anything in the subtle non-physical dimension of the Second World.
15. Primal life force of the breath.
16. "Great Deva" or "Great Shining One." A name of Śiva.
18. The symbol and *mantra* denoting God and the Primal Sound.
19. Loving Gaṇeśa uses this implement to cast *karmas* back on devotees for resolution, never letting up until completion.
20. Loving Gaṇeśa tells of this fruit: "It was given to Me from Lord Śiva's own hand after performing My first wisdom act. It represents the highest spiritual fruition."
22. It's hot in summertime, so Loving Gaṇeśa sits whisking away the past within the minds of devotees with this cooling device.

The Puzzle of the Lord of Spiritual Mysteries

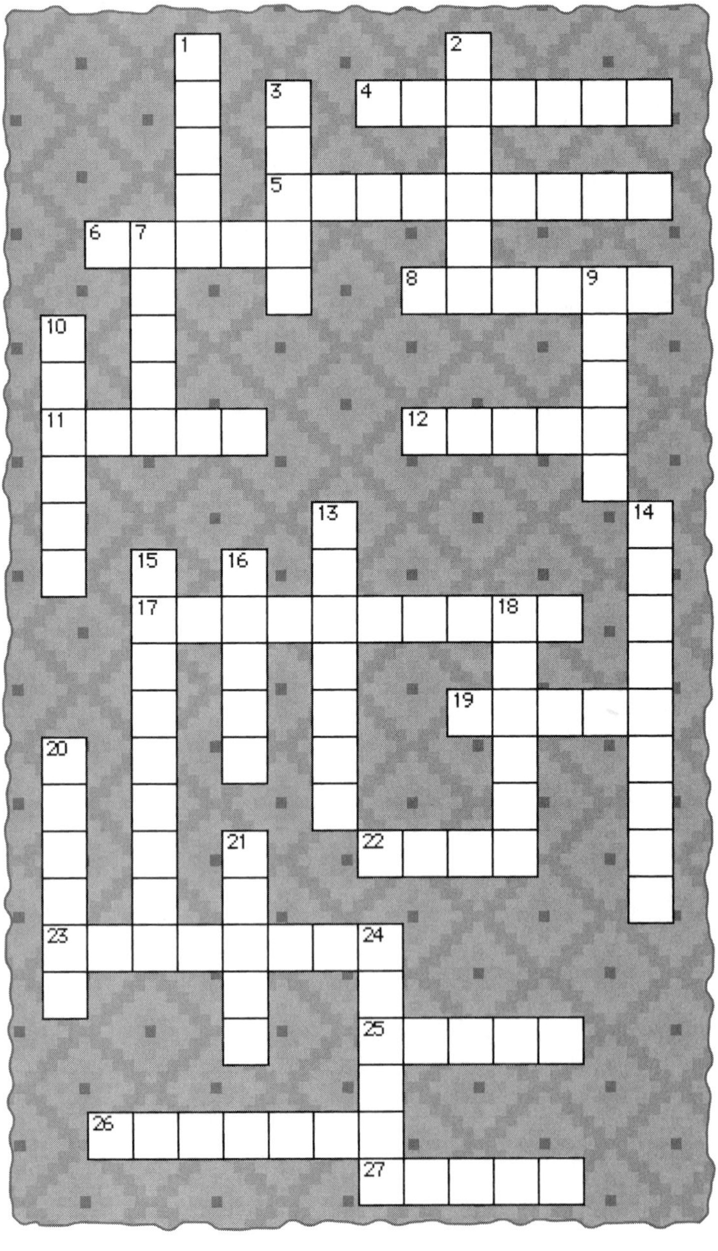

Across

4. Faith.
5. Loving Gaṇeśa, like His brother Murugan, holds this great power. It flashes in the sky during storms, spirit over mind, mind over matter.
6. "A "not spiritual" being living in the Second World on the lower astral plane, sometimes called a "demon."
8. The animal that each Hindu God is depicted as riding on, symbolic of a function of the God.
11. "God." Can refer to the image or *mūrti* installed in a temple or to the Mahādeva whom the murthi represents.
12. A troop of *devas*, especially used in reference to Lord Śiva's attendants under Lord Gaṇeśa's supervision.
17. The last portion of the Vedas. They teach philosophy through people asking questions and wise *ṛishis'* giving answers.
19. Loving Gaṇeśa broke this, His beautiful right tusk in a sacrificial act, using it as a stylus to get the job done. By this act He demonstrates that what we begin we must finish.
22. Inner plane being of light.
23. The ancient Hindu symbol of auspiciousness and good fortune. A square cross with broken arms.
25. The fiery, restless quality of nature.
26. A sweet nut from a palm tree hard as a rock, but soft and white ınside.
27. What He shoots from his bow.

Down

1. Small circle of red powder *(kuṅkuma)* placed between and just above the eyebrows. It symbolizes the opening of the third eye, seeing with superconscious soul vision.
2. Loving Gaṇeśa edits all these scriptures on this and otherplanets.
3. Sacred art of "drawing" intricate decorative patterns at the entrance to a home or temple or at ceremonial sites with the rice powder or colored powdered pulses.
7. Hinduism's revealed scriptures.
9. Loving Gaṇeśa uses this rope-like device to draw close those He loves and save strayed ones in extraordinary ways.
10. Spiritual attainment or power, superconscious abilities, fulfillment.
13. Triple-pointed lance representing Śiva's three-in-one power: Love, Wisdom and Action.
14. Loving Gaṇeśa sits at Lord Śiva's holy feet with *japa mālā* made of these seeds.
15. The *chakra* located at the base of the spine and governing memory, time and space where Loving Gaṇeśa sits inside each person.
16. Sanskṛit word meaning "deed or act;" the principle of cause and effect. Also, the totality of our actions and their concomitant reactions in this and all previous lives.
18. Divine law; the law of being; the way of righteousness or "that which holds one's true nature."
20. Loving Gaṇeśa makes us grow healthy food by the desire for this simple underground vegetable.
21. Loving Gaṇeśa wants us to be like this flower that "comes from the depths of the mud opening into the bud high above the water's edge."
24. The nectar of immortality that Loving Gaṇeśa keeps in his pot.

The Lord Who Is Hidden in All Things

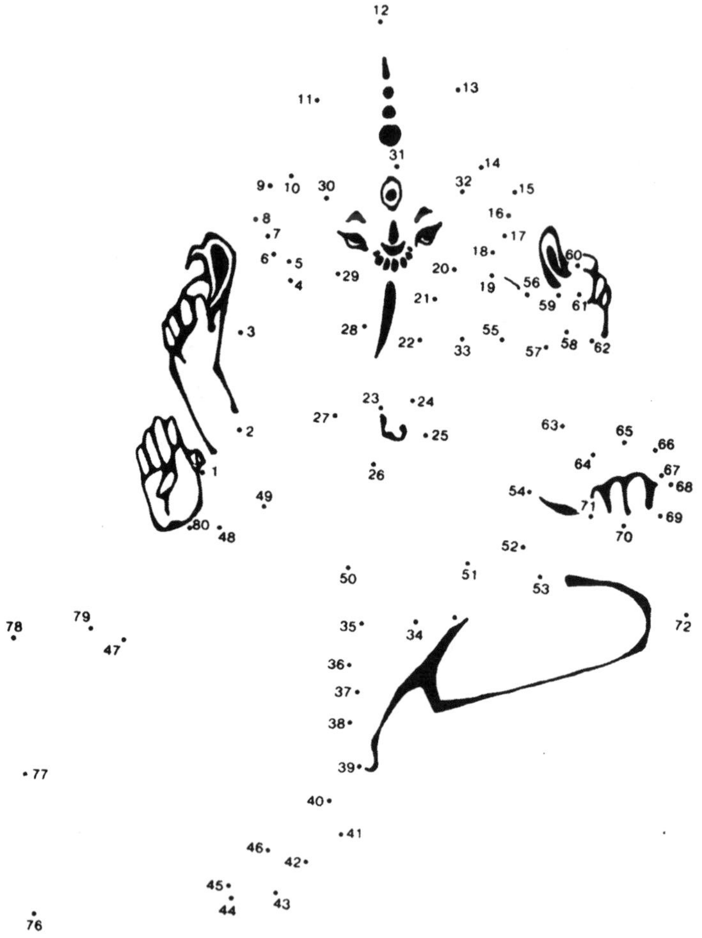

Solution for the Guardian of Bhārat

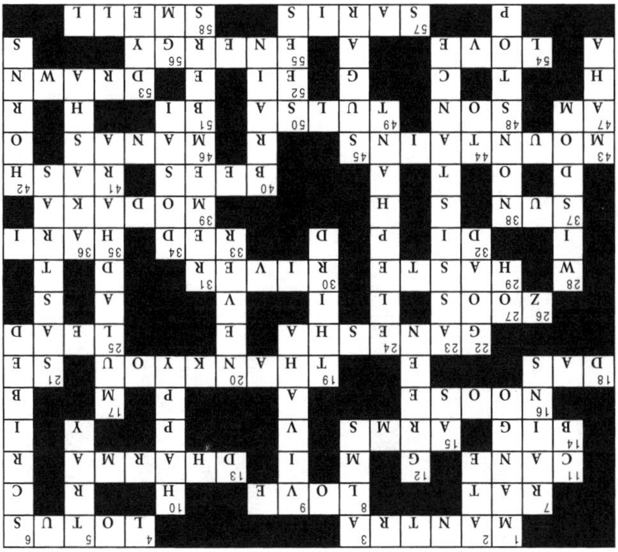

Solution for the Puzzle of Dharma

Solution for the Fruit of Truth

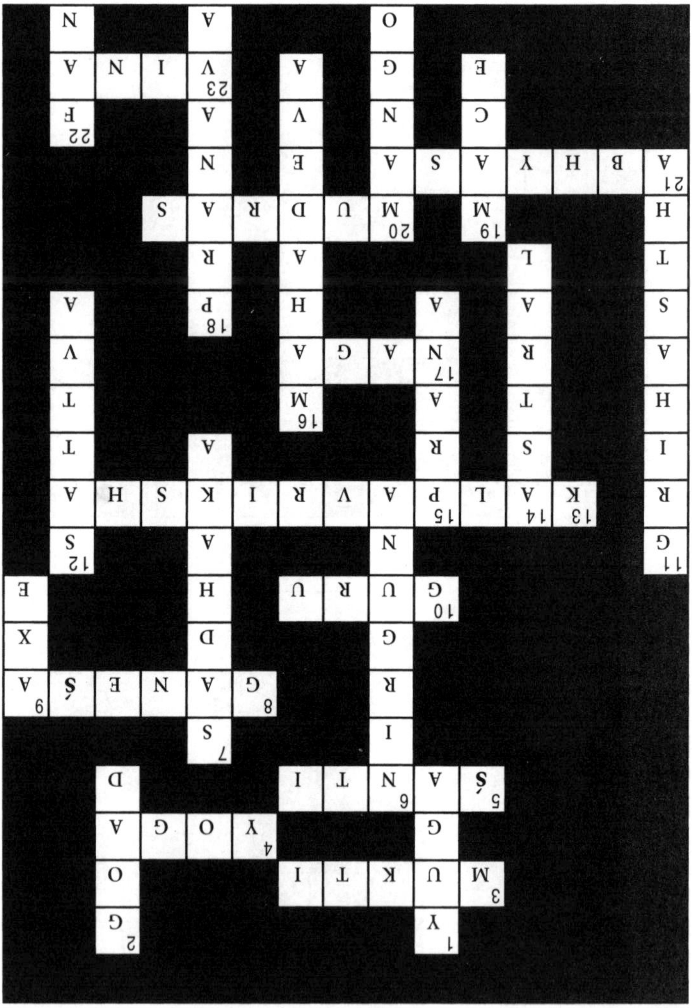

Solution for the Lord of Mysteries

Śākāhāraḥ

शाकाहारः

Vegetarianism

Vegetarianism

UNBEKNOWNST TO US WHEN WE BEGAN THIS BOOK, LOVING GAṆEŚA WAS TO EVENTUALLY INSPIRE SEVERAL CHAPTERS NOT ABOUT His noble self, but on seemingly unrelated subjects, including this chapter on vegetarianism and the one following on *āyurveda*. We were a bit surprised, but somehow it did make sense. After all, food is the source of life. But it should be live food, food with *prāṇa* in it, food direct from the earth. This is life itself for the physical body. I think that the adventures of *prāṇa* in the eating and healing arts are among His great messages. The essence of food when offered to the Gods during *pūjā* holds them close to Earth. Lord Gaṇeśa is especially attentive to diet. He above all wants His devotees to stay well by eating well. So, these two chapters on diet and health will explain exactly how this is done. Read on, be inspired and maintain good health for the natural life span of all humans, 120 years and more. Jaya Gaṇeśa. We thank You, Lord Gaṇeśa, for Your inspiration in inserting these chapters on food for health and happier, longer living.

Vegetarians come in all sizes and shapes, but the elephant is the largest of all, with a sophisticated social life, loving and affectionately caring for its own. Elephants live long, vigorous lives, have a very large brain and, of course, are renowned for their excellent memory. They do not suffer any weakness for not eating meat. In fact, so many muscular and the most intelligent animals—the horse, the cow, giraffe, zebra, rhinoceros, the apes, dolphins and more—are lifelong vegetarians and friends of men. Lean animals, thin and wiry, who are feared by man and beasts alike, are all hunters and killers and eaters of flesh—tigers, sharks, hawks, wolves and the like. Similarly, no one fears a gentle vegetarian, but all have reason to fear the unpredictable meat-eater. Scriptures admonish that it is wise to fear what should be feared.

To awaken and keep open the seven lower *chakras* below the *mūlādhāra,* which only the warrior would need to do, a nonvegetarian diet is considered by some as essential. Keeping awake the consciousness of fear, anger, jealousy, confusion, deception, covert operations of theft and extortion, malice and murder—the states of mind of these seven force centers—is made possible through living a life that takes other life to live. In fact, some Hindu *śāstras* have advised meat-eating for soldiers who necessarily perfected the arts of deception, killed without fear and through devious means conquered their foes in attainment of new lands and royal domains at the expense of the sufferings of others. They performed these deeds in fulfillment of a warrior's way—with not the least restraint of conscience. After conflicts end, the conscience and feelings of remorse naturally arise in the minds of combatants, and they find that their only solace is the worship of Lord Gaṇeśa—*śaraṇam* Gaṇeśa. At this point He lovingly exonerates their instinctive deeds and puts them on the path of *charyā,* righteous living, and they too become vegetarians, driven by the urge to perform personal discipline, *sādhana* and penance, *prāyaśchitta,* to overcome the states of mind their actions provoked, to rid themselves of the pains and pangs of war. *Āyurveda,* too, advises eating meat for certain kinds of ailments for nonvegetarian patients.

How many there are who resent the very mention of becoming a vegetarian, being instinctively repulsed by the idea, for they intuit the road ahead. They sense that once the more *sattvic* diet of pure foods are taken in place of meats (and other dead foods, packaged, processed and cellophane-wrapped) they will feel a great guilt occasioned by their transgressions of *dharma,* as they have so well perfected over the years their *adharmic* ways. *Adharma* means all that stands against Indian spirituality, against the path of the good and the pure and the natural, against *dharma* in all of its intricate dimensions.

In this chapter we will explore a fundamental principle of Sanātana Dharma: vegetarianism, the diet of ancient India, of *yogīs* and Truth seekers, of meditators and cave-dwellers, of mystics, monks and compassionate souls. You may be one or more of these and thus this chapter will be relevant, even though it is also a bit more earthly than the rest of our book. Most books on Gaṇeśa say little or nothing of this key ideal, so we allow ourselves an abundant space through the impelling grace of our loving Gaṇeśa to define, delineate, discuss and defend the concept of not eating another living being to "fatten our own flesh." Bear with us, and if you have not yet become a vegetarian, ponder the possibility. Lord Gaṇeśa is the gatekeeper and knows well the law of *dharma,* which, in its higher expressions, admits of no killing and eating of creatures' flesh. And the elephant Deity is adamant in fulfilling the *dharmic* duties of His office. The inner law is ever so simple—not eating meat, fish, foul or eggs is essential to awaken consciousness into the seven higher *chakras* (the *uttara-chakras),* up to the crown. Nonkilling—and noneating of that which is killed—is a must to pass from realms below, the *adho-chakras,* through Gaṇeśa's first *chakra* gate, the *mūlādhāra.*

Loving Gaṇeśa, the Lord of Dharma, guardian of the true perspective of human life as it should be lived for evolutionary advancement, has declared *ahiṁsā,* which includes vegetarianism, the first obligation. None of the other *dharmas—strī dharma,* the duties of women; *purusha dharma,* the duties of men; *āśrama dharma,* the responsibility of one's stage of life; *varṇa dharma,* one's position in society; and *svadharma,* one's own perfect pattern—even when performed properly will have the same results without fulfilling this virtue. Even *ṛita dharma,* cosmic order, is upset by man's insatiable, aggressive appetites expressed through flesh-consuming.

Vegetarianism, an Ancient Hindu Ethic

Vegetarianism was for thousands of years a principle of health and environmental ethics throughout India. Though Muslim and Christian colonization radically undermined and eroded this ideal, it remains to this day a cardinal ethic of Hindu thought and practice. A subtle sense of guilt persists among Hindus who eat meat, and even they will abstain at special times. There exists an ongoing controversy on this issue on which we hope this chapter will shed some light. For India's ancient thinkers, life is seen as the very stuff of the Divine, an emanation of the Source and part of a cosmic continuum. They further hold that each life form, even water and trees, possesses consciousness and energy. Nonviolence, *ahiṁsā,* the primary basis of vegetarianism, has long been central to the religious traditions of India—especially Hinduism, Buddhism and Jainism. Religion in India has consistently upheld the sanctity of life, whether human, animal or, in the case of the Jains, elemental.

The Sanskṛit for vegetarianism is *śākāhāra,* and one following a vegetarian diet is a *śākāhārī.* The term for meat-eating is *mānsāhāra,* and the meat-eater is called *mānsāhārī.* *Āhāra* means "to consume or eat," *śāka* means "vegetable," and *mānsa* means "meat or flesh." The very word *mānsa,* "meat," conveys a deep appreciation of life's sacredness and an understanding of the law of *karma* by which the consequence of each action returns to the doer. As explained in the 2,000-year-old *Manu Dharma Śāstra,* 5.55, "The learned declare that the meaning of *mānsa* (flesh) is, 'he *(sa)* will eat me *(mām)* in the other world whose flesh I eat here.' " There developed early in India an unparalleled concern for harmony among life forms, and this led to a common ethos based on noninjuriousness and a minimal consumption of natural resources—in other words, to compassion and simplicity. If *Homo sapiens* is to survive his present predicament, he will have to rediscover these two primary ethical virtues.

Is Vegetarianism Integral to Noninjury?

In my book, *Dancing with Śiva,* this question is addressed as follows: "Hindus teach vegetarianism as a way to live with a minimum of hurt to other beings, for to consume meat, fish, fowl or eggs is to participate indirectly in acts of cruelty and violence against the animal kingdom. The abhorrence of injury and killing of any kind leads quite naturally to a vegetarian diet, *śākāhāra.* The meat-eater's desire for meat drives another to kill and provide that meat. The act of the butcher begins with the desire of the consumer. Meat-eating contributes to a mentality of violence, for with the chemically complex meat ingested, one absorbs the slaughtered creature's fear, pain and terror. These qualities are nourished within the meat-eater, perpetuating the cycle of cruelty and confusion. When the individual's consciousness lifts and expands, he will abhor violence and not be able to even digest the meat, fish, fowl and eggs he was formerly consuming. India's greatest saints have confirmed that one cannot eat meat and live a peaceful, harmonious life. Man's appetite for meat inflicts devastating harm on the earth itself, stripping its precious forests to make way for pastures. The *Tirukural* candidly states, 'How can he practice true compassion who eats the flesh of an animal to fatten his own flesh? Greater than a thousand *ghee* offerings consumed in sacrificial fires is not to sacrifice and consume any living creature.' "

Amazingly, I have heard people define vegetarian as a diet which excludes the meat of animals but does permit fish and eggs. But what really is vegetarianism? Vegetarian foods include grains, fruits, vegetables, legumes and dairy products. Natural, fresh foods, locally grown without insecticides or chemical fertilizers are preferred. A vegetarian diet does not include meat, fish, fowl, shellfish or eggs. For good health, even certain vegetarian foods are minimized: frozen and canned foods, highly processed foods, such as white rice, white sugar and white flour; and "junk" foods and beverages—those with abundant chemical additives, such as artificial sweeteners, colorings, flavorings and preservatives.

In my forty years of ministry it has become quite evident that vegetarian families have far fewer problems than those who are not vegetarian. If children are raised as vegetarians, every day they are exposed to nonviolence as a principle of peace and compassion. Every day they are growing up they are remembering and being reminded to not kill. They won't even kill another creature to eat, to feed themselves. And if they won't kill another creature to feed themselves, they will be much less likely to do acts of violence against people.

Five Reasons to Be a Vegetarian

In the past fifty years millions of meat-eaters have made the personal decision to stop eating the flesh of other creatures. There are five major motivations for such a decision.

1. THE DHARMIC/SCRIPTURAL LAW REASON

Ahiṁsā, the law of noninjury, is the first duty in fulfillment of his religious obligations to God and God's creation as defined by Vedic scripture.

2. THE KARMIC CONSEQUENCES REASON

All of our actions including our choice of food have *karmic* consequences. By involving oneself in the cycle of inflicting injury, pain and death, even indirectly by eating other creatures, one must in the future experience in equal measure the suffering caused.

3. THE SPIRITUAL CONSCIOUSNESS REASON

Food is the source of the body's chemistry, and what we ingest affects our consciousness, emotions and experiential patterns. If one wants to live in higher consciousness, in peace and happiness and love for all creatures, then he cannot eat meat, fish, shellfish, fowl or eggs. By ingesting the grosser chemistries of animal foods, one introduces into the body and mind anger, jealousy, fear, anxiety, suspicion and a terrible fear of death, all of which are locked into the flesh of butchered creatures. For these reasons, *śākāhārīs* live in higher consciousness and *mānsāhārīs* abide in lower consciousness.

4. THE HEALTH REASON

Medical studies prove that a vegetarian diet is easier to digest, provides a wider range of nutrients and imposes fewer burdens and impurities on the body. Vegetarians are less susceptible to all the major diseases that afflict contemporary humanity. Thus they live longer, healthier, more productive lives. They have fewer physical complaints, less frequent visits to the doctor, fewer dental problems and smaller medical bills. Their immune system is stronger, their bodies are purer, more refined and skin more beautiful.

5. THE ECOLOGICAL REASON

Planet earth is suffering. In large measure, the escalating loss of species, destruction of ancient rain forests to create pasture lands for livestock, loss of topsoil and the consequent increase of water impurities and air pollution have all been traced to the single fact of meat in the human diet. No single decision that we can make as individuals or as a race can have such a dramatic effect on the improvement of our planetary ecology as the decision to not eat meat. Many seeking to save the planet for future generations have made this decision for this reason and this reason alone.

How to Win an Argument with a Meat-Eater

While their numbers are rapidly growing, vegetarians are still a minority, and it is not unusual to be confronted with a meat-eater who not only protects his own right to eat flesh, but argues aggressively that vegetarians should join him in his carnivorous diet. Carnivores may regard nonmeat-eaters as a strange lot who munch on "rabbit food," and whose diet doesn't have the substance to make them strong, productive human beings. The following presentation is designed to turn the tables on such discussions by showing the devastating effects of meat-eating both on individuals and on our planet. It is based on a richly informative poster entitled, "How to win an argument with a meat-eater," published by Earthsave, an organization based in Felton, California, giving facts from Pulitzer Prize nominee John Robbins' book, *Diet for a New America.* Below are nine separate arguments against meat-eating and in favor of a vegetarian diet. Remember, all that follows is based on research in the USA, where a mere 5% of the human race live. So, to get a sense of how the whole globe is affected, multiply all this by twenty!

1. THE HUNGER ARGUMENT AGAINST MEAT-EATING

Much of the world's massive hunger problems could be solved by the reduction or elimination of meat-eating. The reasons: 1) livestock pasture needs cut drastically into land which could otherwise be used to grow food; 2) vast quantities of food which could feed humans is fed to livestock raised to produce meat.

This year alone, twenty million people worldwide will die of malnutrition. One child dies of malnutrition every 2.3 seconds. One hundred million people could be adequately fed using the land freed if Americans reduced their intake of meat by a mere 10%. Twenty percent of the corn grown in the U.S. is eaten by people. Eighty percent of the corn and 95% of the oats grown in the U.S. is eaten by livestock. The percentage of protein wasted by cycling grain through livestock is calculated by experts as 90%. One acre of land can produce 40,000 pounds of potatoes, or 250 pounds of beef. Fifty-six percent of all U.S. farmland is devoted to beef production, and to produce each pound of beef requires 16 pounds of edible grain and soybeans, which could be used to feed the hungry.

2. THE ENVIRONMENTAL ARGUMENT AGAINST MEAT-EATING

Many of the world's massive environmental problems could be solved by the reduction or elimination of meat-eating, including global warming, loss of topsoil, loss of rain forests and species extinction.

The temperature of the earth is rising. This global warming, known as "the greenhouse effect," results primarily from carbon dioxide emissions from burning fossil fuels, such as oil and natural gas. Three times more fossil fuels must be burned to produce a meat-centered diet than for a meat-free diet. If people stopped eating meat, the threat of higher world temperatures would be vastly diminished.

Trees, and especially the old-growth forests, are essential to the survival of the planet. Their destruction is a major cause of global warming and top soil loss. Both of these effects lead to diminished food production. Meat-eating is the number one driving force for the destruction of these forests. Two-hundred and sixty million acres of U.S. forestland has been cleared for crop land to produce the meat-centered diet. Fifty-five square feet of tropical rain forest is consumed to produce every quarter-pound of rain forest beef. An alarming 75% of all U.S. topsoil has been lost to date. Eighty-five percent of this loss is directly related to livestock raising. Another devastating result of deforestation is the loss of plant and animal species. Each year 1,000 species are eliminated due to destruction of tropical rain forests for meat grazing and other uses. The rate is growing yearly. To keep up with U.S. consumption, 300 million pounds of meat are imported annually from Central and South America. This economic incentive impels these nations to cut down their forests to make more pasture land. The short-term gain ignores the long-term, irreparable harm to the earth's ecosystem. In effect these countries are being drained of their resources to put meat on the table of Americans while 75% of all Central American children under the age of five are undernourished.

3. THE CANCER ARGUMENT AGAINST MEAT-EATING

Those who eat flesh are far more likely to contract cancer than those following a vegetarian diet. The risk of contracting breast cancer is 3.8 times greater for women who eat meat daily compared to less than once a week; 2.8 times greater for women who eat eggs daily compared to once a week; and 3.25 greater for women who eat processed butter and cheese 2 to 4 times a week as compared to once a week. The risk of fatal ovarian cancer is three times greater for women who eat eggs 3 or more times a week as compared with less than once a week. The risk of fatal prostate cancer is 3.6 times greater for men who consume meat, eggs, processed cheese and milk daily as compared with sparingly or not at all.

4. THE CHOLESTEROL ARGUMENT AGAINST MEAT-EATING

Here are facts showing that: 1) U.S. physicians are not sufficiently trained in the importance of the relation of diet to health; 2) meat-eaters ingest excessive amounts of cholesterol, making them dangerously susceptible to heart attacks.

It is strange but true that U.S. physicians are as a rule ill-educated in the single most important factor of health, namely diet and nutrition. Of the 125 medical schools in the U.S., only 30 require their students to take a course in nutrition. The average nutrition training received by the average U.S. physician during four years in school is only 2.5 hours. Thus doctors in the U.S. are ill-equipped to advise their patients in minimizing foods, such as meat, that contain excessive amounts of cholesterol and are known causes of heart attack. Heart attack is the most common cause of death in the U.S., killing one person every 45 seconds. The male meat-eater's risk of death from heart attack is 50%. The risk to men who eat no meat is 15%. Reducing one's consumption of meat, processed dairy products and eggs by 10% reduces the risk of heart attack by 10%. Completely eliminating these products from one's diet reduces the risk of heart attack by 90%.

The average cholesterol consumption of a meat-centered diet is 210 milligrams per day. The chance of dying from heart disease if you are male and your blood cholesterol is 210 milligrams daily is greater than 50%.

5. THE NATURAL RESOURCES ARGUMENT AGAINST MEAT-EATING

The world's natural resources are being rapidly depleted as a result of meat-eating. Raising livestock for their meat is a very inefficient way of generating food. Pound for pound, far more resources must be expended to produce meat than to produce grains, fruits and vegetables. For example, more than half of all water used for all purposes in the U.S. is consumed in livestock production. The amount of water used in production of the average cow is sufficient to float a destroyer (a large naval ship). While 25 gallons of water are needed to produce a pound of wheat, 5,000 gallons are needed to produce a pound of California beef. That same 5,000 gallons of water can produce 200 pounds of wheat. If this water cost were not subsidized by the government, the cheapest hamburger meat would cost more than $35 per pound.

Meat-eating is devouring oil reserves at an alarming rate. It takes nearly 78 calories of fossil fuel (oil, natural gas, etc.) energy to produce one calorie of beef protein and only 2 calories of fossil fuel energy to produce one calorie of soybean. If every human ate a meat-centered diet, the world's known oil reserves would last a mere 13 years. They would last 260 years if humans stopped eating meat altogether. That is 20 times longer, giving humanity ample time to develop alternative energy sources.

Thirty-three percent of all raw materials (base products of farming, forestry and mining, including fossil fuels) consumed by the U.S. are devoted to the production of livestock, as compared with 2% to produce a complete vegetarian diet.

6. THE ANTIBIOTIC ARGUMENT AGAINST MEAT-EATING

Here are facts showing the dangers of eating meat because of the large amounts of antibiotics fed to livestock to control staphylococci (commonly called staph infections), which are becoming immune to these drugs at an alarming rate.

The animals that are being raised for meat in the United States are diseased. The livestock industry attempts to control this disease by feeding the animals antibiotics. Huge quantities of drugs go for this purpose. Of all antibiotics used in the U.S., 55% are fed to livestock. But this is only partially effective because the bacteria that cause disease are becoming immune to the antibiotics. The percentage of staphylococci infections resistant to penicillin, for example, has grown from 13% in 1960 to 91% in 1988. These antibiotics and-or the bacteria they are intended to destroy reside in the meat that goes to market. It is not healthy for humans to consume this meat. The response of the European Economic Community to the routine feeding of antibiotics to U.S. livestock was to ban the importation of U.S. meat. European buyers do not want to expose consumers to this serious health hazard. By comparison, U.S. meat and pharmaceutical industries gave their full and complete support to the routine feeding of antibiotics to livestock, turning a blind eye to the threat of disease to the consumer.

8. THE PESTICIDE ARGUMENT AGAINST MEAT-EATING

Unknown to most meat-eaters, U.S.-produced meat contains dangerously high quantities of deadly pesticides. The common belief is that the U.S. Department of Agriculture protects consumers' health through regular and thorough meat inspection. In reality, fewer than one out of every 250,000 slaughtered animals is tested for toxic chemical residues. That these chemicals are indeed ingested by the meat-eater is proven by the following facts:

A. Ninety-nine percent of U.S. mother's milk contains significant levels of DDT. In stark contrast, only 8% of U.S. vegetarian mother's milk contains significant levels of DDT. This shows that the primary source of DDT is the meat ingested by the mothers.

B. Contamination of breast milk due to chlorinated hydrocarbon pesticides in animal products found in meat-eating mothers versus nonmeat-eating mothers is 35 times higher.

C. The amount of the pesticide Dieldrin ingested by the average breast-fed American infant is 9 times the permissible level.

9. THE ETHICAL ARGUMENT AGAINST MEAT-EATING

Many of those who have adopted a vegetarian diet have done so because of the ethical argument, either from reading about or personally experiencing what goes on daily at any one of the thousands of slaughterhouses in the U.S. and other countries, where animals suffer the cruel process of forced confinement, manipulation and violent death. Their pain and terror is beyond calculation.

The slaughterhouse is the final stop for animals raised for their flesh. These ghastly places, while little known to most meat-eaters, process enormous numbers of animals each year. In the U.S. alone, 660,000 animals are killed for meat every hour. A surprising quantity of meat is consumed by the meat-eater. The average per capita consumption of meat in the U.S., Canada and Australia is 200 pounds per year! The average American consumes in a 72-year lifetime approximately 11 cattle, 3 lambs and sheep, 23 hogs, 45 turkeys, 1,100 chickens and 862 pounds of fish! *Bon appétite!*

People who come in contact with slaughterhouses cannot help but be affected by what they see and hear. Those living nearby must daily experience the screams of terror and anger of the animals led to slaughter. Those working inside must also see and participate in the crimes of mayhem and murder. Most who choose this line of work are not on the job for long. Of all occupations in the U.S., slaughterhouse worker has the highest turnover rate. It also has the highest rate of on-the-job injury.

Humans Have neither Fangs nor Claws

A final and most compelling argument against meat-eating is that humans are physiologically not suited for a carnivorous diet. The book *Food for the Spirit, Vegetarianism in the World Religions,* summarizes this point of view as follows. "Many nutritionists, biologists and physiologists offer convincing evidence that humans are in fact not meant to eat flesh...." The book gives seven facts in support of this view:

1. Physiologically, people are more akin to plant-eaters, foragers and grazers, such as monkeys, elephants and cows, than to carnivora such as dogs, tigers and leopards.
2. For example, carnivora do not sweat through their skin; body heat is controlled by rapid breathing and extrusion of the tongue. Vegetarian animals, on the other hand, have sweat pores for heat control and the elimination of impurities.
3. Carnivora have long teeth and claws for holding and killing prey; vegetarian animals have short teeth and no claws.
4. The saliva of carnivora contains no ptyalin and cannot predigest starches; that of vegetarian animals contains ptyalin for the predigestion of starches.
5. Flesh-eating animals secrete large quantities of hydrochloric acid to help dissolve bones; vegetarian animals secrete little hydrochloric acid.
6. The jaws of carnivora only open in an up and down motion; those of vegetarian animals also move sideways for additional kinds of chewing.
7. Carnivora must lap liquids (like a cat); vegetarian animals take liquids in by suction through the teeth.

Food for the Spirit concludes, "There are many such comparisons, and in each case humans fit the vegetarian physiognomy. From a strictly physiological perspective, then, there are strong arguments that humans are not suited to a fleshy diet."

The Health Benefits of Vegetarianism

It was only recently that smoking became recognized as a health and environmental hazard. As a result of research and education on a habit once believed to be not only harmless but stylish, most major U.S. cities have banned smoking of cigarettes, cigars or pipes in all public places. Smoking has also been outlawed in government offices and completely eliminated from all domestic U.S. air flights. Now, another, even more devastating problem—meat-eating—is under scrutiny. Its threat to personal health and the environment is based on overwhelming evidence amassed by recognized authorities over the past fifty years.

Recently a group of eminent doctors called the Physicians Committee for Responsible Medicine (PCRM), themselves members of the AMA, have gathered to change the U.S. consciousness on human nutrition, particularly among the medical community. The PCRM is a nonprofit organization based in Washington, D.C., consisting of doctors and laypersons working together for compassionate and effective medical practice, research and health promotion. Founded in 1985, the PCRM is supported by over 3,000 physicians and 50,000 laypersons. PCRM president Neal D. Barnard, M.D., is a popular speaker and the author of *The Power of Your Plate.* As stated by the PCRM in their 1991 literature:

> A vegetarian diet has been advocated by everyone from philosophers, such as Plato and Nietzsche, to political leaders, such as Benjamin Franklin and Gandhi, to modern pop icons such as Paul McCartney and Bob Marley. Science is also on the side of vegetarian foods. A multitude of studies have proven the health benefits of a vegetarian diet to be remarkable. Vegetarian is defined as avoiding all animal flesh, including fish and poultry. Vegetarians who avoid flesh, but do eat animal products such as cheese, milk and eggs are ovo-lacto-vegetarians (ovo = egg; lacto = milk, cheese, etc.). The ranks of those who eschew all animal products are rapidly growing; these people are referred to as pure vegetarians or vegans (vee'guns). Scientific research shows that ovo-lacto-vegetarians are healthier than meat-eaters, and vegans are healthier than ovo-lacto-vegetarians.

It should be noted that the Indian Hindu vegetarian tradition has always been lacto-vegetarian, permitting the consumption of milk products.

The PCRM literature lists a host of health benefits of a vegetarian diet, including the following:

1. Preventing cancer: "Numerous epidemiological and clinical studies have shown that vegetarians are nearly 50% less likely to die from cancer than nonvegetarians."
2. Preventing heart disease and lowering blood pressure.
3. Preventing and reversing diabetes.
4. Preventing and alleviating gallstones, kidney stones and osteoporosis.
5. Preventing and alleviating asthma.

The New Four Food Groups

In 1991 the Physicians Committee for Responsible Medicine submitted a proposal to change the official "four food groups" which have been promoted by U.S. nutritionists for the past 35 years. Their proposal reflects the fact that the long-held belief in meat as an essential dietary element is being displaced with new findings on the harmful effects of a meat-centered diet. The *PCRM Update*, May–June 1991, explains:

> On April 8, 1991, PCRM unveiled a proposal to replace the Four Basic Food Groups. The Four Food Groups have been part of U.S. government recommendations since 1956, but promote dietary habits which are largely responsible for the epidemics of heart disease, cancer, stroke and other serious illnesses in this country.... The old four groups were meat, dairy, grains and fruits/vegetables. The "New Four Food Groups" are grains, legumes, vegetables and fruits. Meat and dairy will lose their food group status [by this proposal]. The 'New Four Food Groups' represents a nutrition plan that is based on healthy, fiber-rich plant foods rather than the

> former emphasis on cholesterol-and-fat-laden foods. "The meat and dairy groups were the principal sources of cholesterol and saturated fat, which is the biggest culprit in raising blood cholesterol," says PCRM nutritionist Virginia Messina, M.P.H., R.D. "These foods are simply not necessary in the human diet."

Though others have made similar recommendations to revise the American diet, none have done so with quite the authority of the 3,000 physicians of the PCRM. The committee's president, Dr. Neal D. Barnard—a vegetarian—is associate director of Behavioral Studies at the Institute for Disease Prevention at George Washington University. PCRM members instrumental in formulating the new food groups include Dr. T. Colin Campbell, Professor of Nutritional Biochemistry at Cornell University and Director of the massive China Health Project. Collaborator Dr. Oliver Alabaster is director of the Institute for Disease Prevention at the George Washington University Medical Center. The PCRM attacks the traditional four food groups on three major fronts:

1. "The old four food groups fail to assure nutrient adequacy." It is well known that the old food groups were established according to the 1953 understanding of nutrition. Since that time, the recommended daily allowances (RDA's) for protein, vitamins, minerals, etc., have been extensively revised and expanded. A 1978 study showed that only 9 of the 17 RDA's were met by the typical diet based on the old groups.
2. "The old four food groups fail to adequately address the current dietary problems of our population." The 1977-78 Nationwide Food Consumption Survey "indicates that Americans who eat diets based on the four food groups consume an excessive amount of fat."
3. "The old four food groups serve to misinform consumers about some aspects of nutrition. Two of the

> four food groups—meats and dairy products—are clearly not necessary for health and, in fact, may be detrimental to health.... Populations with the lowest rates of heart disease, colon and breast cancer and obesity consume very little meat or no meat at all."

How did the U.S. end up with such a poor choice of food groups 35 years ago? Inadequate nutritional research, for one thing. But more insidiously, since food guides were first established in 1916, there has been an economically motivated tendency to give animal products a preferred designation. Says a PCRM report: "This element of food guides has persisted until the present time due in part to the intensive lobbying efforts of the food industry, and despite evidence of the adverse health effects of such foods." The situation is similar to the tobacco industry's continued denial of the known harmful effects of smoking. A PCRM poster offers the following description of the four New Food Groups.

1. **WHOLE GRAINS** includes breads, pastas, rice, corn and all other grains. Note the emphasis on whole grains rather than refined grains. Build each of your meals around a hearty grain dish—grains are rich in fiber and other complex carbohydrates, as well as protein, B vitamins and zinc.
2. **VEGETABLES** are packed with nutrients; they provide vitamin C, beta-carotene, riboflavin and other vitamins, iron, calcium and fiber. Dark green, leafy vegetables such as broccoli, collards, kale, mustard and turnip greens, chicory or bok choy are especially good sources of these important nutrients. Dark yellow and orange vegetables such as carrots, winter squash, sweet potatoes and pumpkin provide extra beta-carotene. Include generous portions of a variety of vegetables in your diet.

3. **LEGUMES,** another name for beans, peas and lentils, are all good sources of fiber, protein, iron, calcium, zinc and B vitamins. This group also includes chickpeas, baked and refried beans, soy milk, tofu, tempeh and texturized vegetable protein.
4. **FRUITS** are rich in fiber, vitamin C and beta-carotene. Be sure to include at least one serving each day of fruits that are high in vitamin C—citrus fruits, melons and strawberries are all good choices. Choose whole fruit over fruit juices, which don't contain as much healthy fiber.

Common Dietary Concerns

Those considering a vegetarian diet generally worry about getting enough nutrients, since the belief that meat is a necessary part of keeping strong and healthy is still extremely widespread. Armed with decades of nutritional research data, the PCRM addresses this issue head-on:

> The fact is, it is very easy to have a well-balanced diet with vegetarian foods. Vegetarian foods provide plenty of protein. Careful combining of foods is not necessary. Any normal variety of plant foods provides more than enough protein for the body's needs. Although there is somewhat less protein in a vegetarian diet than a meat-eater's diet, this is actually an advantage. Excess protein has been linked to kidney stones, osteoporosis, and possibly heart disease and some cancers. A diet focused on beans, whole grains and vegetables contains adequate amounts of protein without the 'overdose' most meat-eaters get.

Other concerns are allayed by the PCRM as follows:

1. **CALCIUM** is easy to find in a vegetarian diet. Many dark, green leafy vegetables and beans are loaded with calcium, and some orange juices and cereals are calcium-fortified. Iron is plentiful in whole grains, beans and fruits.
2. **VITAMIN B12:** There is a misconception that without eating meat one cannot obtain sufficient vitamin B_{12}, which is an essential nutrient. This is simply not true. The PCRM advises: "Although cases of B_{12} deficiency are very uncommon, it is important to make sure that one has a reliable source of the vitamin. Good sources include all common multiple vitamins (including vegetarian vitamins), fortified cereals and fortified soy milk."
3. **DURING PREGNANCY** one's nutritional needs increase. The American Dietetic Association has found vegan diets adequate for fulfilling nutritional needs during pregnancy, but pregnant women and nursing mothers should supplement their diets with vitamins B_{12} and D.
4. **VEGETARIAN CHILDREN** also have high nutritional needs, but these, too, are met within a vegetarian diet. A vegetarian menu is "life-extending." As young children, vegetarians may grow more gradually, reach puberty somewhat later, and live substantially longer than do meat-eaters. Do be sure to include a reliable source of vitamin B_{12}. Besides the fortified cereals and soymilk mentioned above, vitamin B_{12} sources that are widely available are multiple vitamins, brewers yeast and other potent dietary supplements.

Those interested in supporting or learning more about the work of the Physicians Committee for Responsible Medicine should write to PCRM, P.O. Box 6322, Washington, D.C., 20015, USA.

Surviving in a Flesh-Eater's World

In Singapore, Malaysia, China and Taiwan, Sri Lanka and India, you can track down vegetarian restaurants by following your nose. There are abundant opportunities for Indian and Oriental fare with plenty of variety. In Europe and North America, however, vegetarian restaurants are still somewhat rare. But according to a new Gallop Poll, a startling one-third of American diners are patronizing fine restaurants that offer vegetarian entrees. The National Restaurant Association (NRA) is advising its members to feature a few vegetarian main-dish items on their menus, NRA president John Farquharson told HINDUISM TODAY. The NRA —spurred on by a rapidly growing vegetarian and healthy-eating market—commissioned the Gallop Poll study of the public's taste for nonmeat fare. The study revealed the following:

1. Thirty-three percent of Americans who dine out will order vegetarian entrees if they appear on the menu.
2. Twenty percent of diners polled said they choose where to dine based on the availability of vegetarian dishes.
3. Eighty-eight percent of those who avoid meat do so as part of an overall fitness diet.

According to a survey done at Disney World in Florida, about 3% of Americans are complete vegetarians and a higher percentage are semi-vegetarians. *Vegetarian Times* research puts the number at 10%, just under the percentage in Great Britain. Numbers continue to rise with no sign of abatement as medical, health care, independent research and consumer groups line up to endorse vegetable-based diets.

Where Do We Eat?

Charles Stahler of the Vegetarian Resources Group told HINDUISM TODAY, "Vegetable courses are popping up in every type of restaurant. Even truck stops have salad bars." White tablecloth restaurants like The Trellis in Williamsburg, Virginia, tantalize diners with entrees like Yukon Gold potatoes with asparagus, plum tomatoes and local greens in vinegarette, or braised green lentils with smoked tomatoes, grilled eggplant and saffron pasta.

Here are some practical tips on dining out:

1. The truth is that vegetarians can travel freely through the world in any country and eat better than meat-eaters, be healthier and live longer.
2. Every time you say "I am a vegetarian. Can you please help me with this menu?" you are promoting the new four food groups and spreading the vegetarian message of a healthier, happier, holier future for all mankind.

3. Indian restaurants, located in most major cities, are often the best source of quality vegetarian meals.
4. Many Chinese restaurants are good choices, though successfully avoiding meat-based sauces and eggs mixed in with the rice often requires careful instruction and developing a rapport with the management.
5. Most pizza shops offer delicious vegetarian options. Strict vegetarians should inquire whether the cheeses used were made with animal rennet. Pizza can also be ordered without cheese. Most pizza shops have salad bars as well, at very low prices.
6. Salad bars at hotels or franchise chains like Sizzler's can offer fulfilling meals at a good price.

7. Recently even McDonald's and Burger King have introduced veggie burgers in a few of their fast-food outlets, as well as fresh green salads. They say they will introduce veggie choices more widely if the response is good. McDonald's has reportedly stopped using animal fats to cook french fries.
8. All through Asia there are many strictly vegetarian Chinese restaurants. To make meat-eaters feel at home, they create fish and various meat dishes out of vegetables. They have developed this to an art form.
9. Japan is probably one of the most difficult places to survive as a vegetarian. Prices are very high, and veggie options are scarce. There are occasional health food stores, and of course fruit and vegetables are available from the market—where you can buy that $4.95 apple! You may want to stock up before you arrive on seeds, nuts and dried fruit. At mealtime, order what you can and supplement the meal with these staples. Even here, however, there are Indian restaurants in the major cities, and, of course, McDonald's.
10. In Paris you can always order a bougatiere, the potato and vegetable garnish that usually goes with meat but which chefs will prepare separately when asked. Order yours cooked in butter or vegetable oil with a little wild rice on the side. It's delicious, fulfilling and with a little french bread on the side it's all you can eat.
11. Healthfood restaurants, or healthfood stores with delis, specializing in full, delicious vegetarian meals are becoming more and more common.
12. In restaurants apparently barren of vegetarian food, choices include a baked potato, rice or pasta with one or two side orders of vegetables and a tossed green salad, and a side order of cottage cheese and olives. Be wary of the soup. They may call it vegetable, but it's probably meat or chicken-based. It's best to ask.

13. The Seventh Day Adventists, an international Protestant Christian denomination, are all vegetarians and have developed a whole industry of Loma Linda vegetarian food products specially designed to fit into the meat-eating world. So, if you are having a picnic for your boss and can't think of other options, you can serve veggie hot dogs, hamburgers and other "meat dishes" that will satisfy the meat-eaters, just as do the Chinese chefs who create simulated meat dishes in their restaurants.
14. When making meal reservations for a restaurant, airplane flight or special reception or banquet, state clearly that you are a vegetarian, either a full vegan (no-eggs or dairy products) or lacto vegetarian (includes dairy) or ovo-lacto vegetarian (includes eggs and dairy). Ask what can be served as a delicious meal and what the cost will be. Especially if you are bringing a large group, this is the time to bargain for a good price, since the cost of vegetables is less than meat.
15. When dining in a restaurant without prior reservations, make it clear to the waiter that you are a vegetarian and ask what he or she recommends. If he has a bright, shiny face, he may be a vegetarian himself. Waiters all over the world are used to having this question asked of them, and they will immediately point out ala carte options or full entrees and may personally work out an excellent lunch or dinner for you and your party. Tip your waiter well and you will gain a friend you can rely on during your next visit.
16. Knowledgeable diners bring their own favorite *garam masalas* in 35 mm film cases, just in case, to make any meal more digestible and enjoyable.

Hidden Meat Products

Many foods contain products derived from the killing of animals. Such ingredients include the following. Quoted definitions are from *Webster's Dictionary.*

1. **GELATIN:** "a tasteless, odorless, brittle mixture of proteins extracted by boiling skin, bones, horns, etc. If dissolved in hot water, forming a jelly-like substance, when cooled is used in the preparation of foods, photographic film, etc."
2. **RENNET:** "The membrane lining of the stomach of an unweaned animal, especially the fourth stomach of a calf: an extract of this membrane or of the stomach contents containing rennin, a coagulating enzyme, and used to curdle milk as in making cheese or junket."
3. **CANE SUGAR** is produced by filtering it through bones.

Dining 35,000 Feet Above the Earth

Every major airline in the world now serves vegetarian meals on every flight. But here are some facts and fallacies that vegetarian travelers should be wary of. Order your vegetarian meal when you make your reservation. Be sure to confirm your meal just before your flight, because your first request may not have made it into the computer. A wide variety of veggie options are available in the sophisticated airline menus these days, unlike the old days when the choices were either meat or vegetarian. Each airline has its own list, which regular travelers will want to explore. In general the choices are:

1. **VEGETARIAN MEAL:** This is a broad category, meaning at least that no meat will be served. If you wish to exclude eggs or dairy, be sure to give special instructions to the airline. To be totally clear, it is best to specify what you do want and what you don't want.
2. **HINDU MEAL:** Some airlines, though not all, offer a "Hindu meal." This is often but not necessarily vegetarian,

and includes curried meat and chicken dishes. Be sure to inquire before selecting this option.

3. **HINDU VEGETARIAN:** This should be a really nice meal, generally rice and one curry, chutney and a sweet, especially on airlines accustomed to serving the sophisticated Hindu traveler. Such airlines are Singapore Airlines, Malaysian Airlines, Air India, United Airlines and a few others.
4. **ASIAN VEGETARIAN MEAL:** This choice will usually include curried vegetables, rice and, if one is fortunate, chutneys and Indian sweets, and Indonesian or Oriental delicacies. It is good to verify with the airline what you may expect to receive.
5. **OVO-LACTO VEGETARIAN MEAL:** This choice will tend toward the Western vegetarian diet—e.g., casserole, pasta, cheese sandwich or omelette, with potatoes, steamed vegetable, simple salad, milk, apple and a bread roll. This and other menus may include jello which, unbeknownst to many vegetarians, is created from gelatin derived from animal products.
6. **LACTO-VEGETARIAN:** This will be similar to the above but without eggs. Strict lacto-vegetarians will not eat most bread, and other bakery products, which are generally made with eggs, and may choose not to eat these items or to ask that they not be included in their meal.
7. **FRUIT PLATE OR FRUIT PLATE WITH CHEESE:** This is the choice of many modern travelers—grapes, melon, apples, cheese, crackers, etc. As no cooking is required, the portions are usually generous. Fruit's high liquid content and digestibility makes it ideal for travel, cutting down on jet lag and the fatigue of long-distance travel. Be careful of the cheese. You may want to bring your own purely vegetarian brand made with vegetable rennet.
8. **SNACKS:** Be sure to accept the snack nuts when they are offered, peanuts, cashews, almonds, and you can always ask for an extra package if you wish. Fruit and vegetable

juices and milk are also usually available for free throughout the flight.

9. **GOODIES FROM HOME:** Seasoned travelers often carry an emergency supply of items brought from home or purchased before the flight—nuts, seeds and dried fruits, etc., even a special meal packed at home by a loving member of the family.

If Your Meal Is Forgotten

If for some reason your vegetarian meal is forgotten (which it is about 20% of the time), do not despair. All is not lost. Tell the stewardess, and ask her politely to pull something together, which she will do from some of the extra meals in the pantry. Explain that you will be happy with a little fruit, salad, etc. Having been trained to be really cooperative, she has the option to gather some vegetables, cheeses, breads, etc., from the first-class kitchen to make you a fine meal. Be sure to thank her and tell her to thank the staff for their extra efforts. Your appreciation will help the next veggie whose meal is overlooked. In addition to praising the stewardess for pulling your meal together, also make a formal written complaint during or after your flight. Most airlines have forms for this purpose. Headquarters appreciates hearing of how they can improve, so don't be shy. They also want to know how their catering service is performing, which in most cases is at fault for neglecting your vegetarian meal if you have confirmed your request before your flight.

Include with the form a letter explaining that vegetarians are as hungry as everyone else and you hope the airline will be more careful in the future in seeing to their needs. Such letters can also be written when your meal was not forgotten, but the vegetarian plate was not so good. We have on occasion written such letters to help airlines and restaurants improve the vegetarian fare. To provide a sample, we include here a well-composed letter to a classy restaurant on Kauai.

A Sample Complaint Letter

Chef Bob Grave
INN ON THE CLIFFS,
WESTIN KAUAI
Kalapaki Beach
Lihue, Kauai 96766

Aloha, Mr. Grave:
I wonder if you could take a moment and help us with a continuing predicament? We have enjoyed bringing our guests from Asia and the Mainland to Inn on the Cliffs. As you know, our Hindu and Buddhist visitors to Kauai do not eat meat, fish or eggs. We appreciate your efforts to provide them with a quality vegetarian cuisine. The dinner we had with a friend and Tokyo-based entrepreneur two months back was superior. He claimed it was among the finest out-of-home dinners he has had—quite a compliment coming from a lifetime vegetarian who has eaten in fine restaurants on every continent.

More recently, however, we brought a family who was on Kauai for a week from Alberta, Canada. This was for lunch. We had not called ahead this time, because your staff handled a spontaneous lunch for our eight-member editorial staff one month back and it was great. So when this party went for lunch our expectations were somewhat shattered by the results. Unfortunately, I was not at that meal, for perhaps our earlier choices could have been discussed with the waiter or yourself and all would have gone better.

Our concern is not for the past, but the future. We will have hundreds of pilgrims and guests in the years ahead. Our stewards prefer to work with one restaurant for these special outings, and the INN has been chosen (we used to do the same thing at the Golden Cape for about fifteen years). I hope you will continue to work with us to create an enjoyable eating experience for these special persons. Toward that end, allow me to share with you the original letter sent to John Gilbert. I do this because I understand he is no longer with Westin Kauai and this information may be useful to you. Here, then, is my letter to him:

Aloha, Mr. Gilbert:
We are a Hindu church and monastery on Kauai, secluded in the Wailua River valley. Since we have the only Hindu temple in the state, several hundred people come to Kauai each year. Many of them are vegetarians. Nor are they ordinary tourists, but heads of government, academics, professionals in medicine and engineering. Last year the Governor's and mayor's offices helped us greet and host a renowned politician and Mahārāja of Kashmir, a lifetime vegetarian. Last night we ate dinner for the first time at Prince Bill's, with guests who had traveled far. For 20 years we have enjoyed bringing our island guests to the Golden Cape, where a truly fine vegetarian meal was available.

So, when our dinners came to the table last night, we were stunned. Basically, we received the garnish and potatoes that go with a fish or meat dinner, minus the entree. It was beautifully arranged, but so meager that our guests did not enjoy the evening. Their discomfort was shared by Mike, our kind but helpless waiter. Believe me, you would have been amazed at the portions served—the superb potatoes in the small crock constituted about 80% of the meal!

May we suggest that at least one of the Westin restaurants confront the vegetarian issue (4% of the American population are vegetarians—that's over nine million people). We want to bring our guests there in the years ahead, and to know they will enjoy a hearty meal. They don't even mind if it costs the same as fresh fish or steak. Vegetarians are healthy folks, with normal appetites. Please do something to make them feel at home at the Westin. You have some of the world's great chefs there, and they will know exactly what to do.

We will continue to phone ahead for all dinner reservations, giving you plenty of time to make arrangements. For lunches, we hope this will not be necessary. Your thoughts on the above will be most appreciated. Mahalo nui loa, Chef Graves, for taking the time to work out a long-term plan!

Yours in peace,

SAIVA SIDDHANTA CHURCH
Rev. Sivasiva Palaniswami

Hindus Were the First Vegetarians

Food for the Spirit, Vegetarianism and the World Religions, observes:

> Despite popular knowledge of meat-eating's adverse effects, the nonvegetarian diet became increasingly widespread among Hindus after the two major invasions by foreign powers, first the Muslims and later the British. With them came the desire to be "civilized," to eat as did the *saheeb.* Those actually trained in Vedic knowledge, however, never adopted a meat-oriented diet, and the pious Hindu still observes vegetarian principles as a matter of religious duty.
>
> That vegetarianism has always been widespread in India is clear from the earliest Vedic texts. This was observed by the ancient traveler Megasthenes and also by Fa-hsien, a Chinese Buddhist monk who, in the fifth century, traveled to India in order to obtain authentic copies of the scriptures. These scriptures unambiguously support the meatless way of life. In the *Mahābhārata,* for instance, the great warrior Bhishma explains to Yudhishṭira, eldest of the Pāṇḍava princes, that the meat of animals is like the flesh of one's own son, and that the

foolish person who eats meat must be considered the vilest of human beings [Anu. 114.11]. The eating of "dirty" food, it warns, is not as terrible as the eating of flesh [Śānti. 141.88] (it must be remembered that the *Brāhmaṇas* of ancient India exalted cleanliness to a divine principle).

Similarly, the *Manusmṛiti* declares that one should "refrain from eating all kinds of meat," for such eating involves killing and leads to karmic bondage *(bandha)* [5.49]. Elsewhere in the Vedic literature, the last of the great Vedic kings, Mahārāja Parikshit, is quoted as saying that "only the animal-killer cannot relish the message of the Absolute Truth *[Śrīmad Bhagavatam* 10.1.4].

Scriptures Against Killing and Meat-Eating

Scriptures of all Hindu denominations speak clearly and forcefully on nonkilling and vegetarianism. In the ancient *Ṛig Veda,* we read: "O vegetable, be succulent, wholesome, strengthening; and thus, body, be fully grown." The *Yajur Veda* summarily dictates: "Do not injure the beings living on the earth, in the air and in the water." The beautiful *Tirukural,* a widely-read 2,000-year-old masterpiece of ethics, speaks of conscience: "When a man realizes that meat is the butchered flesh of another creature, he must abstain from eating it." The *Manu Saṁhitā* advises: "Having well considered the origin of flesh and the cruelty of fettering and slaying of corporeal beings, let one entirely abstain from eating flesh." In the *yoga*-infused verses of the *Tirumantiram,* warning is given of how meat-eating holds the mind in gross, *adharmic* states: "The ignoble ones who eat flesh, death's agents bind them fast and push them quick into the fiery jaws of hell (Naraka, lower consciousness)." The roots of noninjury, nonkilling and nonconsumption of meat are found in the *Vedas, Dharma Śāstras, Tirumurai, Yoga Sūtras* and dozens of other sacred texts of Hinduism. Here is a select collection.

Vedas, Hindu Revealed Scriptures

United your resolve, united your hearts,
may your spirits be at one, that you may long
together dwell in unity and concord.

Ṛig Veda Saṁhitā 10.191.4 *VE,* 854

Protect both our species, two-legged and four-legged. Both food and water for their needs supply. May they with us increase in stature and strength. Save us from hurt all our days, O Powers!

Ṛig Veda Saṁhitā 10.37.11. *VE,* 319

One who partakes of human flesh, the flesh of a horse or of another animal, and deprives others of milk by slaughtering cows, O King, if such a fiend does not desist by other means, then you should not hesitate to cut off his head.

Ṛig Veda Saṁhitā 10.87.16, *FS,* 90

Peaceful be the earth, peaceful the ether, peaceful heaven, peaceful the waters, peaceful the herbs, peaceful the trees. May all Gods bring me peace. May there be peace through these invocations of peace. With these invocations of peace which appease everything, I render peaceful whatever here is terrible, whatever here is cruel, whatever here is sinful. Let it become auspicious, let everything be beneficial to us.

Atharva Veda Saṁhitā 10.191.4

Those noble souls who practice meditation and other yogic ways, who are ever careful about all beings, who protect all animals, are the ones who are actually serious about spiritual practices.

Atharva Veda Saṁhitā 19.48.5. *FS,* 90

If we have injured space, the earth or heaven,
or if we have offended mother or father, from that
may Agni, fire of the house, absolve us and guide us
safely to the world of goodness.

Atharva Veda Saṁhitā 6.120.1. *VE*, 636

You must not use your God-given body for
killing God's creatures, whether they are human,
animal or whatever.

Yajur Veda Saṁhitā 12.32. *FS*, 90

onviolence is all the offerings. Renunciation
is the priestly honorarium. The final purification is
death. Thus all the Divinities are established in this
body.

Kṛishṇa Yajur Veda, Prāṇāgnihotra Upanishad 46-8. *VE*, 413-14

To the heavens be peace, to the sky and the
earth; to the waters be peace, to plants and all trees;
to the Gods be peace, to Brahman be peace, to all
men be peace, again and again—peace also to me! O
earthen vessel, strengthen me. May all beings regard
me with friendly eyes! May I look upon all creatures
with friendly eyes! With a friend's eye may we regard
each other!

Śukla Yajur Veda Saṁhitā 36.17-18. *VE*, 306; 342

Ahiṁsā *is not causing pain to any living being at*
any time through the actions of one's mind, speech
or body.

Atharva Veda, Śaṇḍilya Upanishad

The *Mahābhārata* and *Bhagavad Gītā,* Epic History

The very name of the cows is aghnya, *indicating that they should never be slaughtered. Who, then could slay them? Surely, one who kills a cow or a bull commits the most heinous crime.*

Mahābhārata, Śāntiparva 262.47. *FS,* 94

The purchaser of flesh performs hiṁsā *(violence) by his wealth; he who eats flesh does so by enjoying its taste; the killer does* hiṁsā *by actually tying and killing the animal. Thus, there are three forms of killing: he who brings flesh or sends for it, he who cuts off the limbs of an animal, and he who purchases, sells or cooks flesh and eats it —all of these are to be considered meat-eaters.*

Mahābhārata, Anu. 115.40. *FS,* 90

He who desires to augment his own flesh by eating the flesh of other creatures lives in misery in whatever species he may take his birth.

Mahābhārata, Anu. 115.47. *FS,* 90

One should never do that to another which one regards as injurious to one's own self. This, in brief, is the rule of dharma. *Yielding to desire and acting differently, one becomes guilty of* adharma.

Mahābhārata 18.113.8.

Those high-souled persons who desire beauty, faultlessness of limbs, long life, understanding, mental and physical strength and memory should abstain from acts of injury.

Mahābhārata 18.115.8.

Ahiṁsā *is the highest* dharma.
Ahiṁsā *is the best* tapas. Ahiṁsā *is the greatest gift.* Ahiṁsā *is the highest self-control.* Ahiṁsā *is the highest sacrifice.* Ahiṁsā *is the highest power.* Ahiṁsā *is the highest friend.* Ahiṁsā *is the highest truth.* Ahiṁsā *is the highest teaching.*

Mahābhārata 18.116.37-41.

He who sees that the Lord of all is ever the same in all that is—immortal in the field of mortality—he sees the truth. And when a man sees that the God in himself is the same God in all that is, he hurts not himself by hurting others. Then he goes, indeed, to the highest path.

Bhagavad Gītā 13.27-28. *BgM*, 101

Nonviolence, truth, freedom from anger, renunciation, serenity, aversion to fault-finding, sympathy for all beings, peace from greedy cravings, gentleness, modesty, steadiness, energy, forgiveness, fortitude, purity, a good will, freedom from pride—these belong to a man who is born for heaven.

Bhagavad Gītā 16.2-3. *BgM*, 109

Tirumantiram and other Scriptures

Many are the lovely flowers of worship offered to the guru, *but none lovelier than non-killing. Respect for life is the highest worship, the bright lamp, the sweet garland and unwavering devotion.*

Tirumantiram 197

*Spiritual merit and sin are our own making.
The killer of other lives is an outcast. Match your words with your conduct. Steal not, kill not, indulge not in self-praise, condemn not others to their face.*

Liṅgāyat Vachanas

When mindstuff is firmly based in waves of ahiṁsā, *all living beings cease their enmity in the presence of such a person.*

Yoga Sūtras 2.35. *YP,* 205

Those who are ignorant of real dharma *and, though wicked and haughty, account themselves virtuous, kill animals without any feeling of remorse or fear of punishment. Further, in their next lives, such sinful persons will be eaten by the same creatures they have killed in this world.*

Śrīmad Bhagavatam 11.5.4. *FS,* 90

The Tirukural, Preeminent Ethical Scripture

Perhaps nowhere is the principle of nonmeat-eating so fully and eloquently expressed as in the *Tirukural,* written in the Tamil language by a simple weaver saint in a village near Madras over 2,000 years ago. Considered the world's greatest ethical scripture, it is sworn on in South Indian courts of law. The verses here are from our own translation, assembled in a volume entitled *The Weaver.*

> *It is the principle of the pure in heart never to injure others, even when they themselves have been hatefully injured. What is virtuous conduct? It is never destroying life, for killing leads to every other sin (312, 321).*

> *Harming others, even enemies who harmed you unprovoked, assures incessant sorrow. The supreme principle is this: never knowingly harm any one at any time in any way (313, 317).*

> *What is the good way? It is the path that reflects on how it may avoid killing any living creature. Refrain from taking precious life from any living being, even to save your own life (324, 327).*

> *Worthless are those who injure others vengefully while those who stoically endure are like stored gold. Let him who wishes to be free from affliction's pain avoid inflicting harm on others (155, 206).*

> *How can he practice true compassion who eats the flesh of an animal to fatten his own flesh (251)?*

Riches cannot be found in the hands of the thriftless.
Nor can compassion be found in the hearts of those
who eat meat (252).

Goodness is never one with the minds of
these two: one who wields a weapon and one who
feasts on a creature's flesh (253).

If you ask, "What is kindness and
what is unkind?" it is not killing and killing.
Thus, eating flesh is never virtuous (254).

Life is perpetuated by not eating meat.
The clenched jaws of hell hold those who do (255).

If the world did not purchase and consume meat,
there would be none to slaughter and
offer meat for sale (256).

When a man realizes that meat is
the butchered flesh of another creature, he must
abstain from eating it (257).

Perceptive souls who have abandoned passion
will not feed on flesh abandoned by life (258).

Greater than a thousand ghee *offerings*
consumed in sacrificial fires is to not sacrifice and
consume any living creature (259).

All that lives will press palms together in
prayerful adoration of those who refuse to slaughter
and savor meat (260).

Hindu Religious Leaders Speak on Noninjury

The greatness of a nation and its moral progress can be measured by the way in which its animals are treated.

Mahātma Gāndhi

As long as human society continues to allow cows to be regularly killed in slaughterhouses, there cannot be any question of peace and prosperity.

A.C. Bhaktivedānta Swāmī Prabhupāda

Refrain from killing knowingly even the trifling insects like a louse, a bug or a mosquito. Use no violence even to gain possession of a woman, wealth or kingdom. Never kill any animals even for the purpose of sacrifice. Nonviolence is the greatest of all religions.

Swāmī Sahajānand, Divine Life Society

O lover of meditation, become pure and clean. Observe nonviolence in mind, speech and body. Never break another's heart. Avoid wounding another's feelings. Harm no one. Help all. Neither be afraid nor frighten others.

Swāmī Muktānanda

Someone who believes in violence and continues causing injury to others can never be peaceful himself.

Swāmī Satchidānanda

To be free from violence is the duty of every man. No thought of revenge, hatred or ill will should arise in our minds. Injuring others gives rise to hatred.

Swāmī Śivanānda

The Hindu sage who sees the whole of life... if he does not fight, it is not because he rejects all fighting as futile, but because he has finished his fights. He has overcome all dissensions between himself and the world and is now at rest.... We shall have wars and soldiers so long as the brute in us is untamed.

Dr. S. Rādhākṛishṇan

By ahiṁsā, *Patañjali meant the removal of the desire to kill. All forms of life have an equal right to the air of* māyā. *The saint who uncovers the secret of creation will be in harmony with Nature's countless bewildering expressions. All men may understand this truth by overcoming the passion for destruction.*

Śrī Yukteswar to Paramahansa Yogānanda

If you plant eggplant, you can pluck eggplants. If you sow goodness, you can reap goodness. If you sow evil, you will reap evil. Do good to all. God is there, within you. Don't kill. Don't harbor anger.

Sage Yogaswāmī

The test of ahiṁsā *is the absence of jealousy. The man whose heart never cherishes even the thought of injury to anyone, who rejoices at the prosperity of even his greatest enemy, that man is the* bhakta, *he is the* yogī, *he is the* guru *of all.*

Swāmī Vivekānanda

Strictly speaking, no activity and no industry is possible without a certain amount of violence, no matter how little. Even the very process of living is impossible without a certain amount of violence.

What we have to do is to minimize it to the greatest extent possible.

Mahātma Gāndhi, My Socialism, 34-35.

You do not like to suffer yourself.
How can you inflict suffering on others? Every killing is a suicide. The eternal, blissful and natural state has been smothered by this life of ignorance. In this way the present life is due to the killing of the eternal, pristine Being. Is it not a case of suicide?

Rāmana Maharshi, June 1935

BIBLIOGRAPHY

BgM: Juan Mascaro, *The Bhagavad Gita* (Baltimore, Penguin Books, 1966).

VE: Raimond Panikkar, *The Vedic Experience* (New Delhi, Motilal Banarsidass, 1989).

RM: Arthur Osborne, ed., *The Collected Works of Ramana Maharshi* (London, Rider, 1959).

YP: Rammurti S. Mishra, *The Textbook of Yoga Psychology* (New York, Julian Press, 1963).

TW: Tiruvalluvar, *Tirukural: The Weaver* (English translation by Himalayan Academy, Kapaa, Hawaii, USA).

FS: Steven Rosen, *Food for the Spirit, Vegetarianism and the World Religions* (New York, 1990). Bala Books Inc. 74 Old Westbury Road, Old Westbury, N.Y, 11568

John Robbins, *Diet For a New America* (Walpole, New Hampshire, 1987). Stillpoint Publishing, Box 640, Walpole, NH 03608

Conclusion

Modern meats are killed by chemical treatment of the animals, the hormones of fear and chemistry of death before and during slaughter, killed again by refrigerating them, killed again by grinding them, killed again by preserving them, killed again by packaging them, killed again by freezing them, killed again by storing and shipping them, and finally really killed by cooking them to death. How can such so-called food nourish a human being? Loving Gaṇeśa would never touch it. Why should we ever think of eating meat, fish, foul, eggs, anything with eyes or, as some say, with two or more senses. Hindus who are nonvegetarians are not up to the standard of Loving Gaṇeśa's expectations. But He nevertheless helps them through their fears and angers, toils and troubles and confused states of mind, while listening to the cries and screams, and feeling the heartaches, of beloved creatures suffering because of man's insensitive appetites. The cock-a-doodle-doo who wakes us up in the morning is dinner on the table at night. How gruesome. How ruthless to thus forever close the eyes of an animal, or have someone else do it for them in order that they may buy the carcass, closing their eyes to the fact, which is even worse, and keeping their own eyes closed to that creature's suffering to consume it without conscience during jovial small talk over the dinner table. How easy in turn for such a person to turn and maim or kill a fellow human in the same way in times of stress as a natural reaction, in "justifiable righteousness." As the *Ṛig Veda* (10.87.16) proclaims: "One who partakes of human flesh, the flesh of a horse or of another animal, and deprives others of milk by slaughtering cows, O King, if such a fiend does not desist by other means, then you should not hesitate to cut off his head."

Loving Gaṇeśa is the greatest advocate of *ahiṁsā,* nonhurtfulness, whether it be physical, emotional or mental. He, apart from all the other Gods in the *chakras* above *mūlādhāra,* where He sits, accepts the worship of the *mānsāhārīs,* the yet-to-become-vegetarians, as His own until their reform. So gracious is His grace.

The Vegetarian Vow

Taking a vegetarian vow, *śākāhāra vrata,* is a great aid to getting a fresh start on life's path of *dharma.* Vegetarianism is fundamental to spiritual progress, for all higher consciousness depends on a pure and healthy body. As outlined in *sūtra* 116 of my book *Living with Śiva:* "All ardent souls shall eat a strictly vegetarian diet. They understand that higher consciousness depends on the chemistry of foods consumed and thus forbid themselves to eat meat, fish, shellfish, fowl or eggs. Aum." The vegetarian vow embraces the science of *āyurveda,* as explained in *sūtra* 111, "All ardent souls shall cook and eat in the balanced, varied, time-tested, Indian *āyurvedic,* manner. They take food with their fingers to energize it. One day a week, they may enjoy cuisine from other world cultures. Aum."

The vegetarian vow also means eating a healthy, balanced diet, thus avoiding chemically adulterated foods and minimizing junk foods and frozen foods. These and additional dietary guidelines are given in *sūtras* 112-115, as follows. "Ardent souls avoid junk food. They eat freshly cooked foods and drink unchilled water plentifully and with meals. At least at the main meal, all six tastes (sweet, salty, sour, pungent, bitter and astringent) are served. Aum. All ardent souls should adhere to the *āyurvedic* principles of eating at regular times, only when hungry, always seated, at a moderate pace, never between meals, in a disturbed atmosphere or when emotionally upset. Aum. All ardent souls eat in moderation at each meal. The first portion should not exceed what can be held in two hands cupped together. If still hungry, one more handful may be taken. Eating right is good medicine. Aum. All ardent souls should fast on water, herb teas or fruit juices for one day each week or month, on Friday or the thirteenth day of the dark fortnight. However, they shall avoid prolonged, ascetic fasting. Aum Namaḥ Śivāya." Most importantly, *ahiṁsā,* the great imperative of Hindu *dharma,* demands that *śishyas* adhere to vegetarianism, as stated in *sūtra* 32: "No seekers of truth shall intentionally kill or injure any creature whatsoever. Full of compassion, free of the instinct to kill, they are never a source of fear, pain or hurtfulness. They perceive their oneness with all."

VEGETARIAN VRATA CERTIFICATE

Below is a certificate to formalize and document the vegetarian vow, *śākāhāra vrata.* Photocopied and enlarged for framing, it should be read aloud and signed before respected elders after meditating on the meaning of the vow and setting a firm resolve to follow it diligently in the future for a wholesome, healthier, happier life on the path of Hindu Dharma through the grace of our loving Gaṇeśa.

Aum Loving Gaṇeśa!

Śākāhāra Vrata

शाकाहारव्रत சாக்காஹார விரதம்

The Vegetarian Vow

"O Divine Beings of all three worlds, let us bring our minds to rest in the *darśana* of Him who has one tusk. Let us meditate upon Him who has the form of an elephant with a curved trunk. May He guide us always along the right path.

I, ______________________________ ,
Name of Devotee (Please Print)

believe in You, Loving Gaṇeśa, and in the Gods of our faith and the Hindu Dharma. In love and trust I recognize Your goodness in providing for my every material need. In love and trust I recognize Your goodness in providing for my every material and spiritual need. I accept the principle of *śākāhāra* as the method by which I may acknowledge my compassion, my *karuṇa,* for all living beings. As an act of dedication, I am resolved this day to begin (continue) the regular practice of eating a strict vegetarian diet and not eating meat, fish, shellfish, fowl or eggs."

Signature of devotee: ______________________________

It is Hereby Certified

that this devotee, born in ______________________ on ____________, of the ____________ *nakshatra,* and now residing at ______________________ __________, during a divinely ordained ceremony at ______________________ on the auspicious day of ______________ duly voiced the above vegetarian vow in accordance with the traditions of Hinduism before the Deity, the Mahādevas and the *devas.* This devotee is thus bound eternally and immutably to the compassionate life of noninjury aided by the virtue of *śākāhāra.*

SIGNATURES OF PRIESTS, ELDERS AND OTHERS WITNESSING THIS CEREMONY:

Āyurvedaḥ

आयुर्वेदः

The Science of Life

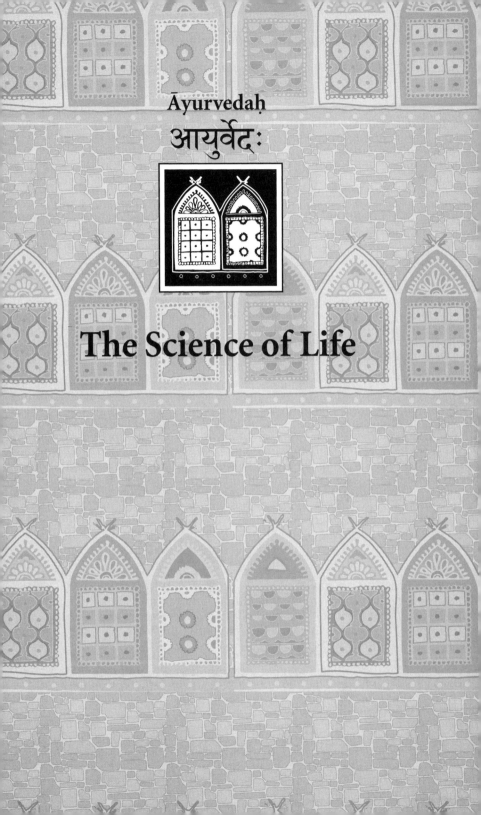

The Science of Life

VERILY, THE FOOD WE EAT IS WHAT WE BECOME. YES, THIS IS A TIME-PROVEN FACT. "THE FOOD WE EAT IS WHAT WE BECOME." It is also a time-proven fact that we live and we are healthy because of what we eat. No need to inject medicines to adjust the symptoms when we can eat the foods that adjust the causes. Food, the *ṛishis* of old wrote, is the best medicine.

There is no greater kitchen than the Amma *nilayam,* which is the real healing center of the home and the community. Amma, mother, is the supreme nurse, the only one in the home that keeps her family healthy by serving what they look forward to, the delicious meals they savor and enjoy. Her kitchen is the only clinic that needs to be entered for the well or ill, unless an arm is broken or other kinds of injuries incurred which need professional expertise. We have here for you the healing center of the New Age. How did we come by it? Well, we transported it from the Old Age to now. It is a precious collection of Asian ingredients that must be in every Hindu home, stored on kitchen shelves in beautiful jars, well labeled, like a shrine to nature's life-giving gifts. It is most pleasing to our Loving Gaṇeśa to see all these items on the shelves. It is His great joy to see them growing in the garden, available to be freshly picked (fifteen square feet of land can help feed an entire family). We must remember that the sun and soil are the best "refrigerator," and that cooling what has been picked diminishes its vitality; freezing even more so. Also, each Amma's garden (her refrigerator out-of-doors and under the sun) must grow the foods that bugs and snails don't like to eat, or grow enough for them to eat, too. They live with us on planet Earth and have the same right to eat as do we. When we grow human food that they don't want to eat, we need no pesticides or other chemicals, which are harmful to our bodies. Amma's garden has within it the foods that grow in the natural soil of the area in which her family lives and the foods that are not bothered by other creatures who live with us that are not human. In the list and explanations below Amma turns her kitchen into a virtual hospital, giving her family what they need in delicious curries. She puts into the menu what is needed to correct the sniffles when *kapha* season comes along. In the summer she cooks with the heat-removing spices. Yes, Amma knows, inspired by loving Gaṇeśa, whom she worships before preparing each and every meal. She does. Read on.

Five Simple Remedies: a Must for Every Home

By Dr. Virender Sodhi, M.D. (Āyurveda), N.D.
Published in HINDUISM TODAY, *July 1994*

Āyurvedic medicine emphasizes that a person must take an active role in his or her own healing process. Natural remedies that harmonize with the body and promote the body's own healing abilities are central to the ancient practice of *āyurveda*. Happily, many of these remedies are easily and inexpensively made at home. These preparations are so simple and so effective that they would be of great benefit to every household any time of the year. The five most important herbs and foods to have on hand year-round are ginger, garlic/onion, black pepper, *trifal* and turmeric. With these, you can create quick and effective remedies for a variety of ailments. A cautionary note: it is important to remember that if you suffer from a serious ailment you should seek the advice of a trained physician.

BLACK PEPPER *Piper nigrum*

Āyurvedic properties: light, dry; taste: pungent, bitter; diuretic; post-digestive taste: bitter; liver stimulant; energy: hot; *dosha* action: decreases *vāta* and *kapha*, increases *pitta*. Pharmacological actions: anti-parasitic; digestive; diuretic; liver stimulant; nervine. [*Dosha* is an *āyurvedic* term for the humors which comprise and govern the body, mind and emotions. *Vāta*, *pitta* and *kapha* are the three *doshas*.]

Black pepper is an excellent herb for sparking the digestive fire, increasing appetite, and cleansing the liver. It promotes hydrochloric acid secretions (which help digest proteins), stimulates the nervous system, and increases circulation to all parts of the body. It also increases sweating (to burn out fevers) and helps expel parasites.

Black pepper helps relieve anorexia, bronchial asthma, bronchitis, cholera, common cold, diarrhea, eye diseases, fevers, frost bite, fungal infections, nervous disorders, painful menstruations, poor circulation, rheumatic conditions, ring worms, skin abscesses, sluggish liver, syphilis, toothaches, and upper respiratory infections. Black pepper provides a quick and easy remedy for the ailments mentioned above. A standard dosage is 500–1,000 mg (approximately ½-1 teaspoon) eaten two to three times a day. This can be boiled in one cup of water, covered to steep, and taken as a tea sweetened with a taste of raw honey. This tea helps relieve the symptoms of cold, flu and painful menstruations. Black pepper powder can be sprinkled on food or mixed with a teaspoon of raw honey and eaten from the spoon. *Pitta* people and those with ulcers should be careful of taking black pepper. It can aggravate ulcers, inflammation and other *pitta* conditions.

GARLIC *Allium sativum*
ONION *Allium cepa*
Āyurvedic properties: heavy, oily; taste: sweet, pungent, bitter, sour, astringent; post-digestive taste: pungent, sweet; energy: heating; *dosha* effects: decreases *vāta*, increases *pitta* and *kapha*. Pharmacological actions: analgesic, antibacterial, antiviral, antifungal, anti-inflammatory, antispasmodic, carminative, cholesterol lowering, diuretic, expectorant.

Onions and garlic have been used for centuries as both food and medicine. They help increase digestive secretions, promote proper fat metabolism and aid in liver detoxification. Garlic and onion help relieve: abscesses, asthma, atherosclerosis, coughs, diabetes, digestive disorders, dysentery, earaches, hemorrhoids, high blood pressure, high cholesterol, hysteria, inflammation, and parasitic conditions.

Onion and garlic have much the same action, but garlic is much more potent that onion. They can both be eaten either raw or cooked for the conditions mentioned above. Dosage depends upon the form. For taking raw, a medium-sized onion can be chopped and eaten as a salad with lemon juice. As a juice, 10–30 cc (a few ounces) of raw onion juice can be mixed with honey. This is an especially helpful remedy for asthma. As onion powder, ½ teaspoon is taken twice a day. Onions can be used in cooking and stir frying for their many therapeutic effects. Cooked onion is particularly good for *vāta*-type people. The dosage for raw garlic is 1–2 cloves eaten once or twice a day. As a dry powder, 500 mg is taken one to three times a day. As garlic oil, 1–2 drops are taken three times a day. Garlic can be used in cooking or stir frying for its therapeutic effects. Neither onions nor garlic should be consumed by those with gallbladder problems or kidney stones. These foods have a contracting action and could increase the pain caused by such conditions. Also, *pittas* should be very cautious when consuming garlic, as it can aggravate gastritis and other *pitta* disorders.

GINGER *Zingiber officinale*

Āyurvedic properties: light, oily; taste: pungent; post-digestive taste: pungent; energy: hot; *dosha* action: decreases *vāta* and *kapha,* increases *pitta.* Pharmacological actions: anti-inflammatory, antimicrobial, aromatic, carminative, cholesterol lowering, free radical scavenger.

In *āyurvedic* medicine, ginger is used to increase the digestive fire—the key to radiant health. It contains enzymes and encourages the body to produce enzymes that help digest fats, carbohydrates, and proteins. Ginger helps relieve: chest pain, cholera, common cold, diarrhea, dizziness, headaches, joint aches and pains, motion sickness, nausea, rheumatism, stomachaches, and vomiting.

Ginger decreases discomfort during pregnancy, including nausea and vomiting, and is also wonderful for postpartum care. In general, it helps alleviate nausea, vomiting, diarrhea, and indigestion. Taken orally, ginger provides an excellent treatment for colds and fever, indigestion, water retention, nausea, elevated cholesterol, liver damage, and many other ailments. Ginger is especially useful for stimulating *kapha* and for aiding *vāta's* poor digestion, aches, and pains. For dosage try ¼ teaspoon dried ginger root powder or ½ to 1 teaspoon freshly grated ginger root in warm water as a tea. This tea can be consumed up to three times per day. You can also sprinkle the above amount of ginger directly onto your food to aid digestion.

Externally, ginger powder can be mixed with water and used as a poultice to stimulate circulation, relieve muscle and joint aches and pains, eliminate headaches and chest pain, and regulate bowel movements. To make a poultice, simply mix ½ to 1 teaspoon of dried ginger root powder with enough warm water to form a paste. This can be spread onto the affected area. When using a poultice, take care to avoid the eyes and mucous membranes. The poultice, as well as any ginger residue left on your hands from making a poultice or a tea, can burn these sensitive areas. Other than this, ginger has no dangerous side effects.

TRIFAL *Terminalia chebula, Terminalia bellinica* and *Phyllanthus emblica*

Āyurvedic properties: light, dry; taste: sweet, sour, astringent, bitter, pungent; post-digestive taste: bitter; energy: warm; *dosha* action: balancing for *vāta, pitta* and *kapha.* Pharmacological actions: adaptogenic, antibacterial, antivirial, antifungal, antiyeast, antihistaminic, anti-inflammatory, antioxidant, antitumor, blood pressure lowering, cholesterol lowering, digestive, diuretic, laxative. *Trifal* (Hindi), known in Sanskṛit as *triphala,* is an ancient *āyurvedic* herbal combination revered for its many therapeutic effects. It is a *rasāyana,* or formula which constantly rejuvenates and balances the body. *Trifal* helps relieve: anemia, bowel toxicity and irregularity, carbohydrate intolerance, chronic lung diseases, constipation, diabetes, eye diseases, high cholesterol, hypertension, indigestion, skin disorders, and yeast infections. *Trifal* is a wonderful preventive remedy that can be taken daily. It is a wonderful intestinal cleanser which gently promotes regularity without irritating the bowels. It first helps digest food, then aids in elimination. As a dry powder, 3,000–6,000 mg (1-2 teaspoons) of *trifal* may be taken one to three times per day. As an extract 500 mg is taken one to three times per day. *Trifal* has no known harmful side effects.

TURMERIC *Curcuma longa*

Āyurvedic properties: light, dry; taste: bitter, astringent; post-digestive taste: bitter; energy: hot; *dosha* action: balances *vāta, pitta,* and *kapha.* Pharmacological actions: anti-allergenic, antibacterial, antiviral (anti-HIV), antifungal, anti-inflammatory, antioxidant, antiparasitic, antispasmodic, anti-tumor, carminative, diuretic.

Turmeric is known as the King of the Spices in *āyurvedic* medicine. A bitter spice, it helps cleanse the liver, purify the blood, and promote good digestion and elimination. It also has a powerful anti-inflammatory action without the unpleasant side effects of anti-inflammatory drugs.

Turmeric helps relieve: acne, allergies, ascites, auto-immune disorders, burns, chicken pox, diabetes, digestive disorders, gallbladder problems, liver damage due to toxic chemical exposure and drug use, liver disorders, skin rashes, tumors and ulcers.

Turmeric is very helpful for all *doshas.* In India, it has been used for thousands of years for its many healing and cleansing properties. It is a wonderful skin cleanser, color enhancer, and food preservative and is widely used for ritual purification. Also, recent studies show that turmeric is effective against cancerous tumors and HIV.

As a dry powder ½–1½ teaspoons of turmeric may be taken two to three times per day. As an extract (8:1) 250 *mg* is taken three times per day. Turmeric has no known harmful side effects and is safe for everyday use.

The Āyurvedic Qualities of Foods

A Quick Reference Drawn from Renowned Sources

The above section presents a basic list of the essential food remedies that every home should have. It is especially designed for householders just getting started in the art of Indian cookery. Below is a more comprehensive directory of dozens of herbs and foods. You may wonder, "What about protein?" The answer is simple, though not obvious. The wonderful herbs, spices, fruits, vegetables and dairy products that *āyurveda* recommends contain more than enough protein for good health. Indeed, protein is not a concern in *āyurveda.* It is hardly even mentioned. The body's need for protein has been highly overrated in modern times, and in fact excess protein creates toxins in the body leading to bone disease. Everything the human body needs is fully contained in a wholesome, fully-balanced, vegetarian diet. Below we have listed and described the *āyurvedic* qualities of the herbs, spices, fruits, vegetables and other foods found in wholesome Hindu homes. Loving Gaṇeśa wants all of His nearly one billion devotees to follow this example.

Spices and Herbs

AJAWAYAN SEEDS *Carum copticum*

Ajawayan is very much an exclusive Asian herb. It is often found only in Indian grocery stores. Ajawayan seeds (also called ajwan) resemble cumin seeds but are smaller in size. They have a distinct aroma, a bitter and pungent taste and, unlike the cooling cumin seed, are heating. As such, this herb is a digestive stimulant, and a strong one at that. It relieves indigestion and colic (intestinal pain) almost miraculously. Ajawayan is often mixed in lentils, beans and leafy vegetable curries to counteract the gas from their digestion. Because of its potent nature, ajawayan is used in small amounts.

ANISE *Pimpinella anisum*

Anise is a sweet and pungent aromatic spice. It has a refreshing, pleasant taste. It is sometimes chewed with cardamom pods after a meal to refresh the breath. Anise seeds have a heating effect on the body and are a good appetizer that enhances *pitta dosha,* destroys mucus accumulations due to *kapha dosha* in the intestines and soothes *vāta dosha.*

ASAFOETIDA *Ferula asafoetida*

Asafoetida has a unique sulphurous odor and pungent taste that takes a little getting used to for those who didn't grow up smelling it. Nevertheless, asafoetida is by far the strongest aid to the gastro-intestinal canal. It stimulates *pitta* (water and fire element), aids food in its movement through the intestines, destroys *ama* (toxins) and eradicates worms in the intestines. It dissipates gas from foods like lentils and beans, making them lighter and more digestible. This crystalized plant resin is also effective against other *vāta* (the air and ether element) disorders, like arthritis and light-headedness.

BASIL LEAVES *Ocimum sanctum*

Every Hindu is aware of the sacredness and medicinal effect of the holy basil, or *tulsi.* It is attributed to Vishṇu for its preserving powers. Wise elders often say that one should eat seven basil leaves each day for good health. Basil leaves are pungent in taste, balancing to *kapha* (the water and earth element) and calming to *vāta.* Basil is effective against respiratory tract diseases, coughs and colds. It is a wonderful tonic for the heart and the immune system, and it clears the mind and breaks up *prāṇic* congestions in the aura. The basil plant itself has a purifying effect on the environment.

BAY LEAVES *Laurus nobilis*

Bay leaves are pungent and aromatic. They give a distinct appetizing flavor to food when they are cooked in oil and mixed into curries or rice dishes. Bay leaves help promote the evacuation of phlegm *(kapha)* from the lungs and throat. They assist *vāta* by encouraging intestinal movement, and they improve *pitta's* catabolic activities.

CARDAMOM SEEDS *Elettaria cardamomum*

For centuries cardamom has been extolled by spice traders for its sweet flavor and smell. It is found in just about all Indian desserts. Cardamom has a sweet, pungent taste and is very calming to the nervous system and the mind. Thus it is a pacifier of *vāta dosha.* It cures *kapha* in the respiratory tract and is known as a tonic for the heart. It stimulates digestion without aggravating the *pitta dosha.* Cardamom pods are often chewed with anise seeds after meals as a breath freshener. This spice combination also counteracts belching and vomiting.

CAYENNE PEPPER *Capsicum annuum*

Cayenne pepper is used either in its fresh green or red chili form, as dried pods or powder. Many hot curry powders and *garam masalas* derive their color and pungency from cayenne. Cayenne pepper is food for the digestive fire. It stimulates appetite, destroys toxic build up, kills worms in the intestines and purifies the blood. It can also "jump-start" weakened organs after an operation. Due to its high *pitta* nature, cayenne pepper is used sparingly, especially during the summer and for people with high *pitta dosha. Āyurveda* generally prefers using black pepper in medicinal formulations when heating action is called for.

CINNAMON BARK *Cinnamomum zeylanicum*

Nearly everybody on this planet can recognize the soothing and refreshing aroma of cinnamon sticks. It is a wonderful spice and medicine with a taste that is pungent, sweet and astringent. Cinnamon is very beneficial to the respiratory and alimentary canal. It regulates *kapha* in the lungs, relieving coughs and colds. Cinnamon also aids in digestion and the assimilation of digested food. It is also strengthening to the heart and kidneys.

CLOVES *Eugenia caryophyllus*

The unmistakable aroma of cloves can be found both in the kitchen and the perfume industry. Cloves are pungent and heating. This herb lends itself both as a pacifier for *kapha* (which governs the lungs, mucus production and bodily functions of assimilation) and *vāta.* It is a stimulator for *pitta.* Clove is used for coughs and colds. It is also well known as a pain reliever. Clove oil, a concoction made from boiling cloves in *ghee* (clarified butter), is a remedy for toothache and is rubbed on joints to soothe rheumatic pains.

CORIANDER *Coriandrum sativum*

The coriander plant offers to Amma's *nilayam* its leaves and seeds. A universal balancer of the *doshas,* its taste is bitter and pungent. No hot Indian coconut chutney or spicy rice is complete without a garnish of fresh coriander leaves (cilantro). It is a household remedy, as its cooling effect mends disorders due to an overstimulated digestive fire. This is why hot foods are garnished with cilantro and almost every blend of *masala* powder contains ground coriander seeds. Coriander aids in the absorption of herbs and food. It is used to heal skin rashes, inflammations and a host of other ailments caused by the aggravation of the body's fire element.

CUMIN SEEDS *Cuminum cyminum*

Cumin seed is another prevalent herb in Indian cooking. The seeds are aromatic and pungent. Acclaimed as an herb of the stomach, it is a well-known digestive stimulant and appetizer. Cumin seeds give character to almost every curry, lentil or chutney. They have the often-needed effect of dissipating gas from complex carbohydrates like *dals.* Cumin seeds are cooling to the body despite their pungency. They are pacifying to *vāta* and *kapha* and a gentle stimulant of *pitta.*

CURRY LEAVES *Murraya konigii*

Curry leaves are an exclusive Indian garnish that give a subtle smell and taste. They are found in almost every non-dessert food. Whole leaves are added to the cooking oil when popping mustard seeds or cumin seeds. Curry leaf is also an appetizer and a digestive stimulant which has a cooling effect. The leaf has a bitter and pungent taste that helps promote movements of the intestines and activates digestive secretions. Its effects are similar to cumin seeds, being pacifying to *vāta* and *kapha* and mildly stimulating to *pitta.*

FENNEL SEEDS *Foeniculum vulgare*

It is a custom in India to serve raw fennel seeds after a sumptuous rice and curry meal. This spice is extolled in *āyurveda* as a universal balancer of *doshas.* The taste is sweet and pungent. It is a digestive rejuvenator, activating proper digestive functions when needed and reducing the digestive fire *(pitta)* when it has been over stimulated. It calms the mind yet prompts alertness. Fennel seeds combine well with coriander seeds and cumin seeds, two other cooling spices.

FENUGREEK SEEDS *Trigonella foenumgraecum*

No *sambar* is complete without fenugreek (methi) seeds. The taste is bitter, pungent and sweet. It is a good pacifier of *vāta* (which governs the colon, nerves and bodily functions of evacuation and movement) and *kapha*. It promotes growth and healing, and it is a rejuvenator. Fenugreek is also a digestion-aiding spice.

GARLIC *Allium sativum*

Garlic's medicinal property is well known by most of the world's medical traditions. *Āyurveda* extols it as a rejuvenator of *vāta*. The whole garlic plant is recommended for use by *āyurveda* as it contains five of the six tastes—sweet, salty, bitter, pungent and astringent—lacking only sour. Garlic reduces *kapha* phlegm production and purifies the blood. Its pungency stimulates digestion.

GINGER ROOT *Zingiber officinale*

Ginger is one of the most widely used spices in Hindu cooking. From curries to desserts, ginger is a must in any kitchen. *Āyurveda* considers ginger as *vishvabhesaj*, "universal medicine." It is used in its fresh form or as dry powder. Its taste is pungent and sweet. Ginger powder, with its more potent drying and digestive stimulant action, is employed to pacify *kapha* and stimulate *pitta*. Fresh ginger is more effective for calming *vāta*. Ginger root is a part of many *āyurvedic* formulations to relieve the conditions of any of the aggravated *doshas*. Paste made from ginger powder is applied externally to relieve aches and pains. Ginger is a wonderful tonic for the whole body, especially the heart and an agitated mind.

MINT *Mentha* sp.

The smooth and slightly pungent taste of mint can often be recognized in Indian chutneys, desserts and teas. There are many types of mints—peppermint, spearmint, thyme and more. Generally they are highly constituted of *ākāśa,* giving them a light, cooling, calming quality. Mints are mild in their actions and are usually used with other herbs to enhance or reduce more aggressive properties. For instance, because of their cooling action, mints are added to hot chutneys. Mints are harmonizing and relaxing to the body and mind.

MUSTARD, BLACK *Brassica nigra*

Black mustard seed is very popular in Hindu cooking. It is popped in hot oil, usually with other spices like cumin seeds or ajawayan, and then added to curry dishes. This process is called tempering. Black mustard seeds assist in the digestion of protein. The pungent seed is a pacifier of both *vāta dosha* and *kapha dosha.* Mustard oil is used to cure rheumatic pains in joints, a *vāta* disorder. Mustard seeds in large amounts cause vomiting, so they must be used cautiously.

NEEM LEAVES *Azadiracta indica*

The neem tree is universally acclaimed the village pharmacy in India. Its various parts are employed in a host of preparations, especially to cure skin problems, purify the blood and cleanse the intestines of parasites and toxins. In cooking, its leaves are used to garnish rice, *rasam* or *sambars.* Neem provides the bitter taste in diet. Neem leaves are high in the *vāta* element, thus they promote all types of movement within the body and mind. Neem stimulates the immune system, enhances healing and has a cooling effect, thus counteracting fevers. It is very beneficial to *pitta* and *kapha doshas* and is used with discretion to calm the *vāta dosha.*

NUTMEG *Myristica fragrans*

Nutmeg is a calming and aromatic spice. It is often taken with milk and cardamom to induce natural sleep. Pungent in taste, it is a good spice to calm the *vāta dosha.* It soothes the nervous system and clears the mind. Nutmeg also helps tremendously with the absorption of digested food and acts as a rejuvenator. Nutmeg is always taken in very small amounts, a pinch at a time, since it can be dulling when taken in excess.

ONION, SMALL RED *Allium cepa*

Small red onions are more pungent than the bigger varieties (which are sweeter) and are more commonly used in Indian cooking. *Āyurveda* generally recommends onions be eaten cooked rather than raw. Cooked onions are pacifying to *vāta* and *kapha.* Onions have a heating effect, thus stimulating the digestive fire. They provide stamina, strength and a general well being to the body.

PEPPER, BLACK *Piper nigrum*

The seeds of the Indian black pepper (known as pepper corns) can probably be found in every kitchen on earth. Black pepper, often used in a powdered state, is a powerful taste enhancer and appetizer. Its pungent taste and heating action not only aids digestion but also burns away toxic waste *(ama)* and mucus build-up in the gastro-intestinal tract. Black pepper is used in salad dressings as an antidote for cold and raw vegetables. Its drying action helps maintain the respiratory system by drying up excess phlegm *(kapha).*

PEPPER, INDIAN LONG *Piper longum*

The Indian long pepper or *pippali* is a close relative of black pepper. Like black pepper, its taste is pungent. It acts to stimulate digestive functions and maintain the respiratory system. However, the Indian long pepper is unique in that it is also a rejuvenator of weakened tissues and biological functions, especially for the lungs. In *āyurvedic* terms it is known as a *rasāyana. Trikatu* is a renowned *āyurvedic* formulation of equal parts Indian long pepper, black pepper and dried ginger that is used to stimulate *pitta* and cleanse the gastrointestinal tract of *ama.*

POPPY SEEDS *Papaver* sp.

Poppy seed, like ajawayan seed, is an exclusive Indian spice. It is used in small quantities. *Āyurvedically,* it is a mind calmer and digestive stimulant. The taste is pungent, astringent and sweet. It is used to assist the small intestines with assimilation. Its heating action also acts as a *vāta dosha* calmer. Thus it is often used in conjunction with nutmeg or valerian to induce sleep. Poppy seeds are sometimes mixed with beans, *dals* and leafy green vegetables to dissipate the gas from their digestion.

SAFFRON *Crocus sativus*

Saffron is definitely one of the most expensive spices. Fortunately, though, it is so potent that it need only be used in small amounts. It is often added to enhance the taste of desserts or rice dishes. Its taste is pungent, bitter and sweet. Saffron is known to be an effective rejuvenator of tissues. It aids in the assimilation of nutrition into all the tissues of the body. It is very balancing to all three *doshas* and emits a cooling and soothing effect for *pitta.* Saffron enhances the effects to the body of other foods and herbs.

SALT, SEA OR ROCK

Unrefined sea salt and rock salt are different from the usual table salt. They have a combination of minerals and are less concentrated compared to table salt. *Āyurveda* recommends these salts. Salt is just as important to the body as water. All the tissues in our body and most biological functions require salt. Salt serves as an appetizer, bringing out the flavor of food and is essential to the proper functioning of digestion and assimilation as a whole. Salt prevents distention in the stomach. Salt is a combination of water and fire. It stimulates *kapha* and *pitta* and pacifies *vāta.*

SESAME SEED *Sesamum indicum*

Sesame seeds are a wonderful rejuvenative food, especially for *vāta.* They have a strong heating effect which soothes the cold quality of *vāta.* However, sesame is usually avoided by people with a high *pitta* constitution. Sesame seeds are very strengthening to the lungs, and help alleviate an aggravated *kapha.*

TAMARIND *Tamarindus indica*

The sweet and sour taste of the tamarind pulp is a famous ingredient in *rasams, sambars* and chutneys. The juice of the tamarind is extracted for cooking by soaking the pulp of the tamarind fruit in water for fifteen minutes, then squeezing out the juice. Tamarind is a mild laxative. It serves as an appetizer and balances high *pitta* distortions caused by overexposure to the sun or pungent foods. Tamarind calms *vāta* but can aggravate the *kapha dosha* if used excessively.

TURMERIC *Curcuma longa*

Turmeric is used both as a spice and a cosmetic. It is a very purifying, cleansing spice and a natural blood purifier and revitalizer. Turmeric has a bitter, astringent and pungent taste and is a general balancer of all three *doshas.* It stimulates *pitta* digestion, alleviates *vāta* aches, pains and anxiety, and it reduces *kapha* congestion. Turmeric also stimulates the immune systems and revitalizes the skin, both being *vāta* functions. It is often used in pickles because of its anti-bacterial, preservative effect.

Anna Gaṇeśa Raṅgoli

An Image of Gaṇapati Made with Herbs And Spices, a Special Sādhana for Gaṇeśa Chaturthī

Below is an image of Gaṇeśa we created in our publications facility. The chart on page 471 shows the ingredients used, all from the inspiration of the Lord of Categories. Nearly all the spices *āyurveda* recommends (from the listings above) went into our *raṅgoli (kolam* in Tamil) of loving Gaṇeśa. We enlarged the drawing (below) on a photocopier, then placed each spice with a spoon into its assigned area. Two sugges-

tions: work from top to bottom to avoid disturbing already placed spices; and put the turmeric on last, no matter where it is located! Other spices with similar color and texture can be substituted for those not yet in your pantry.

Each month on His special day or at least yearly during the Gaṇeśa Chaturthī festival, gather with the entire family and create this *raṅgoli (kolam* in Tamil) of our loving Lord in all the healing foods that He wants us to use daily for the dear children and their parents. Performing this *sādhana* ensures that the proper spices are in the pantry and reminds everyone of the value of their use. It will be fun for the whole family. After Chaturthī day take the health-giving ingredients to a garden or park and offer them to the birds, mice and insects, for they live with us too on planet Earth and are as loved by Gaṇeśa as are we. There are, of course, other ways to make a Chaturthī *raṅgoli* for our Loving Gaṇeśa to enjoy,

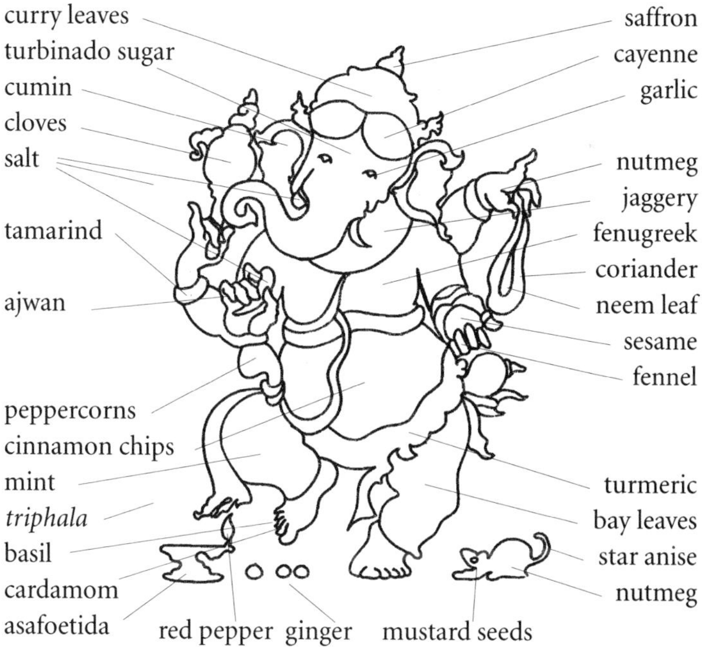

using essential spices and other pantry items that are standard in every Hindu Amma's home, seen in big jars in every kitchen. For example, below is a simpler Gaṇeśa, made with six healing ingredients: the five home remedial foods described by Dr. Sodhi, along with jaggery for Gaṇeśa's happy, ever-giving face. To the right are two *swastikas,* one made with six ingredients and the other with thirty-one.

The Herb of the Day

There are 31 important herbs and spices listed to the right, one for each day of the month. Each day in your home, make it a point to feature the item of the day in your menu in some way. Be creative and enjoy these wonderful foods throughout the year for good health and longevity.

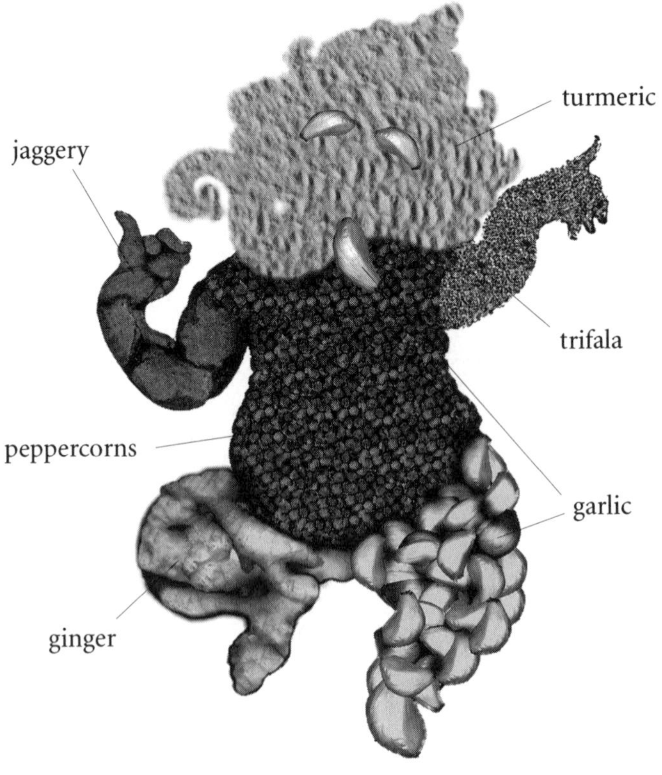

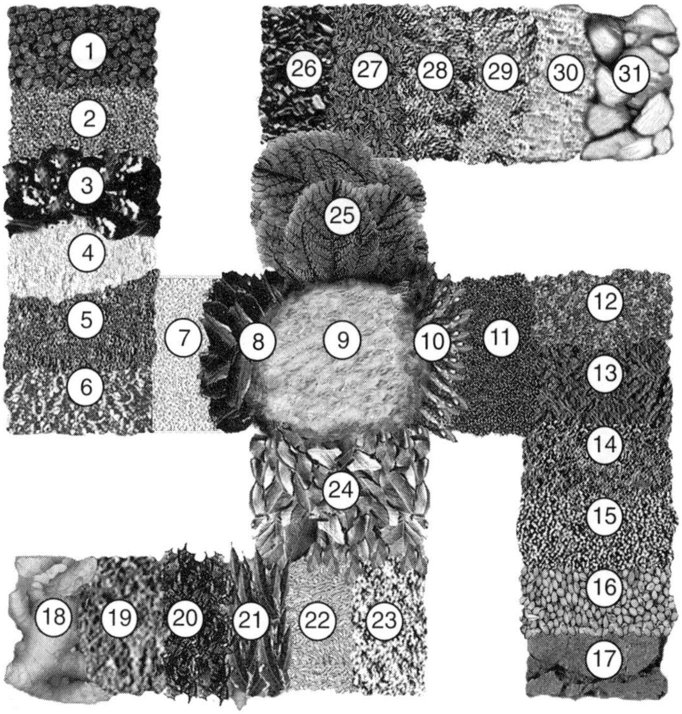

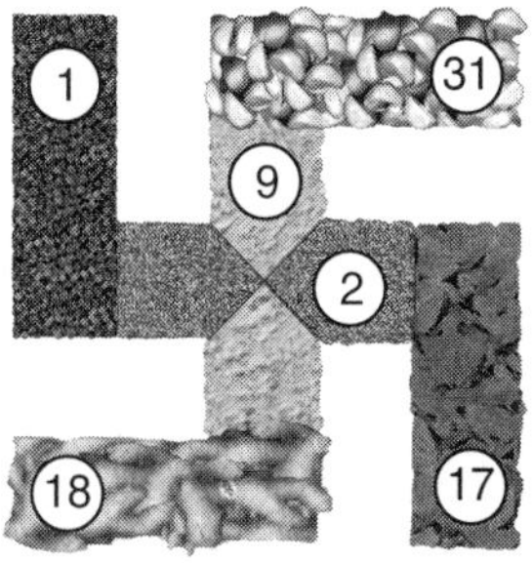

1. peppercorns
2. trifala
3. tamarind
4. turbinado sugar
5. cumin
6. cloves
7. salt
8. curry leaves
9. turmeric
10. red pepper
11. mustard seeds
12. saffron
13. cayenne
14. nutmeg
15. fenugreek
16. coriander
17. jaggery
18. ginger
19. nutmeg
20. star anise
21. neem leaf
22. fennel
23. sesame
24. bay leaves
25. mint
26. cinnamon (chips)
27. ajawan
28. basil
29. cardamom
30. asofoetida
31. garlic

Fruit

APPLES *Malus domestica*

Slightly astringent and cooling, sweet apples are good for *pitta* and *kapha.* Raw apples can help constipation, bleeding gums and cold sores. The juice is useful in gastritis, colitis and bladder infection. Cooked apples can alleviate diarrhea and dysentery.

APRICOTS *Prunus armeniaca*

Sweet, astringent and heating, apricots increase *pitta.* Apricots are taken in large quantity to relieve chronic constipation and to help in anemia.

BANANAS *Musa paradisiaca sapientum*

Sweet and cooling in quality, ripe bananas decrease *vāta* and increase *pitta* and *kapha.* They energize muscle, fat, nerve and reproductive tissues and are used to alleviate constipation, muscle cramps and burning urination. Bananas should not be taken with milk or yogurt.

CHERRIES *Prunus avium*

Sweet, sour, astringent and heating, cherries pacify *vāta* and *kapha,* but may increase *pitta* if taken in large amounts. They are good for mental fatigue, stress, insomnia and effective in premenstrual syndrome and motion sickness.

COCONUTS *Cocos nucifera*

Sweet and cooling, coconut pacifies *vāta* and *pitta* but may aggravate *kapha* when taken in excess. Coconut oil is useful for skin problems such as sunburn. Coconut water can help in stomach disorders and burning urination as well as rashes, such as measles and chicken pox.

DATES *Phoenix dactylifera*

Fresh dates are sweet and cooling. Energizing and nourishing in quality, dates increase each *dosha* and generally promote health. Concoctions of dates and *ghee* can improve digestion, help anemia and relieve fatigue. A poultice of date sugar can soothe a painful muscle. Dates and certain herbs relieve coughs and other ailments of the chest region.

FIGS *Ficus carica*

Fresh figs are sweet and cooling. They calm *vāta* and *pitta* and promote *kapha.* They are a good source of iron and to build up the blood, especially recommended for women in their childbearing years. Figs strengthen the gums, relieve indigestion, heartburn, diarrhea, burning urination and give some relief in asthma. Figs should not be taken with milk or by people suffering from diarrhea or dysentery.

GRAPES *Vitis vinifera*

Grapes are sour, sweet and heating. They stimulate *kapha* and *pitta* and should be used for *vāta* in moderation. Red, purple or black grapes are *tridoshic,* meaning they are balanced in their effect. They are sweet, sour and astringent, with a cooling energy and a gentle laxative effect. Grapes and grape concoctions are taken for problems of urination, chest pain, cough, fever and sexual debility.

GRAPEFRUIT *Citrus paradisi*

Sweet, bitter and cooling, grapefruit subdues *vāta* and increases *pitta* and *kapha.* It encourages healthy intestines and prevents diarrhea, dysentery and other infectious diseases of the digestive tract.

LEMONS *Citrus limonum*

Sour and heating, lemons calm *vāta,* detoxify and balance *pitta* but may stimulate aggravated *pitta* and *kapha doshas.* In *āyurveda,* lemons have great healing value. They are used for high blood pressure, nausea, vomiting, indigestion, gas, morning sickness and kidney stones.

LIMES *Citrus aurantifolia*

Sour and slightly bitter, limes calm *vāta,* but can aggravate *pitta* in excess and stimulate *kapha.* They cool the *pitta*-provoking nature of hot, spicy foods. Lime improves appetite and digestion, relieves heartburn, nausea and hyperacidity.

MANGOS *Mangifera indica*

Ripe mangos are sweet and heating and balance the three *doshas.* Mangos are an energizer and useful to help lactation in women. Green, unripe mangos disturb all three *doshas* unless pickled, in which case they help digestion and improve the flavor of food.

MELONS *Cucumis melo*

Sweet and cooling, melons calm *vāta* and *pitta* but may provoke *kapha.* Melons have a diuretic action. The rind can help with rashes and acne, and chewing melons can relieve bleeding gums. Melons should be eaten alone.

ORANGES *Citrus sinensis*

Sour, sweet and heating, oranges pacify *vāta* and stimulate *kapha* when taken in excess. Sweet oranges are all right for *pitta*, but sour ones provoke this *dosha*. Oranges are useful for bleeding gums, hemorrhoids, bloodshot eyes, hangover, high blood pressure and indigestion.

PAPAYAS *Carica papaya*

Sweet and heating, papayas calm all three *doshas* but should not be taken more than once a week by *pitta* constitutions. They are helpful for cough, asthma, liver and spleen disorders. The enzymes in papayas enhance digestion.

PEACHES *Prunus persica*

Sour, sweet and heating, peaches pacify *vāta* and promote *pitta*. They are used in control of worms and the treatment of kidney stones, high fever and constipation.

PEARS *Pyrus communis*

Sweet, sour and cooling, pears stimulate *vāta*, calm *pitta* and reduce *kapha*. A pear eaten alone can help stop diarrhea. Pears can stimulate the appetite and help inflamed gums.

PINEAPPLES *Ananas comosus*

Sweet, sour and heating, ripe pineapples are soothing to *vāta* and *kapha* and all right for *pitta*. Pineapple is helpful in cases of indigestion and constipation. Its pulp relieves some skin irritations.

PLUMS *Prunus domestica*

Sweet, astringent and cooling, plums increase *kapha*. In small quantities they help the system produce more blood, open the lower digestive tract and clean the stomach. Plums are very useful in subduing excess *vāta* and *pitta*.

POMEGRANATES *Punica granatum*

Sweet, sour and astringent, pomegranates increase *vāta* and decrease *pitta* and *kapha*. They promote the production of red blood cells and are good for anemia, fever and heart conditions. Pomegranates are used to treat nausea, vomiting, rashes and morning sickness. Fresh juice in each nostril can stop a nosebleed, and a drop in the eye can relieve burning.

RASPBERRIES *Rubus strigosus*
Sweet, slightly sour and astringent, raspberries stimulate *vāta* and calm *kapha.* Eating more than two handfuls at a time may cause vomiting. Medicinally, they relieve urinary problems, bleeding gums and hemorrhoids, and are able to slow bleeding and control profuse menstruation.

STRAWBERRIES *Fragaria virginiana*
Sour, sweet, astringent and heating, strawberries in moderation are suitable for all *doshas.* Daily consumption may help in pulmonary tuberculosis or anemia.

WATERMELONS *Citrullus vulgaris*
Sweet and cooling, watermelon provokes *kapha* and *vāta* and relieves *pitta.* It binds the stools and flushes the kidneys. The dried pulp is used in cosmetics to improve the skin.

Vegetables

BEETS *Beta vulgaris*
Sweet and heating, beets increase *pitta.* Their alkaline nature and iron content make them a blood-producing food. Beets and beet tops are excellent for iron or calcium deficiency.

BITTER MELON *Momordica charantia*
Bitter and cooling, bitter melon can provoke *vāta* and soothe *pitta* and *kapha.* It is used to treat fever, anemia, diabetes and worms. Cooked bitter melon is good for cleansing the liver. It is good for pregnant women and diabetics. Drops of juice in the nostrils can relieve migraine.

CARROTS *Daucus carota*

Sweet, pungent and heating, carrots are calming for *vāta* and *kapha* but stimulate *pitta* when taken in excess. Carrots are digestive, laxative and can detoxify the body. They are used to treat anemia, chronic indigestion and cancer.

CUCUMBERS *Cucumus sativus*

Sweet, astringent and cooling, cucumbers increase *kapha.* They work magically on restlessness caused by heat, and the juice gives instantaneous relief to any burning sensation in the stomach. Cucumbers cure constipation and counteract hyperacidity and gastric or duodenal ulcers.

FIDDLENECK FERN TIPS

Fern tips are a delicacy when they are picked fresh. This is an astringent food that is light and easy to digest, very good food for *kapha* people. However it aggravates *vāta* and needs to be eaten with onions and garlic for balancing out the wind element in the body. Fern tips cook in less than five minutes when steamed or boiled. If they are overcooked they become unbearably astringent and unctuous. They should be eaten no more than once or twice a week according to Hawaiian cultural tradition.

MUSHROOMS *Mussirionis*

There are many types of mushrooms. In general they are light and dry, which makes it a good food for *kapha* people. Their astringent and sweet taste also make them pacifying to *pitta*. *Kapha* and *pitta* constituted people may take them raw. However for *vâta*, the mushroom's light and astringent quality makes it aggravating. This quality is somewhat counteracted when mushrooms are cooked. Mushrooms should be eaten in moderation(once or twice a week) as they can be dulling owing to its *tamasic* nature.

RADISHES *Raphanus sativus*

Pungent and heating, radishes are fine for *vāta* and *kapha*. They can improve digestion, help relieve gas, flush the liver and get rid of intestinal worms. The long white *daikon* is especially effective.

SPINACH *Spinacea oleracea*

Pungent, bitter, sweet and cooling, spinach provokes *vāta* and *pitta* but can be calming to *kapha*. Spinach is used to treat asthma and coughs. The juice applied externally can relieve swelling.

TARO ROOT AND LEAF *Colocasia esculenta*

Sweet, pungent and neither hot nor cold, taro root increases *vāta*. The root is unctuous and heavy to digest, but if digested well it gives much strength. It should be cooked with black cumin, red cardamom, ajawayan, garlic or ginger. Taro root cooks in about 40-60 minutes. In cases of dry cough, taro root liquifies the cough and expels mucous. Taro leaf is bitter, sweet and slightly unctuous. Like the root, taro leaves contain oxalic acid in crystal form. If eaten uncooked, these crystals prick the digestive canals, causing painful swelling that can even be deadly. Fortunately, cooking completely breaks down the acid, alleviating the potential hazards. Taro leaf must be steamed (or boiled) for 40-60 minutes. The cooked leaf is easy to digest, subdues *pitta* and strengthens *kapha dosha.* It is best cooked with garlic and cumin seeds, which makes it balancing for *vāta dosha.* Both the root and the leaf should be eaten no more than twice a week.

SWEET POTATOES *Ipomoea batatas*

Heavy, warming, sweet potatoes increase *kapha.* Despite the label "potato," these are not members of the nightshade family. Their leaves may be used as a vegetable. Natives of tropical America, these relatives of the morning glory can be eaten by those who cannot eat white potatoes and are more nutritious. The orange-fleshed varieties are high in beta carotene (vitamin A)—the brighter the orange color, the more nutrition. They are mildly laxative and may create gas.

TURNIPS *Brassica rapa*

Sweet, pungent and cooling, turnips balance all three *doshas.* They purify the system and help it produce more blood. Turnips are prescribed for healing in cases of jaundice, edema, bronchitis, scabies, psoriasis and eczema.

YAMS *Dioscorea*

The true yams (tuberous roots of the lily family and cousins of onions and asparagus) of India, Africa and the Caribbean lack vitamin A. But they are antihelminthic (expel worms) and antihemorrhoidal. They are similar to sweet potatoes in increasing *kapha.* There are hundreds of varieties ranging from sweet to bitter to tasteless. Some are used to make poultices to reduce swelling. The quasi-yams of North America are a moist-fleshed variety of sweet potato.

Nightshade plants (Solanaceae)

Nightshade is in the solanaceae family of flowering plants. It includes the white potato, eggplant, tomato, red pepper, capsicum, tobacco and many garden ornamentals. Belladonna (*Atropa belladonna* or deadly nightshade) is from the same family. Some species, tomatoes among them, accumulate poisonous alkaloids primarily in their leaves, which should not be used. Nightshades are related to the air element. Cases are reported in which individuals have been cured of osteoarthritis simply by abstaining from all nightshade plants. These foods should be taken moderately, once or twice a week, and not mixed with yogurt, milk, melon or cucumber. Individuals with kidney stones, gallstones or gout are advised to refrain from most nightshades because of the high oxalate content. (Kidney stones are calcium oxalate crystals). Other high oxalate foods are: spinach, beet leaves, rhubbarb, parsley, cranberry, nuts, black tea and cocoa.

EGGPLANT *Solanum melongena*

Eggplant is very popular in India, though it is not as highly nutritional as other vegetables. It is somewhat toxic to the system and should not be eaten more than once a week. It is pungent, astringent and heating. It encourages *agni* and detoxifies the colon but should not be eaten by those with kidney or gallstone problems. Eggplant is high in oxalic acid, which causes the formation of calcium oxalate crystals.

POTATOES, WHITE *Solanum tuberosum*

Cool, light and dry, white potatoes aggravate *vāta,* benefit *kapha* and have a neutral effect on *pitta. Pittas* and *kaphas* do best with boiled or stewed potatoes. They should be eaten no more often than three to five days a week. *Pitta* people can eat baked potatoes. *Vāta* people need their potatoes well spiced and moistened. Potatoes, being rich in vitamin C, are an old *āyurvedic* cure for scurvy. An important part of the nutrition is in the skins. Easy to digest, they are recommended for people with nervous indigestion or liver weakness. However, eaten alone, or with fatty condiments or in poor food combinations, the potato may be constipating and *vāta* aggravating. Potatoes are one of the few nightshade plants that can accumulate enough toxins in their edible portion to be overtly toxic. Fortunately, this is easily seen. Wherever the skin has a green shade, the alkaloids solanine and chaconine have accumulated close to the surface. Peeling ⅛ inch or less off these areas will remove the toxins. Potatoes need dark, cool storage.

TOMATOES *Lycopersicon esculentum*
Tomatoes, though among the world's most popular foods, are generally toxic to the human body and should be eaten no more than once or twice a week. They are only recommended in *āyurveda* when cooked with certain spices for healing purposes. Sour and slightly pungent, ripe tomatoes upset all *doshas* when eaten raw, as do green and yellow tomatoes. Therefore, tomatoes must be eaten cooked to maintain good health.

Grains

Grains are classified as sweet by *āyurveda.* They have a grounding, calming effect, smoothing out metabolic functions. Whole grains are more nutritious and balancing than refined grains. *Vātas* and *pittas* benefit from a good helping of grains, while *kaphas* should eat somewhat less. Grains provide the energy for work. In Asia a grain may be 60 percent of a complete meal. Each type of whole grain, such as rice, wheat and millet, has its unique qualities. Sugars mixed with grains may cause gas. Whole grains keep their *prāṇa* for a year. Flour should be eaten within two weeks after grinding, lest it become *tamasic.* Breads become *tamasic* eight hours after they are baked. Refined, highly processed flour should not be eaten, for it coats the intestinal tract with a paste that is constipating and debilitates proper assimilation.

RICE *Oryza sativa*

There are over 40,000 varieties of rice. It is the queen of grains, the staple food for most of humanity, grown in countries throughout the world. *Basmati* is the famous, aromatic long-grained rice from India and Pakistan that balances all three *doshas.* It is very light and cooling. Texmati is an excellent substitute grown in North America. *Āyurveda* recommends unpolished white *basmati* mixed with mung dal, a dish called *khicheri,* as a mono-diet to balance, cleanse and rejuvenate the system. Milled varieties, some of which are parboiled before milling, have reduced nutritional value and increase *kapha* but are more easily assimilated by delicate stomachs. Rice is a miracle food which can be eaten without limitation, even at every meal.

Brown rice refers to any whole rice with only the rough husk removed but the bran and germ intact. Thus, the life force and ability to grow is retained. It is warming, heavy, moist and rough, sweet and astringent. It is balancing for *vāta,* but slightly unbalancing for *pitta* and *kapha.* Its high fiber prevents constipation. Its germ and bran contains proteins, vitamin B and minerals not found in white rice. It should be well cooked and well chewed. Mixing it half and half with barley will cool it for *pittas.* Rice and barley combined, *āyurveda* explains, dispels fatigue.

WHEAT *Triticum*

Wheat is the heaviest, moistest of all grains, excellent for gaining weight and very grounding when served with foods that are cool and moist, like cheese. Wheat is good for *vāta* and *pitta,* but unbalancing for *kapha.* It is well suited for hard physical labor and cold climates. Wheat is the second most widely used grain in the world. Rice is number one. Unfortunately, many people have a severe intolerance for wheat—one in 500 persons in some areas. Studies have traced this to exposure in early infancy, perhaps as young as three weeks. Infants cannot digest grains that early. The wheat is treated as a toxin, and the body develops antibodies which may be triggered as a reaction to the intake of wheat throughout life. Wheat reactions can be complicated by an intolerance for cow's milk, which produces similar symptoms, ranging from mild sluggishness to indigestion, headache, joint pain and moodiness, puffiness in the face and sinus problems. You can test this in your own system by simply abstaining from wheat and dairy for a few months. If such symptoms disappear, you will know your own body's tolerance. A more severe intolerance for the gluten protein in wheat results in malabsorption, bloating, irritability, diarrhea. Severe cases of gluten intolerance is called celiac's disease. Babies do best on mother's milk for even up to two years with the slow introduction of pureed fresh fruits and vegetables. The habitual use of wheat crackers and biscuits as snacks for children also contributes to wheat intolerance.

MILLET *Panicum miliaceum*

This tiny grain is hot, light and dry. It is balancing for *kapha. Vāta* types should not eat it alone as it is too light and dry. Its sweet after-effect balances out its heat for *pitta,* especially if it is cooked with extra water. Millet is high in calcium. The dark millet of India, called *ragi,* is renowned for bestowing endurance. Besides millet, many other small grass seeds, such as *quinoa* and *amaranthus,* are highly nutritious, light and easily digestible alternatives to rice and wheat.

Dals

LENTIL *Lens culinaris*

Red lentils properly prepared are *tridoshic.* They are a source of iron and so a good blood builder and liver cleanser. Lentils are a beneficial food to take during flu and diarrhea.

MUNG *Vigna radiata*

Sweet and astringent with a cooling energy, green mung beans properly cooked are light, easy to digest and balance the three *doshas.* They are good for indigestion, diarrhea, fever and eye problems. Skinless or yellow mung is sweet and cooling. It calms *kapha* and *vāta.*

TUR *Cajanus cajan*

Astringent, sweet and heating, *tur dal* made into a soup is calming for *vāta* and *kapha.* It is good for strengthening muscles and as a blood builder, also great for skin, eyes, bones and joints.

TOFU

Tofu is a bland, protein-rich cheeselike food, coagulated from an extract of soybeans. It is astringent and sweet, cooling and heavy. Its astringence is good for *kapha* but requires extra spicing with garlic, ginger or black pepper to aid digestion. *Vāta* may find tofu constipating and should eat it in moderation. It is a good food for those with a strong *pitta dosha.* Lambodara, the one with the big belly, wants His dear ones to know this about the highly popular tofu. He wishes them all to maintain a balance in life and live many long years of healthful giving.

Tofu may be eaten daily, prepared in soups and other cooked dishes. It should be prepared by warming it with heat or with spices. It should not be served cold and may not digest properly. This is the most difficult way to consume an already chilling food. It is generally steamed, stewed or lightly sauted. It should not be deep-fried or otherwise exposed to excessive heat. Tofu is very sensitive to heat and when excessively heated changes in chemistry to a form that is said to be detrimental to health. Some people are unable, due to allergy to soybeans, to digest tofu in any form. The term is Sino-Japanese: from *to,* meaning "bean," and *fu,* "ferment." Eaten in excess, tofu will increase *kapha.* Loving Gaṇeśa's thrust here is that no matter how good anything is, nothing should be eaten too much, nor too little, but just in the right amount.

URAD *Vigna mungo*

Sweet and cooling, unctuous and heavy, *urad dal* is a calming food for *vāta.* It detoxifies the system, nourishes muscle, bone and reproductive fluids. It helps lactation and energizes the whole body, but is not good for *kapha* or *pitta* disorders.

Milk Products

CHEESE

Among the many kinds of cheeses, aged hard cheeses are the most commonly sold in markets. These cheeses are sour, unctuous, heavy and oily. They are constipating and *tamasic* and should be enjoyed only two or three times a week. Most hard cheeses are made with an enzyme (called rennet) extracted from the intestines of a calf, unless mentioned otherwise. Strictly speaking, such cheeses are nonvegetarian. There are cheeses made using vegetable rennet which can be found in health food stores. Soft cheeses, including cottage cheese, being lighter, sour and sweet, are more suitable for frequent consumption and are truly vegetarian foods. These pacify *pitta.* It is always advisable for *vāta* and *kapha* people to eat cheese with some cayenne, black pepper or dry ginger powder.

GHEE

Sweet and cooling, *ghee,* clarified butter, is highly praised in scripture for its purifying, disinfecting and healing properties. It is the number-one choice for cooking, and much preferred to other oils for frying. *Ghee* enhances memory, lubricates the connective tissue and makes the body flexible. A drop applied to the eyes relieves itching and improves eyesight. Taken in excess, it increases *kapha.*

MILK

Milk is sweet, cooling and increases *kapha.* Milk in its many forms can be nectar for the human constitution. However, in *āyurveda,* "milk" means milk fresh from a contented cow, and not the medicated, homogenized, ultrapasteurized product sold in stores today. A milk fast can relieve many disorders including fever, coughs and hysteria. Milk should be boiled, as it becomes easier to digest. *Āyurveda* recommends milk be taken alone on an empty stomach as a meal in itself. Small babies and those with lactose intolerance should avoid cow's milk.

YOGURT

Sour, astringent and cooling, yogurt increases *pitta* and *kapha.* It has a generally invigorating effect to the system. Yogurt made from raw milk (and a good strain of the lactobacillus bacteria) is most nutritious and provides the necessary ingredients for good assimilation and elimination. Yogurt should always be taken with a little salt, cumin or black pepper.

Oils

Since oil breaks down rapidly when exposed to heat, light or oxygen, it is best to use *ghee* (clarified butter) for all saute needs. The advertised good-for-you polyunsaturated oils (margarine, safflower, corn, sunflower) are actually more prone to degeneration (oxidation) than butter through heating or simple exposure to ultraviolet light (sunlight), causing free radicals. Free radicals are substances with impaired electrons that swim around inside of us, looking for something they can grab onto. When they latch onto something, it's known as oxidation. Free radicals speed the aging process by destroying healthy cells as well as attacking collagen, the cement that holds cells together. Oxidation can "rust" the body as it does metal. This means cardiovascular disease, atherosclerosis (hardening of the arteries) and most of the heart problems of today's society. (The best sources for the body's much needed unsaturated fatty acids [UFA] are: flax seeds, sesame, pumpkin and sunflower seeds, eaten whole or freshly ground.) *Oil assessment by Dr. Devananda Tandavan.*

Sweeteners

HONEY

Sweet, astringent and heating, honey increases *pitta* and reduces *vāta* and *kapha.* Honey has extensive use in *āyurveda,* both as a treatment in itself for heart, throat, chest, lungs, liver and blood, and as a base in which many medicines are prepared and administered to the patient. Honey with warm water is a laxative. With black pepper it is a popular remedy for coughs and colds. Upon heating, honey loses its medicinal quality and actually becomes toxic to the system. From honey is produced the alcoholic beverage spoken of in the *Vedas* as *madhu* (Sanskṛit for honey as well), the health-giving, natural, fermented beverage known in Europe as mead.

JAGGERY *Borassus flabellifer*

Jaggery is a dark, hard brownish sugar made from the flower sap of the palmyra palm tree (the same tree that produces *toddy,* an alcoholic beverage, by a different process). As a sugar it is far superior to processed cane or beet products in both health and taste. It is available in Indian stores around the world. It is sweet in taste and heating in effect, strengthening and heavy, subduing excess *vāta,* but increasing *pitta* and *kapha.* A product from boiling sugarcane juice is often sold as jaggery, but true jaggery is from a different source.

CANE SUGAR *Saccharum officinarum*

Raw cane sugar is sweet and cooling, oily and heavy. It is most calming to *vāta,* moderately calming to *pitta* and aggravates *kapha.* A useable form of raw cane sugar is sucanat, evaporated organic sugar cane juice, which is similar in taste and texture to brown sugar. Freshly pressed sugar cane juice can also be used for beverages or to cook with. Refined white sugar, which is also derived from the sugar beet, is not recommended. Most "brown sugar" is simply refined white sugar with molasses added for color, so it is also not recommended. However, there is another form of processed sugar which is also brown, called Turbinado, which is better than processed sugar for cooking or baking.

Excessive consumption of all types of sugar depletes the immune system. Children given too much sugar or sugar-rich products, such as candy and soft drinks, become hyperactive and lose their abilities of concentration. A little known fact important to strict vegetarians is that white cane sugar is filtered through animal bones during processing.

Āyurveda Sources

Aziz, Khalid, *Step by Step Guide to Indian Cooking.* London, Hamlyn, 1974. Recipes from the five geographical regions of India, including many desserts.

Frawley, Dr. David, *Ayurvedic Healing.* Salt Lake City, Utah, Passage Press, 1989. Detailed methods of constitution balancing and treatment of common diseases.

Jain, S.K., *Dictionary of Indian Folk Medicine and Ethnobotany.* New Delhi, Deep Publications, 1991. A concise glossary of folk uses for over 2,500 Indian plants.

Johari, Harish, *The Healing Cuisine, India's Art of Ayurvedic Cooking.* Rochester, Vermont, Healing Arts Press, 1994. Explains the healing qualities of foods and spices, with vegetarian recipes based on *āyurveda.*

Lad, Usha and Dr. Vasant, *Ayurvedic Cooking for Self Healing,* Albuquerque, New Mexico, The Ayurvedic Press, 1994. Explores health and healing through diet with recipes and their medicinal and *āyurvedic* effect.

Lad, Dr. Vasant, *Āyurveda, The Science of Self-Healing.* Santa Fe, New Mexico, Lotus Press, 1985. Clearly explains the principles and practical applications of *āyurveda.*

Morningstar, Amadea and Desai, Urmila, *The Ayurvedic Cookbook,* Santa Fe, New Mexico, Lotus Press 1990. Over 250 recipes designed to balance each constitution.

Once. Twice. The Rice!

Articles on Rice from Hinduism Today, *May, 1994*

Although it is still unknown exactly when and how people started growing rice, archaeologists have uncovered evidence that rice was present in Indian civilizations at 8,000 BCE, according to Tuk-Tuk Kumar, author of *The History of Rice in India.* She argues that rice husks used to temper clay pottery at Koldihawa and Mahagara sites indicate that a domesticated rice was grown at that time. Other researchers document a slender, wild strain called Indica growing on Himalayan slopes about 4,000 years ago. Extraordinary in yield, nutrition, resistance to disease, adaptability and savor, rice migrated around the globe with little promotion. Today, India's prized aromatic rice, Basmati, is found as far from its birthplace as Kenya and California.

Hinduism's ancient scriptures have many references to rice. Kumar notes that the *Yajur Veda* describes the preparation of rice cakes as a ritual offering. In the *Atharva Veda,* rice, along with barley, are described as "healing balms, the sons of heaven who never die." *Smṛitis* tell how Goddess Devī Lalithāmbikā is known to be especially fond of *payasa annam,* sweet rice. Indeed, husked rice is always present in even the simplest Hindu *pūjā* as one of the offerings. So revered is rice that, if mixed with turmeric powder, it can substitute if necessary for costly items for the *mūrtis* such as dress, ornaments, even flowers.

Rice is also a potent symbol of auspiciousness and fertility. South Indians call rice Anna Lakshmī. *Anna* means "food" and Lakshmī is the Goddess of prosperity. From ancient times, the ever-giving Goddess Dhānya Lakshmī has been depicted holding a few sheaves of rice in Her hand. The most special offering to Lord Gaṇeśa is the *modaka,* a ball of sweet coconut-jaggery fill covered with a thick rice paste. The first food fed a child is rice. In Rajasthan, when a woman first enters her husband's house, a measure of rice is kept on the threshold. This she scatters through her new home inviting prosperity and happiness. In South India, raw rice, mixed with *kuṅkuma* to redden it, is known as *maṅgala akshadai* and showered over newlyweds. At a harvest festival, *Tai Pongal,* rice is ceremoniously cooked, Sūrya, God of the sun, is worshiped and the nature spirits are thanked.

But this reverence for rice is not restricted to India. The Angkabau of Sumatra use special rice plants to denote the Rice Mother, Indoea Padi. The people of Indochina treat ripened rice in bloom like a pregnant woman, capturing its spirit in a basket. Rice growers of the Malay Peninsula often treat the wife of the cultivator as a pregnant woman for the first three days after storing the rice. Even the Sundanese of West Java, who consider themselves Muslims, believe rice is the personification of the rice Goddess Dewi Sri. In Thailand, when you call the family to a meal you say, "Eat rice." In Japan, to goad children to eat all their rice, grains are called "little Buddhas," and girls are told every grain they leave on the plate will become a pock mark on the face of their future husband. In China, the word for rice is the same as food. The Toradja tribals of Indonesia consider rice to be of heavenly origin. So hallowed was the grain, that it was taboo to plant any other crop in the rice fields. The Ahnishinabe Native American Indian tribe of North America say their ancestors saw tracts of wild rice in visions. So they migrated to the central part of USA-Canada, found the rice, and to this day, gather and trade it for their livelihood.

Winona Laduke is of the Ahnishinabe tribe of Native American Indians. She shared in a *Seeds of Change* magazine interview: "I live on the White Earth reservation. I work mostly on the land. In our language, most nouns are animate, whether it is the word for corn, for wild rice, *min-o-*

min, or stone. Having spirit and standing on its own, I'm very careful when I harvest it because I must reckon with that spirit. In our culture, the respect you have when you harvest is what ensures that you are able to continue harvesting. It is not because you're smart or clever, it's because you're respectful and you are worthy of receiving. Before rice, I offer *ah-say-mah,* tobacco, to that plant—that rice. *Min-o-min* was given to us by our Creator."

Dietetically, rice is cherished as a cholesterol-free, protein-calorie cornucopia. Most people in Asia obtain 60 to 80 percent of their calories from rice. Rice becomes a "complete protein," equivalent to beef protein, when eaten with beans or lentils because the enzymes in rice help to process the proteins in the lentil. As a result, rice is rarely served in India without some kind of lentil or dal.

Rice is prepared in many different ways. In the Far East, it is often squeezed into noodles. In South India, it is soaked overnight and made into fluffy *idlis* or thin, crêpe-like *dosas.* In Northern India, it is often cooked with sweetened milk to form *kheer.* People in Gujarat celebrate *Sharad Pūrṇimā* by soaking flattened rice in sweet milk which they drink at night. Drinking this "*dood-powa*" on this night is said to protect health. In Northern India, people celebrate the festival of *Dīpāvalī* with sugar candy, *batasha,* and *khil,* puffed rice.

In addition to its value as a food, rice serves other purposes in Asia. In Japan, every home is floored with elegant rice mats, called *tatami.* Villagers wear rice straw sandals, and the whole nation unwinds daily on a delicate rice wine, *sake.* In rural India, cooked rice is used as a glue. A verse in ancient Tamil literature says women would dress up in elegant sārīs starched with rice *kanji,* the excess water drained after the rice is cooked. Rice flour is used by housewives to make the beautiful religious *kolam* designs each dawn in front of their homes—and at temples for festivals—to ward off negative energies. Ants are allowed to eat the *kolam* (*raṅgoli* in Sanskṛit) as a natural cycle is fulfilled in a display of human kindness for the most defenseless of creatures.

When I was in India in the 1980s I participated in a Guru Mahāsannidhānam parade around the Meenakshi Temple. The parade was preceded by a grand *pūjā* to Lord Gaṇeśa. Walking beside me was the publisher of HINDUISM TODAY, Satguru Sivaya Subramuniyaswami, and the Holiness of the oldest *aadheenam* in India, Madurai Aadheenam, Śrī-la-Śrī Arunagirināthа Śrī Gnanasambanda Desikar Paramacharya Swamigal. There were three or four elephants in front of us, two or three camels, numerous drummers, *nāgasvara* players and other musicians. After the parade, the elephants and other animals enjoyed an abundant dinner of delicious rice.

Editorial: Rice with Spice Is Twice as Nice

Prolog: Behold life's passing into paradise. How like a languid Vedic sacrifice, with days and years poured into flames of soul in rites precise. How randomless, this intertwined device, where lice have cats and cats have mice. How bountifully it folds eternity into each tiny trice, and hugely unconcise, with fire and ice and fifty thousand kinds of rice.

Deep within the granite mountains of Colorado, where you might expect to find a secret Defense Department stockpile of missiles awaiting the end of the Cold War thaw, lies another kind of reserve. It is a dark, clinically sterile cold room, kept meticulously at 42°F. and a relative humidity between 25 and 30. This is not the vault for a lethal chemical gas antidote or a vaccine for some exotic virus. These chambers, maintained by the United States Department of Agriculture, hold one of the strategic guarantors of human survival—16,474 varieties of rice. If that sounds like a lot, it's a mere fraction of the planet's diversity. India alone (where rice is said to have originated) had 50,000 varieties under cultivation over the centuries. Today most of India's rice comes from fewer than ten varieties.

Bill Clinton is not spending all that money to save Uncle Ben's pre-cooked, short-grain, sticky-white, highly-polished, nutrition-free, artificially-enriched rice for future generations. Uncle Ben's is a kind of paradigm of the West's naivete and historical neglect of rice. It opted for quick-cooking, high-yielding grains, while the East bred its strains for taste and texture. To export, the West selected for long shelf life; in the East 90% of all rice is consumed within eight miles of the fields where it is grown. Did you know that rice yields 6,000 pounds per acre and that 25% of the meager 20 pounds of rice each American consumes in a year is imbibed as beer?

"As rice goes, so will go the world's encounter with starvation," Dr. Charles Balach, the Texas-based guru of America's rice breeding program, now retired, told me last week. This is a man who knows his rice. He bred the variety that feeds most American appetites, a task that took him 8 years (15 years can be devoted to manipulating just the right combination of genes). He observes, "Rice has been cultivated for at least 7,000 years in China. Farmers spent generations selectively getting the 'bad' genes out of a strain, and it's very easy for us to introduce those back inadvertently as we try to improve a strain."

That's exactly what happened, says Dr. Robert Dilday of University of Arkansas' Rice Research Center. "Breeders here were going for the high yields. In the process we didn't recognize, and thus we left out, important strengths." Fortunately, there is a germ plasm program and collection, the one mentioned above. "There are thousands of very ordinary varieties there, seemingly useless. But they may hold some special quality we will want in the future, and it will be there. That's the beauty, and the justification, for this massive collection effort."

Dr. Dilday is beguiled by the variants: from the Japanese Super Rice Kernel (twice the length of the longest long grain, akin to a 12-foot-tall person) to the messy Purple Bran that when it flowers "stains your fingers like you were picking blackberries." Then there are killer rices. He doesn't call them that, preferring "allelopathic," the term scientists use to describe the ability of certain plants to produce natural chemicals that suppress or even kill weed growth within an 8–10" radius. A grain that controls its own competition,

Fingers, Forks or Chopsticks?

The world can be divided into three kinds of people: finger-feeders, fork-feeders and chopstick-feeders. Fork-feeders predominate in Europe and North America only. Chopstick-feeders rule most of Eastern Asia. Finger-feeders are the most widespread, prevailing in India, Sri Lanka, Indonesia and much of Africa. Globally, fork-feeders are a minority, outnumbered more than two to one. Chopsticks have a venerable history, dating back to 1200 BCE, while forks first appeared in the 10th century CE in the Byzantine empire. Although forks first entered society on the tables of the rich and well-born, many royalty, including Queen Elizabeth I and Louis XIV, used fingers.

without chemicals? It's a farmer's dream, and breeders have found six of them.

Americans are relative newcomers to rice cultivation, with a mere 300 years spent growing a handful of types. They are partial to wheat. Rice may sustain half the world, but in America it has been an export commodity known only in an insipid encounter with an anonymous soup ingredient or as a rare substitute for potatoes. Not anymore. There is a rice revolution going on in North America, and a smaller one in Europe. Basically, when immigration laws changed to allow more Asians in, millions answered the call. From Thailand, Cambodia, India, Korea and China they brought with them their culture, their clothing, their language and, of course, their penchant for rice.

When a Thai housewife cooked the Texas long-grain (which traces its roots to Indonesia, then Madagascar and thence to South Carolina in the 17th century), she was totally underwhelmed. Where was the taste? What happened to the sweet aromas she was accustomed to? Nothing. Zip. Not only that, who could eat this Yankee carbohydrate with chopsticks? Not even a black belt epicure could handle this dry grain where every pellet was an individual. In India it is said "Rice should be like brothers: close but not stuck together." But Thais were accustomed to rices that, like Thai people, stick together (stickiness is determined by the ratio of two different starches, amylose and amylopectin). Some varieties are so sticky that if you put a chopstick in a bowl, the entire mass comes out together. Thai gourmets and gourmands love that kind. They break it off with their hands, dip it deeply into a spicy gravy. My theory is that cultures that eat with chopsticks evolved sticky kinds, fork-eaters selected very dry specimens, and those of us who eat with our hands developed in-between varieties.

Faced with their finicky family's famished frowns, Asian women forsook all hope of getting decent rice in the US and began importing it. Tons of it. In fact, 39,690,000 pounds last year, nearly 10% of all the rice consumed in America. Farmers who didn't know a Basmati—which means "Queen of Fragrance"—from a Jasmine suddenly woke up to the new reality. Asians had highly sophisticated tastes and would not settle for anything less than grandma had cooked over an open fire. They were even willing to pay a premium for quality, a big one. Aged Basmati sells for nearly $2 a pound! The wheels of free enterprise cranked up. Breeding programs began, expensive ones focused on one goal: produce and market an aromatic rice that equaled that most popular of all imports, Thai Jasmine.

Thai Jasmine is the monarch of short-grained sticky rices. Its smell is alluring, its texture is described as not-too-wet-not-too-dry, and its taste is savory sweet. American breeders imported a Thai strain from the famed International Rice Research Institute in Manila. They crossed it with a high-yielding Philippine stock, added a little of this DNA, a sprinkle of that and after many years celebrated the christening of Jasmine 85. It was to be the import killer. Hundreds of acres went under the Texas plow in 1989. Thai cooks by the thousands eagerly hauled home the first heavy bags of Jasmine 85, steamed it in the old country way, served it up and—"Yuck"—never went back for more.

"What happened?" marketers mourned. "What happened?" southern farmers fretted. "What happened?" rice breeders brooded. No one could explain. It tasted and smelled the same. It cooked the same. It looked the same. It was cheap. Yet it was a giant flop. Spurious stories spread that only US rats would touch it. Thai rodents preferred starvation. Well, that was the story.

This real-life disaster was a turning point in US rice consciousness. Americans, who pride themselves as the world's most efficient rice farmers, realized they couldn't detect differences which Asians readily perceived. They had made the mistake of not putting a single Asian on their select quality committee. "Before this experience, we didn't recognize the subtlety of it. Or maybe we didn't believe it. Now we believe. It started with the Asians, but now the Anglos are picking up on it too," Dr. Bill Webb confided to me.

The search intensifies as imports continue to grow. US researchers now respect the preferences of the strong Asian market, and they have redoubled their efforts to match qualities found in Southeast Asia. In private they confess, "We're no longer trying to replace the rices from India and Pakistan, but to develop a kind of poor-man's Basmati." Nor can they just bring rices in and plant them. It's against the law. Besides, rice adapts itself to climates, to soils and weather patterns, not to mention birds, insects and diseases. All grains must be bred to US conditions. Those who touted the glories of Texas Long Grain now speak wistfully of approximating a Punjabi Basmati or an Italian Arboria. They are breeding Purple Bran, Spanish Bahia, Black Japonica and dozens of others, hoping to capture the burgeoning niche market for specialty, fragrant rices. For the record, our own absolutely favorite rice, one with no equal in all three worlds, is the ruddy, fluffy Red Country rice, known as *urarisi* in Tamil, grown near Jaffna, Sri Lanka.

Epilog: How nice is rice, especially served with spice.
How it can, at meager price, twice or thrice each day suffice.
How gentle and how very free from vice are those whose
fodder, in the main, is rice.

"The editor's jest, full of zest, is the best as he exalts us
to eat the elite. Rice is so nice served with sweetness or spice.
Can we resist this taste treat? Basmati, Bahia, Arboria,
Japonica—twice, thrice a day, cooked in a legion of ways; rice,
we recite, the ambrosial delight, gracing our palate
each day," Kulamātā Tara Katir, Kauai, USA.

Health through Āyurveda

By Dr. Devananda Tandavan, Four Columns
Reprinted from HINDUISM TODAY, *1991*

Āyurveda, the ancient Indian study of life, uses the *tri-dosha* theory to explain human makeup and behavior. It is considered by the ancient seers that man's psychological and physical makeup may be classified as belonging to a specific type of constitution called *prakṛiti*, the underlying or inherent nature of one's being. It is nature that determines how we behave, what we desire, what we enjoy, our physical constitution and how we respond to all of the stresses of living. It further determines our physical, psychological, social and religious patterns of behavior.

The *prakṛiti* is divided into three main *doshas* or forces that help to bind the five elemental forces into living flesh. These *doshas* are *vāta*, *pitta* and *kapha* representing the philosophical elements air, fire and water, respectively. If we know our *prakṛiti* and are well versed in the foods and activities that are natural to or that aggravate the *doshas*, we can maintain a more peaceful and healthy body and mind.

Very few of us have a pure *prakṛiti* of only one *dosha*, most of us have combinations. That is, we all have all three *doshas* within our makeup, but there is usually a prominence of one or two. For perfect health the goal is to have all of the *doshas* balanced within our *prakṛiti*.

There are seven possibilities of constitutional types: V, VP, P, PK, K, VK, VPK balanced (equal force from each *dosha*). What causes these constitutional types? They are determined at the time of conception and depend upon many factors, such as the spiritual state of the parents at conception, the astrology of the moment, physiology, genetics, and the physical health of the parents. Once the constitutional type is set, it is maintained for the balance of one's life.

It is possible by studying the various types to analyze one's own type from the similarities and dissimilarities with the characteristic patterns and varying categories. The difficulty with this is that we have a tendency to choose characteristics that seem to be "better" or of a "higher type."

It is more accurate to learn one's *prakṛiti* through the *āyurvedic* pulse diagnosis. Those who are trained in the method are able to determine which is the basic type and also able to determine if there are any imbalances. It is said that the real masters of this art are able to tell you about your entire past medical history, even to the extent of what surgery has been performed, as well as your present state of balance of the *doshas.*

In order to simplify this rather complex theory, we speak of the *prakṛiti* as a structura; the basis upon which we (in all of our facets) are structured. We also speak of each *dosha* as though it were a truly separate and concrete form of energy with usual effects upon our being. The extensive study of the *prakṛiti* and the *doshas* is only a small part of the vast field of *āyurveda.*

Āyurveda has studied the natural construction of man and his behavior in order to bring his very being into a closer natural harmony with nature. The very ancient science has a great deal to offer to the health of the world today.

Vāta Dosha

In order to be healthy, according to the *āyurvedic* system of medicine, we must have some knowledge of the character of each *dosha* and how to maintain a balance between them. Balance is attained by varying the diet and activities according to the climate, time of day and the individual's nature.

Vāta is the *dosha* that is the base or driver of all motion within the body. It is the nature of the air/ether elements. It governs all biological movement such as breathing, muscular contraction, heartbeats and movement of single pulses through the nerves. It determines metabolism through the motion of the cell substances and controls the thoughts by leading the mind to constant, desirable objects rather than determined ones. *Vāta* is the root cause of the sense of hearing and stimulates the body fire for appetite. It causes the elimination of urine and feces. It distributes *pitta* and *kapha* in the body. It maintains the health and function of the body depending upon its balance. It also governs emotions such as pain, fear, nervousness, anxiety, tremors, and muscle spasms. *Vāta's* physical properties are dry, expanding, light, cold, penetrating, subtle, rough and dispersing. *Vāta* dominates the fall season and is also most prominent between 2AM to 6AM and 2PM to 6PM. During these times, it is not wise to do or ingest anything that may bring about an imbalance of the *vāta* force. It is this time dominance that suggests that we rise from sleep each day before sunrise. *Vāta* is also dominant in the old-age period, that is, "life over fifty."

Vāta's natural seat is in the colon, pelvic cavity, bones, skin, ears and thighs. Imbalance will cause an accumulation of *vāta* in these areas with resulting diseases such as skin rashes and growths, constipation, abundant flatulence, bloating, bone and joint changes, decreasing mobility, impaired hearing, increased fear and memory loss and often confusion. In the fall we are still geared to a preponderance of *pitta*, so the changes in weather, although pleasant, may aggravate the *vāta dosha*, especially if we have a strong *vāta* constitution.

In order to counteract or attempt to balance this, we should always keep warm and protect ourselves from the strong winds and draft. We must avoid cold foods and drinks, supplementing our diet with warmer, heavier and moister foods but decreasing the *vāta*-aggravating foods such as beans, raw foods such as apples and anything from the cabbage family. Decrease pungent, bitter and astringent tastes as these aggravate *vāta:* increase the sweet, salty and sour tastes, as they tend to balance *vāta.* Dairy products are good to take in moderate amounts.

It is advisable to follow very closely to a routine, which may be boring, for this tends to balance or ground *vāta.* Long air travel tends to aggravate *vāta,* and this can be remedied by keeping warm and quiet and by good deep meditation. Alcohol aggravates *vāta,* especially in the artificial atmosphere of air travel. Sure ways to imbalance *vāta* are to worry, eat on the run, get too little sleep, eat dry, frozen or left-over foods, keep on the move or work at night.

Pitta Dosha

Vāta dosha has to do with energy in motion. *Pitta* is the force that balances the kinetic energy of *vāta* and the potential energy of *kapha. Pitta* is of fire/water energy, is dominant in July to October and peaks at noon and midnight. It governs metabolism, the enzymatic and endocrine systems, and has great influence on the mental activities. *Pitta dosha*'s function is pigmentation, digestion, heat, intelligence, sight, hunger, thirst, softness and radiance of the body, cheerfulness and courage. The physical properties of *pitta* are lightly viscid, non-sticky, active, hot to touch and bitter to taste. It is a combination of elemental fire and water. The normal seat is the duodenum (first section of the small intestine), liver and spleen. It also resides in the heart, eyes and skin and accounts for the skin's radiant heat and health.

Deranged or unbalanced *pitta* may bring about changes in sight, digestion and inflammations of the skin. There is a tendency to be overheated and very thirsty. Ulcers, colitis, migraine headaches, hepatitis, allergies and hyperthyroidism are typical *pitta* diseases. *Pitta* people are of medium build and usually thin. They may have many moles or freckles or other skin blemishes. The skin is soft and warm; the hair is thin and silken. Normally these people have a strong digestion and huge appetites. They crave sweet, bitter, astringent tastes and cold drinks. They do not tolerate sun or heat well, as their body temperature is elevated. They are intelligent and sharp and like to be leaders. They are ambitious and have emotional tendencies toward anger, hate and jealousy.

In order to balance *pitta*, one must keep cool by avoiding heat and the warmer parts of the day, as well as the warmer climates. Avoid oils, fried foods, caffeine, salt, alcohol and hot spices. Plenty of grains and moderate dairy products tend to balance *pitta*, as do sweet, bitter and astringent tastes. Lots of fresh air is advised. Remaining calm and serene helps the *pitta* person to remain balanced. The important thing is to keep cool physically and mentally with such aids as cool, shady spots and cooling rinses after showers.

Hot spices and heavy, oily, fried foods aggravate *pitta*. Hard cheeses, sour cream, buttermilk and yogurt are to be used in very small portions, if at all. The cooling spices such as cumin, coriander, saffron, dill, mint and parsley are valuable in the *pitta* diet. Garlic is very aggravating to this constitution, and thus must sadly be avoided. Deranging the *pitta* constitution is easily accomplished—but hardly recommended—by the following: drink plenty of alcohol, eat spicy foods, especially tomatoes, chilies, raw onions and highly salted foods. Engage in frustrating activities, use drugs, especially cocaine, speed or marijuana, and wear tight, hot clothes. Avoid cool, fresh, peaceful places. Repress your feelings and eat as much red meat and salted fish as possible. These unhealthy forces are highly reactive and must be routinely excreted from the body. *Vāta* is eliminated from the body as gas and muscular or nervous energy. *Pitta* is eliminated from the body through acid, bile and perspiration.

Kapha Dosha

The last of the *tridosha* forces is *kapha*, active during March to June and early morning and early evening. Breakfast should be eaten by *pitta* and *vāta* people between 6 and 7AM. However, this is *kapha* time, so *kapha* people should not eat then, as it would increase the *kapha* within the body. *Kapha* is not mucus but produces mucus to eliminate its forces.

Kapha dosha's main function is viscidity, nourishment, binding of the joints, solidarity, fortitude, forbearance, patience and abstinence. Its physical properties are: motionless, viscid, sticky, heavy, sweet, inert, cold, soft, white and *tamasic. Kapha* is a combination of the earth and water elements. The challenge of a *kaphic* person is to overcome inertia and the desire to have and hold on to everything, even old outgrown attitudes and reactions. The natural site of *kapha dosha* is above the diaphragm. Unbalanced *kapha* produces heaviness in the body, drowsiness, numbness, feeling of old age, dyspepsia, sweet taste in the mouth, loss of memory, decrease in sensations and general debility. If the *kapha* is depleted, there is dryness, weakness, thirst and feeling of internal heat and emptiness.

Activities that imbalance *kapha* are: taking long naps after eating, eating lots of fat and oils, overeating, letting inertia take over your body and mind, not exercising, using drugs (especially sedatives and tranquilizers), never skipping desserts (especially ice cream and gooey, sticky ones), enjoying the sedentary TV life daily and interrupting viewing only by eating large meals and excessive snacking of salty and gooey foods.

In order to balance the *kapha dosha*: exercise daily, reduce fatty foods, eliminate iced drinks and foods and excessive amounts of bread and pastries. Also, eat warm, light and dry foods and have a lot of variety in the menus with vegetables, peppers, ginger, garlic, and turmeric. Keep salt consumption low. Most seeds and all nuts should be eliminated from the diet. Popcorn with no fat or salt is excellent.

The diseases common to *kaphic* constitution are: coughs, excess mucus, bronchitis, rheumatic fever, aching joints, pleurisy, pericarditis, sinusitis, nasal congestion, accentuation of greedy tendencies (holding onto things such as repressions, body wastes), lethargy and sloth.

Conclusion

By careful attention to diet, varying it according to the season of the year and the time of the day with special reference to one's constitutional *dosha*, we are able to balance the *doshas*. This balance is the first step to a healthy and disease-free life. If there is such an upset of the *doshic* balance that a disease process is present, treatments using *prāṇāyāma*, massage, cleansing, aromatherapy, herbals, gems and other techniques are available to the *āyurvedic* physician. Remember that mental balance and a balanced diet according to one's constitution are the basis of health.

Food for Thought: What You Eat Affects Mind, Body and Emotions

Reprinted from Hinduism Today, *February, 1992*

Food comes from nature. According to the ancient science of *āyurveda,* nature is a primordial force of life composed in three modes, qualities or principles of manifestation called *guṇas,* meaning "strand or quality." The three *guṇas* are: *sattva,* "beingness;" *rajas,* "dynamism;" and *tamas,* "darkness." *Sattva* is the tranquil energy, *rajas* is active energy and *tamas* is energy that is inert. The nature of *sattva* is quiescent, rarified, translucent, pervasive. The nature of *rajas* is movement, action, emotion. The nature of *tamas* is inertia, denseness, contraction, resistance and dissolution. These *guṇas* are not separate entities, but varied dimensions or frequencies of the single essential life force. Like all things in the universe, the food we eat has one or more of these qualities of energy and affects our mind, body and emotions accordingly. Hence, what we eat is important. *Sattvic* food is especially good for a contemplative life.

Sattvic food makes the mind calm.

Our peaceful friend on the left above is blessing his food before he begins to eat. This sanctifies the naturally pure elements of his meal of fruits, whole grains, cooked vegetables, salad and pure water. Fresh and close to their natural state, his *sattvic* foods are lightly cooked and seasoned. He could also have fresh dairy products, yogurt or cheese made with vegetable rennet. His mind and emotions will be as wholesome as his meal, not disturbed by agitating or dulling elements in his food. His body will be fully nourished by life-giving carbohydrates, protein and vitamins.

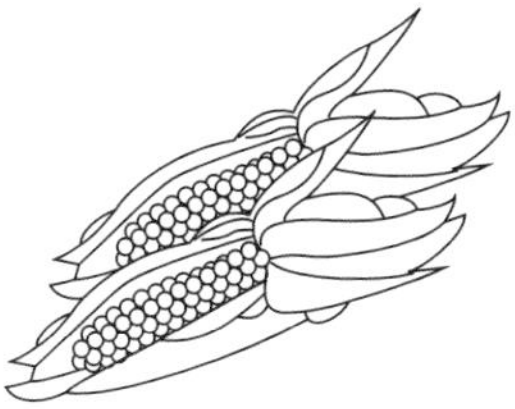

Whole grains and legumes are *sattvic,* such as brown rice, whole wheat, millet, corn, soybeans, lentils, oats and beans.

Freshly picked organically grown vegetables are *sattvic,* such as celery, cauliflower, zucchini, lettuce, green beans, broccoli and asparagus.

Fresh fruits are *sattvic,* such as apples, peaches, oranges, bananas, dates, guavas, berries and papayas.

***Rajasic* food makes the mind restless.** Our active friend in the middle in the drawing is about to enjoy his meal of spicy fish, potatoes, parsley and wine. Though nutritious, this food will excite his mind, emotions and body, causing a continuously restless state. Just as he desires new food and spices to enjoy, he desires ever-changing emotional and intellectual gratification. He will be aggressive with others, not at peace with himself and subject to illness. Fish, foul, eggs, meat (except beef and pork, which are tamasic), coffee, tobacco and spicy foods are all *rajasic*. This diet militates against a calm approach to life.

Fish and meat are *rajasic*, such as salmon, sole, trout, lamb, chicken, turkey, tuna, venison and eggs.

Spices are *rajasic*, such as salt, cayenne, black pepper and ginger. So are onions, radishes and garlic.

Stimulants are *rajasic*, such as coffee, tea, sugar, cola drinks and chocolate. In moderation, beer and wine are *rajasic*.

***Tamasic* food makes the mind dull.** Our lethargic friend on the right in the picture is about to enjoy a standard American meal: cheeseburger and fries, with bourbon on ice to drink. He is unwittingly consuming largely lifeless matter. The patty of beef has been treated with chemicals, frozen, then cooked hours in advance. The cheese was curdled with rennet from calf stomach. The refined white bun provides precious little nutrition. The deep-fried french fries are difficult to digest. The drink will blur his senses. With this heavy load to digest, it is no wonder our friend's mind is a little dull.

Beef and veal are *tamasic* as are preserved meats such as hot dogs, sausages, sardines, bologna, bacon and ham.

Deep-fried foods are *tamasic*, such as french fries. So are foods preserved with salt or by pickling in vinegar.

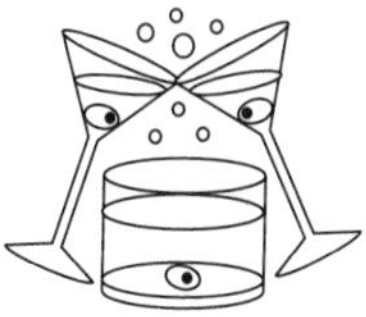

Hard liquor is *tamasic*, such as gin, vodka, arrack, whisky, rum, scotch, martinis and other mixed drinks.

Hindū Sampradāyāḥ

हिन्दूसम्प्रदायाः

Hindu Denominations

Hindu Denominations

WESTERN-EDUCATED PERSONS HAVE LONG BEEN PERPLEXED BY AND SOMETIMES APPREHENSIVE ABOUT THE MYSTERIOUS EAST and its mystical ways. But one hundred years ago a bridge between East and West began to grow as Hindu *swāmīs* and *sants* traveled to the West, and Western seekers journeyed East. Millions discovered an incredible spiritual wealth, and many sought in succeeding years to become a part of it. But, alas, they were firmly held back because of the misconceived, caste-based, *bramanical* imperative, "You have to be born a Hindu to be a Hindu." Lord Gaṇeśa had already set aside this obstacle through the world-renowned Swāmī Vivekānanda Mahārāj, whose views were affirmed by Śrī S. Rādhakṛishṇan, former president of India [see quotes on page 542-543]. It is now and has always been possible for *ardha*-Hindus to fully and formally enter the Hindu faith.

More than zealous *ardha*-Hindus or self-proclaimed Hindus could hope to understand, let alone practice, in one lifetime is contained within the Sanātana Dharma. *Ardha*-Hindus include the Western Hindu attracted to the truths of Hinduism, the Indian person whose family did not offer training in the family's faith and the follower of a *guru* who does not bring his devotees into the fullness that he was given. Whatever their background, *ardha*-Hindus must, for clear direction and a straight path for the future, choose one of the four sects or denominations under the one Hindu banner and a particular *guru* lineage within it. They know that the term *Hinduism,* used mostly in English, or *Sanātana Dharma,* used mostly when speaking Asian languages, does not describe a single religion, but uncounted paths roughly organized in four broad sects. It is, of course, necessary to make an educated choice, and certain study is required. The following information may help in understanding the essential differences and similarities of each of the four major sects: Śaivism, Śāktism, Vaishṇavism and Smārtism, and begin to indicate the many spiritual lineages within each. Here the *guru* can be helpful, for at a certain point within the spiritual life of the devotee, it is necessary to embrace and become an acknowledged member of his sect within it. This is done through the name-giving sacrament, *nāmakaraṇa saṁskāra,* ideally performed by a priest who belongs to the sect or lineage you are entering. How to enter Hinduism is explained in Chapter 24.

Many modern Indian *gurus* have become liberal universalists to their public in order to serve those of all persuasions. But within their heart of hearts they maintain their *guru's* traditions or that of their family. To fathom the *guru's* denomination, if he is hesitant to divulge it, ferret it out by slowly inquiring as to his family lineage and that of his initiating *guru,* as well as the Deity he pays most homage to. Hindu priests, of which there are tens of thousands, are clear and open about the sect for which they perform their services.

In reading on into this chapter take a good look at yourself and how you have evolved into the Eternal Truth, Sanātana Dharma. At the end of this chapter is a Paramparā Vrata, or vow, to your *guru* and his lineage. It is necessary to make a firm commitment to the *guru* lineage of your choice. Commitment impresses the deep inner mind and gives the strength to persevere on the path to the top without distractions and attain the highest goal of one's *dharma.* Incidentally, this chapter came about at the very end of the creation of this book. It was our loving Gaṇeśa Himself who ordered the formal entrance into the Sanātana Dharma for those awakening souls who are close but not yet fully committed. We have discovered through His guidance the fullness of dedication as the following verses explain. Read on!

The *Kulārṇava Tantra,* an authoritative text of the Āgamic tradition, focuses unambiguously on the ultimate quest for God Realization, the highest Self within, calling on us to leave aside our attachments, our desires, our misapprehensions and to live a divine life, a holy life, on this earth and seek for the Self within under the guidance of a *satguru.* Here are a few of its profound verses (translated by Śrī M.P. Pundit in 1916).

> It is only on this earth—and that too in a human body endowed with a soul—that one can choose one's path for spiritual progress. But not all are aware of the precious opportunity afforded by human birth, which is truly the ladder to Liberation. The Self is to be realized only here in this life. If here you do not find it and work out the means for your Liberation, where else is it possible? It is possible nowhere else. It has to be worked out by yourself from within yourself.
>
> Remember, the physical body does not last forever. Age prowls like a leopard; diseases attack like an enemy. Death waits not to see what is done or not done. Before the limbs lose their vitality, before adversities crowd in upon you, take to the auspicious path.
>
> Therefore, choose, then worship a *satguru.* Worship his feet. Cherish the very sandals *(pāduka)* which hold his feet. It is these feet, when remembered, that protect in times of distress, danger or calamity.

On the following five pages is a brief presentation of the major denominations of Hinduism, drawn from *Dancing with Śiva, Hinduism's Contemporary Catechism.*

What Are Hinduism's Principal Sects?

ŚLOKA 6

The Sanātana Dharma, or "eternal faith," known today as Hinduism, is a family of religions that accept the authority of the *Vedas*. Its four principal denominations are Śaivism, Śāktism, Vaishṇavism and Smārtism. Aum.

BHĀSHYA

The world's billion Hindus, one-sixth of the human family, are organized in four main denominations, each distinguished by its Supreme Deity. For Vaishṇavites, Lord Vishṇu is God. For Śaivites, God is Śiva. For Śāktas, Goddess Śakti is supreme. For Smārtas, liberal Hindus, the choice of Deity is left to the devotee. Each has a multitude of *guru* lineages, religious leaders, priesthoods, sacred literature, monastic communities, schools, pilgrimage centers and tens of thousands of temples. They possess a wealth of art and architecture, philosophy and scholarship. These four sects hold such divergent beliefs that each is a complete and independent religion. Yet, they share a vast heritage of culture and belief—*karma, dharma,* reincarnation, all-pervasive Divinity, temple worship, sacraments, manifold Deities, the *guru-śishya* tradition and the *Vedas* as scriptural authority. While India is home to most Hindus, large communities flourish worldwide. The *Vedas* elaborate, "He is Brahmā. He is Śiva. He is Indra. He is the immutable, the supreme, the self-luminous. He is Vishṇu. He is life. He is time. He is the fire, and He is the moon." Aum Namaḥ Śivāya.

What Is the Deeply Mystical Śaiva Sect?

ŚLOKA 7

Śaivism is the world's oldest religion. Worshiping God Śiva, the compassionate One, it stresses potent disciplines, high philosophy, the *guru's* centrality and *bhakti-rāja-siddha yoga* leading to oneness with Śiva within. Aum.

BHĀSHYA

Śaivism is ancient, truly ageless, for it has no beginning. It is the precursor of the many-faceted religion now termed Hinduism. Scholars trace the roots of Śiva worship back more than 8,000 years to the advanced Indus Valley civilization. But sacred writings tell us there never was a time when Śaivism did not exist. Modern history records six main schools: Śaiva Siddhānta, Pāśupatism, Kashmīr Śaivism, Vīra Śaivism, Siddha Siddhānta and Śiva Advaita. Śaivism's grandeur and beauty are found in a practical culture, an enlightened view of man's place in the universe and a profound system of temple mysticism and *siddha yoga.* It provides knowledge of man's evolution from God and back to God, of the soul's unfoldment and awakening guided by enlightened sages. Like all the sects, its majority are devout families, headed by hundreds of orders of *swāmīs* and *sādhus* who follow the fiery, world-renouncing path to *moksha.* The *Vedas* state, "By knowing Śiva, the Auspicious One who is hidden in all things, exceedingly fine, like film arising from clarified butter, the One embracer of the universe—by realizing God, one is released from all fetters." Aum Namaḥ Śivāya.

What Is the Magic and Power of Śāktism?

ŚLOKA 8

Śāktism reveres the Supreme as the Divine Mother, Śakti or Devī, in Her many forms, both gentle and fierce. Śāktas use *mantra, tantra, yantra, yoga* and *pūjā* to invoke cosmic forces and awaken the *kuṇḍalinī* power. Aum.

BHĀSHYA

While worship of the Divine Mother extends beyond the pale of history, Śākta Hinduism arose as an organized sect in India around the fifth century. Today it has four expressions—devotional, folk-shamanic, *yogic* and universalist—all invoking the fierce power of Kālī or Durgā, or the benign grace of Pārvatī or Ambikā. Śākta devotionalists use *pūjā* rites, especially to the *Śrī Chakra yantra,* to establish intimacy with the Goddess. Shamanic Śāktism employs magic, trance mediumship, firewalking and animal sacrifice for healing, fertility, prophecy and power. Śākta *yogīs* seek to awaken the sleeping Goddess Kuṇḍalinī and unite her with Śiva in the *sahasrāra chakra.* Śākta universalists follow the reformed Vedāntic tradition exemplified by Śrī Rāmakṛishṇa. "Left-hand" *tantric* rites transcend traditional ethical codes. Śāktism is chiefly *advaitic,* defining the soul's destiny as complete identity with the Unmanifest, Śiva. Central scriptures are the *Vedas, Śākta Āgamas* and *Purāṇas.* The *Devī Gītā* extols, "We bow down to the universal soul of all. Above and below and in all four directions, Mother of the universe, we bow." Aum Chaṇḍikāyai Namaḥ.

What Is the Devotional Vaishṇava Sect?

ŚLOKA 9

Vaishṇavism is an ancient Hindu sect centering on the worship of Lord Vishṇu and His incarnations, especially Kṛishṇa and Rāma. Largely dualistic, profoundly devotional, it is rich in saints, temples and scriptures. Aum.

BHĀSHYA

The worship of Vishṇu, meaning "pervader," dates back to Vedic times. The Pañcharātra and Bhāgavata sects were popular prior to 300 BCE. Today's five Vaishṇava schools emerged in the middle ages, founded by Rāmānuja, Madhva, Nimbārka, Vallabha and Chaitanya. Vaishṇavism stresses *prapatti,* single-pointed surrender to Vishṇu, or His ten or more incarnations, called *avatāras. Japa* is a key devotional *sādhana,* as is ecstatic chanting and dancing, called *kīrtana.* Temple worship and festivals are elaborately observed. Philosophically, Vaishṇavism ranges from Mādhva's pure dualism to Rāmānuja's qualified nondualism to Vallabha's nearly monistic vision. God and soul are everlastingly distinct. The soul's destiny, through God's grace, is to eternally worship and enjoy Him. While generally nonascetic, advocating *bhakti* as the highest path, Vaishṇavism has a strong monastic community. Central scriptures are the *Vedas, Vaishṇava Āgamas, Itihāsas* and *Purāṇas.* The *Bhagavad Gītā* states, "On those who meditate on Me and worship with undivided heart, I confer attainment of what they have not, and preserve what they have." Aum Namo Nārāyaṇāya.

What Is the Universalistic Smārta Sect?

ŚLOKA 10

Smārtism is an ancient *brāhminical* tradition reformed by Śaṅkara in the ninth century. Worshiping six forms of God, this liberal Hindu path is monistic, nonsectarian, meditative and philosophical. Aum Namaḥ Śivāya.

BHĀSHYA

Smārta means a follower of classical *smṛiti,* particularly the *Dharma Śāstras, Purāṇas* and *Itihāsas.* Smārtas revere the *Vedas* and honor the *Āgamas.* Today this faith is synonymous with the teachings of Ādi Śaṅkara, the monk-philosopher, known as *shaṇmata sthāpanāchārya,* "founder of the six-sect system." He campaigned India-wide to consolidate the Hindu faiths of his time under the banner of Advaita Vedānta. To unify the worship, he popularized the ancient Smārta five-Deity altar—Gaṇapati, Sūrya, Vishṇu, Śiva and Śakti—and added Kumāra. From these, devotees may choose their "preferred Deity," or *Ishṭa Devatā.* Each God is but a reflection of the one Saguṇa Brahman. Śaṅkara organized hundreds of monasteries into a ten-order, *daśanāmī* system, which now has five pontifical centers. He wrote profuse commentaries on the *Upanishads, Brahma Sūtras* and *Bhagavad Gītā.* Śaṅkara proclaimed, "It is the one Reality which appears to our ignorance as a manifold universe of names and forms and changes. Like the gold of which many ornaments are made, it remains in itself unchanged. Such is Brahman, and That art Thou." Aum Namaḥ Śivāya.

THE SPIRITUAL LINEAGE VOW

Below is a certificate that can be photocopied and enlarged (or retypeset) to document the *paramparā vrata.* This sacrament marks the formal entrance into a *guru* lineage of a particular sect of Hinduism, through the acceptance and blessings of established members and the blessings of Gods and *devas* invoked through rites performed by an authorized Hindu priest.

Aum Loving Gaṇeśa!

Paramparā Vrata

परम्परा व्रत பரம்பரை விரதம்

The Holy Lineage Vow

"O Divine Beings of all three worlds, let us bring our minds to rest in the *darśana* of Him who has one tusk. Let us meditate upon Him who has the form of an elephant with a curved trunk. May He guide us always along the right path.

I, ______________________________ ,
Name of Devotee (Please Print)

believe in You, Loving Gaṇeśa, and in the Gods of our faith and the Hindu Dharma. In love and trust I recognize Your goodness in providing for my every material need. I wholeheartedly accept the spiritual guru lineage of *siddhas* of the ______________ Sampradāya and the principles of the *pañcha nitya karmas.* As an act of faith, *śraddhā,* I am resolved this day to be loyal and abiding to the Hindu faith and at this moment vow my full dedication to my beloved *guru,* ______________________, of the ________________ Paramparā."

Signature of devotee: ______________________________

It is Hereby Certified

that this devotee, born in ______________________ on ____________, of the ____________ *nakshatra,* and now residing at______________________ ____________, during a divinely ordained ceremony at ______________________ on the auspicious day of ______________ duly voiced the above spiritual lineage vow in accordance with the traditions of Hinduism before the Deity, the Mahādevas and the *devas.* This devotee is thus bound eternally and immutably to the fulfilling life of one-pointed dedication aided by the virtue of *paramparā bhakti.*

SIGNATURES OF PRIESTS, ELDERS AND OTHERS WITNESSING THIS CEREMONY:

Hindū Katham Bhūyate

हिन्दू कथं भूयते

How to Become a Hindu

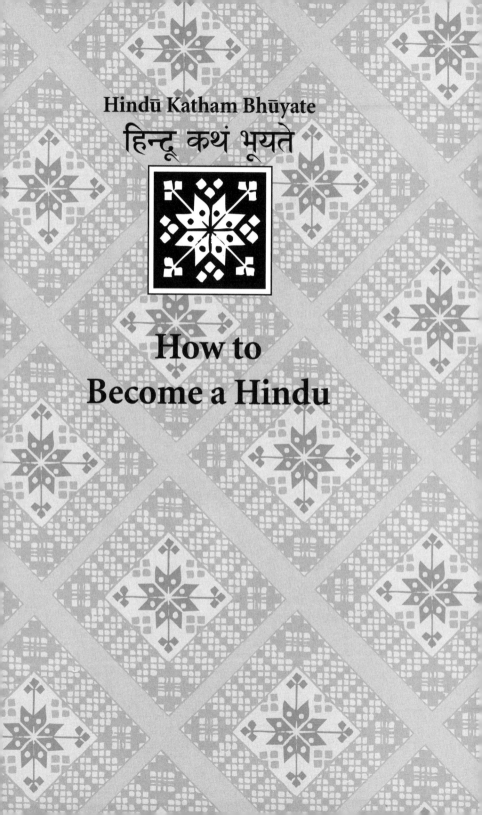

How to Become a Hindu

XENOPHOBIA IS A FOREIGN CONCEPT TO HINDUS, WHO EMBRACE EVEN THOSE WHO ARE UNLIKE THEMSELVES. HOW DO YOU know if you are a Hindu deep inside? if an elder, your guru or a friend has given you a Hindu name? If you have met a *swāmī* or *yogī, paṇḍita* or *satguru* who speaks out the truths you always knew to be the way of the universe? If you feel in your heart of hearts that no other religion suits you better, expresses your native spirituality more profoundly, offers you a way to personally know the Divine within you? Let us analyze and through the process of elimination find out. If you believe, as your *guru* does, in the existence of God everywhere and in all things, you are certainly not a Christian, Muslim or Jew. If you believe in one Supreme God and many Gods, you are certainly not a Christian, Muslim, Jew or Buddhist. The Buddhists don't believe in a personal God. They do not like to use the word *God.* They do not feel the concept of God is part of their deepest understanding. They do not accept a creator, or a knowing God who guides His creation. I was deeply impressed at hearing the Dalai Lama and the head of a Japanese Buddhist tradition make a strong and articulate point of this to several hundred spiritual leaders at the Presidents' Assembly at the Parliament of the World's Religions 1993 centennial in Chicago, when they appealed to the other religions to please not include the use of the word *God* in an important declaration, "Toward a Global Ethic," that all faith leaders were asked to affirm and to sign.

If you believe in the law of *karma,* action receiving its comparable just due, you might be a Buddhist, but then you have the personal God problem. But you are certainly not a Christian, Jew or Muslim, because their doctrines do not include *karma.* If you believe in reincarnation, *punarjanma* "being born again and again," you might be a Buddhist or a Jain, but then there is the God problem again. But again, you are not a Christian, Jew or Muslim, because they adamantly reject these Vedic revelations (though Hasidic Jews do attest to reincarnation).

In summary, your religion is the group that you are the most comfortable with, those who think like you, share the same ideals, according to their similar philosophies. Another point: if you are attracted to Hindu temples, well then certainly you are not a Christian, Buddhist, Jew, Muslim, Shintoist or Taoist. The Parliament of the World's Religions brought all these faiths together, and it became very clear that the religions of the world are happy to be different, unique, not the same. They celebrated these differences, while also affirming an inner oneness. As one of the three presidents of Hinduism at the Presidents' Assembly, along with Swāmī Chidānanda Sarasvatī and Mātājī Amṛitānandamāyī, I can say that each one of the leaders of the world's religions knows who the others are and is not about to change. The whole idea that all religions are one may be true in spirit, but in actuality no. One path or another must be chosen and then lived fully. We don't hear Indian Hindus saying much anymore, "I'm a Christian, I'm a Muslim, I'm a Jew," as they used to proclaim in the '70s. Today they are proudly saying, "I am a Smārta, a Vaishṇavite, a Śākta or a Śaivite." Much of this change is due to the courageous stand that Hindu leaders of all denominations and traditions have taken.

If truly you find you are the Hindu an elder, friend or *guru* saw in you by giving you a Hindu name (they usually give Ānanda or Jyoti for starters), then take the next step and accept the culture, the protocol, the fullness of the world's oldest spiritual tradition, with its *yogas* and its multitudinous wisdoms. Carefully choose the sect within the Sanātana Dharma that you will devote your life to following.

It is important to know that one cannot simply enter the Hindu religion. That is not possible. It is necessary to enter one of Hinduism's specific sects or denominations. Even in these tempestuous times, the subtle differences of Hindu lineages are clearly and methodically demarcated by our priesthoods. Go with your Hindu friends to a Hindu priest in a temple of your choice and arrange for the name-giving sacrament, *nāmakaraṇa saṁskāra.* Your beliefs and way of life have affirmed your inner decision to become a Hindu. This ceremony brings you formally into the Hindu community, recognizing and ratifying your proclamation of loyalty and wholehearted commitment to the Sanātana Dharma and validating, now and forever, your Hindu first and last name.

A model *nāmakaraṇa* certificate is included in this chapter that you can photocopy or retypeset to document the event, signed by the priest and several witnesses, especially members of the society you are entering, who will share your joy in becoming a full-fledged Hindu. Then have your new name made legal on your passport, social security card, driver's license, telephone listing and more.

The certificate marking entrance into the Hindu fold is a legal document giving the name of the temple, home or hall the ceremony was performed in. It is signed by yourself, and by the priest, his assistant and at least three witnesses who are established members of Hinduism. It is proof of your Hindu name which can be used for name changes on other documents, though ideally the name change should be legalized before the *nāmakaraṇa saṁskāra.* In the United States, a legal change by court order is required to obtain a passport and in some states it must be signed by a secretary of state. Each country has its own rules, and for these matters it is best to consult the proper authorities. For strength of character, commitment, loyalty and integrity, a double standard should be avoided at all costs, such as being a Hindu in the home and a non-Hindu to others by using the former name, or using a Hindu on your driver's license but a non-Hindu name on your passport for international travel. This type of behavior reaps no spiritual benefits.

When seeking out a liturgist who will perform the name-giving rite, or *nāmakaraṇa saṁskāra,* it is necessary to approach a priest from within the sect that one wishes to enter. Bring with you to the ceremony an offering basket of incense, fruit, coconut, candy, loose flowers and a beautiful flower garland for Lord Gaṇeśa. *Dakshiṇā,* a love offering for the priest, is traditional in appreciation for his services in bringing you into the Sanātana Dharma sect of your choice. A generous *dakshiṇā,* a sum of $900 or more is appropriate by 1995 standards in the US, depending upon the number of priests attending. It is estimated that such a Vedic ceremony will take one to two hours and require many more hours of strict preparations. The presiding priest would be given US$301 or more, his second helper $201 and other helpers $101. Traditionally, cash is wrapped in a betel leaf or its equivalent, and handed personally to the priests right after the ceremony. Since this is a once-in-a-lifetime happening, the cost of the giving should not be a consideration. Of course, when the rite is performed in a temple, the management should also be given $100 to $200 for the use of their facilities, which would be arranged in advance with the management and could be paid by check. In general, generosity is preferred to miserliness when it comes to rewarding our priests for these enormously important sacred ceremonies and passages. Such appreciation in the form of equitable payment ensures the gratitude and good feelings of the priests for the life ahead. If more than one family member is receiving the *nāmakaraṇa saṁskāra,* the amount paid to the priests and the temple would not necessarily be increased. This depends on the protocol of the particular temple. Any reception held afterwards would, of course, involve additional costs. You may elect to give gifts to the temple, such as a picture of your *guru* and his books and other publications, in thanks for the assistance and services.

Four originals of the *nāmakaraṇa* certificate should be signed: one for temple management to display, one for your records, one for your *guru* and one for legal matters, such as immigration and travel. From your original, many photocopies should be made and sent to friends and relatives. Further, a copy of this significant document proving your membership in the Hindu faith should always be kept with your passport to respond to institutions that ask of your Hindu identity when entering their premises.

The Importance of the Hindu Name

Of all the aspects of fully embracing the Hindu religion, the legal changing of one's name is certainly the most public, requiring adjustment on the part of friends, relatives, neighbors and even business acquaintances. A few approach this with trepidation, but the expected negative reaction—particularly from personal and business acquaintances—seldom materializes. If the immediate family becomes genuinely concerned, this will be overcome by the obvious love, sincerity and depth of conviction of the individual.

Having one's name legally changed is not unusual. Women do it all the time, at marriage. Movie stars rarely use their birth name. Name changes for religious reasons are almost as common. Heavyweight boxer Casius Clay startled the world in 1967 by proclaiming his conversion to Islam and changing his name to Muhammed Ali.

But anyone who has gone through the experience of a religious name change knows that there are real obstacles. Here are a few:

1. Grandma's fears that you are rejecting your family traditions.
2. Business associates: your fears of what they might think.

3. The tendency to use the old name when you are among your non-Hindu friends.
4. The tendency to use the new first name and the old last name.
5. Using the name but not having it made legal.
6. Using the Hindu name with one group and former name with another, a practice of double standard that erodes one's self-image and by which no one will take you seriously.

The most ancient and common source of Hindu names is from the names of God and the Gods. Each child receives a name selected from those of the family's Ishṭa Devatā, or chosen Deity. Such names are called theophoric. The custom of choosing a name from the Gods is among the most ancient, with examples in Persia, Greece, India and the early Indo-European civilizations. In Vedic times there was a Sanskṛit convention for forming patronymics: If Garga was the father, then Gargi was the son, Gargya the grandson and Gargyāyana the greatgrandson.

Hindu names often indicate caste and sect. *Iyer* is for a certain caste of South Indian *brahmins. Sharma* is for a caste of North Indian *brahmins.* The God names *Veṅkateśvara* or *Krishṇa* indicate a follower of Vishṇu. Common names of Śaivites are *Naṭarāja, Mahādevan, Śivaliṅga, Nilakaṇṭha, Subramaniam, Kandiah* and *Kumāra. Dās* or *Dāsa* is a frequently used suffix meaning "slave" and is used by all denominations—hence *Śivadas, Kalidas, Haridas.* Often the first name is chosen according to the syllable mystically related to the individual's *nakshatra,* birth star. There are 108 different such sounds used to begin a name: four for each of the twenty-seven *nakshatras.*

Hindus sometimes change their name during their life as a result of a blessing at a temple or when a holy man initiates them. Swāmī Vivekānanda—who said, "Certainly, there is a great deal in a name!"—was originally named Narendranāth Dutt and had several names as a monk. The Tamil Saint Manikkavasagar was originally named Vathavooran. My *satguru,* Āsān Yogaswāmī, gave new names to many of his devotees, and many of those names were made legal. A good example is myself. Yogaswāmī gave me the name Subramuniya in 1949. Returning to the United States, I had it made legal in the courts in 1950. Such changes of name in Hinduism are considered sacred moments, indicative of spiritual changes taking place on the inside.

The change of name, and using it under all circumstances, is an important sign of religious sincerity to the Hindu community. It shows the willingness to stand up and be counted as a Hindu. Proceed with confidence. Be a hundred-percenter. Don't remain on the fence. It is risky to walk down the middle of the road. Stand up boldly and declare who you are. Realize that if your *guru* gave you a Hindu name, he saw something in you, and that is what attracted you to him. Or if you don't find you hold the basic beliefs of the other religions named above, then "stand strong for Hinduism."

The following paragraphs of this chapter explain what Hinduism is and what is necessary to go through to become a full Hindu of your chosen sect: Śaiva, Vaishṇava, Śākta or Smārta. Thousands of seekers have converted to or adopted Hinduism in modern times, and we have a wonderful book that outlines the entire process in more detail than we have presented below: *Śaivite Names: Satguru Speaks on Becoming a Hindu.* Remember, no one reaches out to convert anyone to the Sanātana Dharma. Hinduism is not and never has been a proselytizing religion. For its strength and that of its devotees, elders, religious leaders and established extended families rely on the soul of the individual to burst forward. What follows is the methodology that was developed in personal lives and through the peerless "wisdom council of elders" as to how, with the blessings of Hindu priests, the witness of observers and the sanction of their *guru,* devotees have irrevocably and of their own volition turned themselves into full members of the Sanātana Dharma, the world's oldest religion on planet Earth.

What Is Hinduism?

Hinduism is India's indigenous religious and cultural system, followed today by nearly one billion adherents, mostly in India, but with large populations in many other countries. Also called Sanātana Dharma, "eternal religion," and Vaidika Dharma, "religion of the *Vedas,*" Hinduism encompasses a broad spectrum of philosophies ranging from pluralistic theism to absolute monism. It is a family of myriad faiths with four primary denominations: Śaivism, Vaishṇavism, Śāktism and Smārtism. These four hold such divergent beliefs that each is a complete and independent religion. Yet, they share a vast heritage of culture and belief: *karma, dharma,* reincarnation, all-pervasive Divinity, temple worship, sacraments, manifold Deities, the many *yogas,* the *guru-śishya* tradition and a reliance on the *Vedas* as scriptural authority.

From the rich soil of Hinduism long ago sprang various other traditions. Among these were Jainism, Buddhism and Sikhism, which rejected the Vedas and thus emerged as completely distinct religions, disassociated from Hinduism, while still sharing many philosophical insights and cultural values with their parent faith.

Not unlike all the other religions of the world, Hinduism has no central headquarters. Neither do the Christians, Jews, Muslims or Buddhists. They all have many who represent and are the secretariates for their various denominations. Hinduism is no different in today's world. It has had many founders in the past and will in the futures of its sects, its teaching lineages within them, each headed by a pontiff. Then there are the exemplary few spiritual beings to whom all flock for upliftment and solace, who have renounced sec-

tarianism, lineage and formalities for the Self and all the greatness it contains.

Critics have claimed Hinduism as not being an organized religion. In truth, they are correct. Islamic and Christian rule in India, Hinduism's central citadel, for 1,200 years eroded greatly upon its perpetuation. Yet it survived. In today's world it may be accused of being a purely unorganized religion, but it's getting better daily. Its temples and active organizations surround the world. Whatever its faults, it has kept the fires of *sādhana* and renunciation, of unabashed spiritual life and *yoga* disciplines, alive. No other faith has done that to the same extent. Hinduism's nearly three million *swāmīs, gurus* and *sādhus* work tirelessly within and upon themselves and then, when ready, serve others, leading them from darkness into light, from death to immortality.

What Makes One a Hindu?

In our discussion of Hindu conversion, the question clearly arises of how Hinduism historically has looked at the matter. Second, what is it exactly that makes a person a Hindu? We will approach the latter question first. To the born Hindu of today, the question of entering Hinduism may appear unnecessary, for by definition Hinduism is a way of life, a culture, both religious and secular. The Hindu is not accustomed to thinking of his religion as a clearly defined system, distinct and different from other systems, for it fills his life. It encompasses all of life. Partly this pure, simple view stems from the relative isolation Hindu communities have enjoyed for centuries, with little interaction with alien faiths to highlight Hinduism's uniqueness. Even more so, it has to do with Hinduism's all-embracing quality which accepts so many variations of belief and practice into itself. But this view ignores the true distinctions between this way of life and those ways of the other great religions of the world. There is no denying that Hinduism is also a distinct world religion.

Those who follow that way of life are Hindus. It is similar to the story in the *Mahābhārata* in which the great King Yudhishṭhira was asked, "What makes a *brahmin*—birth, learning or conduct?" to which he replied, "It is conduct which makes a *brahmin*." Similarly, the modern Hindu may well state that it is conduct, based upon belief in *dharma, karma* and reincarnation, which makes a Hindu. After all, he might muse, is not a true devotee whose heart is filled with faith in and love for his Ishṭa Devatā and who lives the Hindu *dharma* as much a Hindu as his agnostic neighbor, though the first was born in Indonesia or North America and the second in Andra Pradesh?

Sri K. Navaratnam of Sri Lanka, devotee of Paramaguru Siva Yogaswami for some 40 years, in his book *Studies in Hinduism* quotes from the book, *Introduction to the Study of the Hindu Doctrines,* "Hindus are those who adhere to the Hindu tradition, on the understanding that they are duly qualified to do so really effectively, and not simply in an exterior and illusory way; non-Hindus, on the contrary, are those who, for any reason whatsoever, do not participate in the tradition in question." Sri K. Navaratnam enumerates a set of basic beliefs held by Hindus:

1. A belief in the existence of God.
2. A belief in the existence of a soul separate from the body.
3. A belief in the existence of the finitizing principle known as *avidyā* or *māyā.*
4. A belief in the principle of matter—*prakṛiti* or *māyā.*
5. A belief in the theory of *karma* and reincarnation.
6. A belief in the indispensable guidance of a guru to guide the spiritual aspirant towards God Realization.
7. A belief in *moksha,* or liberation, as the goal of human existence.
8. A belief in the indispensable necessity of temple worship...in religious life.
9. A belief in graded forms of religious practices, both in-

ternal and external, until one realizes God.

10. A belief in *ahiṁsā* as the greatest *dharma* or virtue.
11. A belief in mental and physical purity as indispensable factors for spiritual progress.

Śrī Śrī Śrī Jayendra Sarasvatī, 69th Śaṅkarāchārya of the Kamakoti Peetham, Kanchipuram, defines in one of his writings the basic features of Hinduism as follows.

1. The concept of idol worship and the worship of God in his Nirguṇa as well as Saguṇa form.
2. The wearing of sacred marks on the forehead.
3. Belief in the theory of past and future births in accordance with the theory of *karma.*
4. Cremation of ordinary men and burial of great men.

An article in *Hindu Vishva* (Jan./Feb., 1986) cites various common definitions including the following: "He who has perfect faith in the law of *karma,* the law of reincarnation, *avatāra,* ancestor worship, *varṇāshrama dharma, Vedas* and existence of God, he who practices the instructions given in the *Vedas* with faith and earnestness, he who does *snāna, sṛāddha, pitṛi-tarpaṇa* and the *pañcha mahāyajñas,* he who follows the *varṇāshram-dharmas,* he who worships the *avatāras* and studies the *Vedas,* is a Hindu.' "

The Vishva Hindu Parishad's official definition of a Hindu, stated in its Memorandum of Association, Rules and Regulation (1966) is: "'*Hindu*' means a person believing in, following or respecting the eternal values of life, ethical and spiritual, which have sprung up in Bhāratkhand [India] and includes any person calling himself a Hindu."

In the above and other definitions, the three pivotal beliefs for all Hindus are *karma,* reincarnation and the belief in all-pervasive Divinity—forming as they do the crux of day-to-day religion, explaining our past existence, guiding our present life and determining our future union with God.

It is apparent from the pervasiveness of these beliefs today that a large number of non-Hindus qualify as self-declared Hindus already, for many believe in *karma, dharma* and reincarnation, strive to see God everywhere, have some concept of *māyā,* recognize someone as their *guru,* respect temple worship and believe in the evolution of the soul. Many of these beliefs are heretical to most other religions, especially Christianity and the Jewish religion, and those who do believe in *karma* and reincarnation and in union with the Divine have evolved beyond the boundaries of Western religion.

A Summary of What Most Hindus Believe

In the last decade we crafted a simple summary of Hindu belief and distributed hundreds of thousands of pamphlets around the world sharing these. They were printed side-by-side with their Christian counterparts in *Christianity Today* magazine, February 8, 1993, so Christians could better comprehend Hindus. On August, 1995, they were published by the Religious News Service in Washington, DC, for hundreds of American newspapers. These nine beliefs offer a basic summary of Sanātana Dharma's spirituality.

NINE BELIEFS OF HINDUISM

1. Hindus believe in the divinity of the *Vedas,* the world's most ancient scripture, and venerate the *Āgamas* as equally revealed. These primordial hymns are God's word and the bedrock of Sanātana Dharma, the eternal religion which has neither beginning nor end.
2. Hindus believe in a one, all-pervasive Supreme Being who is both immanent and transcendent, both Creator and Unmanifest Reality.
3. Hindus believe that the universe undergoes endless cycles of creation, preservation and dissolution.
4. Hindus believe in *karma,* the law of cause and effect by which each individual creates his own destiny by his

thoughts, words and deeds.

5. Hindus believe that the soul reincarnates, evolving through many births until all *karmas* have been resolved, and *moksha*, spiritual knowledge and liberation from the cycle of rebirth, is attained. Not a single soul will be eternally deprived of this destiny.
6. Hindus believe that divine beings exist in unseen worlds and that temple worship, rituals, sacraments as well as personal devotionals create a communion with these *devas* and Gods.
7. Hindus believe that a spiritually awakened master, or *satguru,* is essential to know the Transcendent Absolute, as are personal discipline, good conduct, purification, pilgrimage, self-inquiry and meditation.
8. Hindus believe that all life is sacred, to be loved and revered, and therefore practice *ahiṁsā,* "noninjury."
9. Hindus believe that no particular religion teaches the only way to salvation above all others, but that all genuine religious paths are facets of God's Pure Love and Light, deserving tolerance and understanding.

FIVE OBLIGATIONS OF ALL HINDUS

1. **WORSHIP, UPĀSANĀ:** Young Hindus are taught daily worship in the family shrine room—rituals, disciplines, chants, *yogas* and religious study. They learn to be secure through devotion in home and temple, wearing traditional dress, bringing forth love of the Divine and preparing the mind for serene meditation.
2. **HOLY DAYS, UTSAVA:** Young Hindus are taught to participate in Hindu festivals and holy days in the home and temple. They learn to be happy through sweet communion with God at such auspicious celebrations. *Utsava* includes fasting and attending the temple on Monday or Friday and other holy days.

3. **VIRTUOUS LIVING, DHARMA:** Young Hindus are taught to live a life of duty and good conduct. They learn to be selfless by thinking of others first, being respectful of parents, elders and *swāmīs,* following divine law, especially *ahiṁsā,* mental, emotional and physical noninjury to all beings. Thus they resolve *karmas.*
4. **PILGRIMAGE, TĪRTHAYĀTRĀ:** Young Hindus are taught the value of pilgrimage and are taken at least once a year for darśana of holy persons, temples and places, near or far. They learn to be detached by setting aside worldly affairs and making God, Gods and *gurus* life's singular focus during these journeys.
5. **RITES OF PASSAGE, SAṂSKĀRA:** Young Hindus are taught to observe the many sacraments which mark and sanctify their passages through life. They learn to be traditional by celebrating the rites of birth, name-giving, head-shaving, first feeding, ear-piercing, first learning, coming of age, marriage and death.

Hinduism Has Always Accepted Adoptives and Converts

It is sometimes claimed that one must be born in a Hindu family in order to be a Hindu, that one cannot adopt or convert to this world's most ancient faith. This is simply not true. The acceptance of outsiders into the Hindu fold has occurred for thousands of years. Groups as diverse as local aborigines and the invading Greeks of Alexander the Great have been brought in. Entering Hinduism has traditionally required little more than accepting and living the beliefs and codes of Hindus. This remains the basic factor in the process, although there are, and always have been, formal ceremonies recognizing an individual's entrance into the religion, particularly the *nāmakaraṇa saṁskāra,* or naming rite in the case of adoptives and converts, and the *vrātyastoma,* oath-taking rite, in the case of those returning to the Hindu faith.

The most compelling testimony to Hinduism's acceptance of non-Hindus into its fold is history. Here we quote the writings of well-known Hindus who present both their own opinions and cite examples from history. Possibly the most thorough exposition of the subject appears in the *Complete Works of Swami Vivekananda* (Volume V, pg. 233), in an interview called "On the bounds of Hinduism," which first appeared in the *Prabuddha Bharata* in April, 1899: "Having been directed by the Editor, writes our representative, to interview Swāmī Vivekānanda on the question of converts to Hinduism, I found an opportunity one evening on the roof of a Ganges houseboat. It was after nightfall, and we had stopped at the embankment of the Rāmakṛishṇa Maṭh, and there the Swāmī came down to speak with me. Time and place were alike delightful. Overhead the stars, and around, the rolling Gaṅgā; and on one side stood the dimly lighted building, with its background of palms and lofty shade-trees. 'I want to see you, Swāmī,' I began, 'on this matter of receiving back into Hinduism those who have been perverted from it. Is it your opinion that they should be received?'

'Certainly,' said the *swāmī,* 'they can and ought to be taken.' He sat gravely for a moment, thinking, and then resumed. 'The vast majority of Hindu perverts to Islam and Christianity are perverts by the sword, or the descendants of these. It would be obviously unfair to subject these to disabilities of any kind. As to the case of born aliens, did you say? Why, born aliens have been converted in the past by crowds, and the process is still going on.'

'In my own opinion, this statement not only applies to aboriginal tribes, to outlying nations, and to almost all our conquerors before the Mohammedan conquest, but also to all those castes who find a special origin in the *Pūraṇas.* I hold that they have been aliens thus adopted.'

'Ceremonies of expiation are no doubt suitable in the case of willing converts, returning to their Mother-Church, as it were; but on those who were alienated by conquest—as in Kashmir and Nepal—or on strangers wishing to join us, no penance should be imposed.'

'But of what caste would these people be, Swāmījī?' I ventured to ask. 'They must have some, or they can never be assimilated into the great body of Hindus. Where shall we look for their rightful place?'

'Returning converts,' said the *swāmī* quietly, 'will gain their own castes, of course. And new people will make theirs. You will remember,' he added, 'that this has already been done in the case of Vaishṇavism. Converts from different castes and aliens were all able to combine under that flag and form a caste by themselves—and a very respectable one, too. From Rāmānuja down to Chaitanya of Bengal, all great Vaishṇava teachers have done the same.'

'Then as to names,' I enquired, 'I suppose aliens and perverts who have adopted non-Hindu names should be named newly. Would you give them caste names, or what?' 'Certainly,' said the Swami thoughtfully, 'there is a great deal in a name!' and on this question he would say no more.

Dr. S. Rādhākṛishṇan confirms the *swāmī's* views in a brief passage from his well-known book *The Hindu View of Life* (page 28-29): "In a sense, Hinduism may be regarded as the first example in the world of a missionary religion. Only its missionary spirit is different from that associated with the proselytizing creeds. It did not regard it as its mission to convert humanity to any one opinion. For what counts is conduct and not belief. Worshipers of different Gods and followers of different rites were taken into the Hindu fold. The ancient practice of *vrātyastoma,* described fully in the *Taṇḍya Brāhmaṇa,* shows that not only individuals but whole tribes were absorbed into Hinduism. Many modern sects accept outsiders. *Dvala's Smṛiti* lays down rules for the simple purification of people forcibly converted to other faiths, or of womenfolk defiled and confined for years, and even of people who, for worldly advantage, embrace other faiths."

How Swāmī Vivekānanda's Wisdom Applies Today

Today, one who holds only a single Hindu name or who appreciates Hinduism's essence but has not accepted its totality is called an *ardha*-Hindu, or "half-Hindu." *Ardha*-Hindus include not only Westerners who have taken a Hindu first name, but Easterners who have taken a Western name, first or last, to disguise their true Hindu name or to render it easier for Westerners to pronounce. Other religions abhor this. For instance, in the Islamic community we would never meet Mohammed Ali Johnson or Joe Mohammed. They are proud to be who they are, abhoring all disguises. They set a good example for us. Hindus, or *ardha*-Hindus, seeking to be ecumenical and all-embracing observe Easter or celebrate Christmas, thinking themselves tolerant. But are they? In fact, they are not, for they do not equally celebrate the Prophet Mohammed's birthday, nor do they observe Jewish or Shinto or Buddhist holy days, or those of other faiths that, as universalists, they profess to proclaim as their own.

People of other religions and those who choose not to commit, who are committed to being non-committal, are called *mlecçha,* outsiders. Those who enter the Sanātana Dharma from other religions or from none at all are considered to be within the caste *(jāti)* of their occupation at the time of entrance. Workers under others are *śudra.* The self-employed are *vaiśyas*—lawyers, bankers, businessmen, arbitrators and government personnel. Lawyers, arbitrators, soldiers and politicians are *kshatriyas.* Religionists, scholars, inventors and visionaries are the *brahmins.*

These converts or adoptives are distinguished by the appellation *Arsha,* derived from *ṛishi,* meaning "seer," an ennobling term closely bound to the *Vedas,* because they have had to fulfill deep study and soul-searching to enter the faith. The seer, their *guru,* sees where the soul is in its evolution and brings it into the proper *dharma,* whatever the place of birth or ethnic-racial background.

Thus, in modern times, the term *Arsha* has encompassed the meaning of *convert* or *adoptive,* a soul brought into the faith by a *satguru, guru* or *swāmī, pundit* or elder who has indoctrinated the devotee to the point of fully entering the Eternal Path through the entrance sacrament, *nāmakaraṇa saṁskāra.* They, therefore, may use the term *Arsha* after their name, as the followers of Sri Rāmānuja use *Iyengar,* generation after generation. Similarly, in India, the designation *Arya,* meaning "noble," is given by the Arya Samaj, the Vishva Hindu Parishad and others to Indians who convert to or reenter the Hindu faith through the *vrātyastoma* or *śuddhi* rites. Another term recommended for those reentering Hinduism, is *Sanātani,* which conveys the meaning of eternal connection to the root religion.

As an example, I had the Arsha evolution in my *prārabdha karma* which was seen by my *satguru,* Sage Yogaswāmī, when I told him that I had adopted the Sanātana Dharma as the first and only religion of my life. Without hesitation he brought me into his Śaiva Hindu tradition. After my *nāmakaraṇa saṁskāra,* my body relaxed and felt secure, like being home. My emotions satisfied because of acceptance, my intellect quieted, its task now done, my spirit welled, its task just begun. A few days later, he gave me my life's mission, of building a bridge for all his devotees to the lands beyond Sri Lankan shores—Malaysia, Singapore, Mauritius, Europe, Canada, the United States, Australia, New Zealand and many other countries—preparing the way for the *visarjana,* the diaspora, of the Sri Lankan Tamil people brought about by the great civil war which started in 1983 and continued beyond 1995. Until his departure he communicated with me, through Kandiah Chettiar who took me to the first meeting, year after year. I was young then and did not understand much of the international impact that was to occur. But in the 1980s and '90s it became quite clear: my *satguru* was the seer of seers and I had been enlisted as a Śivathondar, slave of Śiva, and given a mission that I had not applied for. But in my heart of hearts, soul of souls, spirit of spirits, I understood that it was my duty to fulfill my *guru's* edicts better than his expectations on my individual path to *moksha.* He was a great seer who saw ahead to the future of futures, and as his mission unfolded within me unto this day I wonder how the impact of a forceful slap on the back could have transferred his mission to me. As a knowledgeable *śāstric* priest explained to me in later years, Yogaswāmī put his *saṁskāras* into me and awakened my futuristic *saṁskāras* past this birth. A mystery of mysteries that only the Nāthas of Nāthas of Nātha *ṛishis* could ever explain.

The Steps of Conversion

To gain a clear subconscious for his future religious life, the individual must examine and reject those beliefs of his previous religion or philosophy which differ from those of the sect of Hinduism he wishes to join. Then he must examine and accept the Hindu beliefs which are new to him.

If he was confirmed or otherwise initiated in another religion or ideology, he must effect formal severance from his previous religion or faith before formally entering the Hindu religion through the *nāmakaraṇa saṁskāra,* the name-giving sacrament. Full religious conversion means that one's former religious or philosophical leader is made aware, preferably through a personal meeting with the convert, that the individual is entering a new religion.

Further, ethical conversion means that the parents and relatives, too, understand the momentous change that has taken place. This societal recognition, along with initiation and vow-giving, legal change of name on passport and all documents, signifies true conversion on all levels of being. Nothing less will suffice. Even within Hinduism itself there are formal ceremonies and soul-searching requirements for

Hindus converting from one denomination to another, as when a Śaivite becomes a Vaishṇavite or a Smārta becomes a Śākta, accomplished, in part, in some communities by writing with a golden needle the divine *mantras* on the convert's tongue.

Before explaining the steps of conversion, we want to advise Hindu societies worldwide to make close inquiries of adoptives and converts as to their fulfilling the six steps of conversion which our loving Gaṇeśa has given to us to open the doors to the *ardha*-Hindu into the fullness of the sectarian faith of his or her choice. Detailed below are the procedures for religious reconciliation that we have established in our own fellowship, leading through the process of severance from former faiths and into Hinduism.

1. JOINING A HINDU COMMUNITY

First and most importantly, the devotee mixes socially and earns acceptance into an established Hindu community. The devotee should be worshiping regularly at the community's *satsaṅgas* or temples, making yearly pilgrimages, performing daily *pūjā* and *sādhanas* within the home and seriously striving to live up to the culture defined in the 365 Nandinātha Sūtras of *Living with Śiva*, which is a complete statement of Hindu values and culture.

2. POINT-COUNTERPOINT

The devotee undertakes certain assigned Hindu studies and a formal analysis of former religions, denominations, *sampradāyas* or philosophical systems. He or she writes a point-counterpoint comparing Hinduism with each such school of thought to demonstrate a thorough grasp of the similarities and differences. Part two of this assignment is to complete a written analysis of all former pledges or vows, indicating when and why each point mentioned in those vows was abandoned. This point-counterpoint is then presented to a Hindu elder for his review and comment.

3. SEVERING FROM FORMER MENTORS

If formal severance is required, the devotee returns to the former institution and attends services or lectures for a few weeks. Then, accompanied by a relative or friend as a witness, he or she meets personally with the former mentor. In the case of a married person, the spouse is preferred as a witness. The devotee explains that he will be joining the Hindu religion and wishes to sever ties with this church or institution. For an intimate understanding of severance, I would like to share with you a letter that one of my *kulapati* counselors wrote to a potential convert from Catholicism:

"Your point-counterpoint will do much for you in preparing you to meet your former priest to convince him that an inner transformation has occurred and you are indeed a Hindu soul, not a Catholic. This is a face-to-face meeting with the religious leader of your former faith or his successor. This step is done on a very personal level, as the fire of severance takes place during this confrontation. It cannot be done through the mail or on the telephone. During this meeting, your conviction and clear understanding of both religions will allow your priest to see the thoughtfulness and sincerity of the decision you have made. A letter of release can, many times, be obtained before you leave his office when he sees clearly that you have completely abandoned the Catholic faith. This letter validates your personal release and clears the way for your formal entrance into Hinduism in all three worlds. It is an essential experience and document necessary for your *nāmakaraṇa saṁskāra.*"

We have many letters from Catholic priests, even archbishops, attesting to full conversion to Hinduism on the part of their former paritioners. In the case of formal religions, the devotee requests a letter of release, as an apostate (such as with the Catholic Church) or as inactive (as in most Protestant Christian denominations). If the religious leader grants a verbal severance but will not convey it in writing, the witness to the interview writes a letter stating what took place. This letter is later given to the guiding elder of the Hindu community the devotee seeks to fully join.

Even if there is no granting of severance, verbally or in writing, the conversion is still considered complete, based on the canon law of the Catholic church (and which applies to other faiths in principle, such as Judaism) that someone who adopts another religion is, *ipso facto,* an apostate. In cases where there has been no formal commitment, such as in nonreligious schools of thought, an inner severance may be effected through heartfelt conversation in which the devotee shares his or her true convictions.

4. ADOPTING A HINDU NAME

The devotee then proceeds to have his or her name legally changed and then placed on one's passport, driver's license and all important financial or legal instruments, including credit cards, library cards and bank accounts. Even before formal entrance to Hinduism, devotees are encouraged to begin using their Hindu names at all times.

5. THE NĀMAKARAṆA SAṂSKĀRA

The name-giving sacrament can be held at any Hindu temple. Before the *nāmakaraṇa saṁskāra,* the devotee informs family, relatives and close friends of his or her name change and intended entrance into Hinduism. At the sacred name-giving rite, the Hindu name is received, vows are taken and a certificate is signed, documenting the former name and the new name, place of ceremony and signature of the priest and at least three witnesses. We have included a sample *nāmakaraṇa* certificate on the next page for this purpose.

6. ANNOUNCING THE SEVERANCE AND NAME-GIVING

After the severance and name-giving, the devotee publishes a three-day announcement in a local newspaper stating that the name-change has been completed and he or she has entered the Hindu religion through the *nāmakaraṇa saṁskāra.* The devotee should keep a copy of these announcements and all other documents related to the conversion (such as letters from attorneys and elders) as part of a dossier verifying the name-giving which may be needed in the future, such as when seeking acceptance into a conservative Hindu organization, seeking permanent residency or citizenship in a foreign country or in other cases when the Hindu name may come into question. Similarly, many temples in India and other countries will ask to see the passport or other appropriate proof of Hindu identity before admitting devotees of non-Indian origin for more than casual worship.

NAME-GIVING CERTIFICATE

Below is a certificate that can be photocopied (enlarged) to document a *nāmakaraṇa* held at any temple. This sacrament marks the formal entrance into a particular sect of Hinduism, through the acceptance and blessings of established members and the blessings of Gods and *devas* invoked through rites performed by an authorized Hindu priest.

Aum Gaṇeśa!

Nāmakaraṇa Saṁskāra

नामकरण संस्कार   நாமகரண சம்ஸ்காரம்

Hindu Name-Giving Sacrament

I, ____ ,

Hindu Name of Devotee (Please Print)

formerly known as ______________________________, having declared of my own volition acceptance of the principles of the Sanātana Dharma, and having formally severed all previous non-Hindu religious affiliations, attachments and commitments, hereby humbly petition entrance into the (❑ Śaiva ❑ Vaishṇava ❑ Śākta ❑ Smārta ❑ other) ____________________ sect of the Hindu religion through the traditional *nāmakaraṇa saṁskāra* and plead for recognition by the community of devotees witnessing this sacred rite of this irrevocable adoption of or conversion to Hinduism. I have completed a study of the Hindu teachings and hereby proclaim my acceptance of the following nine beliefs of Hinduism and my promise to fulfill to the best of my ability the *pañcha nitya karmas:* worship, *upāsanā;* holy days, *utsava,* virtuous living, *dharma;* pilgrimage, *tīrthayātrā;* and rites of passage, *saṁskāra.* I now avow to the nine beliefs by reading them aloud. Aum.

1. I believe in the divinity of the *Vedas*, the world's most ancient scripture, and venerate the *Āgamas* as equally revealed. These primordial hymns are God's word and the bedrock of Sanātana Dharma, the eternal religion which has neither beginning nor end.
2. I believe in a one, all-pervasive Supreme Being who is both immanent and transcendent, both Creator and Unmanifest Reality.
3. I believe that the universe undergoes endless cycles of creation, preservation and dissolution.
4. I believe in *karma*, the law of cause and effect by which each individual creates his own destiny by his thoughts, words and deeds.
5. I believe that the soul reincarnates, evolving through many births until all *karmas* have been resolved, and *moksha*, spiritual knowledge and liberation from the cycle of rebirth, is attained. Not a single soul will be eternally deprived of this destiny.
6. I believe that divine beings exist in unseen worlds and that temple worship, rituals, sacraments as well as personal devotionals create a communion with these *devas* and Gods.
7. I believe that a spiritually awakened master, or *satguru*, is essential to know the Transcendent Absolute, as are personal discipline, good conduct, purification, pilgrimage, self-inquiry and meditation.
8. I believe that all life is sacred, to be loved and revered, and therefore practice *ahiṁsā*, "noninjury."
9. I believe that no particular religion teaches the only way to salvation above all others, but that all genuine religious paths are facets of God's Pure Love and Light, deserving tolerance and understanding.

Signature: former name: ____________________ *Hindu name:* ____________________

It is Hereby Certified

that this devotee, born in ____________________ on ____________, and now residing at ______________________________, was at a *nāmakaraṇa samskāra* held at the temple known as ________________________, located in ____________________, on the auspicious day of ____________ duly given a Hindu name in accordance with the traditions of Sanātana Dharma before the Deity, the Mahādevas and the *devas* and the congregation of devotees. This person is thus bound eternally and immutably to the Hindu religion as a member of this most ancient faith with full rights of access to all public Hindu temples, shrines and institutions throughout the world from this day onward. Through this magical Vedic ceremony guardian *devas* have been invoked from the Antarloka to protect, guide and defend this devotee.

______________________________ OFFICIATING PRIEST

______________________________ ELDER WITNESS

______________________________ ASSISTANT PRIEST

______________________________ ELDER WITNESS

______________________________ ELDER WITNESS

The Ceremony of Welcoming Back

It is one of the duties of the Hindu priesthood to stand guard at the gates of Sanātana Dharma and perform the sacred ceremonies for worthy souls to allow them entrance for the first time or reentrance into the Hindu fold in case they strayed into an alien faith and desire to return. The priesthoods of all four major denominations of Sanātana Dharma—Śaivism, Vaishṇavism, Smārtism and Śaktism—are performing the duty, empowered by the Gods, of bringing devotees back into the Hindu fold through a congregation of devotees.

When such souls do return, it is the duty of established followers to shepherd them, blend them in and assist at every opportunity to make them successful members of the international extended family of our venerable faith.

The process of "reconversion" of Hindus previously converted to other faiths has been widely practiced in India throughout this century. In many cases the earlier conversion, generally to Islam or Christianity, occurred several generations ago. Another institution, the Masurāśrama in Bombay, specializes in reconversions through a Śuddhi Śraddhā ceremony, bringing in dozens of new converts each month. Masurāśrama's founder, Dharma Bhaskar Masurkar Mahārāj, set a strong precedent in 1928 when he organized the *śuddhi* ceremony for 1,150 individuals in Goa who were previously converted to Christianity.

In recent decades, two South Indian *āśramas*—Madurai Aadheenam and Kundrakuddi Aadheenam—have brought thousands of Indians back into Hinduism through mass conversion rites. This century the Vishva Hindu Parishad has reportedly brought back into the Hindu fold, beginning in the early 1960s, over one-half million individuals through Śuddhi ceremonies all over India.

VRĀTYASTOMA CERTIFICATE

Below is a *vrātyastoma* certificate that can be photocopied (enlarged) to document this purification ceremony held at any temple. This sacrament marks the formal reentrance into a particular sect of Hinduism, through the acceptance of established members and the blessings of Gods and *devas* invoked through rites performed by an authorized priest.

Aum Gaṇeśa!

Vrātyastoma

व्रात्यस्तोम

விரத்தியாஸ்தோம

Purification Sacrament for Returning to the Eternal Faith

I, ________________________________ ,

Hindu Name of Devotee (Please Print)

having voluntarily declared my acceptance of the principles of the Sanātana Dharma, including a firm belief in all-pervasive Divinity, Satchidānanda, and the Vedic revelations of *karma, dharma* and *puṇarjanma,* and having severed all non-Hindu religious affiliations, attachments and commitments, hereby humbly beg to reenter the ____________ sect of the Hindu religion through the traditional Vrātyastoma, the purificatory vow ceremony, also known as Śuddhi Śraddhā, and plead for gracious permission from the community to return to my cherished Hindu faith. I solemnly promise to live as an example for the next generation. Aum.

Signature of devotee: ________________________________

It is Hereby Certified

that this devotee, born in was duly given the *vrātyastoma* ceremony on the auspicious day of ________________________ at the Hindu temple known as ________________________, in accordance with the traditions of the world's most ancient faith and vowed before the Deity, the Mahādevas and the *devas* faithfulness to the Sanātana Dharma. Thus, this devotee has been eternally and immutably bound to the Hindu religion and is now again recognized as a member of this and all of our communities worldwide with full rights of access to all public Hindu temples, shrines and institutions throughout the world from this day onward.

____

OFFICIATING PRIEST

WITNESSES:

____

ASSISTANT PRIEST

____

CITY & COUNTRY

Breaking the Idol Barrier

An Essay by Rudit J. Emir
From HINDUISM TODAY, *August, 1995*

I grew up in a Christian family. Not only was it Christian, it was Protestant. Protestants tend to be austere in their ritualism and in their portrayal of holy images. The typical church holds a cross, perhaps a statue or painting of Christ. Stained glass windows may depict the life of Christ or of his apostles—that is all. The Catholic propensity for richer symbolism was viewed through my Protestant family's eyes as a strange kind of extravagance, colored by a touch of something almost pagan. I remember looking skeptically at Catholics kneeling in front of statues of saints and burning candles by their images to invoke their blessings.

That's the kind of mind that came in contact with the religious thought and culture of the Hindus. Around the age of sixteen the impact of spiritual India began to enter my life. The influence came first through contemplative literature—the poetry of Rabindranāth Tagore, the *Bhagavad Gītā*, and the *Upanishads*. Though they touched my heart and initiated new stirrings deep within, still, the heart was not blasted wide open. I had not yet met my *guru*.

Then I met Gurudev, Swāmī Chinmayānanda. I was twenty-six, with an unappeased hunger that had begun ten years earlier and had still not been satisfied. Swāmījī blasted my heart wide open as his love-drenched intellect pierced through my rational mind to reach the sanctuary within.

Around that time the symbolic and ritual aspect of Hindu worship also became known to me through *bhajanas* and *kīrtana*, prostrations to the teacher, receiving of *prasāda* from the hands of the *guru*, and the first tentative, uncertain, yet strangely overpowering experiences with a *pādapūjā*, worship of the *guru's* sandals. Still, the Protestant in me affirmed, "I am a Vedāntin, not a Hindu. The ritualistic aspect of the spiritual search is for the Hindu, not for me, a Westerner. I am striving for the essence behind the symbol; the symbol itself I can forego."

My first trip to India, about ten years after I had met Swāmījī, included a few unforgettable visits to temples and some dutiful prostrations in front of idols. I did it out of respect for the spiritual traditions of a country I had grown to revere and out of my intellectual appreciation that each symbol stood for a deeper meaning behind it. But the Protestant in me still persisted in her protest against worship of inanimate stone and wood.

In the fall of 1987 I had the good fortune to participate in a Chinmayā Spiritual Camp at Sidhabari, Himachal Pradesh, at the foothills of the Himālayas. The spiritually charged setting, the meditative stillness of the Himālayas, left my mind in awe. One morning after meditation, I found myself walking toward the temple. After doing my *pranāms* in front of the idols in the sanctuary, I followed the other worshipers to the rear of the temple. I must confess I had no idea what I might find there. As I turned the corner, my eyes fell upon a wooden image of Gaṇeśa. A blast of overpowering emotion almost pushed me to the ground. I was reeling inside. Lord Gaṇeśa, through the idol, had just come alive for me. In fact, He had caught me totally unawares, had taken me by surprise by this unexpectedly powerful announcement of His undeniable presence. "Lord Gaṇeśa what have You done? Of all the idols that I had contemplated upon in my intellectual studies of Hindu symbolism, You of all the many Deities left me quizzical and wondering—You with the strange animal head, the bloated belly, the broken tusk. I could never take You seriously. I wondered how so many Hindus could. And now, what have You done? Among the bevy of beautiful, statuesque, inspiring images of Hindu Gods, dear Lord, You chose to speak to me through the strange, even comical,

form of Gaṇeśa!"

I left the temple as though struck by a bolt of lightning. My mind later pondered over what had transpired. Perhaps my encounter with Gaṇeśa was simply the extension of a fulfilling hour of contemplation that had ended just moments before my visit to the temple. The experience would most likely not be repeated. The next day I decided to test the previous day's newfound reality. As I rounded the corner toward the back of the temple, I found myself talking to Gaṇeśa, half-reverently, half-jokingly (as He had left me with a very intimate, slightly jovial feeling of His presence the day before): "Gaṇeśa, will You really be there for me again? Will you assert Your reality through the dead image of carved wood? Go ahead, prove it to me!"

He did it again. And again and again, for many days afterward.

The Protestant in me no longer protests.

How can she? Not only does Gaṇeśa speak to me through the idol now, He has also proven His presence as the Remover of Obstacles for me.

On my return trip for Sidhabari, I had no train reservations. Gathered in a huddle on the station platform, my friends were valiantly trying to persuade the railway personnel to allow me to use a ticket unused by another passenger. In vain. The conductor's face remained stern; his head continued to shake in an adamant "No!" Departure time was approaching fast. By the minute, it looked less and less likely that I would reach New Delhi in time to meet Swāmījī when he arrived there.

Only one thing to do. "Gaṇeśa !" I cried in my mind, "You must come to help me now! Remove this obstacle!" The very instant I shouted those words in my mind, a smile broke across the conductor's face. "OK," he said, "we'll arrange for a seat."

The Protestant protests no more.

The idol barrier has been broken.

Embracing Hindu Culture

CUES AND CLUES

Those seeking to adopt the Hindu culture fully who have been raised in non-Hindu environments will face many changes. The refinements of Hindu culture must be carefully studied and practiced. Western culture gives freedom to the individual, irrespective of the hurts he may cause to elders, spouse and children. Eastern culture gives freedom within the bounds of duty to elders, spouse and children. The sense of duty is the foundation of Hindu culture, and in performing duty one finds freedom within oneself through the higher accomplishments of *yoga.* Arriving at this state of unity requires study, worship, *sādhana* and effort to mold oneself into the beliefs and culture of the religion you seek to adopt. The gentle Hindu culture is the embodiment of the profound philosophy. Therefore, to become fully Hindu means fully adopting the attitudes, customs and protocol of Hinduism. Of course, the best way to absorb the subtle nuances is to associate with and live among high-minded Hindus and learn from their example.

The Meaning of Culture

Each of the religions of the world has its own culture with many beautiful, refined qualities. Each religious culture naturally embodies the beliefs of that religion as followers live out their convictions and goals at all levels of life. The same is true of philosophies that are nonreligious, such as existentialism, humanism, materialism and communism. They, too, have a culture. Each country has its combined culture as well. Today in the West and in Asia as well there are also many "sub-cultures," some of which are made up of "anti-establishment" "anti-religious" people who consciously defy others by being "uncultured" by the standards of the mainstream society. That is actually part of their culture.

A Few Cultural Cues and Clues

To be cultured, in the highest sense, means to be in control of oneself and exemplify the highest qualities of one's society, religion or philosophy. For Hindus and those of other Eastern faiths, this means to consistently conduct oneself in

accordance with the higher nature. The Hindu culture is a culture of love, respect, honoring others and humbling one's own ego so that the inner nature, which is naturally pure and modest, will shine forth. There are countless ways the Hindu attitudes of compassion, respect and self-effacement are expressed. Below we briefly describe some of the most important for new converts and adoptives to incorporate into their lifestyle.

RESPECT

1. **RESPECT FOR ELDERS:** Respect for elders is a keystone of Hindu culture. This genuine acknowledgment of seniority is demonstrated through endearing customs such as: sitting to the left of elders, bringing gifts on special oc-

casions, not sitting while they are standing, not speaking excessively, not yawning or stretching, not putting one's opinions forward strongly, not contradicting or arguing, seeking their advice and blessings, giving them first choice of seats, inviting them to take their food first or serving them first.

2. **NAME PROTOCOL:** Youngers never use the proper name of their elders. Younger brother, for example, refers to his elder brother as *annai,* or *periannai* (in Tamil), not by name. The elder may use the name of the younger. Children are trained to refer to all adults as auntie or uncle. Adults too refer to each other as elder or younger brother or simply as brother (likewise for women). Only men the same age will occasionally address each other by first name. A Hindu wife never speaks the name of her husband. When referring to him she uses terms such as "my husband," "him" or, for example, "Jothi's father." When addressing *yogīs, swāmis* or *sādhakas,* one uses the title, not personal pronouns, such as *you* or *your* (nor by the name alone). For example, one would never ask, "What do you want?" Instead, one would inquire, "What does *swāmī* want?"
3. **TOUCHING FEET IN RESPECT:** One touches the feet of holy men and women in recognition of their great humility and inner attainment. A dancer or a musician touches the feet of his or her teacher before each lesson. Children prostrate and touch the feet of their mother and father at special times, such as New Year's day, birthdays and before parting for a journey.

Purity

Cleanliness in Western culture tends to be thought of almost entirely as a physical issue. A thing is pure if it lacks "dirt." Eastern culture regards purity as more than just physical. Something may be perfectly clean, yet be impure or polluted by thoughts of another or by undesirable vibrations. Here are several ways purity is preserved in Hindu culture.

1. **PURITY AND FOOD:** Food is central to the concept of purity, for the nature of one's nourishment deeply affects one's physical, mental and emotional nature. In a marketplace, one does not touch food they don't intend to buy. One cooking food for others would never taste of the dish from a spoon and then put the spoon back in the pot.

   Similarly, one would not touch the lips to a water vessel that is also used by others. Nor would one offer something to another from which one has taken a bite or a sip.
2. **SANCTIFIED FOOD OFFERINGS:** However, the opposite of this is true in the case of the *satguru's* food leavings. Food that he has tasted of is revered as sacred *prasāda* or *ucçhishṭa.* This, and the water from the washing of his feet, is sought after and imbibed by all devotees for the great spiritual blessings that it contains toward *moksha.*
3. **FLOWER OFFERINGS:** One does not sniff flowers picked for offering to the Deities—even the smell is for the Gods, not for us. Flowers that fall to the ground should not be offered.
4. **OFFERINGS:** Offerings, such as an *archana* basket, flowers or garlands, are carried with both hands on the right side of the body, so as to not be breathed on. All items are

washed in preparation and, if carried more than a short distance, wrapped or covered.

5. **THE LEFT HAND:** In Asian culture, the left hand is considered impure because it is used for personal hygiene by washing after answering the call of nature. Handing another person anything with the left hand may be considered a subtle insult.
6. **NO SHOES INSIDE THE HOME:** Shoes are considered impure objects. The cultured Hindu never wears shoes or sandals inside a temple or shrine, nor in his own home or the homes of other Hindus. Carrying shoes in the hands from one part of the premises to another is also avoided.
7. **CAUTION WITH FOOTWEAR:** It is very important to apologize immediately if one touched someone with their shoe or sandal. This is done by touching the right hand to where foot touched the other person and then touching one's right hand lightly to the left eye and then the right. This same remedy applies to inadvertently hitting someone with the hand or foot or bumping into them.

EXCHANGE OF PRĀṆA

1. **GIVING AND RECEIVING WITH BOTH HANDS:** Giving and accepting things from one to another, presenting offerings to the Deity, etc., is most properly done with both hands. The reason for this is that with the gift, *prāṇa* is also given through both hands, thus endowing more energy to the object. The recipient of the gift receives it with both hands along with the *prāṇa* from the gracious giver. It is known that this exchange of energies is vital for friendship, harmony and the total release of the gift to the recipient.
2. **NOT POINTING THE FINGER:** Pointing with the forefinger of the right hand or shaking the forefinger in emphasis while talking is never, ever done. This is because the right hand possesses a powerful, aggressive *prāṇic* force,

an energy that moves the forces of the world. Pointing the index finger channels that force into a single stream. The harshness of this energy would be severely felt in the nerve system of the recipient. More properly, rather than pointing or shaking the index finger to give direction or emphasize a verbal statement, the entire hand is used as a pointer, with the palm up and the thumb held alongside the forefinger.

3. **SHAKING HANDS:** The traditional way that Hindu men greet one another is with the *añjali mudrā,* then, with palms still held together, extending their hands to one another, in a two-handed handshake, in a deliberate transfer of *prāṇa.* The hands of one man, usually the less senior, are gently clasped between the other's. Each looks smilingly into the other's face while bowing slightly in humility. This handshake is not firm, but relaxed and gentle.
4. **GREETING WOMEN:** However, Hindu men never shake hands with women in the above manner or in any other way. Women are greeted by only placing hands in *añjali mudrā,* hands in the prayerful gesture.
5. **NOT THROWING THINGS:** Throwing any kind of object from one person to another is considered extremely improper, even if the persons know each other very well. Cultured Hindus consider this crude and even mildly violent, even if done in efficiency or jest.
6. **CARE IN SITTING:** It is improper to ever sit with one's legs outstretched toward a temple, shrine or altar, or even toward another person. This is a grave insult. Crossing one leg over the knee when sitting in a chair should be avoided, though crossing at the ankles is permitted. One must always try to follow the example of traditional elders. Worshiping in the kneeling pose is not acceptable among Hindus.
7. **DOORWAYS:** Conversations are not held inside or through doorways. This is considered inauspicious. Similarly, to

exchange or give or lend an object, one steps inside the room first, or the recipient steps out of the room so that both parties are in the same room.

MODESTY

1. **MODESTY:** Interactions in public between men and women are usually much more restrained in Asian culture than in Western culture. In Asian culture, for the most part, men socialize with men, and women with women. Men never touch women in public, such as helping a woman out of a car, unless the lady is very elderly or infirm.
2. **DISPLAYING AFFECTION:** Married couples in Asia do not hug, hold hands or kiss in public. Even embracing at airports and train stations is considered out of the question. Men, however, frequently walk hand in hand.

THE ROLE OF WOMEN

Women in Hindu society are held in the highest regard, far more respected, in truth, than in the West. But this does not imply the kind of "equality" or participation in public interactions that are common in the West. The qualities traditionally most admired in an Eastern woman are modesty of manner, shyness and self-effacement. Self-assertive or bold tendencies are regarded with circumspection. Feminine refinements are expressed and protected in many customs including the following.

1. **WOMANLY RESERVE:** In mixed company, a Hindu woman will keep modestly in the background and not participate freely in conversation. This, of course, does not apply to situations among family and close friends. When male guests are in the home, women of the household will appear when it is proper for them to do so. Visitors do not expect or ask to meet them. Women are not expected to speak out or make themselves a part of the conversation.

2. **WIFE WALKS BEHIND HUSBAND:** The wife walks a step or two behind her husband, or if walking by his side, a step or two back, always giving him the lead. (In the West, the reverse of this is often true.)
3. **SERVING AT MEALS:** At meals, women follow the ancient custom of serving the men first before eating.
4. **CHAPERONING:** It is customary for a woman to always be accompanied when she leaves the home. Living alone, too, is unusual.
5. **WOMEN IN PUBLIC:** Generally, it is improper for women to speak with strangers on the street, much less strike up a casual conversation. Similarly, drinking or smoking in public, no matter how innocent, is interpreted as a sign of moral laxity.

GUESTS IN THE HOME

1. **HOME VISITS:** Close friends can visit one another anytime without being announced or making arrangements first. When they drop in, at least a refreshing drink is always served.
2. **HOSTING GUESTS:** Children generally leave the room, with a smile, when guests enter. The mother remains close by to serve as needs arise. The father, if present, will speak with the guest. If not present, the mother and a son will fulfill this role, and if no son is present, the mother may act as hostess, but only with the accompaniment of someone close to the family.
3. **WIFE HOME ALONE:** If the lady of the house is home alone and a male visitor comes to see her husband, it is not proper for her to invite him in, nor for him to expect to enter. Rather, he will leave a message and take his leave.
4. **GIVING GIFTS:** Gifts are always given when one stays over night as a guest in someone's home. The value of the gift varies greatly, depending upon circumstance. It is proper

to give a separate gift for the wife and the husband. The wife receives the nicest item.

BODY LANGUAGE

All Hindus know that "Life is meant to be lived joyously!" All is God, and God is everywhere and in all things. This understanding and appreciation is exemplified in every aspect of Hindu deportment.

1. **KINDLY WORDS AND COUNTENANCE:** Hindus strive to keep a pleasant expression on their face, a gentle smile and a kind word for everyone they meet through the day. They know in their heart of hearts that God is everywhere and that all in the Universe is perfect at every point in time. This knowledge gives them strength and courage to face their daily *karmas* positively and graciously.
2. **REFINED GESTURES:** Hindus know that every movement of the body, the face, hands, eyes, mouth, head, etc., has a meaning. They are taught to be sensitive to the thoughts and feelings of others in their body language. It is wise for new adoptives and converts to realize that they are "talking" even when they are not speaking.

Transmitting Hinduism to the Next Generation

It goes without saying that many responsibilities accompany the momentus step of entering the world's most venerable faith. Having walked through this doorway, it becomes the duty of the new adoptive or convert to follow the principles of the Sanātana Dharma to the best of his or her ability. One of the most important duties is to pass the religion on to the next generation through raising children according to the tenets of our faith. In *Dancing with Śiva,* we developed a *Primer for Children.* On the following pages we bring that chapter to you in *Loving Gaṇeśa* with all its five parts: Hinduism A-Z, Five Precepts, Five Obligations, Five Parenting Guidelines and Eight Sacraments.

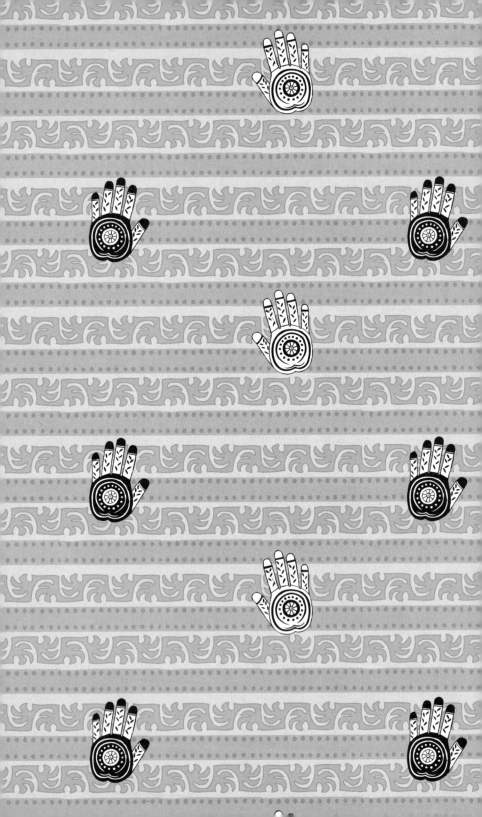

Dharma Ṛiṇam

धर्म-ऋणम्

Religion's Dues

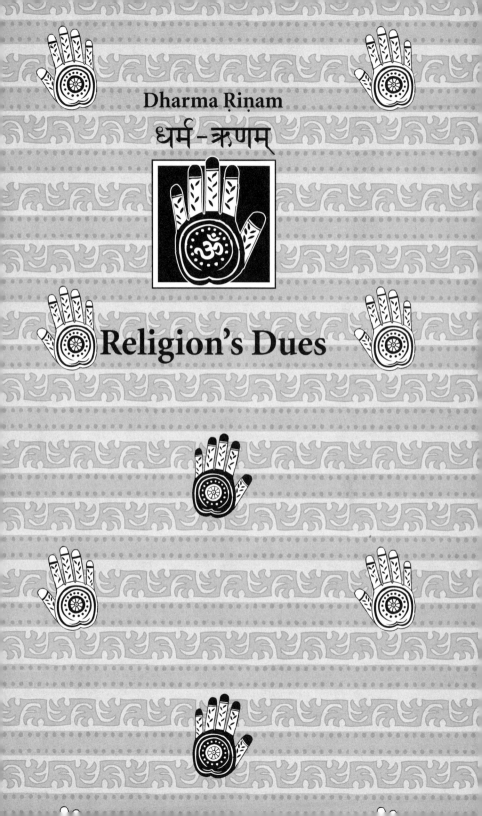

Religion's Dues

YES, BECOMING PART OF A RELIGION IS MUCH LIKE BECOMING PART OF A FAMILY THAT EXISTS TOGETHER UNDER ONE NAME, CONsisting of embodied souls on planet earth, beings of light in the astral world and Gods of the heavenly realms. In Sanātana Dharma, our scriptures say 100% of our wealth should be offered to God, Gods and *guru,* and only thus sanctified a portion used by the devotee for life's needs. For instance, it is without hesitation that our loving Gaṇeśa would claim 100% of the accumulated wealth and daily income of all of His devotees who pray to Him as prescribed by scripture and explained in this book. His generosity is so generous and constantly out-pouring that it has always, through eons of time, amassed a return. Ninety-percent of gifts received are blessed for good usage and returned to His faithful ones; He keeps a tiny portion, just 10%, for His important work.

The remover of obstacles is also the placer of obstacles. It has been testified, too, by many that when only a miniscule portion is given to Him, the rest is taken away by barriers that less-than-generous givers did not expect. Yes, loving Gaṇeśa requires of His devotees 100% dedication and giving before His ever-present grace takes hold in their lives.

We shall now explain how the spiritual practice of tithing, paying monthly religious dues of 10%, creates wealth over time for individuals and families alike—a wealth that is blessed to never gain losses, but to perpetuate itself generation after generation. Read on and learn! Tithing is giving 10%: not a dollar more, not a dollar less; not a rupee more, not a rupee less; not a pound more, not a pound less; not a lira more, not a lira less.

God's Money

Everything from a lump of carbon to a dazzling diamond, a molecule of oxygen to the galactic explosion of a star gone supernova is of the Being of God. We place lesser and greater value upon things usually dependent upon our interests. Ultimately, we would have to say that everything is God's, including what we manufacture from native elements. Indeed, if all the trillions of dollars, rupees, yen, pounds, rubles, deutschmarks and francs, and all the precious metals and gems were gathered and compressed together into one giant cube, any Hindu would readily have to admit that man's money and the planet's minerals are really God's.

So, in the first sense, God's money is the sum of all monetary values. Connecting this idealistic perspective to a practical one, where we as individuals are engaged in the *dharmic* pursuit of wealth, God's money is what we dedicate to God, as our religious dues, to perpetuate His greater spiritual design for our planet. This is also true for our personal use of time. God's time is what we dedicate, as roughly ten percent of our time, toward service that furthers our religion. This is outside of the time spent in our personal spiritual practices: home *pūjā*, scripture reading, *japa*, *sādhana* and meditation.

This chapter is about joyously returning each month ten percent of our earnings and gifts to God for our own spiritual upliftment and economic welfare, and for the support and perpetuation of our Hindu religion, the *Sanātana Dharma,* the "Eternal Path." This is the spiritual practice, the unfolding process of *daśamaṁśa.* In the West it is known as tithe, which also means "a tenth." Among the world religions and faiths, it is an ancient common denominator. In the earliest known historical civilizations of Egyptian, Sumeria and the Indus Valley, all of which were theocracies, "religion-governed," the totality of the annual product of the empire was given to the Gods in their temples, then redistributed to the populace.

Imagine the phenomenal results if the ancient practice of *daśamaṁśa* was fully revitalized today. There are 900 million Hindus worldwide. Some 840 million live in India. A large percentage, say 700 million, are monetarily poor—the per-capita annual income in India is around US$50. Yet even if each offered one dollar (which is only two percent) as God's money every year, that would total 700 million dollars annually for Hindu institutions from the poor sector alone. If a full ten percent was paid, the amount would be $3.5 billion. The remaining 200 million Hindus worldwide, ranging from low to extremely high incomes (paying an average of 400 dollars), in giving God's money would provide an annual fund pool of $80 billion. Every year, this ancient spiritual undertaking of God's money, religion's dues, would give Hinduism some 83.5 billion dollars. Since *daśamaṁśa* is paid by each individual to the institution of his choice, the distribution of the money would be fairly evenly widespread.

Hinduism, balancing on the edge of the 21st century, urgently needs this monetary strength. Hinduism is incalculably rich in religious knowledge, mystic ceremony and spiritual experience. This inner treasure house of Hinduism will never diminish. But the great periphery that touches every Hindu's life does need constant sustenance. Our temples should look like exquisitely wrought jewelry, worthy earthly abodes for God and the Gods and spiritually enrapturing for devotees. Our monasteries and lecture halls, schools and cultural centers should glow with inviting beauty and radiate the best the Hindu mind can offer to the world. All Hindus should be well-educated in their faith and have every facility available for advancing spiritually, socially, economically and culturally. In the past, the present and into the future the practice of *daśamaṁśa* has no equal in instilling closeness to God through our *dharma* of gaining wealth, and in a steady provisioning of our religion. It is a proven system needed now.

In this brief presentation, we can only outline the benefits an individual or an organizational body will gain from giving God's money. I have managed my institutions for thirty-five years on a tithing basis. It achieves results of people's lives unfolding into a greater spirituality, financial security and religious fellowship. These are day-by-day rewards, not easily summed up in a few sentences. But it distills down to the fact that members, largely because they practice *daśamaṁśa,* are happy, healthy, at peace within themselves and among themselves and energetically enthusiastic about advancing their religion. They have cultivated a deep sense of selflessness that recognizes God in all dimensions of their lives. The practice of God's money, religion's dues, has become a doorway into tangible inner experience.

Hinduism has always celebrated the merits of giving, both of wealth and knowledge. The householder gives to the children, the poor and the *sādhus;* the children give to the parents in old age, the elderly give to the community; the student and *sādhus* give to the *guru,* and the *guru* gives to all. It is so much a part of our soul nature to give. Every time we give, more of our soul nature is expressed. Yet when it comes to our hard-earned money which in Hinduism we call *artha,* "wealth," it is sometimes difficult to give, especially on a regular basis and to a society or institution we may not have a voice in governing. Nevertheless, it is our *dharma* to give of our *artha.* Only by our generous contributions individually and as a group will Hinduism flourish and grow from strength to strength. That the scriptures are crystal clear on.

The powerful man should give to one in straights;
let him consider the road that lies ahead!
Riches revolve like a chariot's wheels,
coming to one man now, then to another.

Ṛig Veda, 10.117.5. *VE,* 850-851

To not give generously and regularly is to be unduly self-interested, a condition that will cloud our divine nature and make us feel guilty and stressful. The practice of *daśamaṁśa* will do just the opposite: create positive *karma* of abundance and financial opportunity, cultivate family and community bonding and enhance healthy states of mind. And, a group that is jointly paying religious dues will enjoy a fulfillment, accomplishment and spiritual joy that is collective.

It may interest our readers to know the genesis of this chapter. Some time ago my staff at Himalayan Academy gathered together all the published material they could find on tithing. It came from many sources worldwide, including scripture and citations from Hindu history. Some unusual knowledge was uncovered, such as the case of the Chettiar salt merchants of Tamil Nadu, South India, who 400 years ago began dedicating one eighth or 12% of their earnings to Lord Palani (Murugan) of the Palani Hills Temple. Recorded testimony of the merchants state that because of the payment of 12% of religious dues, called *makimai* in Tamil, their businesses prospered to the extent that even the *mahārāja* took favorable notice.

Hindu Children

Here is a story that demonstrates the spirit of *daśamaṁśa*. A businessman in Texas had made several large gifts to the temple and to local charities. Few calls for funds ever failed to receive a willing response. His generosity to community causes was well known to many people who were identified with the organizations he supported. One evening he was introduced as the speaker at a banquet. The chairman told of a number of instances when that man's generosity had helped to make financial campaigns successful. When the Texas businessman arose to begin his address he was evidently embarrassed. "I want to make it clear that I do not deserve credit for what I give to my temple or to any cause in our community," he began. "The way I look at it is that I have contributed none of my own money. The money all belongs to God; for, you see, I am a tither, having in early childhood taken my *daśama bhāga vrata.*"

Most tithers are humble about their regular habit of setting aside a tenth of their income, especially if they had started the habit at an early age. For they truly have come to feel that they are but the stewards of God's money and pay their religion's dues with a full heart and gratitude for their abundance, whether large or small. A California financier related the story of how he began the habit of tithing. He was one of four boys, all about twelve years of age, who were received into membership of a Hindu society. At the conclusion of the *pūjā,* the priest remarked to one of the leading officials, "It was a great and holy service this morning wasn't it, sir?"

"To what do you refer?" the official inquired. "Why, those four boys surrendering themselves to our Gods," the priest replied. The official commented as he walked away, "They didn't bring fruit and flowers as an offering nor did they give anything to the *hundi.*"

This particular boy overheard the conversation between the priest and the temple official. When he was able to talk to the priest alone, the boy inquired what he would be expected to give when coming to *pūjās* and for the support of the temple. The priest then explained that every Hindu should bring fruit and flowers when coming to a *pūjā* and that it is a spiritual privilege to pay one-tenth of their income to God in appreciation of His blessings. The priest asked how much the boy was earning. He replied that his part-time wages were only $35.00 each week. The priest suggested that the lad think of $3.50 a week as his contribution for the support of the temple and that he should take the *daśama bhāga vrata* before he begins to set aside his *daśamaṁśa.* The priest went on to explain that in Sanskṛit *vrata* means vow or pledge, *daśama* means tenth, and *bhāga* means part or share. *Daśamaṁśa* means tithe and *tithe* means a tenth. Immediately setting aside the tithe as soon as money is received sanctifies the remaining balance. Once the money has thus been blessed it would be difficult to use it for a profligate, *adharmic* purpose, the priest explained. The lad was pleased to hear that *daśamaṁśa* was an ancient religious practice of giving one-tenth of one's income back to God and the Gods to perpetuate their work on Earth.

The priest went on to explain that this is a custom as old as our Hindu religion and that many other religions practice it as well. Thus the taking of the *daśama bhāga vrata* and then beginning to pay *daśamaṁśa,* religion's dues, is a very important part of every modern Hindu's life. The boy prostrated before God, Gods and a picture of his *guru* and then took his *vrata* without hesitation. A few elders listened, and they smiled. All were pleased to see the brightness on his face as he put the envelope with the $3.50 into the *hundi* before he left the temple *maṇḍapa.* He was now truly one of the congregation in his heart and in the hearts of all.

Now the pattern was set and the boy began the life-long habit of setting aside one-tenth of his income for God's work. As a seasoned businessman, he declared that he had never ceased to tithe. He felt that he was helped personally more by tithing than by any other habit which he had observed throughout his life. It is important to notice that this financier began tithing as a boy. Many of the men and women who tithe in this generation say that they, also, began the practice in their early youth.

Tithing ought to begin in childhood. If boys and girls have the example of their parents to encourage them, the decision to tithe will not be a difficult one to make. Even if parents do not tithe, children readily respond to the suggestion that God has given us so much that it is only right that we should set aside a portion of all we receive and bring it as an offering to the temple for its support. This is one way of thanking God and the Gods for Their goodness. And, this is the only way that we truly bless the remaining nine-tenths. Yes, the pattern of a lifetime can best be set by carefully teaching a young person to begin tithing with the first money he or she is given or earns.

Paying Religion's Dues Monthly

Included in the sacred act of tithing is not only laying aside the specified amount of the *daśamaṁśa,* but also the idea of regular monthly giving to the temple or Hindu organization the tither has chosen to support. Many Hindus have never learned to give systematically. They follow no plan in facing their responsibility to the temple they worship in, the society they belong to or the community they live in. Tithing provides a spiritual plan for meeting these responsibilities. The key is to regularly, on a monthly schedule, set aside in a special saving account or envelope one-tenth of one's income as soon as it is received. Then, again on a monthly schedule, give that sum to a religious organization of one's own choosing.

Forego Gratification

Most Hindus give if they are specifically asked for a contribution and their name is published. Others give generously if they hear the temple needs an extra amount to pay a deficit. Many such persons feel virtuous if they are enabled to pull the temple out of what they think is a "financial hole." They fail to consider that the deficit would not have been necessary if they, and others, had voluntarily and regularly contributed their share during the first week of each month. Some Hindus give only if they like the priest, others if they are supporting some phase or all of a special festival. Still others only give out of a sense of appreciation for prayers being answered.

We were acquainted with a negligent Hindu in London who never failed to boast about how he had helped to erect a temple though he had not attended a *pūjā* for many years. Yet, he often bragged that he had helped build the temple. I came to believe he had given the major amount for the building. He had left such an impression with so many people. But one day someone took it upon themself to look into the past financial records of the temple and discovered that the man had contributed the "magnanimous" total of $101! All this time he had avoided his responsibilities to the Gods and to their temple by giving the false impression that he had given so much that he should not be expected to contribute any more.

Because of his carelessness in giving, that man had lost the vital power which is available through faith in God and our Gods. He actually thought he had given a proper sum, but his lack of system in regular sharing had distorted his values. Because he did not begin giving to his religion when he was young, he did not understand the true nature of sharing. This caused him to lose vast opportunities for joy in his Hindu experience throughout his life.

The Rediscovery of Tithing

Our young generation of modern Hindus are awakening to an awareness of the need for a fuller and more dedicated life in God consciousness. The trends in current civilization in this technological age indicate that we must go deeper into our faith and into ourselves if we are to spiritually unfold and experience the bliss that is ours to enjoy. Thoughtful, contemporary Hindus are made aware every day of the conflicting forces which war in the world during this time in the *Kali Yuga*. They know that it is a time which cries out for a more complete surrender of money, time and talents to the will of God and our Gods. They are also well aware that it is the religious institutions that keep the knowledge of Hinduism alive in the world and that the temples provide open doors for devotees. Many Hindus conclude that they must teach their children the spiritual merits of tithing from their gifts and later from their earnings.

Money has assumed a place of increasing importance in the life of everyone this century. With each passing year fewer people live the kind of existence in which they themselves produce the necessities of life. Money has become the buying power to satisfy almost every physical demand. Even the farmer has come to rely upon money. Only a few decades ago the tiller of the soil raised the food which fulfilled the needs of his family. The power to work his fields came from animals which themselves had their subsistence in the land. But now he needs money to operate a farm. He buys rather than raises much of his food. Money pays for the electric power to operate his machinery and for the fuel to run his tractor. His clothing is bought at a store, and his recreation is purchased by the investment he makes in radio or television.

What has happened in recent years to the farmer has long been the experience of millions of workers who earn their livelihood in the factory or the office. For many people the possession of money has become an end in itself in life. The growing importance of money has turned the focus of attention from the true source of the world's goods. The man who worked the fields to produce the necessities for sustenance was in a position to observe the creating and sustaining power of God and the Gods in his life. When he was dependent upon the rainfall, the sun and the fertile earth for his well-being, it was natural to recognize loving Gods. But such recognition becomes more difficult when money is the source of one's physical and psychological satisfaction. It is harder to see God and the Gods at work in the product of a machine or a factory. Then man is tempted to give his worshipful devotion to a pay envelope or a check book. That means money to him. It is the source of his personal comforts and pleasures.

A New Standard Is Needed

The need for a new standard by which faithful Hindus may test their acknowledgment of God's providential care has led many Hindus to a rediscovery of tithing. In this technological age people are tempted to believe that their skills and ingenuity which produce material commodities come from themselves alone. They either assume the absence of God's power in the world, or God and the Gods are pushed back so far in their mind that no vital contact is felt with these great beings or even their own Divinity. Everyone will agree that a new standard is needed to put God consciousness first.

When Hindu children recognize God's creative gifts by setting aside a tithe from their gift or income immediately upon receiving it, before any money is spent for themselves or others, they express their conviction that God is the giver of all that they have. Each young person inwardly admits that the product of the mine or the fertile field can only be explained by the long creative process which is the direct result of the existence of God and the Gods that Hindus extoll. The money that the computer engineer, the baker or the manufacturer earns has its ultimate source in those elements which man did not and could not create. Each occupation or profession engaging the efforts of mankind deals with factors beyond the range of man's ability to make.

Children who pay their tithe learn that God continues to be the owner of the material possessions entrusted to them. They know that the final title to property or money does not rest with the individual, but with God. They learn that people may be stewards of worldly possessions for many years; yet, inevitably they must surrender that stewardship at the end of their earthly life. The trust is then placed upon some other person. They slowly come to realize through experience that people do not own the material world; they are merely its stewards.

Honor God by Sharing

American-born William Colgate was a tither throughout his long and successful business career. He gave not merely one-tenth of the earnings of Colgate's Soap Products; he gave two-tenths, then three-tenths and finally five-tenths of all his income to the work of God in the world. During the latter days of his life, he revealed the origin of his devotion to the principle of tithing. When he was sixteen years old, he left home to find employment in New York City. He had previously worked in a soap manufacturing shop. When he told the captain of the canal boat he was traveling on that he planned to make soap in New York the man gave him this advice: "Someone will soon be the leading soap maker in New York. You can be that person. But you must never lose sight of the fact that the soap you make has been given to you by God. Honor Him by sharing what you earn. Begin by tithing on all you receive." William Colgate felt the urge to tithe because he recognized that God was the giver of all that he possessed, not only of opportunity, but even of the elements used in the manufacture of his products.

Questions on Religious Dues

How can tithing help eliminate debt? My finances are a mess. Tithing helps to establish order in mind and affairs; and when order exists, debt is vanquished. All conditions that are not in divine order are eliminated. New avenues of supply open up. Intuition is strengthened. Giving opens the door for receiving.

Shall I tithe before my debts are paid? Tithing is the best-known and most practical method of consecrating your finances to God. You can tithe your way out of debt if you do it through prayer and in the spirit of love and understanding. Practiced properly, tithing will help solve the conditions that create debt. This has been accomplished by thousands of others; it can be done by you. The tithes that you lay at God's lotus feet in loving consecration may be likened to drops of water that, drawn up by the sun, form rain clouds and descend again to earth in refreshing showers.

Do I tithe on the money I borrow to consolidate debt? No. Nor should you use borrowed money for any purpose other than that for which it was secured.

If I am tithing and my debt becomes heavy, should I stop? A few do tithe for years, and when their expenses become heavy stop in order to meet their bills. In stopping tithing their desires increase and debts are piled so high that there seems to be no way out.

Would it be wiser for me to wait before deciding to tithe? If you feel an inner urge to tithe, now is the time to make a start. Those who wait until they feel they have abundance to spare usually never begin.

Tithing and Your Standard of Living

Won't tithing change my accustomed standard of living? In Hinduism, one's standard of living is measured by the four aims: *artha* (wealth), *kāma* (enjoyment), *dharma* (virtuous conduct) and *moksha* (liberation). *Dharma* governs *artha* and *kāma* so that they are not overly self-centered. Tithing is a *dharmic* act. Your standard of living will be spiritually higher, and in many cases the tither's standards are raised culturally and financially as well.

I should look to God, Gods and guru *to care for me rather than my money. Is that correct?* When your first thought upon receiving your income is to share it with God, your whole being is flooded with divine love. Desires that keep you reaching out after things beyond your means no longer tempt you. A balance is established between pursuing *artha* and *kāma* and the following of *dharma.*

Will my income improve if I depend totally on God to help? As you tithe faithfully and your affairs become established in divine order, your visible supply will increase. You will be able to avoid debt and to learn to live as befits a child of God. The tithe always returns to you, the tither, as further prosperity and abundance for you and for your loved ones. You can't give anything away but that it eventually comes back to you, even God's money.

Religious Dues and the Law of *Karma*

Then tithing is an act of faith. Is this correct? Tithing is an act of faith. When you give love with your religious dues, you become receptive to God's blessing of love. Tithing is a positive use of the law of *karma.* When you give freely and joyously with the consciousness of plenty, you draw back to yourself abundance and many happy experiences. This spirit of giving magnetizes the unseen *devas* of the inner worlds who then can give to you by opening opportunities for you.

Will I be convinced once I experience the positive effects of* karma *in my life as a result of tithing? People are most aware of the negative *karmic* effects in their life. But when they become free in their giving, they are able to give more of their soul self with their gifts, and experience more in return. In conforming to the divine law of *karma,* wonderful things occur in their lives.

Is this a way to use the law of* karma *to our best advantage? *Karmic* effects (being either positive, negative or mixed) are created unknowingly by most Hindus and knowingly by some. To use this law to your best advantage, ask for divine guidance and wisdom in spending your money. You will be delighted to see how much more you can do with it and all that will return to you.

Tithing for the Self-Employed

Is there one key to successful tithing for the self-employed? Yes. It is to separate one's business finances from one's family finances. This is done by maintaining two checking accounts, one for the business and one for the family.

How do the self-employed calculate their tithe? An owner or partner tithes on the income he receives from the business. Firstly, he tithes on his monthly draw from the business. Secondly, he tithes on his share of any net profits earned for the year which exceed his monthly draw.

Please give an example to illustrate this concept for someone who owns his own business. Firstly, the owner of a sole proprietorship draws $2,500 a month from the business by writing a check on his business account, depositing it in his personal account, then writing a tithing check for $250. Secondly, in January the year-end financial statements for the business are completed and show a net profit after taxes of $45,000. Having already drawn $30,000 during the year, the net profit exceeds his monthly draw by $15,000. Therefore, he needs to tithe $1,500 on this amount. To do this he draws an extra $1,500 from the business, deposits it in his personal account and writes a tithing check for the full $1,500.

What is the importance of a monthly draw from the business? Drawing monthly from the business is a form of income for the family on which they can tithe regularly.

If my business is not earning a profit, should I still tithe? It is even more important to be tithing on one's family income if one's business is not doing well.

How do I adjust my tithe if the amount I have drawn from the business during the year exceeds my share of the business's net profit? This is carried forward and adjusted from one year to the next. For example, say in 1995 your year's draw exceeds your share of the net profit by $10,000. In 1996 your profit share exceeds your draw by $8,000, and in 1997 your profit share exceeds your draw by $15,000. The extra tithe at the end of 1995 is zero, 1996 is zero and 1997 is 10% of the $13,000, or $1,300.

Tithing and the Hindu Institution

I have not even been giving a dollar or a rupee to the temple recently. Now I am being encouraged to tithe? When you ceased to give, did you not feel as though you had closed an inner door? Many devotees give a little something as a means of opening the way into a larger measure of loving, living and giving even though they do not tithe.

How do I decide where to pay my religious dues? The most obvious choice is the Hindu leader or institution that is most relevant to your spiritual life and represents the tradition you find solace in. This benefactor could be in your community, or 10,000 miles away. Or there may be a temple in your community that you and your family worship at that would be strengthened and encouraged by your support. If you are not blessed with such an association and do not know exactly where your religious dues would best be used to promote Sanātana Dharma, you can begin by giving to one or more Hindu Heritage Endowment funds of your choice, or create a new fund to benefit one or more institutions of your choice. HHE is a very special foundation designed to support India's diverse spiritual paths and traditions. Begin right away paying ten percent of your income to HHE. Then in the months ahead find the exact institution or project that you feel most inclined to strengthen by your strength.

With this in mind, should I look carefully into each institution? Yes! Tithing is like investing in the stock market for a secure return. Religious leaders have a duty to perform in spending the money wisely, as do corporate presidents.

Is there a responsibility on the giver as well as the receiver? Yes! Both are stewards of God's money. Wisely choose a worthy temple, Hindu church, temple or institution that you feel good about paying your tithe to.

My tithe will not be much to begin with. Will the leaders judge me because of this? A religious leader does not or should not judge the offerings of devotees. Hindus give according to their means. If a devotee's circumstances dictate a small tithe, then that tithe is worth great value to God, for the wealthy can easily afford to tithe. Tithing is totally fair; for each one is paying his religious dues of ten percent of his income, small or large. Tithing can also be applied to time and talents. For example, if a devotee is a carpenter or seamstress, those talents may help a local Hindu institution. After the dues are paid, further religious giving can take place, of sponsoring temple construction and supporting other religious endeavors. There is a big difference between *daśamaṁśa,* which is a debt, and religious giving from the remaining 90%.

Tithing and Hindu Leaders

Should a spiritual leader be at the institution's helm? Not necessarily, though spiritual leadership is preferred. Many large Hindu institutions are doing great work without spiritual leadership within the organization. But they usually look for spiritual guidance from outside the organization. Internal spiritual leadership has the advantage of being much more intimate. The leader provides personal guidance, counsel and stability, working to keep the spiritual work peaceful, harmonious and productive.

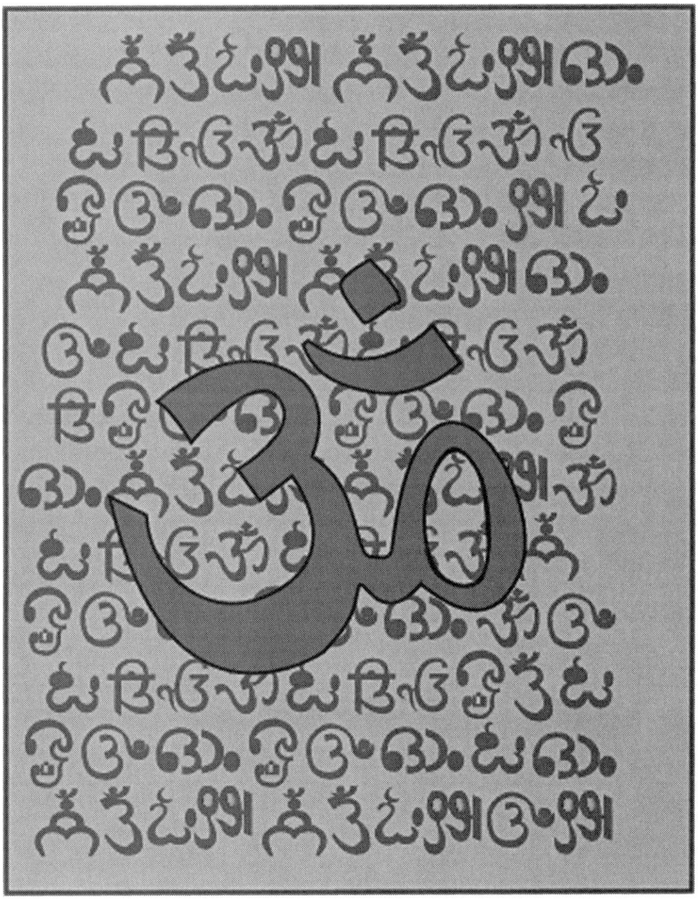

What is the nature of Hindu leadership? Traditional leadership in Hindu institutions is hierarchical. The monarch gave his suggestions to the head of the nearby monastery of a physical, economic nature. The head of the monastery took his suggestions on how to interpret and fulfill them from his *guru* if he was living, or from his own divine Self. The hierarchical system has never failed Hinduism since time began. It exists today and will in the future, despite the popular democratic alternative.

What is a good example of a large Hindu tithing institution? Perhaps the best example is the Swāmīṇārāyan Fellowship, whose leader, Śrī Śrī Śrī Pramukh Swāmī Mahārāj, was given the Renaissance Award by HINDUISM TODAY and named 1995 Hindu of the Year. He has earned a permanent place in the Hindu timeline. His congregation of tens of thousands all pay their religious dues through *daśamaṁśa.* With so many dedicated Fellowship devotees paying their tithe to their *guru,* and on top of that giving gold each year in measure equal to his weight and selflessly contributing vast quantities of their time and encouraging their children to do the same, it all adds up to a truly powerful force in the world. On the strength of a tithing membership, they built a $4 million temple in the middle of London, inaugurated in August of 1995. They support a strict monastic order of 500 *swāmīs,* run numerous social services and are single-handedly educating millions of people all over the world in the cultural sophistications of Hindu India's wonderful traditions. If more Hindus were to follow their tithing example, Hinduism would be even stronger than it is today. We look forward to an abundant future in the decades to come.

Can we conclude by saying that an organization must properly spend the funds entrusted to it? A feeling of God-is-present-here and a responsible sense of Hindu tolerance and ministry should be apparent in the organization before the tithe is committed. Then, once you have considered well and chosen, be loyal. Don't discipline the leaders of the organization by withdrawing the tithe if disappointments come. Those in the ministry are human, doing their best to deal with individual and group *karmas.* Remember that God's Mind is present in all our affairs.

Does tithing include produce grown on one's property? Pay your tithe freely, with loving Gaṇeśa in your heart, to the temple or institution of your choice. Give also a tenth of any food you grow: one coconut for every ten, one banana for every ten. This is only proper, for the one coconut, one banana are not your own. They belong to God.

Have Your Children Declare Their *Vrata* Now

Now is the time for the children to be brought forward by their parents into a greater depth of religious life. If they believe in the divine laws of *Sanātana Dharma* and have faith in the principle of *daśamaṁśa,* then they are ready to take their *daśama bhāga vrata.* Have your Hindu children repeat this vow and begin a new adventure in the Hindu experience. If you, as an adult, have not already taken the vow yourself, there is no better time than now. Those taking the vow should repeat the following paragraph in the home shrine or temple before God and the Gods, family, *guru* or a respected elder. Repeat the *daśama bhāga vrata,* the vow to pay religion's dues, three times and create a covenant to tithe. We have enclosed here a *vrata* certificate to document the vow taking. It can be photocopied and enlarged, signed and then framed or kept safely with other valuable papers.

> *O Divine Beings of all three worlds, let us bring our minds to rest in the* darśana *of Him who has one tusk. Let us meditate upon Him, who has the form of an elephant with a curved trunk. May He guide us always along the right path. I believe in You, Loving Gaṇeśa, and the Gods of our faith and in the Hindu Dharma. In love and trust I recognize Your goodness in providing for my every material need. I accept the principle of daśamaṁśa, religion's dues, as the method by which I may acknowledge my gratitude to You, and share in helping You fulfill and perpetuate Your work on Earth. As an act of dedication, I am resolved this day to begin (or continue) the regular practice of tithing.*

Announce Your Intent to Tithe

After you have made your *vrata,* tell the trustees of your temple, Hindu church or society about the decision to pay your *daśamaṁśa,* your religious dues, to their organization during the first week of each month. They will be pleased that they have been chosen by you as its steward and be able to plan your contributions into their yearly budgets.

Aum Loving Gaṇeśa!

Daśama Bhāga Vrata

दशमभागव्रत தசமபாக விரதம்

The Tithing Vow

"O Divine Beings of all three worlds, let us bring our minds to rest in the *darśana* of Him who has one tusk. Let us meditate upon Him who has the form of an elephant with a curved trunk. May He guide us always along the right path.

I, ______________________________ ,
Name of Devotee (Please Print)

believe in You, Loving Gaṇeśa, and in the Gods of our faith and the Hindu Dharma. In love and trust I recognize Your goodness in providing for my every material and spiritual need. I wholeheartedly accept the principle of *daśamamśa* (paying one-tenth of my income as religion's dues) as the method by which I may acknowledge my gratitude to You and share in helping You fulfill and perpetuate Your work on earth. As an act of dedication, I am resolved this day to begin (or continue) the regular practice of tithing."

Signature of devotee: ______________________________

It is Hereby Certified

that this devotee, born in ______________________ on ____________, of the ____________ *nakshatra*, and now residing at ______________________ ________, during a divinely ordained ceremony at ______________________ on the auspicious day of ____________ duly voiced the above tithing vow in accordance with the traditions of Hinduism before the Deity, the Mahādevas and the *devas*. This devotee is thus bound eternally and immutably to the abundant life of spiritual giving, aided by the virtue of *daśamaṁśa*.

SIGNATURES OF PRIESTS, ELDERS AND OTHERS WITNESSING THIS CEREMONY:

Bālaka Pustakam
बालकपुस्तकम्

A Children's Primer

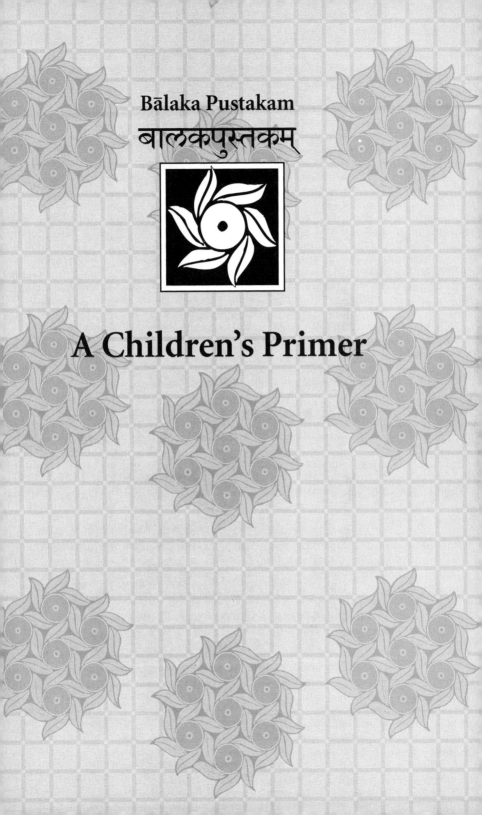

Phalgun

A Children's Primer

Z IS FOR *ZEAL* AND *A* IS FOR *AUM,* AND EVERYTHING IN BETWEEN IS WHAT THIS CHAPTER IS ALL ABOUT, A PRIMER FOR CHILDREN. THE poster "Hinduism A to Z" has been found pasted on refrigerators in kitchens, in nurseries and family rooms in homes all over the world. This presentation was the result of the demand of Hindu parents worldwide who called for a common religious code to teach their sons and daughters. They asked, "What is the minimum I must do to dispatch my duty to my religion and my children?" The World Hindu Federation of Nepal discussed this need at its international conference in Bali in late 1992, and shared their concern with me at that time. In response, I told the Bali Mahāsaṅgha that I would work with my research staff to prepare the minimal duties for parents to pass on the Sanātana Dharma to the next generation. The result was ten *ślokas* summarizing the five essential Hindu beliefs, and the five corresponding observances performed in expression of those beliefs. *Āchāryas* concur that these are enough to know and follow to be a good Hindu. We first published these in *Hinduism Today*'s March, 1993, edition, along with the extremely popular primer for children covering Hinduism from A to Z. Both of these are assembled here as *A Children's Primer.* In this section you will also find an illustrated summary of the essential Hindu *saṁskāras,* or rites of passage. These sacraments are vital to Hindus, for whom life is a sacred journey and every crucial step is acknowledged through traditional ceremony. The modern Hindu child raised up with these precepts, practices and sacraments will be a fully functioning human being, one who is tolerant, devotional, fair, fearless, obedient, secure, happy, selfless, detached and traditional.

Hinduism A to Z

Dharma Varṇamālā

धर्मवर्णमाला

A CHILDREN'S PRIMER ON HINDU THOUGHT AND IDEALS, COVERING DHARMA FROM A TO Z AND FEATURING A UNIQUE INITIAL ALPHABET DESIGNED WITH INDIAN MOTIFS.

A is for Aum, the three-syllabled mantra that represents the Sacred Mystery in sound and vibration.

B is for bhakti, deep devotion and love for the Divine which softens even hearts of stone.

C is for culture, the beauty of Hindu music, fine arts, drama, dance, literature and architecture.

D is for dharma, which is righteousness, cosmic order and duty, leading us on the right path.

E is for Earth, our lovely blue planet, which we treat as sacred, protecting all its wonderful creatures.

F is for family, the precious cornerstone of Hindu life, culture, service and tradition.

G is for guru, our enlightened master who, knowing Truth himself, can guide us there.

H is for haṭha yoga, healthful physical science for vitality, energy-balancing and meditation.

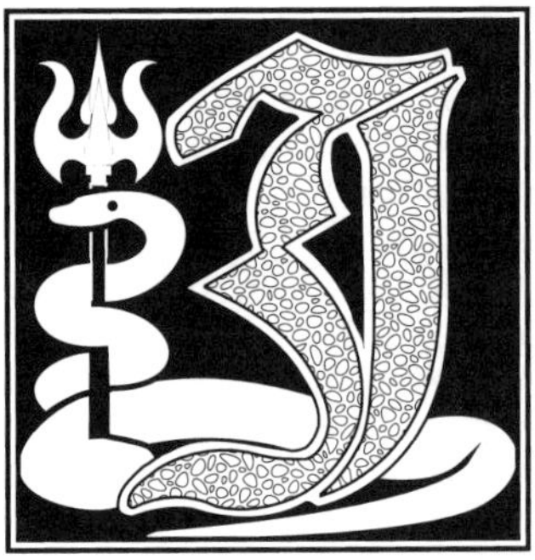

I is for India, Bhārata, Motherland to one-sixth of humanity, Holy Land for Hindus everywhere.

J is for japa, repetitive, prayerful mantras which quiet emotion and empower the mind.

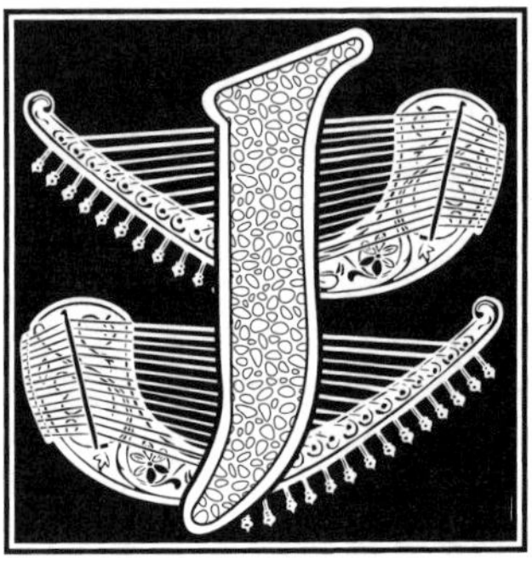

K is for karma, the law of cause and effect by which we determine our experience and destiny.

L is for lotus, the heart's inner shrine, where God dwells, ever serene, ever perfect.

M is for mauna, not talking, the inner silence known when words, thoughts and actions are stilled.

N is for non-attachment, the art of living the simple life, without too many needs or desires.

O is for open-mindedness, the Hindu's tolerant freedom of thought, inquiry and belief.

P is for pūjā, mystic worship of the Divine in our home shrine and holy temples and places.

Q is for quest, seeking to know, "Who am I? Where did I come from? Where am I going?"

R is for reincarnation, our immortal soul's journey from birth to rebirth. We do not fear death.

S is for saṁskāras, sacraments sanctifying life's passages: name-giving, marriage, death and more.

T is for tilaka, forehead marks worn in honor of our unique and varied lineages.

U is for utsava, our many home and temple festivals, full of bhakti, fun, feasting, and family sharing.

V is for Vedas, our oldest and holiest book, the word of God recorded in 100,000 Sanskṛit verses.

W is for wealth (artha), one of life's four goals, along with love, dharma and enlightenment.

X is for xerophily, the ability of certain plants and animals to thrive in India's hot, arid plains.

Y is for yoga, union of the soul with God which brings release from worldly bondage.

Z is for zeal, the fervor with which we perform service, go on pilgrimage and greet our holy religious leaders.

Five Precepts

Pañcha Śraddhā

पञ्चश्रद्धा

THESE FIVE ŚLOKAS CONSTITUTE THE MINIMAL HINDU BELIEFS. BY TEACHING THESE TO SONS AND DAUGHTERS, PARENTS WORLDWIDE PASS ON THE SANĀTANA DHARMA TO THEIR CHILDREN.

सर्व ब्रह्म 1. *Sarva Brahma:* God is All in all

The dear children are taught of one Supreme Being, all-pervasive, transcendent, creator, preserver, destroyer, manifesting in various forms, worshiped in all religions by many names, the immortal Self in all. They learn to be tolerant, knowing the soul's divinity and the unity of all mankind.

मन्दिर 2. *Mandira:* Holy Temples

The dear children are taught that God, other divine beings and highly evolved souls exist in unseen worlds. They learn to be devoted, knowing that temple worship, fire-ceremonies, sacraments and devotionals open channels for loving blessings, help and guidance from these beings.

कर्म 3. *Karma:* Cosmic Justice

The dear children are taught of *karma,* the divine law of cause and effect by which every thought, word and deed justly returns to them in this or a future life. They learn to be compassionate, knowing that each experience, good or bad, is the self-created reward of prior expressions of free will.

संसार मोक्ष 4. *Saṁsāra-Moksha:* Liberation

The dear children are taught that souls experience righteousness, wealth and pleasure in many births, while maturing spiritually. They learn to be fearless, knowing that all souls, without exception, will ultimately attain Self Realization, liberation from rebirth and union with God.

वेद गुरु 5. *Veda, Guru:* Scripture, Preceptor

The dear children are taught that God revealed the *Vedas* and *Āgamas,* which contain the eternal truths. They learn to be obedient, following the precepts of these sacred scriptures and awakened *satgurus,* whose guidance is absolutely essential for spiritual progress and enlightenment.

Five Practices

Pañcha Kriyā

पञ्चक्रिया

THESE FIVE ŚLOKAS OUTLINE THE MINIMAL HINDU PRACTICES THAT PARENTS TEACH THEIR CHILDREN IN ORDER TO NURTURE FUTURE CITIZENS WHO ARE STRONG, SECURE, RESPONSIBLE, TOLERANT AND TRADITIONAL.

उपासना 1. *Upāsanā:* Worship

The dear children are taught daily worship in the family shrine room—rituals, disciplines, chants, *yogas* and religious study. They learn to be secure through devotion in home and temple, wearing traditional dress, bringing forth love of the Divine and preparing the mind for serene meditation.

उत्सव 2. *Utsava:* Holy Days

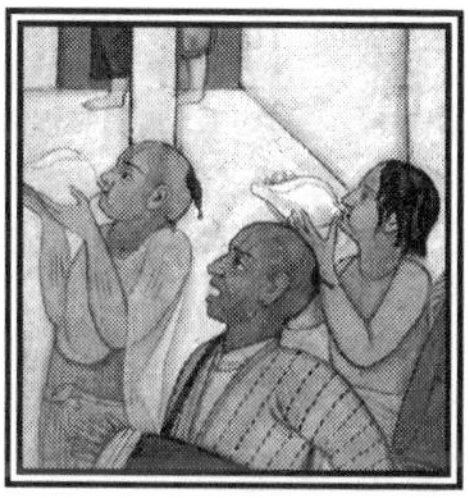

The dear children are taught to participate in Hindu festivals and holy days in the home and temple. They learn to be happy through sweet communion with God at such auspicious celebrations. *Utsava* includes fasting and attending the temple on Monday or Friday and other holy days.

धर्म 3. *Dharma:* Virtuous Living

The dear children are taught to live a life of duty and good conduct. They learn to be selfless by thinking of others first, being respectful of parents, elders and *swāmīs,* following divine law, especially *ahiṁsā,* mental, emotional and physical noninjury to all beings. Thus they resolve *karmas.*

तीर्थयात्रा 4. *Tīrthayātrā:* Pilgrimage

The dear children are taught the value of pilgrimage and are taken at least once a year for *darśana* of holy persons, temples and places, near or far. They learn to be detached by setting aside worldly affairs and making God, Gods and *gurus* life's singular focus during these journeys.

संस्कार 5. *Saṁskāra:* Rites of Passage

The dear children are taught to observe the many sacraments which mark and sanctify their passages through life. They learn to be traditional by celebrating the rites of birth, name-giving, head-shaving, first feeding, ear-piercing, first learning, coming of age, marriage and death.

Five Parenting Guidelines

Pañcha Kuṭumba Sādhana

पञ्चकुटुम्ब साधन

1. Good Conduct—*Dharmāchāra:* Loving fathers and mothers, knowing they are the greatest influence in a child's life, behave the way their dear children should when adults. They never anger or argue before young ones. Father in a *dhotī*, mother in a *sārī* at home, all sing to God, Gods and *guru.*

2. Home Worship—*Dharma Svagṛiha:* Loving fathers and mothers establish a separate shrine room in the home for God, Gods and guardian *devas* of the family. Ideally it should be large enough for all the dear children. It is a sacred place for scriptural study, a refuge from the *karmic* storms of life.

3. Talking About Religion—*Dharma Sambhāshana:* Loving fathers and mothers speak Vedic precepts while driving, eating and playing. This helps dear children understand experiences in right perspective. Parents know many worldly voices are blaring, and their *dharmic* voice must be stronger.

4. Continuing Self-Study—*Dharma Svādhyāya:* Loving fathers and mothers keep informed by studying the *Vedas, Āgamas* and sacred literature, listening to *swāmīs* and *paṇḍitas.* Youth face a world they will one day own, thus parents prepare their dear children to guide their own future progeny.

5. Following a Spiritual Preceptor—*Dharma Saṅga:* Loving fathers and mothers choose a preceptor, a traditional *satguru,* and lineage to follow. They support their lineage with all their heart, energy and service. He in turn provides them clear guidance for a successful life, material and religious.

Eight Rites of Passage

Asht̤ a Saṁskāra

अष्टसंस्कार

SACRAMENTS ARE PERFORMED TO CELEBRATE AND SANCTIFY LIFE'S CRUCIAL JUNCTURES, INFORM FAMILY AND COMMUNITY, AND SECURE INNER-WORLD BLESSINGS. HERE ARE EIGHT OF THE ESSENTIAL RITES.

Nāmakaraṇa Saṁskāra
This is the Hindu name-giving ceremony, performed in the home or the temple 11 to 41 days after birth. The father whispers the auspicious new name in the infant's right ear.

Annaprāśana Saṁskāra
The first feeding of solid food is a sacred event performed by the father in the temple or home. The choice of food offered to a child at this crucial time is said to help forge his or her destiny.

Karṇavedha Saṁskāra
The ear-piercing ceremony, given to both boys and girls, performed in the temple or the home, generally on the child's first birthday. Health and wealth benefits derive from this ancient rite.

Chūḍākaraṇa Saṁskāra
The head is shaven and smeared with sandalwood paste in this rite performed in the temple or home before age four. It is a very happy day for the child. The shaven head denotes purity and egolessness.

Vidyārambha Saṁskāra
The official beginning of primary education. In this rite, performed in the home or temple, the child scribes his or her first letter of the alphabet in a tray of unbroken, uncooked, saffron rice.

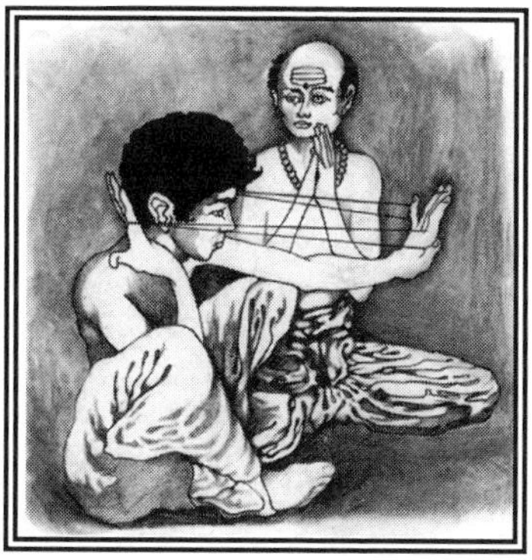

Upanayana Saṁskāra
The ceremonial investment of the "sacred thread" and inititation into Vedic study, performed in the home or temple, usually between the ages of 9 and 15, after which a youth is considered "twice born."

Vivāha Saṁskāra
The marriage ceremony, performed in a temple or wedding hall around the sacred *homa* fire. Lifetime vows, Vedic prayers and seven steps before God and Gods consecrate the union of husband and wife.

Antyeshṭi Saṁskāra
The funeral rite includes preparation of the body, cremation, home-cleansing and dispersal of ashes. The purifying fire releases the soul from this world that it may journey unhindered to the next.

Conclusion

Nirvahaṇam

निर्वहणम्

NOW WE HAVE TOLD HIS STORY AND HAVE BEEN REWARDED WITH THE KINDLY RESPONSES OF EMINENT, SCHOLARLY *SWĀMĪS, satgurus* and religionists who have had so many generous comments and remarks to make as to its 99% perfection. We know that we could have done 1% better, but rest in the feeling that we did our humble best. Praying to our loving Gaṇeśa is a must for each Hindu and *ardha*-Hindu to be able to succeed and then sustain their enterprises. For this beloved God looks far into the future and expects family wealth not to be a temporary prosperity for one generation or two, but a sustainable fortune for ten and then more and more generations into the future of futures. So, a prayer now and again is worth the praying. The wealth of knowledge is immense about this founder of Hinduism, the pope of it all (the God that even Śiva-Brahmā-Vishṇu Himself proclaimed He must worship before success is assured, so the stories inform us). We had not hoped to capture all His glorious subtleties within these few pages, just enough to know how to proceed in His worship, receive His love and commence well-thought-out plans with His grace. This mystic God knows no bounds. He is the channel to all the 330 million Gods and Supreme God of the *Vedas*. To be sure, Gaṇeśa is boundless and as competent as gravity, responding to our every need just a little faster than the speed of light. Believe it. It's true. We affectionately conclude *Loving Gaṇeśa*, remembering the patron of culture, protector of travelers, the door opener and the guardian of destiny.

Glossary

Śabdāvalī

शब्दावली

aadheenam: ஆதீனம் "Ownership, possession, dependence; Śaiva monastery." A Śaivite Hindu monastery-temple complex in the South Indian, Śaiva Siddhānta tradition. The *aadheenam* head, or pontiff, is called the *guru mahāsannidhānam* or *aadheenakartar.*

abhaya mudrā: अभयमुद्रा The hand pose common in Hindu icons, betokening "fear not," in which the fingers of the right hand are raised and the palm faces forward. See: *mudrā.*

abhimāna: अभिमान Egoism.

abhisheka: अभिषेक "Sprinkling; ablution." Ritual bathing of the Deity's image with water, curd, milk, honey, *ghee,* rosewater, etc. A special form of *pūjā* prescribed by Āgamic injunction. Also performed in the inauguration of religious and political monarchs and other special blessings. See: *pūjā.*

abhyāsa: अभ्यास्य Dedicated striving and practice.

ablution: *Snāna.* A washing of the body, especially as a religious ceremony.

Absolute: Lower case (absolute): real, not dependent on anything else, not relative. Upper case (Absolute): Ultimate Reality, the unmanifest, unchanging and transcendent Paraśiva—utterly nonrelational to even the most subtle level of consciousness. It is the Self God, the essence of man's soul. Same as *Absolute Being* and *Absolute Reality.*

absorption: To take in and make part of an existent whole. Known in Sanskṛit as *saṁhāra,* absorption is one of God's five powers (*pañchakṛitya*), synonymous with *destruction* or *dissolution,* but with no negative or frightful implications. All form issues from God and eventually returns to Him. See: *Naṭarāja.*

abstain: To hold oneself back, to refrain from or do without. To avoid a desire, negative action or habit.

abyss: A bottomless pit. The dark states of consciousness into which one may fall as a result of serious misbehavior; the seven *chakras* (psychic centers), or *talas* (realms of consciousness), below the *mūlādhāra chakra,* which is located at the base of the spine. See: *chakra, loka.*

āchārya: आचार्य A highly respected teacher. The wise one who practices what he preaches. A title generally bestowed through *dīkshā* and ordination, such as in the Śivāchārya priest tradition.

acidic: A substance which is acid forming or which contains an excess of acid-forming substances. The opposite of alkaline.

actinic: Spiritual, creating light. From the Greek *aktis,* meaning "ray." Of or pertaining to consciousness in its pure, unadulterated state.

actinodic: Spiritual-magnetic; a mixture of odic and actinic force. Actinic refers to consciousness in its pure, unadulterated state. Odic energy, the force of attraction and repulsion between people, people and their things, manifests as masculine (aggressive) and feminine (passive), arising from the *piṅgalā* and *iḍā* currents.

adage: An old saying that has been popularly accepted as truth.

adept: Highly skilled; expert. In religion, one who has mastered certain spiritual practices or disciplines. An advanced *yogī.*

adharma: अधर्म Opposite of *dharma.* Thoughts, words or deeds that transgress divine law. Unrighteousness, irreligiousness; demerit. See: *dharma, pāpa, sin.*

adopt: To take an idea, principle, or even a religion and henceforth live with it and use it as one's own.

adulate: To praise and flatter highly.

advaita: अद्वैत "Nondual; not two." Nonduality or monism. The philosophical doctrine that Ultimate Reality consists of a one principle substance, or God. Opposite of *dvaita,* dualism. Advaita is the primary philosophical stance of the Vedic *Upanishads,* and of Hinduism, interpreted differently by the many *ṛishis, gurus, paṇḍitas* and philosophers. See: *Vedānta.*

adversity: A state of misfortune, difficulty and trouble; the cause of such.

advocate: To speak or write in support of; to be in favor of.

affirmation: *Dṛidhavāchana* ("firm statement"). A positive declaration or assertion. A statement repeated regularly while concentrating on the meaning and mental images invoked, often used to attain a desired result.

affirmation of faith: A brief statement of one's faith and essential beliefs.

affliction: Pain; suffering; distress.

affluence: An abundance of riches; wealth; opulence.

Āgama: आगम "That which has come down." An enormous collection of Sanskṛit scriptures which, along with the *Vedas,* are revered as *śruti* (revealed scripture). The *Āgamas* are the primary source and authority for ritual, *yoga* and temple construction. Each of the major denominations—Śaivism, Vaishṇavism and Śāktism—has its unique *Āgama* texts.

agarbhatti: अगर्भत्ति "Stick incense (Gujarati)." See: *Incense.*

agni: अग्नि "Fire." 1) One of the five elements, *pañchabhūta.* 2) God of the element fire, invoked through Vedic ritual known as *yajña, agnikāraka, homa* and *havana.* The God *Agni* is the divine messenger who receives prayers and oblations and conveys them to the heavenly spheres. See: *yajña.*

ahaṁkāra: अहंकार "I-maker." Personal ego. The mental faculty of individuation; sense of duality and separateness from others. Sense of I-ness, "me" and "mine." *Ahaṁkāra* is characterized by the sense of I-ness *(abhimāna),* sense of mine-ness, identifying with the body *(madīyam),* planning for one's own happiness *(mamasukha)*, brooding over sorrow *(mamaduḥkha)*, and possessiveness *(mama idam)*. See: *āṇava mala, ego.*

***alaṅkāra:* अलंकर** "Ornamentation." Adornment worn by the Deity.

alkaline: Any mineral salt substance that can neutralize acids. Technically, having a pH greater than 7. The opposite of acidic.

***ahiṁsā:* अहिंसा** "Noninjury," nonviolence or nonhurtfulness. Refraining from causing harm to others, physically, mentally or emotionally. *Ahiṁsā* is the first and most important of the *yamas* (restraints). It is the cardinal virtue upon which all others depend.

***ajapa:* अजप** "Non-recitation." Silent incantation of a *mantra*. See: *japa.*

***ājñā chakra:* आज्ञाचक्र** "Command wheel." The third-eye center. See: *chakra.*

***ākāśa:* आकाश** "Space." The sky. Free, open space. Ether, the fifth and most subtle of the five elements—earth, air, fire, water and ether. Empirically, the rarified space or ethereal fluid plasma that pervades the universes, inner and outer. Esoterically, mind, the superconscious strata holding all that exists and all that potentially exists, wherein all happenings are recorded and can be read by clairvoyants. It is through psychic entry into this transcendental *ākāśa* that cosmic knowledge is gathered, and the entire circle of time—past, present and future—can be known. See: *mind (universal).*

***akshata:* अक्षत** "Unbroken." Unmilled, uncooked rice, often mixed with turmeric, offered as a sacred substance during *pūjā*, or in blessings for individuals at weddings and other ceremonies. See: *pūjā.*

all-pervasive: Diffused throughout or existing in every part of the universe.

***ama:* अम** Toxic wastes that accumulate in the body, primarily due to poor digestion and assimilation. In *āyurvedic* living, *ama* is removed periodically through cleansing tonics and procedures. *Amata* is sickness, disease.

***āmra:* आम्र** "Mango."

***amṛita:* अमृत** "Immortality." Literally, "without death *(mṛita)*." The nectar of divine bliss which flows down from the *sahasrāra chakra* when one enters very deep states of meditation.

***amṛitakumbha:* अमृतकुम्भ** "Pot of immortality." This icon held by Loving Gaṇeśa holds the divine *amṛita* that flows from the *sahasrāra chakra* during deep meditation. It is the nectar of immortality.

***ananasa:* अननस** "Pineapple."

***ānanda:* आनन्द** "Bliss." The pure joy—ecstasy or enstasy—of God-consciousness or spiritual experience. In its highest sense, *ānanda* is expressed in the famous Vedic description of God: *sat-chit-ānanda*, "existence-consciousness-bliss"—the divine or superconscious mind of all souls. See: *God Realization.*

***āṇava mala:* आणवमल** "Impurity of smallness; finitizing principle." The individualizing veil of duality that enshrouds the soul. It is the source of finitude and ignorance, the most basic of the three bonds *(āṇava, karma, māyā)* which temporarily limit the soul. The presence of *āṇava mala* is what causes the misapprehension about the nature of God, soul and world, the notion of being separate and distinct from God and the universe. See: *evolution of the soul, grace, mala, soul.*

añjali mudrā: अञ्जलिमुद्रा "Reverence gesture." Also called *praṇāmāñjali.* A gesture of respect and greeting, in which the two palms are held softly together and slightly cupped. Often accompanied by the verbal salutation "*namaskāra,*" meaning "reverent salutation." See: *mudrā, namaskāra.*

aṅkuśa: अंकुश Goad, the elephant prod, symbol of Lord Gaṇeśa's power to remove obstacles from the devotee's path, and to spur the dullards onward.

annaprāśana: अन्नप्राशन "Feeding." The childhood sacrament of first solid food. See: *saṁskāra.*

anorexia: Generally a lack of appetite for food. Specifically, an eating disorder, chiefly in young women, characterized by aversion to food and obsession with weight loss, excessive exercise, even self-induced starvation.

Antarloka: अन्तर्लोक "Inner or in-between world." The astral plane. See: *loka.*

antaryāmin: अन्तर्यामिन् "Inner controller." The conscience, the knowing voice of the soul.

anthology: A choice collection of prose or poetry excerpts.

antyavachana: अन्त्यवचन "Final word." Colophon.

antyeshṭi: अन्त्येष्टि "Last rites." Funeral. See: *death, saṁskāra.*

anubhava: अनुभव "Perception, apprehension; experience." Personal experience; understanding; impressions on the mind not derived from memory.

anugraha śakti: अनुग्रहशक्ति "Graceful or favoring power." Revealing grace. God Śiva's power of illumination, through which the soul is freed from the bonds of *āṇava, karma* and *māyā* and ultimately attains liberation, *moksha.* See: *āṇava mala, grace, Naṭarāja.*

anukramaṇikā: अनुक्रमणिका "Succession, arrangement." An index for a book.

apostate: One who has abandoned what he formerly believed in.

Appar: அப்பர் "Father." Endearing name for Tirunavukarasu (ca 700), one of four Tamil saints, Samayāchāryas, who reconverted errant Śaivites who had embraced Jainism. Calling himself the servant of God's servants, he composed magnificent hymns in praise of Śiva. See: *Nayanar.*

Āraṇyaka: आरण्यक "Forest treatise." Third section of each of the four *Vedas.* Texts containing esoteric, mystical knowledge, largely on the inner meanings and functions of the Vedic *yajña,* or fire ceremonies. See: *Vedas.*

āratī: आरती "Light." The circling or waving of a lamp—usually fed with *ghee,* camphor or oil—before a holy person or the temple Deity at the high point of *pūjā.* The flame is then presented to the devotees, each passing his or her hands through it and bringing them to the eyes three times, thereby receiving the blessings. *Āratī* can also be performed as the briefest form of *pūjā.* See: *archana, pūjā.*

archana: अर्चन A special, personal, abbreviated *pūjā* done by temple priests in which the name, birthstar and family lineage of a devotee are recited to invoke individual guidance and blessings. *Archana* also refers to chanting the names of the Deity, which is a central part of every *pūjā.* See: *pūjā.*

ardent: Intensely enthusiastic or devoted; warm or intense in feeling.

***ardha*-Hindu:** अर्धहिन्दु "Half-Hindu." A devotee who has adopted Hindu belief and culture to a great extent but has not formally entered the religion through ceremony and taking a Hindu first and last name. Also refers to Easterners born into the faith who adopt non-Hindu names.

arduous: Difficult; requiring much labor, energy or strain.

Ārsha: आर्ष "Of seers." Relating to or deriving from *ṛishis.* Of sacred lineage.

artha: अर्थ "Goal or purpose; wealth, property, money." Also has the meaning of utility, desire. See: *dharma, purushārtha.*

Arunagirinathar: அருணகிரிநாதர் South Indian Śaivite poet saint (ca 1500).

***aruhu* grass:** அறுகம்புல் Tamil name for a common type of grass sacred to Lord Gaṇeśa, used as an offering in *archana* and for making wreaths for the Deity image. Also known by the Tamil *hariali,* in Sanskṛit it is known as *dūrvā,* and botanically as *Cynodon dactylon.* See: *dūrvā.*

Ārya: आर्य "Honorable or respectable one; a master, lord."

āsān: ஆசான் "Teacher; master." A title for a respected *guru.*

ascetic: A person who leads a life of contemplation and rigorous self-denial, shunning comforts and pleasures for religious purposes.

ash: See: *vibhūti.*

ashṭavibhūti: अष्टविभूति "Eight powers." Supernormal *siddhis* mentioned in numerous texts: 1) *animā:* to be as small as an atom; 2) *mahimā:* to become infinitely large; 3) *laghimā:* super-lightness, levitation; 4) *prāpti:* pervasiveness, extension, to be anywhere at will; 5) *prakāmya:* fulfillment of desires; 6) *vashitva:* control of natural forces; 7) *iśititva:* supremacy over nature; 8) *kāma-avasayitva:* complete satisfaction. See: *siddhi.*

Ashṭavināyaka: अष्टविनायक "The Eight [obstacle] removers." Eight Gaṇeśa *mūrtis* that attract thousands of pilgrims each year at eight temples in Mahā-அருணகிரிநாதர் "Teacher; master." A title for a respected *guru.*

ascetic: A personMahad and Pali.

āśrama: आश्रम "Place of striving." From *śram,* "to exert energy." Hermitage; order of the life. Holy sanctuary; the residence and teaching center of a *sādhu,* saint, *swāmī,* ascetic or *guru;* often includes lodging for students. Also names life's four stages.

āśrama dharma: आश्रमधर्म "Laws of each order of life." See: *dharma.*

astral: Of the subtle, nonphysical sphere (astral plane) which exists between the physical and causal planes. See: *astral plane.*

astral body: The subtle, nonphysical body *(sūkshma śarīra)* in which the soul functions in the astral plane, the inner world also called Antarloka. The astral body includes the *prāṇic* sheath *(prāṇamaya kośa),* the instinctive-intellectual sheath *(manomaya kośa)* and the cognitive sheath *(vijñānamaya kośa)*—with the *prāṇic* sheath dropping off at the death of the physical body. See: *soul.*

astral plane: From the word *astral,* meaning "of the stars." Belonging to the subtle, non-physical dimension of the Second World. "Astral forces" exist in the Second World but can be felt psychically in the First. See: *loka.*

astringent: A substance that contracts body tissue and/or checks secretions, capillary bleeding, etc. In a more general sense, anything having a harsh or biting quality, such as food with an astringent taste.

astrology: Science of celestial influences. See: *jyotisha.*

asura: **असुर** "Evil spirit; demon." (Opposite of *sura: "deva;* God.") A being of the lower astral plane, Naraka. *Asuras* can and do interact with the physical plane, causing major and minor problems in people's lives. *Asuras* do evolve and are not permanently in this state. See: *Naraka.*

asuric: Of the nature of an *asura,* "not spiritual."

atheism: The rejection of all religion or religious belief, or simply the belief that God or Gods do not exist.

ātman: **आत्मन्** "The soul; the breath; the principle of life and sensation." The soul in its entirety—as the soul body *(ānandamaya kośa)* and its essence (Parāśakti and Paraśiva). One of Hinduism's most fundamental tenets is that we are the *ātman,* not the physical body, emotions, external mind or personality. See: *Paramātman, soul.*

ātmārtha pūjā: **आत्मार्थपूजा** "Personal worship rite." Home *pūjā.* See: *pūjā.*

atone: To make amends or reconcile. See: *pāpa, penance, sin.*

attainment: Something which has been acquired, achieved or reached through effort. Spiritual accomplishment.

attire: Clothes, especially rich or fine apparel; finery.

attitude: Disposition. State of mind. Manner of carrying oneself, acting, thinking or feeling revealing one's disposition, opinions and beliefs. See: *conscience.*

Aum: ॐ or **ओम्** Often spelled *Om.* The mystic syllable of Hinduism, placed at the beginning of most sacred writings. A symbol of loving Gaṇeśa. As a *mantra,* it is pronounced *aw* (as in *law*), *oo* (as in *zoo*), *mm.* The dot above, called *anusvāra,* represents the Soundless Sound, Paranāda. In common usage in several Indian languages, *aum* means "yes, verily" or "hail." See: *nāda.*

aura: The luminous colorful field of subtle energy radiating within and around the human body, extending out from three to seven feet. The colors of the aura change constantly according to the ebb and flow of one's state of consciousness, thoughts, moods and emotions. See: *mind (five states).*

auspicious: Favorable, of good omen, foreboding well. *Maṅgala.* One of the central concepts in Hindu life. Astrology defines a method for determining times that are favorable for various human endeavors. See: *jyotisha.*

austerity: Self-denial and discipline, physical or mental, performed for various reasons including acquiring powers, attaining grace, conquering the instinctive nature and burning the seeds of past *karmas.* See: *penance, tapas.*

authority: Influence, power or right to give commands, enforce obedience, take action or make final decisions.

Auvaiyar: ஔவையார் A woman saint of Tamil Nadu (ca 200 BCE), a contemporary of Saint Tiruvalluvar, devotee of Lord Gaṇeśa and Kārttikeya, or

Murugan, and one of the greatest literary figures in ancient India. As a young girl, she prayed to have her beauty removed so she would not be forced into marriage and could devote her full life to God. She was a great *bhakta* who wrote exquisite ethical works, some in aphoristic style and some in four-line verse. Among the most famous are *Atti Chudi, Konrai Ventan, Ulaka Niti, Muturai,* and *Nalvali.* Her Tamil primer is studied by children to this day. A second Saint Auvaiyar may have lived around the seventh century.

avasthā: अवस्था "Condition, state of consciousness or experience." In Vedic perceptions of consciousness, *avasthā* refers to four states of being discussed in the *Māṇḍūkya Upanishad*: *jāgrat* (or *vaiśvānara*), "wakefulness;" *svapna* (or *taijasa*), "dreaming;" *sushupti*, "deep sleep;" and *turīya*, "the fourth," a state of superconsciousness. A fifth state, "beyond *turīya*," is *turīyātīta.*

avatāra: अवतार "Descent." A God born in a human (or animal) body. A central concept of Śāktism, Smārtism and Vaishṇavism. See: *incarnation, Ishṭa Devatā, Vaishṇavism.*

avidyā: अविद्या "Spiritual ignorance." Wrongful understanding of the nature of reality. Mistaking the impermanent for the everlasting.

awareness: *Sākshin*, or *chit.* Individual consciousness, perception, knowing; the witness of perception, the "inner eye of the soul." The soul's ability to sense, see or know and to be conscious of this knowing. See: *consciousness.*

āyurveda: आयुर्वेद "Science of life." A holistic system of medicine and health native to ancient India. The aims of *āyurveda* are *āyus*, "long life," and *ārogya*, "diseaselessness," which facilitate progress toward ultimate spiritual goals. Health is achieved by balancing energies (especially the *doshas*, bodily humors) at all levels of being. See: *dosha.*

Bāla Gaṇapati: बालगणपति A name and traditional *mūrti*, or form, of Gaṇeśa meaning the "small (or young) one." He holds five kinds of sweets: banana, mango, sugar cane, jackfruit and *modaka.*

bālasthāpana: भालस्थापन "New or initial establishing." The religious rites of firmly determining and blessing the site of a new temple.

Ballaleśvara: बल्ललेश्वर "Lord of Ballala [a young devotee]." The Gaṇeśa *mūrti* enshrined at the Pali Temple of Mahārāshṭra.

barbiturates: Dangerous, habit-forming drugs—depressants, sedatives.

begrudgingly: To give with ill will or reluctance.

betel leaf: The leaf of the piper betel plant, of the Piperaceae family, enjoyed after meals as a digestive and breath freshener, mixed with areca nut and lime. Known in Sanskṛit as *tambula,* and in Hindi as *pān.* Betel leaves are also a traditional wrapping material for monetary payments or gifts, such as the *dakshiṇā* given a priest at the conclusion of a rite.

betoken: To be a token or sign of; indicate; show.

Bhagavad Gītā: भगवद् गीता "Song of the Lord." One of the most popular of

Hindu writings, a conversation between Lord Kṛishṇa and Arjuna on the brink of the great battle at Kurukshetra. In this central episode of the epic *Mahābhārata* (part of the sixth book), Kṛishṇa illumines the warrior-prince Arjuna on *yoga,* asceticism, *dharma* and the manifold spiritual path. See: *Itihāsa, Mahābhārata.*

Bhagnadanta: भग्नदन्त "He of broken tusk." A name of loving Gaṇeśa.

bhajana: भजन Spiritual song. Individual or group singing of devotional songs, hymns and chants. See: *kīrtana.*

bhakta: भक्त "Devotee." A worshiper. One who is surrendered in the Divine.

bhakti: भक्ति "Devotion." Surrender to God, Gods or *guru. Bhakti* extends from the simplest expression of devotion to the ego-decimating principle of *prapatti,* which is total surrender. *Bhakti* is the foundation of all denominations of Hinduism, as well as *yoga* schools throughout the world. See: *bhakti yoga, darśana, prapatti, prasāda, sacrifice, surrender, yajña.*

Bhakti Gaṇapati: भक्तिगणपति "Dear to devotees" is a popular *mūrti,* unique in that He holds a coconut and a bowl of pudding, mango and banana.

bhakti yoga: भक्तियोग "Union through devotion." *Bhakti yoga* is the practice of devotional disciplines, worship, prayer, chanting and singing with the aim of awakening love in the heart and opening oneself to God's grace. From the beginning practice of *bhakti* to advanced devotion, called *prapatti,* self-effacement is an intricate part of Hindu, even all Indian, culture. See: *prapatti, sacrifice, surrender.*

bhaṅgima: भंगिम "Posture." The position of the limbs, as in describing a *mūrti.*

Bhārata: भारत The ancient and original name of India and its constitutional name in Hindi: Bhāratavarsha "land of Bhārat," a legendary monarch and sage.

Bhāratkhand: "Continent, or land, of Bhārat: India."

bhava: भव Concentrated feeling, emotion, mature *bhakti.*

Bhūloka: भूलोक "Earth world." The physical plane. See: *loka.*

bhūmikā: भूमिका "Earth; ground; soil." Preface; introduction to a book. From *bhū,* "to become, exist; arise, come into being."

bīja mantra: बीजमन्त्र "Seed syllable." A Sanskṛit sound associated with a specific Deity used for invocation during mystic rites.

bilva: बिल्व "Bael." *Aegle marmelos* Correa, also called Bengal quince, Indian quince, golden apple, holy fruit, stone apple, bel, bela, sirphal, maredoo and other dialectal names in India. It is sometimes called elephant apple, which leads to confusion with the *kapittha,* a related fruit of that name. A tree 40-50 feet tall, bilva grows in central and southern India, and in Myanmar, Pakistan and Bangladesh. It is a very sacred tree mentioned in writings dating back beyond 800 BCE. The leaves are one of the most precious offerings in Śiva *pūjā.* The fruit is prized in *āyurveda* for its medicinal qualities.

bindu: बिन्दु "A drop, small particle, dot." 1) The seed or source of creation. 2) Small dot worn on the forehead between the eyebrows, or in the middle of the forehead, made of red powder *(kuṁkuma)*, sandalpaste, clay, cosmetics or other substance. It is a sign that one is a Hindu. Mystically, it represents the "third eye," or the "mind's eye," which sees things that the physical eyes cannot see. See: *tilaka.*

blessing: Good wishes; benediction. Seeking and giving blessings is extremely central in Hindu life, nurtured in the precepts of *kāruṇya* (grace), *śakti* (energy), *darśana* (seeing the divine), *prasāda* (blessed offerings), *pūjā* (invocation), *tīrthayātrā* (pilgrimage), *dīkshā* (initiation), *śaktipāta* (descent of grace), *saṁskāras* (rites of passage), *sānnidhya* (holy presence) and *sādhana* (inner-attunement disciplines).

bodily humor: Commonly, the fluids of the body, an English equivalent of the *āyurvedic* term *dosha,* which names three fundamental interbalancing principles or constituents of the human constitution. See: *āyurveda, dosha.*

bond (bondage): See: *evolution of the soul, mala, pāśa.*

bone-gathering: Part of Hindu funeral rites. About twelve hours after cremation, family men return to the cremation site to collect the remains. Some Hindus return the ashes and bones to India for deposition in the Gaṅga. Or they may be put into any ocean or river. See: *cremation, death.*

boon: *Varadāna.* A welcome blessing, a benefit received. An unexpected benefit or bonus. See: *blessing, grace.*

bountiful: Giving abundantly and without restraint; plentiful.

Brahmā: **ब्रह्मा** The name of God in His aspect of Creator. Śaivites consider Brahmā, Vishṇu and Rudra to be three of five aspects of Śiva. Smārtas group Brahmā, Vishṇu and Śiva as a holy trinity in which Śiva is the destroyer. *Brahmā* the Creator is not to be confused with 1) *Brahman,* the Transcendent Supreme of the *Upanishads;* 2) *Brāhmaṇa,* Vedic texts; 3) *brāhmaṇa,* the Hindu priest caste (also spelled *brāhmin*). See: *Brahman, Parameśvara.*

brahmachārī: **ब्रह्मचारी** An unmarried male spiritual aspirant who practices continence, observes religious disciplines, including *sādhana,* devotion and service and who may be under simple vows. Also names one in the student stage, age 12–24, or until marriage. See: *āśrama dharma.*

brahmachāriṇī: **ब्रह्मचारिणी** Feminine counterpart of *brahmachārī.* See: *nunk.*

brahmacharya: **ब्रह्मचर्य** Sexual purity—restraint of lust and the instinctive nature. See: *yama-niyama.*

Brahman: **ब्रह्मन्** "Supreme Being; expansive spirit." From the root *bṛih,* "to grow, increase, expand." Name of God or Supreme Deity in the *Vedas,* where He is described as 1) the Transcendent Absolute, 2) the all-pervading energy and 3) the Supreme Lord or Primal Soul. These three correspond to Śiva in His three perfections. Thus, Śaivites know Brahman and Śiva to be one and the same God. —***Nirguṇa Brahman:*** God "without qualities *(guṇa),*" i.e., formless, Absolute Reality, Parabrahman, or Paraśiva—totally transcending *guṇa* (quality), manifest existence and even Parāśakti, all of which exhibit perceivable qualities. —***Saguṇa Brahman:*** God "with qualities;" Śiva in His perfections of Parāśakti and Parameśvara—God as superconscious, omnipresent, all-knowing, all-loving and all-powerful. The term Brahman is not to be confused with 1) *Brahmā,* the Creator God; 2) *Brāhmaṇa,* Vedic texts, nor with 3) *brāhmaṇa,* Hindu priest caste (English spelling: *brāhmin*). See: *Parameśvara, Parāśakti, Paraśiva.*

Brāhmaṇa: **ब्राह्मण** 1) One of four primary sections of each *Veda;* concerned mainly with details of *yajña,* or sacrificial fire worship, and specific duties and rules of conduct for priests, but also rich in philosophical lore. 2) The first of the four *varṇas,* or social classes, comprising pious souls of exceptional learning, including priests, educators and humanity's visionary guides. Also spelled *brāhmin.* See: *brāhmin, varṇa dharma, Vedas.*

Brahmaṇaspati: **ब्रह्मणस्पति** "Divine artisan." Lord of the Holy Word.

Brahmāṇḍa: **ब्रह्माण्ड** "Egg of God." The cosmos; inner and outer universe. See: *loka, three worlds, world.*

brahmarandhra: **ब्रह्मरन्ध्र** "Door of Brahman." See: *door of Brahman.*

Brahma Sūtra(s): **ब्रह्मसूत्र** Also known as the *Vedānta Sūtras,* composed by Bādarāyaṇa (ca 400 BCE) as the first known systematic exposition of Upanishadic thought. Its 550 aphorisms are so brief as to be virtually unintelligible without commentary. It was through interpretations of this text, as well as the *Upanishads* themselves and the *Bhagavad Gītā,* that later schools of Vedānta expressed and formulated their own views of the Upanishadic tenets. See: *Upanishad, Vedānta.*

brāhmin (brāhmaṇa): **ब्राह्मण** "Mature or evolved soul." The class of pious souls of exceptional learning. From *Brāhman,* "growth, expansion, evolution, development, swelling of the spirit or soul." The mature soul is the exemplar of wisdom, tolerance, forbearance and humility.

brāhminical tradition: The hereditary religious practices of the Vedic *brāhmins,* such as reciting *mantras,* and personal rules for daily living.

Bṛihaspati: **बृहस्पति** "Lord of Prayer." Vedic preceptor of the Gods and Lord of the Word, sometimes identified with Lord Gaṇeśa. See: *Gaṇeśa.*

bronchitis: Chronic or acute inflammation of the mucous membrane of the bronchial tubes.

Buddha: **बुद्ध** "The enlightened." Usually refers to Siddhārtha Gautama (ca 624–544 BCE), a prince born of the Śākya clan—a Śaivite Hindu tribe that lived in eastern India on the Nepalese border. He renounced the world and became a monk. After his enlightenment he preached the doctrines upon which followers later founded Buddhism. See: *Buddhism.*

Buddhi* and *Siddhi: **बुद्धि सिद्धि** "Wisdom and attainment (or fulfillment);" names of the two symbolic consorts of Lord Gaṇeśa.

buddhi: **बुद्धि** "Intellect, reason, logic." The intellectual or disciplined mind. It is a faculty of *manomaya kośa,* the instinctive-intellectual sheath. See: *intellectual mind, kośa, mind (individual).*

Buddhism: The religion based on the teachings of Siddhārtha Gautama, known as the Buddha (ca 624–544 BCE). He refuted the idea of man's having an immortal soul and did not preach of any Supreme Deity. Instead he taught that man should seek to overcome greed, hatred and delusion and attain enlightenment through realizing the Four Noble Truths and following the Eightfold Path. See: *Buddha.*

camphor: *Karpūra.* An aromatic white crystalline solid derived from the wood of camphor trees (or prepared synthetically from pinene), prized as fuel in temple *āratī* lamps. See: *āratī, pūjā.*

cajan: Rectangular panels of woven palm fronds used as roof, wall and fencing material.

caste: A hierarchical system, called *varṇa dharma* (or *jāti dharma),* established in India in ancient times, which determined the privileges, status, rights and duties of the many occupational groups, wherein status is determined by heredity. There are four main classes *(varṇas)*—*brāhmin, kshatriya, vaiśya* and *śūdra*—and innumerable castes, called *jāti.* See: *varṇa dharma.*

causal plane: Highest plane of existence, Śivaloka. See: *loka, three worlds.*

celebrant: A person who performs a religious rite.

celestial: "Of the sky or heavens." Of or relating to the heavenly regions or beings. Highly refined, divine.

ceremony: A formal rite established by custom or authority as proper to special occasions. From the Latin *caerimonia,* "awe; reverent rite."

chaitanya: चैतन्य "Spirit, consciousness, especially higher consciousness; Supreme Being."A widely used term, often preceded by modifiers, e.g., *sākshī chaitanya,* "witness consciousness," or *bhakti chaitanya,* "devotional consciousness," or Śivachaitanya, "God consciousness." See: *chitta, consciousness, mind (five states), Śiva consciousness.*

chakra: चक्र "Wheel." A) In iconography, a disk-shaped weapon, among the icons of Loving Gaṇeśa and of Lord Vishṇu as well. It is a symbol of the sun and of the mind. Wielded as a weapon, it is the intellect divinely empowered. B) Metaphysically, any of the nerve plexes or centers of force and consciousness located within the *inner bodies* of man. In the physical body there are corresponding nerve plexuses, ganglia and glands. The seven principal *chakras* can be seen psychically as colorful, multi-petaled wheels or lotuses. They are situated along the spinal cord from the base to the cranial chamber. Additionally, seven *chakras,* barely visible, exist below the spine. They are seats of instinctive consciousness, the origin of jealousy, hatred, envy, guilt, sorrow, etc. They constitute the lower or hellish world, called *Naraka* or *pātāla.* Thus, there are 14 major *chakras* in all. The seven upper *chakras,* from lowest to highest, are: 1) ***mūlādhāra*** (base of spine): memory, time and space; 2) ***svādhishṭhāna*** (below navel): reason; 3) ***maṇipūra*** (solar plexus): willpower; 4) ***anāhata*** (heart center): direct cognition; 5) ***viśuddha*** (throat): divine love; 6) ***ājñā*** (third eye): divine sight; 7) ***sahasrāra*** (crown of head): illumination, Godliness. The seven lower *chakras,* from highest to lowest, are 1) ***atala*** (hips): fear and lust; 2) ***vitala*** (thighs): raging anger; 3) ***sutala*** (knees): retaliatory jealousy; 4) ***talātala*** (calves): prolonged mental confusion; 5) ***rasātala*** (ankles): selfishness; 6) ***mahātala*** (feet): absence of conscience; 7) ***pātāla*** (located in the soles of the feet): murder and malice.

chāmara: **चामर** "Fly-whisk fan."

chandana: **चन्दन** "Sandalwood paste." One of the sacred substances offered during *pūjā* and afterwards distributed to devotees as a sacrament *(prasāda).* See: *sandalwood.*

chandra: **चन्द्र** "The moon." Of central importance in Hindu astrology and in the calculation of the festival calendar. Considered the ruler of emotion.

Chintāmaṇi: **चिन्तामणि** "Jewel of consciousness." The Gaṇeśa *mūrti* enshrined at the Thevoor Temple near Pune, Mahārāshṭra.

chit: **चित्** "Consciousness," or "awareness." Philosophically, "pure awareness; transcendent consciousness," as in *Sat-chit-ānanda.* In mundane use, *chit* means "to perceive; be conscious." See: *awareness, chitta, consciousness, mind (universal).*

chitta: **चित्त** "Mind; consciousness." Mind-stuff. On the personal level, it is that in which mental impressions and experiences are recorded. Seat of the conscious, subconscious and superconscious states, and of the three-fold mental faculty, called *antaḥkaraṇa,* consisting of *buddhi, manas* and *ahaṁkāra.* See: *consciousness, mind (individual), mind (universal).*

cholera: A broad group of intestinal diseases, especially Asiatic cholera, an acute and severe infectious disease caused by bacteria (Vibrio cholerae) and characterized by profuse diarrhea, intestinal pain and dehydration.

chūḍākaraṇa: **चूडाकरण** Head-shaving sacrament. See: *saṁskāra.*

çhuri: **छुरि** "Dagger." A rare weapon among Gaṇeśa's icons. Its sharp blade is likened to the "razor's edge," the narrow path spiritual aspirants must walk.

circumambulate: *Pradakshiṇa.* To walk around, usually clockwise. See: *pradakshiṇa, pūjā.*

clairaudience: "Clear-hearing." Psychic or divine hearing, *divyaśravana.* The ability to hear the inner currents of the nervous system, the *Aum* and other mystic tones. Hearing in one's mind the words of inner-plane beings or earthly beings not physically present. Also, hearing the *nādanāḍī śakti* through the day or while in meditation. See: *clairvoyance, nāda.*

clairvoyance: "Clear-seeing." Psychic or divine sight, *divyadṛishṭi.* The ability to look into the inner worlds and see auras, *chakras, nāḍīs,* thought forms, nonphysical people and subtle forces. The ability to see from afar or into the past or future—*avadhijñāna,* "knowing beyond limits." Also the ability to separate the light that illumines one's thoughts from the forms the light illumines.

clear white light: See: *light.*

cognition: Knowing; perception. Knowledge reached through intuitive, superconscious faculties rather than through intellect alone.

commitment: Dedication or engagement to a long-term course of action.

commune: To communicate closely, sharing thoughts, feelings or prayers in an intimate way. To be in close rapport.

compatible: Capable of combining well; getting along, harmonious.

compromise: A settlement in which each side gives up some demands or makes concessions; a weakening, as of one's principles.

concentration: Uninterrupted and sustained attention.

concoction: A compound made by combining various ingredients.

confidentiality: The ability to keep confidences or information told in trust; not divulging private or secret matters.

conscience: The inner sense of right and wrong, sometimes called "the knowing voice of the soul." However, the conscience is affected by the individual's training and belief patterns, and is therefore not necessarily a perfect reflection of *dharma.*

conscious mind: The external, everyday state of consciousness. See: *mind.*

consciousness: *Chitta* or *chaitanya.* 1) A synonym for mind-stuff, *chitta;* or 2) the condition or power of perception, awareness, apprehension. There are myriad gradations of consciousness, from the simple sentience of inanimate matter to the consciousness of basic life forms, to the higher consciousness of human embodiment, to omniscient states of superconsciousness, leading to immersion in the One universal consciousness. Five classical "states" of awareness are discussed in scripture: 1) wakefulness *(jāgrat),* 2) "dream" *(svapna)* or astral consciousness, 3) "deep sleep" *(sushupti)* or sub-superconsciousness, 4) the superconscious state beyond *(turīya* "fourth") and 5) the utterly transcendent state called *turīyātīta* ("beyond the fourth"). See: *awareness, chitta, chaitanya, mind (all entries).*

consort: Spouse, especially of a king or queen, God or Goddess. Among the Gods there are actually no sexes or sexual distinctions, though Hinduism traditionally portrays these great beings in elaborate human-like depictions in mythological folk narratives. Matrimony and human-like family units among the Gods are derived from educational tales designed to illustrate the way people should and should not live. See: *Śakti.*

contemplation: Religious or mystical absorption beyond meditation. See: *rāja yoga, samādhi.*

contemplative: Inclined toward a spiritual, religious, meditative way of life.

contempt: Attitude that considers someone or something as low, worthless.

continence (continent): Restraint, moderation or, most strictly, total abstinence from sexual activity. See: *brahmacharya.*

contradiction: A statement in opposition to another; denial; a condition in which things tend to be contrary to each other.

convert: To change from one religion or philosophy to another. A person who has so changed.

covenant: A binding agreement to do or keep from doing certain things.

covet: To want ardently, especially something belonging to another. To envy.

cranial *chakras:* The *ājñā,* or third-eye center, and the *sahasrāra,* at the top of the head near the pineal and pituitary glands. See: *chakra.*

creator: He who brings about creation. Śiva as one of His five powers. See: *Naṭarāja, Parameśvara.*

creed: *Śraddhādhāraṇā.* An authoritative formulation of the beliefs of a religion. Historically, creeds have arisen to protect doctrinal purity when religions are transplanted into foreign cultures.

cremation: *Dahana.* Burning of the dead. Cremation is the traditional system of disposing of bodily remains, having the positive effect of releasing the soul most quickly from any lingering attachment to the earth plane. In modern times, cremation facilities are widely available in nearly every country, though gas-fueled chambers generally take the place of the customary wood pyre.

creole: Any one of numerous mixed languages, such as the French Creole spoken in Louisiana, USA; or that of Mauritius.

crown *chakra*: *Sahasrāra chakra.* The thousand-petaled cranial center of divine consciousness. See: *chakra.*

culture: Development or refinement of intellect, emotions, interests, manners, and tastes. The ideals, customs, skills and arts of a people or group that are transmitted from one generation to another. Culture is refined living that arises in a peaceful, stable society. Hindu culture arises directly out of worship in the temples.

dāḍima: **दाडिम** "Pomegranate."

dakshiṇā: **दक्षिणा** A fee or gift to a priest given at the completion of any rite; also given to *gurus* as a token of appreciation for their infinite spiritual blessings.

dakshiṇāyane: **दक्षिणायन** "Southern way." Names the half-year, *ayana,* beginning with summer solstice, when the sun begins its apparent southward journey.

dāna: **दान** Generosity, giving. See: *yama-niyama.*

***daṇḍa*:** **दण्ड** "A stick, or staff of support." The staff carried by a *sādhu* or *sannyāsin,* representing the *tapas* which he has taken as his only support, and the vivifying of *sushumṇā* and consequent Realization he seeks. *Daṇḍa* also connotes "penalty or sanction." This sign of authority is one of the icons of loving Gaṇeśa. See: *sannyāsin.*

darśana: **दर्शन** "Vision, sight." Seeing the Divine. Beholding, with inner or outer vision, a temple image, Deity, holy person or place, with the desire to inwardly contact and receive the grace and blessings of the venerated being or beings. Also: "point of view," doctrine or philosophy.

Daśanāmī: **दशनामी** "Ten names." Ten monastic orders organized by Ādi Śaṅkara (ca 800): Āraṇya, Vāna, Giri, Pārvata, Sāgara, Tīrtha, Āśrama, Bhārati, Pūrī and Sarasvatī. Also refers to *sannyāsins* of these orders, each of whom bears his order's name, with *ānanda* often attached to the religious name. For example, Rāmānanda Tīrtha. Traditionally, each order is associated with one of the main Śaṅkarāchārya *pīṭhas.* See: *Smārta, Śaṅkara.*

day of Brahmā: One *kalpa,* or period, in the infinitely recurring periods of the universe's creation, preservation and dissolution. One day of Brahma is equal to 994 *mahāyugas* (a *mahāyuga* is one cycle of the four *yugas:* Satya, Tretā, Dvāpara and Kali). This is calculated as 4,294,080,000 years. After each day of Brahmān occurs a *pralaya* (or *kalpanta,* "end of an eon"), when both the physical and subtle worlds are absorbed into the causal world. This state of withdrawal or "night of Brahmā," continues for the length of an entire *kalpa* until creation again issues forth.

death: Death is a rich concept for which there are many words in Sanskṛit, such as: *mahāprasthāna,* "great departure;" *samādhimaraṇa,* dying consciously while in the state of meditation; *mahāsamādhi,* "great merger, or absorption," naming the departure of an enlightened soul. Hindus know death to be the soul's detaching itself from the physical body and continuing on in the subtle body *(sūkshma śarīra)* with the same desires, aspirations and occupations as when it lived in a physical body. See: *reincarnation.*

decorum: Propriety and good taste in behavior, speech, dress, etc.

deformity: Condition of being disfigured or made ugly in body, mind or emotions.

Deity: "God." Can refer to the image or *mūrti* installed in a temple or to the Mahādeva the *mūrti* represents. See: *mūrti, pūjā.*

demean: To lower in status or character; degrade.

demureness: Decorous; modest; shy; reserved.

denomination: A name for a class of things, especially for various religious groupings, sects and subsects. See: *guru paramparā, sampradāya.*

deprivations: Forced conditions of loss or neediness.

destiny: Final outcome. The seemingly inevitable or predetermined course of events. See: *karma.*

deter: To keep one from doing something by instilling fear, anxiety, doubt, etc.

detractor: One who discredits, slanders or disparages someone else.

deva: **देव** "Shining one." A being living in the higher astral plane, in a subtle, nonphysical body. *Deva* is also used in scripture to mean "God or Deity." See: *Mahādeva.*

devonic: Angelic, heavenly. Of the nature of the higher worlds, in tune with the refined energies of the higher *chakras* or centers of consciousness.

Devanāgarī: **देवनागरी** "Divine writing of townspeople." The alphabetic script in which Sanskṛit, Prākṛit, Hindi and Marāṭhi are written. A descendant of the Northern type of the Brāhmī script. It is characterized by the connecting, horizontal line at the top of the letters. See: *Sanskṛit.*

Devī: **देवी** "Goddess." A name of Śakti, used especially in Śāktism. See: *Śakti, Śāktism.*

devotee: A person strongly dedicated to something or someone, such as to a God or a *guru.* The term *disciple* implies an even deeper commitment. See: *guru bhakti, guru-śishya system.*

dhanush: धनुष् "Bow." Anything bow shaped; a bow for shooting arrows.

dharma: धर्म From *dhṛi,* "to sustain; carry, hold." Hence *dharma* is "that which contains or upholds the cosmos." *Dharma* is a complex and all-inclusive term with many meanings, including: divine law, law of being, way of righteousness, religion, duty, responsibility, virtue, justice, goodness and truth. Essentially, *dharma* is the orderly fulfillment of an inherent nature or destiny. Relating to the soul, it is the mode of conduct most conducive to spiritual advancement, the right and righteous path. There are four principal kinds of *dharma,* as follows. They are known collectively as ***—chaturdharma:*** "four religious laws." 1) ***—ṛita:*** "Universal law." The inherent order of the cosmos. The laws of being and nature that contain and govern all forms, functions and processes, from galaxy clusters to the power of mental thought and perception. 2) ***—varṇa dharma***: "Law of one's kind." Social duty. *Varṇa* can mean "race, tribe, appearance, character, color, social standing, etc." *Varṇa dharma* defines the individual's obligations and responsibilities within the nation, society, community, class, occupational subgroup and family. An important part of this *dharma* is religious and moral law. See: *jāti, varṇa dharma.* 3) ***—āśrama dharma:*** "Duties of life's stages." Human *dharma.* The natural process of maturing from childhood to old age through fulfillment of the duties of each of the four stages of life—*brahmachārī* (student), *gṛihastha* (householder), *vānaprastha* (elder advisor) and *sannyāsa* (religious solitaire)—in pursuit of the four human goals: *dharma* (righteousness), *artha* (wealth), *kāma* (pleasure) and *moksha* (liberation). See: *āśrama dharma.* 4) ***—svadharma***: "Personal law." One's perfect individual pattern through life, according to one's own particular physical, mental and emotional nature. *Svadharma* is determined by the sum of past *karmas* and the cumulative effect of the other three *dharmas.* It is the individualized application of *dharma,* dependent on personal *karma,* reflected on one's race, community, physical characteristics, health, intelligence, skills and aptitudes, desires and tendencies, religion, *sampradāya,* family and *guru.*

Dharma Śāstra: धर्मशास्त्र "Religious law book." A term referring to all or any of numerous codes of Hindu civil and social law composed by various authors. The best known and most respected are those by Manu and Yājñavalkya, thought to have been composed as early as 600 BCE. The *Dharma Śāstras,* along with the *Artha Śāstras,* are the codes of Hindu law, parallel to the Muslim Sharia, the Jewish *Talmud,* each of which provides guidelines for kings, ministers, judicial systems and law enforcement agencies. These spiritual-parliamentary codes differ from British and American law, which separate religion from politics. (Contemporary British law is influenced by Anglican Christian thought, just as American democracy was, and is, profoundly affected by the philosophy of its non-Christian, Deistic founders.) The *Dharma Śāstras* also speak of much more, including creation, initiation, the stages of life, daily rites, duties of husband and wife, caste, Vedic study, penances and transmigration. The *Dharma Śāstras* are part of the *Smṛiti* literature, included in the *Kalpa Vedāṅga,* and are widely available today in many languages. See: *Deism, Manu Dharma Śāstras, Smṛiti.*

dhotī: धोती (Hindi) A long, unstitched cloth wound about the lower part of the body, and sometimes passed between the legs and tucked into the waist. A traditional Hindu apparel for men.

Ḍhuṇḍhi Gaṇapati: ढुण्ढिगणपति "The sought after," enshrined in Varāṇasi, has four arms, holding an axe, prayer beads, tusk and a pot of gems.

Dhumravarṇa: धुम्रवर्ण "Smoke-colored." Gaṇeśa's aspect as the conqueror of *abhimāna,* pride.

dhvaja: ध्वज "Flag." Part of the pageantry of Hinduism, orange or red flags and banners, flown at festivals and other special, occasions symbolize the victory of *Sanātana Dharma.* See: *festival.*

dhyāna: ध्यान "Meditation." See: *internalized worship, meditation, rāja yoga.*

diaspora: The dispersion of people with a common origin, background, beliefs, etc., such as the distribution of Jews when driven out of Israel.

dīkshā: दीक्षा "Initiation." Action or process by which one is entered into a new realm of spiritual knowledge and practice by a teacher or preceptor through the transmission of blessings. Denotes initial or deepened connection with the teacher and his lineage and is usually accompanied by ceremony. Initiation, revered as a moment of awakening, may be bestowed by a touch, a word, a look or a thought. Most Hindu schools, and especially Śaivism, teach that only with initiation from a *satguru* is enlightenment attainable. Sought after by all Hindus is the *dīkshā* called *śaktipāta,* "descent of grace," which, often coming unbidden, stirs and arouses the mystic *kuṇḍalinī* force.

dilute: To change or weaken by mixing with something else.

dīpastambha: दीपस्तम्भ A standing lamp found in the temple, shrine room or home. It is made of metal, with several wicks fed by *ghee* or special oils. Used to light the home and used in *pūjā.* Part of temple and shrine altars, the standing lamp is sometimes worshiped as the divine light, Parāśakti or Parajyoti. Returning from the temple and lighting one's *dīpastambha* courts the accompanying *devas* to remain in the home and channels the vibration of the temple sanctum sanctorum into the home shrine.

discrimination: *Viveka.* Act or ability to distinguish or perceive differences. In spirituality, the ability to distinguish between right and wrong, real and apparent, eternal and transient.

diuretic: A substance or drug tending to increase excretion of urine.

divisive: Causing division, especially causing disagreement or dissension.

dominion: Rulership; domain. **—hold dominion over:** To be king, ruler, lord, or master of (a world, realm, etc).

door of Brahman: *Brahmarandhra;* also called *nirvāna chakra.* An aperture in the crown of the head, the opening of *sushumṇā nāḍī* through which *kuṇḍalinī* enters in ultimate Self Realization, and the spirit escapes at death.

Only the spirits of the truly pure leave the body in this way. *Saṁsārīs* take a downward course. See: *jñāna, kuṇḍalinī.*

dormant: Sleeping; inactive; not functioning.

dosha: दोष "Bodily humor; individual constitution." Refers to three bodily humors, which according to *āyurveda* regulate the body, govern its proper functioning and determine its unique constitution. These are *vāta,* the air humor; *pitta,* the fire humor; and *kapha,* the water humor. *Vāta* has its seat in the intestinal area, *pitta* in the stomach, and *kapha* in the lung area. They govern the creation, preservation and dissolution of bodily tissue. *Vāta* humor is metabolic, nerve energy. *Pitta* is the catabolic, fire energy. *Kapha* is the anabolic, nutritive energy. The three *doshas (tridosha)* also give rise to the various emotions and correspond to the three *guṇas,* "qualities:" *sattva* (quiescence—*vāta*), *rajas* (activity—*pitta*) and *tamas* (inertia—*kapha*). See: *āyurveda, kapha, pitta, vāta.*

dossier: A comprehensive collection of documents about a subject or person.

dualism: Opposite of monism. Any doctrine which holds that there are two eternal and distinct realities in the universe, e.g., God-world, good-evil.

Durga Gaṇapati: दुर्गगणपति "The savior" is an eight-armed *mūrti* distinguished by the flag of victory, bow and arrow and strand of prayer beads.

dūrvā: दूर्वा A type of grass, also called *aruhu* and *harali,* sacred to Gaṇeśa, traditionally offered to Him in *pūjā. Cynodon dactylon.* See: *aruhu grass.*

dvaita-advaita: द्वैत अद्वैत "Dual-nondual; twoness-not twoness." Among the most important terms in the classification of Hindu philosophies. *Dvaita* and *advaita* define two ends of a vast spectrum. ***—dvaita:*** The doctrine of dualism, according to which reality is ultimately composed of two irreducible principles, entities, truths, etc. God and soul, for example, are seen as eternally separate. **—dualistic:** Of or relating to dualism, concepts, writings, theories which treat dualities (good-and-evil, high-and-low, them-and-us) as fixed, rather than transcendable. **—pluralism:** A form of dualism which emphasizes three or more eternally separate realities, e.g., God, soul and world. ***—advaita:*** The doctrine of nondualism or monism, that reality is ultimately composed of one whole principle, substance or God, with no independent parts. In essence, all is God. **—monistic theism:** A dipolar view which encompasses both monism and dualism. See: *monistic theism.*

Dvija Gaṇapati: द्विजगणपति "The twice-born." A name and traditional *mūrti,* or form, of Gaṇeśa. He holds a scripture, a staff and a *japa mālā,* reminding devotees of the need for disciplined striving.

Dvimukha Gaṇapati: द्विमुखगणपति The unmistakable "double-faced" *mūrti* of Lord Gaṇeśa. He holds a noose, goad, broken tusk and a pot of gems.

dysentery: Any of a number of intestinal inflammations causing abdominal pain and diarrhea.

earrings: Decorative jewelry worn in the ears by Hindu women and many men. Ear-piercing for earrings is said to bring health (right ear) and wealth (left ear).

ecumenical: Universal. —**ecumenism:** the principles or practices of promoting cooperation and better understanding among differing faiths.

eczema: A noncontagious skin disorder of unknown cause, characterized by inflammation, itching and the formation of scales.

edampuri: एदम्पुरि "Left-turning." A term for images of Gaṇeśa in which the trunk is turning to the Deity's left. This is the common form. Cf: *valampuri.*

edict: An official public order issued by an authority.

effulgent: Having great brightness; radiance; brilliant; full of light.

ego: The external personality or sense of "I" and "mine." Broadly, individual identity. In Śaiva Siddhānta and other schools, the ego is equated with the *tattva* of *ahaṁkāra,* "I-maker," which bestows the sense of I-ness, individuality and separateness from God. See: *āṇava mala.*

Ekadanta Gaṇapati: एकदन्तगणपति He of "single tusk" is the four-armed Gaṇeśa *mūrti* holding axe, beads, *laddu* (sweet) and His broken tusk.

Ekākshara Gaṇapati: एकाक्षरगणपति He of "single-letter" (गं *gaṁ)* sits in lotus pose upon Mūshika, offering the boon-giving gesture, *abhaya mudrā.*

eloquent: Vivid, forceful, fluent, graceful and persuasive speech or writing.

enchantment: A magic spell; a bewitching, captivating power.

endowment: Funds that are invested for the purpose of providing a permanent income to a charitable institution such as a temple, *āśrama,* school, orphanage or hospital, or to a family or business. The principal is held perpetually inviolate, with only the income from the investment of the funds being available for expenditure.

enlightened: Having attained enlightenment, Self Realization. A *jñānī* or *jīvanmukta.* See: *enlightenment, jñāna, Self Realization.*

enlightenment: For Śaiva monists, Self Realization, *samādhi* without seed *(nirvikalpa samādhi);* the ultimate attainment, sometimes referred to as Paramātma *darśana,* or as *ātma darśana,* "Self vision" (a term which appears in Patañjali's *Yoga Sūtras).* Enlightenment is the experience-nonexperience resulting in the realization of one's transcendent Self—Paraśiva—which exists beyond time, form and space. See: *God Realization, kuṇḍalinī, Self Realization.*

enmity: Bitter attitude or feelings of an enemy; hostility; antagonism.

enstasy: A term coined in 1969 by Mircea Eliade to contrast the Eastern view of bliss as "standing inside oneself" (enstasy) with the Western view as ecstasy, "standing outside oneself." A word chosen as the English equivalent of *samādhi.* See: *samādhi, rāja yoga.*

entanglements: Involvements in difficulty; being tangled or confused.

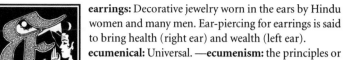

enzyme: Any one of various proteins, formed in plant and animal cells or made synthetically, that acts as an organic catalyst in initiating or speeding up specific chemical reactions.

equivocal: Uncertain; undecided; doubtful.

ephemeral: Transient, temporary, not lasting.

eradicate: To "root out," destroy, get rid of.

erukku: Tamil name for flower (Botanically *Calotropis)* sacred to Lord Gaṇeśa. *Erukku* flowers are strung together and placed 'round the crown and neck of Gaṇeśa during worship ceremonies, especially at festival times.

ether: *Ākāśa.* Space, the most subtle of the five elements. See: *ākāśa, tattva.*

ethical restraints: See: *yama-niyama.*

ethical observances: See: *yama-niyama.*

ethics: The code or system of morals of a nation, people, religion, etc. See: *dharma, pañcha nitya karmas, puṇya.*

esoteric: Beyond the understanding of all but a few, or the initiated.

evil: That which is bad, morally wrong, causing harm, pain, misery. In Western religions, evil is often thought of as a moral antagonism with God. Hindus hold that evil, known in Sanskṛit as *pāpa, pāpman* or *dushṭā,* is the result of unvirtuous acts *(pāpa* or *adharma)* caused by the instinctive-intellectual mind dominating and obscuring deeper, spiritual intelligence. The evil-doer is viewed as a young soul, ignorant of the value of right thought, speech and action, unable to live in the world without becoming entangled in *māyā.* —**intrinsic evil:** Inherent, inborn badness. Hinduism holds that there is no intrinsic evil, and the real nature of man is his divine, soul nature, which is goodness. See: *hell, karma, pāpa, sin.*

evolution of the soul: *Adhyātma prasāra.* In Śaiva Siddhānta, the soul's evolution is a progressive unfoldment, growth and maturing toward its inherent, divine destiny, which is complete merger with Śiva. In its essence, each soul is ever perfect. But as an individual soul body emanated by God Śiva, it is like a small seed yet to develop. As an acorn needs to be planted in the dark underground to grow into a mighty oak tree, so must the soul unfold out of the darkness of the *malas* to full maturity and realization of its innate oneness with God. The soul is not created at the moment of conception of a physical body. Rather, it is created in the Śivaloka. It evolves by taking on denser and denser sheaths—cognitive, instinctive-intellectual and *prāṇic*—until finally it takes birth in physical form in the Bhūloka. Then it experiences many lives, maturing through the reincarnation process. Thus, from birth to birth, souls learn and mature. See: *mala, moksha, reincarnation, saṁsāra, viśvagrāsa.*

exemplify: To show by being an example of.

existentialist: Adjective of "existentialism"—the doctrine that concrete individual existence takes precedence over abstract, conceptual essence.

experience: From the Latin *experior,* "to prove; put to the test." Living through an event; personal involvement. In Sanskṛit, *anubhava.* See: *anubhava.*

extol: To praise highly; laud.

faith: Trust or belief. Conviction. From the Latin *fidere,* "to trust." *Faith* in its broadest sense means "religion, *dharma.*" More specifically, it is the essential element of religion—the belief in phenomena beyond the pale of the five senses, distinguishing it sharply from rationalism. Faith is established through intuitive or transcendent experience of an individual, study of scripture and hearing the testimony of the many wise *ṛishis* speaking out the same truths over thousands of years. The Sanskṛit equivalent is *śraddhā.*

family: *Kuṭumba* or *kula.* The Hindu social unit. The core is the joint family, consisting of several generations of kindred living together under the same roof or in a joining compound. The main characteristics of the joint family are that its members 1) share a common residence, 2) partake of food prepared in the same kitchen, 3) hold their property in common and, 4) ideally, profess the same religion, sect and *sampradāya.* Each individual family of husband, wife and children is under the guidance of the head of the joint family. All work together unselfishly to further the common good. Each joint family extends out from its home to include a second level of connections as an "extended family *(bṛihatkuṭumba* or *mahākuṭumba).*"

fast: To abstain from all or certain foods, as in observance of a vow or holy day. Hindus fast in various ways. A simple fast may consist of merely avoiding certain foods for a day or more, such as when nonvegetarians abstain from fish, fowl and meats. A moderate fast would involve avoiding heavier foods, or taking only juices, teas and other liquids. Such fasts are sometimes observed only during the day, and a normal meal is permitted after sunset. Serious fasting, which is done under supervision, involves taking only water for a number of days and requires a cessation of most external activities.

fellowship: Companionship. Mutual sharing of interests, beliefs or practice. A group of people with common interests and aspirations.

festival: A time of religious celebration and special observances. Festivals generally recur yearly, their dates varying slightly according to astrological calculations. They are characterized by acts of piety (elaborate *pūjās,* penance, fasting, pilgrimage) and rejoicing (songs, dance, music, parades, storytelling and scriptural reading).

First World: The physical universe, called Bhūloka, of gross or material substance in which phenomena are perceived by the five senses. See: *loka.*

five classical duties: See: *pañcha nitya karmas.*

five-fold God consciousness: See: *Śiva consciousness.*

Five Letters: See: *Namaḥ Śivāya.*

five parenting guidelines: See: *pañcha kuṭumba sādhana.*

five practices: See: *pañcha nitya karma.*

five precepts: See: *pañcha śraddhā.*

folk-shamanic: Of or related to a tribal or village tradition in which the mystic priest, shaman, plays a central role, wielding powers of magic and spirituality. Revered for his ability to influence and control nature and people, to cause good and bad things to happen, he is the intermediary between man and divine forces. The term *shaman* is from the Sanskṛit *śramaṇa,* "ascetic," akin to *śram,* "to exert." See: *Śāktism, trance.*

forehead marks: See: *bindu, tilaka, tripuṇḍra.*

forestall: To obstruct or hinder by doing something ahead of time.

forfeiting: Giving up something due to a crime or fault or neglect of duty.

four stages of *dharma:* See: *dharma.*

four traditional goals: *Chaturvarga,* "four-fold good," or *purushārtha,* "human wealths or purposes"—duty *(dharma),* wealth *(artha),* love *(kāma)* and liberation *(moksha).* See: *purushārtha.*

fundamentalist: Any religious or philosophical group or individual marked by extreme dogmatism and intolerance. Fundamentalists believe in a literal interpretation of their scripture as *the* exclusive truth, the one and only way which all souls must follow to attain salvation, and in allegiance to their messiah as the one true representative of God. A religious fanatic.

funeral rites: See: *cremation, bone-gathering.*

gadā: **गदा** "Mace." A rough-headed club, one of the icons of Gaṇeśa, representing His power to cast *karmas* back on devotees until fully resolved.

gaja: **गज** The elephant, king of beasts, representative of Lord Gaṇeśa and sign of royalty and power. Many major Hindu temples keep one or more elephants.

Gajānana: **गजानन** "Elephant-faced." A popular name of Gaṇeśa, which appears in the *Mudgala Purāṇa,* as the vanquisher of *lobha,* greed.

Gaṁ Mantra: **गंमन्त्र** The seed sound, or *bīja mantra,* of Loving Gaṇeśa. *Bīja mantras,* being one-lettered, represent the essence of more complex sound combinations. *Gaṁ* is the root sound within the *mūlādhāra chakra.*

gaṇa(s): **गण** "Multitude, troop; number; a body of followers or attendants." A troop of demigods—God Śiva's attendants, *devonic* helpers under the supervision of Lord Gaṇeśa. See: *Gaṇapati, Gaṇeśa.*

Gaṇapati: **गणपति** "Leader of the *gaṇas.*" A name of *Gaṇeśa.*

Gaṇapati Upanishad: **गणपति उपनिषद्** A later *Upanishad* on Lord Gaṇeśa, not connected with any *Veda;* date of composition is unknown. It is a major scripture for the Gaṇapatians, a minor Hindu sect which reveres Gaṇeśa as Supreme God and is most prevalent in India's Maharashtra state. See: *Gaṇeśa.*

gandha: **गन्ध** "Smell, odor, fragrance." *Gandha* is the fifth of five *tanmātras,* "primal substances," from which the gross elements, *mahābhūtas* (or *pañch-bautikas),* arise in the evolution of the *tattvas.* Smell is the *tanmātra* corresponding to the earth element, *pṛithivī.* See: *tanmātra.*

Gaṇanāthas: **गणनाथ** "Lords of hosts." As a singular term *Gaṇanātha* refers to Lord Gaṇeśa. Plural it refers to the many divine beings who help in guiding the flow of consciousness under the direction of the Mahādevas.

Gaṇeśa: **गणेश** "Lord of Categories." (From *gaṇ,* "to count or reckon," and *Īśa,* "lord.") Or: "Lord of attendants *(gaṇa),*" synonymous with *Gaṇapati.* Gaṇeśa is a Mahādeva, the beloved elephant-faced Deity honored by Hindus of every sect. He is the Lord of Obstacles (Vighneśvara), revered for His great wisdom and invoked first before any undertaking, for He knows all intricacies of each soul's *karma* and the perfect path of *dharma* that makes action successful. He sits on the *mūlādhāra chakra* and is easy of access.

Gaṇeśa Chaturthī: **गणेश चतुर्थी** Birthday of Lord Gaṇeśa, a ten-day festival of August-September that culminates in a spectacular parade called *Gaṇeśa Visarjana.* It is a time of rejoicing, when all Hindus worship together.

Gaṇeśa Visarjana: **गणेश विसर्जन** "Gaṇeśa departure." A parade usually occurring on the 11th day after Gaṇeśa Chaturthī, in which the Gaṇeśa *mūrtis* made for the occasion are taken in procession to a body of water and ceremoniously immersed and left to dissolve. This represents Gaṇeśa's merging with the ocean of consciousness. See: *Gaṇeśa.*

Ganges *(Gaṅgā):* **गंगा** India's most sacred river, 1,557 miles long, arising in the Himalayas above Hardwar under the name Bhagīratha, and being named Gaṅgā after joining the Alakanada (where the Sarasvatī is said to join them underground). It flows southeast across the densely populated Gangetic plain, joining its sister Yamunā (or Jumnā) at Prayaga (Allahabad) and ending at the Bay of Bengal.

Gangetic: Near to or on the banks of the Ganges river in North India.

Gāritra: **गारित्र** "Grains." E.g., wheat or barley.

gāyatrī: **गायत्री** According with the *gāyatrī* verse form, an ancient meter of 24 syllables, generally as a triplet with eight syllables each. From *gāya,* "song." —***Gāyatrī:*** The Vedic Gāyatrī Mantra personified as a Goddess, mother of the four *Vedas.*

Gāyatrī Mantra: **गायत्रीमन्त्र** 1) Famous Vedic *mantra* used in *pūjā* and personal chanting. *Om [bhūr bhuvaḥ svaḥ] tatsavitur vareṇyam, bhargo devasya dhīmahi, dhiyo yo naḥ prachodayāt.* "[O Divine Beings of all three worlds,] we meditate upon the glorious splendor of the Vivifier divine. May He Himself illumine our minds" *(Ṛig Veda* 3.62.10 VE). This sacred verse is also called the Sāvitrī Mantra, being addressed to Savitri, the Sun as Creator, and is considered a universal mystic formula so significant that it is called Vedamātṛi, "mother of the *Vedas.*" 2) Any of a class of special *tantric mantras* called Gāyatrī. Each addresses a particular Deity.

ghaṇṭā: **घण्टा** "Bell." Akin to *ghaṇṭ,* "to speak." An important implement in Hindu worship *(pūjā),* used to chase away *asuras* and summon *devas* and Gods. See: *pūjā.*

ghee: **घी** Hindi for clarified butter; *ghṛita* in Sanskṛit. Butter that has been boiled and strained. An important sacred substance used in temple lamps and offered in fire ceremony, *yajña.* It is also used as a food with many *āyurvedic* virtues. See: *yajña.*

Girijātmaja: गिरिजात्मज "Mountain born." The Gaṇeśa *mūrti* enshrined at the Lenyadhri Cave Temple of Mahārāshṭra.

Goddess: Female representation or manifestation of Divinity; Śakti or Devī. *Goddess* can refer to a female perception or depiction of a causal-plane being (Mahādeva) in its natural state, which is genderless, or it can refer to an astral-plane being residing in a female astral body. To show the Divine's transcendence of sexuality, sometimes God is shown as having qualities of both sexes, e.g., Ardhanārīśvara, "half-woman God;" or Lord Naṭarāja, who wears a feminine earring in one ear and a masculine one in the other.

God Realization: A term naming the direct and personal experience of the Divine within oneself. It can refer to either 1) *savikalpa samādhi* ("enstasy with form") in its various levels, from the experience of inner light to the realization of Satchidānanda, the pure consciousness or primal substance flowing through all form, or 2) *nirvikalpa samādhi* ("enstasy without form"), union with the transcendent Absolute, Paraśiva, the Self God, beyond time, form and space. In *Loving Gaṇeśa,* the term *God Realization* is used to name both of the above *samādhis,* whereas *Self Realization* refers only to *nirvikalpa samādhi.* See: *samādhi, Self Realization.*

Gods: Mahādevas, "great beings of light." In *Living with Śiva,* the plural form of *God* refers to extremely advanced beings existing in their self-effulgent soul bodies in the causal plane. The meaning of *Gods* is best seen in the phrase, "God and the Gods," referring to the Supreme God—Śiva—and the Mahādevas who are His creation. See: *Mahādeva.*

goshṭa: गोषट "Cow pen; nitch." Also names a small, alcove shrine.

grace: "Benevolence, love, giving," from the Latin *gratus,* "beloved, agreeable." God's power of revealment, *anugraha śakti* ("kindness, showing favor"), by which souls are awakened to their true, Divine nature. Grace in the unripe stages of the spiritual journey is experienced by the devotee as receiving gifts or boons, often unbidden, from God. The mature soul finds himself surrounded by grace. He sees all of God's actions as grace, whether they be seemingly pleasant and helpful or not. See: *prapatti.*

guṇa: गुण "Strand; quality." The three constituent principles of *prakṛiti,* primal nature. The three *guṇas* are as follows. —***sattva:*** "Purity," quiescent, rarified, translucent, pervasive, reflecting the light of Pure Consciousness. —***rajas:*** "Passion," inherent in energy, movement, action, emotion, life. —***tamas:*** "Darkness," inertia, density, the force of contraction, resistance and dissolution. The *guṇas* are integral to Hindu thought, as all things are composed of the combination of these qualities of nature, including *āyurveda,* arts, environments and personalities. See: *āyurveda, prakṛiti, tattva.*

guru: गुरु "Weighty one," indicating a being of great knowledge or skill. A term used to describe a teacher or guide in any subject, such as music, dance, sculpture, but especially religion. For clarity, the term is often preceded by a qualifying prefix. Hence, terms such as *kulaguru* (family teacher), *vīṇāguru (vīṇā* teacher) and *satguru* (spiritual preceptor). According to the *Advayatāraka Upanishad* (14–18), *guru* means "dispeller *(gu)* of darkness *(ru)*." See: *guru bhakti, guru-śishya system, satguru.*

guru bhakti: गुरुभक्ति Devotion to the teacher. The attitude of humility, love and ideation held by a student in any field of study. In the spiritual realm, the devotee strives to see the *guru* as his higher Self. By attuning himself to the *satguru's* inner nature and wisdom, the disciple slowly transforms his own nature to ultimately attain the same peace and enlightenment his *guru* has achieved. See: *guru, satguru, guru-śishya system.*

guru lineage: See: *guru paramparā.*

guru paramparā: गुरुपरंपरा "Preceptorial succession" (literally, "from one to another"). A line of spiritual *gurus* in authentic succession of initiation; the chain of mystical power and authorized continuity, passed from *guru* to *guru*. Cf: *sampradāya.*

guru-śishya system: गुरुशिष्य "Master-disciple system."An important education system of Hinduism whereby the teacher conveys his knowledge and tradition to a student. The principle of this system is that knowledge, especially subtle or advanced knowledge, is best conveyed through a strong human relationship based on ideals of the student's respect, commitment, devotion and obedience, and on personal instruction by which the student eventually masters the knowledge the *guru* embodies. See: *guru, guru bhakti, satguru.*

Hanumān: हनुमान् (Hindi) "With large jaws." The powerful monkey God-King of the epic, *Rāmāyaṇa,* and the central figure in the famous drama, *Hanumān-Nāṭaka.* The perfect devoted servant to his master, Rāma, this popular Deity is the epitome of *dasya bhakti.*

Hari: हरि "Vishṇu." See: *Brahmā, Vishṇu.*

Haridrā Gaṇapati: हरिद्रागणपति "The golden one" holds four prevalent icons: noose, goad, tusk and *modaka.*

haṭha yoga: हठयोग "Forceful *yoga.*" *Haṭha yoga* is a system of physical and mental exercise developed in ancient times as a means of preparing the body and mind for meditation. See: *kuṇḍalinī, nāḍī, yoga.*

heaven: The celestial spheres, including the causal plane and the higher realms of the subtle plane, where souls rest and learn between births, and mature souls continue to evolve after *moksha. Heaven* is often used by translators as an equivalent to the Sanskṛit *Svarga.* See: *loka.*

hell: *Naraka.* An unhappy, mentally and emotionally congested, distressful area of consciousness. Hell is a state of mind that can be experienced on the plane of physical existence or in the sub-astral plane (Naraka) after the death of the physical body. It is accompanied by the tormented emotions of hatred, remorse, resentment, fear, jealousy and self-condemnation. However, in the Hindu view, the hellish experience is not permanent, but a temporary condition of one's own making. See: *asura, loka.*

Heramba Gaṇapati: हेरम्बगणपति "Protector of the weak" is a five-faced *mūrti* of Gaṇeśa. He rides a lion and gestures protection and blessing.

hereditary: Ancestral. Passed down through family lines. For example, it is Hindu family *dharma* for the son to be taught everything that the father knows and the daughter to learn everything the mother knows. Thus they inherit knowledge, control of mind and emotions, as well as property.

higher nature, lower nature: Expressions indicating man's refined, soulful qualities on the one hand, and his base, instinctive qualities on the other. See: *mind (five states).*

Himālayas: हिमालय "Abode of snow." The mountain system extending along the India-Tibet border and through Pakistan, Nepal and Bhutan.

Himālayan Academy: The educational institution of Śaiva Siddhānta Church, founded by Saguru Sivaya Subramuniyaswami in 1957.

Hindu: हिन्दु A follower of, or relating to, Hinduism. See: *Hinduism.*

Hinduism (Hindu Dharma): हिन्दुधर्म India's indigenous religious and cultural system, followed today by nearly one billion adherents, mostly in India, but with large populations in many other countries. Also called Sanātana Dharma, "eternal religion" and Vaidika Dharma, "religion of the *Vedas.*" Hinduism is the world's most ancient religion and encompasses a broad spectrum of philosophies ranging from pluralistic theism to absolute monism. It is a family of myriad faiths with four primary denominations: Śaivism, Vaishṇavism, Śāktism and Smārtism. These four hold such divergent beliefs that each is a complete and independent religion. Yet, they share a vast heritage of culture and belief—*karma, dharma,* reincarnation, all-pervasive Divinity, temple worship, sacraments, manifold Deities, the *guru-śishya* tradition and a reliance on the *Vedas* as scriptural authority.

Hinduism Today: The international, monthly newspaper published on nearly every continent by Himalayan Academy and founded in 1979 by Satguru Sivaya Subramuniyaswami.

holy ash: See: *tilaka, tripuṇḍra, vibhūti.*

humors (or bodily humors): See: *āyurveda, bodily humor, dosha.*

huṇḍi: हुण्डि "Offering box," from *hun,* "to sacrifice." A strong box inside Hindu temples into which devotees place their contributions.

icçhā śakti: इच्छाशक्ति "Desire; will." See: *Śakti, triśūla.*

icon: A sacred image, usually of God or a God. English for *mūrti.* See: *mūrti.*

iḍā nāḍī: इडानाडी "Soothing channel." The feminine psychic current flowing along the spine. See: *kuṇḍalinī, nāḍī, piṅgalā.*

ikshukārmuka: इक्षुकार्मुक "Sugar cane bow." A weapon or icon held by loving Gaṇeśa.

ikshukāṇḍa: इक्षुकाण्ड "Sugar cane."

immanent: Indwelling; present and operating within. Relating to God, *imma-*

nent means present in all things and throughout the universe, not aloof or distant.

implore: To ask or beg for earnestly.

incarnation: Endowment with a human body. The soul's taking of physical birth. In some schools, God is believed to incarnate in human form to help humanity. This is called *avatāra.* See: *avatāra, reincarnation.*

incense: *Dhūpa.* Substance that gives off pleasant aromas when burned, usually made from natural substances such as tree resin. A central element in Hindu worship rites, waved gently before the Deity as an offering, especially after ablution. Hindi terms include *sugandhi* and *lobāna.* A popular term for stick incense is *agarbatti* (Gujarati). See: *pūjā.*

individuality: Quality that makes one person or soul other than, or different from, another. See: *ahaṁkāra, ego, āṇava mala, soul.*

Indra: **इन्द्र** "Ruler." Vedic God of rain and thunder, warrior king of the *devas.*

indriya: **इन्द्रिय** "Agent, sense organ." The five agents of perception *(jñānendriyas):* hearing *(śrotra),* touch *(tvak),* sight *(chakshus),* taste *(rasana)* and smell *(ghrāṇa);* and the five agents of action *(karmendriyas):* speech *(vāk),* grasping, by means of the hands *(pāṇi),* movement *(pāda),* excretion *(pāyu)* and generation *(upastha).* See: *kośa, soul, tattva.*

Indus Valley: Region of the Indus River, now in Pakistan, where in 1924 archeologists discovered the remains of a high civilization which flourished between 5000 and 1000 BCE. There, a "seal" was found with the effigy of Śiva as Paśupati, "lord of animals," seated in a *yogic* posture. Neither the language of these people nor their exact background is known. They related culturally and carried on an extensive trade with peoples of other civilizations, far to the West, using sturdy ships that they built themselves. For centuries they were the most advanced civilization on earth. See: *Śaivism.*

initiation (to initiate): To enter into; to admit as a member. In Hinduism, initiation from a qualified preceptor is considered invaluable for spiritual progress. See: *dīkshā, sannyāsa dīkshā.*

instinctive: "Natural or innate." From the Latin *instinctus,* "to impel, instigate." The drives and impulses that order the animal world and the physical and lower astral aspects of humans—for example, self-preservation, procreation, hunger and thirst, as well as the emotions of greed, hatred, anger, fear, lust and jealousy. See: *mind (individual), mind (three phases).*

instinctive mind: *Manas chitta.* The lower mind, which controls the basic faculties of perception, movement, as well as ordinary thought and emotion. *Manas chitta* is of the *manomaya kośa.* See: *mind (three phases).*

intellect: The power to reason or understand; power of thought; mental acumen. See: *buddhi, intellectual mind.*

intellectual mind: *Buddhi chitta.* The faculty of reason and logical thinking. It is the source of discriminating thought, rather than the ordinary, impulsive thought processes of the lower or instinctive mind, called *manas chitta. Buddhi chitta* is of the *manomaya kośa.* See: *buddhi, mind (individual).*

internalize: To take something inside of oneself.
internalized worship: *Yoga.* Worship or contact with God and Gods via meditation and contemplation rather than through external ritual. This is the *yogī's* path, preceded by the *charyā* and *kriyā pādas.* See: *meditation, yoga.*
intrinsic: Essential; inherent. Belonging to the real nature of a being or thing. **—intrinsic evil:** See: *evil.*
intuition (to intuit): Direct understanding or cognition, which bypasses the process of reason. Intuition is a far superior source of knowing than reason, but it does not contradict reason. See: *cognition, mind (five states).*
invincible: That which cannot be overcome; unconquerable.
invocation (to invoke): A "calling or summoning," as to a God, saint, etc., for blessings and assistance. Also, a formal prayer or chant. See: *mantra.*
ipso facto: "By the fact itself." A result accomplished by the deed itself. E.g. in some faiths declaring oneself apostate means *ipso facto* excommunication.
Iraivan: இறைவன் "Worshipful one; divine one." One of the most ancient Tamil names for God. See: *San Mārga Sanctuary.*
Iraivan Temple: See: *San Mārga Sanctuary.*
Itihāsa: इतिहास "So it was." Epic history, particularly the *Rāmāyaṇa* and *Mahābhārata* (of which the famed *Bhagavad Gītā* is a part). This term sometimes refers to the *Purāṇas,* especially the *Skānda Purāṇa* and the *Bhāgavata Purāṇa* (or *Śrīmad Bhāgavatam*). See: *Mahābhārata, Rāmāyaṇa, Smṛiti.*
Īśa: ईश "Ruler, lord or sovereign."
Ishṭa Devatā: इष्टदेवता "Cherished or chosen Deity." The Deity that is the object of one's special pious attention.

jaggery: An Anglo-Indian term for the dark, coarse sugar made from the sap of certain palms, especially the palmyra or fan-palm (Borassus flabelliforris).
jāgrat: जाग्रत् "Wakefulness." The state of mind in which the senses are turned outward. Conscious mind. One of four states of consciousness, *avasthās,* described in the *Māṇḍūkya Upanishad.* See: *avasthā, consciousness.*
jai: जय "Victory!"
Jainism: (Jaina) जैन An ancient non-Vedic religion of India made prominent by the teachings of Mahāvīra ("great hero"), ca 500 BCE. The Jain *Āgamas* teach reverence for all life, vegetarianism and strict renunciation for ascetics. Jains focus great emphasis on the fact that all souls may attain liberation, each by his own effort. Their worship is directed toward their great historic saints, called Tīrthaṅkaras ("ford-crossers"), of whom Mahāvīra was the 24th and last. Jains number about six million today, living mostly in India.
jambira: जम्बिर "Lime."
jambu: जम्बु "Rose apple."
japa: जप "Recitation." Practice of concentratedly repeating a *mantra,* often while counting the repetitions on a *mālā* or strand of beads. It is recom-

mended as a cure for pride and arrogance, anger and jealousy, fear and confusion. It fills the mind with divine syllables, awakening the divine essence of spiritual energies.

japa mālā: "Garland." A strand of beads for holy recitation, *japa,* usually made of *rudrāksha, tulasī,* sandalwood or crystal.

jaṭāmukuṭa: जटामुकुट "Crown of matted hair."

jātakarma: जातकर्म "Rite of birth." See: *saṁskāra.*

jāti: जाति "Birth; genus; community or caste." See: *varṇa dharma.*

jaṭharāgni: जठराग्नि The physical, digestive fire within the body.

jīva: जीव "Living, existing." From *jīv,* "to live." The individual soul, *ātman,* during its embodied state, bound by the three *malas (āṇava, karma* and *māyā).* The *jīvanmukta* is one who is "liberated while living." See: *ātman, evolution of the soul, purusha, soul.*

jñāna: ज्ञान "Knowledge; wisdom." The matured state of the soul. It is the wisdom that comes as an aftermath of the *kuṇḍalinī* breaking through the door of *Brahman* into the realization of Paraśiva, Absolute Reality. *Jñāna* is the awakened, superconscious state *(kāraṇa chitta).* It is the fruition of the progressive stages of *charyā, kriyā* and *yoga* in the Śaiva Siddhānta system of spiritual unfoldment. See: *God Realization, Self Realization, samādhi.*

jñāna pāda: ज्ञानपाद "Stage of wisdom." According to the Śaiva Siddhānta *ṛishis, jñāna* is the last of the four successive *pādas* (stages) of spiritual unfoldment. It is the culmination of the third stage, the *yoga pāda.* Also names the knowledge section of each *Āgama.* See: *jñāna, pāda.*

jñāna śakti: ज्ञानशक्ति "Knowing power." The universal force of wisdom. See: *Śakti, triśūla.*

jñānendriya: ज्ञानेन्द्रिय "Agent of perception." See: *indriya.*

jurisdiction: A sphere of authority; the territorial range of authority.

jyoti: ज्योति "Light."

jyotisha: ज्योतिष From *jyoti,* "light." "The science of the lights (or stars)." Hindu astrology, the knowledge and practice of analyzing events and circumstances, delineating character and determining auspicious moments, according to the positions and movements of heavenly bodies. In calculating horoscopes, *jyotisha* uses the sidereal (fixed-star) system, whereas Western astrology uses the tropical (fixed-date) method.

kadalīphala: कदलीफल "Banana fruit."

Kailāsa: कैलास "Crystalline" or "abode of bliss." The four-faced Himalayan peak in Western Tibet; the earthly abode of Lord Śiva. Associated with Mount Meru, the legendary center of the universe, it is an important pilgrimage destination for all Hindus, as well as for Tibetan Buddhists. Kailāsa is represented in Śāktism by a certain three-dimensional form of the *Śrī Chakra yantra* (also called *kailāsa chakra).*

Kailāsa Paramparā: कैलासपरंपरा A spiritual lineage of *siddhas,* a major stream of the Nandinātha Sampradāya, proponents of the ancient philosophy of monistic Śaiva Siddhānta, of whom Sivaya Subramuniyaswami is the current representative. See: *Yogaswāmī.*

kalaśa: कलश "Water pot; pitcher; jar." In temple rites, a pot of water, *kalaśa,* topped with mango leaves and a husked coconut represents the Deity during special *pūjās. Kalaśa* also names the pot-like spires that adorn temple roofs.

Kali Yuga: कलियुग "Dark Age." The Kali Yuga is the last age in the repetitive cycle of four phases of time the universe passes through. It is comparable to the darkest part of the night, as the forces of ignorance are in full power and many of the subtle faculties of the soul are obscured. See: *yuga.*

kalpavṛiksha: कल्पवृक्ष "Wish-fulfilling tree." An important symbol in Hindu theology.

kāma: काम "Pleasure, love; desire." Cultural, intellectual and sexual fulfillment. One of four human goals, *purushārtha.* See: *purushārtha.*

kamaṇḍalu: कमण्डलु Small water vessel, such as that carried by *sannyāsins.*

kapittha: कपित्थ "On which monkey's dwell." The wood apple tree, *Limonia acidissima,* native to the dry plains of India and Ceylon and cultivated along roads and edges of fields and occasionally in orchards. The *kapittha* fruit, also known as elephant apple, monkey fruit and *kath bel,* is tough shelled, astringent and renowned for its *āyurvedic* potencies.

kāraṇaloka: The causal plane, also called Śivaloka, existing deep within the Antarloka at a higher level of vibration, it is a world of superconsciousness and extremely refined energy. See: *loka.*

karaṇḍa mukuṭa: करण्ड मुकुट "Basket-shaped crown." A headdress or crown-shaped like a conical basket with the narrow end upwards, often topped with a series of smaller flattened spheres, worn by the Deities.

karma: कर्म "Action, deed." One of the most important principles in Hindu thought, *karma* refers to 1) any act or deed; 2) the principle of cause and effect; 3) a consequence or "fruit of action" *(karmaphala)* or "after effect" *(uttaraphala),* which sooner or later returns upon the doer. What we sow, we shall reap in this or future lives. Selfish, hateful acts *(pāpakarma* or *kukarma)* will bring suffering. Benevolent actions *(puṇyakarma* or *sukarma)* will bring loving reactions. *Karma* is a neutral, self-perpetuating law of the inner cosmos, much as gravity is an impersonal law of the outer cosmos. *Karma* is threefold: *sañchita, prārabdha* and *kriyamāna.* —***sañchita karma:*** "Accumulated actions." The sum of all *karmas* of this life and past lives. —***prārabdha karma:*** "Actions begun; set in motion." That portion of *sañchita karma* that is bearing fruit and shaping the events and conditions of the current life, including the nature of one's bodies, personal tendencies and associations. —***kriyamāna karma:*** "Being made." The *karma* being created and added to *sañchita* in this life by one's thoughts, words and actions, or in the inner worlds between lives. See: *mala, moksha, sin, soul.*

karma yoga: कर्मयोग "Union through action." Selfless service. See: *yoga.*

karmendriya: **कर्मेन्द्रिय** "Agent of action." See: *indriya.*

karṇavedha: **कर्णवेध** "Ear-piercing." See: *saṁskāra.*

karpūra: **कर्पूर** "Camphor." The white resinous exudation of the camphor tree burned in *āratī* lamps during *pūjā.* See: *āratī.*

Kārttikeya: **कार्त्तिकेय** Child of the Pleiades, from *Kṛittikā,* "Pleiades." A son of Śiva. A great Mahādeva worshiped in all parts of India and the world. Also known as Murugan, Kumāra, Skanda, Shaṇmukhanātha, Subrahmaṇya and more, He is the God who guides that part of evolution which is religion, the transformation of the instinctive into a divine wisdom through *yoga.* He holds the holy *vel* of *jñāna śakti,* His Power to vanquish ignorance.

karuṇā: **करुणा** "Compassionate; loving, full of grace."

Kauai: Northernmost of the Hawaiian islands; 555 sq. mi., pop. 50,000.

Kauai Aadheenam: Monastery-temple complex founded by Sivaya Subramuniyaswami in 1970; international headquarters of Śaiva Siddhānta Church.

kavacha: **कवच** "Armor; covering." A decorative mask-like covering, usually made of silver or gold, that adorns the face, hands or entire Deity image.

kavadi: காவடி A penance offered to Lord Murugan-Kārttikeya, especially during Tai Pusam, consisting of carrying in procession a heavy, beautifully decorated, wooden object from which pots of milk hang which are to be used for His *abhisheka.* The participant's tongue and other parts of the body are often pierced with small silver spears or hooks. See: *penance.*

keśānta: **केशान्त** "Beard-shaving." See: *saṁskāra.*

khaḍga: **खड्ग** "Sword." A powerful symbol in Hindu iconography, depicting the power of the Gods to aid devotees in overcoming human weaknesses.

kheṭaka: **खेटक** "Shield." As a religious icon, it represents protection, divine security and the upholding of *dharma.*

kīrtana: **कीर्तन** "Praising." Devotional singing and dancing in celebration of God, Gods and *guru.* An important form of congregational worship in many Hindu denominations. See: *bhajana.*

kolam: கோலம் Traditional household and priestly art of "drawing" intricate decorative patterns at the entrance to a home or temple or at the site of a religious ceremony. Known as *raṅgoli* in Sanskṛit. *Kolam* designs are made with rice powder mixed to a watery paste, and sometimes with flowers and various-colored powdered pulses.

konrai: கொன்றை The Golden Shower tree, *Cassia fistula;* symbol of Śiva's cascading, abundant, golden grace.

kośa: **कोश** "Sheath; vessel, container; layer." Philosophically, five sheaths through which the soul functions simultaneously in the various planes or levels of existence. ***—annamaya kośa:*** "Sheath composed of food." The physical or odic body. ***—prāṇamaya kośa:*** "Sheath composed of *prāṇa* (vital force)." Also known as the *prāṇic* or health body, or the etheric body or etheric double. ***—manomaya kośa:*** "Mind-formed sheath." The lower astral body, from *manas,* "thought, will, wish." The instinctive-intellectual sheath of ordinary thought, desire and emotion. ***—vijñānamaya kośa:*** "Sheath of cognition." The mental or cognitive-intuitive sheath, also called the actinodic sheath. —***ānandamaya kośa:*** "Body of bliss." The intuitive-superconscious sheath or actinic-causal body. *Ānandamaya kośa* is not a sheath in the same sense as the four outer *kośas.* It is the soul itself, a body of light, also called *kāraṇa śarīra,* causal body, and *karmāśaya,* holder of *karmas* of this and all past lives. *Ānandamaya kośa* is that which evolves through all incarnations and beyond until the soul's ultimate, fulfilled merger, *viśvagrāsa,* in the Primal Soul, Parameśvara. Then *ānandamaya kośa* becomes Śivamayakośa, the body of God Śiva.

kraal: An enclosure for livestock (Afrikaans); the herd itself.

Kṛishṇa: कृष्ण "Black." Also related to *kṛishṭiḥ,* meaning "drawing, attracting." One of the most popular Gods of the Hindu pantheon. He is worshiped by Vaishṇavas as the eighth *avatāra,* incarnation, of Vishṇu. He is best known as the Supreme Personage depicted in the *Mahābhārata,* and specifically in the *Bhagavad Gītā.* For Gauḍīya Vaishṇavism, Kṛishṇa is the Godhead.

kriyā: क्रिया "Action." In a general sense, *kriyā* can refer to doing of any kind. Specifically, it names religious action, especially rites or ceremonies. In *yoga* terminology, *kriyā* names involuntary physical movements caused by the arousal of the *kuṇḍalinī.* See: *pāda.*

kriyā pāda: क्रियापाद् "Stage of religious action; worship." The stage of worship and devotion, second of four progressive stages of maturation on the Śaiva Siddhānta path of attainment. See: *pāda.*

kriyā śakti: क्रियाशक्ति "Action power." The universal force of doing. See: *Śakti, triśūla.*

krodha: क्रोध "Anger." The emotion of the second *chakra* below the *mūlādhāra,* called *vitala.* Scripture describes it as one of the gates to hell.

kshetra: क्षेत्र "Place." Any property or region; often naming a sacred place.

kshatriya: क्षत्रिय "Governing; sovereign." The social class of lawmakers, law-enforcers and military. See: *varṇa dharma.*

Kshipra Gaṇapati: क्षिप्रगणपति A name and traditional *mūrti,* or form, of Gaṇeśa. "He who is immediate (or quick)." He holds a *kalpavṛiksha* sprig and a pot of gems.

Kshipra Prasāda Gaṇapati: क्षिप्रप्रसाद् गणपति "The quick rewarder" presides from a *kusha*-grass throne holding pomegranate, noose, goad and more.

kukarma: कुकर्म "Unwholesome acts" or the fruit therefrom. See: *karma, pāpa.*

kulaguru: कुलगुरु "Family preceptor or teacher." The *kulaguru* guides the joint and extended family, particularly through the heads of families, and provides spiritual education. He may or may not be a *satguru.*

kumārī: कुमारी "Ever youthful." A young virgin girl, particularly age 10-12.

Kulārṇava Tantra: कुलार्णवतन्त्र A leading scripture of the Kaula school of Śāktism. It comprises 17 chapters totaling 2,058 verses which focus on ways to liberation, with notable chapters on the *guru-śishya* relationship.

Kumāra: कुमार "Virgin youth; ever-youthful." A name of Lord Kārttikeya as an eternal bachelor. See: *Kārttikeya.*

kumbha: कुम्भ Another name for *kalaśa,* a pot of water on which a husked coconut is nested on five mango leaves to represent the Deity; integral to certain sacred Hindu rites.

kumbhābhisheka: कुम्भाभिषेक "Water pot ablution." The formal consecration of a new temple and its periodic reconsecration, usually at twelve-year intervals. The rites culminate when the priests pour sanctified water over the temple spires, which resemble an inverted pot, or *kumbha.*

kukarma: "Unwholesome acts," or the fruit therefrom. See: *karma, pāpa.*

kuṇḍalinī: कुण्डलिनी "She who is coiled; serpent power." The primordial cosmic energy in every individual which, at first, lies coiled like a serpent at the base of the spine and eventually, through the practice of *yoga,* rises up the *sushumṇā nāḍī.* As it rises, the *kuṇḍalinī* awakens each successive *chakra. Nirvikalpa samādhi,* enlightenment, comes as it pierces through the door of Brahman at the core of the *sahasrāra* and enters! See: *chakra, samādhi, nāḍī.*

kuṅkuma: कुंकुम "Saffron; red." The red powder, made of turmeric and lime, worn by Hindus as the *pottu,* dot, at the point of the third eye on the forehead. Names the saffron plant, *Crocus sativus,* and its pollen.

kuttuvilaku: குத்துவிளக்கு A standing lamp *(dīpastambha* in Sanskṛit) found in the temple, shrine room or home. See: *dīpastambha.*

lactation: The secretion of milk from a mammary gland.

laḍḍu: लड्डु A sweet made with milk, flour and sugar in South India, and with chickpea flour, *ghee* and sugar in North India.

Lakshmī: लक्ष्मी "Mark or sign," often of success or prosperity. Śakti, the Universal Mother, as Goddess of wealth. The mythological consort of Vishṇu. Usually depicted on a lotus flower. Prayers are offered to Lakshmī for wealth, beauty and peace. —***Dhānya Lakshmī:*** *"Bestower of wealth."* See: *Goddess, Śakti.*

Lakshmī Gaṇapati: लक्ष्मीगणपति A name and traditional *mūrti,* or form, of Gaṇeśa. "Lord of abundance." Flanked by Wisdom and Achievement (Buddhi and Siddhi) and holds a green parrot, *śukhi.*

Lambodara: लम्बोदर "Large belly." A name of Lord Gaṇeśa cited in the *Mudgala Purāṇa* as the conqueror of *krodha,* anger.

left-handed: *Vāma mārga.* A term describing certain *tantric* practices where the instincts and intellect are transcended, and detachment is sought through practices and behavior which are contrary to orthodox social behavior. See: *tantra, tantric, tantrism.*

Letters Five: See: *Namaḥ Śivāya.*

liberal Hinduism: A synonym for Smārtism and the closely related neo-Indian religion. The latter form carries forward basic Hindu cultural values—such as dress, diet and the arts—while allowing religious values to subside. Neo-Indian religion encourages Hindus to follow any combination of theological, scriptural, *sādhana* and worship patterns, regardless of sectarian or religious origin. See: *Smārtism, universalist.*

liberation: *Moksha,* release from the bonds of *pāśa,* after which the soul is liberated from *saṁsāra* (the round of births and deaths). In Śaiva Siddhānta, *pāśa* is the three-fold bondage of *āṇava, karma* and *māyā,* which limit and confine the soul to the reincarnational cycle so that it may evolve. *Moksha* is freedom from the fettering power of these bonds, which do not cease to exist, but no longer have the power to fetter or bind the soul. See: *mala, moksha, reincarnation, Self Realization.*

light: In an ordinary sense, a form of energy which makes physical objects visible to the eye. In a religious-mystical sense, light also illumines inner objects (i.e., mental images). **—clear white light:** Inner light at a high level of intensity, very clear and pure. When experienced fully, it is seen to be permeating all of existence, the universal substance of all form, inner and outer, pure consciousness, Satchidānanda. This experience, repeated at regular intervals, can yield "a knowing greater than you could acquire at any university or institute of higher learning." See: *Śiva consciousness, tattva.*

līlā: लीला "Play." Ease or facility in doing. A term used to describe God's Divine cosmic drama of creation, preservation, dissolution, concealment and revelation.

liturgy: The proper, prescribed forms of ritual.

lobha: लोभ "Greed." One of the principal obstacles on the path, counteracted by *dāna* (selfless giving) and *aparigraha,* greedlessness. See: *Gajānana.*

loka: लोक "World, habitat, realm, or plane of existence." From *loc,* "to shine, be bright, visible." A dimension of manifest existence; cosmic region. Each *loka* reflects or involves a particular range of consciousness. The three primary *lokas* are 1) ***—Bhūloka:*** "Earth world." The world perceived through the five senses, also called the gross plane, as it is the most dense of the worlds. Sometimes referred to as the First World. 2) ***—Antarloka:*** "Inner or in-between world." Known in English as the subtle or astral plane, the intermediate dimension between the physical and causal worlds, where souls in their astral bodies sojourn between incarnations and when they sleep. Also referred to as the Second World. 3) ***—Śivaloka:*** "World of Śiva," and of the Gods and highly evolved souls. The causal plane, also called Kāraṇaloka, existing deep within the Antarloka at a higher level of vibration, it is a world of superconsciousness and extremely refined energy. It is the plane of creativity and intuition, the quantum level of the universe, where souls exist in self-effulgent bodies made of actinic particles of light. It is here that God and Gods move and lovingly guide the evolution of all the worlds and shed their ever-flowing grace. Its vibratory rate is that of the *viśuddha, ājñā* and *sahasrāra chakras* and those above. Also referred to as the Third World. See: *three worlds.*

macrocosm: "Great world or universe." See: *microcosm-macrocosm, three worlds.*

madhukumbha: **मधुकुम्भ** "Honey vessel."

madhyama vāk: **मध्यम** "Intermediate word." See: *vāk.*

Madurai: City in the South Indian state of Tamil Nadu; home of one of the world's most spectacular Śaivite temples, called Meenakshi-Sundaresvara.

mahā: **महा** A prefix meaning "great."

Mahā Gaṇapati: **महागणपति** "The great one." A classical *mūrti* accompanied by one of His *śaktis.* He holds a pomegranate, blue lily and a pot of gems.

Mahābhārata: **महाभारत** "Great Epic of India." The world's longest epic poem. It revolves around the conflict between two kingdoms, the Pāṇḍavas and Kauravas, and their great battle of Kurukshetra near modern Delhi in approximately 1424 BCE. Woven through the plot are countless discourses on philosophy, religion, astronomy, cosmology, polity, economics and many stories illustrative of simple truths and ethical principles. The *Bhagavad Gītā* is one section of the work. The *Mahābhārata* is revered as scripture by Vaishṇavites and Smārtas. See: *Bhagavad Gītā.*

Mahādeva: **महादेव** "Great shining one; God." Referring either to God Śiva or any of the highly evolved beings who live in the Śivaloka in their natural, effulgent soul bodies. God Śiva in His perfection as Primal Soul is one of the Mahādevas, yet He is unique and incomparable in that He alone is uncreated, the Father-Mother and Destiny of all other Mahādevas. He is called Parameśvara, "Supreme God." He is the Primal Soul, whereas the other Gods are individual souls. See: *Gods, Parameśvara, Śiva.*

mahākāraṇa: **महाकारण** The Great Causal." See: *vāk.*

mahāparaśu: **महापरशु** "Large axe."

mahāpralaya: **महाप्रलय** "Great dissolution." Total annihilation of the universe at the end of a *mahākalpa.* It is the absorption of all existence, including time, space and individual consciousness, all the *lokas* and their inhabitants into God Śiva, as the water of a river returns to its source, the sea. Then Śiva alone exists in His three perfections, until He again issues forth creation. During this incredibly vast period there are many partial dissolutions, *pralayas,* when either the Bhūloka and/or the Antarloka are destroyed.

Mahārāshṭra: **महाराष्ट्र** Central state of modern India whose capital is Bombay. Area 118,717 square miles, population 63 million.

mahāsamādhi: **महासमाधि** "Great enstasy." The death, or dropping off of the physical body, of a great soul, an event occasioned by tremendous blessings. Also names the shrine in which the remains of a great soul are entombed. ***Mahāsamādhi*** **day** names the anniversary of a great soul's transition. See: *cremation, death.*

mahārāja: **महाराज** "Great king." Indian monarch. Title of respect for political or (in modern times) spiritual leaders.

mahātala: **महातल** Sixth netherworld. Region of consciencelessness. See:

chakra.

mahātmā: **महात्मा** "Great soul." Honorific title given to people held in high esteem, especially saints. See: *ātman.*

mahāvākya: **महावाक्य** "Great saying." A profound aphorism from scripture or a holy person. Most famous are four Upanishadic proclamations: *Prajanam Brahma* ("Pure consciousness is God"—*Aitareya U.), Aham Brahmāsmi* ("I am God"—*Bṛihadāraṇyaka U.), Tat tvam asi* ("Thou art That"—*Çhandogya U.)* and *Ayam ātma Brahma* ("The soul is God"—*Māṇḍūkya U.).*

Mahodara: **महोदर** "He of big belly." Gaṇeśa's aspect as the dispeller of *moha,* infatuation or delusion.

mala: **मल** "Impurity." An important term in Śaivism referring to three bonds, called *pāśa—āṇava, karma,* and *māyā*—which limit the soul, preventing it from knowing its true, divine nature. See: *liberation, pāśa.*

mālā: **माला** "Garland." A strand of beads for holy recitation, *japa,* usually made of *rudrāksha, tulasī,* sandalwood or crystal. Also a flower garland.

mamatā: **ममता** "Egoity, self-interest, selfishness."

manas: **मनस्** "Mind; understanding." The lower or instinctive mind, seat of desire and governor of sensory and motor organs, called *indriyas. Manas* is termed the undisciplined, empirical mind. *Manas* is characterized by desire, determination, doubt, faith, lack of faith, steadfastness, lack of steadfastness, shame, intellection and fear. It is a faculty of *manomaya kośa,* the lower astral or instinctive-intellectual sheath. See: *awareness, indriya, instinctive mind, kośa, mind (individual).*

maṇḍapa: **मण्डप** From *maṇḍ,* "to deck, adorn." Temple precinct; a temple compound, open hall or chamber. In entering a large temple, one passes through a series of *maṇḍapas,* each named according to its position, e.g., *mukhamaṇḍapa,* "facing chamber." In some temples, *maṇḍapas* are concentrically arranged. See: *temple.*

mandira: **मन्दिर** Temple or shrine; abode." See: *temple.*

Māṇḍūkya Upanishad: **माण्डूक्य उपनिषद्** A "principal" *Upanishad* (belonging to the *Atharva Veda)* which, in 12 concise verses, teaches of Aum and the four states *(avasthā)* of awareness: waking *(viśva),* dreaming *(taijasa),* dreamless sleep *(prājña)* and transcendent, spiritual consciousness *(turīya).*

maṇipūra chakra: **मणिपूरचक्र** "Wheeled city of jewels." Solar-plexus center of willpower. See: *chakra.*

Manikkavasagar: மாணிக்கவாசகர் "He of ruby-like utterances." Tamil saint who contributed to the medieval Śaivite renaissance (ca 850). He gave up his position as prime minister to follow a renunciate life. His poetic *Tiruvasagam,* "holy utterances"—a major Śaiva Siddhānta scripture (part of the eighth *Tirumurai)* and a jewel of Tamil literature—express his aspirations, trials and *yogic* realizations.

mānsāhārī: **मांसाहारी** "Meat-eater." Those who follow a non-vegetarian diet. See: *meat-eater, vegetarian.*

mantra: **मन्त्र** "Mystic formula." A sound, syllable, word or phrase endowed with special power, usually drawn from scripture. *Mantras* are chanted loudly during *pūjā* to invoke the Gods and establish a force field. To be truly effective, such *mantras* must be given by the preceptor through initiation.

Markali Pillaiyar: மார்கழிப் பிள்ளையார் A month-long, December-January (Markali) festival to Gaṇeśa in the form of Lord Pillaiyar, the Noble Child. Worship, prayer and other spiritual disciplines are commenced during this special period of *sādhana*, and the home is cleaned thoroughly each day.

mārga: **मार्ग** "Path; way." From *mārg*, "to seek." See: *pāda.*

materialism (materialistic): The doctrine that matter is the only reality, that all life, thought and feelings are but the effects of movements of matter, and that there exist no worlds but the physical. See: *worldly.*

materialist: One who believes that physical comfort, pleasure and wealth are the only or the highest goals of life, that matter is the only reality.

mātṛikākshara: **मातृकाक्षर** A letter of the Sanskṛit alphabet, numbering 51.

mātsarya: **मात्सर** "Jealousy."

maya: **मय** "Consisting of; made of," as in *manomaya*, "made of mind."

māyā: **माया** "She who measures;" or "mirific energy." The substance emanated from Śiva through which the world of form is manifested. Hence all creation is also termed *māyā*. It is the cosmic creative force, the principle of manifestation, ever in the process of creation, preservation and dissolution. *Māyā* is a key concept in Hinduism, originally meaning "supernatural power; God's mirific energy," often translated as "illusion." See: *loka, mind (universal).*

mayūra: **मयूर** "Peacock." The *vāhana*, or mount, of Lord Kārttikeya, symbolizing effulgent beauty and religion in full glory. The peacock is able to control powerful snakes, such as the cobra, symbolizing the soulful domination of the instinctive elements—or control of the *kuṇḍalinī*, which is *yoga*. See: *Kārttikeya, vāhana.*

Mayūreśvara: **मयूरेश्वर** "Peacock Lord." The Gaṇeśa *mūrti* enshrined at the Morgaon Temple south of Pune, Mahārāshṭra.

meat-eater: *Mānsāhārī*. Those who follow a nonvegetarian diet. See: *vegetarianism.*

meditation: *Dhyāna*. Sustained concentration. Meditation describes a quiet, alert, powerfully concentrated state wherein new knowledge and insights are awakened from within as awareness focuses one-pointedly on an object or specific line of thought. See: *rāja yoga, yoga.*

mediumship: Act or practice of serving as a channel through which beings of inner worlds communicate with humans. See: *folk-shamanic, trance.*

menses: A woman's monthly menstruation period, during which, by Hindu tradition, she rests from her usual activities and forgoes public and family religious functions.

mentor: One who advises, teaches, instructs, either formally or informally.

merge: To lose distinctness or identity by being absorbed. To unite or become one with.

merger of the soul: See: *evolution of the soul, viśvagrāsa.*

metabolism: The system of physical and chemical processes occurring within a living cell or organism that are necessary for the maintenance of life. The life processes, consisting of anabolism (the changing of food into living tissue) and catabolism (the degeneration of living tissue).

microcosm-macrocosm: "Little world" or "miniature universe" as compared with "great world." *Microcosm* refers to the internal source of something larger or more external (macrocosm). In Hindu cosmology, the outer world is a macrocosm of the inner world, which is its microcosm and is mystically larger and more complex than the physical universe and functions at a higher rate of vibration and even a different rate of time. The microcosm precedes the macrocosm. Thus, the guiding principle of the Bhūloka comes from the Antarloka and Śivaloka. Consciousness precedes physical form. In the *tantric* tradition, the body of man is viewed as a microcosm of the entire divine creation. "Microcosm-macrocosm" is embodied in the terms *piṇḍa* and *aṇḍa.* See: *quantum, tattva, tantra.*

millennium: A period of 1,000 years. **millennia:** Plural of millennium.

mind (five states): A view of the mind in five parts. **—conscious mind:** *Jāgrat chitta* ("wakeful consciousness"). The ordinary, waking, thinking state of mind in which the majority of people function most of the day. **—subconscious mind:** *Saṁskāra chitta* ("impression mind"). The part of mind "beneath" the conscious mind, the storehouse or recorder of all experience (whether remembered consciously or not)—the holder of past impressions, reactions and desires. Also, the seat of involuntary physiological processes. **—subsubconscious mind:** *Vāsanā chitta* ("mind of subliminal traits"). The area of the subconscious mind formed when two thoughts or experiences of the same rate of intensity are sent into the subconscious at different times and, intermingling, give rise to a new and totally different rate of vibration. This subconscious formation later causes the external mind to react to situations according to these accumulated vibrations, be they positive, negative or mixed. **—superconscious mind:** *Kāraṇa chitta.* The mind of light, the all-knowing intelligence of the soul. At its deepest level, the superconscious is Parāśakti, or Satchidānanda, the Divine Mind of God Śiva. **—subsuperconscious mind:** *Anukāraṇa chitta.* The superconscious mind working through the conscious and subconscious states, which brings forth intuition, clarity and insight. See: *chitta, consciousness, saṁskāra.*

mind (individual): At the microcosmic level of individual souls, mind is consciousness and its faculties of memory, desire, thought and cognition. Individual mind is *chitta* (mind, consciousness) and its three-fold expression is called *antaḥkaraṇa,* "inner faculty" composed of: 1) *buddhi* ("intellect, reason, logic," higher mind); 2) *ahaṁkāra* ("I-maker," egoity); 3) *manas* ("lower mind," instinctive-intellectual mind, the seat of desire).

mind (three phases): A perspective of mind as instinctive, intellectual and superconscious. **—instinctive mind.** *Manas chitta,* the seat of desire and governor of sensory and motor organs. **—intellectual mind.** *Buddhi chitta,* the faculty of thought and intelligence. —**superconscious mind:** *Kāraṇa chitta,* the strata of intuition, benevolence and spiritual sustenance. Its most refined essence is Parāsakti, or Satchidānanda, all-knowing, omnipresent consciousness, the One transcendental, self-luminous, divine mind common to all souls. See: *consciousness, mind (five states).*

mind (universal): In the most profound sense, mind is the sum of all things, all energies and manifestations, all forms, subtle and gross, sacred and mundane. It is the inner and outer cosmos. Mind is *māyā.* It is the material matrix. It is everything but That, the Self within, Paraśiva. See: *chitta, consciousness, māyā.*

mlecçha: म्लेच्छ "One who speaks indistinctly (like a foreigner)." A foreigner, barbarian; who does not conform to Hindu culture; a non-Hindu.

moda: मोद् "Arrogance." Gaṇeśa's aspect as the conquerer of *mamata,* egoity.

modaka: मोदक "Sweets." A round lemon-sized sweet made of rice, coconut, sugar, etc. It is a favorite treat of Gaṇeśa. Esoterically, it corresponds to *siddhi* (attainment or fulfillment), the gladdening contentment of pure joy, the sweetest of all things sweet. See: *Gaṇeśa.*

modakapātra: मोदकपात्र "Bowl of sweets." The *modaka,* loving Gaṇeśa's favorite sweet, represents all good things, especially *moksha,* liberation.

moha: मोह "Infatuation, delusion."

moksha: मोक्ष "Liberation." Release from transmigration, *saṁsāra,* the round of births and deaths, which occurs after *karma* has been resolved and *nirvikalpa samādhi*—realization of the Self, Paraśiva—has been attained. Same as *mukti.* See: *kuṇḍalinī, liberation.*

monastic: A monk or nunk (based on the Greek *monos,* "alone"). A man or woman who has withdrawn from the world and lives an austere, religious life, either alone or with others in a monastery. (Not to be confused with *monistic,* having to do with the doctrine of monism.) A monastery-dweller is a *maṭhavāsi,* and *sādhu* is a rough equivalent for mendicant. See: *sannyāsin.*

monism: "Doctrine of oneness." 1) The philosophical view that there is only one ultimate substance or principle. 2) The view that reality is a unified whole without independent parts. See: *advaita.*

monistic theism: Advaita Īśvaravāda. Monism is the doctrine that reality is a one whole or existence without independent parts. Theism is the belief that God exists as a real, conscious, personal Supreme Being. Monistic theism is the dipolar doctrine, also called panentheism, that embraces both monism and theism, two perspectives ordinarily considered contradictory or mutually exclusive, since theism implies dualism. Monistic theism simultaneously accepts that God has a personal form, that He creates, pervades and *is* all that exists—and that He ultimately transcends all existence and that the soul is, in essence, one with God. See: *advaita, theism.*

monistic: Expressive of the belief that reality is of one kind or substance.

monotheism: "Doctrine of one God." Contrasted with polytheism, meaning belief in many Gods. The term *monotheism* covers a wide range of philosophical positions, from exclusive (or pure) monotheism, which recognizes only one God (such as in Semitic faiths), to inclusive monotheism, which also accepts the existence of other Gods. Generally speaking, the denominations of Hinduism are inclusively monotheistic in their belief in a one Supreme God, and in their reverence for other Gods, or Mahādevas.

mṛidaṅga: मृदङ्ग A kind of Indian drum, barrel-shaped and two-headed.

mṛigi mudrā: मृगि मुद्रा "Deer gesture." The right hand is held in the shape of the profile of a deer's head: the thumb, second finger and third finger touching to form the upper jaw, and the first and fourth fingers kept straight, forming the ears. During *pūjā* a flower is held in this *mudrā* (in the "deer's mouth," facing outward) to sprinkle water and waft food essences toward the Deity.

mudgara: मुद्गर "A hammer or mallet." An icon of arts and crafts, also a weapon in Hindu iconography.

mudrā: मुद्रा "Seal." Esoteric hand gestures which express specific energies or powers. Usually accompanied by precise visualizations, *mudrās* are a vital element of ritual worship *(pūjā)*, dance and *yoga.* Among the best-known *mudrās* are: 1) *abhaya mudrā* (gesture of fearlessness), in which the fingers are extended, palm facing forward; 2) *añjali mudrā* (gesture of reverence); 3) *jñāna mudrā* (also known as *chin mudrā* and *yoga mudrā*), in which the thumb and index finger touch, forming a circle, with the other fingers extended; 4) *dhyāna mudrā* (seal of meditation), in which the two hands are open and relaxed with the palms up, resting on the folded legs, the right hand atop the left with the tips of the thumbs gently touching. See: *abhaya mudrā, añjali mudrā, haṭha yoga, namaskāra.*

mūlādhāra chakra: मूलाधारचक्र The center located at the base of the spine and governing memory, time and space. The first of seven nerve plexes or centers of force and consciousness in the psychic nerve system of man, located along the spinal column from its base to the cranial chamber. Loving Gaṇeśa, seated on the four petalled *mūlādhāra,* rules memory and knowledge as gatekeeper to the six *chakras* above and the guard of the seven below.

mūlaka: मूलक "Radish."

mūrti: मूर्ति "Form; manifestation, embodiment, personification." An image or icon of God or a God used during worship. *Mūrtis* range from aniconic *(avyakta,* "nonmanifest"), such as the Śivaliṅga, to *vyakta* "fully manifest," e.g., anthropomorphic images such as Naṭarāja. In-between is the partially manifest *(vyaktāvyakta),* e.g., the *mukha liṅga,* in which the face of Śiva appears on the Śivaliṅga. Other Deity representations include symbols, e.g., the banyan tree, and geometric icons such as *yantras* and *maṇḍalas.* *Svayambhū* names a *mūrti* discovered in nature and not carved or crafted by human hands. Another important term for the Deity icon or idol is *pratimā,* "reflected image." See: *Ishṭa Devatā.*

Murugan: முருகன் "Beautiful one," a favorite name of Kārttikeya among the Tamils of South India, Sri Lanka and elsewhere. See: *Kārttikeya.*

mūshika: **मूषिक** From *mūsh,* "to steal." The mouse, Lord Gaṇeśa's mount, traditionally associated with abundance. Symbolically, the mouse carries Lord Gaṇeśa's grace into every corner of the mind. See: *Gaṇeśa, vāhana.*

nāda: **नाद्** "Sound; tone, vibration." Metaphysically, the mystic sounds of the Eternal, of which the highest is the transcendent or Soundless Sound, Paranāda, the first vibration from which creation emanates. From Paranāda comes Praṇava, Aum, and further evolutes of *nāda.* These are experienced by the meditator as the *nādanāḍī śakti,* "the energy current of sound," heard pulsing through the nerve system as a constant high-pitched *hum,* much like a *tambūra,* an electrical transformer, a swarm of bees or a *śruti* box. Most commonly, *nāda* refers to ordinary sound. See: *Aum.*

nāḍī: **नाडी** "Conduit." A nerve fiber or energy channel of the subtle (inner) bodies of man. It is said there are 72,000. These interconnect the *chakras.* The three main *nāḍīs* are named *iḍā, piṅgalā* and *sushumṇā.* ***—iḍā:*** Also known as *chandra* ("moon") *nāḍī,* it is pink in color and flows downward, ending on the left side of the body. This current is feminine in nature and is the channel of physical-emotional energy. ***—piṅgaḷā:*** Also known as *sūrya* ("sun") *nāḍī,* it is blue in color and flows upward, ending on the right side of the body. This current is masculine in nature and is the channel of intellectual-mental energy. ***—sushumṇā:*** The major nerve current which passes through the spinal column from the *mūlādhāra chakra* at the base to the *sahasrāra* at the crown of the head. It is the channel of *kuṇḍalinī.* Through *yoga,* the *kuṇḍalinī* energy lying dormant in the *mūlādhāra* is awakened and made to rise up this channel through each *chakra* to the *sahasrāra chakra.* See: *chakra, kuṇḍalinī, rāja yoga, tantrism.*

nāga: **नाग** "Snake," often the cobra; symbol of the *kuṇḍalinī* coiled on the four petals of the *mūlādhāra chakra.* See: *kuṇḍalinī, mūlādhāra chakra.*

nāgapāśa: **नागपाश** "Snake cord," worn by Gaṇeśa in His various *mūrtis,* both as a waist band and as a sacred thread *(yajñopavīta),* representing mastery of the life forces, transmutation of instinctiveness into spirituality.

nāgasvara: **नागस्वर** "Snake note." A double-reed woodwind about three feet long, similar to an oboe, but more shrill and piercing, common in South India, played at Hindu *pūjās* and processions with the *tavil,* a large drum.

naivedya: **नैवेद्य** Food offered to the Deity at the temple or home altar. An important element in *pūjā.* See: *prasāda, pūjā.*

nakshatra: **नक्षत्र** "Star cluster." Central to astrological determinations, the *nakshatras* are 27 star-clusters, constellations, which lie along the ecliptic, or path of the sun. An individual's *nakshatra,* or birth star, is the constellation the moon was aligned with at the time of birth. See: *jyotisha.*

namaḥ: **नमः** "Adoration (or homage) to.

Namaḥ Śivāya: **नमः शिवाय** "Adoration (or homage) to Śiva." The supreme *mantra* of Śaivism, known as the *Pañchākshara* or "five letters." *Na* is the Lord's veiling grace; *Ma* is the world; *Śi* is Śiva; *Vā* is His revealing grace; *Ya* is the soul. The letters also represent the physical body: *Na* the legs, *Ma* the stomach, *Śi* the shoulders, *Vā* the mouth and *Ya* the eyes. Embodying the essence of Śaiva Siddhānta, it is found in the center of the central *Veda* (the *Yajur*) of the original three *Vedas (Ṛig, Yajur* and *Sāma). (Kṛishṇa Yajur Veda, Taittirīya Saṁhitā* 4.5.8).

nāmakaraṇa: नामकरण "Name giving." See: *saṁskāra.*

namaskāra: नमस्कार "Reverent salutations." Traditional Hindu verbal greeting and *mudrā* where the palms are joined together and held before the heart or raised to the level of the forehead. The *mudrā* is also called *añjali.*

namaste: नमस्ते "Reverent salutations to you." A traditional verbal greeting. A form of *namas,* meaning "bowing, obeisance." See: *namaskāra.*

Nandī: नन्दी "The joyful." A white bull with a black tail, the *vāhana,* or mount, of Lord Śiva, symbol of the powerful instinctive force tamed by Him. Nandī is the perfect devotee, the soul of man, kneeling humbly before God Śiva, ever concentrated on Him. The ideal and goal of the Śiva *bhakta* is to behold Śiva in everything. See: *vāhana.*

Nandinātha Sampradāya: नन्दिनाथसंप्रदाय See: *Nātha Sampradāya.*

Naraka: नरक Abode of darkness. Literally, "pertaining to man." The lower worlds. Equivalent to the Western term *hell,* a gross region of the Antarloka. Naraka is a congested, distressful area where demonic beings and young souls may sojourn until they resolve the darksome *karmas* they have created. Here beings suffer the consequences of their own misdeeds in previous lives. *Naraka* is understood as having seven regions, called *tala,* corresponding to the states of consciousness of the seven lower *chakras* as follows: 1) Put, "childless"—*atala chakra,* "wheel of the bottomless region." Fear and lust (located in the hips). 2) Avīchi, "joyless"—*vitala chakra:* "wheel of negative region." Center of anger (thighs). 3) Saṁhāta, "abandoned"—*sutala chakra:* "Great depth." Region of jealousy (knees). 4) Tāmisra, "darkness"—*talātala chakra:* "wheel of the lower region." Realm of confused thinking (calves). 5) Ṛijīsha, "expelled"—*rasātala chakra:* "wheel of subterranean region." Selfishness (ankles). 6) Kuḍmala, "leprous"—*mahātala chakra:* "wheel of the great lower region." Region of consciencelessness (feet). The intensity of "hell" begins at this deep level. 7) Kākola, "black poison"—*pātāla chakra,* "wheel of the fallen or sinful level." Region of malice (soles of the feet). See: *hell, loka, purgatory (also, individual tala entries).*

nārikela: नारिकेल "Coconut." In front of Gaṇeśa shrines the world over, husked coconuts are broken as an act of prayer, symbolizing the ego's shattering to reveal the soul's innate sweet, pure nature. The coconut circled by five mango leaves nested on a pot or water is worshiped as a Deity image, especially Lord Gaṇeśa, during certain *pūjā* rites.

Naṭarāja: नटराज "King of Dance, or King of Dancers." God as the Cosmic Dancer. Perhaps Hinduism's richest and most eloquent symbol, Naṭarāja represents Śiva, the Primal Soul, Parameśvara, as the power, energy and life of all that exists. This is Śiva's intricate state of Being in Manifestation. See: *nāda, Parameśvara, Parāśakti, Paraśiva.*

Natchintanai: நற்சிந்தனை The collected songs of Sage Yogaswāmī (1872–1964) of Jaffna, Sri Lanka, extolling the power of the *satguru,* worship of Lord Śiva, the path of *dharma* and the attainment of Self Realization.

Nātha: नाथ "Master, lord; adept." Names an ancient Himalayan tradition of Śaiva-yoga mysticism, whose first historically known exponent was Nandikeśvara (ca 250 BCE). *Nātha*—Self-Realized adept—refers to the extraordinary ascetic masters of this school. The *Nāthas* are considered the source of *haṭha* as well as *rāja yoga.*

Nātha Sampradāya: नाथसंप्रदाय "Traditional doctrine of knowledge of masters." *Sampradāya* means a living stream of tradition or theology. Nātha Sampradāya is a philosophical and *yogic* tradition of Śaivism whose origins are unknown. This oldest of Śaivite *sampradāyas* existing today consists of two major streams: the Nandinātha and the Ādinātha. See: *Kailāsa Paramparā, Nātha, Śaivism, sampradāya.*

Nayanar: நாயனார் "Teacher." The 63 canonized Tamil saints of South India, as documented in the *Periyapurāṇam* by Sekkilar (ca 1140). All but a few were householders, recognized as outstanding exemplars of devotion to Lord Śiva. Several contributed to the Śaiva Siddhānta scriptural compendium called *Tirumurai.*

negative attachment: A fear, worry or doubt of the future or a lingering regret about the past that keeps one from "flowing with the river of life," living fully in the moment as an independent, spiritual being, facing each experience in the light of understanding.

nervine: An ingestive substance that strengthens activity of the nervous system, such as stimulants and sedatives.

nīlapadma: नीलपद्म "Blue water lily."

Nirguṇa Brahman: निर्गुणब्रह्मन् "God without qualities." See: *Brahman.*

nityavāk: नित्यवाक् "The eternal Word." An expression from the *Vedas* describing the primal sound, the Word, the first impulse of creation. See: *vāk.*

nivedana: निवेदन "Announcement." The dedication of a book.

niyama: नियम "Restraint." See: *yama-niyama.*

nondualism: "Not two." Refers to monistic philosophy. See: *advaita, monism, monistic theism, Vedānta.*

Nṛitya Gaṇapati: नृत्यगणपति A name and traditional *mūrti,* or form, of Gaṇeśa. "He who is dancing," a four-armed golden *mūrti* under a *kalpavṛiksha,* wish-fulfilling, tree.

nurture: To raise or promote development, train; educate or foster.

occult: Hidden, or kept secret; revealed only after initiation.

olai: ஓலை "Leaf." An ancient form of Indian books used in South India, made of strips of fronds from the palmyra *(triṇḍruma)* and talipot (*tālapatra,* "fan-leaf") palms. Prepared birch bark *(bhūrja patra)* was the medium in the North. These books are small in size, averaging about 2 inches high and 8 inches wide and up to 11 or 12 inches thick, wound with string and generally protected in colored cloth.

old soul: One who has reincarnated many times, experienced much and is therefore farther along the path. Old souls may be recognized by their qualities of compassion, self-effacement and wisdom. See: *soul.*

Om: ओम् "Yes, verily." The most sacred *mantra* of Hinduism. An alternate transliteration of *Aum* (the sounds A and U blend to become O). See: *Aum.*

Oṁkāra: ओंकार A name of God as the source, or creator, of Primal Sound, Aum. See: *Aum.*

omnipotent: All-powerful. Able to do anything.

omnipresent: Present everywhere and in all things.

omniscient: Having infinite knowledge, all-knowing.

ordain (ordination): To give someone the duties and responsibilities, authority and spiritual power of a religious office, such as priest, minister or *satguru,* through religious ceremony or mystical initiation. See: *dīkshā.*

orifice of Brahman: See: *door of Brahman.*

pada: पद् "A step, pace, stride; footstep, trace."

pāda: पाद् "The foot (of men and animals); quarter-part, section; stage; path." Names the four major sections of the Āgamic texts and the corresponding stages of practice and unfoldment on the path to *moksha.*)—***charyā pāda:*** "Good conduct stage." The first stage where one learns to live righteously, serve selflessly, performing *karma yoga.* Traditional acts of *charyā* include cleaning the temple, lighting lamps and collecting flowers for worship. Worship at this stage is mostly external. —***kriyā pāda:*** "Religious action; worship stage." Stage of *bhakti yoga,* of cultivating devotion through performing *pūjā* and regular daily *sādhana.* A central practice of the *kriyā pāda* is performing daily *pūjā.* —***yoga pāda:*** Having matured in the *charyā* and *kriyā pādas,* the soul now turns to internalized worship and *rāja yoga* under the guidance of a *satguru.* It is a time of *sādhana* and serious striving when realization of the Self is the goal. —***jñāna pāda:*** "Stage of wisdom." Once the soul has attained Realization, it is henceforth a wise one, who lives out the life of the body, shedding blessings on mankind. This stage is also called the San Mārga, "true path." See: *jñāna, yoga.*

pāda pūjā: पादपूजा "Foot worship." Ceremonial worship of the *guru's* sandals or holy feet, often through ablution with precious substances and offering of fruit and flowers. After the ceremony, the water of the bath, the fruit and other precious substances are partaken of as *prasāda* by the devotees. See: *guru, guru bhakti, pādukā, prasāda, ucçhishṭa.*

padma: पद्म The lotus flower, *Nelumbo nucifera,* symbol of spiritual development and the *chakras.* Because it grows out of mud and rises to perfect purity and glory, it is an apt representation of spiritual unfoldment.

padmāsana: पद्मासन "Lotus posture." The most famous *haṭha yoga āsana,* the optimum pose for sustained meditation. The legs are crossed, the soles of the feet upward, resembling a lotus flower. In this pose the intellectual-emotional energies are balanced and quieted. See: *rāja yoga, yoga.*

pādukā: पादुका "Sandals." *Śrī Pādukā* refers to the sandals of the preceptor, the traditional icon of the *guru,* representing his holy feet and worshiped as the source of grace. *Pādukā* also names one of Vīra Śaivism's eight aids *(ashṭāvaraṇa)* to faith—the practice of drinking the water from the ceremonial washing of the Śivaliṅga or the *guru's* feet. See: *guru bhakti, prasāda, satguru, ucçhishṭa.*

panasa phala: पनसफल "Jackfruit."

Pancha Gaṇapati: पञ्चगणपति A name and *mūrti* of Gaṇeśa with five *(pañcha)* heads. Gaṇeśa in this form is worshiped especially during the Pañcha Gaṇapati festival, December 20-25, a time of gift-giving, celebration and renewal of harmony in personal relationships.

Pañchākshara Mantra: पञ्चाक्षरमन्त्र "Five-lettered chant." Śaivism's most sacred *mantra, Namaḥ Śivaya,* "Homage to Siva." See: *Namaḥ Śivāya.*

pañcha kriya(s): पञ्चक्रिय "Five duties." See: *pañcha nitya karma(s).*

pañcha kuṭumba sādhana: पञ्चकुटुम्ब साधन "Five family disciplines" or parenting guidelines for raising children as strong, secure, responsible, tolerant and traditional citizens. 1) ***dharmāchāra:*** Good conduct. 2) ***dharma svagṛiha:*** Home worship. 3) ***dharma sambhāshana:*** Talking about religion. 4) ***dharma svādhyāya:*** Continuing self-study. 5) ***dharma saṅga:*** Following a spiritual preceptor.

pañchāṅga: पञ्चाङ्ग "Five limbs." The traditional Hindu sacred calendar, so named for its five basic elements: *tithi* (lunar day), *nakshatra* (asterism), *kāraṇa* (half lunar day), *yoga* (sun-moon angle) and *vāra* (week day). *Pañchāṅgas* are used by priests, astrologers and lay persons to determine the optimum times for various types of actitivies.

pañcha mahāyajñas: पञ्चमहायज्ञ The five daily *yajñas,* or sacrifices, of the householder (outlined in the *Dharma Śāstras): —**brahma yajña:*** (also called *Veda yajña* or *ṛishi yajña*) "Homage to the seers." Accomplished through studying and teaching the *Vedas. —**deva yajña:*** "Homage to Gods and elementals." Recognizing the debt due to those who guide nature, and the feeding of them by pouring into the fire. This is the *homa* sacrifice. ***—pitṛi yajña* (or *pitṛi tarpana):*** "Homage to ancestors." Offering of cakes *(piṇḍa)* and water to the family line and the progenitors of mankind. ***—bhūta***

yajña: "Homage to beings." Placing food-offerings, *bali,* on the ground, intended for animals, birds, insects, wandering outcastes and beings of the invisible worlds. ***—manushya yajña:*** "Homage to men." Feeding guests and the poor, the homeless and the student. *Manushya yajña* includes all acts of philanthropy, such as tithing and charity. The Vedic study is performed in the morning. The other four *yajñas* are performed just before taking one's noon meal.

pañcha nitya karma(s): पञ्चनित्यकर्म "Five constant duties." A traditional regimen of religious practice for Hindus: 1) *dharma* (virtuous living), 2) *upāsanā* (worship), 3) *utsava* (holy days), 4) *tīrthayātrā* (pilgrimage) and 5) *saṁskāras* (sacraments.) See: *dharma, festival, pilgrimage, saṁskāra.*

pañcha śraddhā: पञ्चश्रद्धा "Five faiths, or precepts." A concise summary of Hindu belief exactly correlated to the "five constant practices," *pañcha nitya karmas.* The *pañcha śraddhā* are 1) *sarva* Brahman: God is All in all, soul is divine; 2) *mandira:* belief in temples and divine beings; 3) *karma:* cosmic justice; 4) *saṁsāra–moksha:* rebirth brings enlightenment and liberation; 5) *Vedas* and *satguru:* the necessity of scripture and preceptor. See: *pañcha nitya karma.*

paṇḍita: पण्डित See: *pundit.*

pantheon: The array of all Gods of a people or religious denomination.

pāpa: पाप "Wickedness; sin, crime." 1) Bad or evil. 2) Wrongful action. 3) Demerit earned through wrongdoing. Pāpa includes all forms of wrongdoing, from the simplest infraction to the most heinous crime. Each act of *pāpa* carries its *karmic* consequence, *karmaphala,* "fruit of action," for which scriptures delineate specific penance for expiation. See: *evil, karma, penance, puṇya, sin.*

Paramātman: परमात्मन् "Supreme Self," or "transcendent soul." Paraśiva, Absolute Reality, the one transcendent Self of every soul. Contrasted with *ātman,* which includes all three aspects of the soul: *Paraśiva, Parāśakti* and *ānandamaya kośa.* See: *Paraśiva, Self, soul.*

paramount: Ranking higher than any other in importance.

Parameśvara: परमेश्वर "Supreme Lord or Ruler." God Śiva in the third perfection as Supreme Mahādeva, Śiva-Śakti, mother of the universe. In this perfection as Personal, father-mother God, Śiva is a person—who has a body, with head, arms and legs, etc.—who acts, wills, blesses, gives *darśana,* guides, creates, preserves, reabsorbs, obscures and enlightens. See: *Naṭarāja.*

paramparā: परंपरा "Uninterrupted succession." Lineage. See: *guru paramparā.*

parārtha pūjā: परार्थपूजा "Public liturgy and worship." See: *pūjā.*

Parāśakti: पराशक्ति "Supreme power; primal energy." God Śiva's second perfection, which is impersonal, immanent, and with form—the all-pervasive, Pure Consciousness and Primal Substance of all that exists. There are many other descriptive names for Parāśakti—Satchidānanda ("existence-consciousness-bliss"), light, silence, divine mind, superconsciousness and more. The attainment of Parāśakti is called *savikalpa samādhi.* See: *Śiva.*

***Paraśiva:* परशिव** "Transcendent Śiva." The Self God, Śiva in His first perfection, Absolute Reality. God Śiva as *That* which is beyond the grasp of consciousness, transcends time, form and space and defies description. Attainment of this is called Self Realization or *nirvikalpa samādhi.* See: *samādhi, Śiva.*

***paraśu:* परशु** "Axe."

***Paraśvadha:* परश्वध** "Battleaxe."

***Paravāk:* परवाक्** "The Primal Word." See: *vāk.*

***Pārvatī:* पार्वती** "Mountain's daughter." One of many names for the Universal Mother. Prayers are offered to Her for strength, health and eradication of impurities. Mythologically, Pārvatī is wedded to Śiva. See: *Goddess, Śakti.*

***pāśa*: पाश** "Tether; noose." The whole of existence, manifest and unmanifest. That which binds or limits the soul and keeps it (for a time) from manifesting its full potential. *Pāśa* refers to the soul's three-fold bondage of *āṇava, karma* and *māyā.* See: *liberation, mala, Pati-paśu-pāśa.*

***Pāshāṇadāraṇa:* पाषाणदारण** "Pick axe."

***paśyānti vāk:* पश्यान्ति वाक्** "The word that perceives." See: *vāk.*

***pātāla:* पाताल** "Fallen or sinful region." The seventh *chakra* below the *mūlādhāra,* centered in the soles of the feet. Corresponds to the seventh and lowest astral netherworld beneath the earth's surface, called Kākola ("black poison") or Pātāla. This is the realm in which misguided souls indulge in destruction for the sake of destruction, of torture, and of murder for the sake of murder. *Pātāla* also names the netherworld in general, and is a synonym for *Naraka.* See: *chakra, loka, Naraka.*

***Patañjali:* पतञ्जलि** A Śaivite Nātha *siddha* (ca 200 BCE) who codified the ancient *yoga* philosophy which outlines the path to enlightenment through purification, control and transcendence of the mind. One of the six classical philosophical systems *(darśanas)* of Hinduism, known as Yoga Darśana. His great work, the *Yoga Sūtras,* comprises 200 aphorisms delineating *ashṭāṅga* (eight-limbed), *rāja* (kingly) or *siddha* (perfection) *yoga.* Still today it is the foremost text on meditative *yoga.* See: *rāja yoga, yoga.*

***pāṭ haśāla:* पाठशाल** "Place of lessons." A school for training temple priests.

***Pati:* पति** "Master; lord; owner." A name for God Śiva indicating His commanding relationship with souls as caring ruler and helpful guide. In Śaiva Siddhānta the term is part of the analogy of cowherd *(pati),* cows *(paśu,* souls) and the tether *(pāśa—āṇava, karma* and *māyā)* by which cows are tied. See: Pati-*paśu-pāśa, Śiva.*

***Pati-paśu-pāśa:* पति पशु पाश** Literally: "master, cow and tether." These are the three primary elements (*padārtha,* or *tattvatrayī)* of Śaiva Siddhānta philosophy: God, soul and world—Divinity, man and cosmos—seen as a mystically and intricately interrelated unity. Pati is God, envisioned as a cowherd. *Paśu* is the soul, envisioned as a cow. *Pāśa* is the all-important force or fetter by which God brings souls along the path to Truth. See: *pāśa, Śaiva Siddhānta, soul.*

***pātra:* पात्र** Worthy; literally, a "recepticle" as in a drinking vessel. The condition of being a fit recepticle for.

patronymic: A name derived from the name of a father or ancestor, especially through a suffix or prefix indicating descent.

pāyasa: पायस "Prepared with milk." Tapioca or rice pudding.

penance: *Prāyaśchitta.* Atonement, expiation. An act of devotion *(bhakti),* austerity *(tapas)* or discipline *(sukṛitya)* undertaken to soften or nullify the anticipated reaction to a past action. Penance is uncomfortable *karma* inflicted upon oneself to mitigate one's *karmic* burden caused by wrongful actions *(kukarma).* It includes such acts as prostrating 108 times, fasting, self-denial, or carrying *kavadi* (public penance), as well as more extreme austerities, or *tapas.* See: *evil, kavadi, pāpa, sin.*

perpetuate: Cause to continue or be remembered; to keep from being lost.

Periyapurāṇam: பெரிய புராணம் Twelfth book of the *Tirumurai.* Story of the 63 Śaiva Nayanar saints of Tamil Nadu, written by Sekkilar (CA 1140).

phala: फल "fruit."

pilgrimage: *Tīrthayātrā.* "Journeying to a holy place." Pilgrimage. One of the five sacred duties *(pañcha nitya karmas)* of the Hindu is to journey periodically to one of the innumerable holy spots in India or other countries. Preceded by fasting and continence, it is a time of austerity and purification, when all worldly concerns are set aside and God becomes one's singular focus. See: *pañcha nitya karma.*

piṅgalā: पिंगला "Tawny channel." The masculine psychic current flowing along the spine. See: *kuṇḍalinī, nāḍī, rāja yoga.*

pitṛi tarpaṇa: पितृ तर्पण "Libations to ancestors." A sacred rite of offering water to deceased ancestors. One of the five daily sacrifices prescribed in the *Dharma Śāstras.* See: *pañcha mahāyajñas.*

pitta: पित्त "Bile; fire." One of the three bodily humors, called *doshas, pitta* is known as the fire humor. It is the *āyurvedic* principle of bodily heat-energy. *Pitta dosha* governs nutritional absorption, body temperature and intelligence. See: *āyurveda, dosha.*

plague: To distress, afflict, trouble or torment.

poultice: A soft, moist mass of medicative substances, usually folded into a cloth bandage, for external application to a wound or inflammation.

polytheism: Belief in or worship of many Gods. See: *monotheism.*

pontiff: A high priest, a spiritual leader endowed with great authority.

prabhāvalī: प्रभावली "Luminous circle." The ornate arch, made of stone or metal, that stands just behind and above Deity images in temples and shrines. It connotes the cycle of creation, preservation and destruction. At the top of the arch is the fierce face of Mahākāla, the God of time, who transcends form and ultimately claims everything.

pradakshiṇā: प्रदक्षिणा "Moving to the right." Worshipful circumambulation, walking clockwise around the temple sanctum or other holy place, with the intention of shifting the mind from worldly concerns to awareness of the Divine. *Clockwise* has esoteric significance in that the *chakras* of *mūlādhāra* and above spin clockwise, while those below spin counterclockwise, taking one down into the lower regions of selfishness, greed, conflict and turmoil.

prakṛiti: प्रकृति "Primary matter; nature." In the 25-*tattva* Sāṅkhya system—which concerns itself only with the tangible spectrum of creation—*prakṛiti,* or *pradhāna,* is one of two supreme beginningless realities: matter and spirit, *prakṛiti* and *purusha,* the female and male principles. *Prakṛiti* is the manifesting aspect, as contrasted with the quiescent unmanifest—*purusha,* which is pure consciousness. In Śāktism, *prakṛiti,* the active principle, is personified as Devī, the Goddess, and is synonymous with Māyā. Prakṛiti is thus often seen, and depicted so in the *Purāṇas,* as the Divine Mother, whose love and care embrace and comfort all beings. In Śaivite cosmology, *prakṛiti* is the 24th of 36 *tattvas,* the potentiality of the physical cosmos, the gross energy from which all lower *tattvas* are formed. Its three qualities are *sattva, rajas* and *tamas.* See: *purusha, tattva.*

prāṇa: प्राण Vital energy or life principle. Literally, "vital air," from the root *praṇ,* "to breathe." *Prāṇa* in the human body moves in the *prāṇamaya kośa* as five primary life currents known as *vāyus,* "vital airs or winds." These are *prāṇa* (outgoing breath), *apāṇa* (incoming breath), *vyāṇa* (retained breath), *udāṇa* (ascending breath) and *samāṇa* (equalizing breath). Each governs crucial bodily functions, and all bodily energies are modifications of these. Usually *prāṇa* refers to the life principle, but sometimes denotes energy, power or the animating force of the cosmos. See: *kośa, tattva.*

praṇāma: प्रणाम "Obeisance; to bow down." Reverent salutation in which the head or body is bowed. ***—ashṭāṅga praṇāma:*** "Eight-limbed obeisance." The full body form for men, in which the hands, chest, forehead, knees and feet touch the ground. (Same as *śashṭāṇga praṇāma.*) ***—pañchāṅga praṇāma:*** "Five-limbed obeisance." The woman's form of prostration, in which the hands, head and legs touch the ground (with the ankles crossed, right over the left). A more exacting term for prostration is *praṇipāta,* "falling down in obeisance." See: *bhakti, namaskāra, prapatti.*

Praṇava: प्रणव "Humming." The mantra *Aum,* denoting God as the Primal Sound. It can be heard as the sound of one's own nerve system, like the sound of an electrical transformer or a swarm of bees. The meditator is taught to inwardly transform this sound into the inner light which lights the thoughts, and bask in this blissful consciousness. Praṇava is also known as the sound of the *nādanāḍī śakti.* See: *Aum, Śiva Consciousness.*

prāṇāyāma: प्राणायाम "Breath control." See: *rāja yoga.*

prapatti: प्रपत्ति "Throwing oneself down." *Bhakti*—total, unconditional submission to God, often coupled with the attitude of personal helplessness, self-effacement and resignation. A term especially used in Vaishṇavism to name a concept extremely central to virtually all Hindu schools. See: *bhakti, grace, pāda, surrender.*

prārabdha karma: प्रारब्धकर्म "Action that has been unleashed or aroused." See: *karma.*

prasāda: **प्रसाद** "Clarity, brightness; grace." 1) The virtue of serenity and graciousness. 2) Food offered to the Deity or the *guru,* or the blessed remnants of such food. 3) Any propitiatory offering. See: *sacrament.*

praśnottara: **प्रश्नोत्तर** "Question-answer *(praśna-uttara).*" A term used in *Dancing with Śiva* for *catechism,* an interrogatory summation of religious doctrine.

precept: A commandment meant as a rule of action or conduct.

preceptor: Highly respected teacher and head of a spiritual order and clan; the equivalent of the word *satguru.*

preside: To be chairman at a gathering, in a position of authority within a group. To have charge of; to dominate.

Primal Soul: The uncreated, original, perfect soul—Śiva Parameśvara—who emanates from Himself the inner and outer universes and an infinite plurality of individual souls whose essence is identical with His essence. God in His personal aspect as Lord and Creator, depicted in many forms: Naṭarāja by Śaivites, Vishṇu by Vaishṇavites, Devī by Śāktas. See: *Naṭarāja, Parameśvara.*

prostration: See: *praṇāma.*

Primal Sound: In Hinduism, sound is the first manifestation, even before light, in the creative scheme of things. The Primal Sound is also known as *Praṇava,* the sound of the *mula mantra,* "Aum." See: *Praṇava.*

pṛithivī tattva: **पृथिवी तत्त्व** "Earth element." See: *tanmātra, tattva.*

protocol: Customs of proper etiquette and ceremony, especially in relation to religious or political dignitaries. See: *culture.*

psoriasis: A chronic skin disease characterized by scaly, reddish patches.

psychic: "Of the psyche or soul." Sensitive to spiritual processes and energies. Inwardly or intuitively aware of nonphysical realities; able to use powers such as clairvoyance, clairaudience and precognition. Nonphysical, subtle; pertaining to the deeper aspects of man. See: *clairaudience, clairvoyance.*

pūjā: **पूजा** "Worship, adoration." An Āgamic rite of worship performed in the home, temple or shrine, to the *mūrti* (Deity image), *śrī pādukā* (holy sandals), or other consecrated object, or to a person, such as the *satguru.* Its inner purpose is to purify the atmosphere around the object worshiped, establish a connection with the inner worlds and invoke the presence of God, Gods or one's *guru.* During *pūjā,* the officiant *(pujārī)* recites various chants praising the Divine and beseeching divine blessings, while making offerings in accordance with established traditions. *Pūjā,* the worship of a *mūrti* through water, lights and flowers in temples and shrines, is the Āgamic counterpart of the Vedic *yajña* rite, in which offerings are conveyed through the sacred *homa* fire. These are the two great streams of adoration and communion in Hinduism. ***—ātmārtha pūjā:*** *Kāraṇa Āgama,* v. 2, states: *Ātmārtha cha parārtha cha pūjā dvividhamuchyate,* "Worship is two-fold: for the benefit of oneself and for the benefit of others." *Ātmārtha pūjā* is done for oneself and immediate family, usually at home in a private shrine. ***—parārtha pūjā:*** "*Pūjā* for others." *Parārtha pūjā* is public *pūjā,* performed by authorized or ordained priests in a public shrine or temple.

pujārī: पुजारी "Worshiper." A general term for Hindu temple priests, as well as anyone performing *pūjā*. *Pujārī* (sometimes *pūjārī*) is the Hindi form of the Sanskṛit *pūjaka; pūsārī* in Tamil. *Archaka* is another term for priest used in the southern tradition. *Purohita* is a Smārta *brāhmin* priest who specializes in domestic rites. See: *pūjā*.

pundit *(paṇḍita):* पण्डित A Hindu religious scholar or theologian, a man well versed in philosophy, liturgy, religious law and sacred science.

punarjanma: पुनर्जन्म "Reincarnation." From *punaḥ*, "again and again," and *janma*, "taking birth." See: *reincarnation*.

puṇya: पुण्य "Holy; virtuous; auspicious." 1) Good or righteous. 2) Meritorious action. 3) Merit earned through right thought, word and action. *Puṇya* includes all forms of doing good, from the simplest helpful deed to a lifetime of conscientious beneficence. Each act of *puṇya* carries its *karmic* consequence, *karmaphala*, "fruit of action"—the positive reward of actions, words and deeds that are in keeping with *dharma*. See: *karma, pāpa, penance*.

Purāṇa: पुराण "Ancient." Hindu folk narratives containing ethical and cosmological teachings relative to Gods, man and the world. They revolve around five subjects: primary creation, secondary creation, genealogy, cycles of time and history. There are 18 major *Purāṇas* which are designated as either Śaivite, Vaishṇavite or Śākta.

Pure Consciousness: See: *Parāśakti*.

purusha: पुरुष "The spirit that dwells in the body/in the universe." Person; spirit; man. Metaphysically, the soul, neither male nor female. Also used in Yoga and Sāṅkhya for the transcendent Self. A synonym for *ātman*. *Purusha* can also refer to the Supreme Being or Soul, as it sometimes does in the *Upanishads*. In the *Ṛig Veda* hymn "Purusha Sūkta," Purusha is the cosmic man, having a thousand heads, a thousand eyes, a thousand feet and encompassing the earth, spreading in all directions into animate and inanimate things. In the Sāṅkhya system, *purusha* is one of two supreme, beginningless realities: spirit and matter, *purusha* and *prakṛiti*, the male and female principles. It is the quiescent unmanifest, pure consciousness, contrasted with *Prakṛiti*, the manifesting, primal nature from which the cosmos unfolds. See: *ātman, jīva, prakṛiti, soul, tattva*.

purushārtha: पुरुषार्थ "Human wealth or purpose." The four pursuits in which humans may legitimately engage, a basic principle of Hindu ethics. ***—dharma:*** "Righteous living." The fulfillment of virtue, good works, duties and responsibilities, restraints and observances—performing one's part in the service and upliftment of society. This includes pursuit of truth under a *guru* of a particular *paramparā* and *sampradāya*. See: *dharma*. ***—artha:*** "Wealth." Material welfare and abundance, money, property, possessions. *Artha* is the pursuit of wealth, guided by *dharma*. It includes the basic needs—food, money, clothing and shelter—and extends to the wealth required to maintain a comfortable home, raise a family, fulfill a successful career and perform religious duties. See: *yajña.* **—*kāma:*** "Pleasure, love; enjoyment." Earthly love, aesthetic and cultural fulfillment, pleasures of the world (including sexual), the joys of family, intellectual satisfaction. Enjoyment of happiness, security, creativity, usefulness and inspiration. **—*moksha:*** "Liberation." Freedom from rebirth through the ultimate attainment, realization of the Self God, Paraśiva. The spiritual attainments and superconscious joys, attending renunciation and *yoga* leading to Self Realization. *Moksha* comes through the fulfillment of *dharma, artha* and *kāma* in the current or past lives, so that one is no longer attached to worldly joys or sorrows. See: *liberation, moksha.*

pushpaśara: पुष्पशर "Flower arrow." A weapon wielded by loving Gaṇeśa.

quantum: Quantity or amount. In science's quantum theory: a fixed basic unit, usually of energy. **—quantum particles of light:** Light understood not as a continuum, but as traveling bundles each of a same intensity. Deeper still, these particles originate and resolve themselves in a one divine energy. **—at the quantum level (of the mind):** Deep within the mind, at a subtle energy level.

quatrain: A stanza or poem of four lines.

quell: To quiet, subdue or put an end to.

Rādhākṛishṇan, Dr. S.: राधाकृष्णन् (1888-1975) The president of India from 1962 to 1967, a scholar, philosopher, prolific writer, compelling speaker and effective spokesman of Hinduism. Along with Vivekānanda, Tagore, Aurobindo and others, he helped bring about the current Hindu revival. He made Hinduism better known and appreciated at home and abroad, especially in the intellectual world. He was a foremost proponent of panentheism. See: *Vedānta.*

rāga: राग "That which enraptures." In the structure of melody in Indian music, a specific collection of sounds or notes. *Rāga* is similar to "scale" in Western notation but *rāga* includes the unique emotional or mystical mood created when the melody is heard.

rajas: रजस् "Passion; activity." See: *guṇa.*

rāja yoga: राजयोग "King of *yogas.*" Also known as *ashṭāṅga yoga,* "eight-limbed *yoga.*" The classical *yoga* system of eight progressive stages to Illumination as described in various *yoga Upanishads,* the *Tirumantiram* and, most notably, the *Yoga Sūtras* of Patañjali. The eight stages are: *yama* (restraints), *niyama* (observances), *āsana* (posture), *prāṇāyāma* (breath control) *pratyāhara* (withdrawal), *dhāraṇa* (concentration), *dhyāna* (meditation) and *samādhi* (enstasy, mystic oneness). See: *enstasy, samādhi, yoga.*

Rāma: राम Venerated hero of the *Rāmāyaṇa* epic, and one of the two most popular incarnations of Vishṇu, along with Kṛishṇa. His worship is almost universal among Vaishṇavas, and extensive among Smārtas and other liberal Hindus. He was a great worshiper of Śiva, and a Śiva temple, called Rāmeśvaram, was built in his name at the southern tip of India.

***Rāmakṛishṇa:* रामकृष्ण** (1836–1886) One of the great saints and mystics of modern Hinduism, and an exemplar of monistic theism—fervent devotee of Mother Kālī and staunch monist who taught oneness and the pursuit of *nirvikalpa samādhi*, realization of the Absolute. He was *guru* to the great Swāmī Vivekānanda (1863–1902), who internationalized Hindu thought and philosophy.

***Rāmānuja:* रामानुज** Philosopher (1017–1137), saint, great *bhakta*, founder of one of five major Vaishṇava schools, and considered the greatest critic of *advaita*. In his famous *Śrī Bhāshya* on the *Brahma Sūtras*, he countered Śaṅkara's absolute monism point-by-point with his qualified monism, called *Viśishṭādvaita Vedānta*. See: *Vedānta*.

***Rāmāyaṇa:* रामायण** "Life of Rāma." One of India's two grand epics *(Itihāsa)* along with the *Mahābhārata*. It is Valmiki's tragic love story of Rāma and Sītā, whose exemplary lives have helped set high standards of dignity and nobility as an integral part of Hindu *dharma*. Astronomical data in the story puts Rāma's reign at about 2015 BCE. See: *Rāma*.

***raṅgoli:* रङ्गोलि** Traditional household and priestly art of "drawing" intricate decorative patterns at the entrance to a home or temple or at the site of a religious ceremony. Known as *kolam* in Tamil. *Raṅgoli* designs are made with rice powder mixed to a watery paste, and sometimes with flowers and various-colored powdered pulses.

***rasātala:* रसातल** "Subterranean region." The fifth *chakra* below the *mūlādhāra*, centered in the ankles. Corresponds to the fifth astral netherworld beneath the earth's surface, called Ṛijīsha ("expelled") or Rasātala. Region of selfishness, self-centeredness and possessiveness. *Rasā* means "earth, soil; moisture." See: *chakra, loka, Naraka*.

***rasāyana:* रसायन** "Rejuvenative." A food which rejuvenates and balances the *doshas*, *āyurvedic* super-foods and herbal preparations such as *chywanprash* (made from *amala* fruit) and *triphala*.

***ratnakumbha:* रत्नकुम्भ** "Pot of gems."

reaction: A response to an action.

reconciliation: To harmonize quarrels or mend differences. A tithing reconciliation is a written accounting of income and tithing.

reincarnate: Taking birth in another body, having lived and died before.

reincarnation: "Re-entering the flesh." *Punarjanma;* metempsychosis. The process wherein souls take on a physical body through the birth process. The cycle of reincarnation ends when *karma* has been resolved and the Self God (Paraśiva) has been realized. This condition of release is called *moksha*. Then the soul continues to evolve and mature, but without the need to return to physical existence. See: *karma, moksha, saṁsāra, soul*.

religion: From Latin *religare,* "to bind back." Any system which advocates the belief in and worship of a Supreme Being or Power. Religion is a structured vehicle for soul advancement which often includes theology, scripture, spiritual and moral practices, priesthood and liturgy. See: *Hinduism.*

remorse: Deep guilt or regret over a wrong one has committed.

renunciate: One who has given up worldly life; a monk. See: *sannyāsin.*

restraints: See: *yama-niyama.*

Ṛig Veda: ऋग्वेद् "*Veda* of verse *(ṛik).*" The first and oldest of the four *Veda* compendia of revealed scriptures *(śruti),* including a hymn collection *(Saṁhitā),* priestly explanatory manuals *(Brāhmaṇas),* forest treatises *(Āraṇyakas)* elaborating on the Vedic rites, and philosophical dialogs *(Upanishads).* The oldest and core portion is the *Saṁhitā,* believed to date back, in its oral form, as far as 8,000 years. It embodies prayerful hymns of praise and invocation to the Divinities of nature and to the One Divine. The *Ṛig Veda Saṁhitā,* which in length equals Homer's *Iliad* and *Odyssey* combined, is the most important Vedic hymn collection, for it lends a large number of its hymns to the other three *Veda Saṁhitās* (the *Sāma, Yajur* and *Atharva).* Chronologically, after the *Saṁhitās* came the *Brāhmaṇas,* followed by the *Āraṇyakas,* and finally the *Upanishads,* also called the *Vedānta,* meaning "*Veda's* end." See: *śruti, Vedas.*

Ṛiṇamochana Gaṇapati: ऋणमोचनगणपति "The remover of bondage" is unique in that He holds a rose apple, goad, noose and His broken tusk.

ṛishi: ऋषि "Seer." A term for an enlightened being, emphasizing psychic perception and visionary wisdom.

rite (or ritual): A religious ceremony. See: *sacrament, sacrifice, saṁskāra.*

rites of passage: Sacraments marking crucial stages of life. See: *saṁskāra.*

Rudra: रुद्र् "Controller of terrific powers;" or "red, shining one." The name of Śiva as the God of dissolution, the universal force of reabsorption. *Rudra-Śiva* is revered both as the "terrifying one" and the "lord of tears," for He wields and controls the terrific powers which may cause lamentation among humans. See: *Naṭarāja.*

rudrāksha: रुद्राक्ष "Eye of Rudra; or red-eyed." Refers to the third eye, or *ājñā chakra.* Marble-sized, multi-faced, reddish-brown seeds from the *Eleocarpus ganitrus,* or blue marble tree, which are sacred to Śiva and a symbol of His compassion for humanity. Garlands, *rudrāksha mālā,* of larger seeds are worn around the neck by monks, and nonmonastics, both men and women, often wear a single bead on a cord at the throat. Smaller beads (usually numbering 108) are strung together for *japa* (recitation). See: *japa, mantra.*

rudrāksha mālā: रुद्राक्षमाला "Garland of Śiva's tears." A strand of prayer beads, usually 108, to count the repetitions of a sacred *mantra.* Gaṇeśa holding a *japa mālā* reminds us all to perform our daily *japa yoga.*

śabda kośa: शब्दकोश "Sheath of sounds, or words." Vocabulary; a dictionary or glossary of terms.

sacrament: 1) Holy rite, especially one solemnized in a formal, consecrated manner which is a bonding between the recipient and God, Gods or *guru.* This includes rites of passage *(saṁskāra),* ceremonies sanctifying crucial events or stages of life. 2) *Prasāda.* Sacred substances, blessed in ceremony or by a holy person. See: *saṁskāra.*

sacred thread: *Yajñopavīta.* See: *upanayana.*

sacrifice: *Yajña.* 1) Giving offerings to a Deity as an expression of homage and devotion. 2) Giving up something, often one's own possession, advantage or preference, to serve a higher purpose. The literal meaning of *sacrifice* is "to make sacred," implying an act of worship. It is the most common translation of the term *yajña.* See: *surrender.*

sādhaka: साधक "Accomplished one; a devotee who performs *sādhana.*" A serious aspirant who has undertaken spiritual disciplines, is usually celibate and under the guidance of a *guru.* He wears white and may be under vows, but is not a *sannyāsin.* See: *sādhana.*

sādhana: साधन "Effective means of attainment." Religious or spiritual disciplines, such as *pūjā, yoga,* meditation, *japa,* fasting and austerity. The effect of *sādhana* is the building of willpower, faith and confidence in oneself and in God, Gods and *guru.* See: *pāda, rāja yoga, spiritual unfoldment.*

Sadāśiva: सदाशिव "Ever-auspicious." A name of the Primal Soul, Śiva, a synonym for Parameśvara, which is expressed in the physical being of the *satguru. Sadāśiva* especially denotes the power of revealing grace, *anugraha śakti,* the third *tattva,* after which emerge Śiva's other four divine powers. This five-fold manifestation or expression of God's activity in the cosmos is depicted in Hindu *mantras,* literature and art as the five-faced Sadāśivamūrti. See: *Parameśvara, tattva.*

sādhu: साधु "Virtuous one; straight, unerring." A holy person dedicated to the search for God. A *sādhu* may or may not be a *yogī* or a *sannyāsin,* or be connected in any way with a *guru* or legitimate lineage. *Sādhus* usually have no fixed abode and travel unattached from place to place, often living on alms.

Saguṇa Brahman: सगुणब्रह्मन् Brahman "with qualities." Describes Śiva's perfections of Satchidānanda and Maheśvara, the Primal Soul and His Divine Mind—that part of God which is divine, all-knowing, all-loving, all-powerful and omnipotent. See: *Brahman.*

sahasrāra chakra: सहस्रारचक्र "Thousand-spoked wheel." The cranial psychic force center. See: *chakra.*

Śaiva: शैव Of or relating to Śaivism or its adherents, of whom there are about 400 million in the world today. Same as *Śaivite.* See: *Śaivism.*

Śaiva Ātmārtha Pūjā: शैव आत्मार्थ पूजा See: *pūjā.*

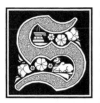

Śaiva Siddhānta: शैवसिद्धान्त "Final conclusions of Śaivism." The most widespread and influential Śaivite school today, predominant especially among the Tamil people in Sri Lanka and South India. It is the formalized theology of the divine revelations contained in the twenty-eight *Śaiva Āgamas.* For Śaiva Siddhāntins, Śiva is the totality of all, understood in three perfections: Parameśvara (the Personal Creator Lord), Parāśakti (the substratum of form) and Paraśiva (Absolute Reality which transcends all). Souls and world are identical in essence with Śiva, yet also differ in that they are evolving. A pluralistic stream arose in the middle ages from the teachings of Aghoraśiva and Meykandar, which denies that souls ever attain perfect sameness or unity with Śiva. See: *Śaivism.*

Śaiva Siddhānta Church (Dharmasabhā): **शैव सिद्धान्त धर्मसभा** "Church of God Siva's Revealed Truth," founded in 1949 by Satguru Sivaya Subramuniyaswami.

Śaiva Siddhānta Yoga Order: Ecclesiastical body of lifetime renunciate *swāmīs.* This *saṅgam* was founded by Satguru Sivaya Subramuniyaswami in 1949.

Śaivism (Śaiva): **शैव** The religion followed by those who worship Śiva as supreme God. Oldest of the four denominations of Hinduism. The earliest historical evidence of Śaivism is from the 8,000-year-old Indus Valley civilization in the form of the famous seal of Śiva as Lord Paśupati, seated in a *yogic* pose. In the *Rāmāyaṇa,* dated astronomically at 2000 BCE, Lord Rāma worshiped Śiva, as did his rival Rāvaṇa. Buddha in 624 BCE was born into a Śaivite family, and records of his time speak of the Śaiva ascetics who wandered the hills looking much as they do today.

Śaivite (Śaiva): **शैव** Of or relating to Śaivism or its adherents, of whom there are about 400 million in the world today. See: *Śaivism.*

Śaivite saints: See: *Nayanar.*

śākāhāra: **शाकाहार** "Vegetarian diet." From *śāka,* "vegetable;" and *āhāra,* "eating; taking food." See: *meat-eater, vegetarian, yama-niyama.*

Śākta: **शाक्त** Of or relating to *Śāktism.* A follower of the Śākta Hindu religion. See: *Śāktism.*

Śakti: **शक्ति** "Power, energy." The active power or manifest energy of Śiva that pervades all of existence. Its most refined aspect is Parāśakti, or Satchidānanda, the pure consciousness and primal substratum of all form. This pristine, divine energy unfolds as *icçhā śakti* (the power of desire, will, love), *kriyā śakti* (the power of action) and *jñāna śakti* (the power of wisdom, knowing), represented as the three prongs of Śiva's *triśūla,* or trident. From these arise the five powers of revealment, concealment, dissolution, preservation and creation. In Śaiva Siddhānta, Śiva is All, and His divine energy, Śakti, is inseparable from Him. This unity is symbolized in the image of Ardhanārīśvara, "half-female God." In popular, village Hinduism, the unity of Śiva and Śakti is replaced with the concept of Śiva and Śakti as separate entities. Śakti is represented as female, and Śiva as male. Śakti is most easily experienced by devotees as the sublime, bliss-inspiring energy that emanates from a holy person or sanctified Hindu temple. See: *Parāśak-*

ti, Śāktism.

Śaktis: **शक्ति** "Consorts." Loving Gaṇeśa is often seen with two female consorts, or *śaktis.* They represent *iḍā* and *piṅgalā,* the two life currents, emotion and intellect, that hold us close to Earth.

Śakti Gaṇapati: **शक्तिगणपति** "The powerful" is four-armed and seated with *Śakti* on His knee. He holds a garland and gestures *abhaya mudrā.*

Śāktism (Śākta): **शाक्त** "Doctrine of power." The religion followed by those who worship the Supreme as the Divine Mother—Śakti or Devī—in Her many forms, both gentle and fierce. Śāktism is one of the four primary denominations of Hinduism. See: *Śakti, tantrism.*

śālipallava: **शालिपल्लव** "Rice sprig."

samādhi: **समाधि** "Enstasy," which means "standing within one's Self." "Sameness; contemplation; union, wholeness; completion, accomplishment." *Samādhi* is the state of true *yoga,* in which the meditator and the object of meditation are one. *Samādhi* is of two levels. The first is *savikalpa samādhi* ("enstasy with form or seed"), identification or oneness with the essence of an object. Its highest form is the realization of the primal substratum or pure consciousness, Satchidānanda. The second is *nirvikalpa samādhi* ("enstasy without form or seed"), identification with the Self, in which all modes of consciousness are transcended and Absolute Reality, Paraśiva, beyond time, form and space, is experienced. This brings in its aftermath a complete transformation of consciousness. See: *kuṇḍalinī, Paraśiva, rāja yoga, Self Realization.*

sampradāya: **संप्रदाय** "Traditional doctrine of knowledge." A living stream of tradition or theology within Hinduism, passed on by oral training and initiation. The term derives from the verb *sampradā,* meaning "to give, grant, bestow or confer on; to hand down by tradition; to bequeath." See: *guru paramparā.*

saṁsāra: **संसार** "Flow." The phenomenal world. Transmigratory existence, fraught with impermanence and change. The cycle of birth, death and rebirth; the total pattern of successive earthly lives experienced by a soul.

saṁskāra: **संस्कार** "Impression, activator; sanctification, preparation." 1) The imprints left on the subconscious mind by experience (from this or previous lives), which then color all of life, one's nature, responses, states of mind, etc. 2) A sacrament or rite done to mark a significant transition of life. These make deep and positive impressions on the mind of the recipient, inform the family and community of changes in the lives of its members and secure inner-world blessings. See: *mind (five states), sacrament.*

Sanātana Dharma: **सनातनधर्म** "Eternal religion" or "everlasting path." It is a traditional name for the Hindu religion. See: *Hinduism.*

Sanātani: **सनातनि** "Of the eternal." A Hindu, a follower of the eternal path.

sanctified waters: See: *pāda pūjā, prasāda, ucçhishṭa.*

sandalwood: *Chandana.* The Asian evergreen tree *Santalum album.* Its sweetly fragrant heartwood is ground into the fine, tan-colored paste distributed as *prasāda* in Śaivite temples and used for sacred marks on the forehead, *tilaka.* Sandalwood is also prized for incense, carving and fine cabinetry.

saṅgama: सङ्गम "Association; fellowship." Also *saṅga.* Coming together in a group, especially for religious purposes.

saṅkalpa: संकल्प "Will; purpose; determination." A solemn vow or declaration of purpose to perform any ritual observance. Most commonly, *saṅkalpa* names the mental and verbal preparation made by a temple priest as he begins rites of worship. During the *saṅkalpa,* he informs all three worlds what he is about to do. He recites the name of the Deity, and the present time and place according to precise astrological notations and announces the type of ritual he is about to perform. Once the *saṅkalpa* is made, he is bound to complete the ceremony. See: *pūjā.*

Śaṅkara: शङ्कर "Conferring happiness; propitious." A name of Śiva.

Śaṅkara: शङ्कर One of Hinduism's most extraordinary monks (788–820) and preeminent *guru* of the Smārta Sampradāya. He is noted for his monistic philosophy of Advaita Vedānta, his many scriptural commentaries, and establishing ten orders of *sannyāsins* with pontifical headquarters at strategic points across India. He only lived 32 years, but traveled throughout India and transformed the Hindu world in that time. See: *Vedānta.*

Saṅkaṭ ahara Gaṇapati: संकटहरगणपति "The dispeller of sorrow," seated on a red lotus flower, holds a bowl of pudding, and displays *varada mudrā.*

śaṅkha: शङ्ख "Conch." The water-born conch symbolizes the origin of existence, which evolves in spiraling spheres. In ancient days its sound signaled battle's victory, today it heralds the high point of *pūjā* in Hindu temples. In the Deity's hands it stands for protection from evil, sounding the sacred.

San Mārga: सन्मार्ग "True path." A term especially important in *Śaiva Siddhānta.* 1) In general, the straight spiritual path leading to the ultimate goal, Self Realization, which does not detour into unnecessary psychic exploration or pointless development of *siddhis. San Mārgī* names a person who is "on the path," as opposed to *saṁsārī,* one engrossed in worldliness. 2) *San Mārga* is also an alternate term for the *jñāna pāda.* See: *liberation, pāda.*

San Mārga Sanctuary: A sanctuary at Kauai Aadheenam on the Garden Island of Kauai, Hawaii, centered around a ½-mile straight path to the Supreme God, Śiva (Parameśvara-Parāśakti-Paraśiva) and the Iraivan Temple enshrining a massive 700-pound, single-pointed quartz crystal.

sānnidhya: सान्निध्य "(Divine) presence; nearness, proximity." The radiance and blessed presence of *śakti* within and around a temple or a holy person.

sannyāsa: संन्यास "Renunciation." "Throwing down or abandoning." *Sannyāsa* is the repudiation of the *dharma,* including the obligations and duties, of the householder and the acceptance of the even more demanding *dharma* of the renunciate. See: *sannyāsin.*

sannyāsin: संन्यासिन् "Renouncer." One who has taken *sannyāsa dīkshā,* a formal rite, or less often an informal blessing, entering the devotee into renunciate monasticism, binding him for life to certain vows which include chastity, poverty and obedience, and directing him on the path to Self Realization. A Hindu monk, *swāmī*, and one of a world brotherhood (or holy order) of *sannyāsins*. See: *swāmī*.

Sanskṛit: संस्कृत "Well-made; perfected." The classical sacerdotal language of ancient India, considered a pure vehicle for communication with the celestial worlds. It is the primary language in which Hindu scriptures are written, including the *Vedas* and *Āgamas*. Employed today as a liturgical, literary and scholarly language, but no longer used as a spoken tongue.

sant: सन्त "Saint." A Hindi or vernacular term derived from the Sanskṛit *sat*, meaning "truth; reality."

śānti: शान्ति "Peace."

śara: शर "Arrow." Loving Gaṇeśa has power over thought and each one hits its mark. Bow drawn, arrow aimed, He teaches us to precisely begin beginnings all with good intentions.

śaraṇa: शरण "Refuge."

Sarasvatī: सरस्वती "The flowing one." Śakti, the Universal Mother; Goddess of the arts and learning, mythological consort of the God Brahmā. Sarasvatī, the river Goddess, is usually depicted wearing a white *sārī* and holding a *vīṇā*, sitting upon a swan or lotus flower. Prayers are offered to her for refinements of art, culture and learning. *Sarasvatī* also names one of seven sacred rivers (Sapta Sindhu) mentioned in the *Ṛig Veda*, but which now flows underground. See: *Goddess, Śakti*.

sārī: (Hindi, साड़ी) The traditional outer garment of a Hindu woman, consisting of a long, unstitched piece of cloth, usually colorful cotton or silk, wrapped around the body, forming an ankle-length skirt, and around the bosom and over the shoulder.

śaśikalā: शशिकला "Period of the moon." Specifically, the moon that adorns Lord Śiva's hair, the crescent moon of the dark fortnight's second day.

śāstra: शास्त्र "Sacred text; teaching." 1) Any religious or philosophical treatise, or body of writings. 2) A department of knowledge, a science; e.g., the *Dharma Śāstras* on religious law, *Artha Śāstras* on politics.

Śatapatha Brāhmaṇa: शतपथब्राह्मण "Priest manual of 100 paths." A supplement of *Śukla Yajur Veda* on theology, philosophy and modes of worship.

satguru (sadguru): सद्गुरु "True weighty one." A spiritual preceptor of the highest attainment—one who has realized the ultimate Truth, Paraśiva, through *nirvikalpa samādhi*—a *jīvanmukta* able to lead others securely along the spiritual path. He is always a *sannyāsin*, an unmarried renunciate. All Hindu denominations teach that the grace and guidance of a living *satguru* is a necessity for Self Realization. He is recognized and revered as the embodiment of God, Sadāśiva, the source of grace and of liberation. See: *guru bhakti, guru, guru-śishya system*.

sattva guṇa: सत्त्वगुण "Purity." The quality of goodness or purity. See: *guṇa*.

Satya Mantra: सत्य मन्त्र "Sacred syllable of truth." Aum. See: *Aum*.

scabies: A contagious skin disease caused by a parasitic mite that burrows under the skin, deposits eggs and causes intense itching.

Second World: The astral or subtle plane. Here the soul continues its activities in the astral body during sleep and after the physical body dies. It is the in-between world which includes the Devaloka and the Narakaloka. The Second world exists "within" the First World or physical plane. See: *loka.*

secular humanism: A system that rejects religious faith and worship and holds that one need not look beyond man for life's ethical meaning.

secular: Not sacred or religious; temporal or worldly.

seer: Visionary; *ṛishi.* A wise being or mystic who sees beyond the limits of ordinary perception. See: *ākāśa, ṛishi.*

Self (Self God): God Śiva's perfection of Absolute Reality, Paraśiva—That which abides at the core of every soul. See: *Paramātman, Paraśiva.*

self-declared *sannyāsin:* Paramadeśī sannyāsin. See: *sannyāsa dīkshā.*

self-effacement: Modest, retiring behavior; giving all credit to God, preceptor and other persons and not accepting praise for one's accomplishments.

self-erasement: The process of wiping out or eradicating the personal ego and the dross of the past, lodged in the memory patterns of the subconscious.

Self Realization: Direct knowing of the Self God, Paraśiva. Self Realization is known in Sanskṛit as *nirvikalpa samādhi;* "enstasy without form or seed;" the ultimate spiritual attainment (also called *asamprajñata samādhi).* Esoterically, this state is attained when the mystic *kuṇḍalinī* force pierces through the *sahasrāra chakra* at the crown of the head. See: *God Realization, liberation, kuṇḍalinī, Paraśiva, rāja yoga, samādhi.*

sentāmarai: செந்தாமரை "Red lotus flower."

severance: A breaking off or separation.

Shaṇmukha: षण्मुख "Six-faced." A name for Lord Murugan or Kārttikeya, denoting the multiplicity of His divine functions. See: *Kārttikeya.*

shrouded: Covered, protected, screened, veiled, sheltered.

shaṭkoṇa: षट्कोण "Six-pointed star," formed by two interlocking triangles, the upper one representing Śiva's transcendent Being, and the lower one Śiva's manifest energy, Śakti. The *shaṭkoṇa* is part of Lord Kārttikeya's *yantra.* See: *Kārttikeya.*

siddha yoga: सिद्धयोग "*Yoga* of perfected attainment, or of supernatural powers." 1) A term used in the *Tirumantiram* and other Śaiva scriptures to describe the *yoga* which is the way of life of adepts after attaining of Paraśiva. *Siddha yoga* involves the development of magical or mystical powers, or *siddhis,* such as the eight classical powers. It is a highly advanced *yoga* which seeks profound transformation of body, mind and emotions and the ability to live in a flawless state of God Consciousness. 2) The highly accomplished practices of certain alchemists. See: *siddha yogī, siddhi.*

Siddhi* and *Buddhi: सिद्धि बुद्धि "Attainment and Wisdom;" names of the two symbolic consorts of Lord Gaṇeśa.

siddhi: सिद्धि "Power, accomplishment; perfection." Extraordinary powers of the soul, developed through consistent meditation and deliberate, grueling, often uncomfortable *tapas,* or awakened naturally through spiritual maturity and *yogic sādhana.* Through the repeated experience of Self Realization, *siddhis* naturally unfold according to the needs of the individual. Before Self Realization, the use or development of *siddhis* is among the greatest obstacles on the path because it cultivates *ahaṁkāra,* I-ness, and militates against the attainment of *prapatti,* complete submission to the will of God, Gods and *guru.* See: *ashṭavibhūti.*

Siddhidātā: सिद्धिदाता "Giver of success, fulfillment," a name of Lord Gaṇeśa.

Siddhi Gaṇapati: सिद्धिगणपति A name and traditional *mūrti,* or form, of Gaṇeśa, "the accomplished one," who holds a bouquet of flowers, an axe, mango, sugarcane and, in His trunk, a sesame sweet.

Sikhism: "Disciple." Religion of nine million members founded in India about 500 years ago by the saint Guru Nānak. A reformist faith which rejects idolatry and the caste system, its holy book is the *Ādi Granth,* and main holy center is the Golden Temple of Amritsar.

sin: Intentional transgression of divine law. Akin to the Latin *sous,* "guilty." Hinduism does not view sin as a crime against God, but as an act against *dharma*—moral order—and one's own self. It is thought natural, if unfortunate, that young souls act wrongly, for they are living in nescience, *avidya,* the darkness of ignorance. Sin is an *adharmic* course of action which automatically brings negative consequences. The term *sin* carries a double meaning, as do its Sanskṛit equivalents: 1) a wrongful act, 2) the negative consequences resulting from a wrongful act. In Hinduism, there are no such concepts as *inherent* or *mortal sin.* See: *aura, evil, karma, pāpa.*

sindūra: सिन्दूर "Red lead, vermillion." *(Sindūr* in Hindi.) A red powder used to make the forehead mark *(pottu,* or *tilaka)* on the Deity image. See: *tilaka.*

Sinha Gaṇapati: सिंहगणपति "The lion-like one" rides a lion and holds another in one hand. He also holds a *vīṇā,* a lotus and pot of jewels.

śishya: शिष्य "A pupil or disciple," especially one who has proven himself and has formally been accepted by a *guru.*

Śiva: शिव "The auspicious, gracious or kindly one." Supreme Being of the Śaivite religion. God Śiva is All and in all, simultaneously the creator and the creation, both immanent and transcendent. As personal Deity, He is creator, preserver and destroyer. He is a one being, perhaps best understood in three perfections: Parameśvara (Primal Soul), Parāśakti (pure consciousness) and Paraśiva (Absolute Reality). See: *Parameśvara, Parāśakti, Paraśiva, Naṭarāja, Śaivism.*

Śivāchārya: शिवाचार्य The hereditary priests of the Śaiva Siddhānta tradition. The title of Ādiśaiva Brāhmins. An Ādiśaiva priest who has received the necessary training and *dīkshās* to perform public Śiva temple rites known as Āgamic *nitya parārtha pūjā.* A fully qualified Śivāchārya is also known as *archaka. Śivāchārya,* too, names the family clan of this priest tradition. See: *Brahmā.*

Śiva consciousness: Śivachaitanya. A broad term naming the experience or state of being conscious of Śiva in a multitude of ways, such as in the five expressed in the following meditation. **Vital Breath: *prāṇa.*** Experience the inbreath and outbreath as Śiva's will within the body. Become attuned to the ever-present pulse of the universe, knowing that nothing moves but by His divine will. **All-Pervasive Energy: *śakti.*** Become conscious of the flow of life within the body. Realize that it is the same universal energy within every living thing. Practice seeing the life energy within another's eyes. **Manifest Sacred Form: *darśana.*** Hold in your mind a sacred form, such as Naṭarāja, Śivaliṅga or the *satguru*—who is Sadāśiva—and think of nothing else. See every form as a form of our God Śiva. **Inner Light: *jyoti.*** Observe the light that illumines the thoughts. Concentrate only on that light, as you might practice being more aware of the light on a TV screen than of its changing pictures. **Sacred Sound: *nāda.*** Listen to the constant high-pitched *ee* sounding in the head. It is like the tone of an electrical transformer, a hundred *tamburas* distantly playing or a humming swarm of bees. See: *jñāna, mind (five states).*

Śivaliṅga: शिवलिङ्ग "Mark, or sign, of Śiva." The most prevalent icon of Śiva, found in virtually all Śiva temples. A rounded, elliptical, aniconic image, usually set on a circular base, or *pīṭha.* The Śivaliṅga is the simplest and most ancient symbol of Śiva, especially of Paraśiva, God beyond all forms and qualities. The *pīṭha* represents Parāśakti, the manifesting power of God. Liṅgas are usually of stone (either carved or naturally existing, *svayambhū,* such as shaped by a swift-flowing river), but may also be of metal, precious gems, crystal, wood, earth or transitory materials such as ice. See: *mūrti, Śaivism.*

Śivaloka: शिवलोक "Realm of Śiva." See: *loka.*

Śiva-Śakti: शिवशक्ति Father-Mother God, both immanent and transcendent. A name for God Śiva encompassing His unmanifest Being and manifest energy. See: *Parameśvara, Śiva.*

Śivāya: शिवाय "To Siva."

Skanda: स्कन्द "Quicksilver; leaping one." One of Lord Kārttikeya's oldest names, and His form as scarlet-hued warrior God. See: *Kārttikeya.*

śloka: श्लोक A verse, phrase, proverb or hymn of praise, usually composed in a specified meter. Especially a verse of two lines, each of sixteen syllables. *Śloka* is the primary verse form of the Sanskṛit epics, *Mahābhārata* and *Rāmāyaṇa.* See: *sūtra.*

Smārta: स्मार्त "Of or related to *smṛiti,*" the secondary Hindu scriptures. Of or related to Smārtism; a follower of Smārtism. See: *Smārtism.*

Smārtism: स्मार्त "Sect based on the secondary scriptures *(smṛiti).*" The most liberal of the four major denominations of Hinduism, an ancient Vedic *brāhminical* tradition (ca 700 BCE) which from the 9th century onward was guided and deeply influenced by the Advaita Vedānta teachings of the reformist Ādi Śaṅkara. Its adherents rely mainly on the classical *smṛiti* literature, especially the *Itihāsas (Rāmāyaṇa* and *Mahābhārata,* the latter of which includes the *Bhagavad Gītā*), *Purāṇas* and *Dharma Śāstras*. These are regarded as complementary to and a means to understanding the *Vedas*. See: *Daśanāmi, Śaṅkara.*

smṛiti: **स्मृति** "That which is remembered; the tradition." Hinduism's nonrevealed, secondary but deeply revered scriptures, derived from man's insight and experience. *Smṛiti* speaks of secular matters—science, law, history, agriculture, etc.—as well as spiritual lore, ranging from day-to-day rules and regulations to superconscious outpourings. 1) The term *smṛiti* refers to a specific collection of ancient Sanskṛitic texts. 2) In a general sense, *smṛiti* may refer to any text other than *śruti* (revealed scripture) that is revered as scripture within a particular sect.

snāna: **स्नान** "Bathing." Ceremonial ablution, especially in sacred waters, traditionally presribed as an obligatory Hindu duty.

soul: The real being of man, as distinguished from body, mind and emotions. The soul—known as *ātman* or *purusha*—is the sum of its two aspects, the form or body of the soul and the essence of the soul—Pure Consciousness *(Parāśakti* or *Satchidānanda)* and Absolute Reality *(Paraśiva).* See: *ātman, Paramātman, spiritual unfoldment.*

spiritual unfoldment: The unfoldment of the spirit, the inherent, divine soul of man. The gradual expansion of consciousness as *kuṇḍalinī śakti* slowly rises through the *sushumṇā*. The term *spiritual unfoldment* indicates this slow, imperceptible process, likened to a lotus flower's emerging from bud to effulgent beauty. See: *kuṇḍalinī, liberation, pāda, sādhana.*

spurious: Illegitimate, not true or genuine.

śraddhā: **श्रद्धा** "Faith; belief." See: *pañcha śraddhā.*

śrāddha: **श्राद्ध** Relating to commemorative ceremonies for the deceased, held one week, one month after death, and annually thereafter, according to tradition. See: *death, bone-gathering, saṁskāra.*

Śrī Chakra: **श्रीचक्र** See: *yantra.*

Śrī Laṅkā **श्रीलङ्का** ஸ்ரீ லங்கா "Venerable lion." Island country off the southeast tip of India, formerly called Ceylon, 80% Buddhist, home to several million Tamil Śaivites who live mostly in the arid north. It was a British colony until independence in 1948 as a member of the Commonwealth; became a republic in 1972; 25,000 square miles, 15 million population.

Śrī Rudram: **श्रीरुद्रम्** "Hymn to the wielder of terrific powers." Preeminent Vedic hymn to Lord Śiva as the God of dissolution, chanted daily in Śiva temples throughout India. It is in this long prayer, located in the *Yajur Veda, Taittirīya Saṁhitā*, in the middle of the first three *Vedas*, that the Śaivite *mantra* Namaḥ Śivāya first appears.

sṛishṭi: **सृष्टि** "Creation."

Sṛishṭi Gaṇapati: **सृष्टिगणपति** "The creator God" rides a mouse and holds a noose, goad, His broken tusk (representing selfless sacrifice) and a mango.

śruti: **श्रुति** "That which is heard." Hinduism's revealed scriptures, of supreme theological authority and spiritual value. They are timeless teachings transmitted to *ṛishis*, or seers, directly by God thousands of years ago. *Śruti* is thus said to be *apaurusheya*, "impersonal." *Śruti* consists of the *Vedas* and the *Āgamas*, preserved through oral tradition and eventually written down in Sanskṛit. Among the many sacred books of the Hindus, these two bodies of knowledge are held in the highest esteem. For countless centuries *śruti* has been the basis of philosophical discussion, study and commentary, and this attention has given rise to countless schools of thought. It is also the subject of deep study and meditation, to realize the wisdom of the ancients within oneself. Most *mantras* are drawn from *śruti*, used for rites of worship, both public and domestic, as well as personal prayer and *japa*. See: *Āgamas, smṛiti, Vedas.*

sthapati: स्थपति From *stha*, "building or place," and *pati*, "lord or father." A master architect of Āgamic temples. A *sthapati* must be well versed in the *Śilpa Śāstras*, experienced in all aspects of temple construction, pious, mystically trained, and a good administrator, for he has a team of *śilpīs* working under him, stone cutters, carvers, sculptors, wood workers, etc.

sthūla: स्थूल "Gross; physical." See: *vāk.*

subatomic: Of the inner parts of atoms; anything smaller than an atom.

subconscious mind: *Saṁskāra chitta.* See: *aura, conscience, mind (five states).*

sub-subconscious: *Vāsanā chitta.* Area of the subconscious where past experiences mix and merge, forming new images, reactions and beliefs. See: *mind (five states)*

substratum: A substance or element which lies beneath and supports another.

subsuperconscious mind: *Anukāraṇa chitta.* See: *mind (five states).*

śuddhi: शुद्धि "Purification." Also, *śraddha śuddhi*, "purification of faith." The rite of accepting back into the Hindu fold individuals who have been converted to other faiths or otherwise require purification to rejoin the Hindu congregation. An alternate term to *vrātyastoma*, "oath affirmation."

śūdra: शूद्र "Worker, servant." The social class of skilled artisans, workers and laborers. See: *varṇa dharma.*

śuka: शुक "Parrot."

sukarma: सुकर्म See: *karma, puṇya.*

sukhāsana: सुखासन "Pleasant or easy pose." Often applies to any comfortable seating pose. More specificially, a synonym for the *swāstikāsana*, in which the legs are crossed, the feet tucked under the knees.

sūkshma: सूक्ष्म "Subtle." See: *vāk.*

śuṇḍā: शुण्डा "Elephant trunk."

Sundarar: சுந்தரர் One of the four Tamil Samayāchāryas (ca 800), and composer of devotional hymns to God Śiva, which form the seventh book of the *Tirumurai*. In these, he pleads forth-rightly to Śiva for material as well as spiritual abundance. See: *Nayanar.*

superconscious mind: *Kāraṇa chitta.* See: *mind (five states;three phases).*

supplicate (supplication): To ask for humbly. To earnestly pray for.

supreme: Highest in rank, power, authority.

Supreme God: Highest God, the source or creator of all other Gods, beings and all manifestation.

surrender: Giving up or yielding. Surrender to the Divine is called *prapatti,* a complete giving over of oneself to God's will in total trust and abandonment. See: *bhakti, prapatti, sacrifice.*

Sūrya: सूर्य "Sun." One of the principal Divinities of the *Vedas,* also prominent in the epics and *Purāṇas.* Śaivites revere Sūrya, the Sun God each morning as Śiva Sūrya. Smārtas and Vaishṇavas revere the golden orb as Sūrya Nārāyaṇa. As the source of light, the sun is the most readily apparent image of Divinity available to man. As the giver of life, Sūrya is worshiped during harvest festivals everywhere. Esoterically, the sun represents the point where the manifest and unmanifest worlds meet or unite. In *yoga,* the sun represents the masculine force, *piṅgalā.* Sūrya also signifies the Self within.

sushumṇā nāḍī: सुषुम्णानाडी "Most gracious channel." Central psychic nerve current within the spinal column. See: *kuṇḍalinī, nāḍī, samādhi.*

sushupti: सुषुप्ति "Deep sleep." A state more refined than the ordinary dream state, the perceptions of which are often too subtle to be remembered upon awakening. This is the state of visionary dreams. One of the four *avasthās* described in the *Māṇḍūkya Upanishad.* See: *avasthā, consciousness.*

sūtra: सूत्र "Thread." An aphoristic verse; the literary style consisting of such maxims. From 500 BCE, this style was widely adopted by Indian philosophical systems and eventually employed in works on law, grammar, medicine, poetry, crafts, etc. Each *sūtra* is often accompanied by a commentary called *bhāshya.*

svadharma: स्वधर्म "One's own way." See: *dharma.*

svādhishṭhāna: स्वाधिष्ठान "One's own base." See: *chakra.*

svādhyāya: स्वाध्याय "Self-reflection; scriptural study." See: *yama-niyama.*

svapna: स्वप्न "Dream." Astral consciousness. The sleeping-dreaming state of subtle perception and experience. One of the four states of consciousness, *avasthās,* described in the *Māṇḍūkya Upanishad.* See: *avasthā, consciousness.*

svayambhū mūrti: स्वयम्भूमूर्ति "Self-existent image." A Deity image discovered in nature, and not carved or crafted by human hands. See: *mūrti.*

swāmī: स्वामी "Lord; owner." He who knows or is master of himself. A respectful title for a Hindu monk, usually a *sannyāsin.* The term *swāmī* is sometimes applied more broadly to include nonmonastics dedicated to spiritual work. See: *monastic, sannyāsin.*

swastika: स्वस्तिक "It is well." The ancient Hindu symbol of auspiciousness and good fortune, representing the sun and often associated with Gaṇeśa. The right-angled arms of the *swastika* denote the indirect way in which Divinity is reached—through intuition and not by intellect—and how life is filled with change and indirection. It has been a prominent icon in many cultures. See: *mūrti.*

taijasa: **तैजस** "Full of light." A term for the dreaming state, equivalent to *svapna.* See: *avasthā, svapna.*

tāla: **ताल** "Time measure." In Indian music, the organization of time into meter and rhythmic pulse with sometimes complex subdivisions. *Tāla* is similar to "time signature" in Western notation except that *tāla* includes the unique emotional or mystical mood.

talātala chakra: **तलातल चक्र** "Lower region." The fourth *chakra* below the *mūlādhāra,* centered in the calves. Region of chronic mental confusion and unreasonable stubbornness. Corresponds to the fourth astral netherworld beneath the earth's surface, called Tāmisra ("darkness") or Talātala. This state of consciousness is born of the sole motivation of self-preservation. See: *chakra, loka, Naraka.*

taṁbūrā: **तंबूरा** (Hindi) A long-necked, four-stringed fretless lute that provides a drone accompaniment for a singer or instrumentalist.

Tamil: தமிழ் A Dravidian language and Caucasian race of South India.

Tamil Nadu: தமிழ் நாடு State in South India, 50,000 square miles, population 55 million. Land of countless holy scriptures, saints, sages and over 40,000 magnificent temples, including Chidambaram, Madurai, Palani Hills and Rāmeśvaram.

tanmātrā: **तन्मात्रा** "Primal matter." The five fundamental subtle "substances" of the five gross elements, *mahābhūtas.* The five *tanmātras* and their corresponding elements are: 1) *śabda* (sound), *ākāśa* (ether); 2) *sparśa* (touch), *vāyu* (air); 3) *rūpa* (sight), *tejas* (fire); 4) *rasa* (taste), *apas* (water); 5) *gandha* (smell), *pṛithivī* (earth).

tantra: **तन्त्र** "Loom, methodology." 1) Most generally, a synonym for *śāstra,* "scripture." 2) A synonym for the Āgamic texts, especially those of the Śākta faith, a class of Hindu scripture providing detailed instruction on all aspects of religion, mystic knowledge and science. The *tantras* are also associated with the Śaiva tradition. 3) A specific method, technique or spiritual practice within the Śaiva and Śākta traditions. See: *tantrism.*

tantric (tāntrika): **तान्त्रिक** Adjectival form for practices prescribed in the Tantra traditions. The name of a follower of any of the *tantric* traditions. See: *tantra, tantrism.*

tantrism: The enlightenment path outlined in the *Tantra* scriptures. 1) Tantrism is sometimes considered a parallel stream of history and tradition in Hinduism, running alongside and gradually interweaving with the Vedic *brāhminical* tradition. 2) Tantrism refers to traditions, mainly within Śaivism and Śāktism, that focus on the arousal of the *kuṇḍalinī* force, and which view the human body as a vehicle of the Divine and an instrument for liberation. Tantrism's ultimate aim is a channeling of the *kuṇḍalinī* life force through the *sushumṇā,* the gracious channel, upwards into the *sahasrāra chakra* and beyond, through the door of *brahman (brahmarandhra)* into Paraśiva, either before or at the time of death. The stress is on the transformation of all spheres of consciousness, spiritual, psychic, emotional and material. It is a path of *sādhana*. 3) —***Śākta Tantrism:*** Brings a strong emphasis on the worship of the feminine force. Depending on the school, this may be symbolic or literal in rites involving sexual intercourse, etc. Śākta Tantrism's main principle is the use of the material to gain the spiritual. In certain schools, historically, this implies embracing that which is normally forbidden and manipulating the forces to attain transcendent consciousness rather than lower consciousness. See: *Śāktism, kuṇḍalinī, rāja yoga, tantra.*

tapas: तपस् "Heat, fire." 1) Purificatory spiritual disciplines, severe austerity, penance and sacrifice. The endurance of pain, suffering, through the performance of extreme penance, religious austerity and mortification. By comparison, *sādhana* is austerity of a simple, sustained kind, while *tapas* is austerity of a severe, psyche-transforming nature. *Tapas* is extreme bodily mortification, long term *sādhanas,* such as meditating under a tree in one place for 12 years, taking a lifetime vow of silence and never speaking or writing, or standing on one leg for a prescribed number of years. Scriptures generally warn against extreme asceticism which would bring harm to the body. 2) On a deeper level, *tapas* is the intense inner state of *kuṇḍalinī* "fire" which stimulates mental anguish and separates the individual from society. The individual can *mollify* this heated condition by continuing his regular *sādhana* as outlined by the *guru.* The fires of self-transformation may be stimulated by the practice of *tapas,* or come unbidden. One can "do" *tapas,* but the true *tapas* is a condition of being and consciousness which is a state of grace, bringing positive change, transformation and purification of one's nature. *Guru bhakti* is the only force that can cool the fires of *tapas.* See: *kuṇḍalinī, penance, sādhana.*

Taruṇa Gaṇapati: तरुणगणपति A name and traditional *mūrti,* or form, of Gaṇeśa, "the youthful one," with eight arms, holding noose, goad, *modaka,* wood apple, rose apple, tusk, paddy and sugar cane.

tattva: तत्त्व "That-ness" or "essential nature." *Tattvas* are the primary principles, elements, states or categories of existence, the building blocks of the universe. *Ṛishis* describe this emanational process as the unfoldment of thirty-six *tattvas,* stages or evolutes of manifestation, descending from subtle to gross. At *mahāpralaya,* cosmic dissolution, they enfold into their respective sources, with only the first two *tattvas* surviving the great dissolution. See: *mahāpralaya.*

temple: A place consecrated for, and dedicated to, the worship of God or Gods. Hindus revere their temples as sacred, magical places in which the three worlds most consciously commune—structures especially built and consecrated to channel the subtle spiritual energies of inner-world beings. The temple's psychic atmosphere is maintained through regular worship ceremonies *(pūjā)* invoking the Deity, who uses His installed image *(mūrti)* as a temporary body to bless those living on the earth plane. See:

darśana, pilgrimage.

tenet: A principle, doctrine, or belief held as a truth, as by some group.

theism: Belief that God exists as a real, conscious, personal Supreme Being, creator and ruler of the universe. May also include belief in the Gods.

third eye: The inner organ of psychic vision, located above and between the two physical eyes at the location of the *ājñā chakra.* See: *ājñā chakra, chakras.*

Third World: See: *loka.*

three worlds: The three worlds of existence, *triloka,* are the primary hierarchical divisions of the cosmos. 1) Bhūloka: "Earth world," the physical plane. 2) Antarloka: "Inner or in-between world," the subtle or astral plane. 3) Śivaloka: "World of Śiva," and of the Gods and highly evolved souls; the causal plane, also called Kāraṇaloka. See: *loka.*

tila gola: तिलगोल "Sesame ball." A type of Indian sweet.

tilaka: तिलक Marks made on the forehead or the brow with clay, ashes or sandalwood paste as an indication of sectarian affiliation. Vaishṇavas wear a vertical v-shaped *tilaka* made from clay. The Śaivite *tilaka,* called *tripuṇḍra,* consists of three horizontal strips of holy ash with a dot near the middle, or between the eyebrows. See: *bindu, Hinduism.*

tīrtha: तीर्थ "Passageway; ford." A bathing *ghat* or place of pilgrimage, especially on the banks of sacred waters. Also refers to water offered in *pūjā.*

tīrthayātrā: तीर्थयात्रा "Journeying to a holy place." Pilgrimage. One of the five sacred duties *(pañcha nitya karmas)* of the Hindu is to journey periodically to one of the innumerable holy spots in India or other countries. Preceded by fasting and continence, it is a time of austerity and purification, when all worldly concerns are set aside and God becomes one's singular focus. See: *pañcha nitya karmas, pañcha śraddhā.*

Tirukural: திருக்குறள் "Holy couplets." A treasury of Hindu ethical insight and a literary masterpiece of the Tamil language, written by Śaiva Saint Tiruvalluvar (ca 200 BCE) near present-day Madras. See: *Tiruvalluvar.*

Tirumantiram: திருமந்திரம் "Holy incantation." The Nandinātha Sampradāya's oldest Tamil scripture; written ca 200 BCE by Ṛishi Tirumular. It is the earliest of the *Tirumurai,* and a vast storehouse of esoteric *yogic* and *tantric* knowledge. It contains the essence of *rāja yoga* and *siddha yoga,* and the fundamental doctrines of the 28 *Śaiva Siddhānta Āgamas,* which in turn are the heritage of the ancient pre-historic traditions of Śaivism.

Tirumular: திருமூலர் An illustrious *siddha yogī* and *ṛishi* of the Nandinātha Sampradāya's Kailāsa Paramparā who came from the Himalayas (ca 200 BCE) to Tamil Nadu to compose the *Tirumantiram.* In this scripture he recorded the tenets of Śaivism in concise and precise verse form, based upon his own realizations and the supreme authority of the *Śaiva Āgamas* and the *Vedas.* Tirumular was a disciple of Maharishi Nandinātha. See: *Tirumantiram, Kailāsa Paramparā, Vedānta.*

Tiruvalluvar: திருவள்ளுவர் "Holy weaver." Tamil weaver and householder saint (ca 200 BCE) who wrote the classic Śaivite ethical scripture

Tirukural. See: *Tirukural.*

tithing: *Daśamāṁśa.* "One-tenth sharing." Religion's dues. The spiritual discipline, often a *vrata,* of paying one tenth of one's gainful and gifted income to a religious organization of one's choice, thus sustaining spiritual education and upliftment on earth. The Sanskṛit equivalent is *daśamāṁśa,* called *makimai* in the Tamil tradition. See: *tithing vow.*

tithing vow: *Daśama bhāga vrata.* "One-tenth-part vow." A promise that tithers make before God, Gods and their family or peers to tithe regularly each month—for a specified time, or for life.

trance: In general, a condition of altered consciousness, accompanied by a lack of awareness to physical surroundings, neither a state of wakefulness nor sleep. In a religious sense it is a state of intense concentration, introspection or meditation. In spiritualism, trance describes the phenomenon in which an individual leaves the physical body, and a disincarnate being enters or takes control of the body, often giving forth verbal messages to others in attendance, as in a seance. Trance can be either voluntary or involuntary.

transcendent: Surpassing the limits of experience or manifest form. In Śaiva Siddhānta, a quality of God Śiva as Absolute Reality, Paraśiva, the Self. Distinguished from immanent. See: *Paraśiva.*

transliteration: Writing words, sentences, etc., in the corresponding characters of another alphabet.

translucent: Partially transparent; allowing some light to shine through.

tribhaṅga: त्रिभंग "Three bends." A standing pose in which the body's center line passes through the left (or right) eye, the middle of the chest, and between the heels. The hips are shifted to the right (or left), the upper torso to the left (or right), and the head leans to the right (or left).

tribal: Relating to, or having the character of a tribe, a group, clan or village often related by ancestry, race or allegiance to a common leader or lineage.

trikaṭu: त्रिकटु "Three tastes." A renowned *āyurvedic* formulation of equal parts Indian long pepper, black pepper and dried ginger that is used to stimulate *pitta* and cleanse the gastro-intestinal tract of *ama.* See: *āyurveda.*

Trimukha Gaṇapati: त्रिमुखगणपति The contemplative "three-faced" Lord sits on a golden lotus flower, telling His beads, gesturing protection and blessings.

tṛiṇa: तृण "Grass."

tripuṇḍra: त्रिपुण्ड्र "Three marks." The Śaivite sectarian mark, consisting of three horizontal lines of *vibhūti* (holy ash) on the brow, often with a dot *(bindu)* at the third eye. The three lines represent the soul's three bonds: *āṇava, karma* and *māyā.* Holy ash, made of burnt cow dung, is a reminder of the temporary nature of the physical body and the urgency to strive for spiritual attainment and closeness to God. See: *bindu, tilaka, vibhūti.*

triśūla: त्रिशूल "Trident."A three-pronged spear or trident wielded by Lord Śiva and certain Śaivite ascetics. Also held by loving Gaṇeśa, it symbolizes God's three fundamental *śaktis* or powers—*icçhā* (desire, will, love), *kriyā* (action) and *jñāna* (wisdom).

Tṛitīyākshi: **तृतीयाक्षि** "The third eye." See: *third eye.*

Truth: When capitalized, ultimate knowing which is unchanging. Lower case (truth): honesty, integrity; virtue.

Tryakshara Gaṇapati: **त्र्यक्षरगणपति** "The Lord of three letters" (A-U-M) has fly whisks in His ears. He is often seen holding a tasty *modaka* in His trunk.

turīya: **तुरीय** "The fourth." The superconscious state beyond waking, dreaming and deep sleep. One of the four states of consciousness, *avasthās,* described in the *Māṇḍūkya Upanishad.* See: *avasthā, consciousness.*

turīyātīta: **तुरीयातीत** "Beyond the fourth." The utterly transcendent, superconscious state. A state of *samādhi.* See: *avasthā, consciousness.*

turmeric: A plant of India, *Curcuma longa,* of the ginger family whose powdered rhizome is a prized seasoning and yellow dye. It has rich *āyurvedic* properties, is used in holy ritual and serves also to make *kuṅkuma.*

ucçhishṭa: **उच्छिष्ट** "Leavings; remainder." Religiously, the precious leavings from the *guru's* food plate or the waters from the bathing of his feet or sandals (or of a Deity) which are ingested by devotees as *prasāda.* See: *prasāda, satguru.*

Ucçhishṭa Gaṇapati: **उच्छिष्टगणपति** A name and traditional *mūrti,* or form, of Gaṇeśa as "Lord of offerings (of that which has been offered and blessed)." A six-armed *mūrti,* He sits with His *śakti,* holding a *vīṇā* and a *japa mālā.*

udarabandha: **उदरबन्ध** "Waist band."

Uddaṇḍa Gaṇapati: **उद्दण्डगणपति** "The enforcer of *dharma*" is a ten-armed *mūrti* holding a pot of gems, sugar cane, lotus, a mace and more.

Umā: **उमा** "O do not." A name for Śakti said to derive from the exclamation addressed to Pārvatī by her mother in the *Śiva Purāṇa,* beseeching her to not practice austerities. ***Umāsundarī:*** "Goddess of beauty."

unctuous: Having the characteristic of an oil or ointment; slippery.

unmanifest: Not evident or perceivable. Philosophically, akin to *transcendent.* God Śiva is unmanifest in His formless perfection, Paraśiva. See: *Paraśiva.*

unwavering: Not having any doubt or indecision.

upadeśa: **उपदेश** "Advice; religious instruction." Often given in question-and-answer form from *guru* to disciple. The *satguru's* spiritual discourses.

upanayana: **उपनयन** "Bringing near." A youth's formal initiation into Vedic study under a *guru,* traditionally as a resident of his *āśrama,* and the investiture of the sacred thread *(yajñopavīta or upavīta),* signifying entrance into one of the three upper castes. The *upanayana* is among twelve *saṁskāras* prescribed in the *Dharma Śāstras* and explained in the *Gṛihya Sūtras.* See: *saṁskāra.*

Upanishad: **उपनिषद्** "Sitting near devotedly." The fourth and final portion of the *Vedas,* expounding the secret, philosophical meaning of the Vedic hymns. The *Upanishads* are a collection of profound texts which are the source of Vedānta and have dominated Indian thought for thousands of years. They are philosophical chronicles of *ṛishis* expounding the nature of God, soul and cosmos, exquisite renderings of the deepest Hindu thought. See: *śruti, Vedas, Vedānta.*

upāsanā: **उपासना** "Sitting near." Worship or contemplation of God. One of the *pañcha nitya karmas.* "five constant duties." See: *pañcha nitya karmas.*

Ūrdhva Gaṇapati: **ऊर्ध्वगणपति** "The elevated one" sits with one of His *śaktis* on His left knee. His six hands hold a sprig of paddy, a lotus and more.

utkuṭakāsana: **उत्कुटकासन** "Sitting on the hams," usually with one or both knees raised. The name of a common *bhaṅgima,* or pose, of Lord Gaṇeśa.

utsava: **उत्सव** "Festival." Religious celebrations or holy days and their observance in the home and temple. *Utsava* is one of the five constant duties, *pañcha nitya karmas.* See: *festival, pañcha nitya karmas.*

uttarāyana: **उत्तरायन** "Northern way." The half-year, *ayana,* beginning with winter solstice, when the sun begins its apparent northward journey.

vāhana: **वाहन** "Bearing, carrying or conveying." Each Hindu God is depicted as riding an animal/bird *vāhana,* which is symbolic of a function of the God. For example, Śiva rides the bull, Lord Murugan rides the peacock and Lord Gaṇeśa rides the mouse.

Vaidika Dharma: **वैदिकधर्म** "The way of the *Vedas.*" An alternate term for *Hinduism.* See: *Hinduism.*

vaidyuta: **वैद्युत** "Proceeding from lightning." Electric energy.

vaikharī vāk: **वैखरी वाक्** "The faculty of speech." See: *vāk.*

Vaishṇava: **वैष्णव** Of or relating to Vishṇu; same as Vaishṇavite. A follower of Lord Vishṇu or His incarnations, such as Kṛishṇa or Rāma. See: *Vaishṇavism.*

Vaishṇavism (Vaishṇava): **वैष्णव** One of the four major religions, or denominations of Hinduism, representing roughly half of the world's one billion Hindus. It gravitates around the worship of Lord Vishṇu as Personal God, His incarnations and their consorts. Vaishṇavism stresses the personal aspect of God over the impersonal, and *bhakti* (devotion) as the true path to salvation. Foremost among Vaishṇava scriptures are the *Vaishṇava Āgamas, Rāmāyaṇa, Bhagavad Gītā* and *Bhāgavata Purāṇa.*

Vaishṇavite: A follower of Vishṇu or His incarnations. See: *Vaishṇavism.*

vaiśvānara: **वैश्वानर** "Referring to all human beings." A term referring to the waking state of beings in general, the cosmic soul in the conscious mind. *Vaiśvānara* is one of the four states of consciousness, *avasthās.* It is a name for *agni,* as the fire that controls body, mind and emotions in the waking state. Also an alternate term for *jāgrat,* wakefulness. See: *avasthā, jāgrat.*

vaiśya: **वैश्य** "Landowner; merchant." The social class of bankers, businessmen, industrialists; employers. Merchant class, originally those whose business was trade as well as agriculture. See: *varṇa dharma.*

vajra: वज्र "Lightning bolt." Also *vajratriśūla.* A symbol of spiritual power. Usually two tridents, without staffs, joined together with the two sets of three prongs pointing away from one another at 180°. *Vajra* can also refer to the single trident.

vāk: वाक् "Speech." Theologically, it is through the supreme Vāk (or Paravāk), the "Primal Word" of the *Vedas,* and its various aspects, that creation issues forth. Vāk, the word, is said to descend in four cosmic steps or levels: *mahākāraṇa,* the great causal; *kāraṇa,* the causal, the mind principle; *sūkshma,* the vital life force; and *sthūla,* physical matter. These correspond to the four states, *avasthās,* of consciousness: *jāgrat,* wakefulness; *svapna,* dreaming; *sushupti,* deep sleep; and *turīya,* the fourth. Related to the human microcosm in the *tantrika* tradition, *vāk* is correlated to the *chakras.* Paravāk, the great causal, *mahākāraṇa,* is said to center in the base of the spinal column in the *mūlādhāra chakra,* the abode of Gaṇapati as Brahmaṇaspati, Master of the Word. *Pasyānti vāk,* "the word that perceives," is located in the navel center, *maṇipūra chakra. Madhyama vāk,* the intermediate word, is centered between the navel and the throat, from whence speech, *easyharī vāk,* is expressed. Gaṇapati as Brahmaṇaspati is the Master of the Word, the Lord of Satya Mantra. And so, the *Tantra* conceives Him having His abode in the *mūlādhāra* of beings, from where speech originates in the form of Paravāk.

Vakratuṇḍa: वक्रतुण्ड "He of crooked trunk." An aspect of Lord Gaṇeśa cited in the *Mudgala Purāṇa* as the conqueror of *matsara,* jealousy.

valampuri: वलम्पुरि "Right-turning." A term for the rather rare images of Gaṇeśa in which the trunk is turning to the Deity's right. Cf: *edampuri.*

vāma: वाम 1) "Pleasant; beautiful; benignant; striving after"—as in Vāmadeva, a name of Śiva. 2) "Left; crooked; acting in the opposite way"—as in *vāma mārga,* the left-handed *tantric* path." See: *left-handed, tantrism.*

vanakkam: வணக்கம் The Tamil equivalent to *namaskāra.*

Varada Gaṇapati: वरदगणपति "The boon-giver" is the *mūrti* distinguished by the prominent third eye, dish of honey and crowning crescent moon.

varada mudrā: वरदमुद्रा "Boon-giving gesture." A hand pose shown by the Gods or a *guru,* in which the palm hangs loose at the wrist, facing the benefactor, with the fingers pointing downward, usually outstretched.

Varada Vināyaka: वरदविनायक "Lord of boons." The Gaṇeśa *mūrti* enshrined at the Mahad Hamlet Temple of Mahārāshṭra.

Vārāṇasī: वाराणसी Also known as Kāśī or Banāras. One of the most holy of Śaivite cities, and among the oldest cities in the world. Located in North India on the Ganges River. Hindus consider it highly sanctifying to die in Kāśī, revering it as a gateway to *moksha.*

varṇa dharma: वर्णधर्म "The way of one's kind." The hereditary social class system, generally referred to as *caste,* established in India in ancient times. Within *varṇa dharma* are the many religious and moral codes which define human virtue. *Varṇa dharma* is social duty, in keeping with the principles of good conduct, according to one's community, which is generally based on the craft or occupation of the family. Strictly speaking it encompasses two interrelated social hierarchies: 1) *varṇa,* which refers to the four classes: *brāhmin, kshatriya, vaiśya* and *śūdra;* and 2) *jāti,* the myriad occupational subgroups, or guilds, which in India number over 3,000. Hence this *dharma* is sometimes called *jāti dharma.* The class-caste system is still very much a part of Indian life today. Many modern Hindus propose that social status is now (and was originally) more properly determined by a person's skills and accomplishments than by birth. Mobility between *jātis,* or castes, within Hindu communities worldwide is limited but not impossible, and is accomplished through marrying into a new *jāti,* or changing professions through persistence, skill and education. *Śāstrīs* say that once a person breaks out of his *varṇa* or *jāti* of birth and changes "caste," it takes three generations for his family to become fully established in that new strata of society, provided the continuity is unbroken.

varṇāśrama dharma: **वर्णाश्रमधर्म** "The way of one's caste and stage of life." Names the social structure of four classes *(varṇa),* hundreds of castes *(jāti)* and four stages of life *(āśramas).* It is the combined principles of *varṇa dharma* and *āśrama dharma.* See: *āśrama dharma, dharma.*

Vasishṭ ha: **वसिष्ठ** Disciple of Maharishi Nandikeśvara (Nandinātha) (ca 250 BCE) along with Patañjali and Vyāghrapāda (as recorded in Pāṇini's book of grammar). Also the name of several other famous sages, including the *ṛishi* attributed with composing the hymns of the *Ṛig Veda's* seventh *maṇḍala,* another who plays a central role in the epics and certain *Purāṇas* and *Upanishads,* and a third who expounds the ancient *yogic* wisdom to Lord Rāma in the 29,000-verse *Yoga Vāsishṭha.*

vāta: **वात** "Movement." *Vāyu,* "air-ether." One of the three bodily humors, called *dosha, vāta* is known as the air humor. Principle of movement in the body. *Vāta dosha* governs such functions as breathing and movement of the muscles and tissues. See: *āyurveda, dosha.*

Veda: **वेद** "Wisdom." Sagely revelations which comprise Hinduism's most authoritative scripture. They, along with the *Āgamas,* are *śruti,* "that which is heard." The *Vedas* are a body of dozens of holy texts known collectively as the *Veda,* or as the four *Vedas: Ṛig, Yajur, Sāma* and *Atharva.* In all they include over 100,000 verses, as well as additional prose. Each *Veda* has four sections: *Saṁhitās* (hymn collections), *Brāhmaṇas* (priestly manuals), *Āraṇyakas* (forest treatises) and *Upanishads* (enlightened discourses). See: *Āraṇyaka, Brāhmaṇa, śruti, Upanishad.*

Vedānta: **वेदान्त** "Ultimate wisdom" or "final conclusions of the *Vedas.*" Vedānta is the system of thought embodied in the *Upanishads* (ca 1500-600 BCE), which give forth the ultimate conclusions of the *Vedas.* Through history there developed numerous Vedānta schools, ranging from pure dualism to absolute monism. The first and original school is Advaita Īsvaravāda, "monistic theism" or panentheism, exemplified in the Vedānta-Siddhānta of Ṛishi Tirumular (ca 250 BCE) of the Nandinātha Sampradāya in his *Tirumantiram,* which is a perfect summation of both the *Vedas* and the *Āgamas.* See: *monistic theism, panentheism, Tirumantiram.*

Vedic-Āgamic: Simultaneously drawing from and complying with both of Hinduism's revealed scriptures *(śruti), Vedas* and *Āgamas,* which represent two complementary, intertwining streams of history and tradition. The difference between Siddhānta and Vedānta is traditionally described in the following way. While the *Vedas* depict man looking for God, the *Āgamas* hold the perspective of God looking to help man.

vegetarian: *Śākāhāra.* Of a diet which excludes meat, fish, fowl and eggs. Vegetarianism is a principle of health and environmental ethics that has been a keystone of Indian life for thousands of years. Vegetarian foods include grains, fruits, vegetables, legumes and dairy products. A person following a vegetarian diet is called a *śākāhārī.* A nonveggie is called *mānsāhārī.* See: *guṇa, yama-niyama.*

veiling grace: *Tirobhāva śakti.* The divine power that limits the soul's perception by binding or attaching the soul to the bonds of *āṇava, karma,* and *māyā*— enabling it to grow and evolve as an individual being. See: *grace.*

vel: வேல் "Spear, lance." The symbol of Lord Kārttikeya's divine authority as Lord of *yoga* and commander of the *devas.* (Known as *śūla* in Sanskṛit.)

venerate: To look upon with feelings of deep respect or reverence.

vermillion: Bright red.

vestments: The clothing, especially official robes or other garb, worn by religious persons, often as a sign of their spiritual position or ordination.

vibhūti: विभूति "Resplendent, powerful." Holy ash, prepared by burning cow dung along with other precious substances, milk, *ghee,* honey, etc. It symbolizes purity and is one of the main sacraments given at *pūjā* in all Śaivite temples and shrines. Śaivites wear three stripes on the brow as a distinct sectarian mark, as do many Smārtas. *Vibhūti* is also a synonym for *siddhi,* supernormal powers developed through *yoga* practice. See: *tilaka. tripuṇḍra.*

vidyā: विद्या "Knowledge, learning, science." The power of understanding gained through study and meditation. Contrasted with *avidyā,* ignorance.

vidyārambha: विद्यारंभ "Commencement of learning." See: *saṁskāra.*

Vighnarāja Gaṇapati: विघ्नराजगणपति "The Lord of obstacles" is bedecked in jewels. His special implements are the conch, discus and flower arrow. Gaṇeśa's aspect as the conqueror of *mamata,* egoity.

Vighneśvara: विघ्नेश्वर "Lord of Obstacles." A name for Lord Gaṇeśa describing His power to both remove and create obstacles to guide souls along the right path. See: *Gaṇeśa.*

Vijaya Gaṇapati: विजयगणपति "The victorious one" rides the mouse and holds four primary symbols: the broken tusk, goad, noose and mango.

Vikaṭa: विकट "Deformed; having an unusual size or aspect." A name of Gaṇeśa cited in the *Mudgala Purāṇa* as the conqueror of *kāma,* lust.

vīṇā: वीणा Large South Indian popular musical instrument usually having seven strings and two calabash gourd resonance boxes.

Vināyaka: **विनायक** "Remover." A name of Lord Gaṇeśa, meaning the remover of obstacles (sometimes preceded by *vighna,* "obstacle"). See: *Gaṇeśa.*

Vināyaka Ahaval: விநாயகர் அகவல் "Poem to Vināyaka." Famous Tamil poem in praise of Gaṇeśa by the 8th-century woman saint, Auvaiyar.

Vināyaka Vratam: விநாயக விரதம் A 21-day festival to Lord Gaṇeśa beginning on the full-moon day of November-December. An important festival in Tamil Nadu and in Tamil communities worldwide, when special *pūjās* are conducted in Gaṇeśa temples, and devotees make a vow *(vrata),* such as to attend the daily *pūjā,* or to fast by taking only one meal a day.

Vīra Gaṇapati: **वीरगणपति** "The valiant warrior" is a *mūrti* recognized by His sixteen hands, holding every variety of weapon: mace, bow, axes and more.

visarjana: **विसर्जन** "Departure." See: *Gaṇeśa Chaturthī.*

Vishṇu: **विष्णु** "All-pervasive." Supreme Deity of the Vaishṇavite religion. God as personal Lord and Creator, the All-Loving Divine Personality, who periodically incarnates and lives a fully human life to reestablish *dharma* whenever necessary. In Śaivism, Vishṇu is Śiva's aspect as Preserver. See: *Vaishṇavism.*

visualize (visualization): To imagine, create mental images. Exercising the power of thought to create the future.

vitala: **वितल** "Region of negation." Region of raging anger and viciousness. The second *chakra* below the *mūlādhāra,* centered in the thighs. Corresponds to the second astral netherworld beneath the earth's surface, called Avīchi ("joyless") or Vitala. See: *chakra, loka, Naraka.*

vivāha: **विवाह** "Marriage." See: *saṁskāras.*

Vivekānanda, Swāmī: **विवेकानन्द** Disciple of Śrī Rāmakṛishṇa who was overtaken by an ardent love of Hinduism and a missionary zeal that drove him onward. He attained *mahāsamādhi* at age 39 (1863–1902). Most notable among his achievements was a trip around the world on which he gave brilliant lectures, especially in Europe and America, that created much respect for Hinduism. In India he founded the Rāmakṛishṇa Mission which thrives today internationally with over 100 centers and nearly 1,000 *sannyāsins.* He is credited, along with Tagore, Aurobindo, Rādhākṛishṇan and others, with sparking the modern Hindu revival.

vow: See: *vrata.*

vrata: **व्रत** "Vow, religious oath." Often a vow to perform certain disciplines over a period of time, such as penance, fasting, specific *mantra* repetitions, worship or meditation. *Vratas* extend from the simplest personal promise to irrevocable vows made before God, Gods, *guru* and community.

vrātyastoma: **व्रात्यस्तोम** "Vow pronouncement." The traditional purification rite, outlined in the *Taṇḍya Brāhmaṇa,* to welcome back into a Hindu community those who have become impure. It is performed for Hindus returning to India from abroad and for those who have embraced other faiths.

vṛiksha: **वृक्ष** "Tree."

wealth: *Artha.* Abundance; financial stability. See: *purushārtha.*

wood apple: The *kapittha* fruit. See: *kapittha.*

world: In Hindu theology, *world* refers to 1) ***loka:*** a particular region of consciousness or plane of existence. 2) ***māyā:*** The whole of manifest existence; the phenomenal universe, or cosmos, including the mental and spiritual, physical realms of existence, depending on its use. Also denoted by the terms *prakṛiti* and Brahmāṇḍa. 3) ***pāśa:*** In Śaivism, the term *world* is often used to translate the term *pāśa* in the Āgamic triad of fundamentals—Pati, *paśu, pāśa,* "God, soul, world." It is thus defined as the "fetter" *(pāśa)* that binds the soul, veiling its true nature and enabling it to grow and evolve through experience as an individual being. In this sense, the world, or *pāśa,* is three-fold, comprising *āṇava* (the force of individuation), *karma* (the principle of cause and effect) and *māyā* (manifestation, the principle of matter, Śiva's mirific energy, the sixth *tattva).* See: *Brahmāṇḍa, microcosm-macrocosm, tattva.*

worldly: Materialistic, unspiritual. Devoted to or concerned with the affairs or pleasures of the world, especially excessive concern to the exclusion of religious thought and life. Connoting ways born of the lower *chakras:* jealousy, greed, selfishness, anger, guile, etc. —**worldliness:** The state or quality of being worldly.

yajña: **यज्ञ** "Worship; sacrifice." One of the most central Hindu concepts—sacrifice and surrender through acts of worship, inner and outer. 1) A form of ritual worship especially prevalent in Vedic times, in which oblations—*ghee,* grains, spices and exotic woods—are offered into a fire according to scriptural injunctions while special *mantras* are chanted. The element fire, *Agni,* is revered as the divine messenger who carries offerings and prayers to the Gods.

yajñopavīta: **यज्ञोपवीत** "Sacred thread." See: *upanayana.*

Yajur Veda: **यजुर्वेद** "Wisdom of sacrificial formulas." One of the four compendia of revelatory texts called *Vedas (Ṛig, Sāma, Yajur* and *Atharva).* When used alone, the term *Yajur Veda* generally refers to this *Veda's* central and oldest portion—the *Saṁhitā,* "hymn collection." Of this there are two recensions: 1) the *Kṛishṇa* ("black") *Yajur Veda* (so-called because the commentary, *Brāhmaṇa,* material is mixed with the hymns); and 2) the *Śukla* ("white or clear") *Yajur Veda* (with no commentary among the hymns). See: *Vedas.*

yama-niyama: **यम नियम** The first two of the eight limbs of *rāja yoga,* constituting Hinduism's fundamental ethical codes, the ten *yamas* and ten *niyamas* are the essential foundation for all spiritual progress. The *yamas* are the ethical restraints; the *niyamas* are the religious practices. Here are the ten traditional *yamas* and ten *niyamas*. ***—yamas:*** 1) ***ahiṁsā:*** "Noninjury." 2) ***satya:*** "Truthfulness." 3) ***asteya:*** "Nonstealing." 4) ***brahmacharya:*** "Sexual purity." 5) ***kshamā:*** "Patience." 6) ***dhṛiti:*** "Steadfastness." 7) ***dayā:*** "Compassion." 8) ***ārjava:*** "Honesty, straightforwardness." 9) ***mitāhāra:*** "Moderate appetite." 10) ***śaucha:*** "Purity." ***—niyamas:*** 1) ***hrī:*** "Remorse." 2) ***santosha:*** "Contentment." 3) ***dāna:*** "Giving." 4) ***āstikya:*** "Faith." 5) **Īśvarapūjana:** "Worship of the Lord." 6) ***siddhānta śravaṇa:*** "Scriptural listening." 7) ***mati:*** "Cognition." 8) ***vrata:*** "Sacred vows." 9) ***japa:*** "Recitation." 10) ***tapas:*** "Austerity." See: *rāja yoga.*

yantra: यन्त्र "Vessel; container." A mystic diagram composed of geometric and alphabetic figures—usually etched on small plates of gold, silver or copper. Sometimes rendered in three dimensions in stone or metal. The purpose of a *yantra* is to focus spiritual and mental energies according to computer-like *yantric* pattern, be it for health, wealth, childbearing or the invoking of one God or another. It is usually installed near or under the temple Deity.

yoga: योग "Union." From *yuj,* "to yoke, harness, unite." The philosophy, process, disciplines and practices whose purpose is the yoking of individual consciousness with transcendent or divine consciousness. One of the six *darśanas,* or systems of orthodox Hindu philosophy. *Yoga* was codified by Patañjali in his *Yoga Sūtras* (ca 200 BCE) as the eight limbs *(ashṭāṅga)* of *rāja yoga.* It is essentially a one system, but historically, parts of *rāja yoga* have been developed and emphasized as *yogas* in themselves. Prominent among the many forms of *yoga* are *haṭha yoga* (emphasizing bodily perfection in preparation for meditation), *kriyā yoga* (emphasizing breath control), as well as *karma yoga* (selfless service) and *bhakti yoga* (devotional practices) which could be regarded as an expression of *rāja yoga's* first two limbs *(yama* and *niyama).* See: *bhakti yoga, haṭha yoga, rāja yoga.*

yogadaṇḍa: योगदण्ड "Meditation staff." A curved arm rest used during meditation, usually made of wood and attached to a staff about two feet long.

Yoga Gaṇapati: योगगणपति "The meditator" is a special *mūrti* of Gaṇeśa, seated in *yogic* pose holding a *yoga* staff and a strand of prayer beads.

yoga pāda: योगपाद The third of the successive stages in spiritual unfoldment in Śaiva Siddhānta, wherein the goal is Self Realization. See: *pāda, yoga.*

Yogaswāmī: யோகசுவாமி "Master of *yoga.*" Sri Lanka's renowned spiritual master (1872–1964); a *siddha* of the Nandinātha Sampradāya's Kailasa Paramparā who initiated Satguru Sivaya Subramuniyaswami in 1949. See: *Kailāsa Paramparā.*

yogī: योगी One who practices *yoga,* especially *kuṇḍalinī* or *rāja yoga.*

yuga: युग "Period, age." One of four ages which chart the duration of the world according to Hindu thought: Satya (or Kṛita), Tretā, Dvāpara and Kali. In the first period, *dharma* reigns supreme, but as the ages revolve, virtue diminishes and ignorance and injustice increase. At the end of the Kali Yuga, which we are in now, the cycle begins again with Satya Yuga.

Index

Anukramaṇikā

अनुक्रमणिका